Garfield
FAT CAT 3-PACK
VOLUME 3

BY
JIM DAVIS

BALLANTINE BOOKS · NEW YORK

2007 Ballantine Books Trade Paperback Edition

Published in the United States by Ballantine Books, an imprint of The Random House Publishing Group, a division of Random House, Inc., New York.

BALLANTINE and colophon are registered trademarks of Random House, Inc.

ISBN: 978-0-345-48088-0

Printed in the United States of America

www.ballantinebooks.com

First Colorized Edition: October 2007

9 8 7 6 5 4 3

Garfield
sits around the house

BY JIM DAVIS

Ballantine Books • **New York**

A GARFIELD NIGHT...

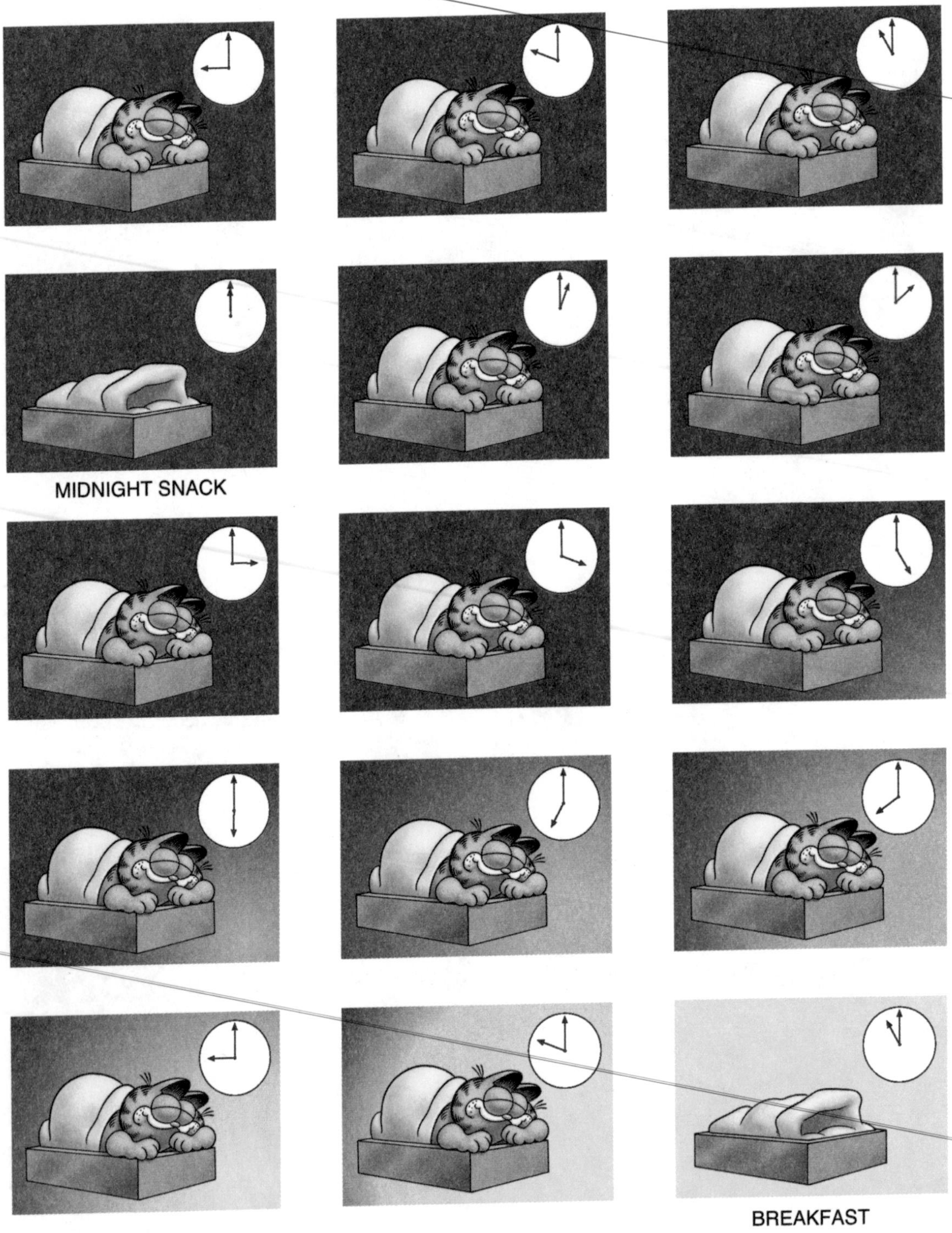
MIDNIGHT SNACK
BREAKFAST

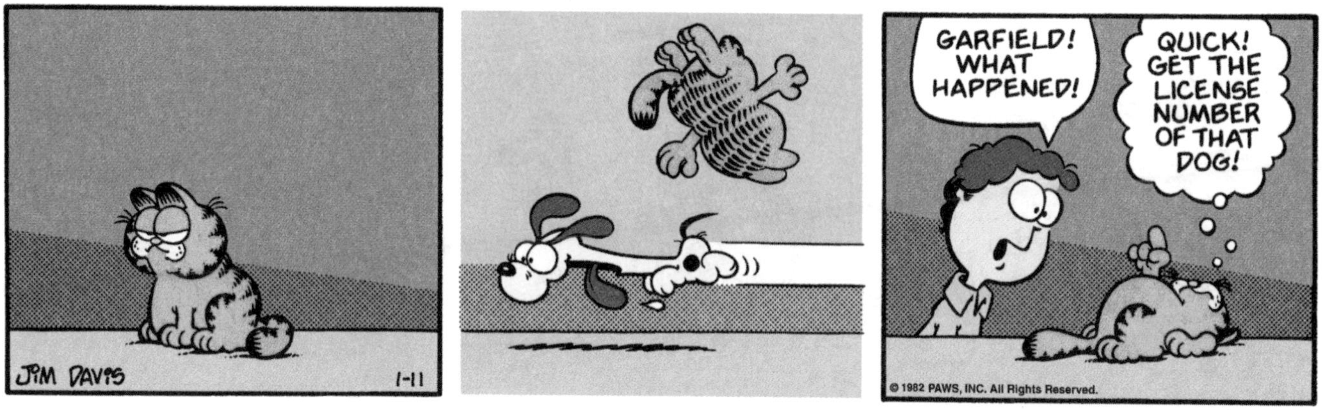
JIM DAVIS
1-11
GARFIELD! WHAT HAPPENED!
QUICK! GET THE LICENSE NUMBER OF THAT DOG!
© 1982 PAWS, INC. All Rights Reserved.

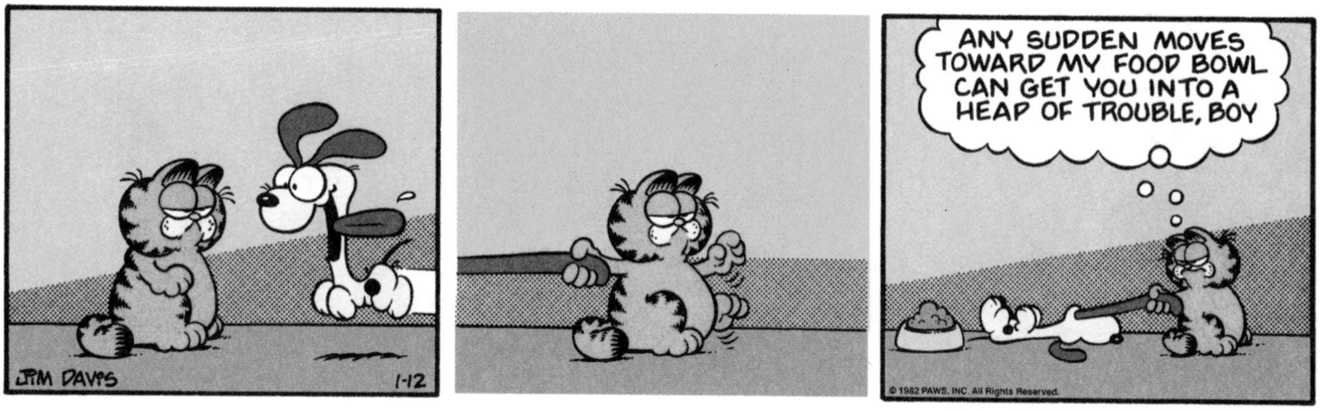
JIM DAVIS
1-12
ANY SUDDEN MOVES TOWARD MY FOOD BOWL CAN GET YOU INTO A HEAP OF TROUBLE, BOY
© 1982 PAWS, INC. All Rights Reserved.

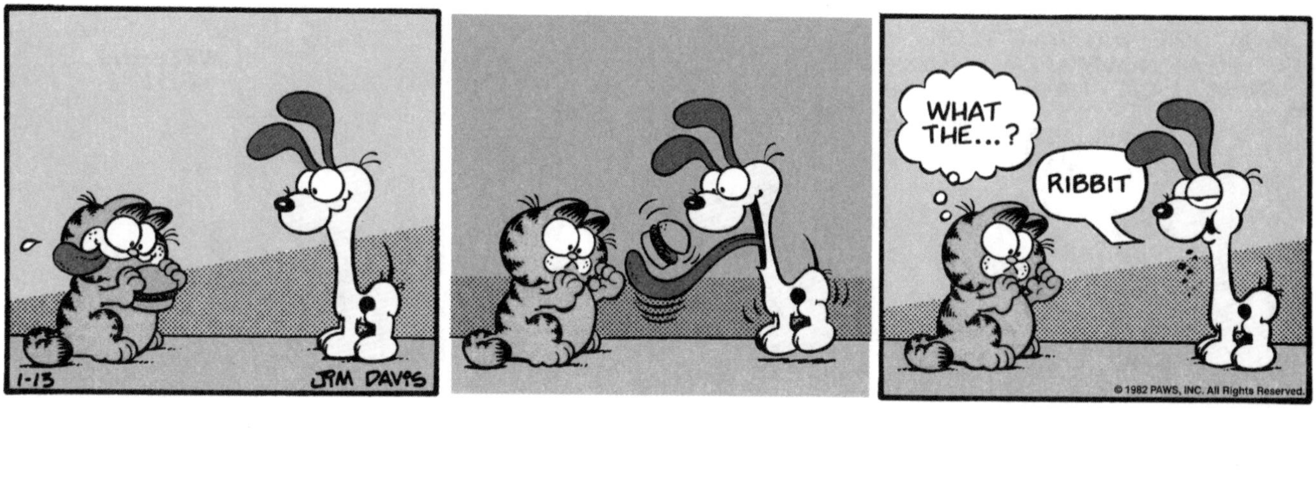
1-13
JIM DAVIS
WHAT THE...?
RIBBIT
© 1982 PAWS, INC. All Rights Reserved.

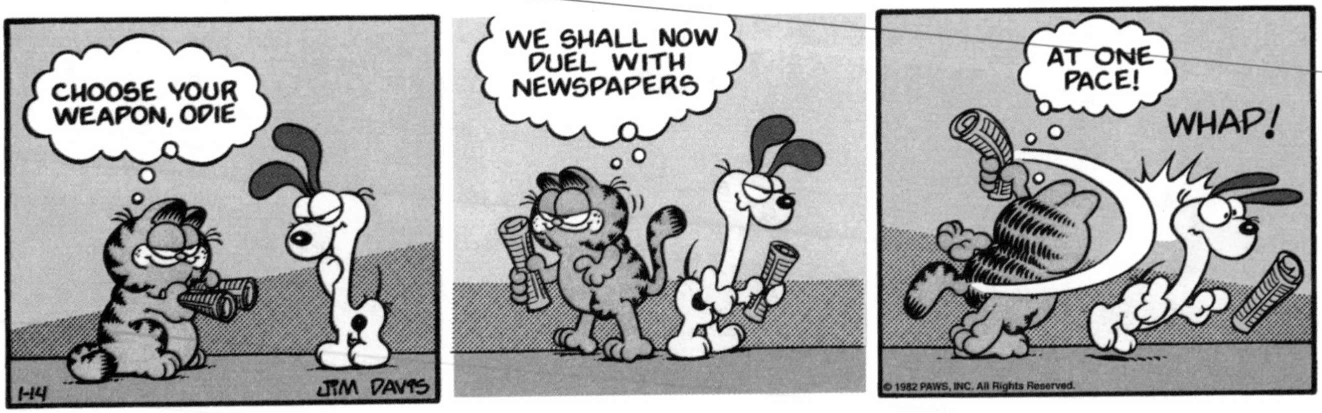
CHOOSE YOUR WEAPON, ODIE
1-14
JIM DAVIS
WE SHALL NOW DUEL WITH NEWSPAPERS
AT ONE PACE!
WHAP!
© 1982 PAWS, INC. All Rights Reserved.

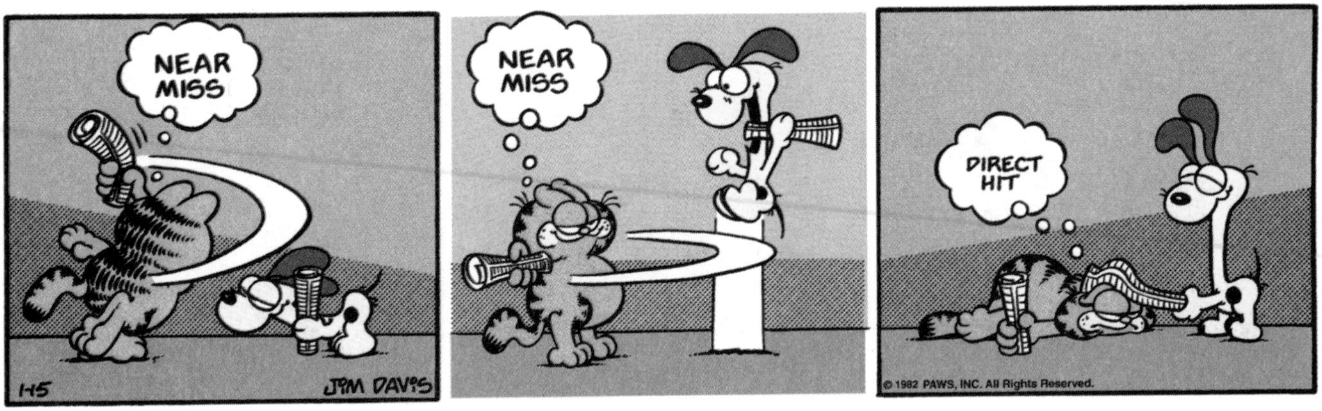
NEAR MISS
1-15
JIM DAVIS
NEAR MISS
DIRECT HIT
© 1982 PAWS, INC. All Rights Reserved.

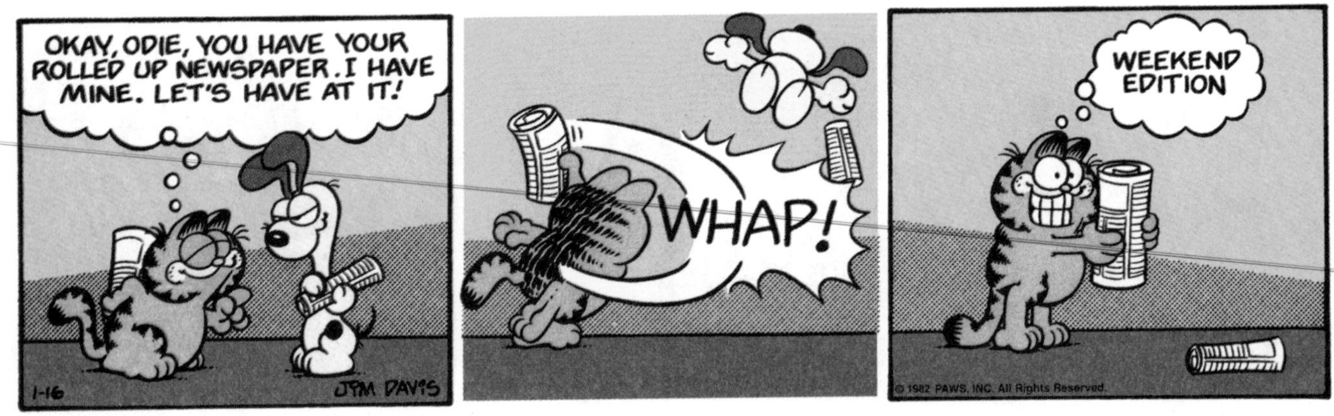
OKAY, ODIE, YOU HAVE YOUR ROLLED UP NEWSPAPER. I HAVE MINE. LET'S HAVE AT IT!
1-16
JIM DAVIS
WHAP!
WEEKEND EDITION
© 1982 PAWS, INC. All Rights Reserved.

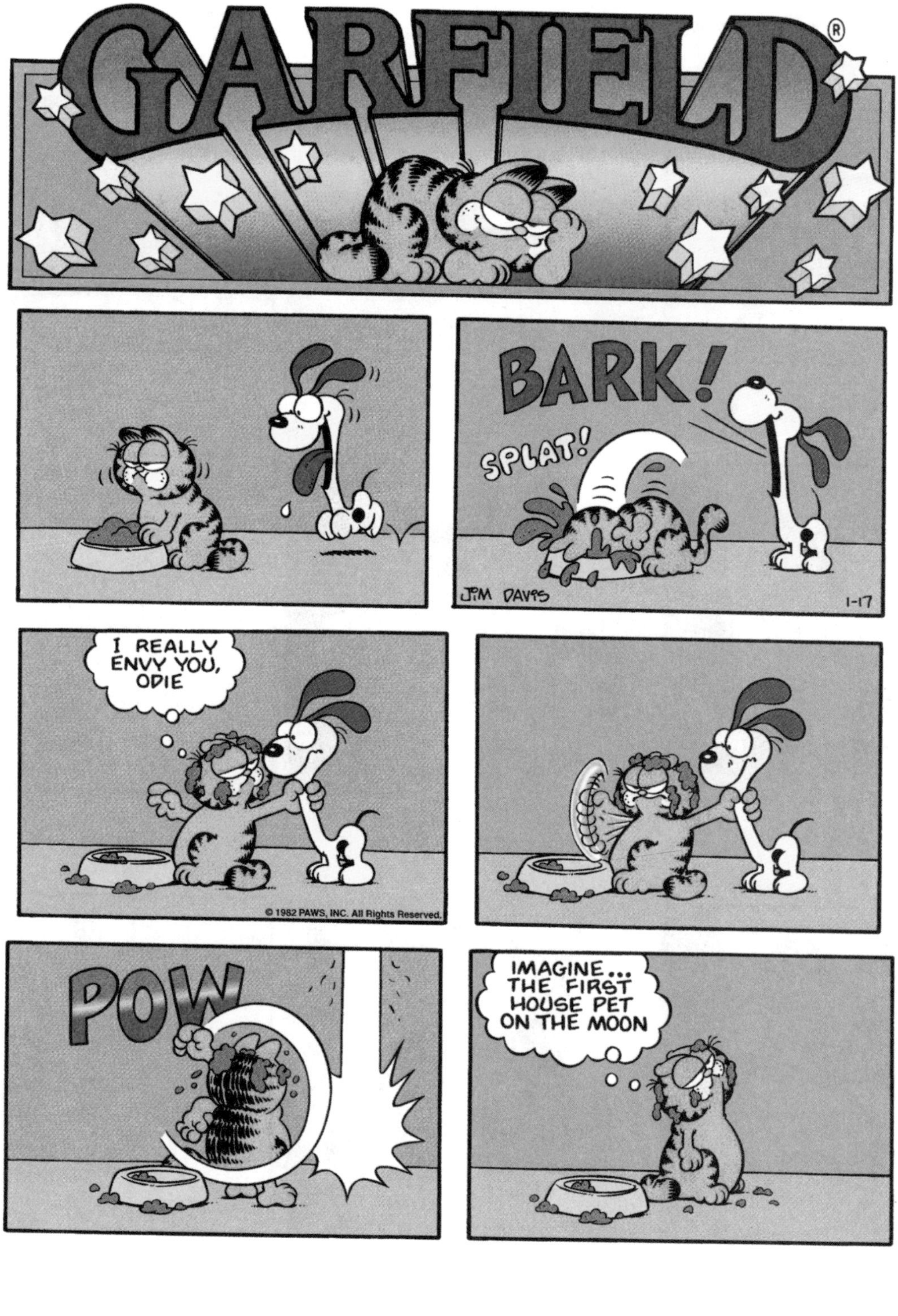
GARFIELD®
BARK!
SPLAT!
JIM DAVIS
1-17
I REALLY ENVY YOU, ODIE
© 1982 PAWS, INC. All Rights Reserved.
POW
IMAGINE... THE FIRST HOUSE PET ON THE MOON

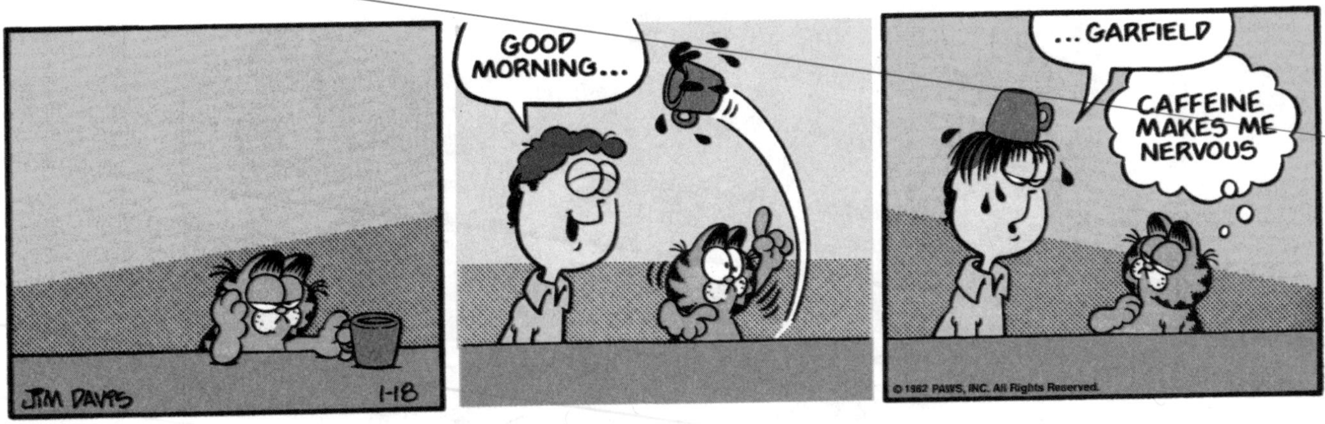
JIM DAVIS
1-18
GOOD MORNING...
...GARFIELD
CAFFEINE MAKES ME NERVOUS
© 1982 PAWS, INC. All Rights Reserved.

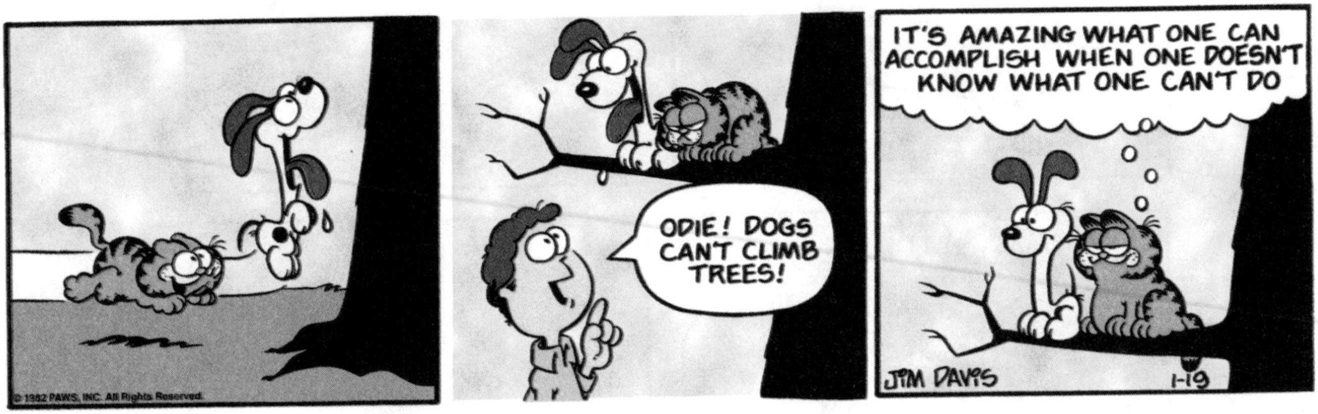
© 1982 PAWS, INC. All Rights Reserved.
ODIE! DOGS CAN'T CLIMB TREES!
IT'S AMAZING WHAT ONE CAN ACCOMPLISH WHEN ONE DOESN'T KNOW WHAT ONE CAN'T DO
JIM DAVIS
1-19

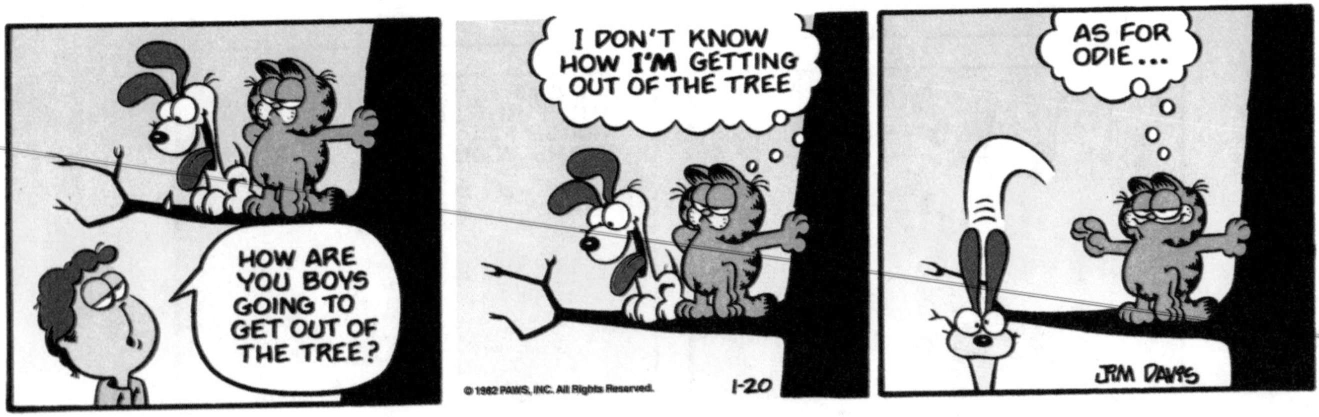
HOW ARE YOU BOYS GOING TO GET OUT OF THE TREE?
I DON'T KNOW HOW **I'M** GETTING OUT OF THE TREE
© 1982 PAWS, INC. All Rights Reserved.
1-20
AS FOR ODIE...
JIM DAVIS

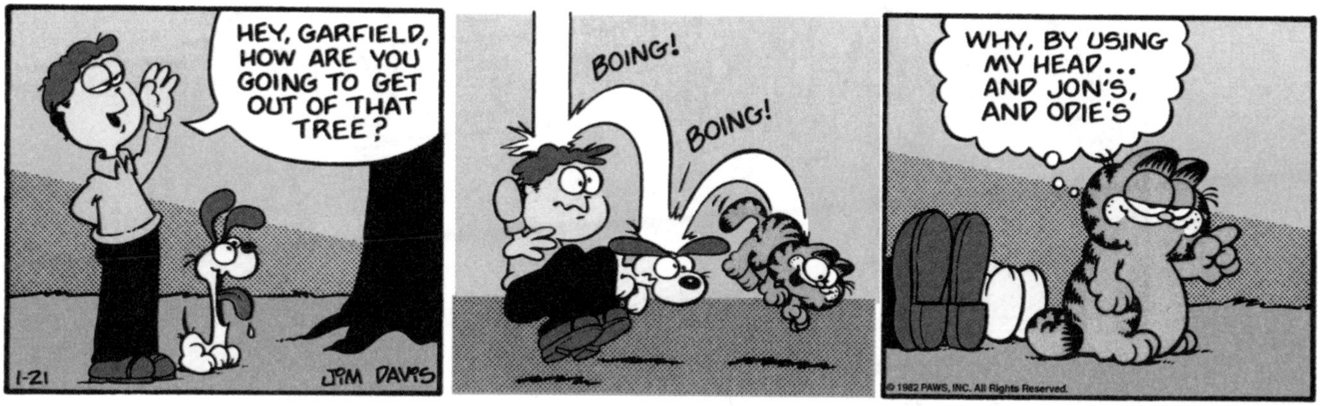
HEY, GARFIELD, HOW ARE YOU GOING TO GET OUT OF THAT TREE?
1-21
JIM DAVIS
BOING!
BOING!
WHY, BY USING MY HEAD... AND JON'S, AND ODIE'S
© 1982 PAWS, INC. All Rights Reserved.

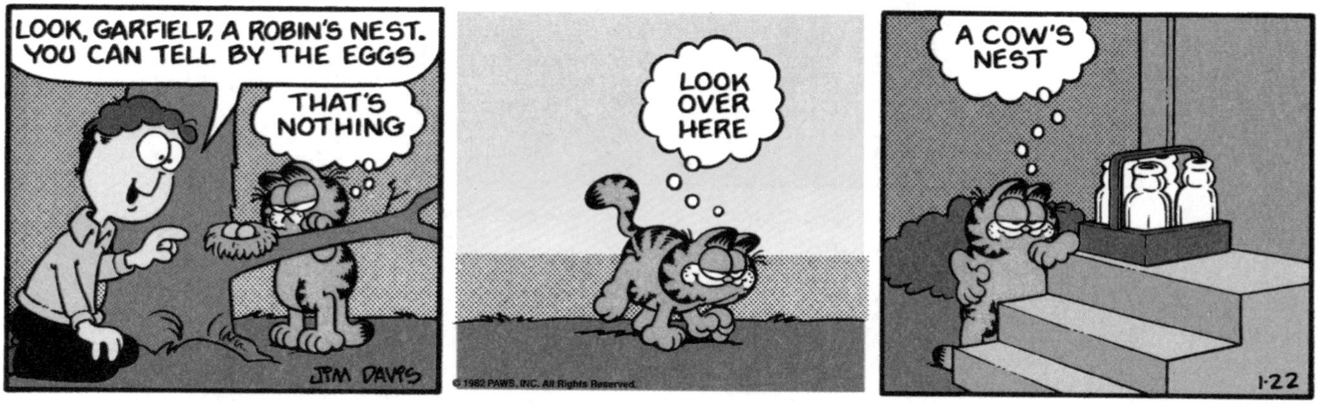
LOOK, GARFIELD, A ROBIN'S NEST. YOU CAN TELL BY THE EGGS
THAT'S NOTHING
JIM DAVIS
LOOK OVER HERE
© 1982 PAWS, INC. All Rights Reserved.
A COW'S NEST
1-22

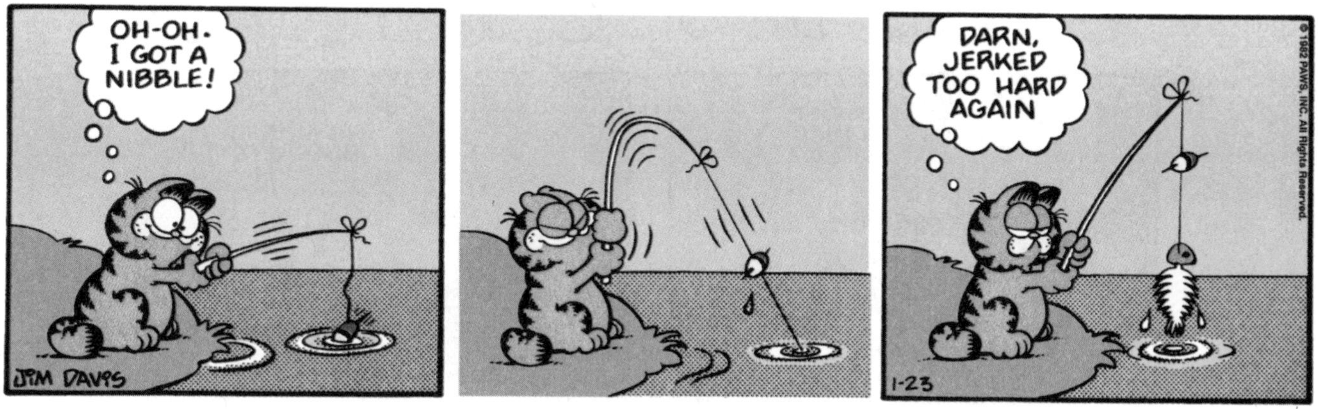
OH-OH. I GOT A NIBBLE!
JIM DAVIS
DARN, JERKED TOO HARD AGAIN
1-23
© 1982 PAWS, INC. All Rights Reserved.

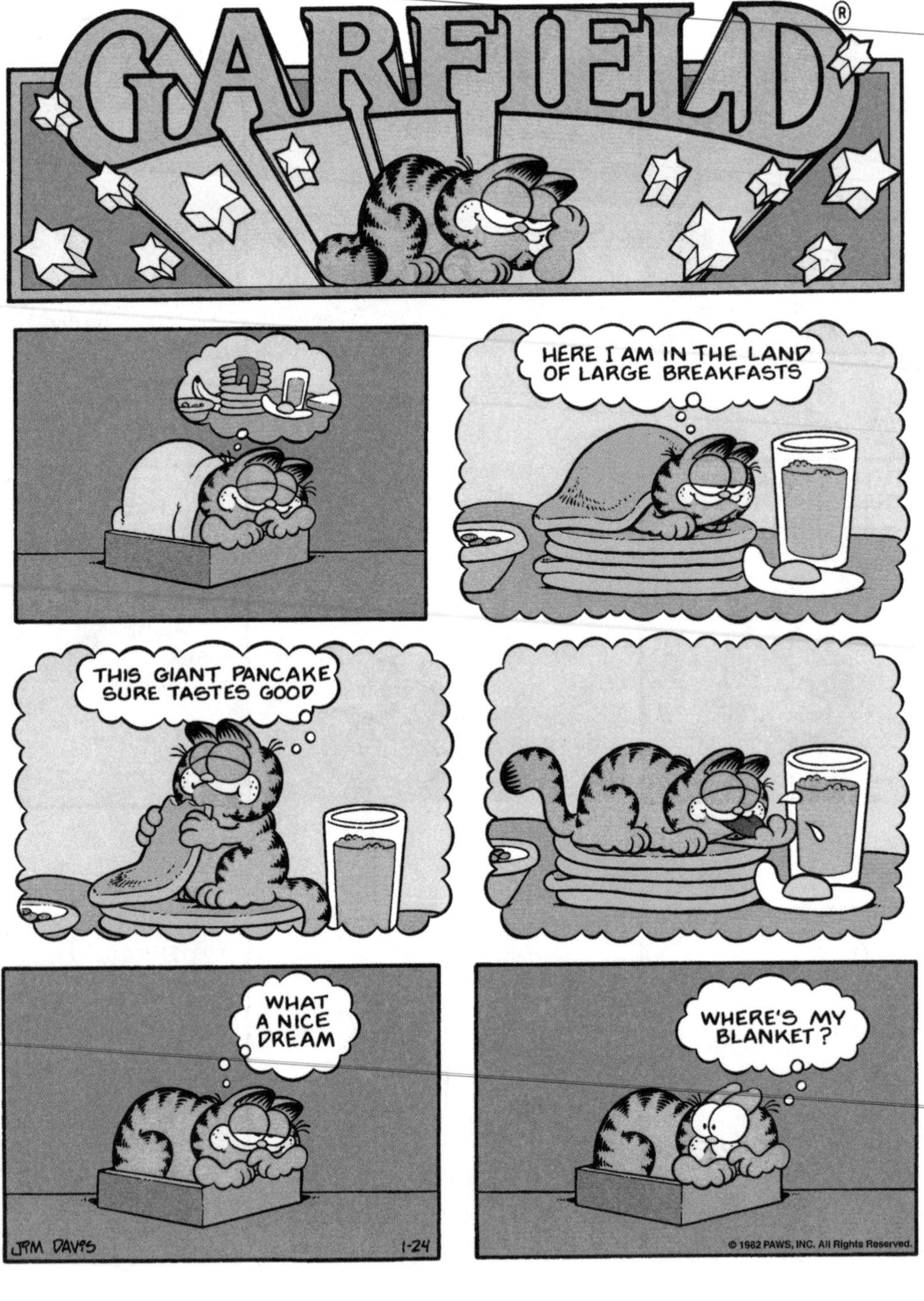
GARFIELD®
HERE I AM IN THE LAND OF LARGE BREAKFASTS
THIS GIANT PANCAKE SURE TASTES GOOD
WHAT A NICE DREAM
WHERE'S MY BLANKET?
JIM DAVIS
1-24
© 1982 PAWS, INC. All Rights Reserved.

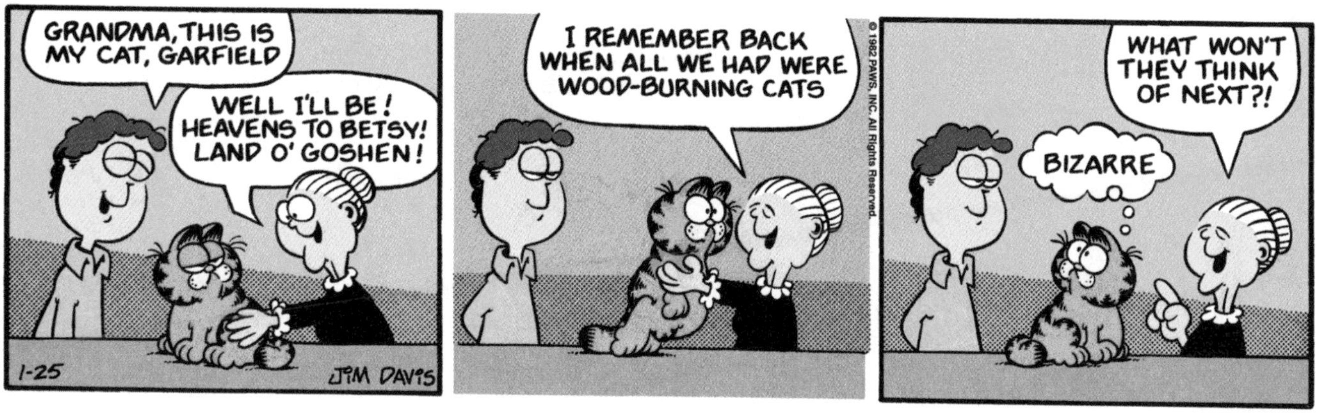
GRANDMA, THIS IS MY CAT, GARFIELD
WELL I'LL BE! HEAVENS TO BETSY! LAND O' GOSHEN!
1-25
JIM DAVIS
I REMEMBER BACK WHEN ALL WE HAD WERE WOOD-BURNING CATS
© 1982 PAWS, INC. All Rights Reserved.
BIZARRE
WHAT WON'T THEY THINK OF NEXT?!

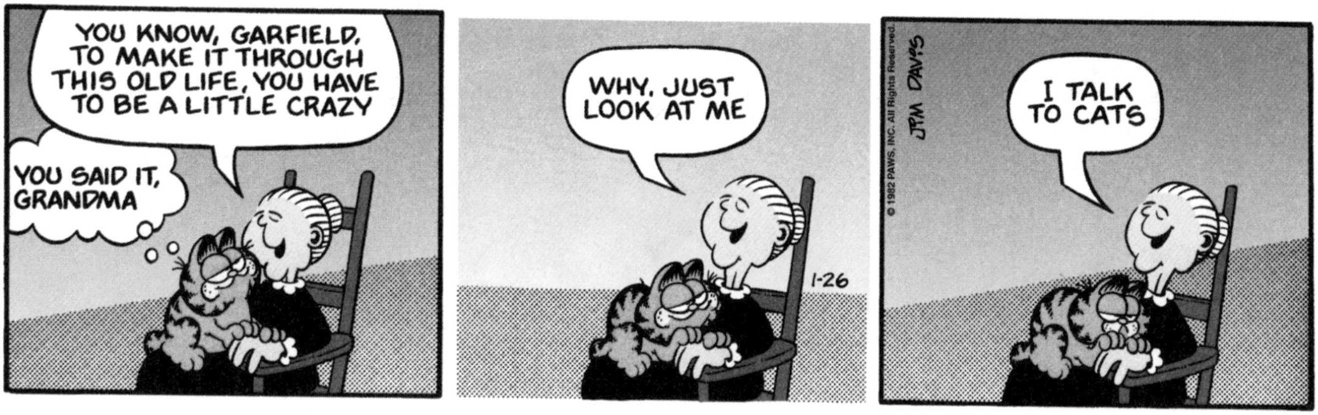
YOU KNOW, GARFIELD, TO MAKE IT THROUGH THIS OLD LIFE, YOU HAVE TO BE A LITTLE CRAZY
YOU SAID IT, GRANDMA
WHY, JUST LOOK AT ME
1-26
© 1982 PAWS, INC. All Rights Reserved.
JIM DAVIS
I TALK TO CATS

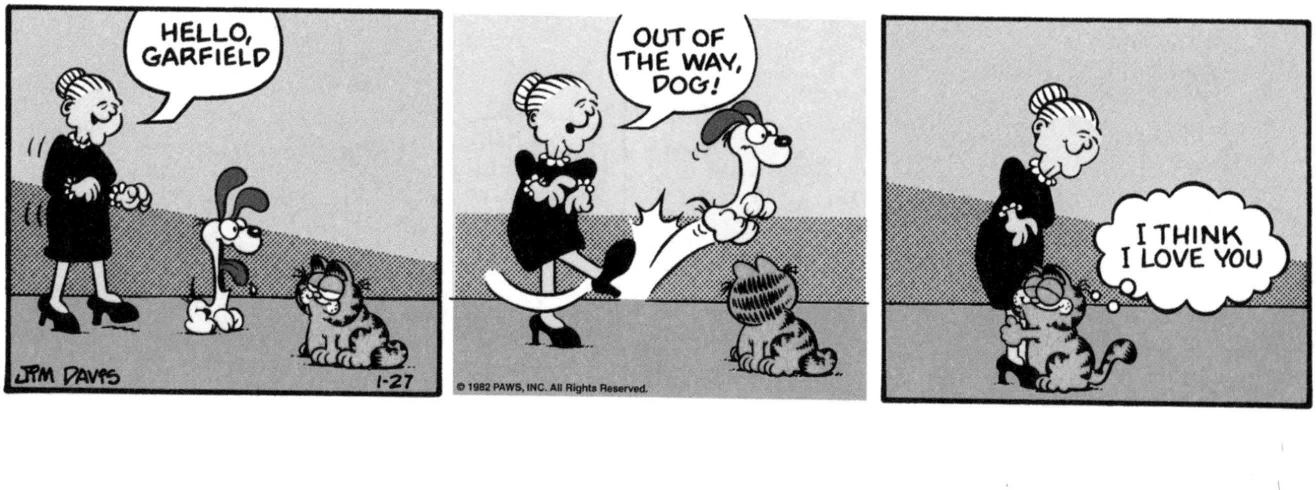
HELLO, GARFIELD
JIM DAVIS
1-27
OUT OF THE WAY, DOG!
© 1982 PAWS, INC. All Rights Reserved.
I THINK I LOVE YOU

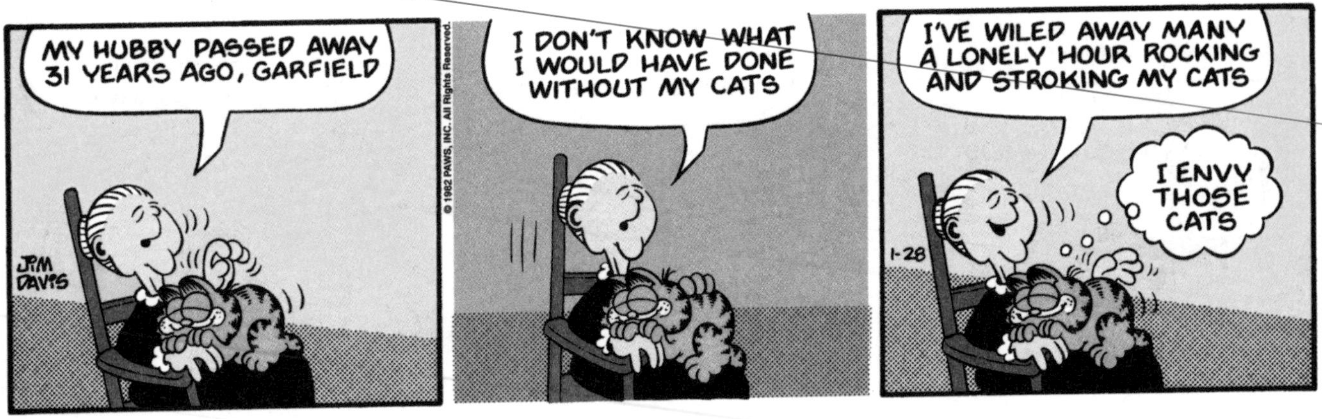
MY HUBBY PASSED AWAY 31 YEARS AGO, GARFIELD
JIM DAVIS
© 1982 PAWS, INC. All Rights Reserved.
I DON'T KNOW WHAT I WOULD HAVE DONE WITHOUT MY CATS
I'VE WILED AWAY MANY A LONELY HOUR ROCKING AND STROKING MY CATS
I ENVY THOSE CATS
1-28

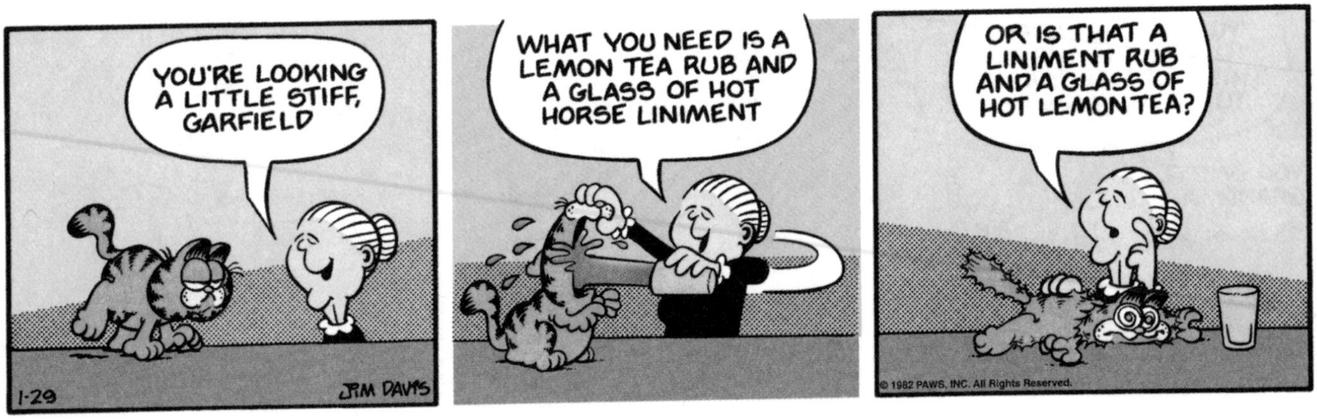
YOU'RE LOOKING A LITTLE STIFF, GARFIELD
1-29
JIM DAVIS
WHAT YOU NEED IS A LEMON TEA RUB AND A GLASS OF HOT HORSE LINIMENT
OR IS THAT A LINIMENT RUB AND A GLASS OF HOT LEMON TEA?
© 1982 PAWS, INC. All Rights Reserved.

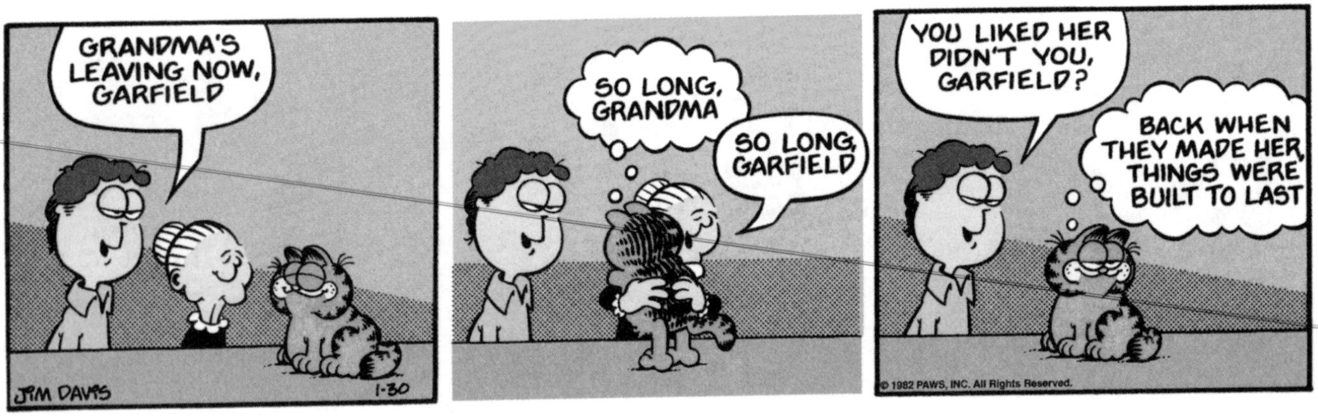
GRANDMA'S LEAVING NOW, GARFIELD
JIM DAVIS
1-30
SO LONG, GRANDMA
SO LONG, GARFIELD
YOU LIKED HER DIDN'T YOU, GARFIELD?
BACK WHEN THEY MADE HER, THINGS WERE BUILT TO LAST
© 1982 PAWS, INC. All Rights Reserved.

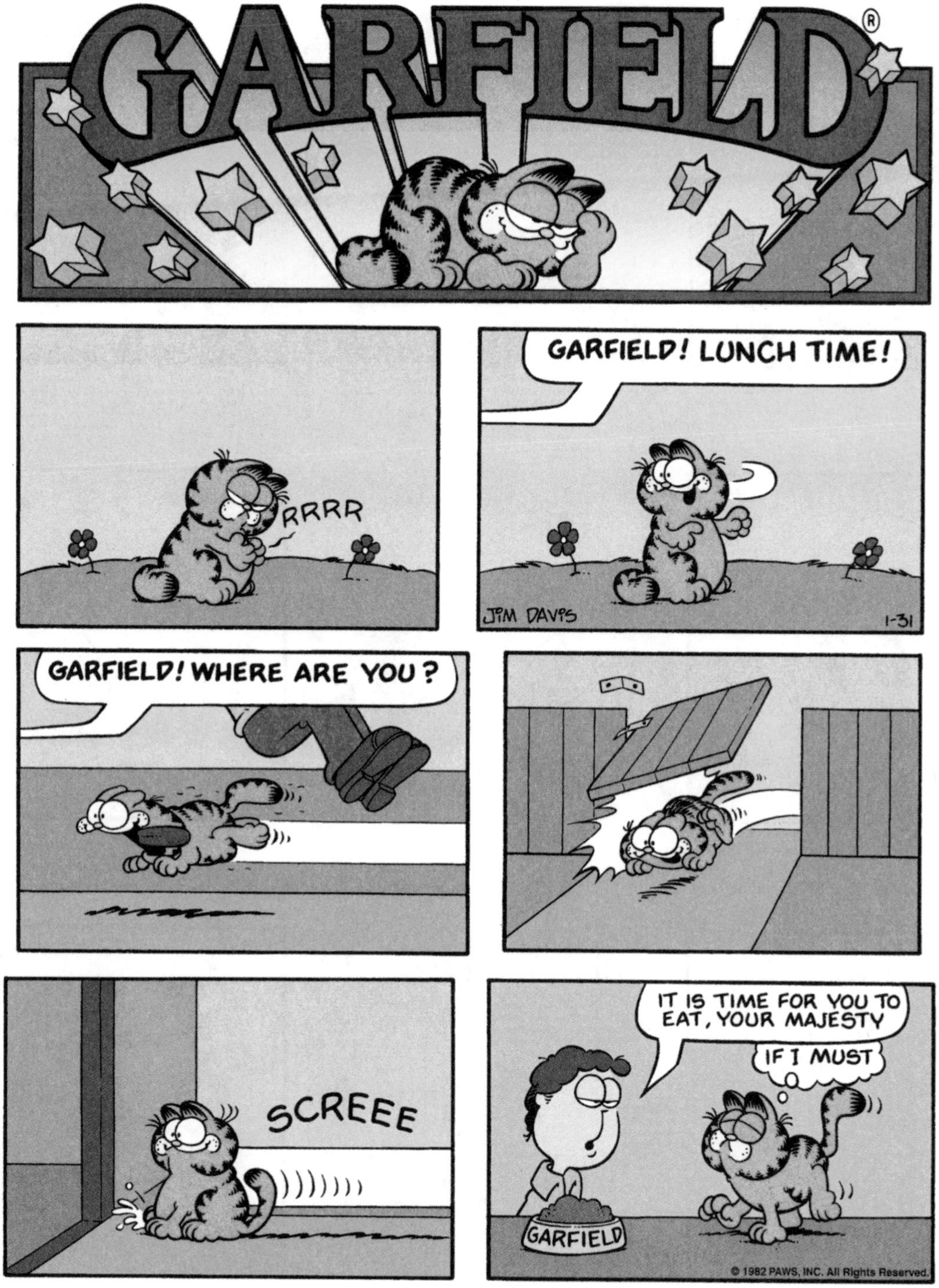
GARFIELD®
RRRR
GARFIELD! LUNCH TIME!
JIM DAVIS
1-31
GARFIELD! WHERE ARE YOU?
SCREEE
IT IS TIME FOR YOU TO EAT, YOUR MAJESTY
IF I MUST
GARFIELD
© 1982 PAWS, INC. All Rights Reserved.

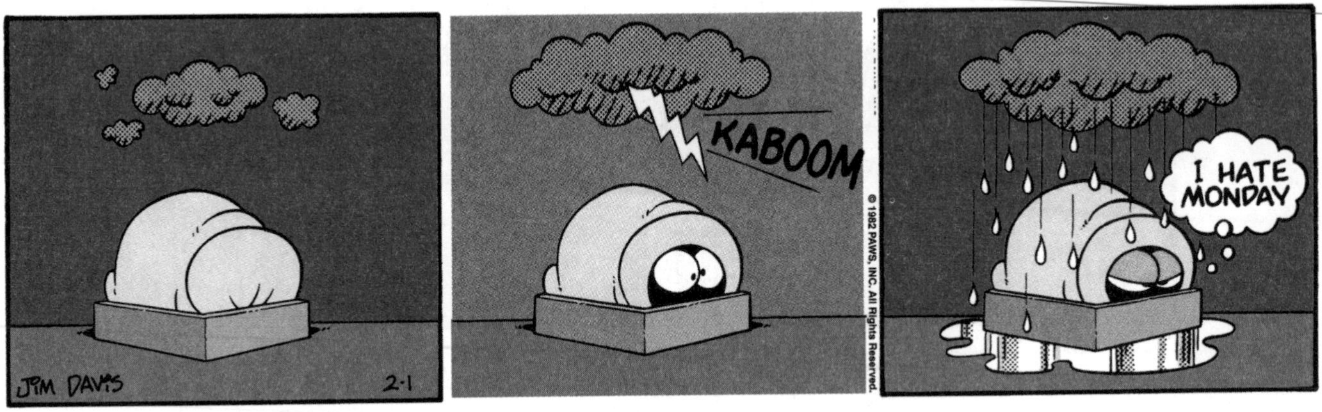
JIM DAVIS
2-1
KABOOM
© 1982 PAWS, INC. All Rights Reserved.
I HATE MONDAY

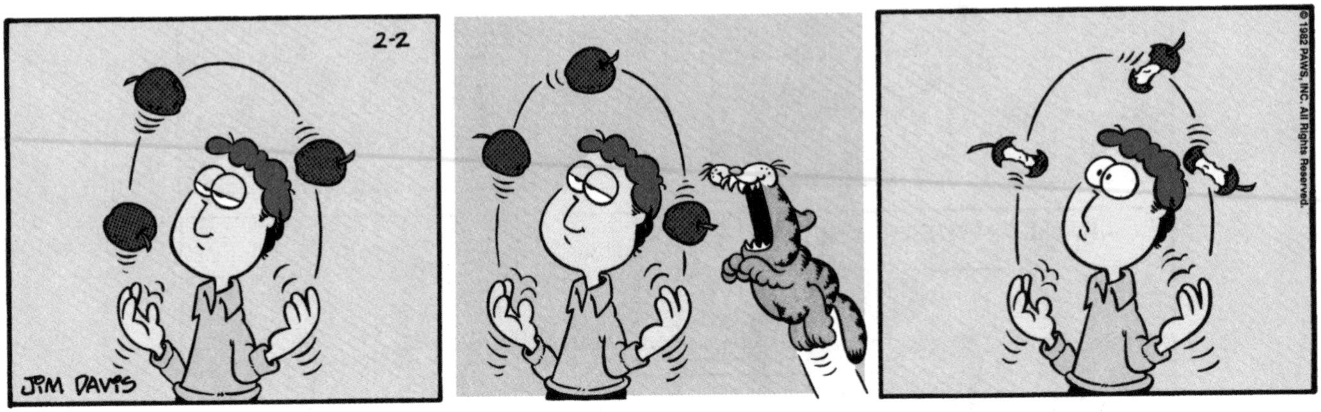
2-2
JIM DAVIS
© 1982 PAWS, INC. All Rights Reserved.

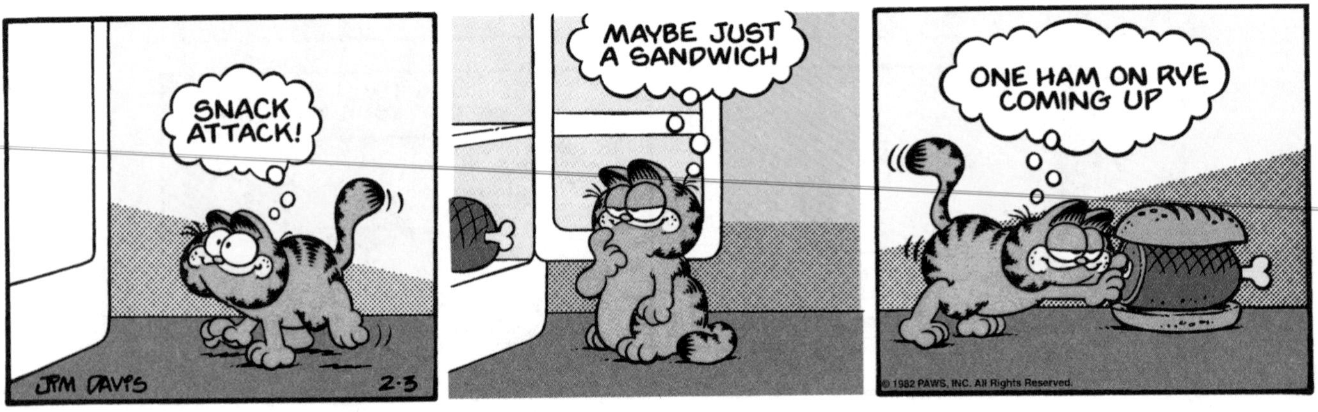
SNACK ATTACK!
JIM DAVIS
2-3
MAYBE JUST A SANDWICH
ONE HAM ON RYE COMING UP
© 1982 PAWS, INC. All Rights Reserved.

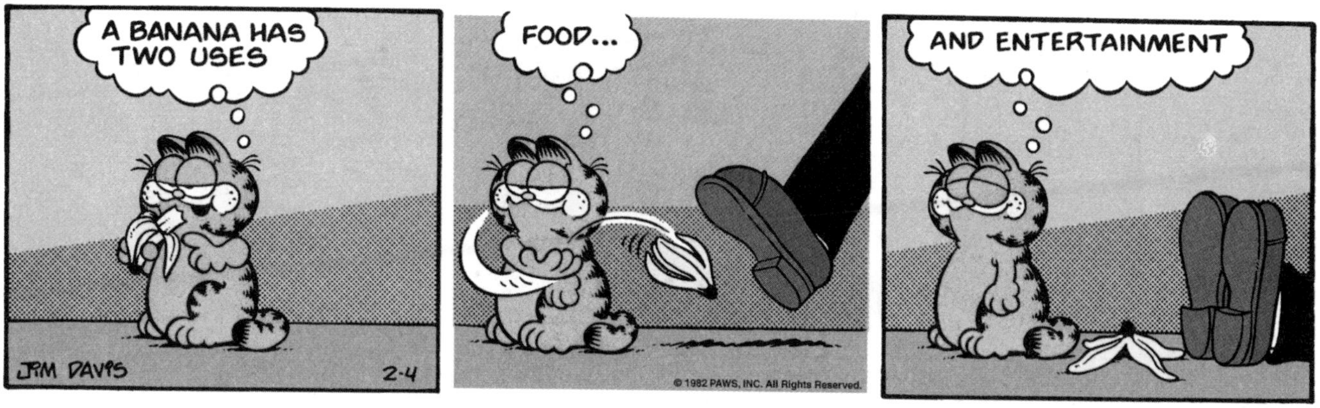
A BANANA HAS TWO USES
JIM DAVIS 2-4
FOOD...
© 1982 PAWS, INC. All Rights Reserved.
AND ENTERTAINMENT

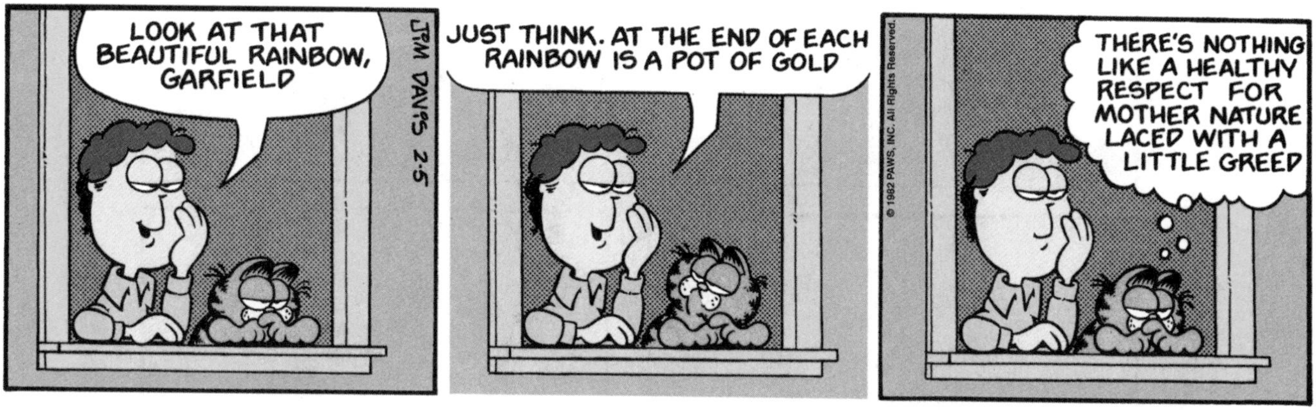
LOOK AT THAT BEAUTIFUL RAINBOW, GARFIELD
JIM DAVIS 2-5
JUST THINK. AT THE END OF EACH RAINBOW IS A POT OF GOLD
© 1982 PAWS, INC. All Rights Reserved.
THERE'S NOTHING LIKE A HEALTHY RESPECT FOR MOTHER NATURE LACED WITH A LITTLE GREED

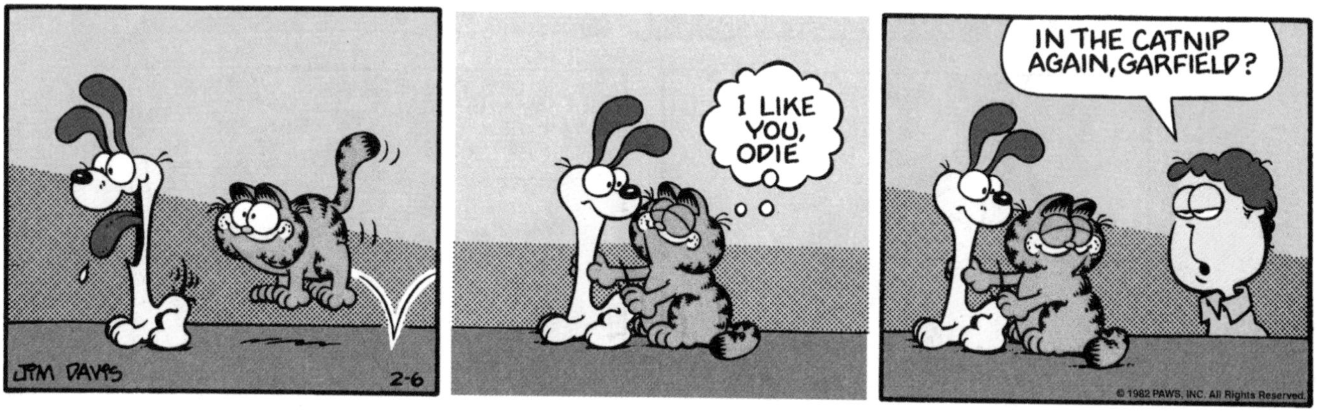
JIM DAVIS 2-6
I LIKE YOU, ODIE
IN THE CATNIP AGAIN, GARFIELD?
© 1982 PAWS, INC. All Rights Reserved.

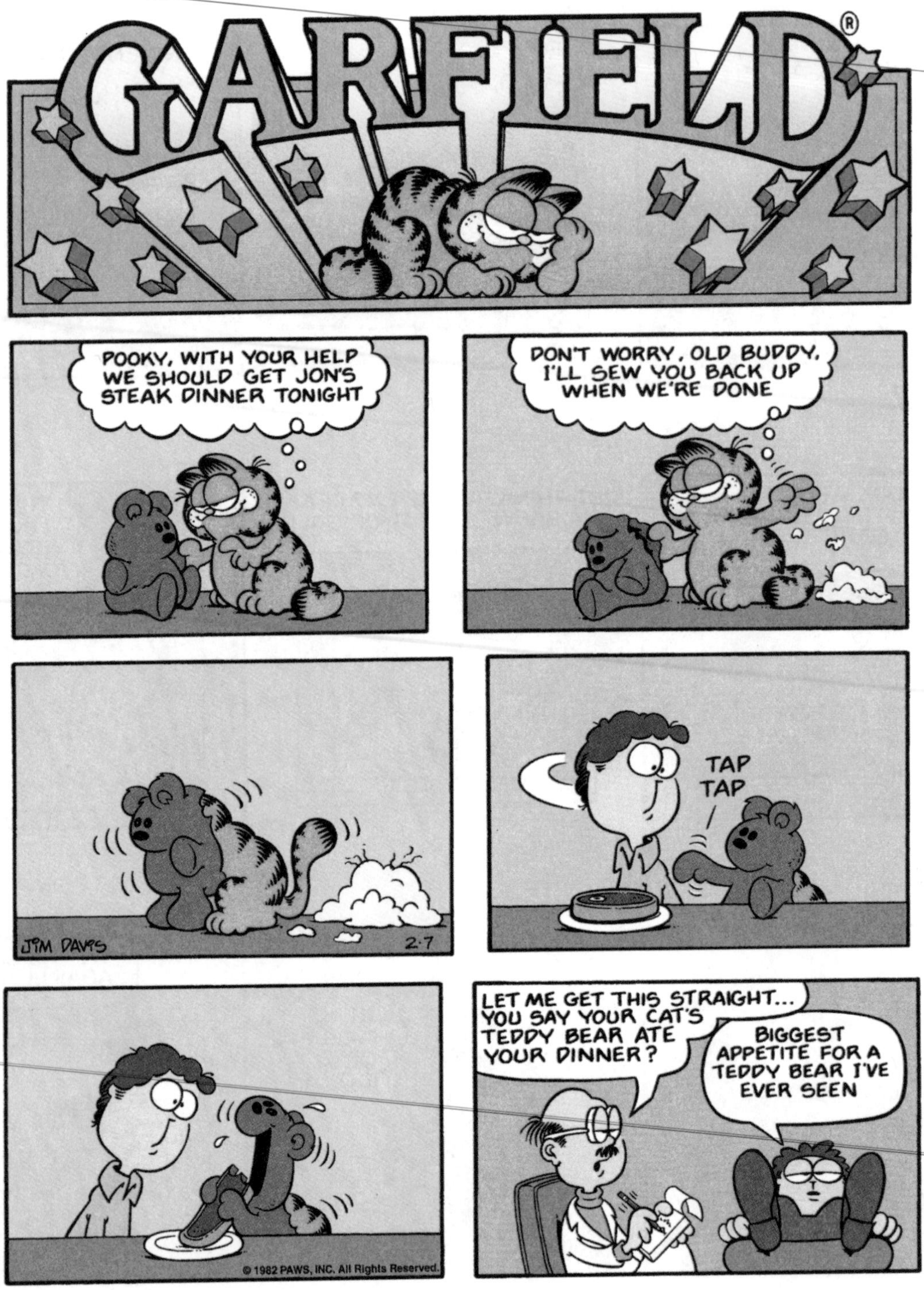
GARFIELD®
POOKY, WITH YOUR HELP WE SHOULD GET JON'S STEAK DINNER TONIGHT
DON'T WORRY, OLD BUDDY, I'LL SEW YOU BACK UP WHEN WE'RE DONE
JIM DAVIS 2-7
TAP TAP
LET ME GET THIS STRAIGHT... YOU SAY YOUR CAT'S TEDDY BEAR ATE YOUR DINNER?
BIGGEST APPETITE FOR A TEDDY BEAR I'VE EVER SEEN
© 1982 PAWS, INC. All Rights Reserved.

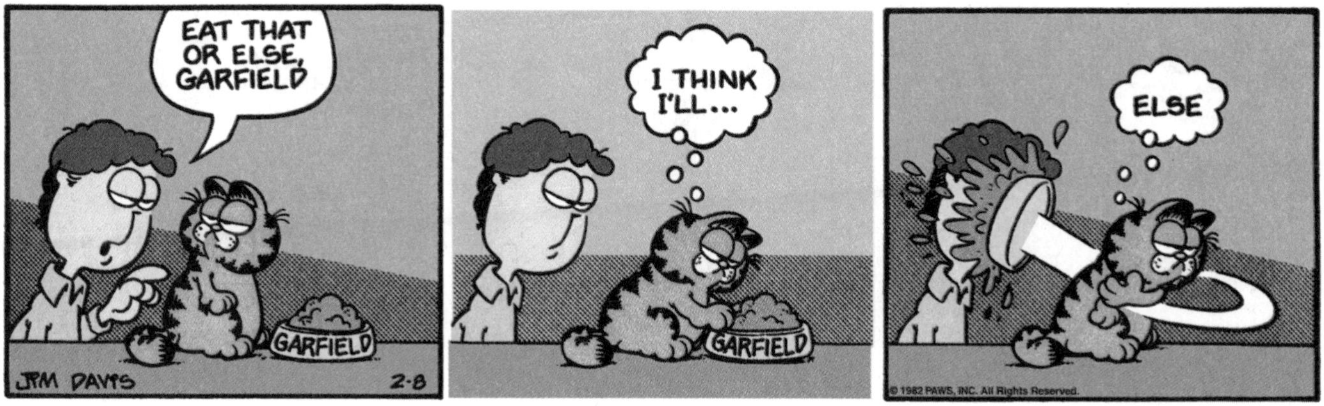
EAT THAT OR ELSE, GARFIELD
GARFIELD
JIM DAVIS
2-8
I THINK I'LL...
GARFIELD
ELSE
© 1982 PAWS, INC. All Rights Reserved.

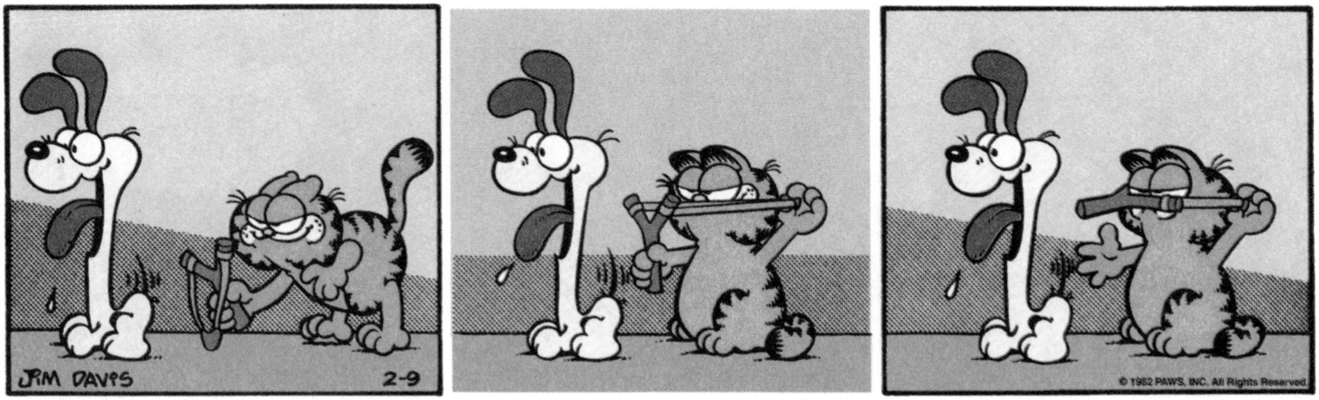
JIM DAVIS
2-9
© 1982 PAWS, INC. All Rights Reserved.

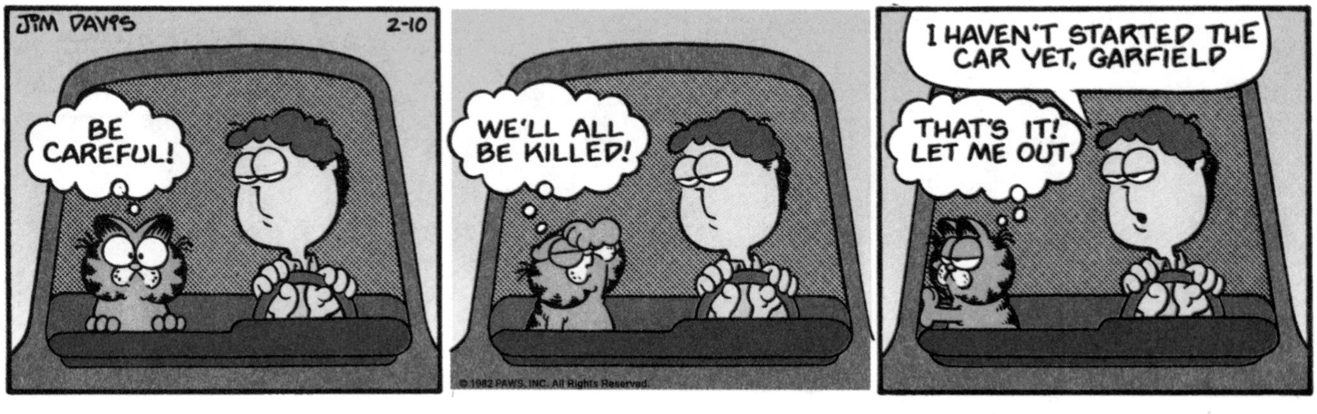
JIM DAVIS
2-10
BE CAREFUL!
WE'LL ALL BE KILLED!
© 1982 PAWS, INC. All Rights Reserved.
I HAVEN'T STARTED THE CAR YET, GARFIELD
THAT'S IT! LET ME OUT

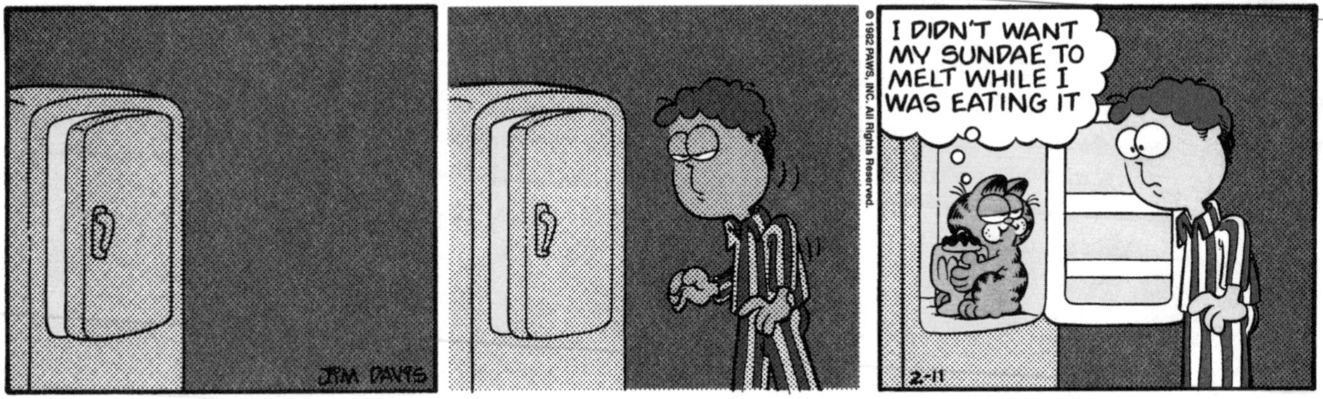
JIM DAVIS
© 1982 PAWS, INC. All Rights Reserved.
I DIDN'T WANT MY SUNDAE TO MELT WHILE I WAS EATING IT
2-11

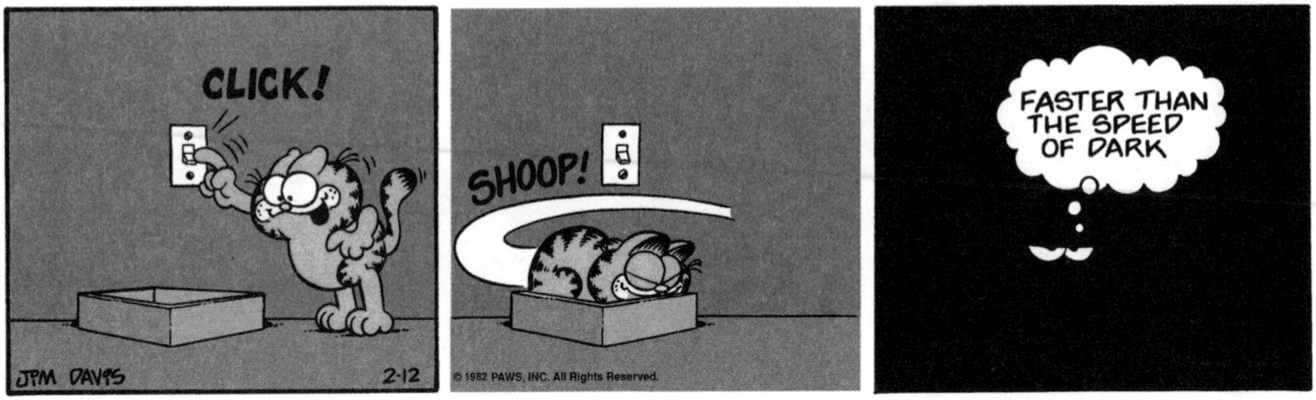
CLICK!
JIM DAVIS
2-12
SHOOP!
© 1982 PAWS, INC. All Rights Reserved.
FASTER THAN THE SPEED OF DARK

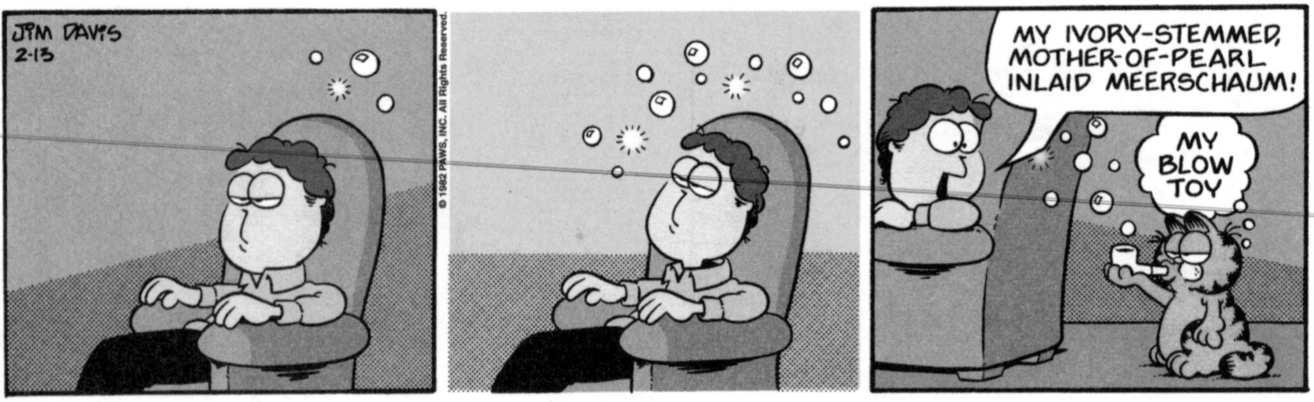
JIM DAVIS
2-13
© 1982 PAWS, INC. All Rights Reserved.
MY IVORY-STEMMED, MOTHER-OF-PEARL INLAID MEERSCHAUM!
MY BLOW TOY

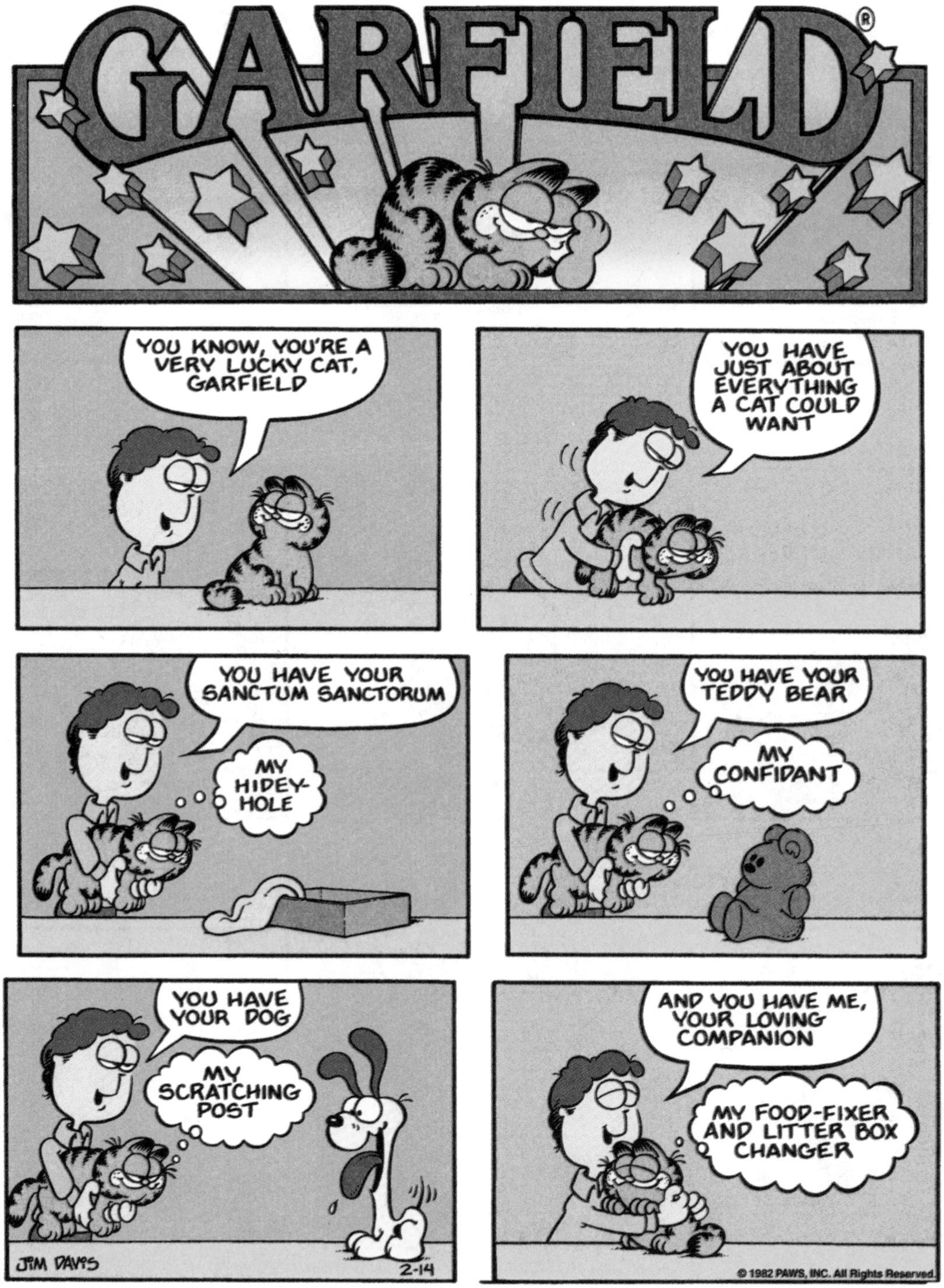
GARFIELD
YOU KNOW, YOU'RE A VERY LUCKY CAT, GARFIELD
YOU HAVE JUST ABOUT EVERYTHING A CAT COULD WANT
YOU HAVE YOUR SANCTUM SANCTORUM
MY HIDEY-HOLE
YOU HAVE YOUR TEDDY BEAR
MY CONFIDANT
YOU HAVE YOUR DOG
MY SCRATCHING POST
AND YOU HAVE ME, YOUR LOVING COMPANION
MY FOOD-FIXER AND LITTER BOX CHANGER
JIM DAVIS
2-14
© 1982 PAWS, INC. All Rights Reserved.

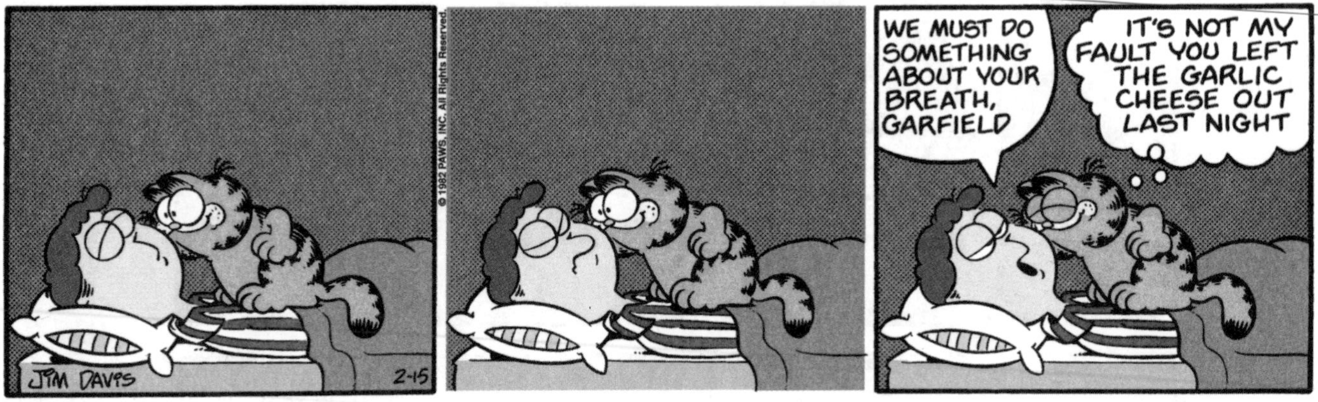
JIM DAVIS
2-15
© 1982 PAWS, INC. All Rights Reserved.
WE MUST DO SOMETHING ABOUT YOUR BREATH, GARFIELD
IT'S NOT MY FAULT YOU LEFT THE GARLIC CHEESE OUT LAST NIGHT

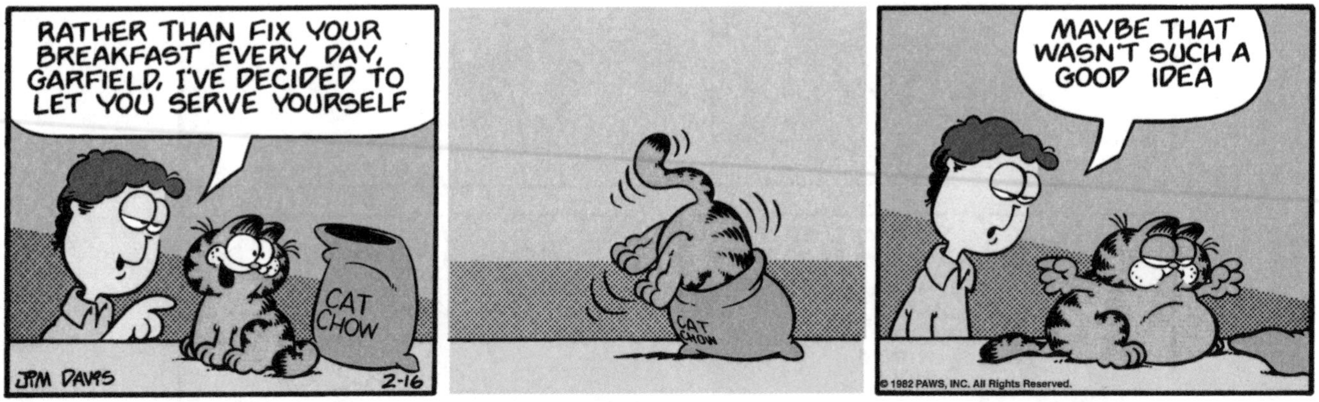
RATHER THAN FIX YOUR BREAKFAST EVERY DAY, GARFIELD, I'VE DECIDED TO LET YOU SERVE YOURSELF
CAT CHOW
JIM DAVIS
2-16
CAT CHOW
MAYBE THAT WASN'T SUCH A GOOD IDEA
© 1982 PAWS, INC. All Rights Reserved.

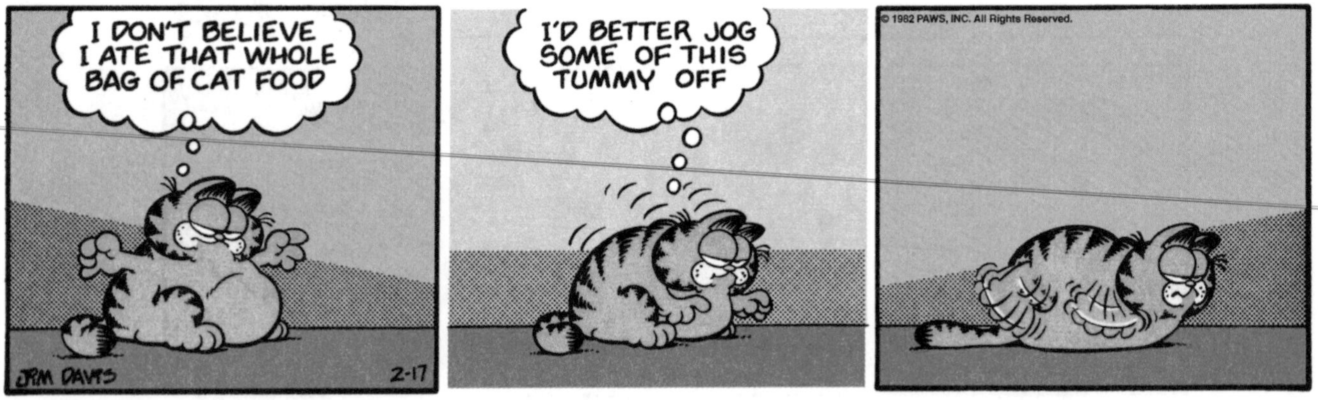
I DON'T BELIEVE I ATE THAT WHOLE BAG OF CAT FOOD
JIM DAVIS
2-17
I'D BETTER JOG SOME OF THIS TUMMY OFF
© 1982 PAWS, INC. All Rights Reserved.

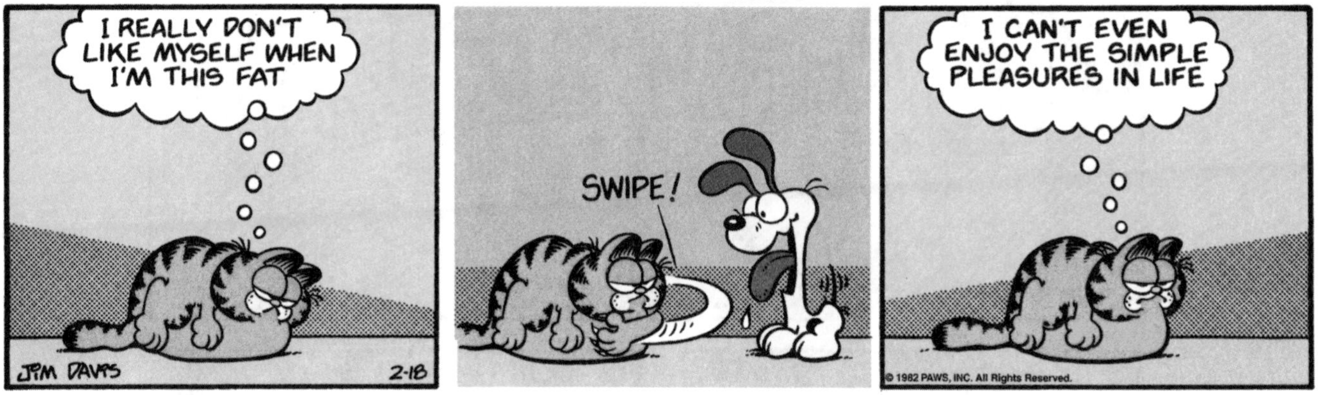
I REALLY DON'T LIKE MYSELF WHEN I'M THIS FAT
JIM DAVIS
2-18
SWIPE!
I CAN'T EVEN ENJOY THE SIMPLE PLEASURES IN LIFE
© 1982 PAWS, INC. All Rights Reserved.

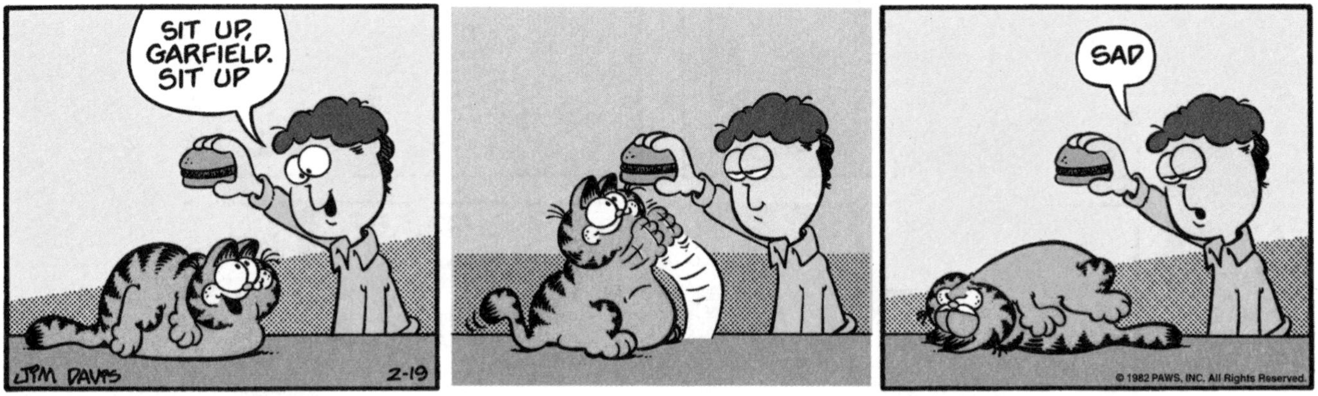
SIT UP, GARFIELD. SIT UP
JIM DAVIS
2-19
SAD
© 1982 PAWS, INC. All Rights Reserved.

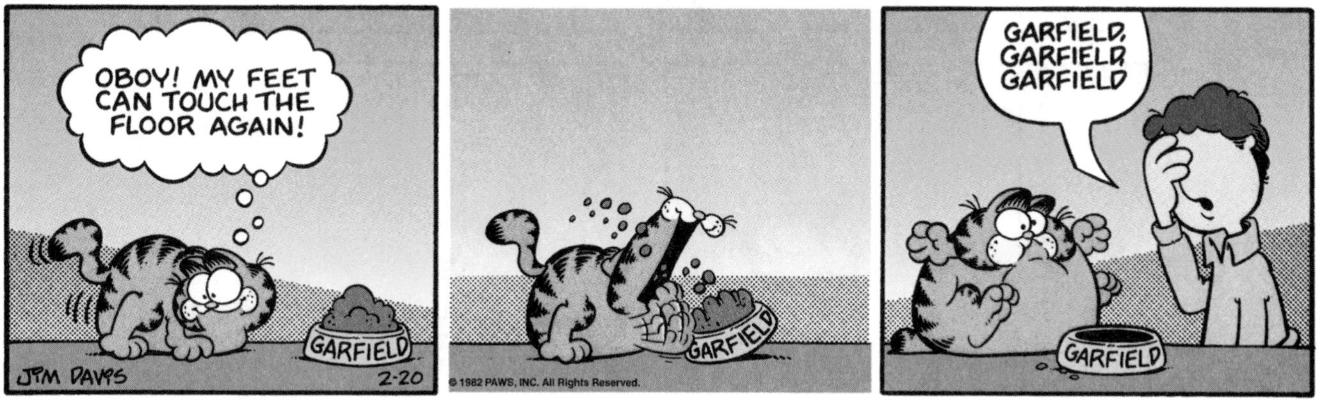
OBOY! MY FEET CAN TOUCH THE FLOOR AGAIN!
GARFIELD
JIM DAVIS
2-20
GARFIELD
© 1982 PAWS, INC. All Rights Reserved.
GARFIELD, GARFIELD, GARFIELD
GARFIELD

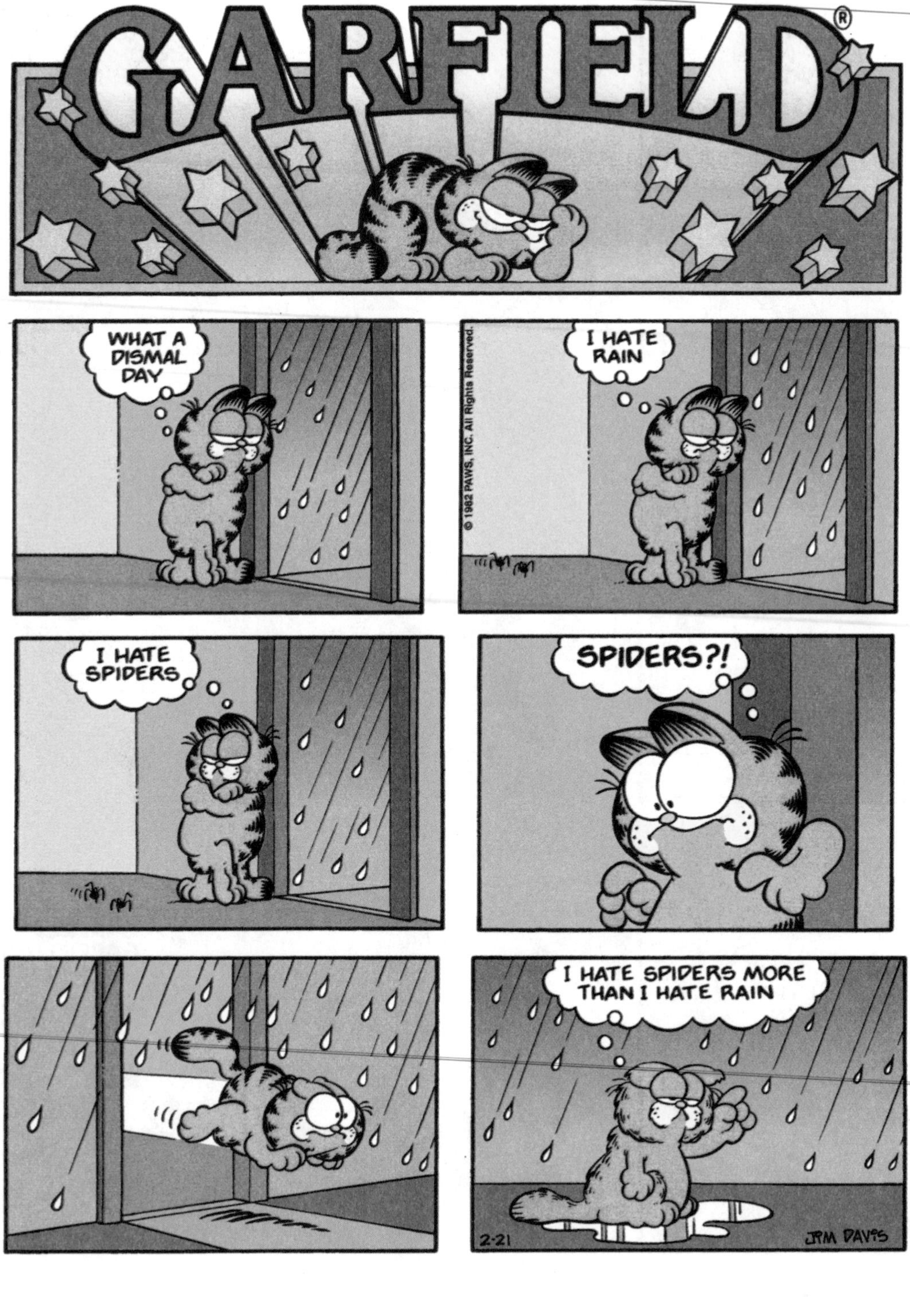
GARFIELD®
WHAT A DISMAL DAY
I HATE RAIN
© 1982 PAWS, INC. All Rights Reserved.
I HATE SPIDERS
SPIDERS?!
I HATE SPIDERS MORE THAN I HATE RAIN
2-21
JIM DAVIS

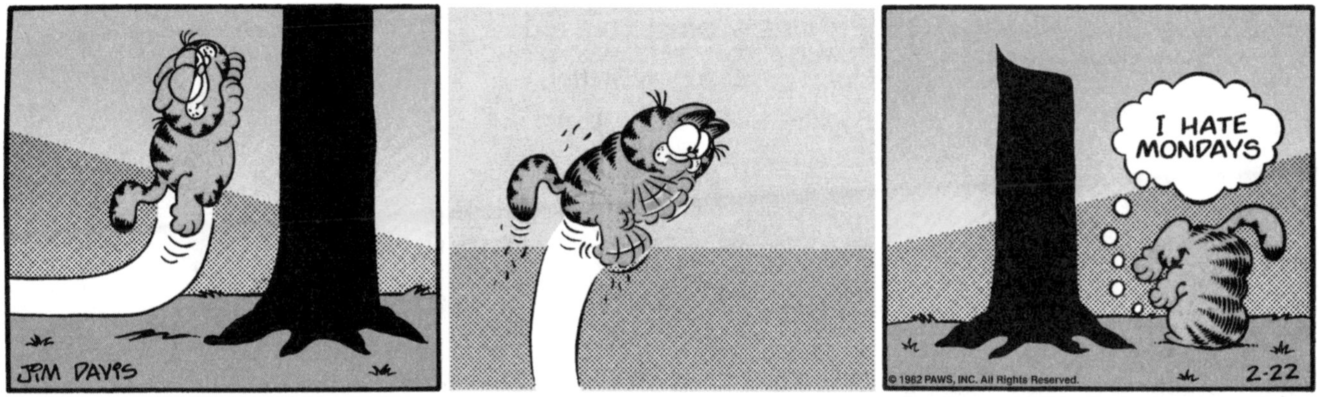
JIM DAVIS
I HATE MONDAYS
© 1982 PAWS, INC. All Rights Reserved.
2-22

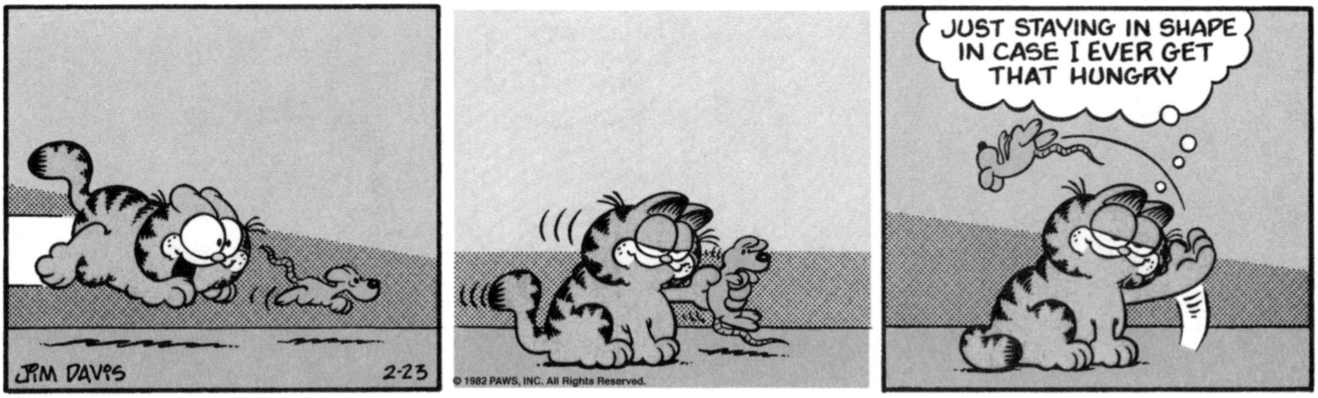
JIM DAVIS
2-23
© 1982 PAWS, INC. All Rights Reserved.
JUST STAYING IN SHAPE IN CASE I EVER GET THAT HUNGRY

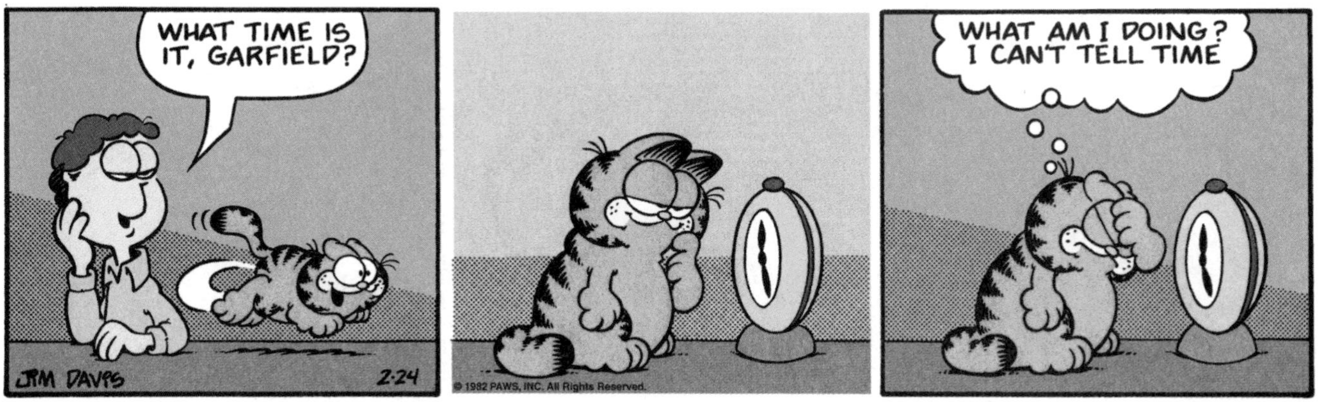
WHAT TIME IS IT, GARFIELD?
JIM DAVIS
2-24
© 1982 PAWS, INC. All Rights Reserved.
WHAT AM I DOING? I CAN'T TELL TIME

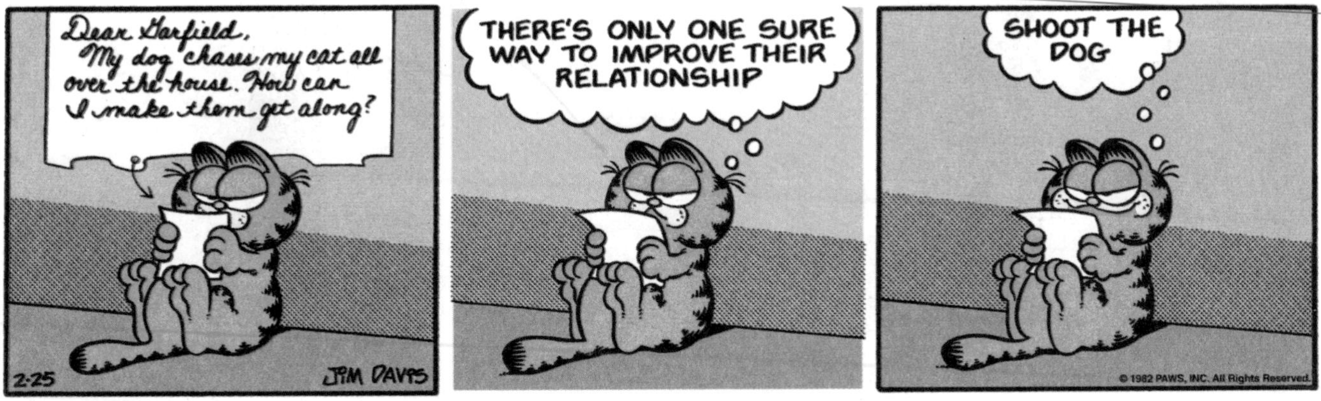
Dear Garfield,
My dog chases my cat all over the house. How can I make them get along?
2-25
JIM DAVIS
THERE'S ONLY ONE SURE WAY TO IMPROVE THEIR RELATIONSHIP
SHOOT THE DOG
© 1982 PAWS, INC. All Rights Reserved.

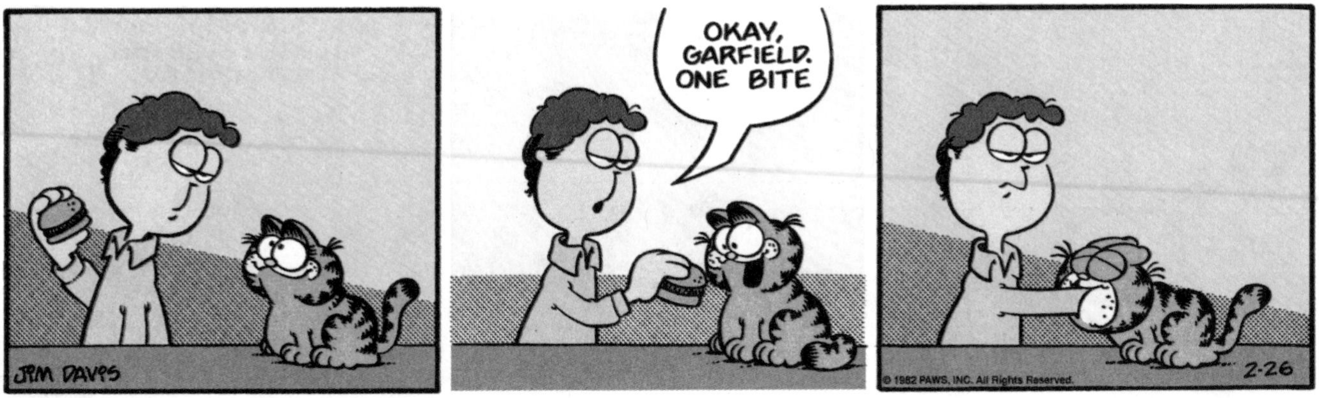
JIM DAVIS
OKAY, GARFIELD. ONE BITE
© 1982 PAWS, INC. All Rights Reserved.
2-26

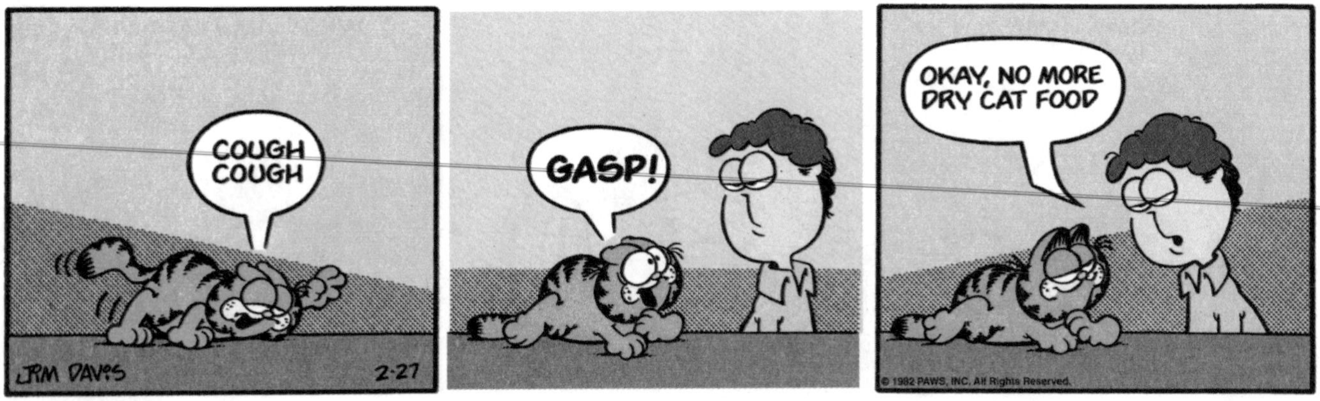
COUGH COUGH
JIM DAVIS
2-27
GASP!
OKAY, NO MORE DRY CAT FOOD
© 1982 PAWS, INC. All Rights Reserved.

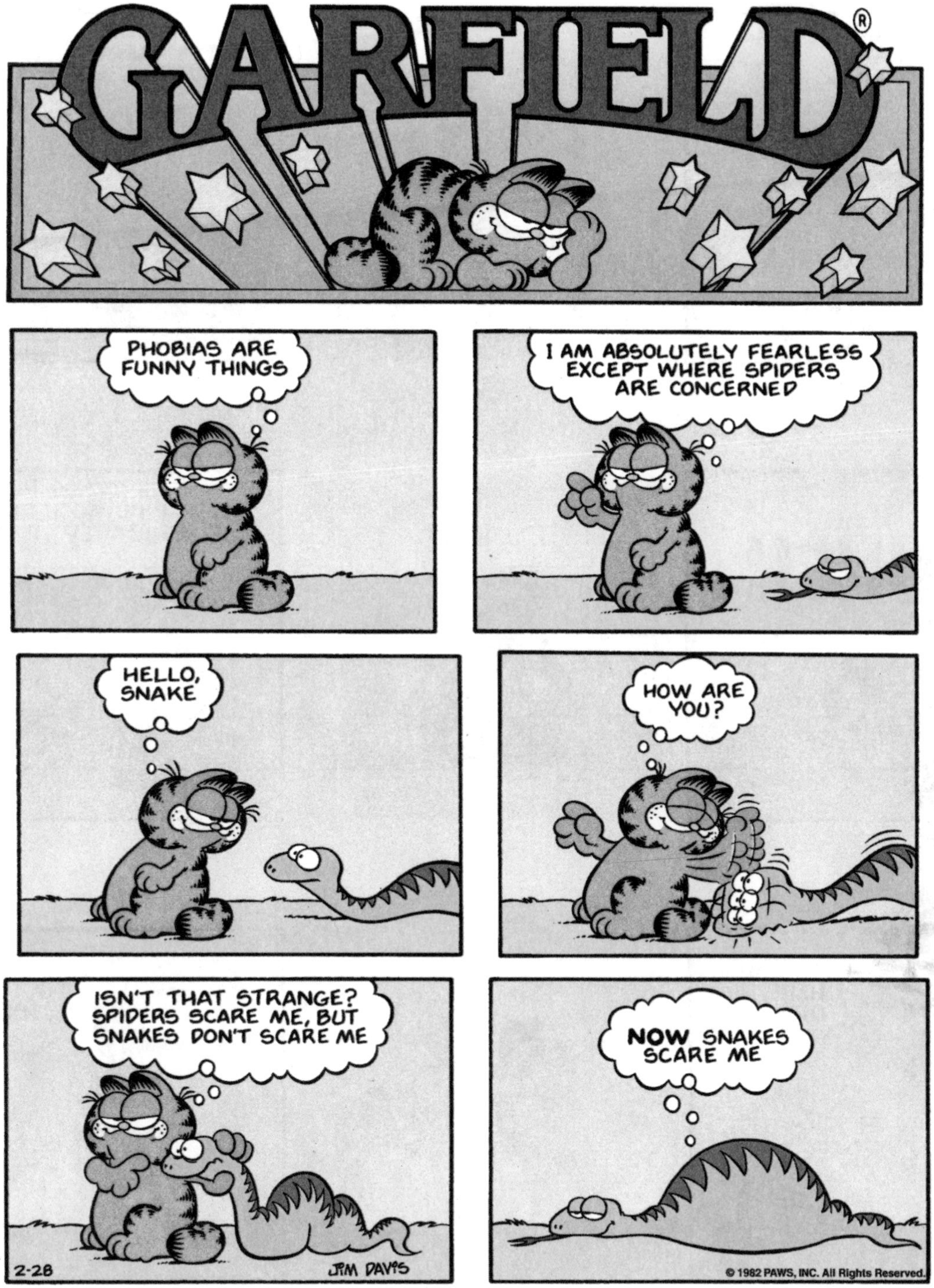
GARFIELD®
PHOBIAS ARE FUNNY THINGS
I AM ABSOLUTELY FEARLESS EXCEPT WHERE SPIDERS ARE CONCERNED
HELLO, SNAKE
HOW ARE YOU?
ISN'T THAT STRANGE? SPIDERS SCARE ME, BUT SNAKES DON'T SCARE ME
NOW SNAKES SCARE ME
2-28
JIM DAVIS
© 1982 PAWS, INC. All Rights Reserved.

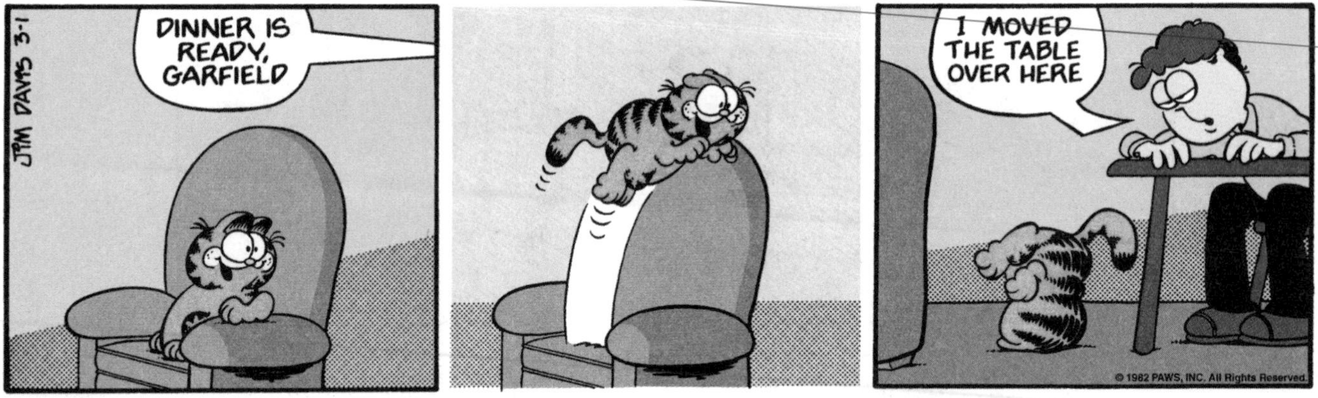
JIM DAVIS 3-1
DINNER IS READY, GARFIELD
I MOVED THE TABLE OVER HERE
© 1982 PAWS, INC. All Rights Reserved.

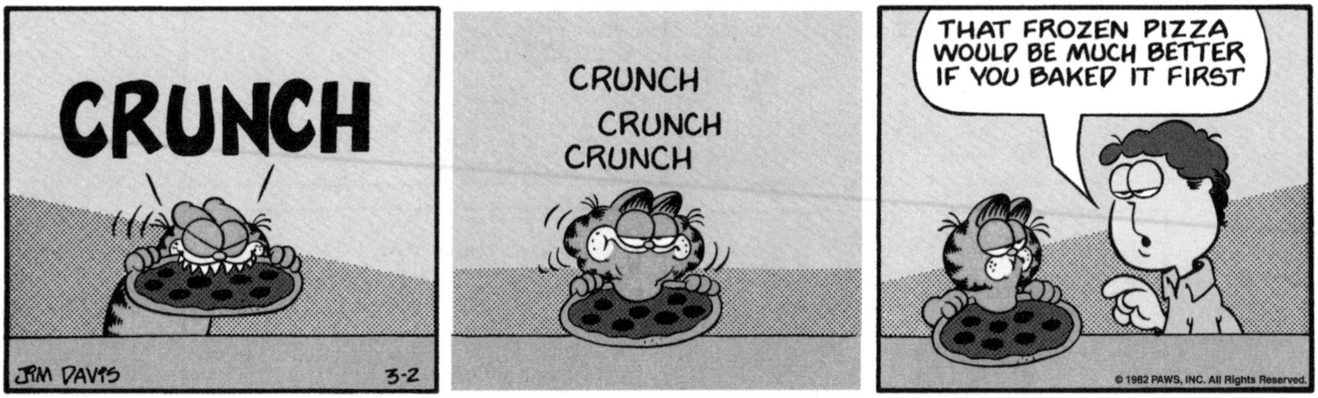
CRUNCH
JIM DAVIS 3-2
CRUNCH
CRUNCH
CRUNCH
THAT FROZEN PIZZA WOULD BE MUCH BETTER IF YOU BAKED IT FIRST
© 1982 PAWS, INC. All Rights Reserved.

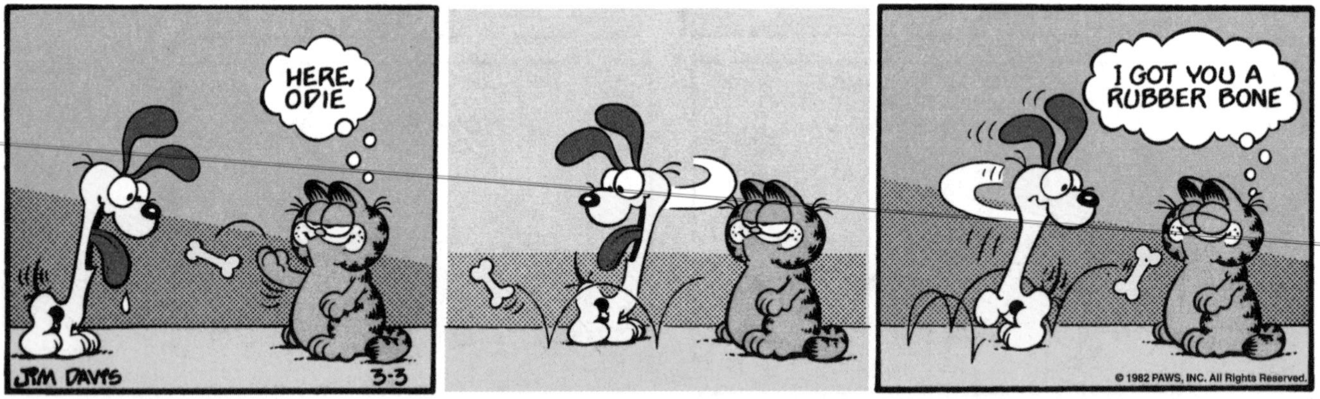
HERE, ODIE
JIM DAVIS 3-3
I GOT YOU A RUBBER BONE
© 1982 PAWS, INC. All Rights Reserved.

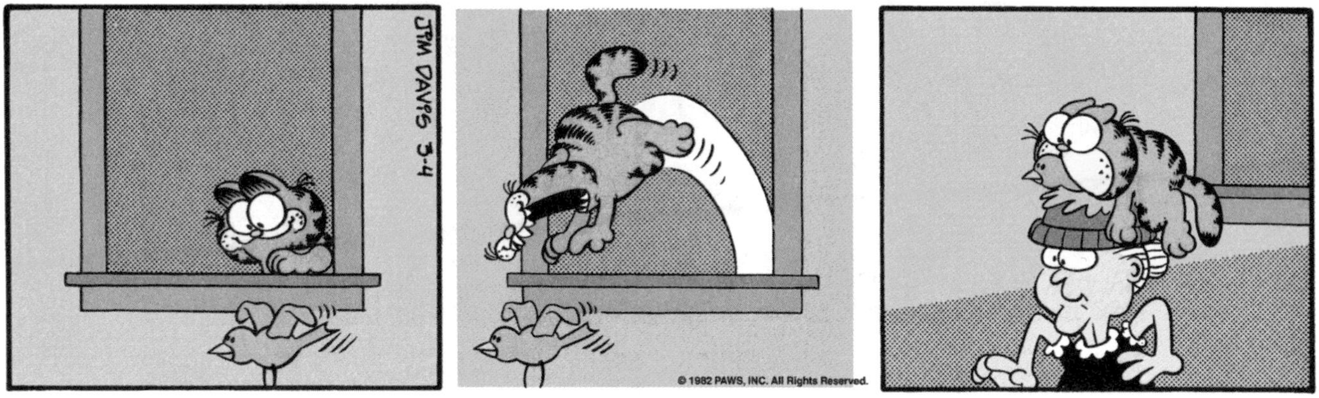
JIM DAVIS 3-4
© 1982 PAWS, INC. All Rights Reserved.

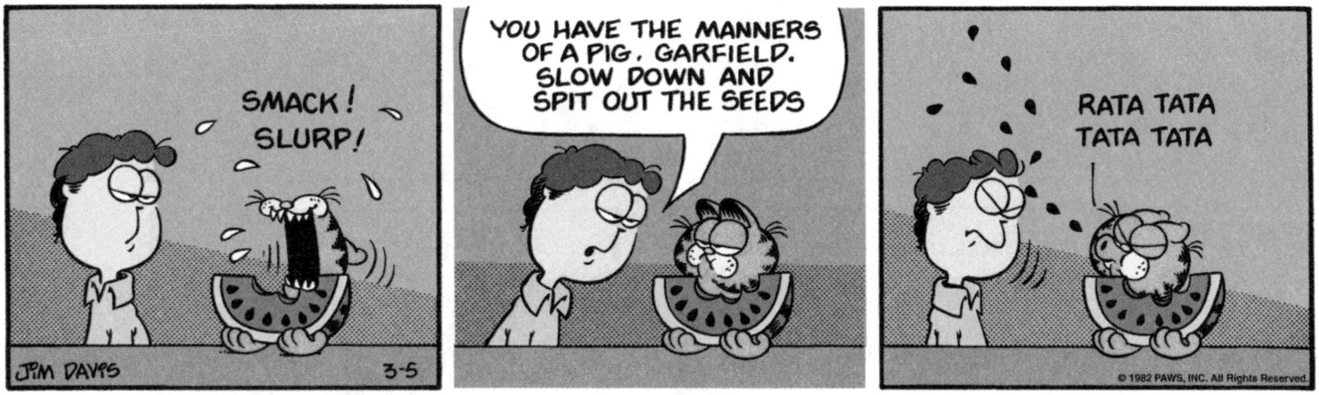
SMACK! SLURP!
JIM DAVIS 3-5
YOU HAVE THE MANNERS OF A PIG, GARFIELD. SLOW DOWN AND SPIT OUT THE SEEDS
RATA TATA TATA TATA
© 1982 PAWS, INC. All Rights Reserved.

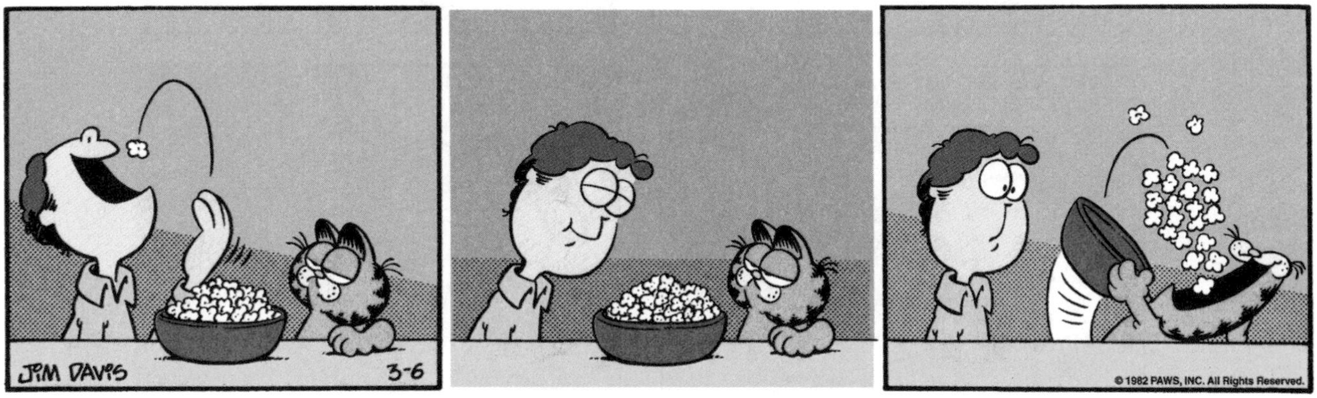
JIM DAVIS 3-6
© 1982 PAWS, INC. All Rights Reserved.

GARFIELD®
WHAT DO YOU THINK, GARFIELD?
DON'T ASK
THERE'S NOTHING LIKE CAMPING OUT IN COLD WEATHER
THAT'S FOR SURE
JIM DAVIS
3-7
AS THE TEMPERATURE DROPS, THE CIRCULATION GETS GOING
AND THE FEET GET NUMB
© 1982 PAWS, INC. All Rights Reserved.
THIS IS NATURE AT HER BEST!
I'D SETTLE FOR LESS
WE HAVE EVERYTHING... OUR FIRE, OUR SHELTER...
OUR COFFEE ON A STICK

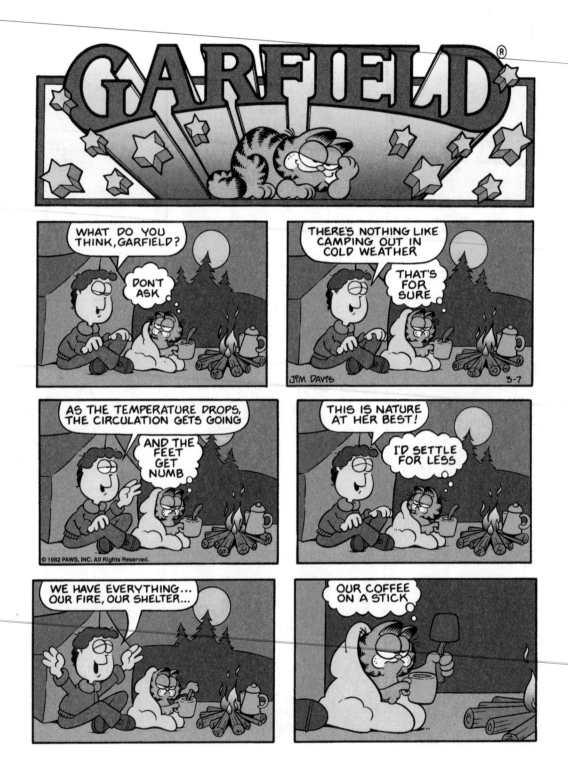

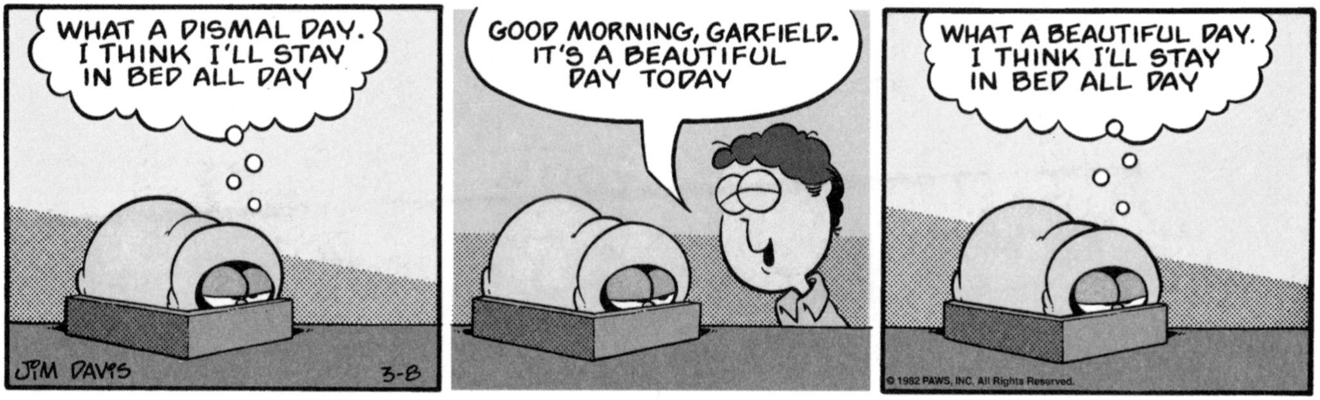
WHAT A DISMAL DAY. I THINK I'LL STAY IN BED ALL DAY
JIM DAVIS
3-8
GOOD MORNING, GARFIELD. IT'S A BEAUTIFUL DAY TODAY
WHAT A BEAUTIFUL DAY. I THINK I'LL STAY IN BED ALL DAY
© 1982 PAWS, INC. All Rights Reserved.

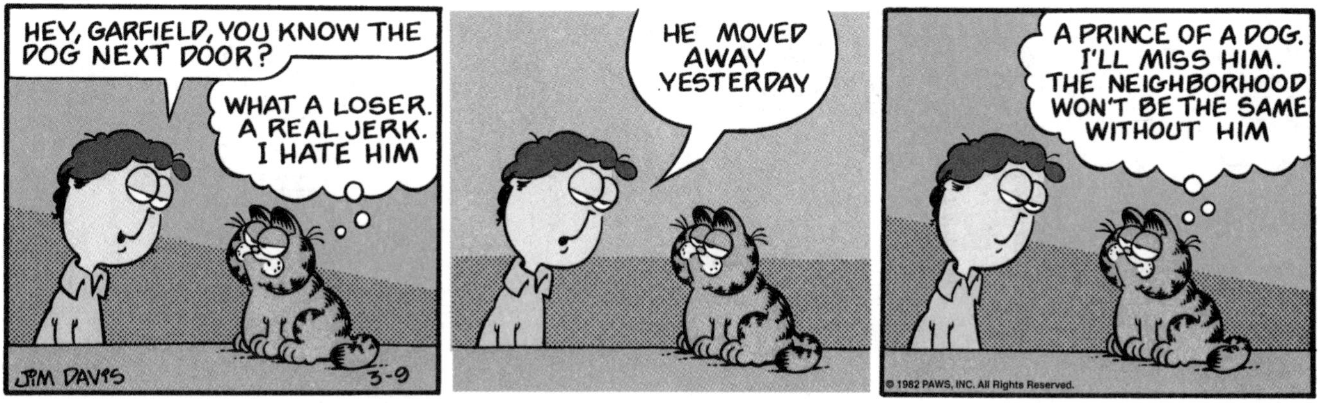
HEY, GARFIELD, YOU KNOW THE DOG NEXT DOOR?
WHAT A LOSER. A REAL JERK. I HATE HIM
JIM DAVIS
3-9
HE MOVED AWAY YESTERDAY
A PRINCE OF A DOG. I'LL MISS HIM. THE NEIGHBORHOOD WON'T BE THE SAME WITHOUT HIM
© 1982 PAWS, INC. All Rights Reserved.

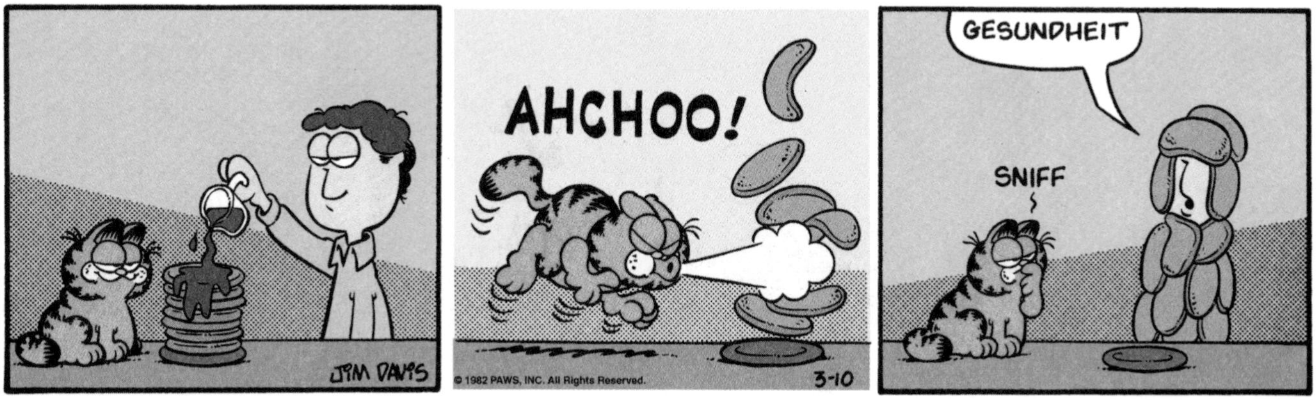
JIM DAVIS
AHCHOO!
© 1982 PAWS, INC. All Rights Reserved.
3-10
GESUNDHEIT
SNIFF

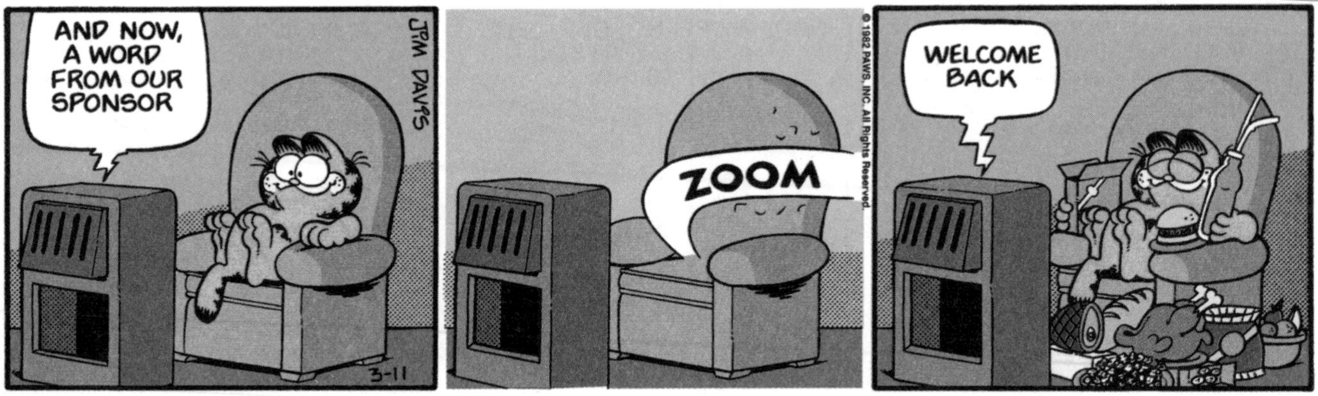
AND NOW, A WORD FROM OUR SPONSOR
JIM DAVIS
3-11
© 1982 PAWS, INC. All Rights Reserved.
ZOOM
WELCOME BACK

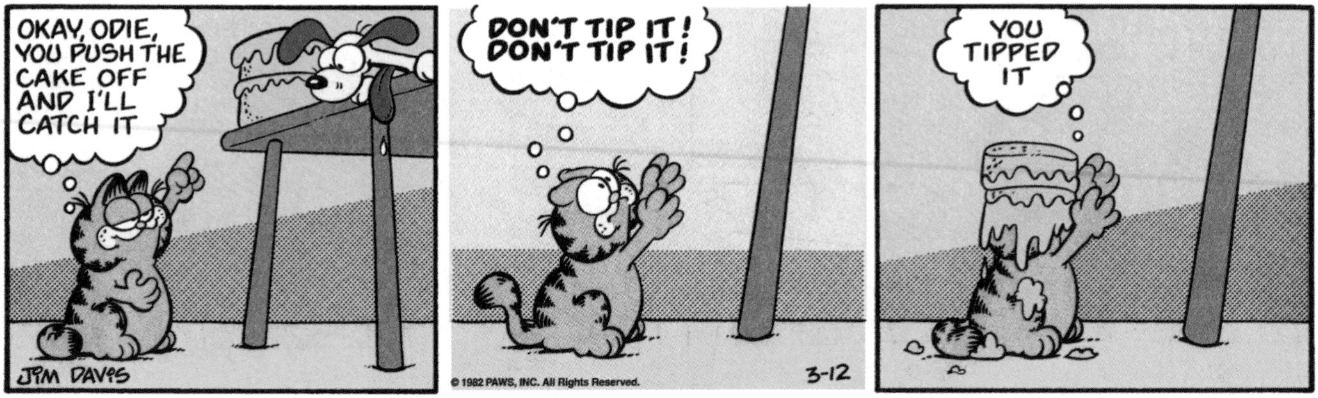
OKAY, ODIE, YOU PUSH THE CAKE OFF AND I'LL CATCH IT
JIM DAVIS
DON'T TIP IT! DON'T TIP IT!
© 1982 PAWS, INC. All Rights Reserved.
3-12
YOU TIPPED IT

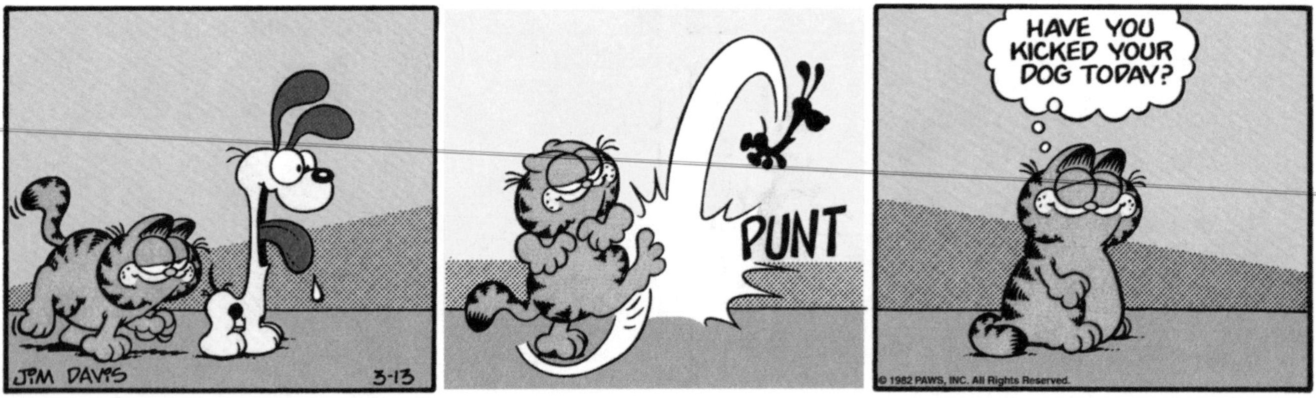
JIM DAVIS
3-13
PUNT
HAVE YOU KICKED YOUR DOG TODAY?
© 1982 PAWS, INC. All Rights Reserved.

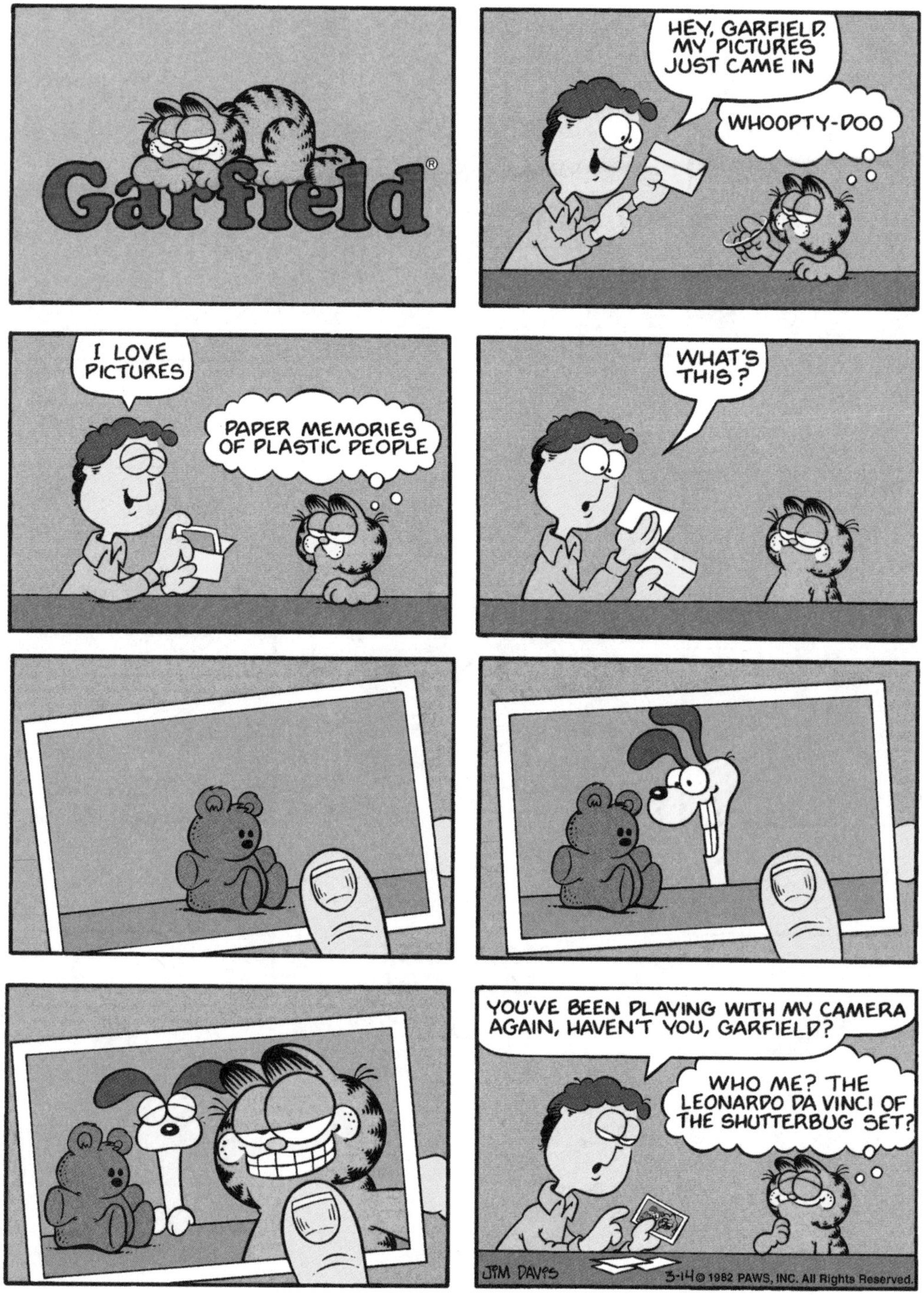
Garfield®
HEY, GARFIELD. MY PICTURES JUST CAME IN
WHOOPTY-DOO
I LOVE PICTURES
PAPER MEMORIES OF PLASTIC PEOPLE
WHAT'S THIS?
YOU'VE BEEN PLAYING WITH MY CAMERA AGAIN, HAVEN'T YOU, GARFIELD?
WHO ME? THE LEONARDO DA VINCI OF THE SHUTTERBUG SET?
JIM DAVIS
3-14 © 1982 PAWS, INC. All Rights Reserved.

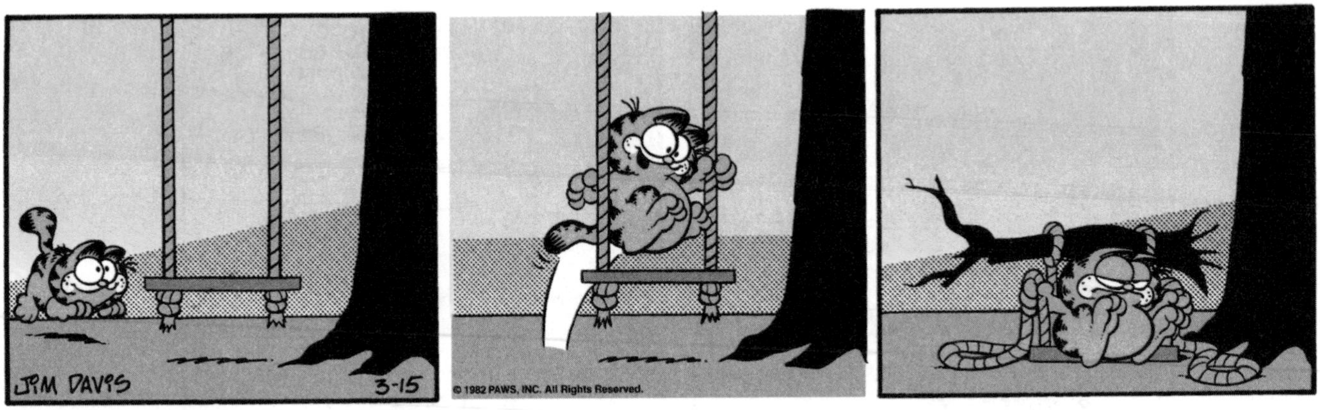
JIM DAVIS
3-15
© 1982 PAWS, INC. All Rights Reserved.

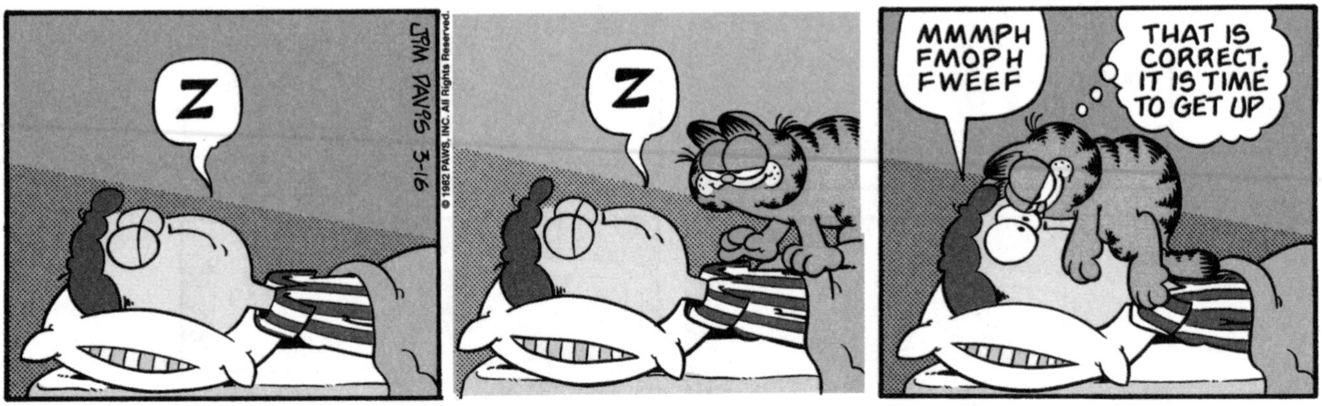
JIM DAVIS 3-16
© 1982 PAWS, INC. All Rights Reserved.
Z
Z
MMMPH FMOPH FWEEF
THAT IS CORRECT. IT IS TIME TO GET UP

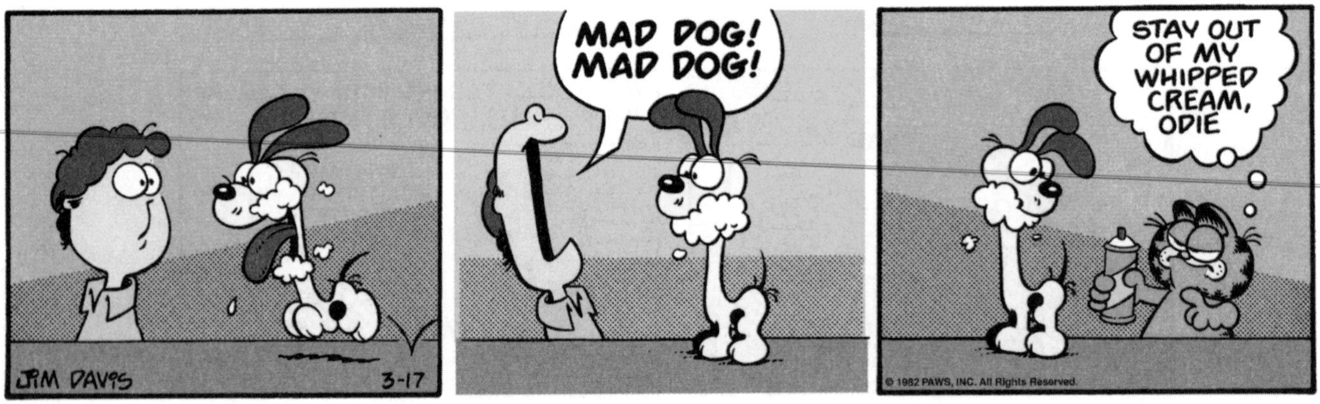
JIM DAVIS
3-17
MAD DOG! MAD DOG!
STAY OUT OF MY WHIPPED CREAM, ODIE
© 1982 PAWS, INC. All Rights Reserved.

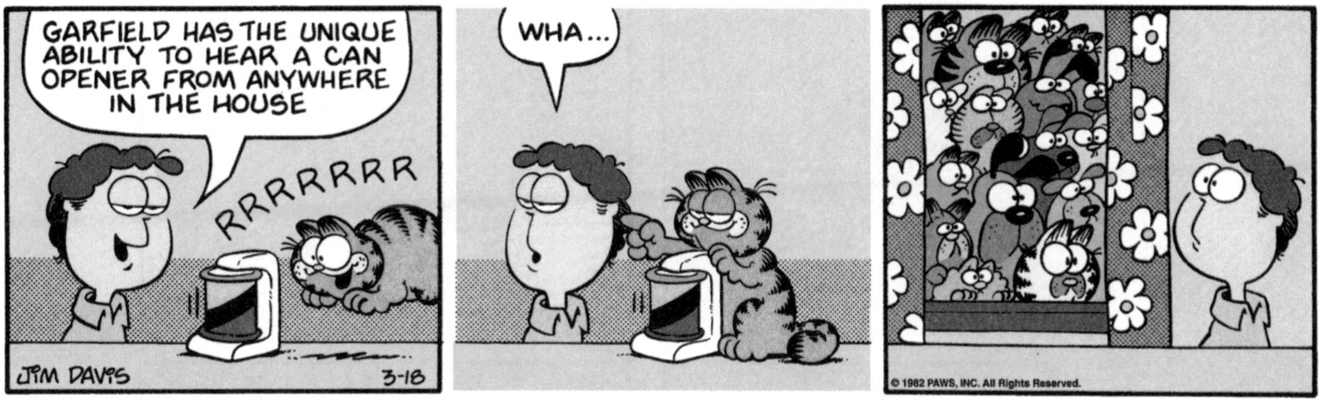
GARFIELD HAS THE UNIQUE ABILITY TO HEAR A CAN OPENER FROM ANYWHERE IN THE HOUSE
RRRRRRR
JIM DAVIS
3-18
WHA...
© 1982 PAWS, INC. All Rights Reserved.

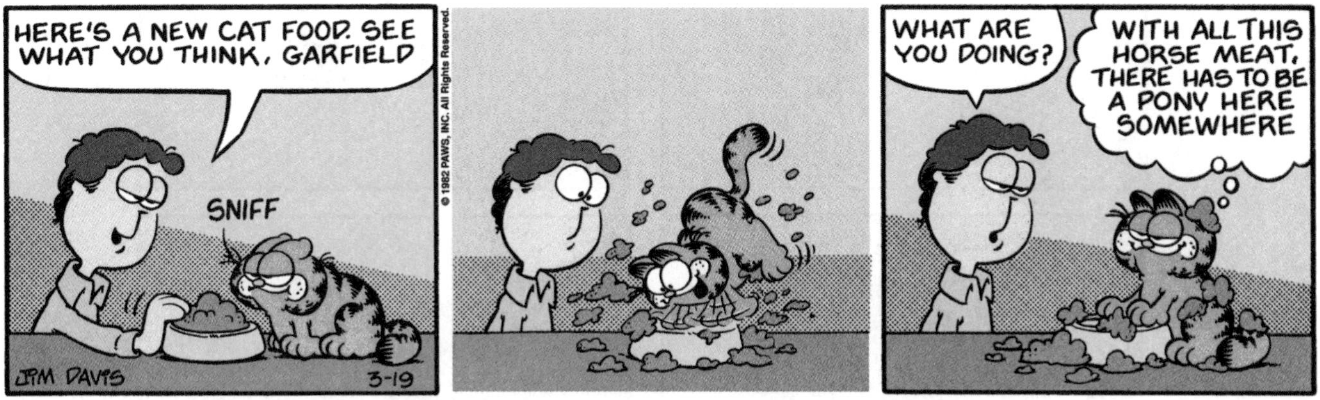
HERE'S A NEW CAT FOOD. SEE WHAT YOU THINK, GARFIELD
SNIFF
JIM DAVIS
3-19
© 1982 PAWS, INC. All Rights Reserved.
WHAT ARE YOU DOING?
WITH ALL THIS HORSE MEAT, THERE HAS TO BE A PONY HERE SOMEWHERE

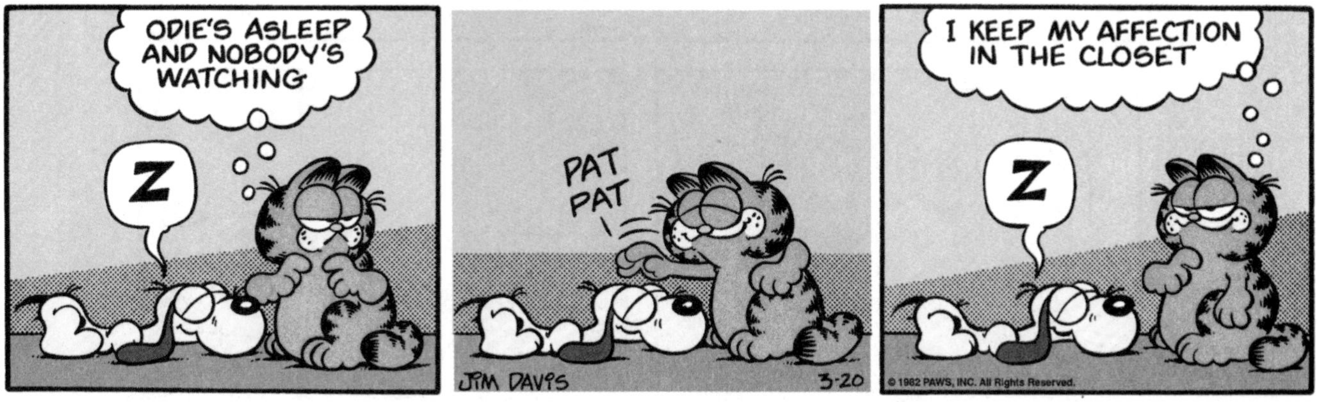
ODIE'S ASLEEP AND NOBODY'S WATCHING
Z
PAT PAT
JIM DAVIS
3-20
I KEEP MY AFFECTION IN THE CLOSET
Z
© 1982 PAWS, INC. All Rights Reserved.

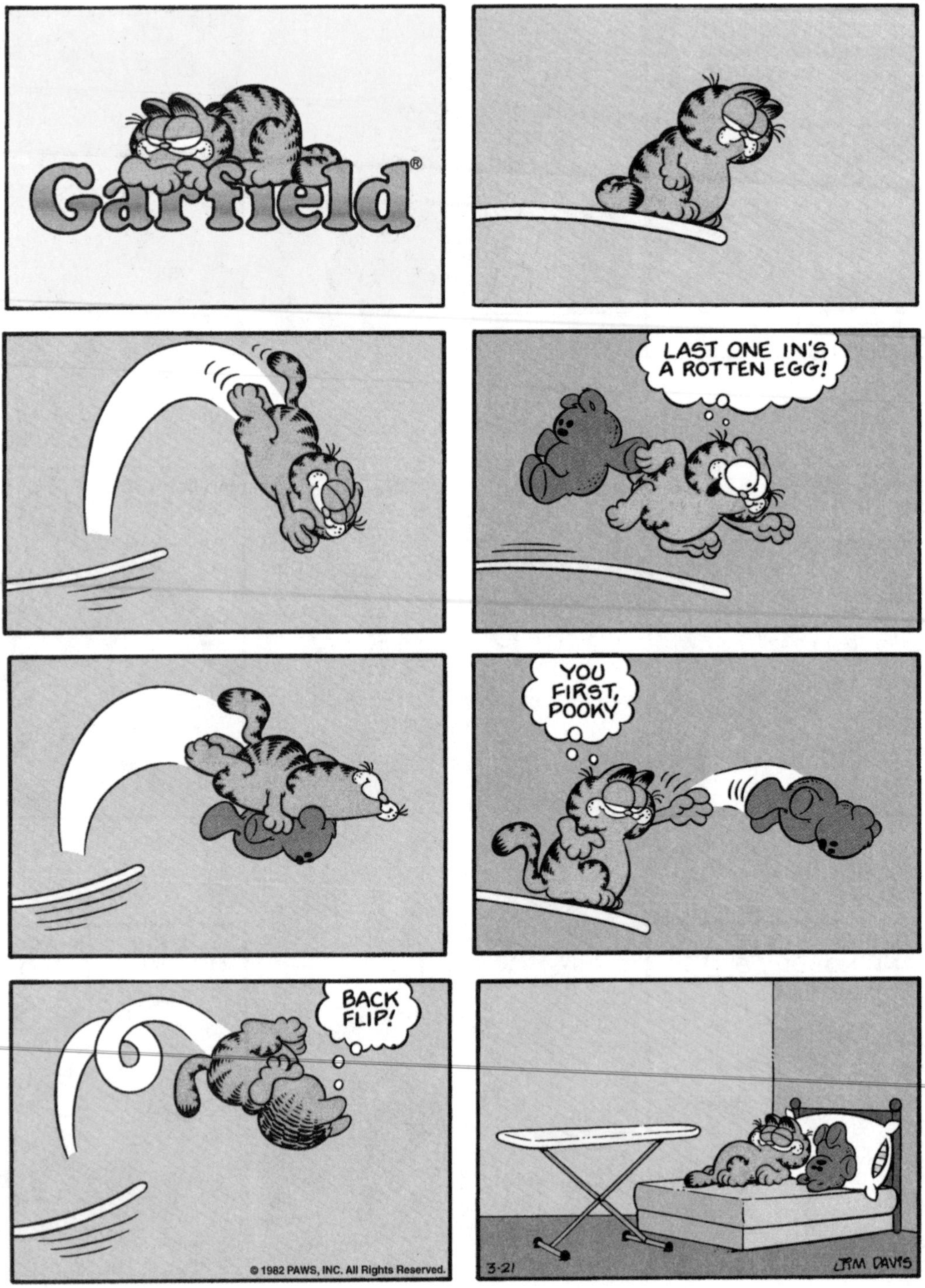
Garfield®
LAST ONE IN'S A ROTTEN EGG!
YOU FIRST, POOKY
BACK FLIP!
© 1982 PAWS, INC. All Rights Reserved.
3-21
JIM DAVIS

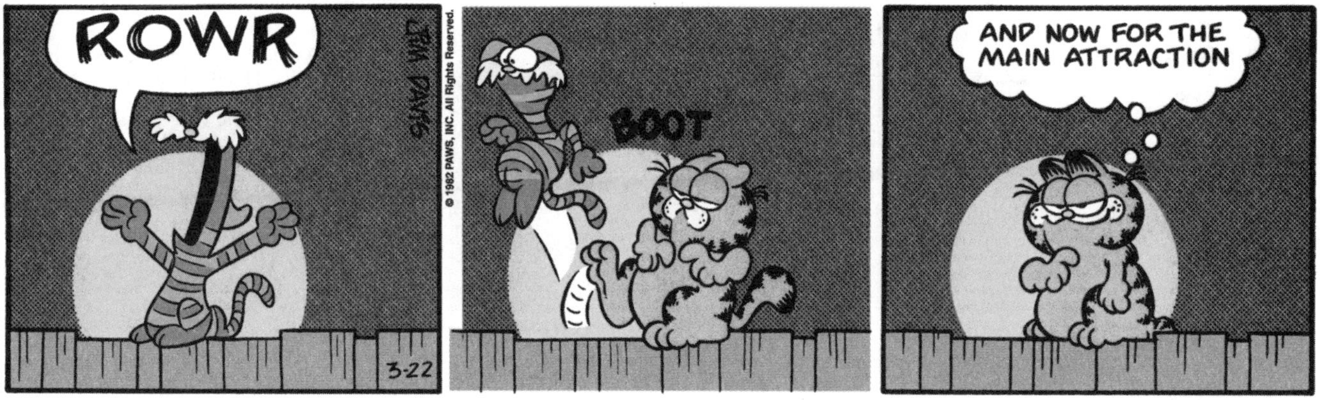
ROWR
JIM DAVIS
3-22
© 1982 PAWS, INC. All Rights Reserved.
BOOT
AND NOW FOR THE MAIN ATTRACTION

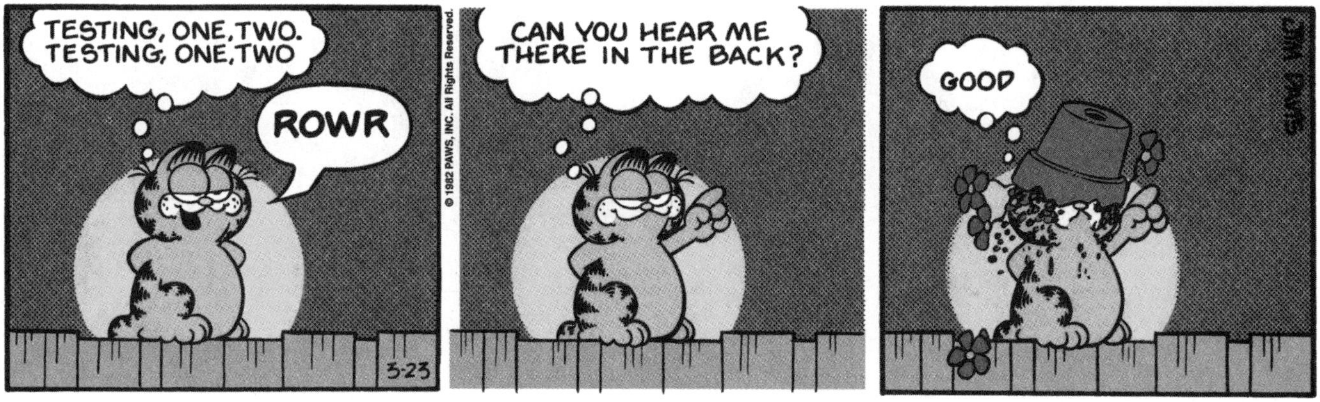
TESTING, ONE, TWO. TESTING, ONE, TWO
ROWR
3-23
© 1982 PAWS, INC. All Rights Reserved.
CAN YOU HEAR ME THERE IN THE BACK?
GOOD
JIM DAVIS

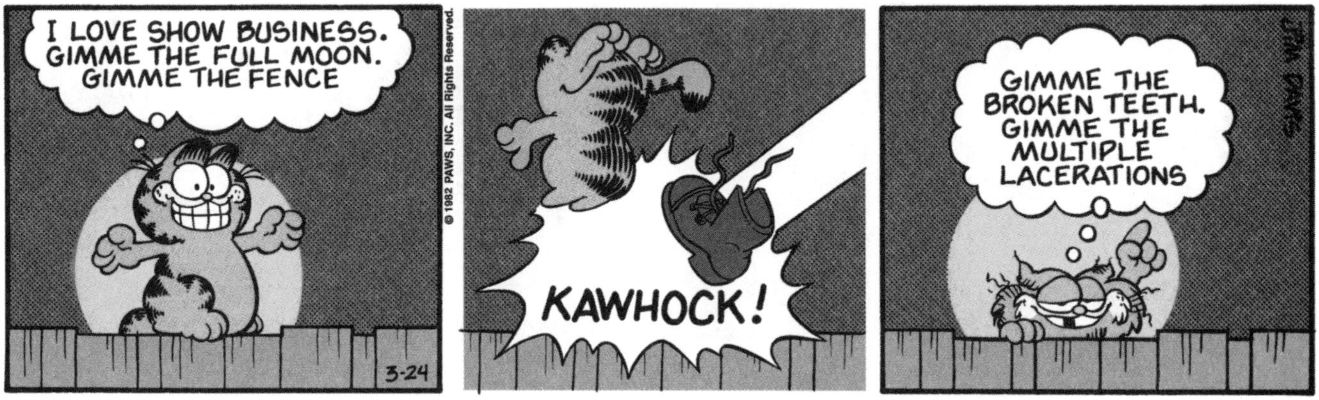
I LOVE SHOW BUSINESS. GIMME THE FULL MOON. GIMME THE FENCE
3-24
© 1982 PAWS, INC. All Rights Reserved.
KAWHOCK!
JIM DAVIS
GIMME THE BROKEN TEETH. GIMME THE MULTIPLE LACERATIONS

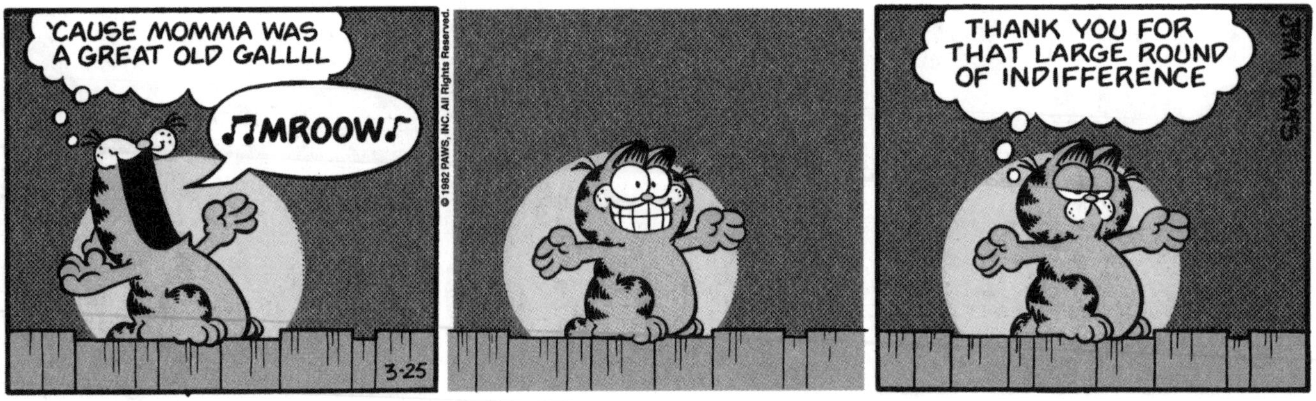
'CAUSE MOMMA WAS A GREAT OLD GALLLL
♫MROOW♪
3-25
© 1982 PAWS, INC. All Rights Reserved.
THANK YOU FOR THAT LARGE ROUND OF INDIFFERENCE
JIM DAVIS

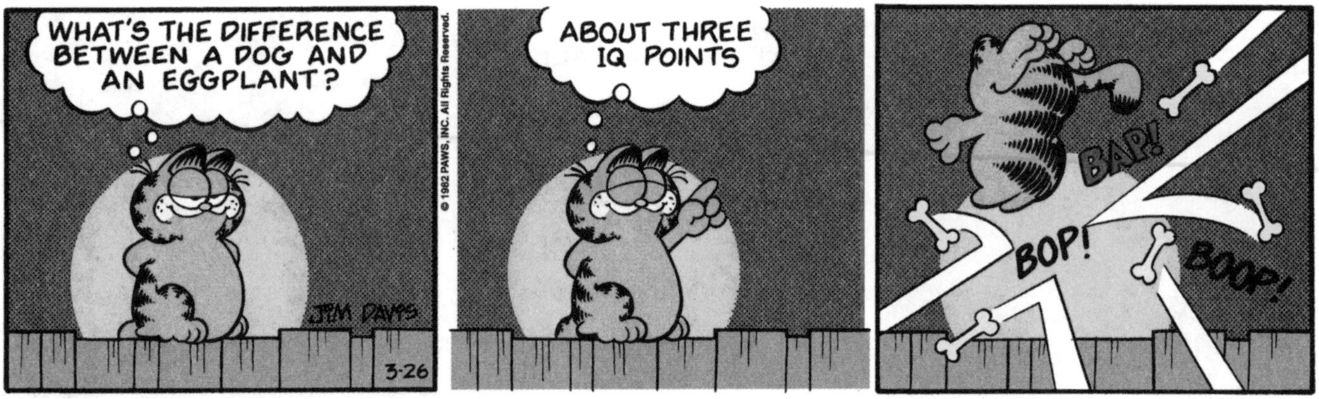
WHAT'S THE DIFFERENCE BETWEEN A DOG AND AN EGGPLANT?
JIM DAVIS
3-26
© 1982 PAWS, INC. All Rights Reserved.
ABOUT THREE IQ POINTS
BAP!
BOP!
BOOP!

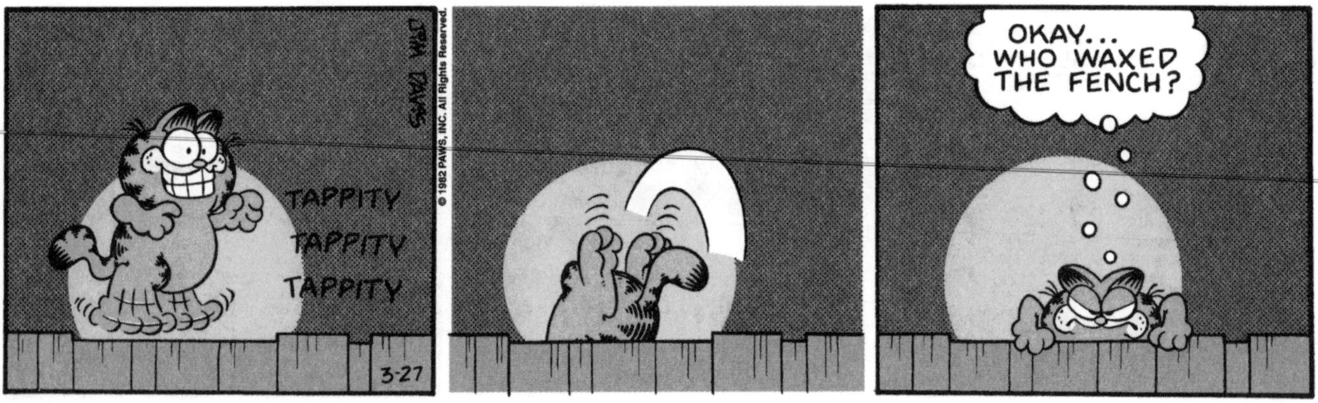
TAPPITY
TAPPITY
TAPPITY
3-27
JIM DAVIS
© 1982 PAWS, INC. All Rights Reserved.
OKAY... WHO WAXED THE FENCE?

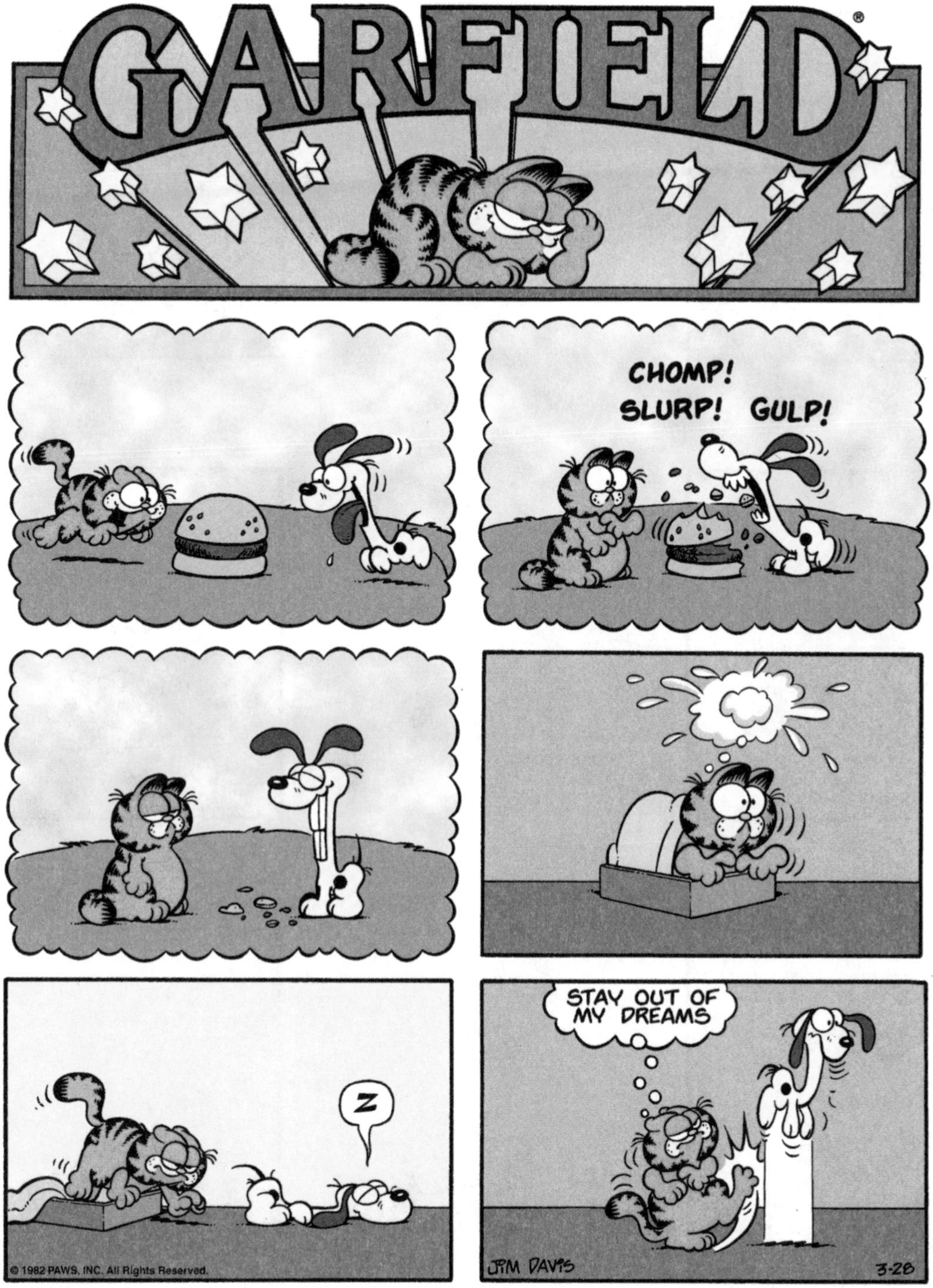
GARFIELD®
CHOMP!
SLURP! GULP!
Z
STAY OUT OF MY DREAMS
© 1982 PAWS, INC. All Rights Reserved.
JIM DAVIS
3-28

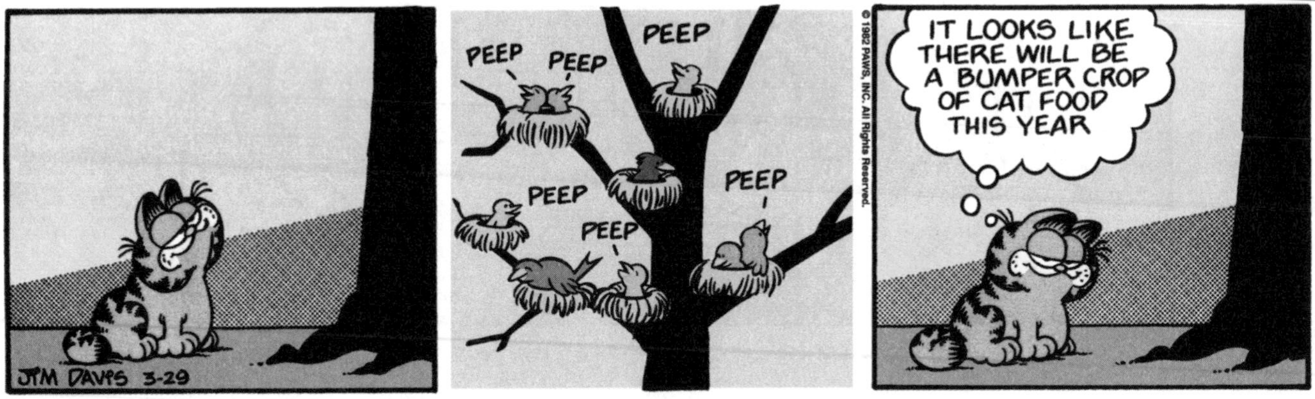
JIM DAVIS 3-29
PEEP PEEP
PEEP
PEEP
PEEP
PEEP
© 1982 PAWS, INC. All Rights Reserved.
IT LOOKS LIKE THERE WILL BE A BUMPER CROP OF CAT FOOD THIS YEAR

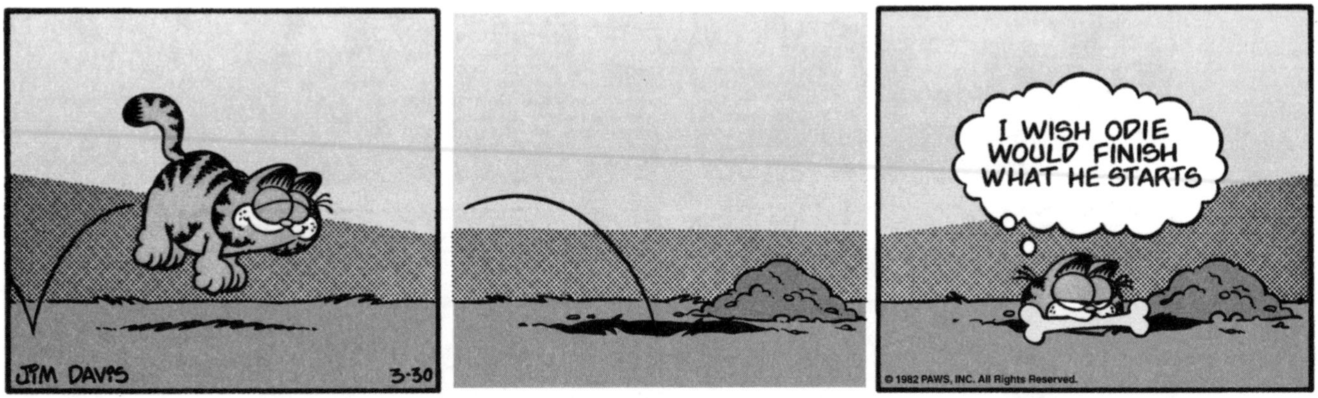
JIM DAVIS 3-30
I WISH ODIE WOULD FINISH WHAT HE STARTS
© 1982 PAWS, INC. All Rights Reserved.

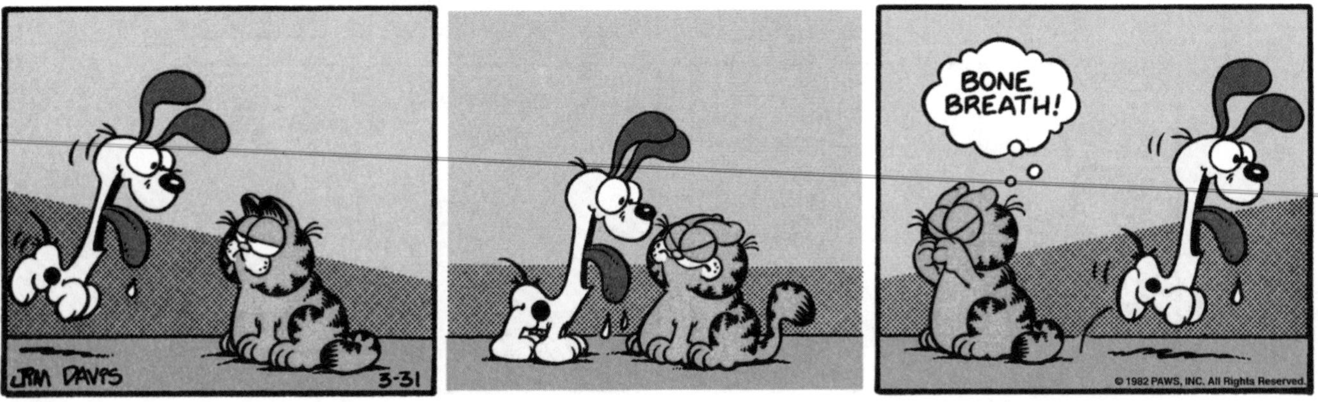
JIM DAVIS 3-31
BONE BREATH!
© 1982 PAWS, INC. All Rights Reserved.

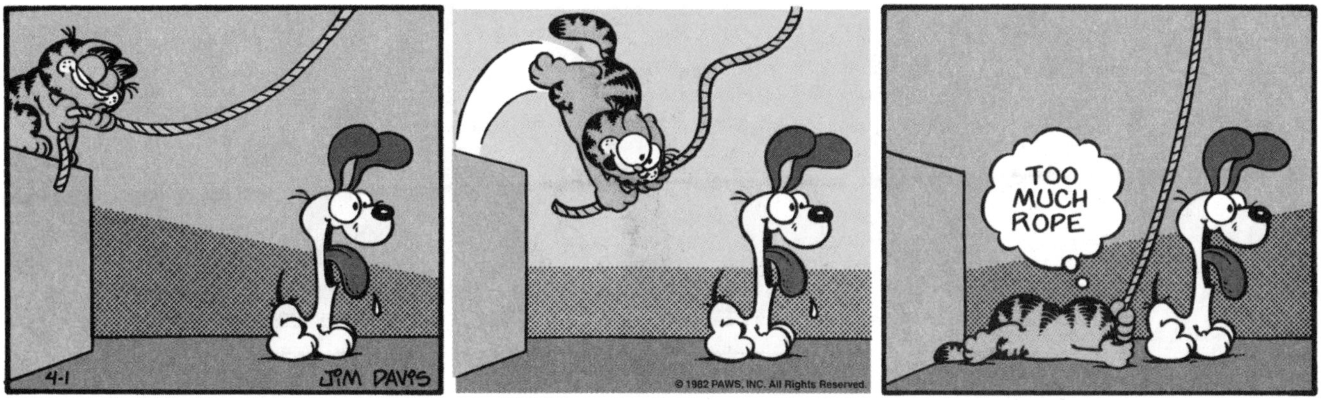
4-1
JIM DAVIS
© 1982 PAWS, INC. All Rights Reserved.
TOO MUCH ROPE

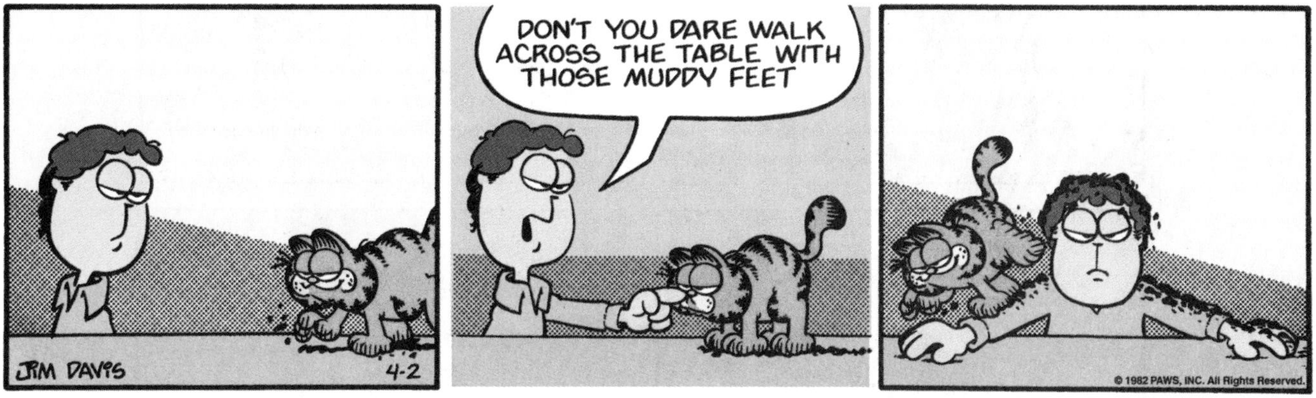
JIM DAVIS
4-2
DON'T YOU DARE WALK ACROSS THE TABLE WITH THOSE MUDDY FEET
© 1982 PAWS, INC. All Rights Reserved.

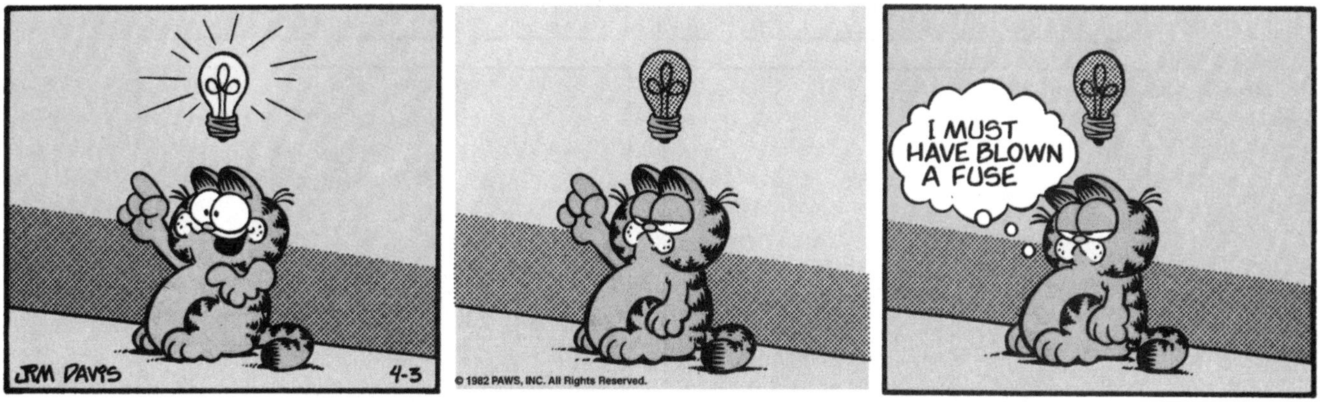
JIM DAVIS
4-3
© 1982 PAWS, INC. All Rights Reserved.
I MUST HAVE BLOWN A FUSE

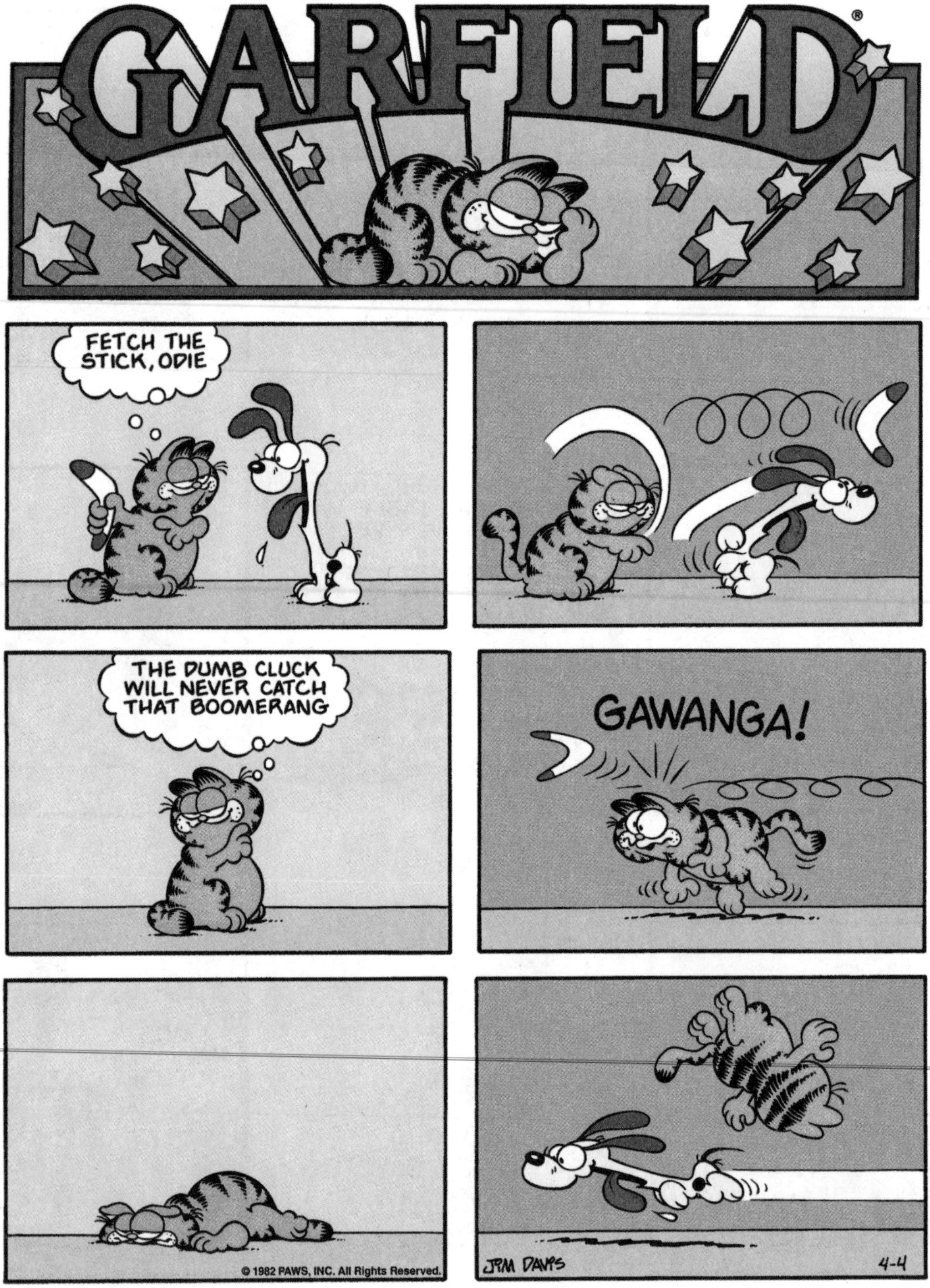
GARFIELD
FETCH THE STICK, ODIE
THE DUMB CLUCK WILL NEVER CATCH THAT BOOMERANG
GAWANGA!
JIM DAVIS
4-4

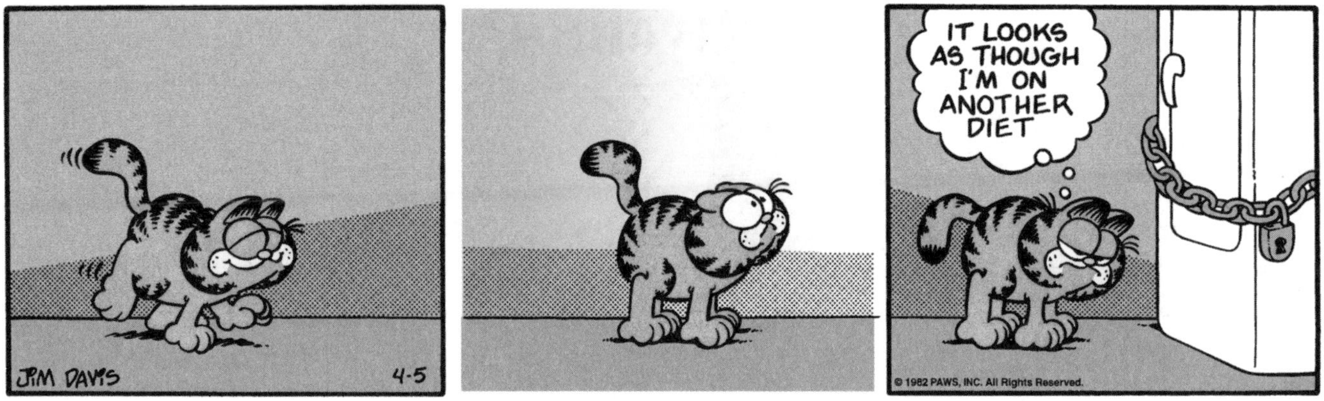
JIM DAVIS
4-5
IT LOOKS AS THOUGH I'M ON ANOTHER DIET
© 1982 PAWS, INC. All Rights Reserved.

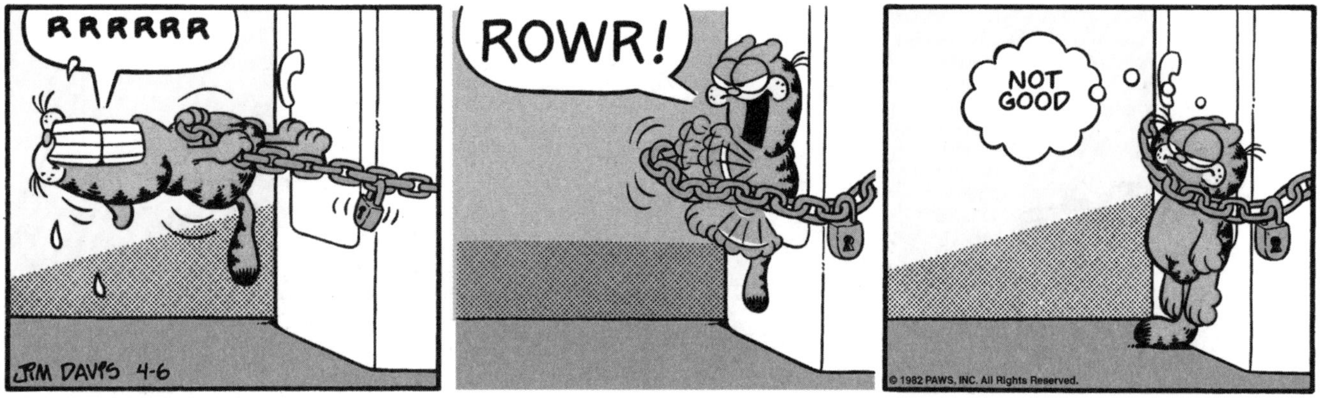
RRRRRRR
JIM DAVIS 4-6
ROWR!
NOT GOOD
© 1982 PAWS, INC. All Rights Reserved.

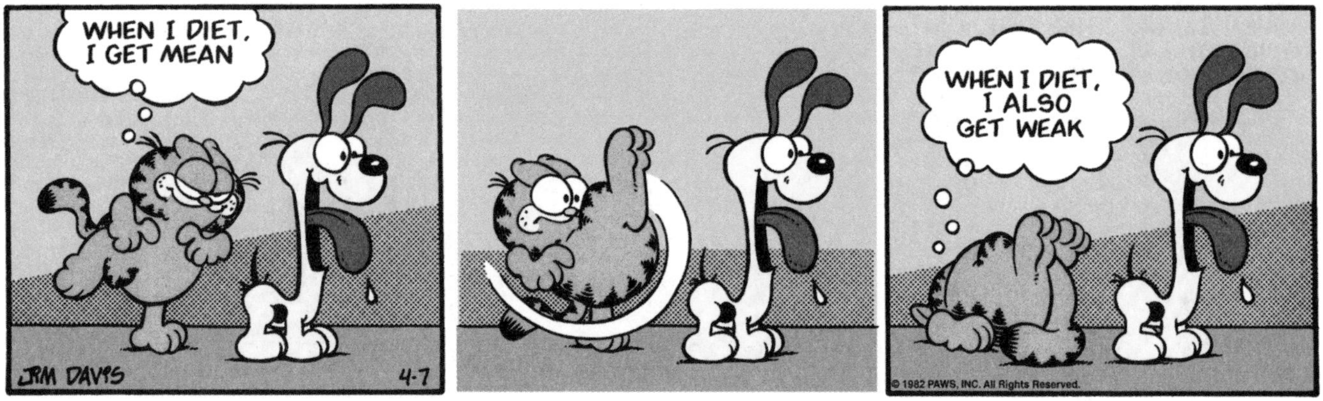
WHEN I DIET, I GET MEAN
JIM DAVIS
4-7
WHEN I DIET, I ALSO GET WEAK
© 1982 PAWS, INC. All Rights Reserved.

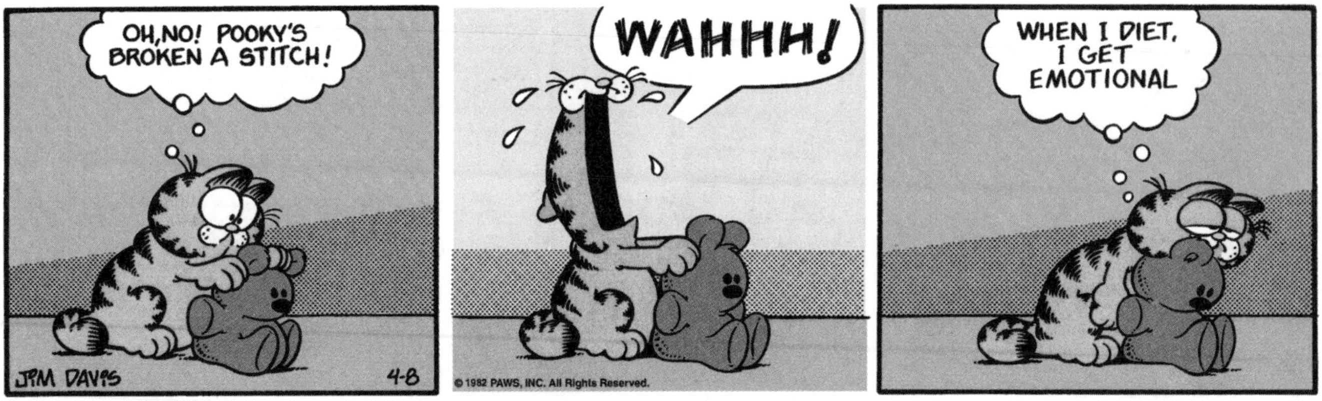
OH, NO! POOKY'S BROKEN A STITCH!
WAHHH!
WHEN I DIET, I GET EMOTIONAL
JIM DAVIS
4-8
© 1982 PAWS, INC. All Rights Reserved.

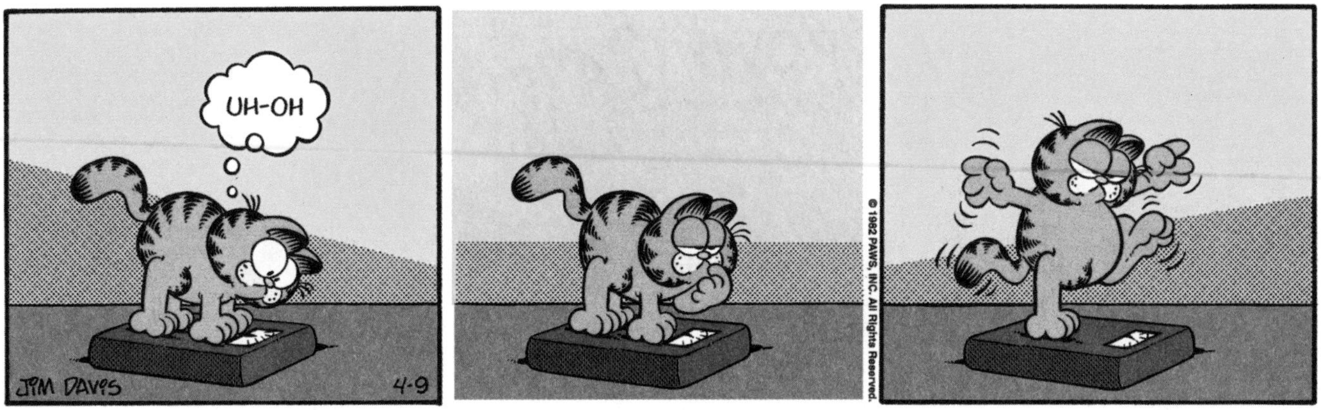
UH-OH
JIM DAVIS
4-9
© 1982 PAWS, INC. All Rights Reserved.

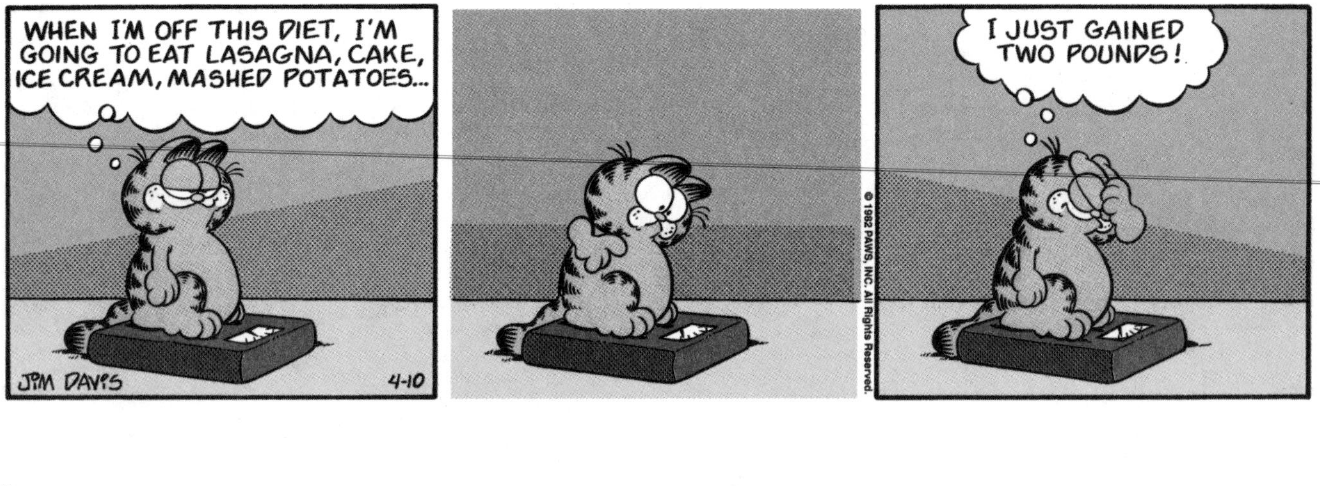
WHEN I'M OFF THIS DIET, I'M GOING TO EAT LASAGNA, CAKE, ICE CREAM, MASHED POTATOES...
I JUST GAINED TWO POUNDS!
JIM DAVIS
4-10
© 1982 PAWS, INC. All Rights Reserved.

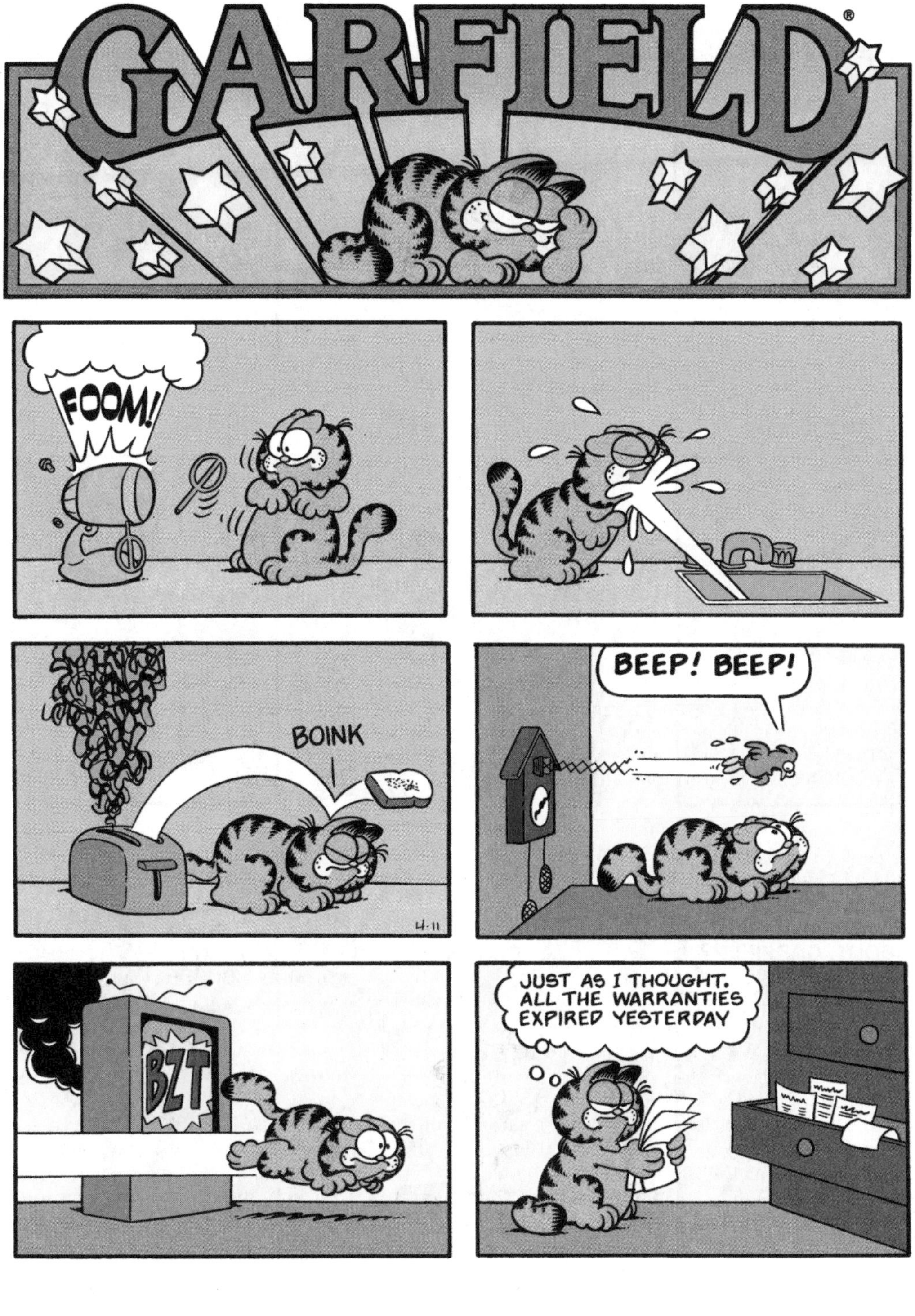
GARFIELD
FOOM!
BOINK
BEEP! BEEP!
BZT
JUST AS I THOUGHT. ALL THE WARRANTIES EXPIRED YESTERDAY

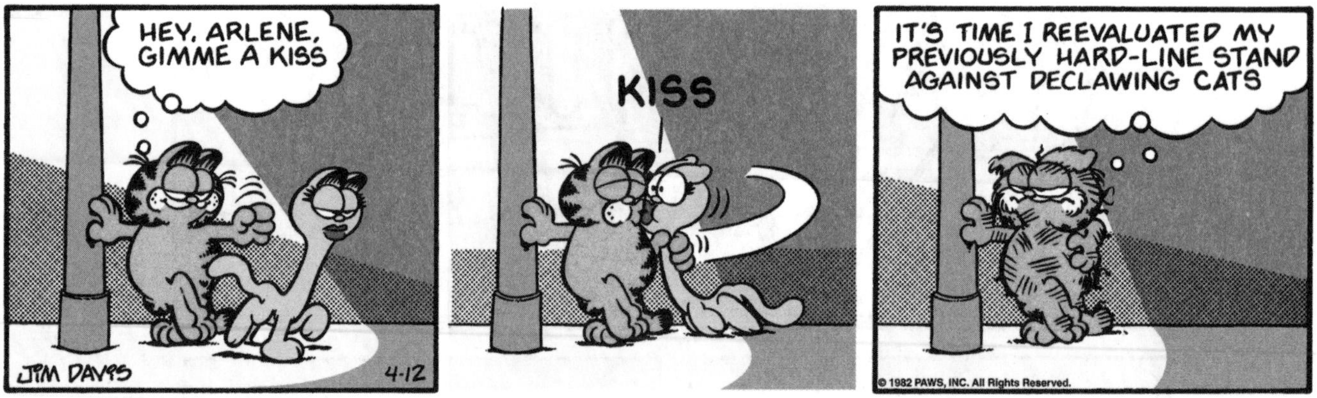
HEY, ARLENE, GIMME A KISS
JIM DAVIS
4-12
KISS
IT'S TIME I REEVALUATED MY PREVIOUSLY HARD-LINE STAND AGAINST DECLAWING CATS
© 1982 PAWS, INC. All Rights Reserved.

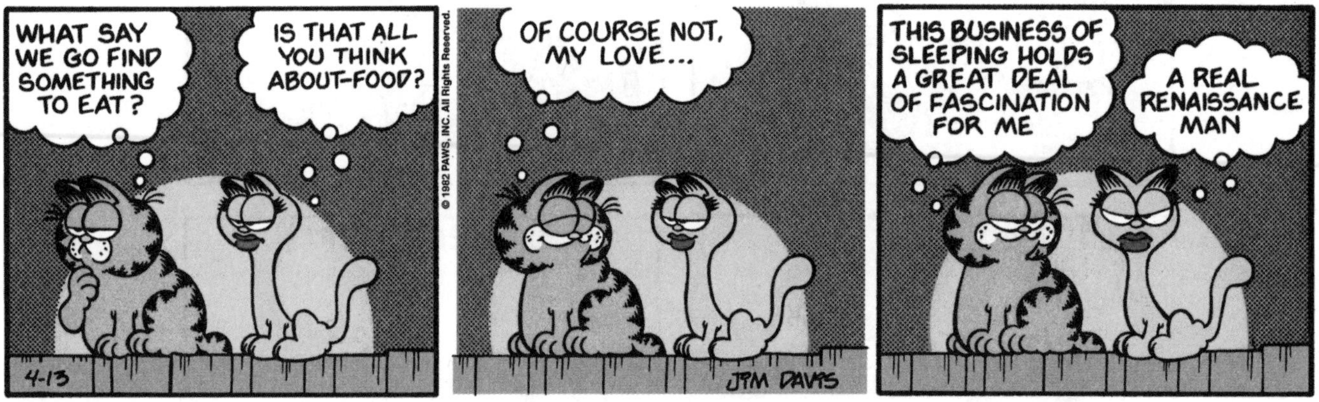
WHAT SAY WE GO FIND SOMETHING TO EAT?
IS THAT ALL YOU THINK ABOUT-FOOD?
4-13
© 1982 PAWS, INC. All Rights Reserved.
OF COURSE NOT, MY LOVE...
JIM DAVIS
THIS BUSINESS OF SLEEPING HOLDS A GREAT DEAL OF FASCINATION FOR ME
A REAL RENAISSANCE MAN

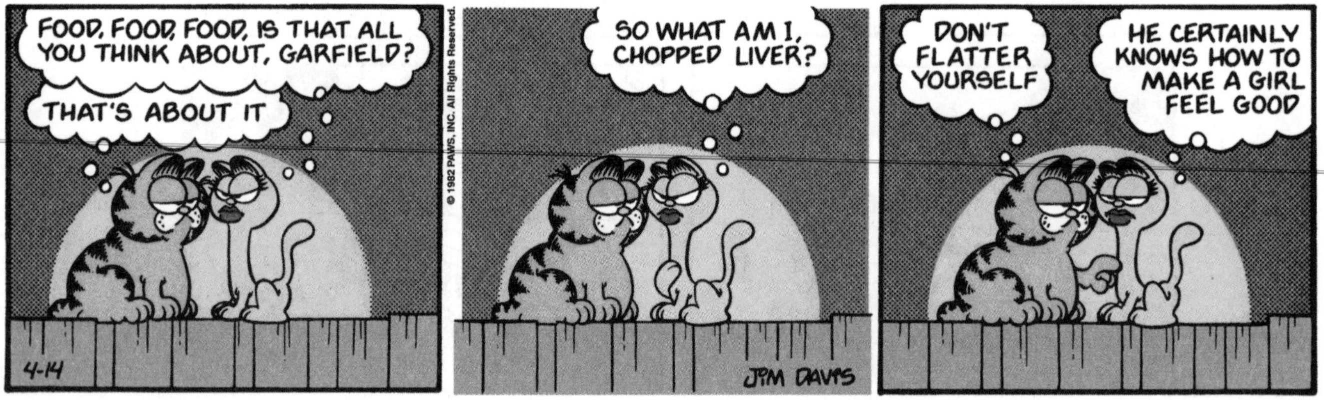
FOOD, FOOD, FOOD, IS THAT ALL YOU THINK ABOUT, GARFIELD?
THAT'S ABOUT IT
4-14
© 1982 PAWS, INC. All Rights Reserved.
SO WHAT AM I, CHOPPED LIVER?
JIM DAVIS
DON'T FLATTER YOURSELF
HE CERTAINLY KNOWS HOW TO MAKE A GIRL FEEL GOOD

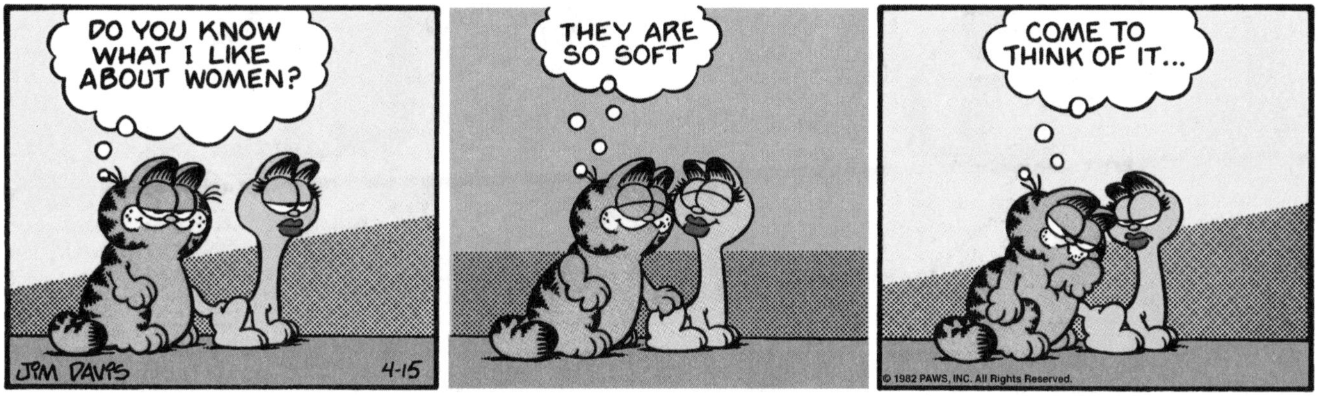
DO YOU KNOW WHAT I LIKE ABOUT WOMEN?
THEY ARE SO SOFT
COME TO THINK OF IT...
JIM DAVIS
4-15
© 1982 PAWS, INC. All Rights Reserved.

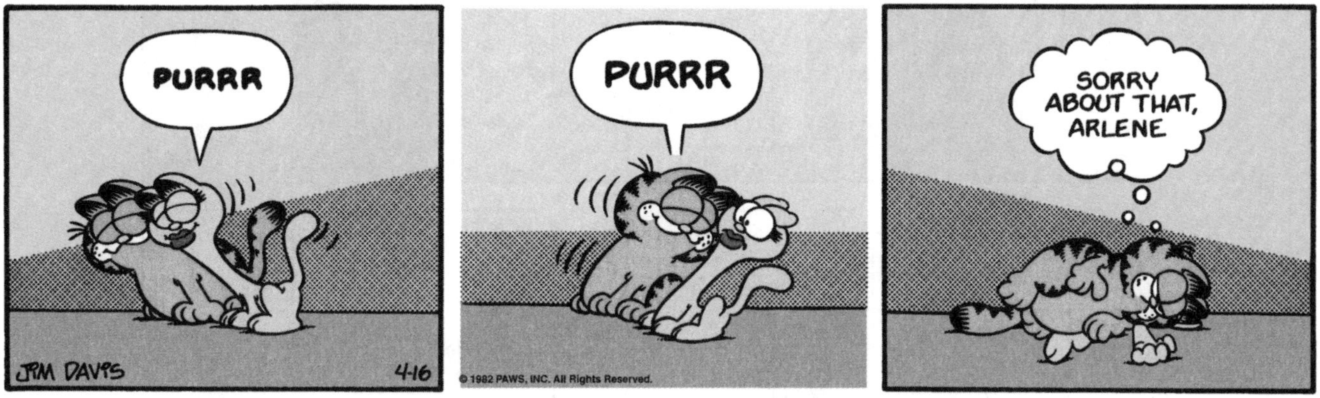
PURRR
PURRR
SORRY ABOUT THAT, ARLENE
JIM DAVIS
4-16
© 1982 PAWS, INC. All Rights Reserved.

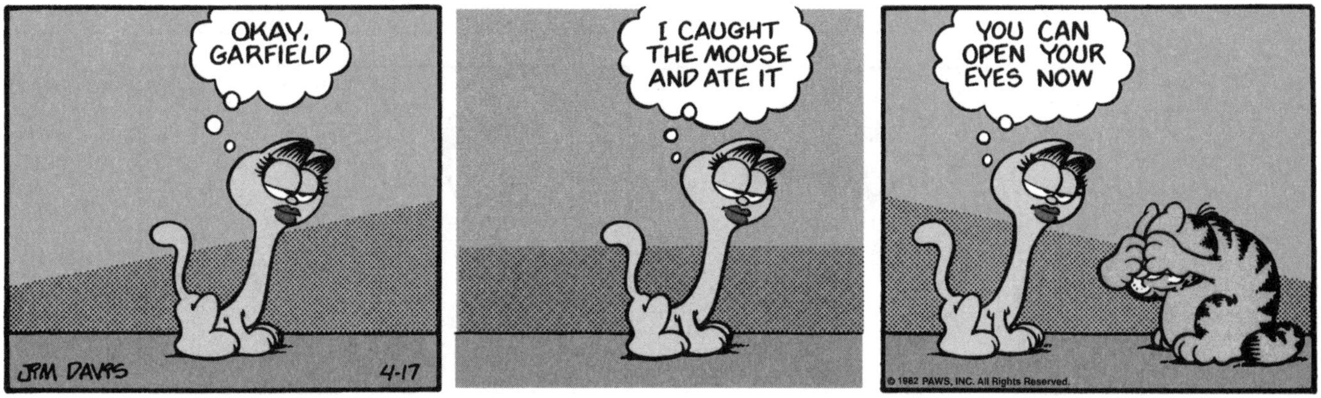
OKAY, GARFIELD
I CAUGHT THE MOUSE AND ATE IT
YOU CAN OPEN YOUR EYES NOW
JIM DAVIS
4-17
© 1982 PAWS, INC. All Rights Reserved.

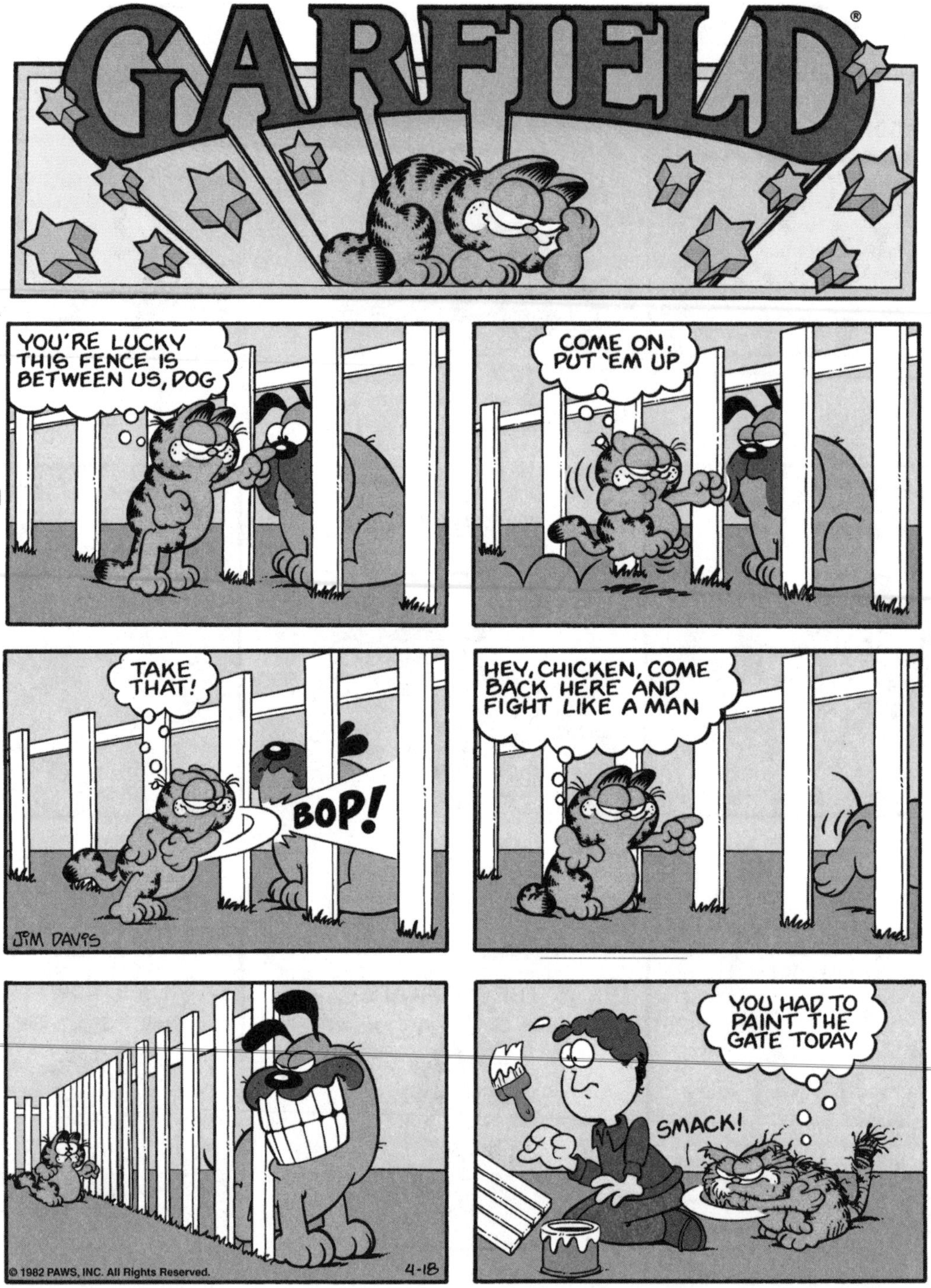
GARFIELD®
YOU'RE LUCKY THIS FENCE IS BETWEEN US, DOG
COME ON, PUT 'EM UP
TAKE THAT!
BOP!
JIM DAVIS
HEY, CHICKEN, COME BACK HERE AND FIGHT LIKE A MAN
© 1982 PAWS, INC. All Rights Reserved.
4-18
YOU HAD TO PAINT THE GATE TODAY
SMACK!

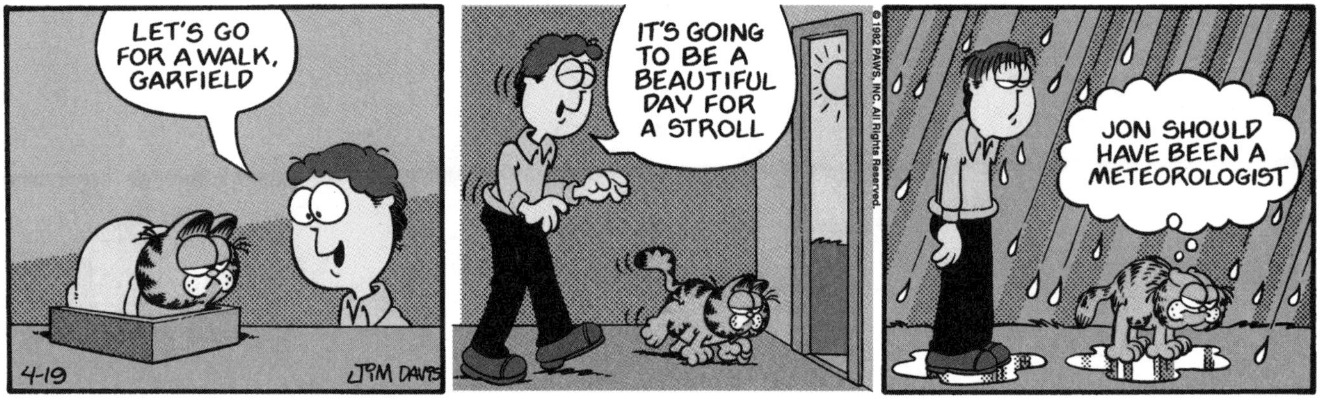
LET'S GO FOR A WALK, GARFIELD
4-19
JIM DAVIS
IT'S GOING TO BE A BEAUTIFUL DAY FOR A STROLL
© 1982 PAWS, INC. All Rights Reserved.
JON SHOULD HAVE BEEN A METEOROLOGIST

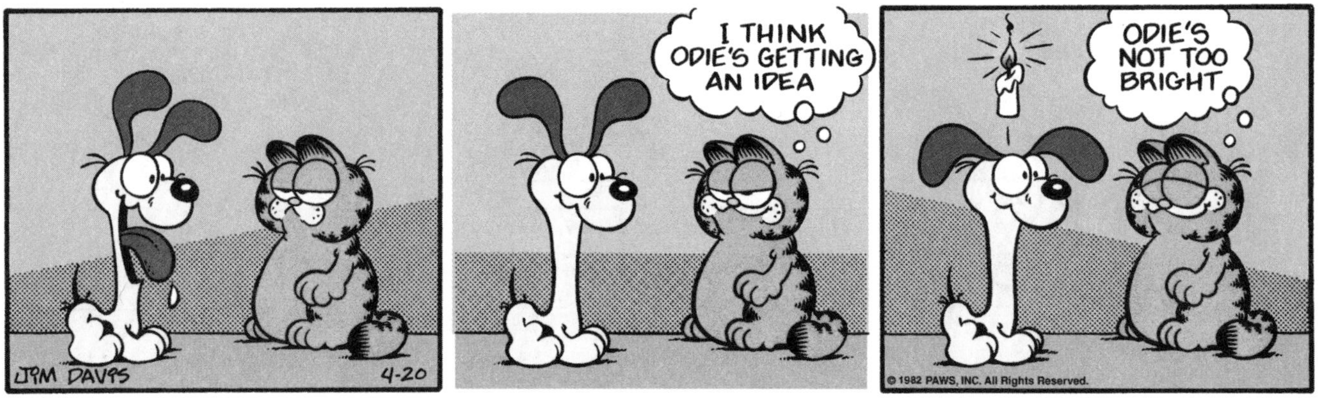
JIM DAVIS
4-20
I THINK ODIE'S GETTING AN IDEA
ODIE'S NOT TOO BRIGHT
© 1982 PAWS, INC. All Rights Reserved.

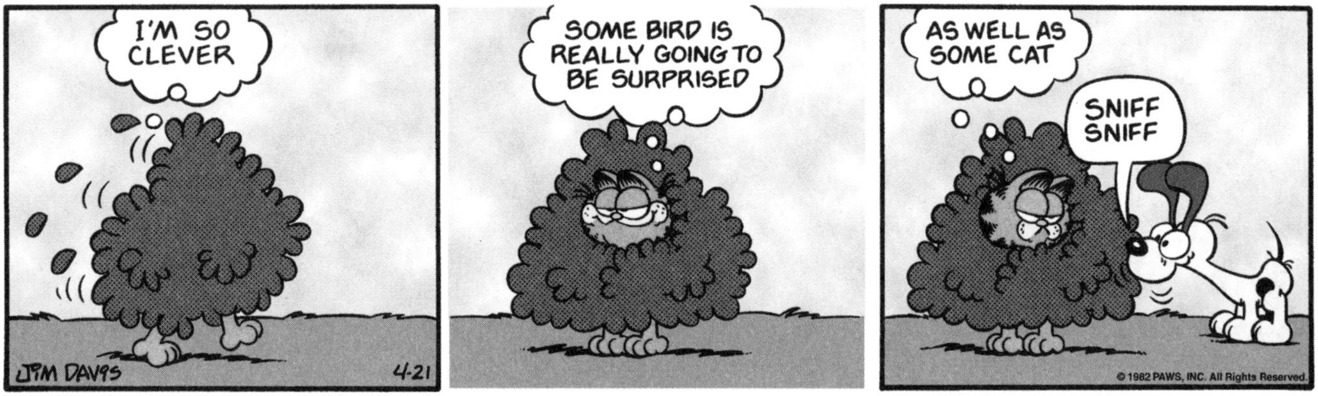
I'M SO CLEVER
JIM DAVIS
4-21
SOME BIRD IS REALLY GOING TO BE SURPRISED
AS WELL AS SOME CAT
SNIFF SNIFF
© 1982 PAWS, INC. All Rights Reserved.

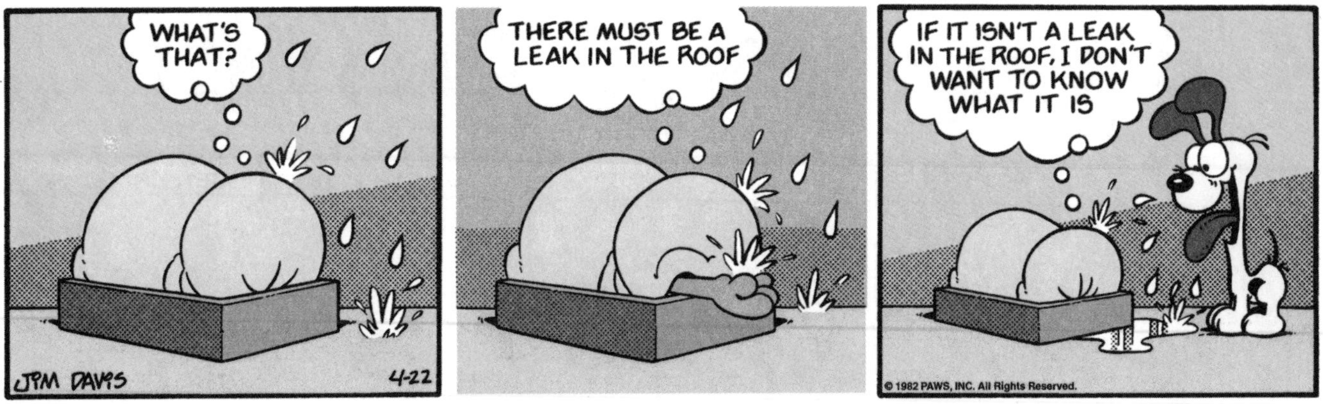
WHAT'S THAT?
JIM DAVIS
4-22
THERE MUST BE A LEAK IN THE ROOF
IF IT ISN'T A LEAK IN THE ROOF, I DON'T WANT TO KNOW WHAT IT IS
© 1982 PAWS, INC. All Rights Reserved.

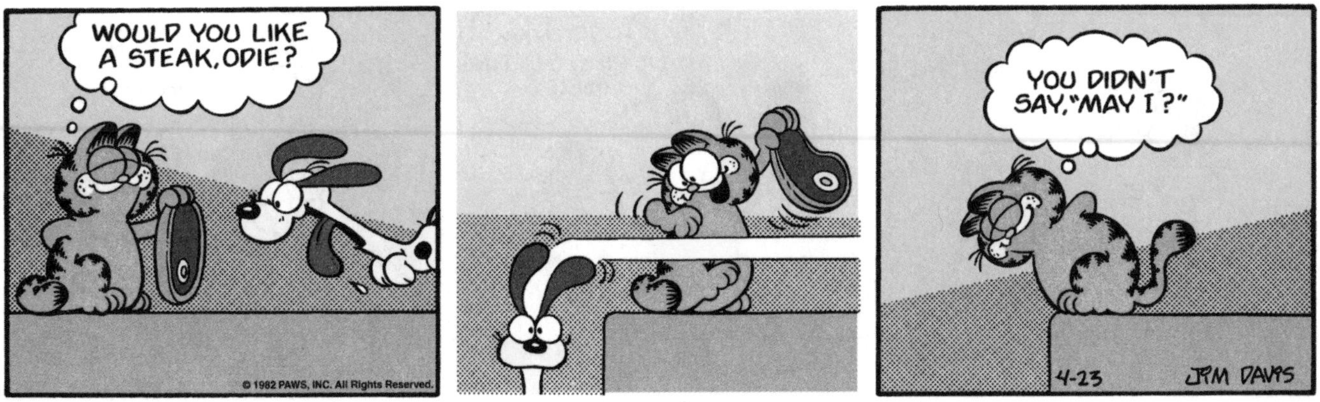
WOULD YOU LIKE A STEAK, ODIE?
© 1982 PAWS, INC. All Rights Reserved.
YOU DIDN'T SAY, "MAY I?"
4-23
JIM DAVIS

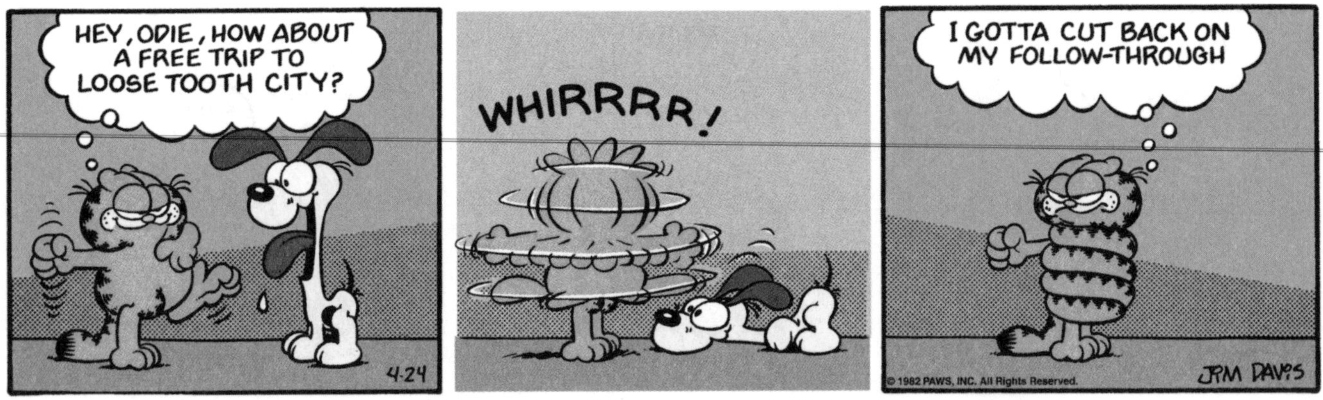
HEY, ODIE, HOW ABOUT A FREE TRIP TO LOOSE TOOTH CITY?
4-24
WHIRRRR!
I GOTTA CUT BACK ON MY FOLLOW-THROUGH
© 1982 PAWS, INC. All Rights Reserved.
JIM DAVIS

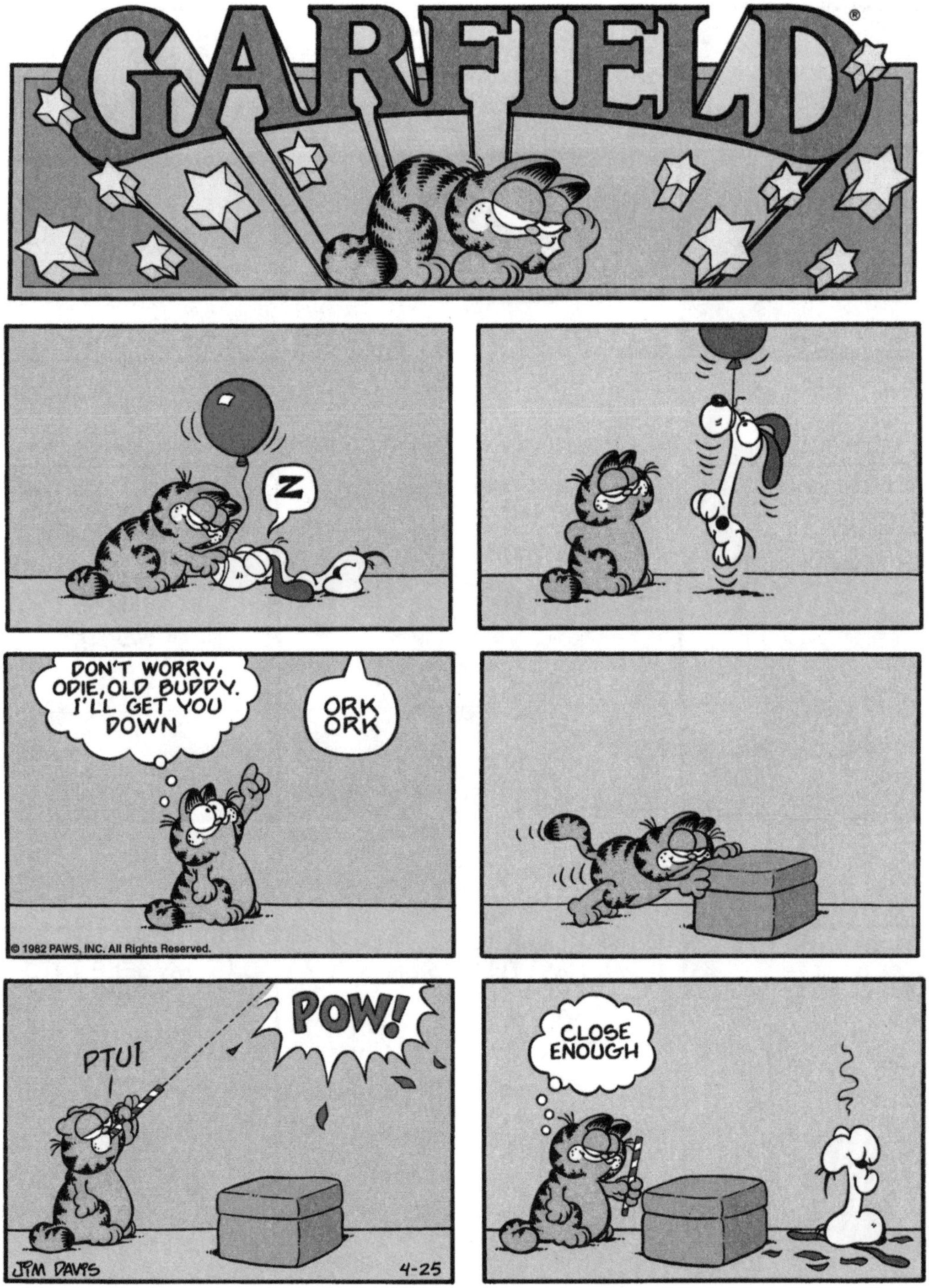
GARFIELD
Z
DON'T WORRY, ODIE, OLD BUDDY. I'LL GET YOU DOWN
ORK ORK
PTUI
POW!
CLOSE ENOUGH
JIM DAVIS
4-25

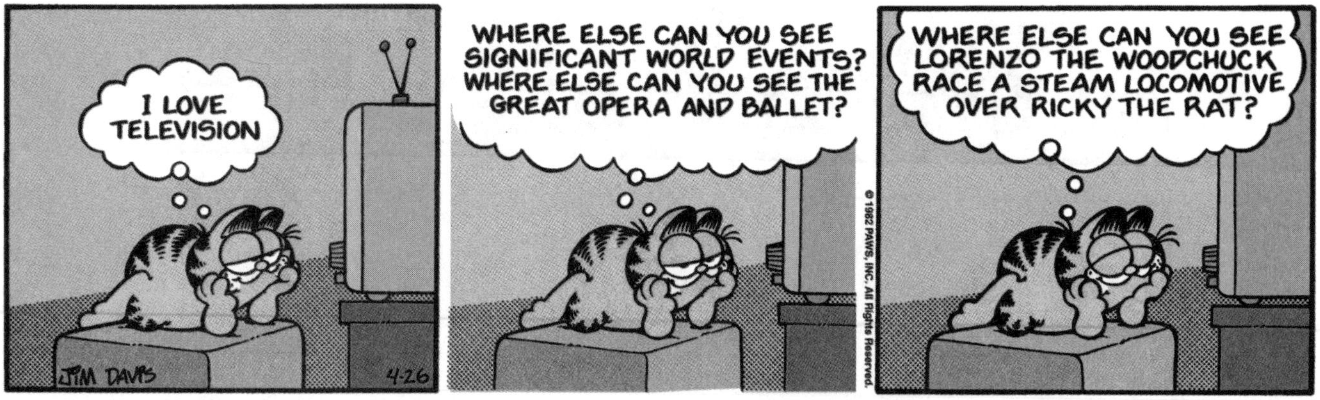
I LOVE TELEVISION
JIM DAVIS
4-26
WHERE ELSE CAN YOU SEE SIGNIFICANT WORLD EVENTS? WHERE ELSE CAN YOU SEE THE GREAT OPERA AND BALLET?
© 1982 PAWS, INC. All Rights Reserved.
WHERE ELSE CAN YOU SEE LORENZO THE WOODCHUCK RACE A STEAM LOCOMOTIVE OVER RICKY THE RAT?

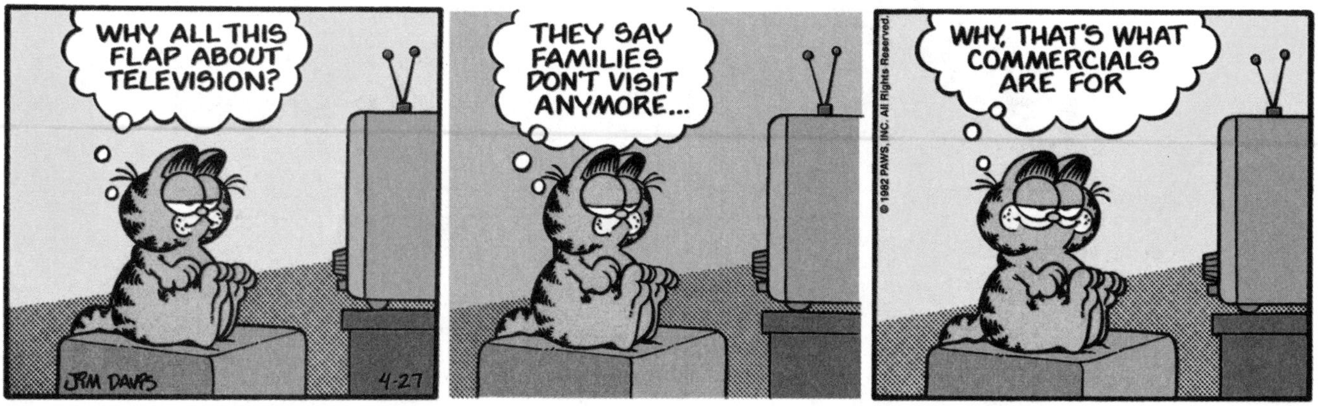
WHY ALL THIS FLAP ABOUT TELEVISION?
JIM DAVIS
4-27
THEY SAY FAMILIES DON'T VISIT ANYMORE...
© 1982 PAWS, INC. All Rights Reserved.
WHY, THAT'S WHAT COMMERCIALS ARE FOR

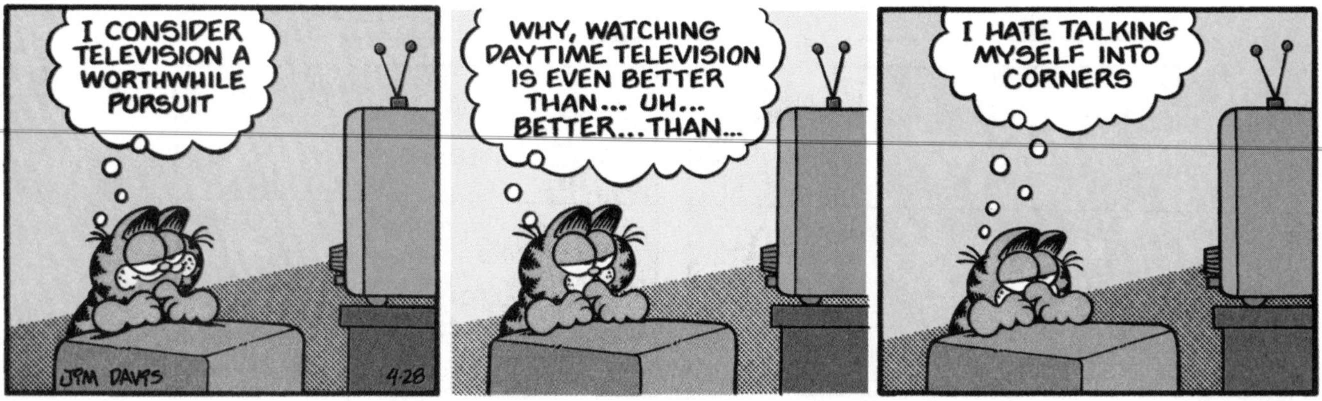
I CONSIDER TELEVISION A WORTHWHILE PURSUIT
JIM DAVIS
4-28
WHY, WATCHING DAYTIME TELEVISION IS EVEN BETTER THAN... UH... BETTER...THAN...
I HATE TALKING MYSELF INTO CORNERS

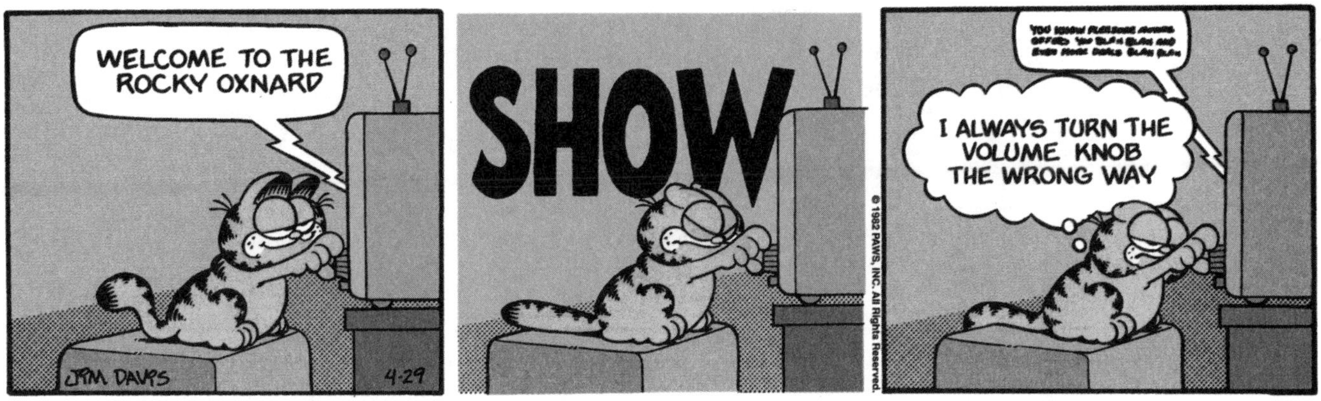
WELCOME TO THE ROCKY OXNARD
JIM DAVIS
4-29
SHOW
© 1982 PAWS, INC. All Rights Reserved.
I ALWAYS TURN THE VOLUME KNOB THE WRONG WAY

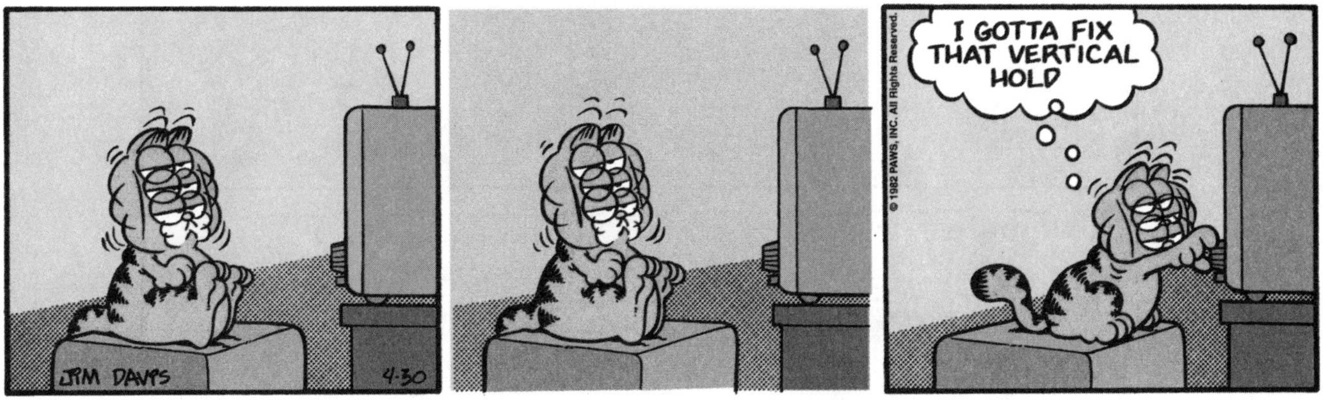
JIM DAVIS
4-30
© 1982 PAWS, INC. All Rights Reserved.
I GOTTA FIX THAT VERTICAL HOLD

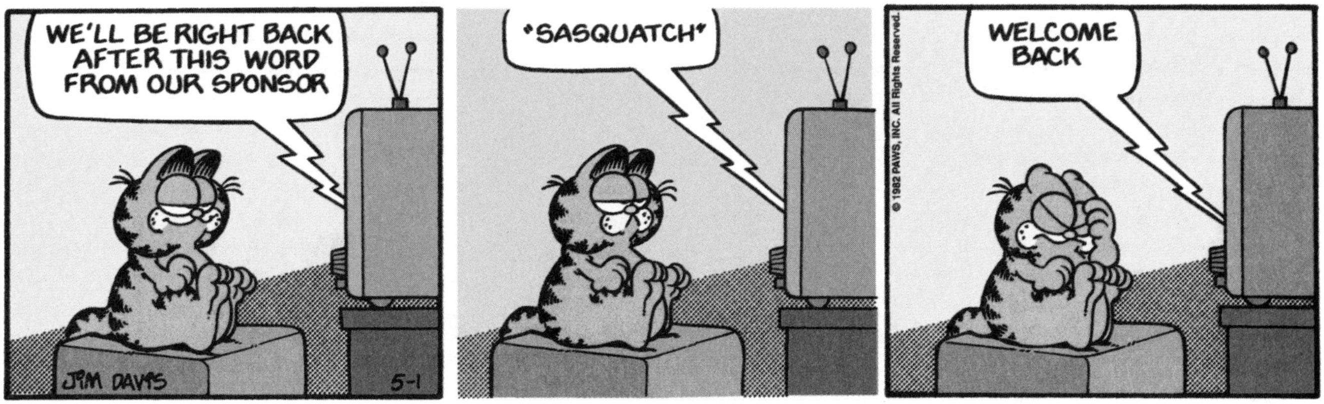
WE'LL BE RIGHT BACK AFTER THIS WORD FROM OUR SPONSOR
JIM DAVIS
5-1
SASQUATCH
© 1982 PAWS, INC. All Rights Reserved.
WELCOME BACK

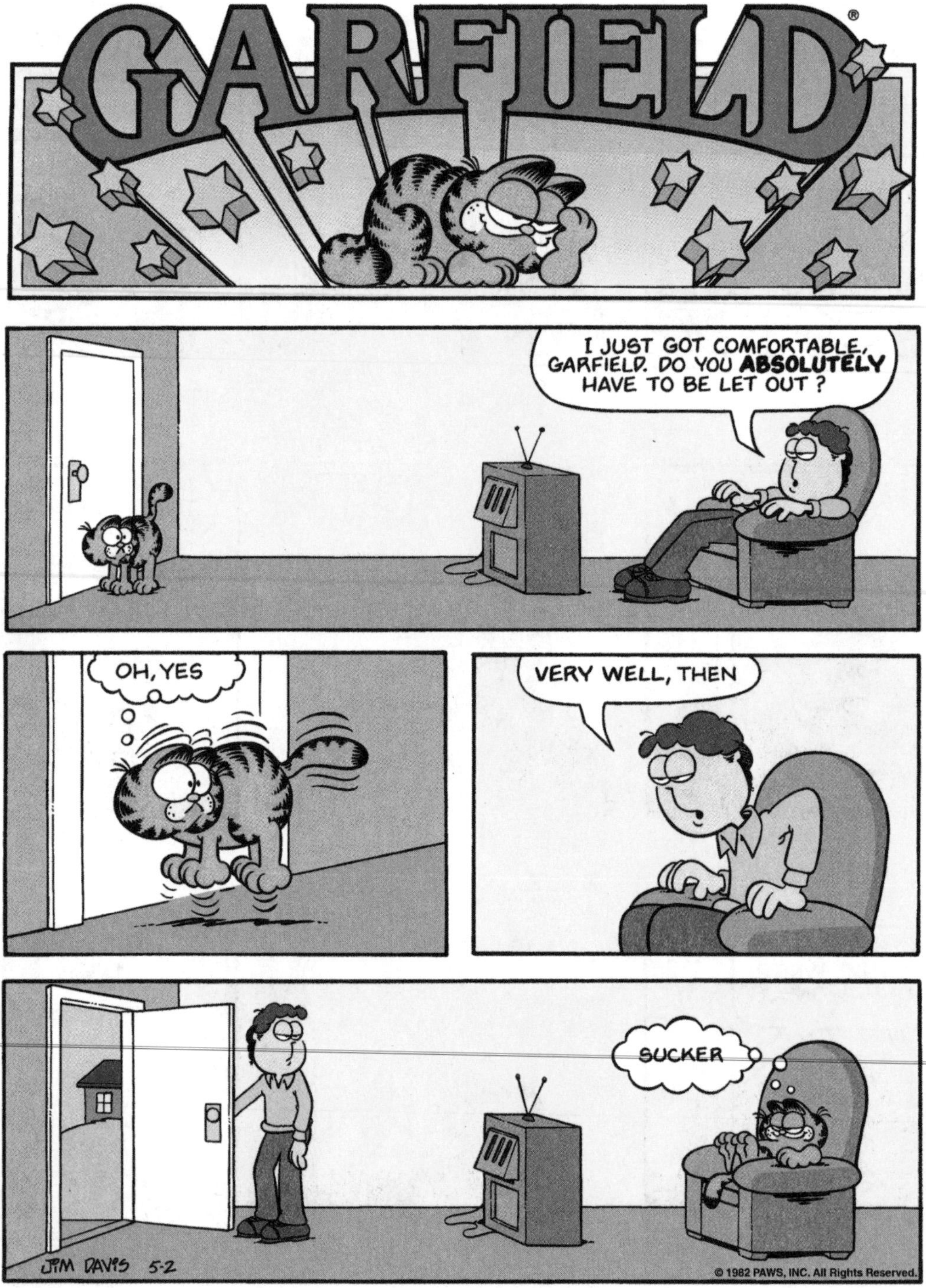
GARFIELD
I JUST GOT COMFORTABLE, GARFIELD. DO YOU ABSOLUTELY HAVE TO BE LET OUT ?
OH, YES
VERY WELL, THEN
SUCKER
JIM DAVIS 5-2
© 1982 PAWS, INC. All Rights Reserved.

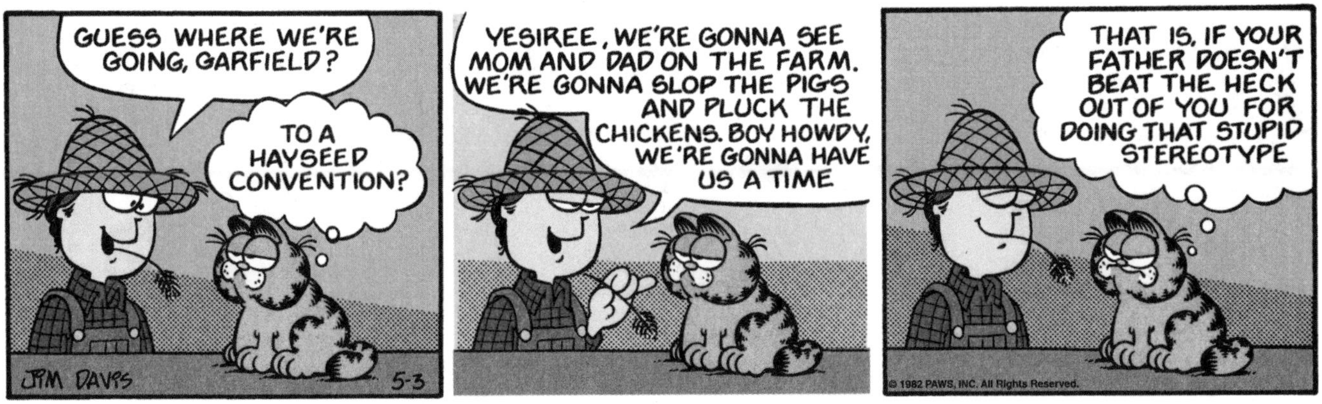
GUESS WHERE WE'RE GOING, GARFIELD?
TO A HAYSEED CONVENTION?
JIM DAVIS
5-3
YESIREE, WE'RE GONNA SEE MOM AND DAD ON THE FARM. WE'RE GONNA SLOP THE PIGS AND PLUCK THE CHICKENS. BOY HOWDY, WE'RE GONNA HAVE US A TIME
THAT IS, IF YOUR FATHER DOESN'T BEAT THE HECK OUT OF YOU FOR DOING THAT STUPID STEREOTYPE
© 1982 PAWS, INC. All Rights Reserved.

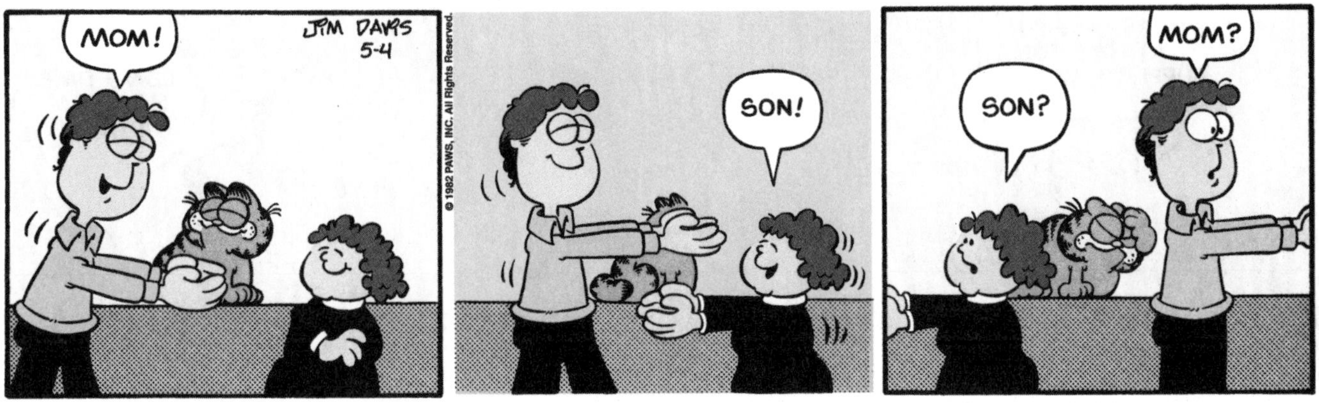
MOM!
JIM DAVIS
5-4
© 1982 PAWS, INC. All Rights Reserved.
SON!
SON?
MOM?

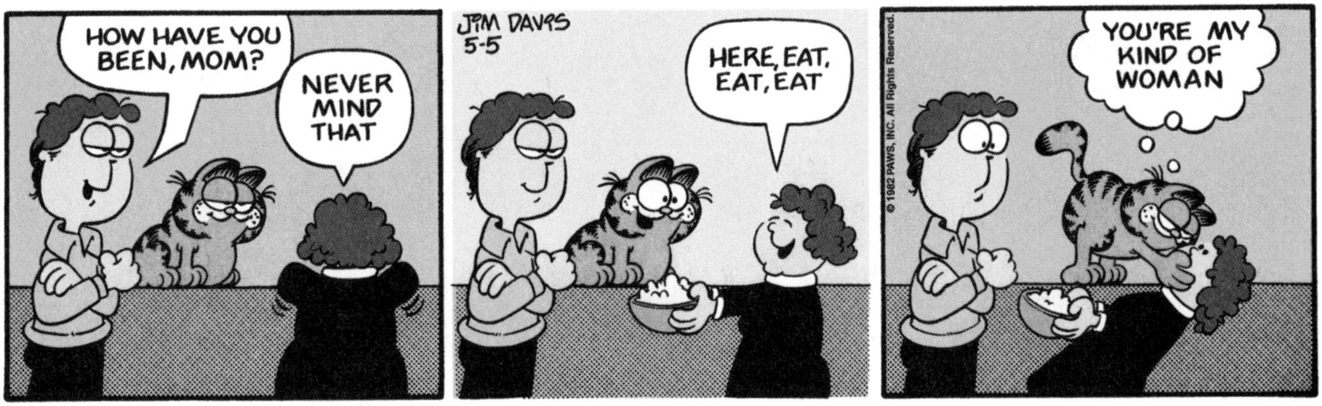
HOW HAVE YOU BEEN, MOM?
NEVER MIND THAT
JIM DAVIS
5-5
HERE, EAT, EAT, EAT
© 1982 PAWS, INC. All Rights Reserved.
YOU'RE MY KIND OF WOMAN

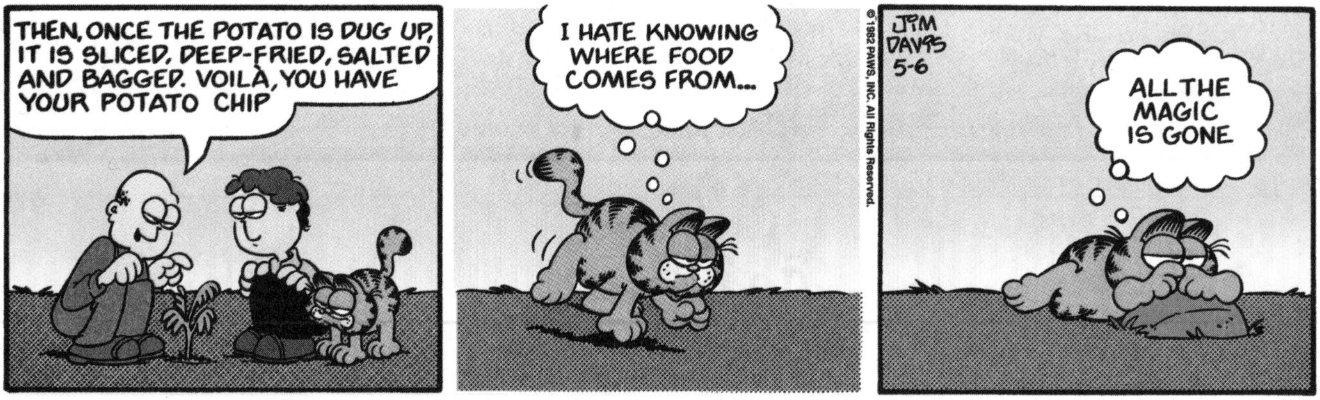
THEN, ONCE THE POTATO IS DUG UP, IT IS SLICED, DEEP-FRIED, SALTED AND BAGGED. VOILÀ, YOU HAVE YOUR POTATO CHIP
I HATE KNOWING WHERE FOOD COMES FROM...
© 1982 PAWS, INC. All Rights Reserved.
JIM DAVIS 5-6
ALL THE MAGIC IS GONE

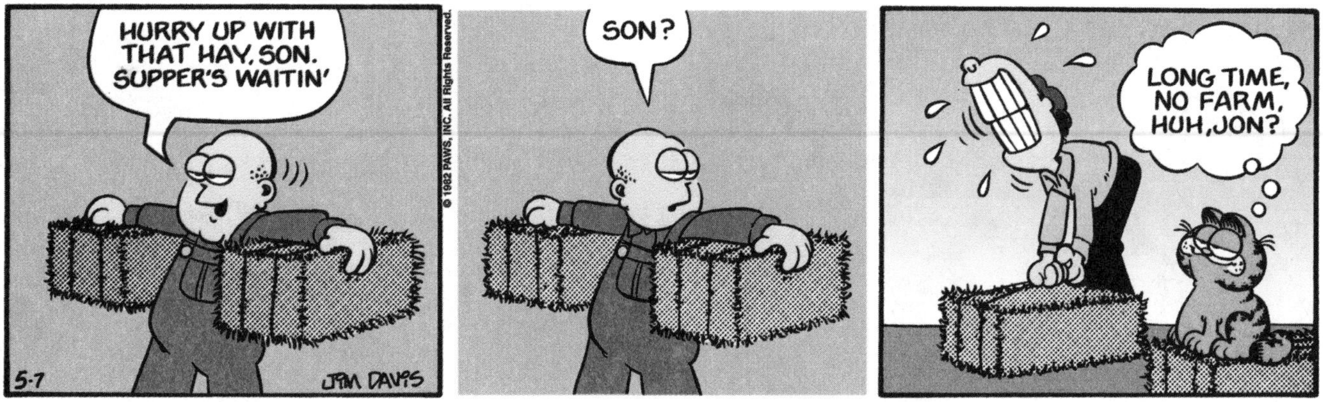
HURRY UP WITH THAT HAY, SON. SUPPER'S WAITIN'
5-7
JIM DAVIS
© 1982 PAWS, INC. All Rights Reserved.
SON?
LONG TIME, NO FARM, HUH, JON?

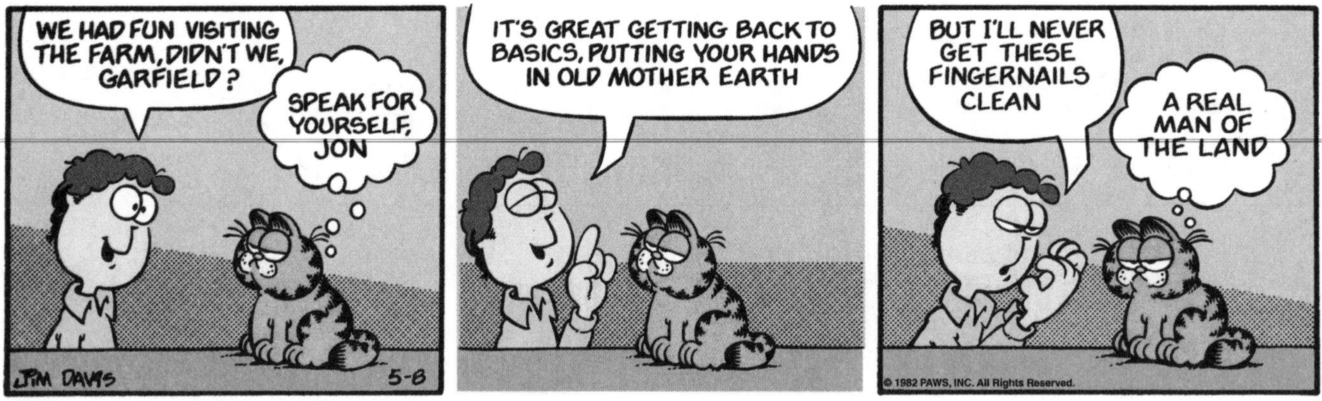
WE HAD FUN VISITING THE FARM, DIDN'T WE, GARFIELD?
SPEAK FOR YOURSELF, JON
JIM DAVIS
5-8
IT'S GREAT GETTING BACK TO BASICS, PUTTING YOUR HANDS IN OLD MOTHER EARTH
BUT I'LL NEVER GET THESE FINGERNAILS CLEAN
A REAL MAN OF THE LAND
© 1982 PAWS, INC. All Rights Reserved.

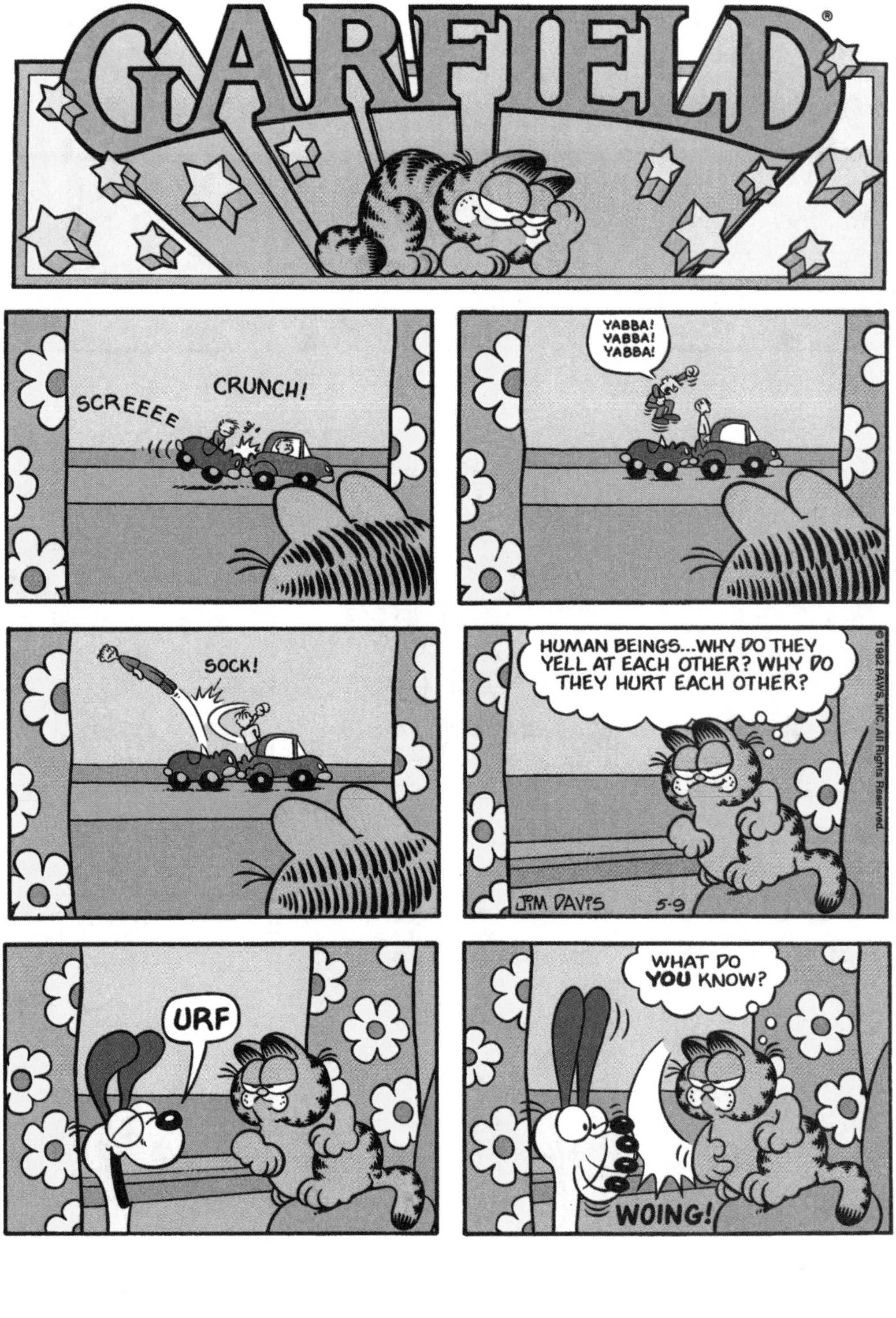
GARFIELD®
SCREEEE
CRUNCH!
YABBA! YABBA! YABBA!
SOCK!
HUMAN BEINGS...WHY DO THEY YELL AT EACH OTHER? WHY DO THEY HURT EACH OTHER?
© 1982 PAWS, INC. All Rights Reserved.
JIM DAVIS 5-9
URF
WHAT DO YOU KNOW?
WOING!

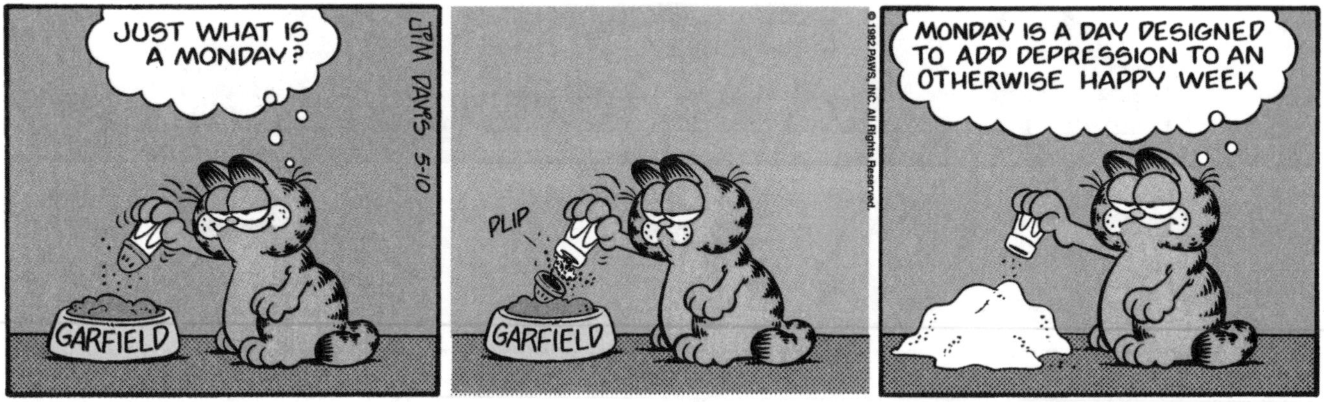
JUST WHAT IS A MONDAY?
JIM DAVIS 5-10
GARFIELD
PLIP
GARFIELD
© 1982 PAWS, INC. All Rights Reserved.
MONDAY IS A DAY DESIGNED TO ADD DEPRESSION TO AN OTHERWISE HAPPY WEEK

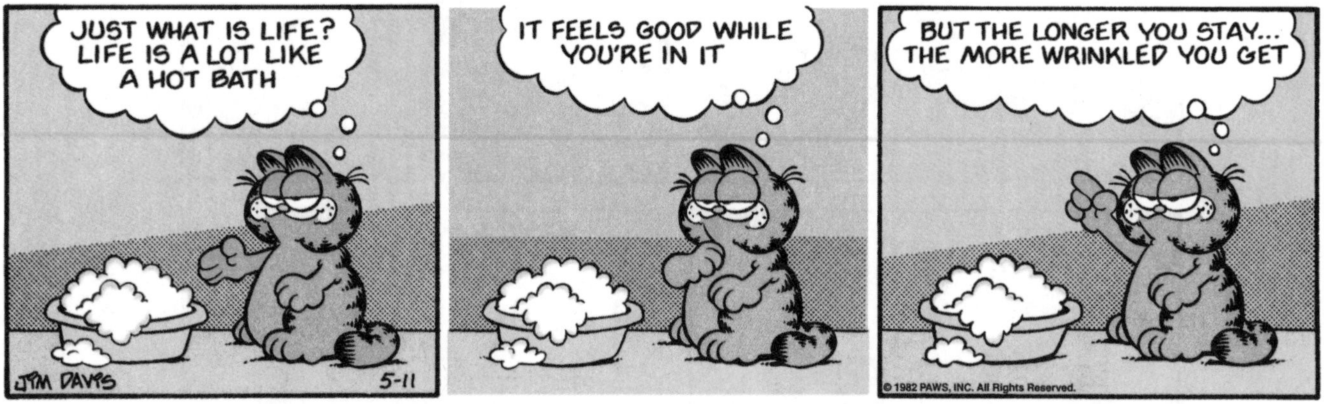
JUST WHAT IS LIFE? LIFE IS A LOT LIKE A HOT BATH
JIM DAVIS
5-11
IT FEELS GOOD WHILE YOU'RE IN IT
BUT THE LONGER YOU STAY... THE MORE WRINKLED YOU GET
© 1982 PAWS, INC. All Rights Reserved.

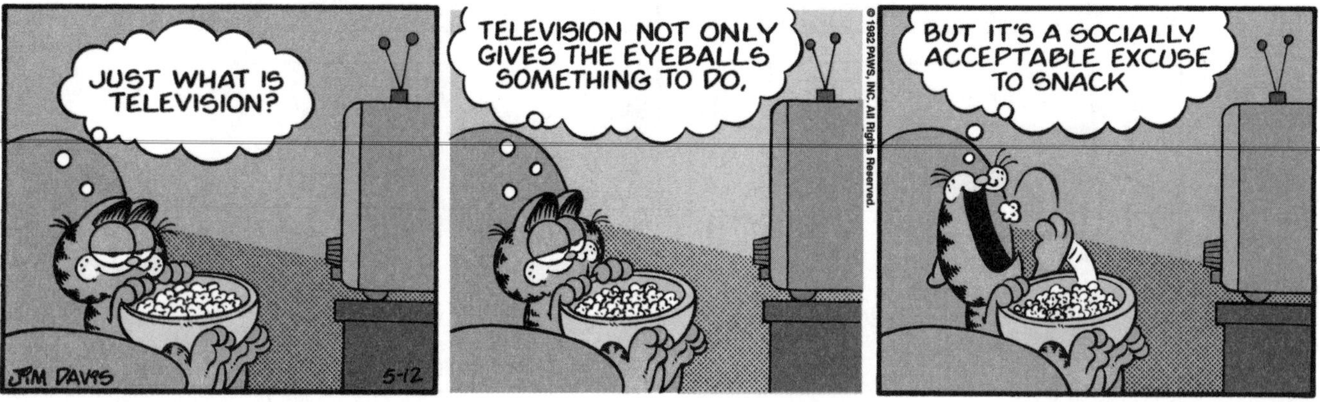
JUST WHAT IS TELEVISION?
JIM DAVIS
5-12
TELEVISION NOT ONLY GIVES THE EYEBALLS SOMETHING TO DO,
© 1982 PAWS, INC. All Rights Reserved.
BUT IT'S A SOCIALLY ACCEPTABLE EXCUSE TO SNACK

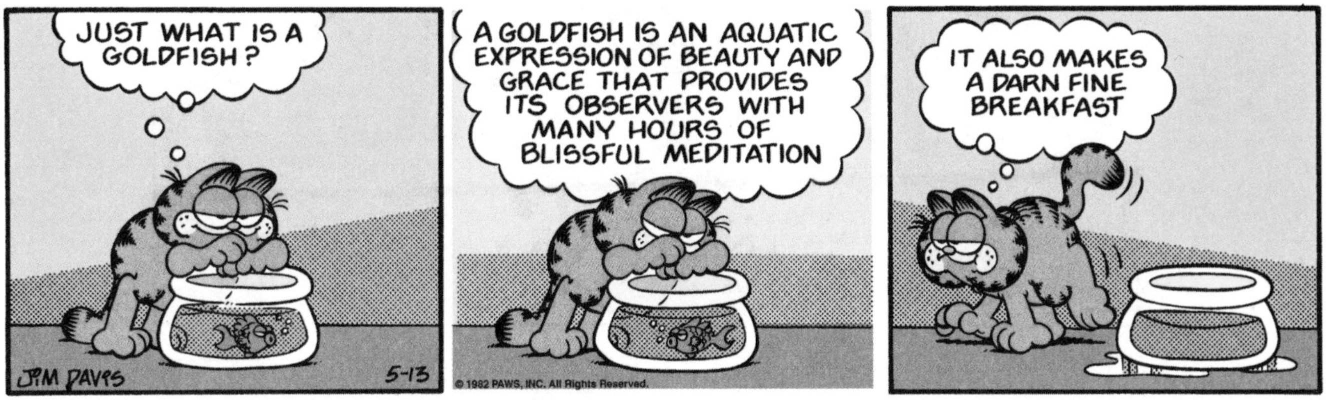
JUST WHAT IS A GOLDFISH?
JIM DAVIS
5-13
A GOLDFISH IS AN AQUATIC EXPRESSION OF BEAUTY AND GRACE THAT PROVIDES ITS OBSERVERS WITH MANY HOURS OF BLISSFUL MEDITATION
© 1982 PAWS, INC. All Rights Reserved.
IT ALSO MAKES A DARN FINE BREAKFAST

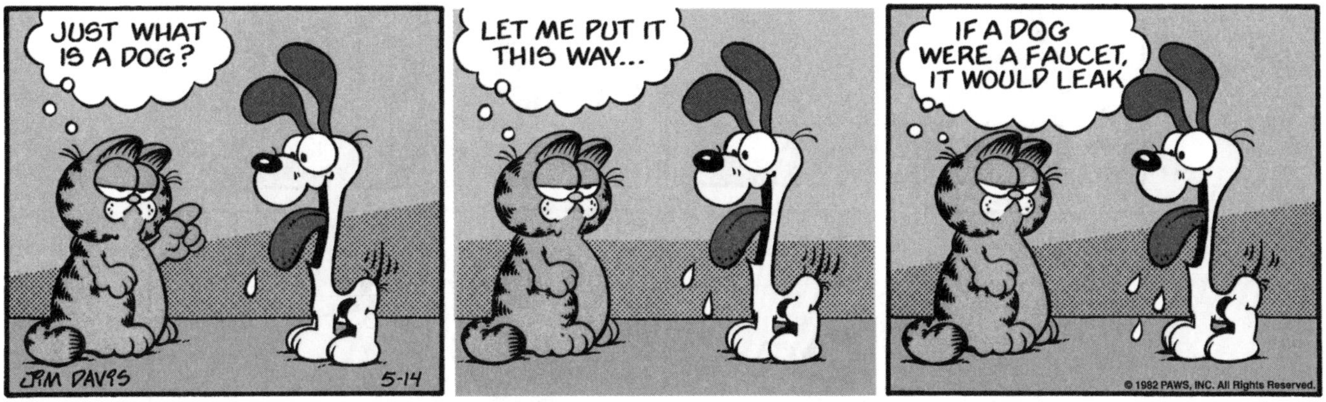
JUST WHAT IS A DOG?
JIM DAVIS
5-14
LET ME PUT IT THIS WAY...
IF A DOG WERE A FAUCET, IT WOULD LEAK
© 1982 PAWS, INC. All Rights Reserved.

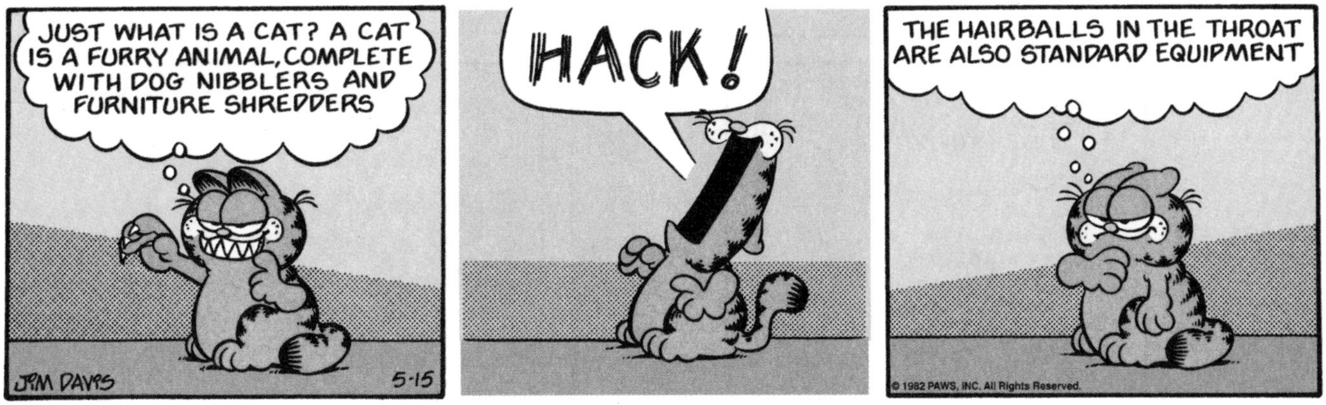
JUST WHAT IS A CAT? A CAT IS A FURRY ANIMAL, COMPLETE WITH DOG NIBBLERS AND FURNITURE SHREDDERS
JIM DAVIS
5-15
HACK!
THE HAIRBALLS IN THE THROAT ARE ALSO STANDARD EQUIPMENT
© 1982 PAWS, INC. All Rights Reserved.

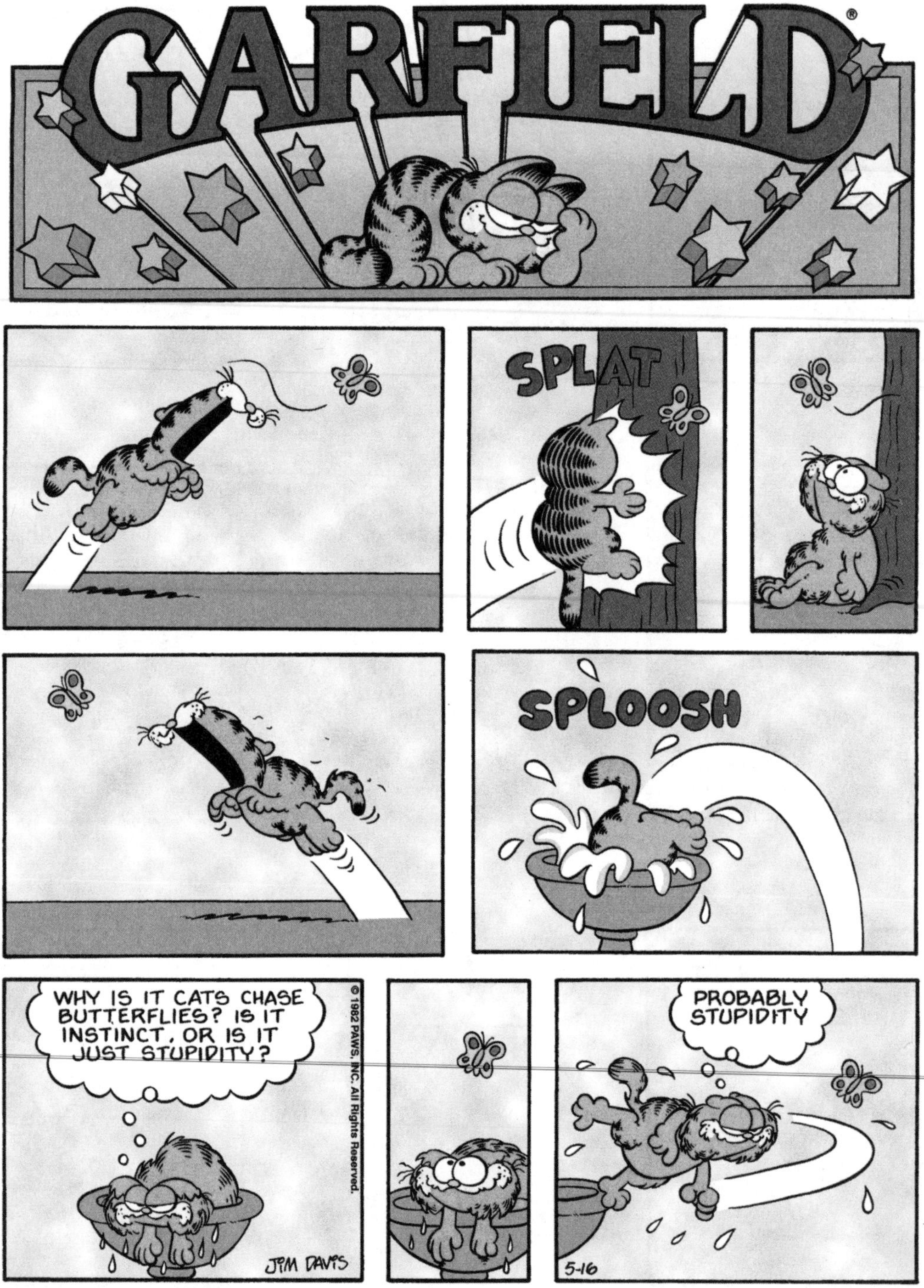
GARFIELD
SPLAT
SPLOOSH
WHY IS IT CATS CHASE BUTTERFLIES? IS IT INSTINCT, OR IS IT JUST STUPIDITY?
© 1982 PAWS, INC. All Rights Reserved.
JIM DAVIS
PROBABLY STUPIDITY
5-16

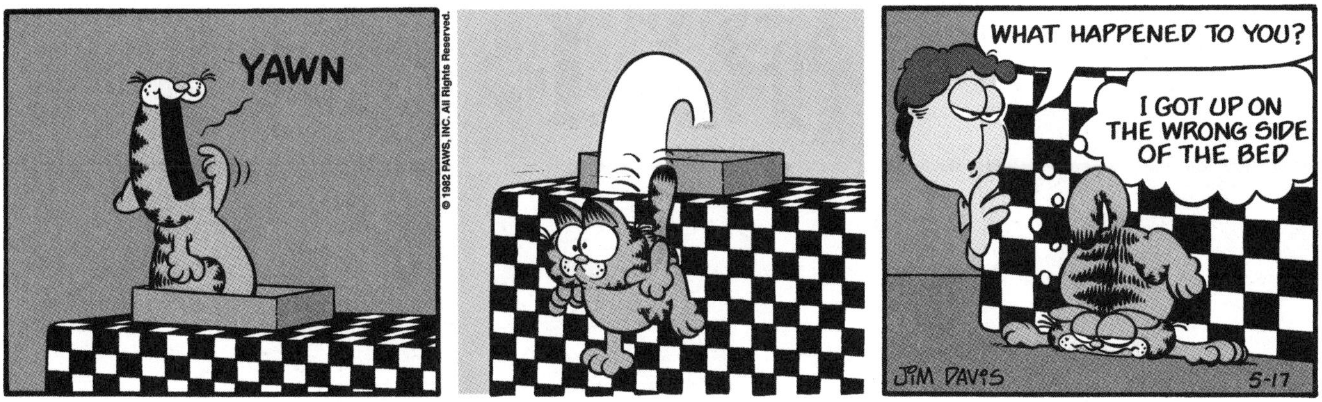
YAWN
© 1982 PAWS, INC. All Rights Reserved.
WHAT HAPPENED TO YOU?
I GOT UP ON THE WRONG SIDE OF THE BED
JIM DAVIS
5-17

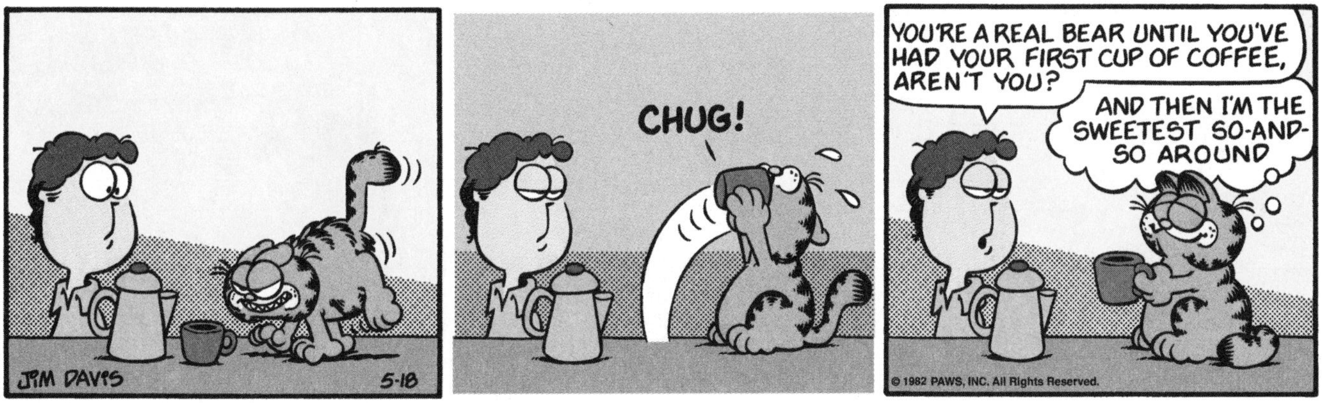
JIM DAVIS
5-18
CHUG!
YOU'RE A REAL BEAR UNTIL YOU'VE HAD YOUR FIRST CUP OF COFFEE, AREN'T YOU?
AND THEN I'M THE SWEETEST SO-AND-SO AROUND
© 1982 PAWS, INC. All Rights Reserved.

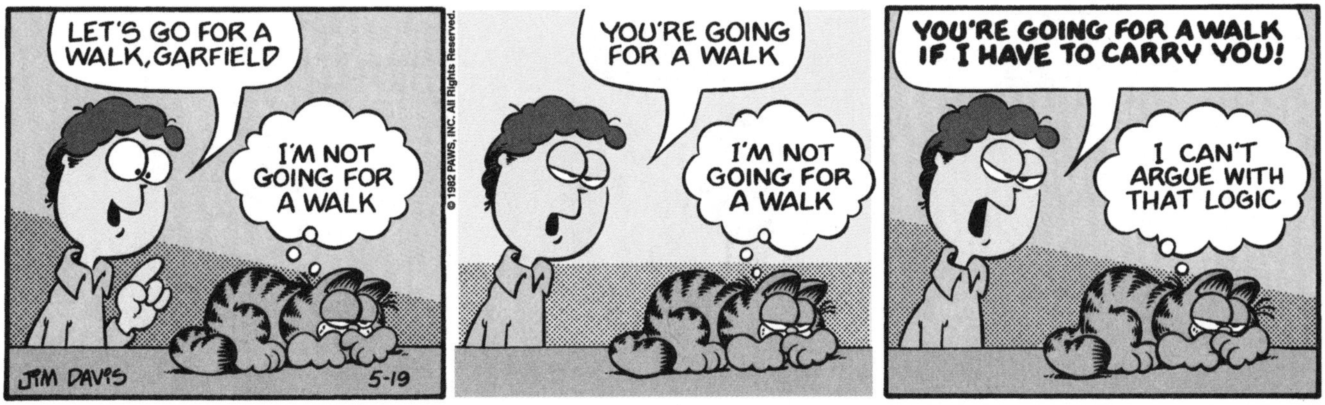
LET'S GO FOR A WALK, GARFIELD
I'M NOT GOING FOR A WALK
JIM DAVIS
5-19
© 1982 PAWS, INC. All Rights Reserved.
YOU'RE GOING FOR A WALK
I'M NOT GOING FOR A WALK
YOU'RE GOING FOR A WALK IF I HAVE TO CARRY YOU!
I CAN'T ARGUE WITH THAT LOGIC

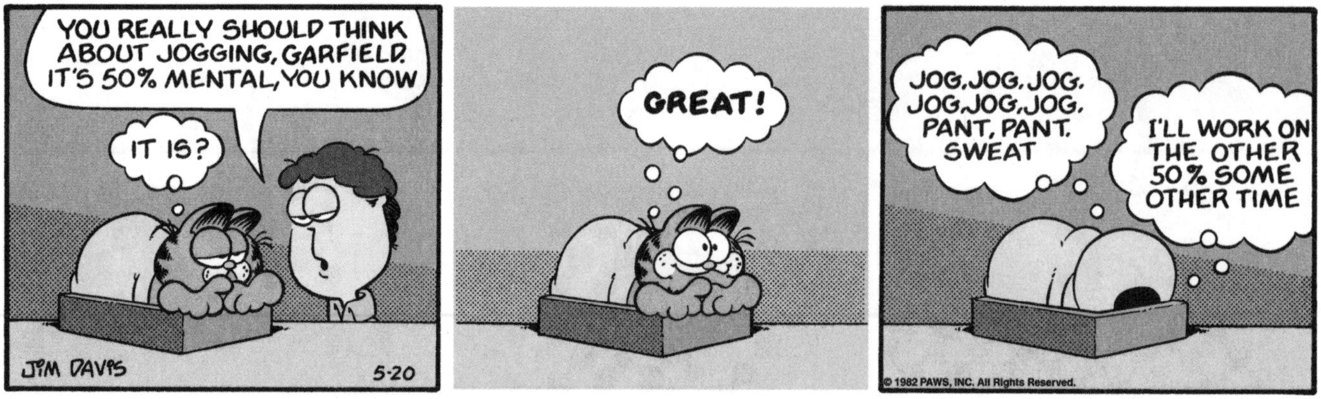
YOU REALLY SHOULD THINK ABOUT JOGGING, GARFIELD. IT'S 50% MENTAL, YOU KNOW
IT IS?
GREAT!
JOG, JOG, JOG, JOG, JOG, JOG, PANT, PANT, SWEAT
I'LL WORK ON THE OTHER 50% SOME OTHER TIME
JIM DAVIS 5-20
© 1982 PAWS, INC. All Rights Reserved.

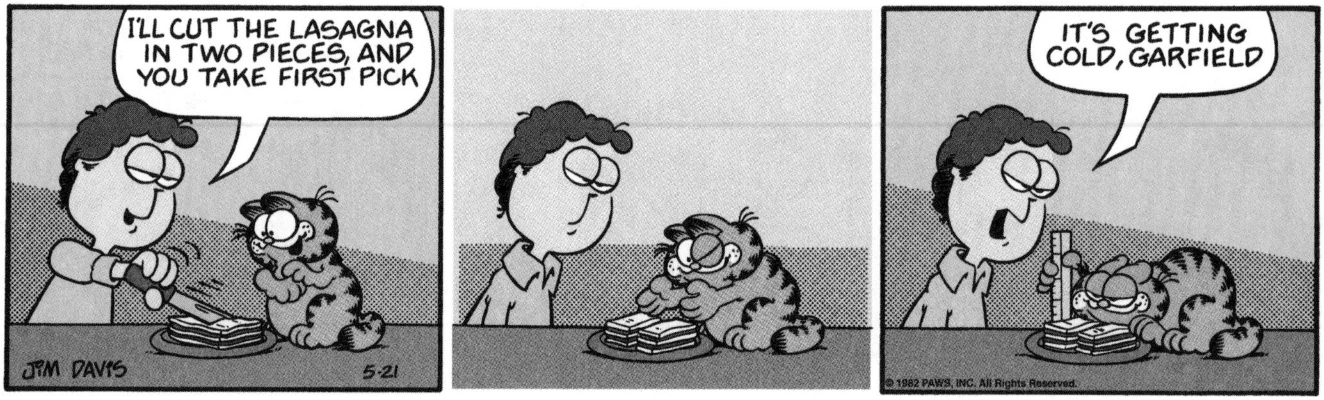
I'LL CUT THE LASAGNA IN TWO PIECES, AND YOU TAKE FIRST PICK
IT'S GETTING COLD, GARFIELD
JIM DAVIS 5-21
© 1982 PAWS, INC. All Rights Reserved.

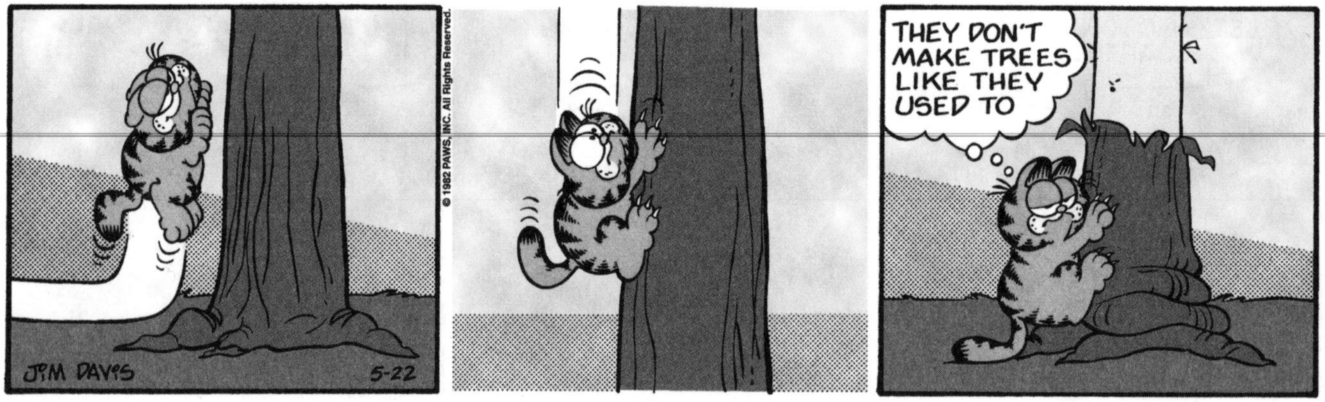
JIM DAVIS 5-22
© 1982 PAWS, INC. All Rights Reserved.
THEY DON'T MAKE TREES LIKE THEY USED TO

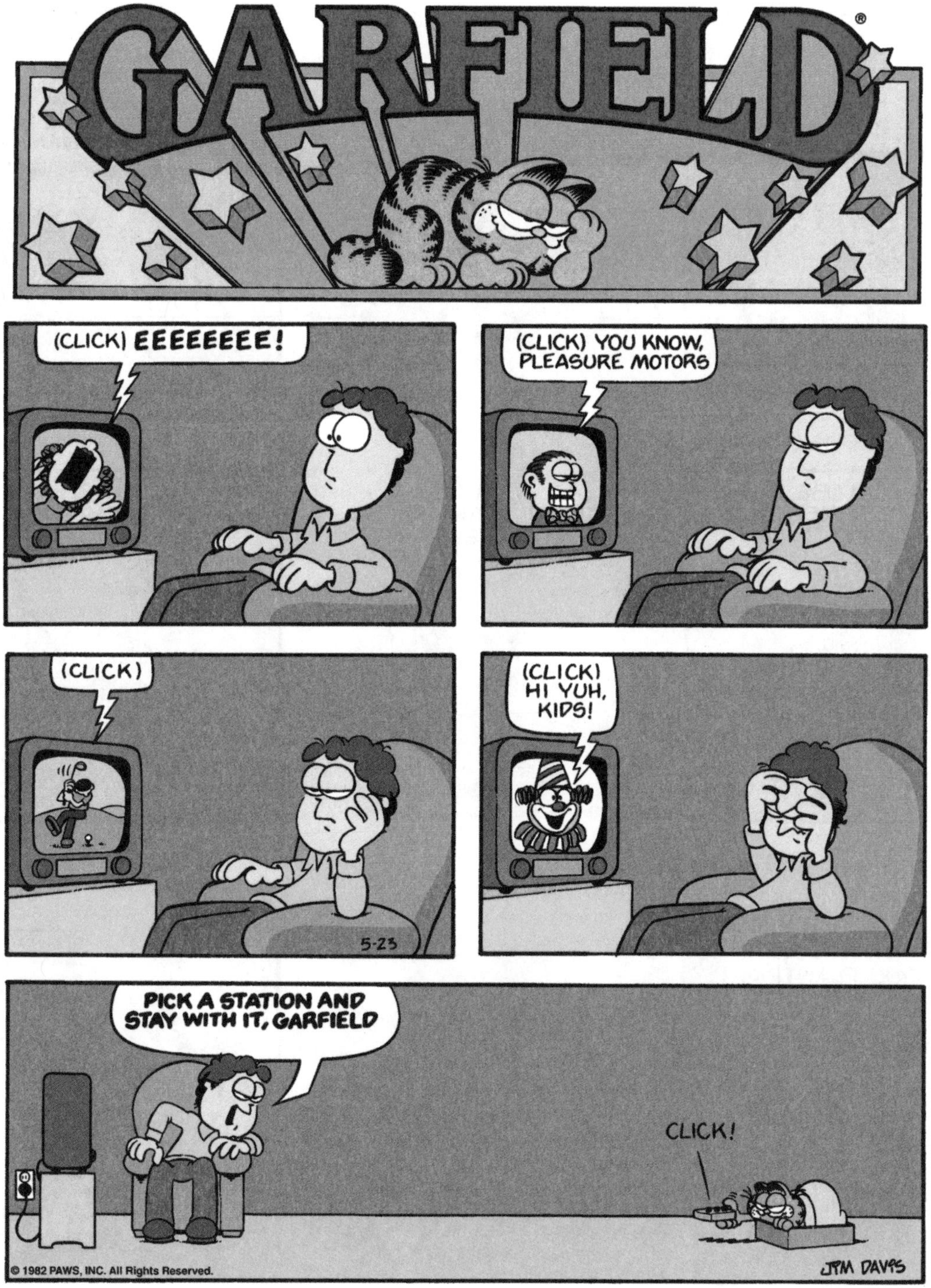
GARFIELD®
(CLICK) EEEEEEEE!
(CLICK) YOU KNOW, PLEASURE MOTORS
(CLICK)
(CLICK) HI YUH, KIDS!
5-23
PICK A STATION AND STAY WITH IT, GARFIELD
CLICK!
© 1982 PAWS, INC. All Rights Reserved.
JIM DAVIS

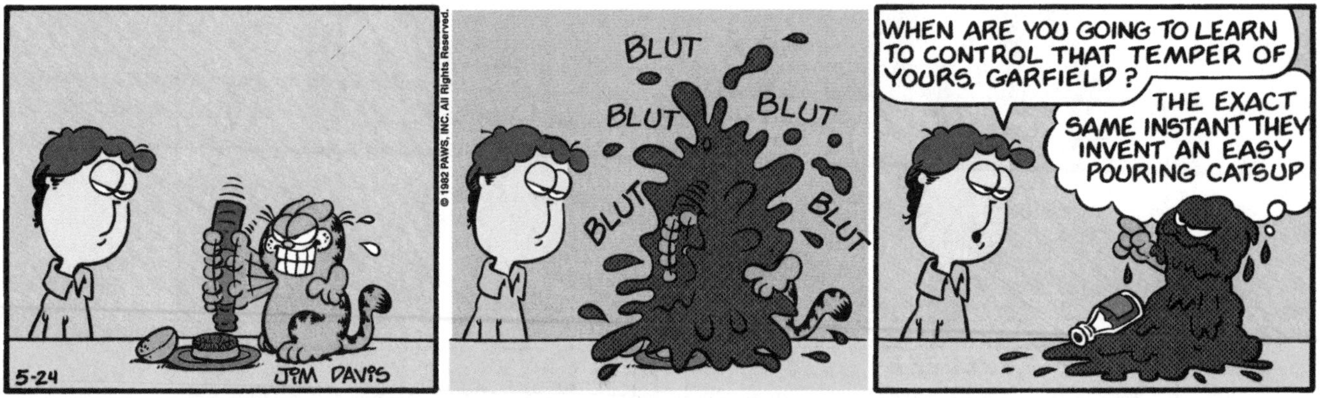
5-24
JIM DAVIS
© 1982 PAWS, INC. All Rights Reserved.
BLUT
BLUT
BLUT
BLUT
BLUT
WHEN ARE YOU GOING TO LEARN TO CONTROL THAT TEMPER OF YOURS, GARFIELD?
THE EXACT SAME INSTANT THEY INVENT AN EASY POURING CATSUP

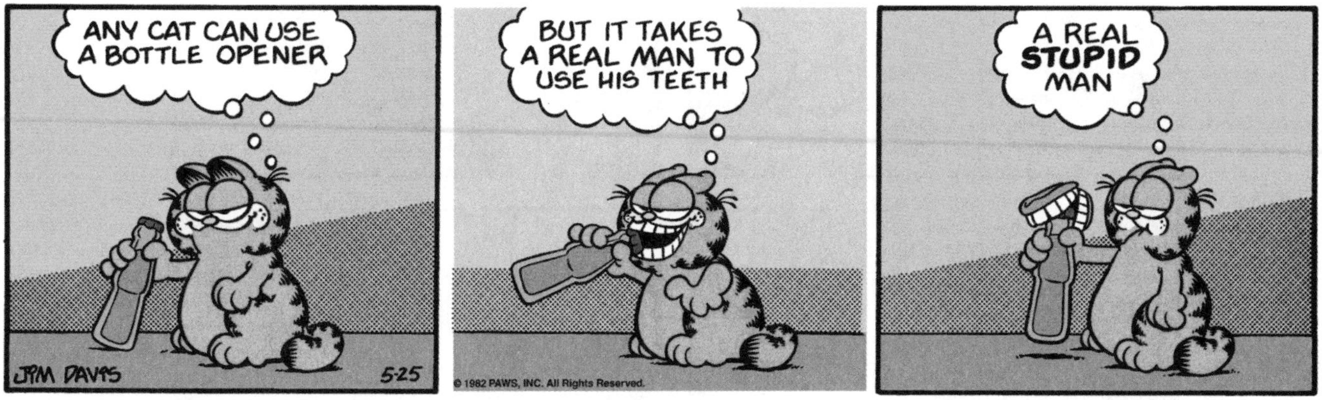
ANY CAT CAN USE A BOTTLE OPENER
JIM DAVIS
5-25
BUT IT TAKES A REAL MAN TO USE HIS TEETH
© 1982 PAWS, INC. All Rights Reserved.
A REAL **STUPID** MAN

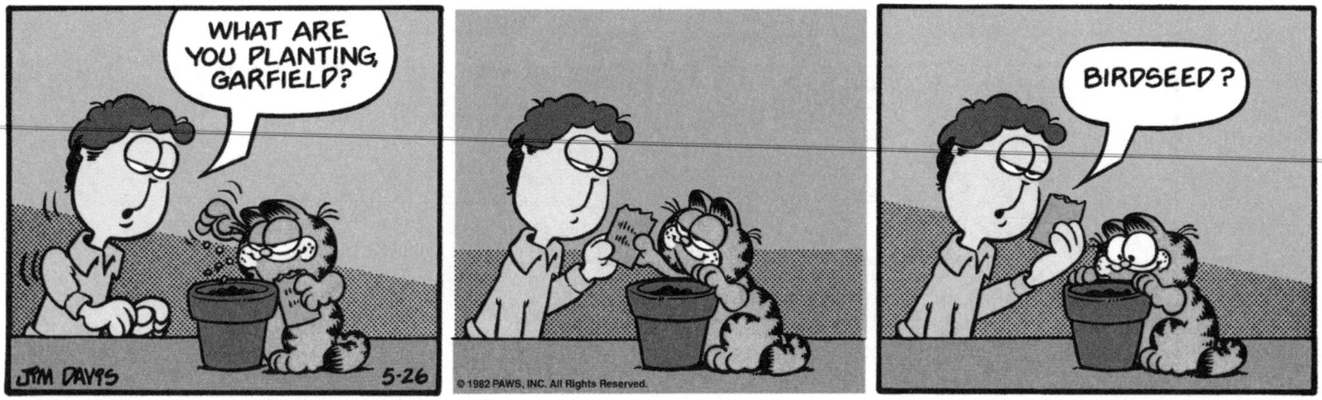
WHAT ARE YOU PLANTING, GARFIELD?
JIM DAVIS
5-26
© 1982 PAWS, INC. All Rights Reserved.
BIRDSEED?

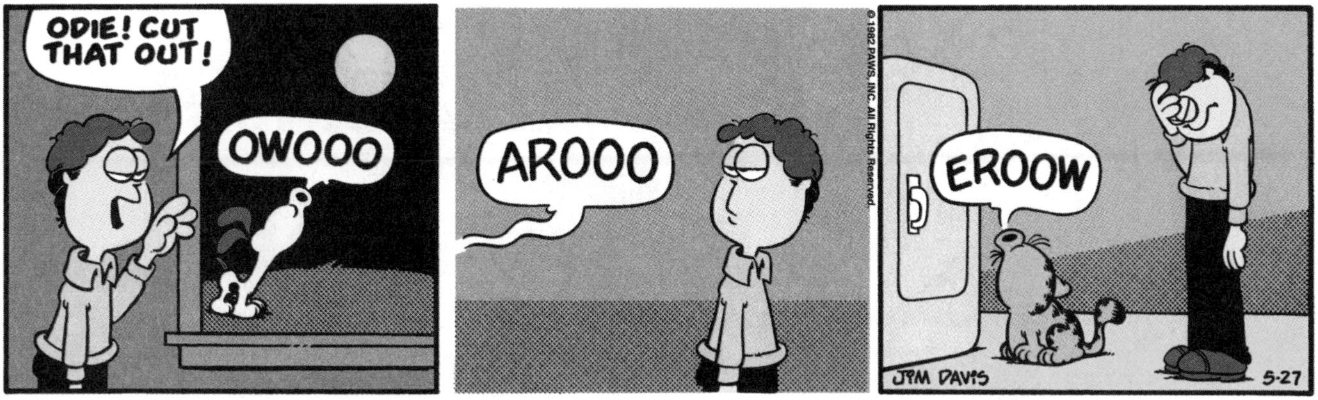
ODIE! CUT THAT OUT!
OWOOO
AROOO
© 1982 PAWS, INC. All Rights Reserved.
EROOW
JIM DAVIS
5-27

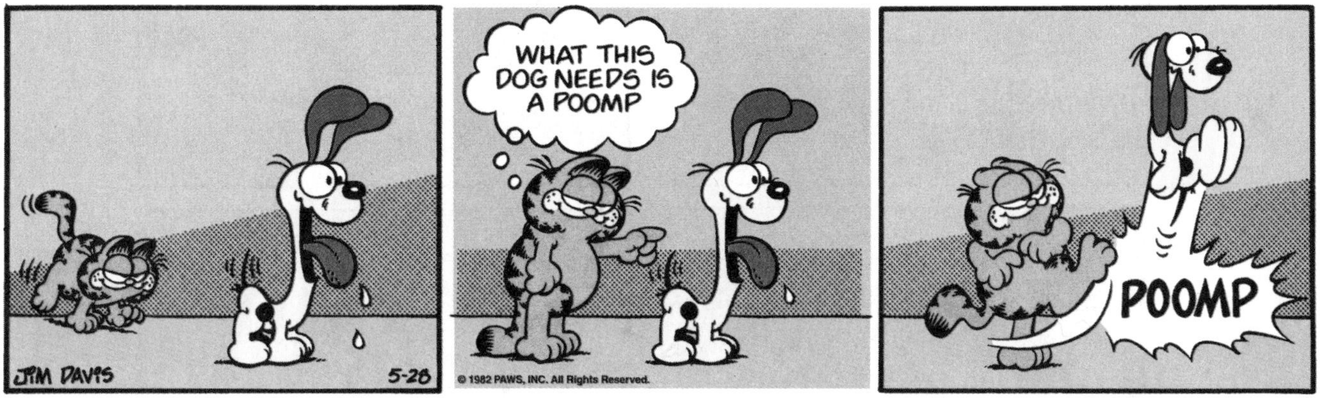
JIM DAVIS
5-28
WHAT THIS DOG NEEDS IS A POOMP
© 1982 PAWS, INC. All Rights Reserved.
POOMP

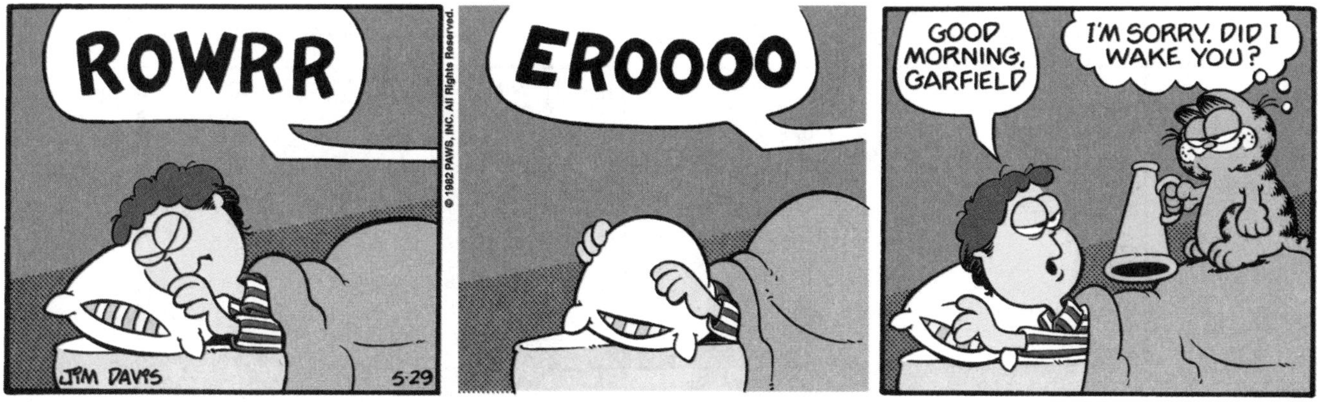
ROWRR
JIM DAVIS
5-29
© 1982 PAWS, INC. All Rights Reserved.
EROOOO
GOOD MORNING, GARFIELD
I'M SORRY. DID I WAKE YOU?

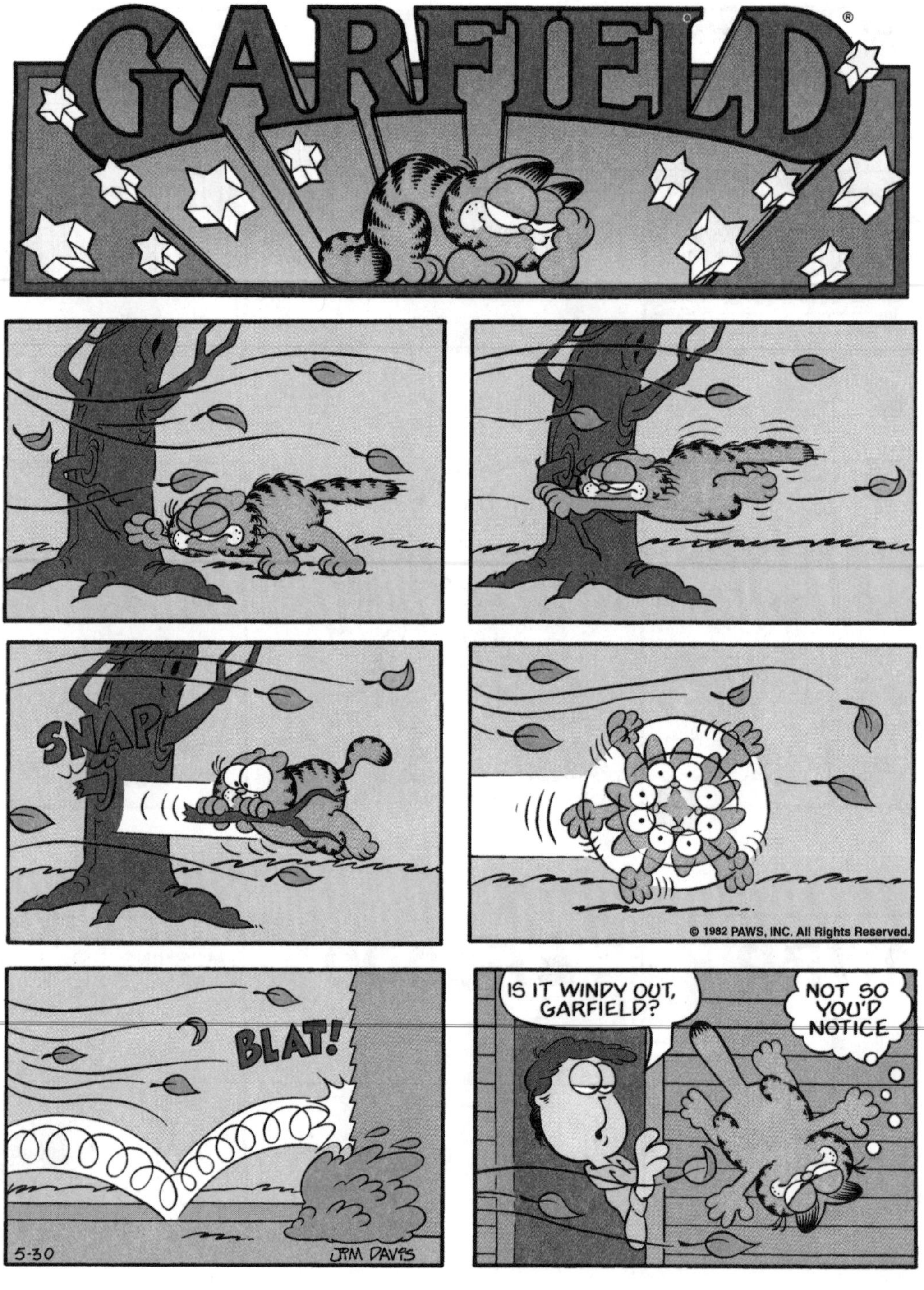
GARFIELD®
SNAP
© 1982 PAWS, INC. All Rights Reserved.
BLAT!
5-30
JIM DAVIS
IS IT WINDY OUT, GARFIELD?
NOT SO YOU'D NOTICE

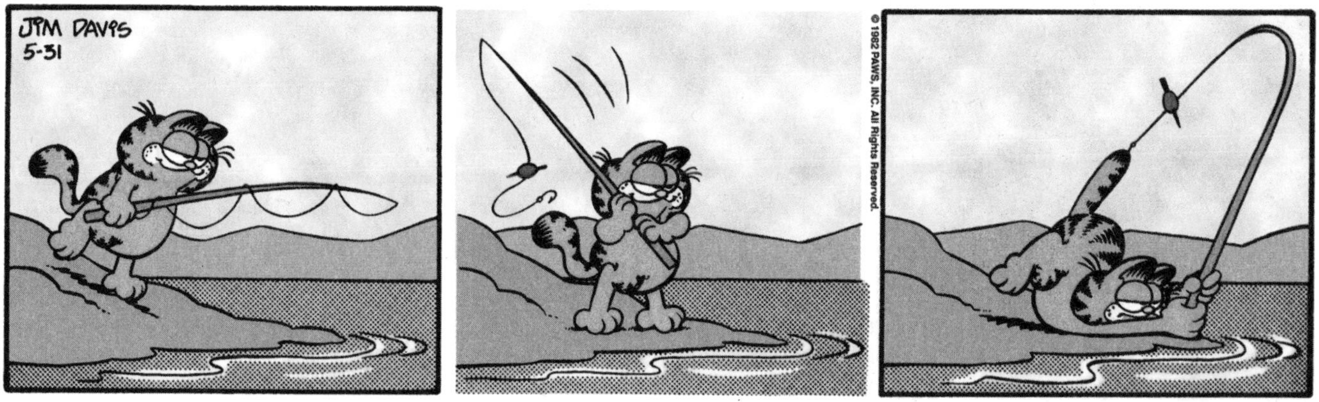
JIM DAVIS
5-31
© 1982 PAWS, INC. All Rights Reserved.

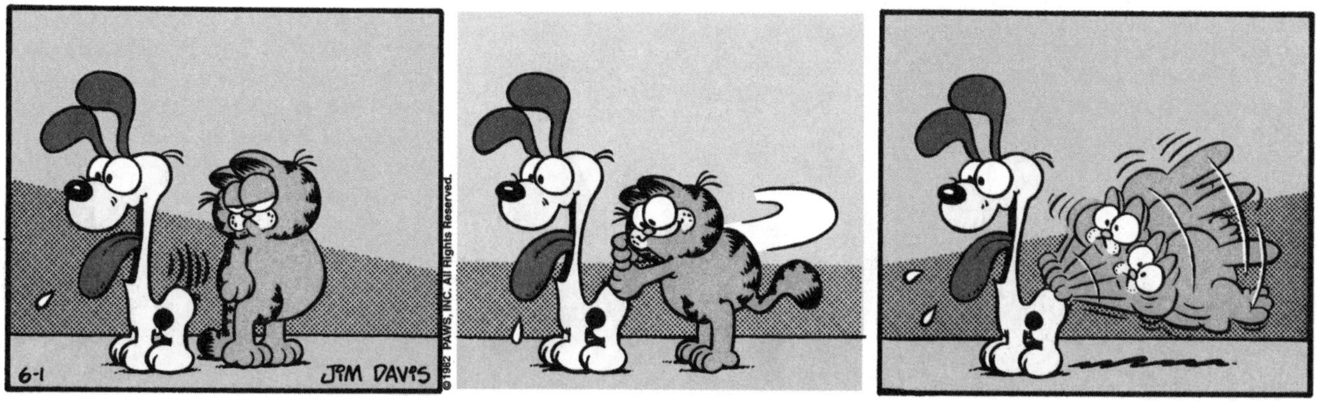
6-1
JIM DAVIS
© 1982 PAWS, INC. All Rights Reserved.

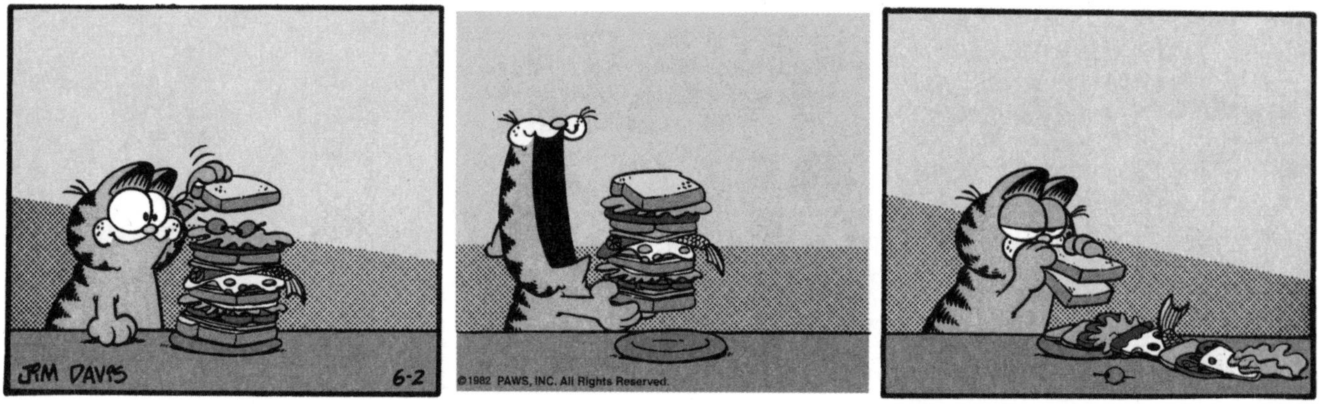
JIM DAVIS
6-2
©1982 PAWS, INC. All Rights Reserved.

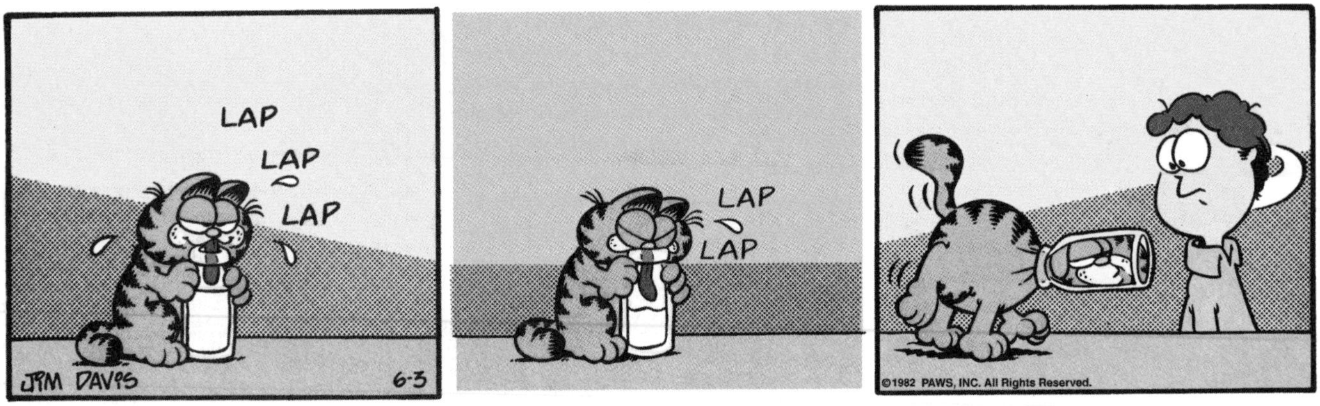
LAP
LAP
LAP
JIM DAVIS
6-3
LAP
LAP
©1982 PAWS, INC. All Rights Reserved.

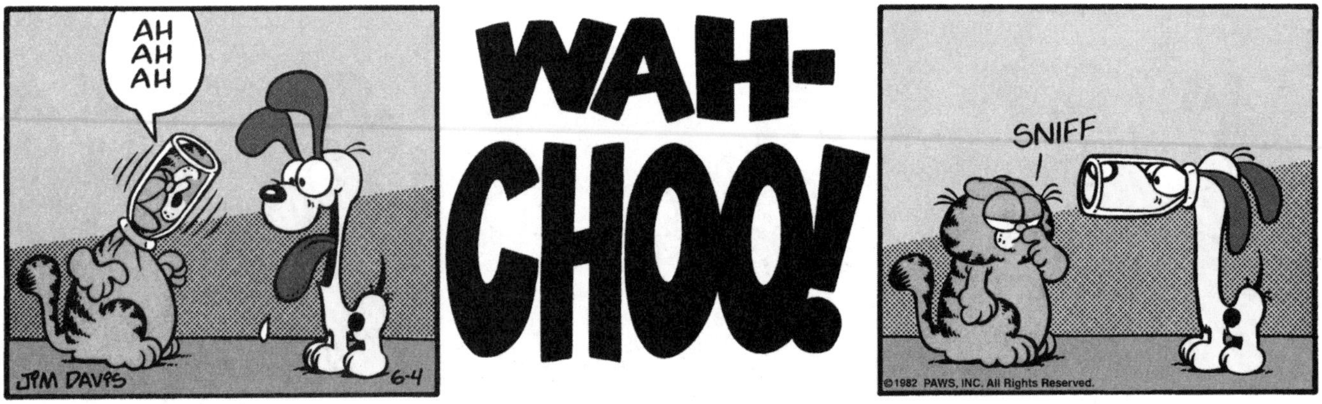
AH
AH
AH
JIM DAVIS
6-4
WAH-
CHOO!
SNIFF
©1982 PAWS, INC. All Rights Reserved.

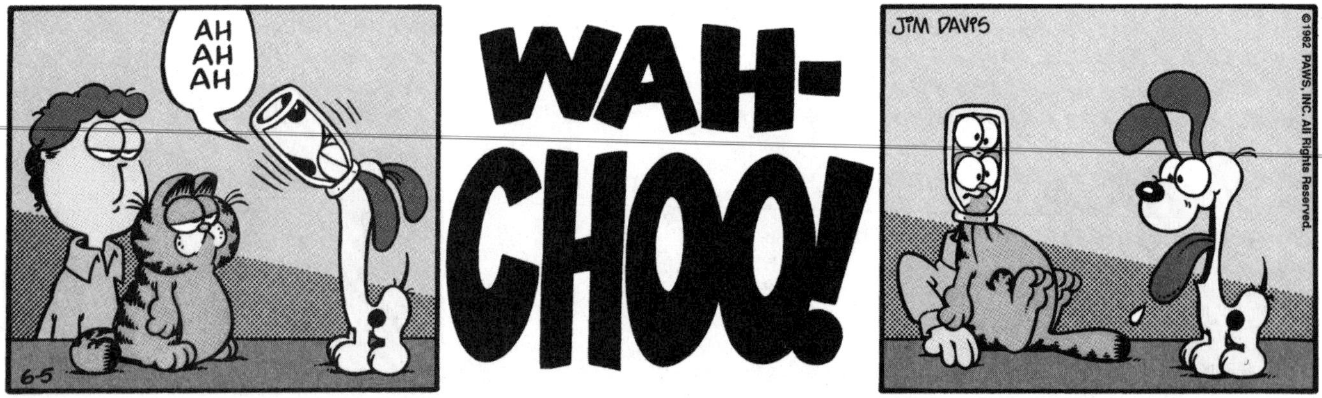
AH
AH
AH
6-5
WAH-
CHOO!
JIM DAVIS
©1982 PAWS, INC. All Rights Reserved.

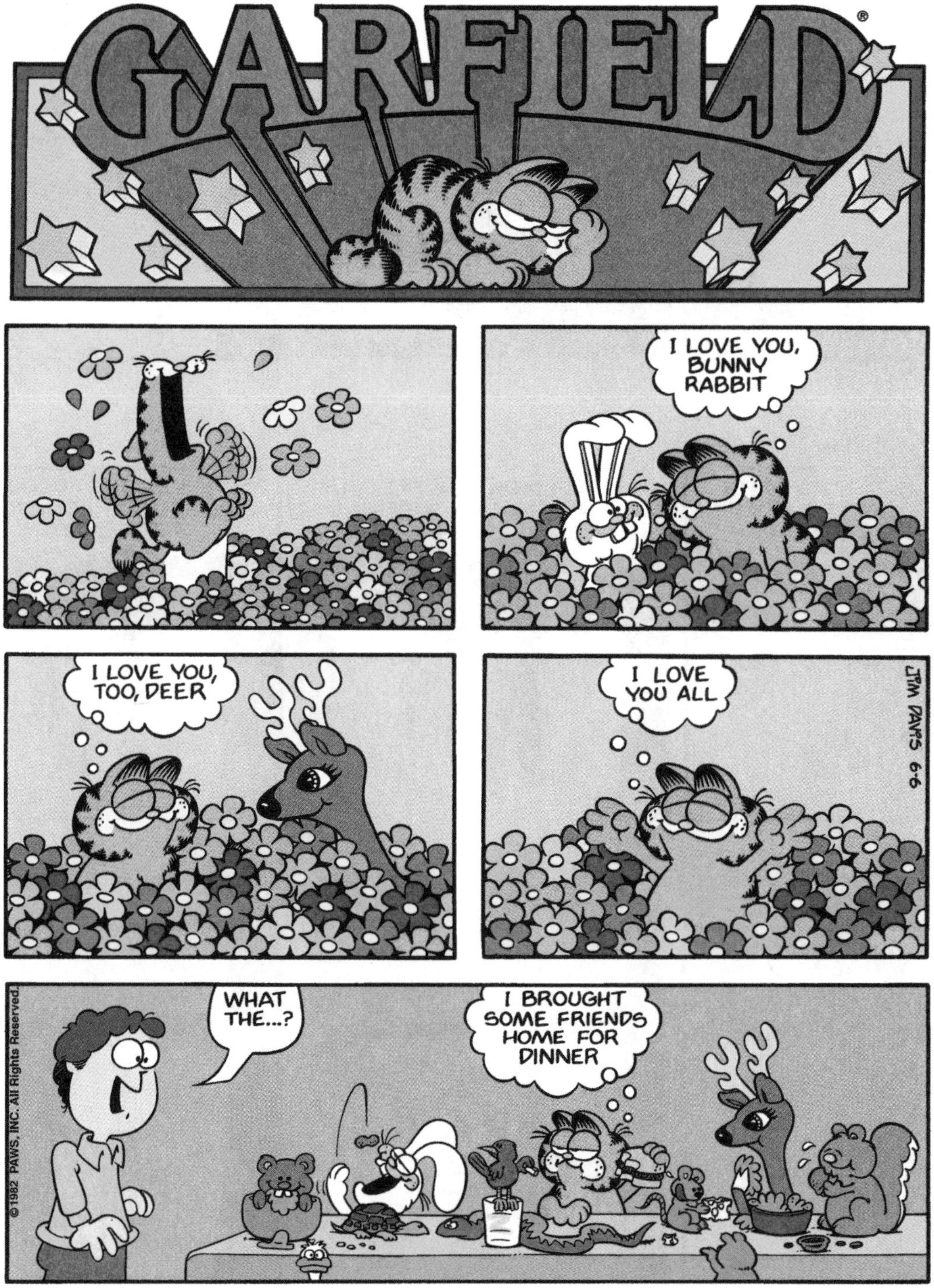
GARFIELD
I LOVE YOU, BUNNY RABBIT
I LOVE YOU, TOO, DEER
I LOVE YOU ALL
JIM DAVIS 6-6
©1982 PAWS, INC. All Rights Reserved.
WHAT THE...?
I BROUGHT SOME FRIENDS HOME FOR DINNER

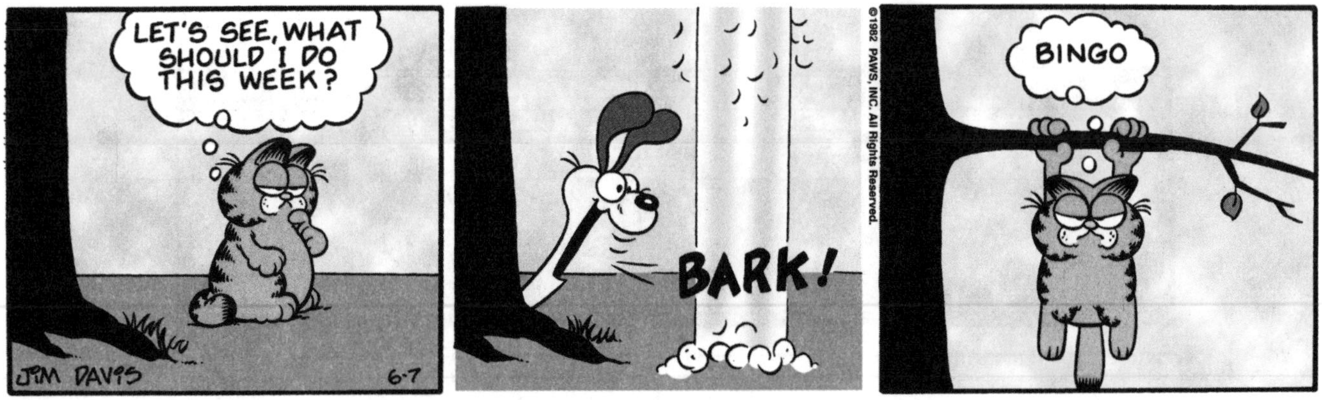
LET'S SEE, WHAT SHOULD I DO THIS WEEK?
JIM DAVIS
6-7
©1982 PAWS, INC. All Rights Reserved.
BARK!
BINGO

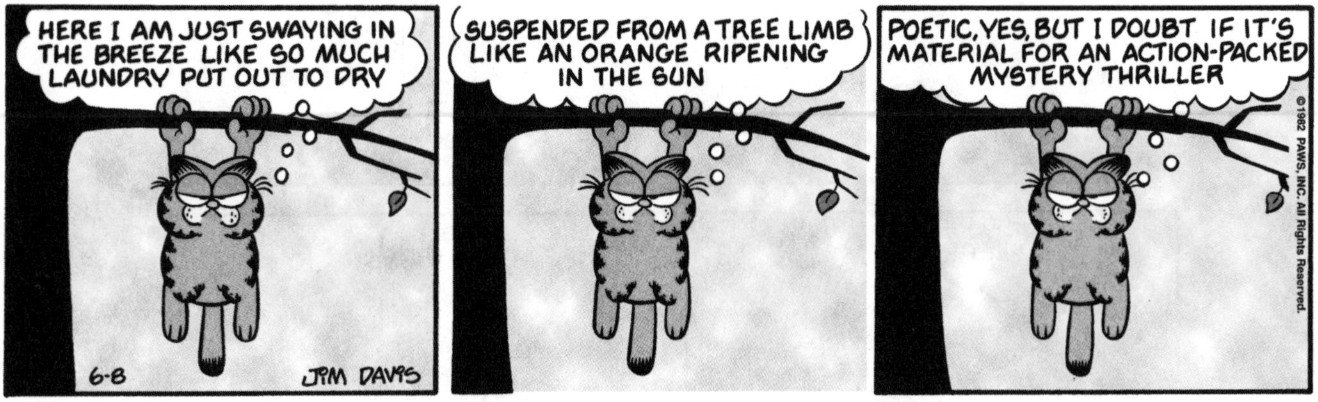
HERE I AM JUST SWAYING IN THE BREEZE LIKE SO MUCH LAUNDRY PUT OUT TO DRY
6-8
JIM DAVIS
SUSPENDED FROM A TREE LIMB LIKE AN ORANGE RIPENING IN THE SUN
POETIC, YES, BUT I DOUBT IF IT'S MATERIAL FOR AN ACTION-PACKED MYSTERY THRILLER
©1982 PAWS, INC. All Rights Reserved.

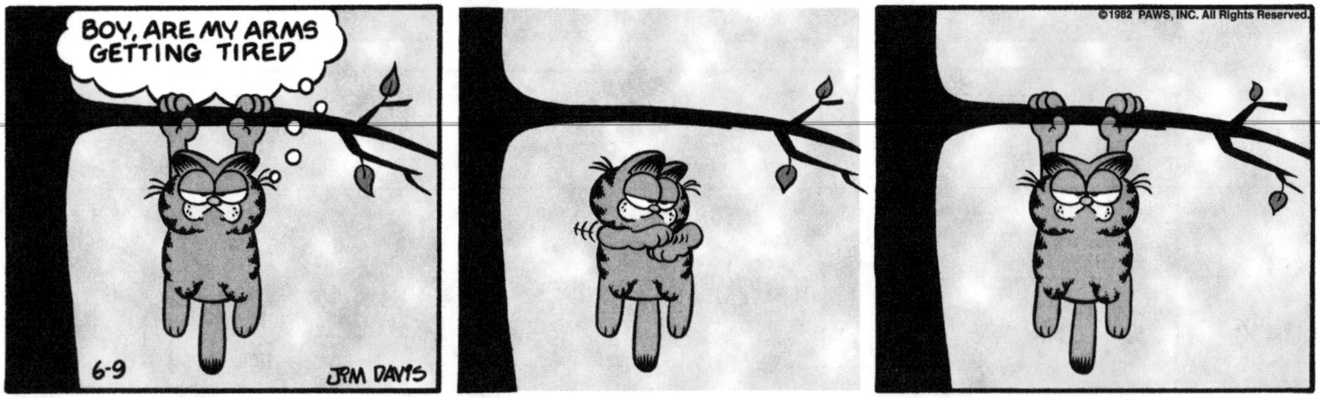
BOY, ARE MY ARMS GETTING TIRED
6-9
JIM DAVIS
©1982 PAWS, INC. All Rights Reserved.

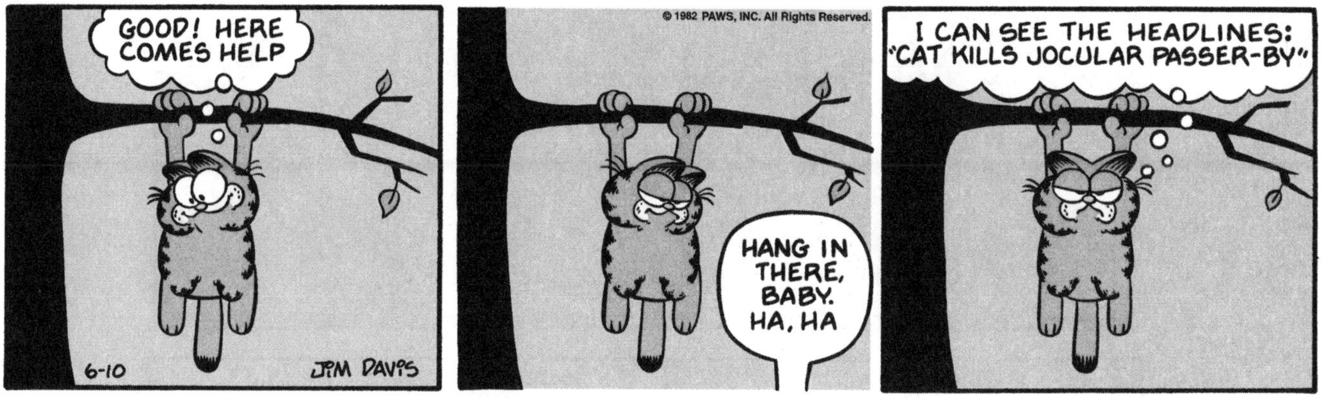
GOOD! HERE COMES HELP
6-10
JIM DAVIS
© 1982 PAWS, INC. All Rights Reserved.
HANG IN THERE, BABY. HA, HA
I CAN SEE THE HEADLINES: "CAT KILLS JOCULAR PASSER-BY"

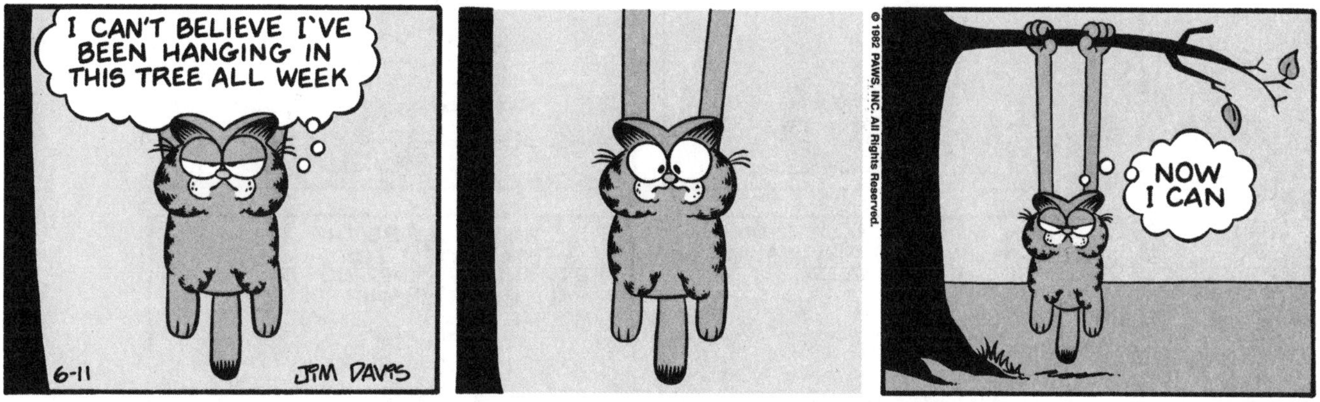
I CAN'T BELIEVE I'VE BEEN HANGING IN THIS TREE ALL WEEK
6-11
JIM DAVIS
© 1982 PAWS, INC. All Rights Reserved.
NOW I CAN

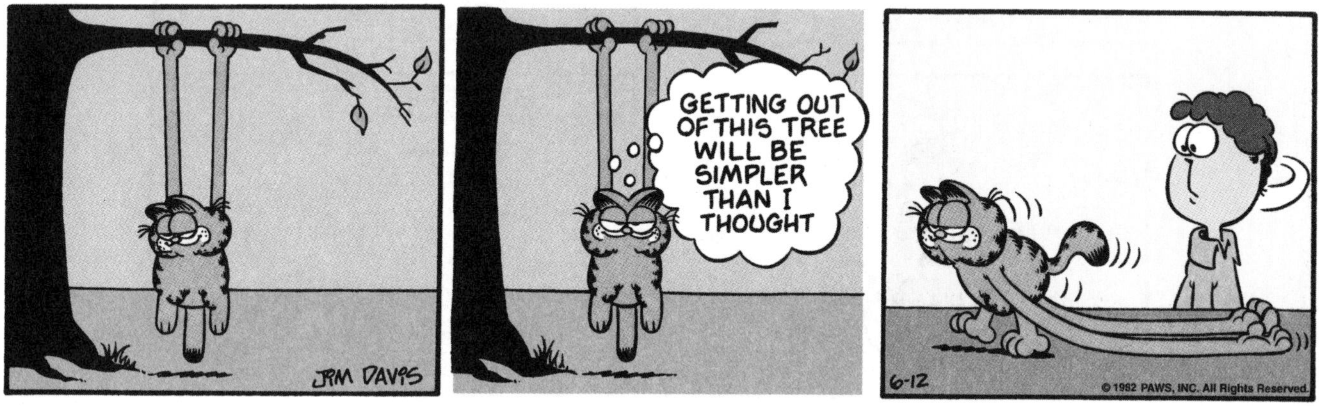
JIM DAVIS
GETTING OUT OF THIS TREE WILL BE SIMPLER THAN I THOUGHT
6-12
© 1982 PAWS, INC. All Rights Reserved.

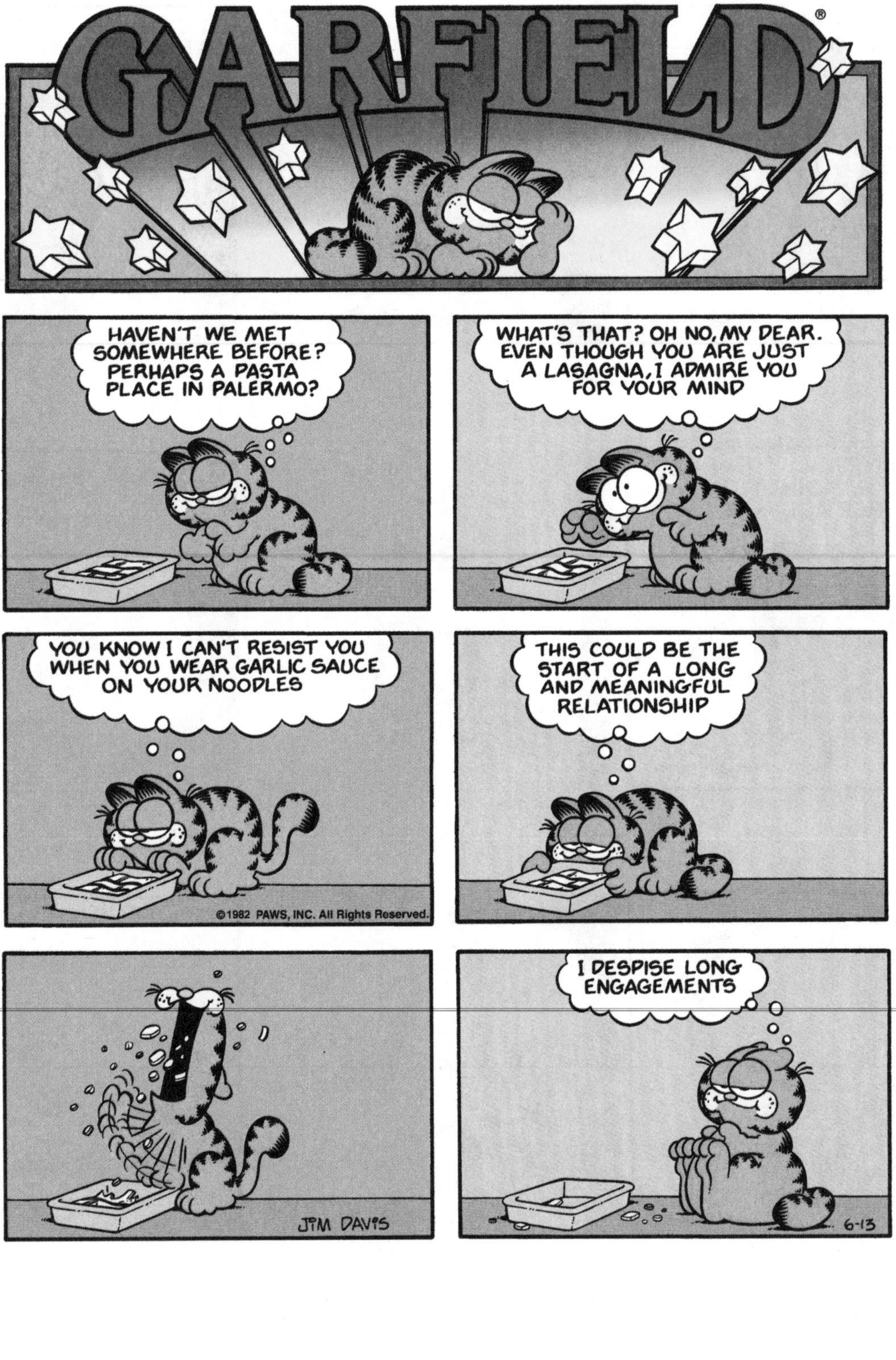
GARFIELD
HAVEN'T WE MET SOMEWHERE BEFORE? PERHAPS A PASTA PLACE IN PALERMO?
WHAT'S THAT? OH NO, MY DEAR. EVEN THOUGH YOU ARE JUST A LASAGNA, I ADMIRE YOU FOR YOUR MIND
YOU KNOW I CAN'T RESIST YOU WHEN YOU WEAR GARLIC SAUCE ON YOUR NOODLES
©1982 PAWS, INC. All Rights Reserved.
THIS COULD BE THE START OF A LONG AND MEANINGFUL RELATIONSHIP
JIM DAVIS
I DESPISE LONG ENGAGEMENTS
6-13

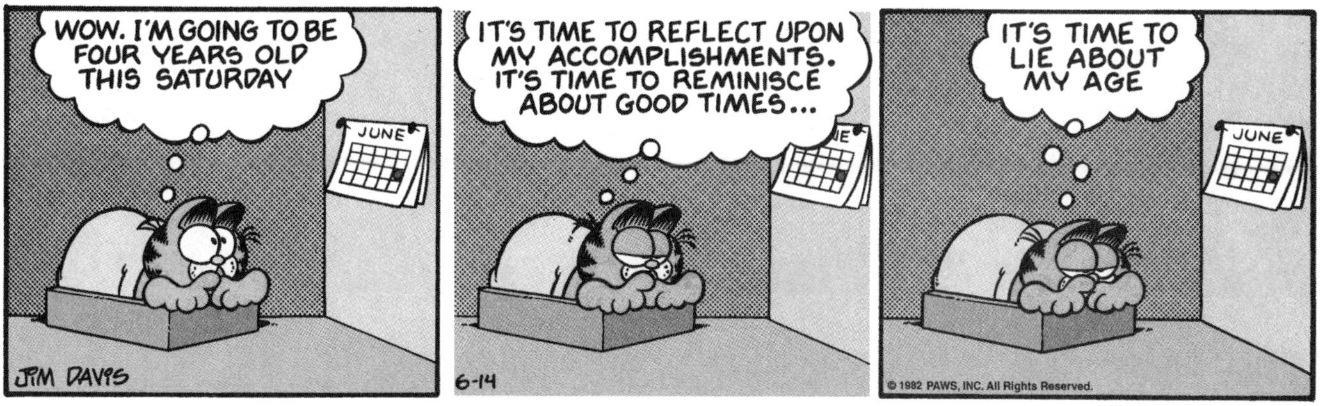
WOW. I'M GOING TO BE FOUR YEARS OLD THIS SATURDAY
JUNE
JIM DAVIS
IT'S TIME TO REFLECT UPON MY ACCOMPLISHMENTS. IT'S TIME TO REMINISCE ABOUT GOOD TIMES...
6-14
IT'S TIME TO LIE ABOUT MY AGE
JUNE
© 1982 PAWS, INC. All Rights Reserved.

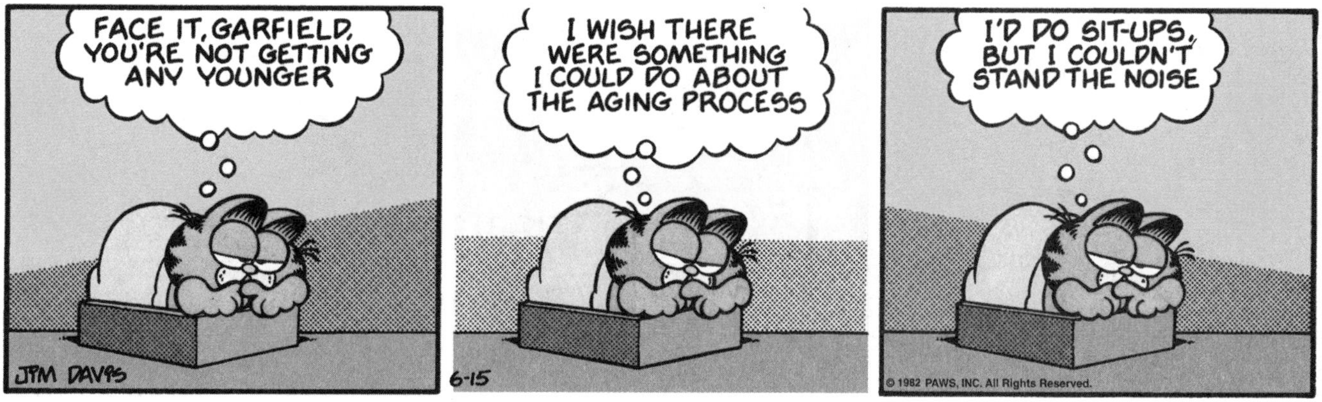
FACE IT, GARFIELD, YOU'RE NOT GETTING ANY YOUNGER
JIM DAVIS
I WISH THERE WERE SOMETHING I COULD DO ABOUT THE AGING PROCESS
6-15
I'D DO SIT-UPS, BUT I COULDN'T STAND THE NOISE
© 1982 PAWS, INC. All Rights Reserved.

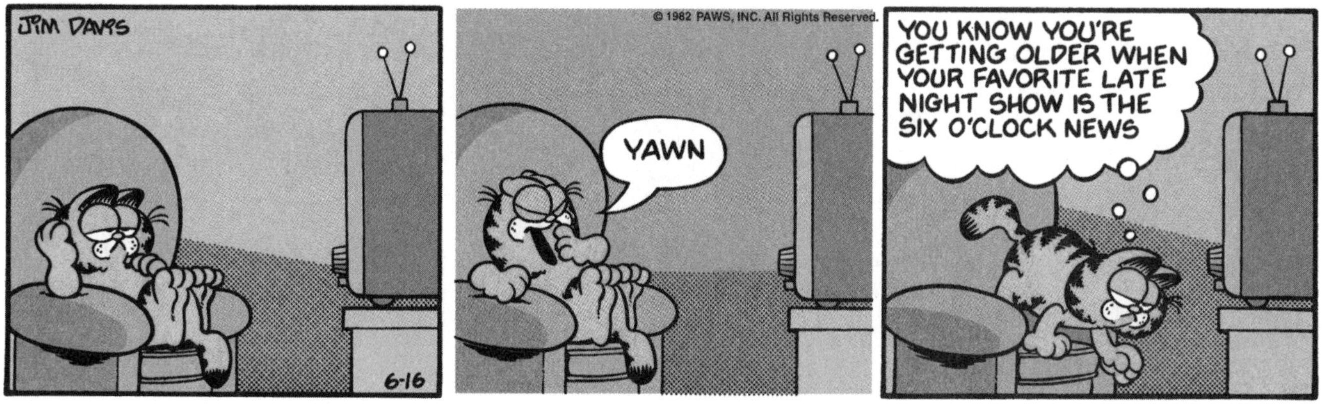
JIM DAVIS
6-16
© 1982 PAWS, INC. All Rights Reserved.
YAWN
YOU KNOW YOU'RE GETTING OLDER WHEN YOUR FAVORITE LATE NIGHT SHOW IS THE SIX O'CLOCK NEWS

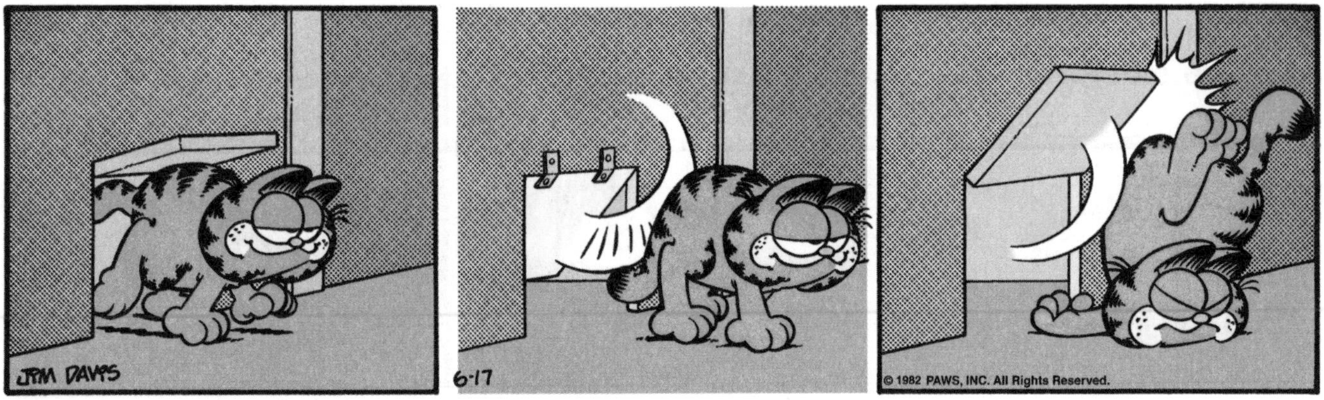
JIM DAVIS
6-17
© 1982 PAWS, INC. All Rights Reserved.

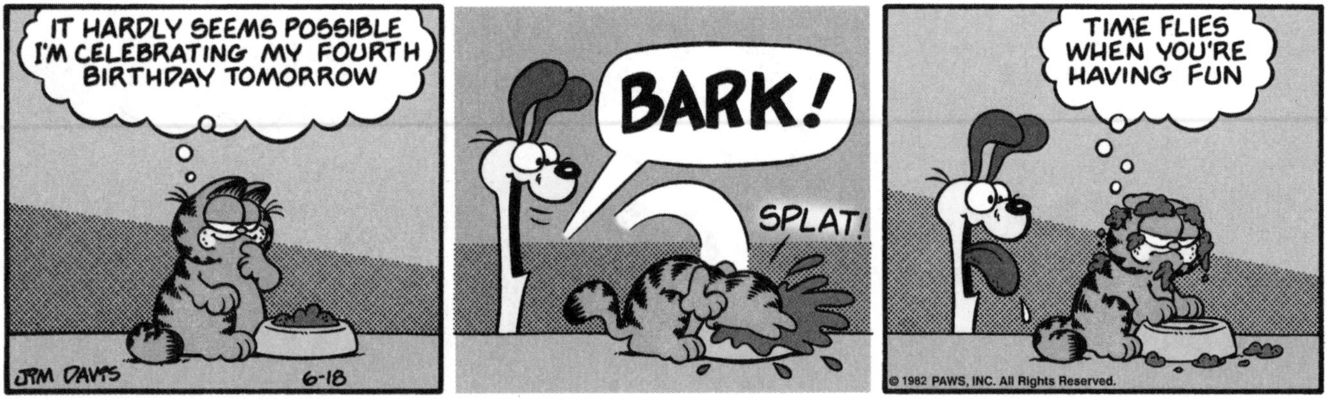
IT HARDLY SEEMS POSSIBLE I'M CELEBRATING MY FOURTH BIRTHDAY TOMORROW
JIM DAVIS
6-18
BARK!
SPLAT!
TIME FLIES WHEN YOU'RE HAVING FUN
© 1982 PAWS, INC. All Rights Reserved.

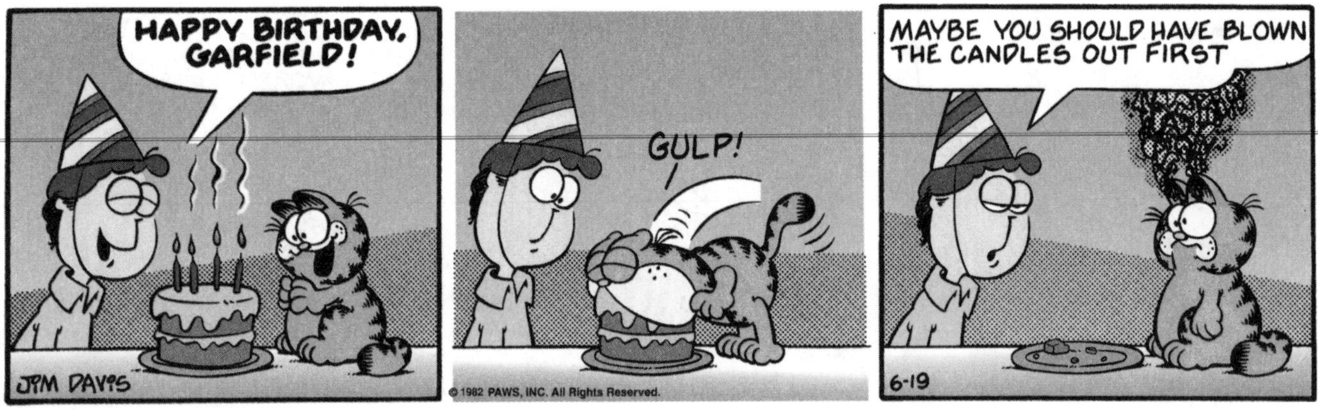
HAPPY BIRTHDAY, GARFIELD!
JIM DAVIS
GULP!
© 1982 PAWS, INC. All Rights Reserved.
MAYBE YOU SHOULD HAVE BLOWN THE CANDLES OUT FIRST
6-19

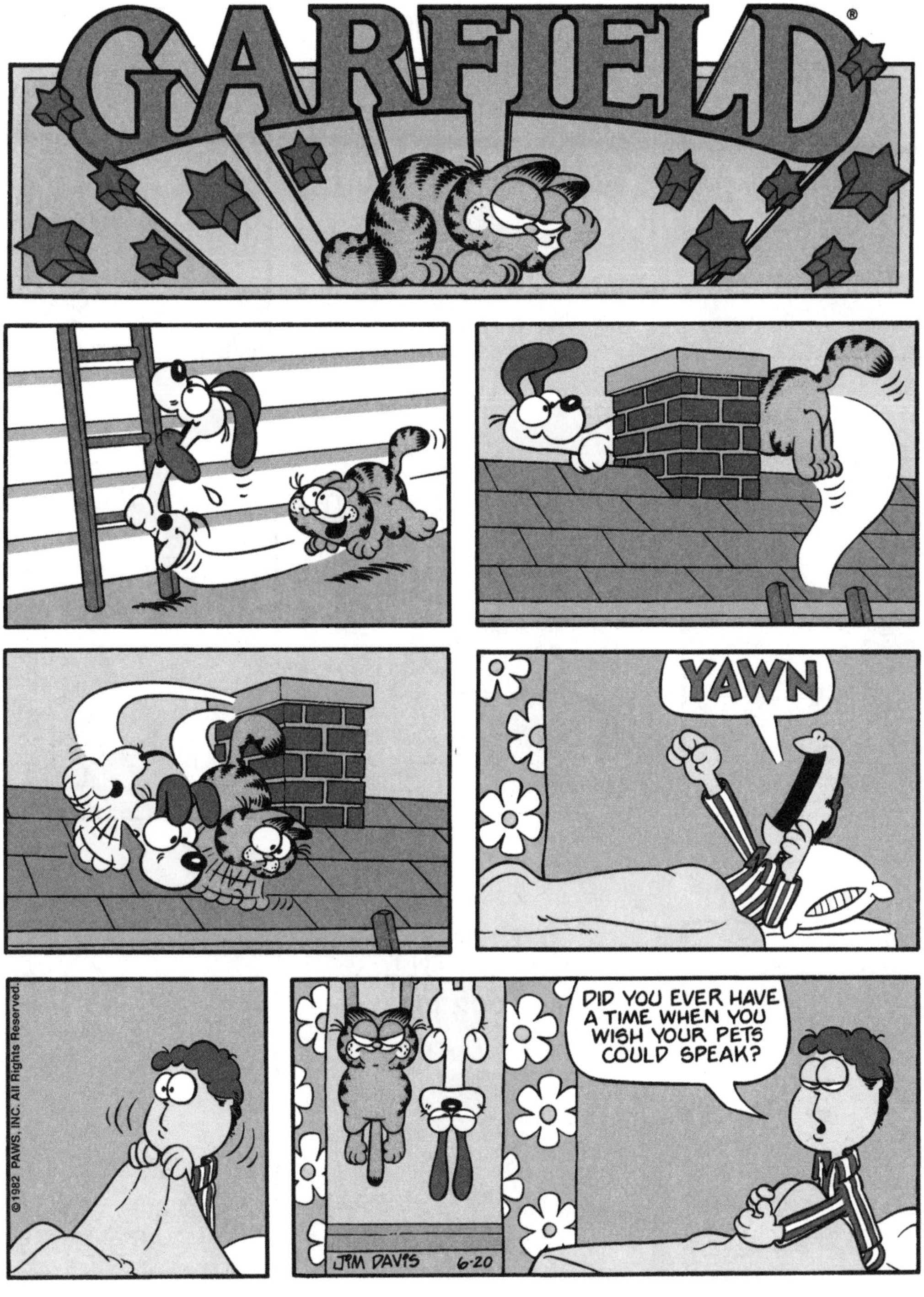
GARFIELD®
YAWN
DID YOU EVER HAVE A TIME WHEN YOU WISH YOUR PETS COULD SPEAK?
JIM DAVIS 6-20

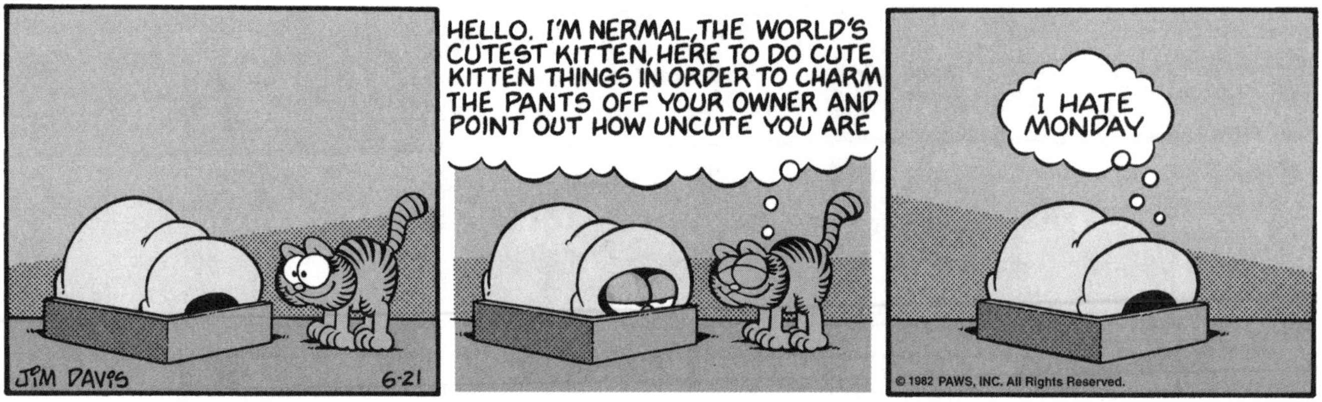
JIM DAVIS
6-21
HELLO. I'M NERMAL, THE WORLD'S CUTEST KITTEN, HERE TO DO CUTE KITTEN THINGS IN ORDER TO CHARM THE PANTS OFF YOUR OWNER AND POINT OUT HOW UNCUTE YOU ARE
I HATE MONDAY
© 1982 PAWS, INC. All Rights Reserved.

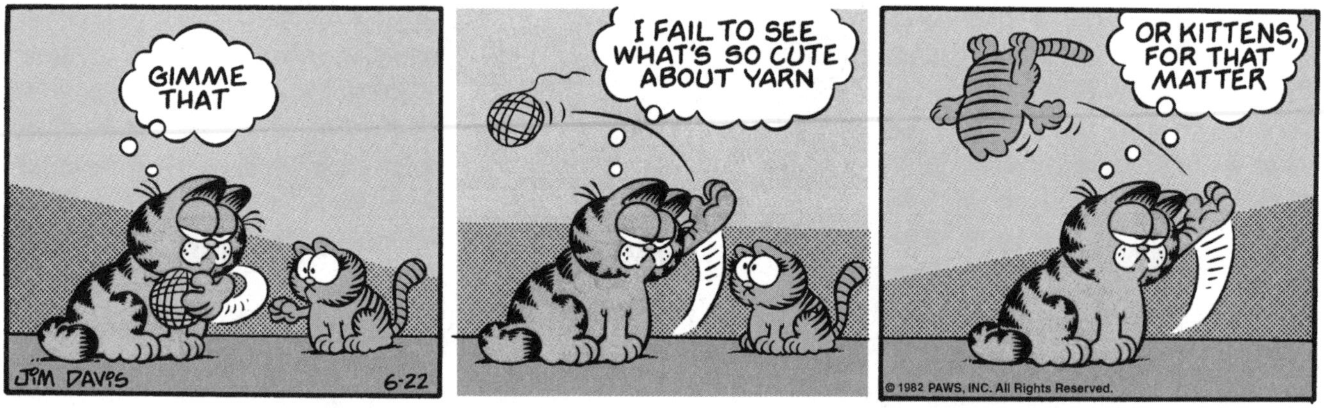
GIMME THAT
JIM DAVIS
6-22
I FAIL TO SEE WHAT'S SO CUTE ABOUT YARN
OR KITTENS, FOR THAT MATTER
© 1982 PAWS, INC. All Rights Reserved.

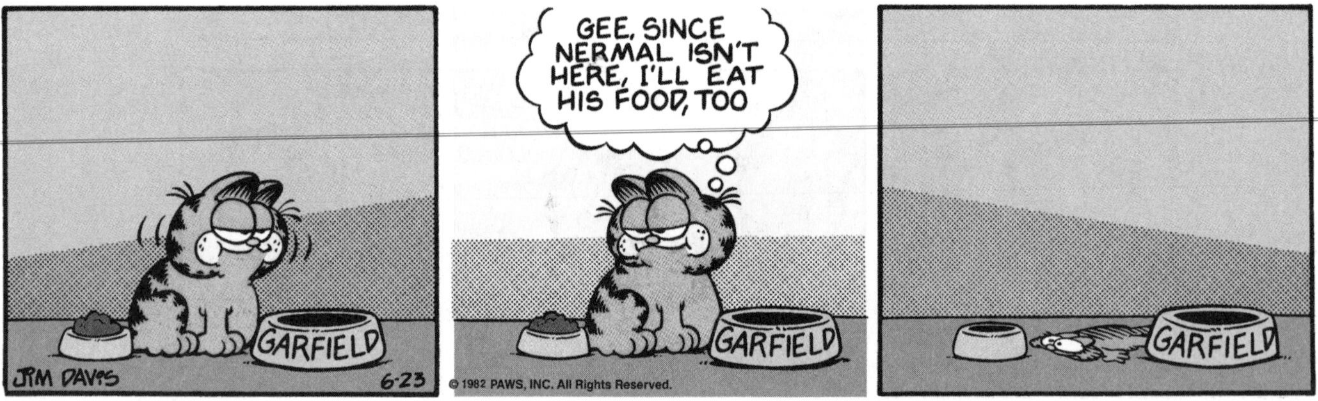
GARFIELD
JIM DAVIS
6-23
GEE, SINCE NERMAL ISN'T HERE, I'LL EAT HIS FOOD, TOO
GARFIELD
© 1982 PAWS, INC. All Rights Reserved.
GARFIELD

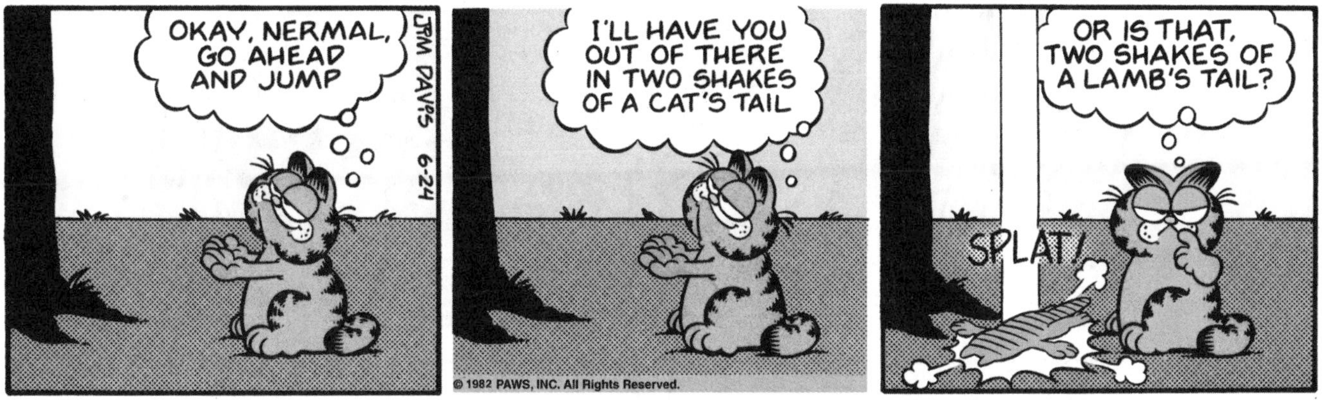
OKAY, NERMAL, GO AHEAD AND JUMP
JIM DAVIS 6-24
I'LL HAVE YOU OUT OF THERE IN TWO SHAKES OF A CAT'S TAIL
© 1982 PAWS, INC. All Rights Reserved.
OR IS THAT, TWO SHAKES OF A LAMB'S TAIL?
SPLAT!

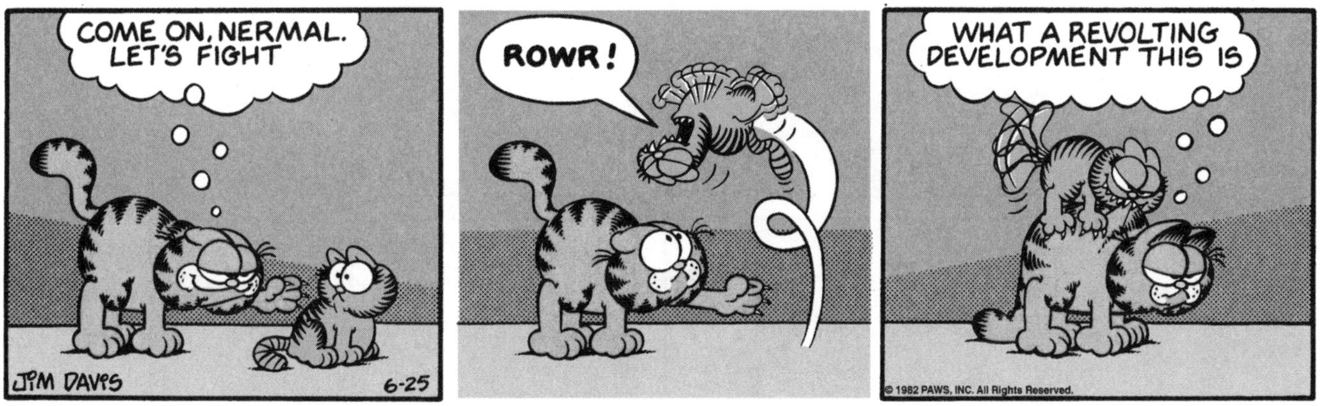
COME ON, NERMAL. LET'S FIGHT
JIM DAVIS
6-25
ROWR!
WHAT A REVOLTING DEVELOPMENT THIS IS
© 1982 PAWS, INC. All Rights Reserved.

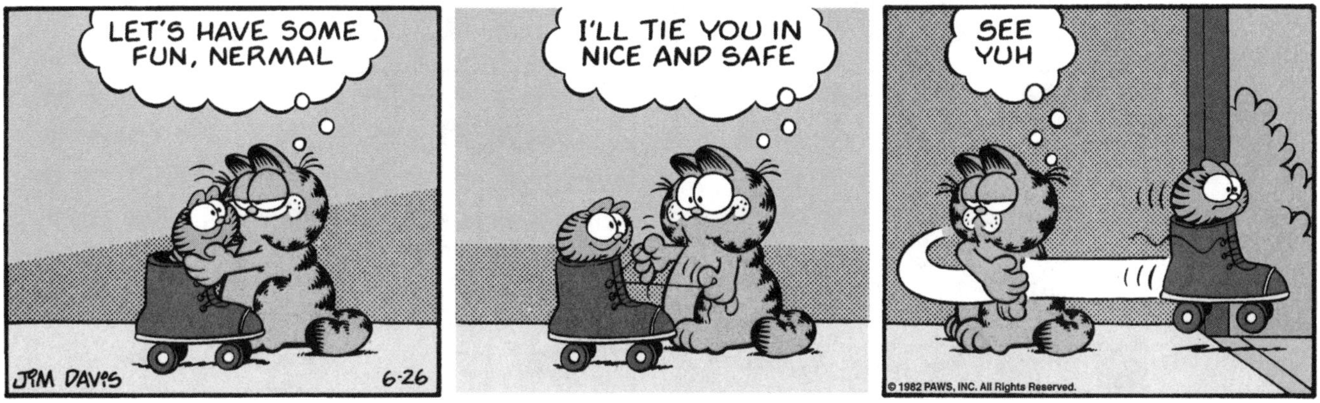
LET'S HAVE SOME FUN, NERMAL
JIM DAVIS
6-26
I'LL TIE YOU IN NICE AND SAFE
SEE YUH
© 1982 PAWS, INC. All Rights Reserved.

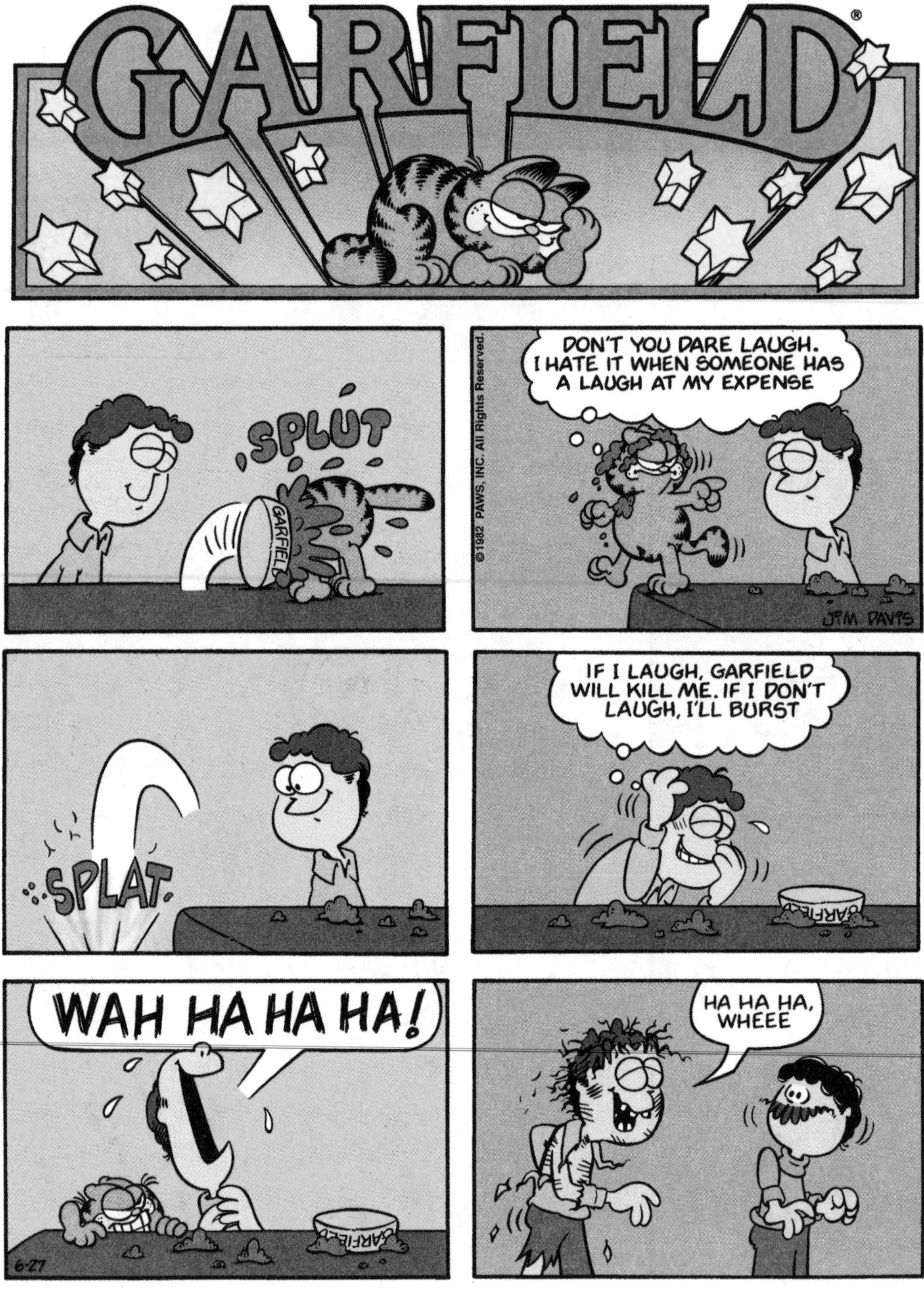
GARFIELD
SPLUT
GARFIELD
©1982 PAWS, INC. All Rights Reserved.
DON'T YOU DARE LAUGH. I HATE IT WHEN SOMEONE HAS A LAUGH AT MY EXPENSE
JIM DAVIS
SPLAT
IF I LAUGH, GARFIELD WILL KILL ME. IF I DON'T LAUGH, I'LL BURST
GARFIELD
WAH HA HA HA!
GARFIELD
6-27
HA HA HA, WHEEE

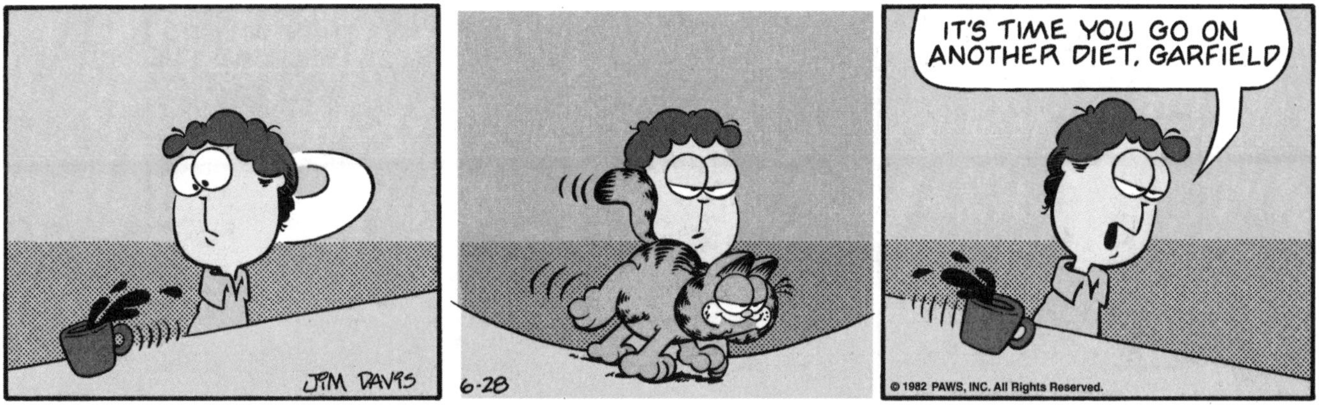
JIM DAVIS
6-28
IT'S TIME YOU GO ON ANOTHER DIET, GARFIELD
© 1982 PAWS, INC. All Rights Reserved.

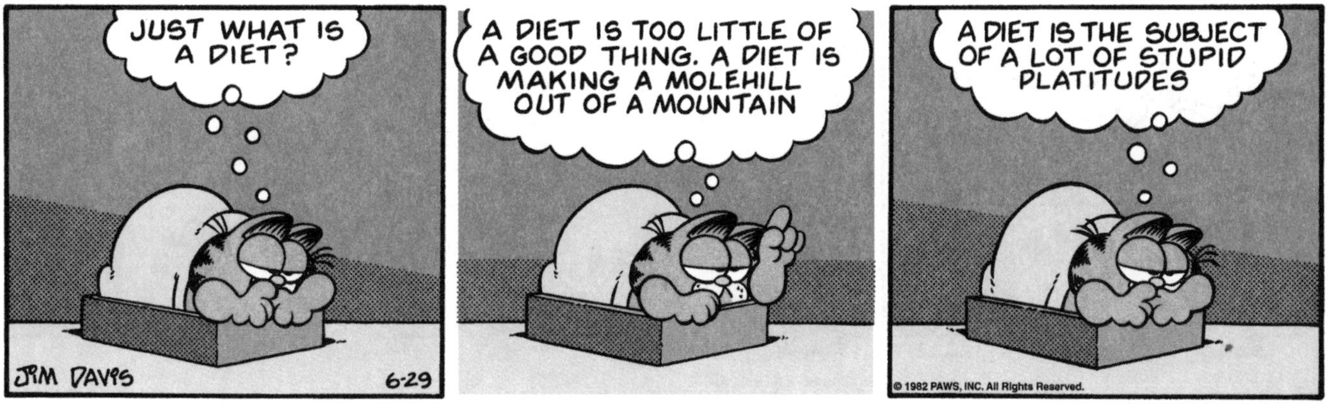
JUST WHAT IS A DIET?
JIM DAVIS
6-29
A DIET IS TOO LITTLE OF A GOOD THING. A DIET IS MAKING A MOLEHILL OUT OF A MOUNTAIN
A DIET IS THE SUBJECT OF A LOT OF STUPID PLATITUDES
© 1982 PAWS, INC. All Rights Reserved.

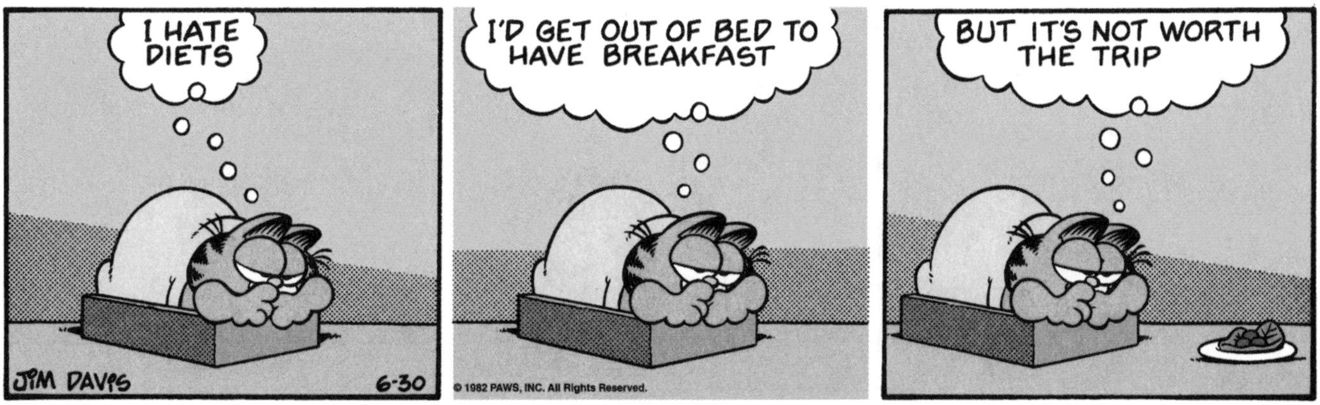
I HATE DIETS
JIM DAVIS
6-30
I'D GET OUT OF BED TO HAVE BREAKFAST
© 1982 PAWS, INC. All Rights Reserved.
BUT IT'S NOT WORTH THE TRIP

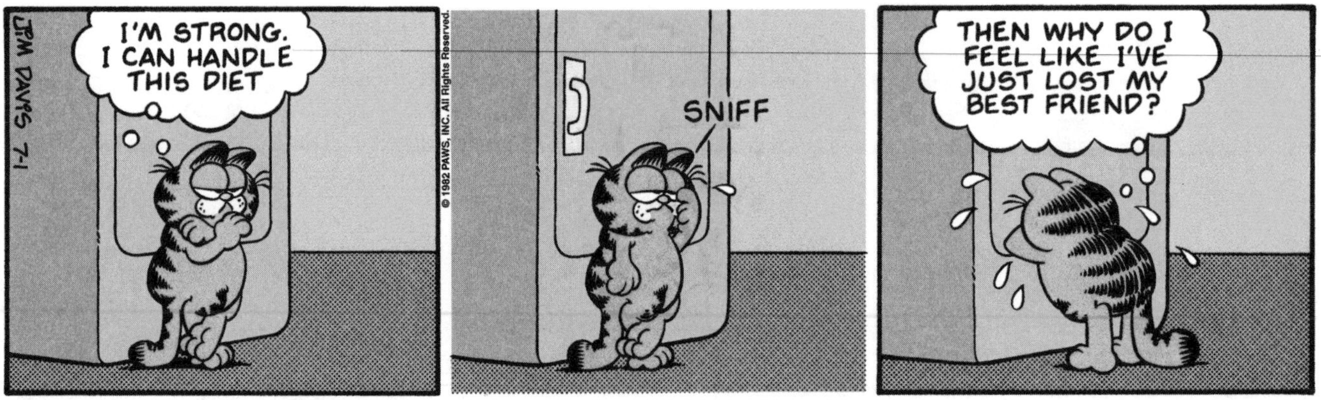
JIM DAVIS 7-1
I'M STRONG. I CAN HANDLE THIS DIET
© 1982 PAWS, INC. All Rights Reserved.
SNIFF
THEN WHY DO I FEEL LIKE I'VE JUST LOST MY BEST FRIEND?

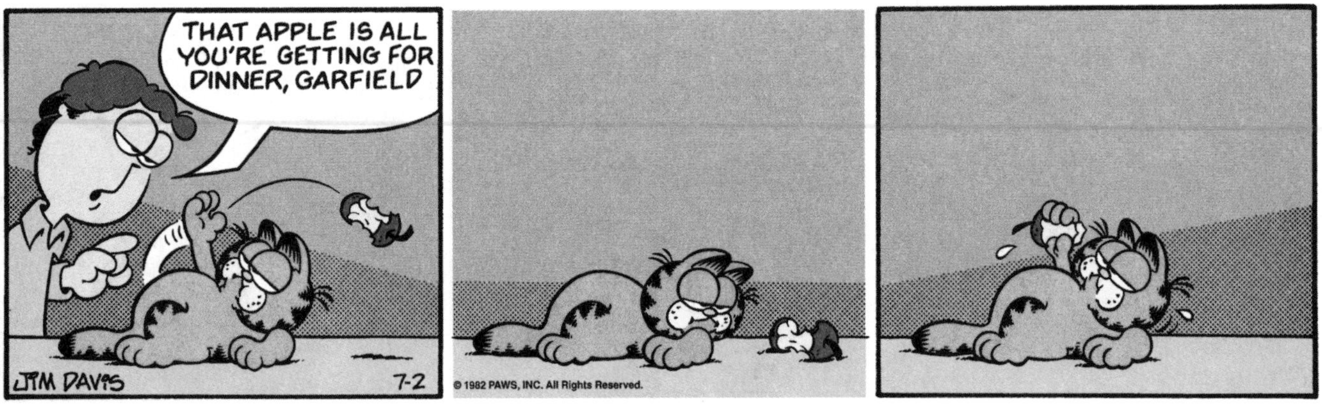
THAT APPLE IS ALL YOU'RE GETTING FOR DINNER, GARFIELD
JIM DAVIS 7-2
© 1982 PAWS, INC. All Rights Reserved.

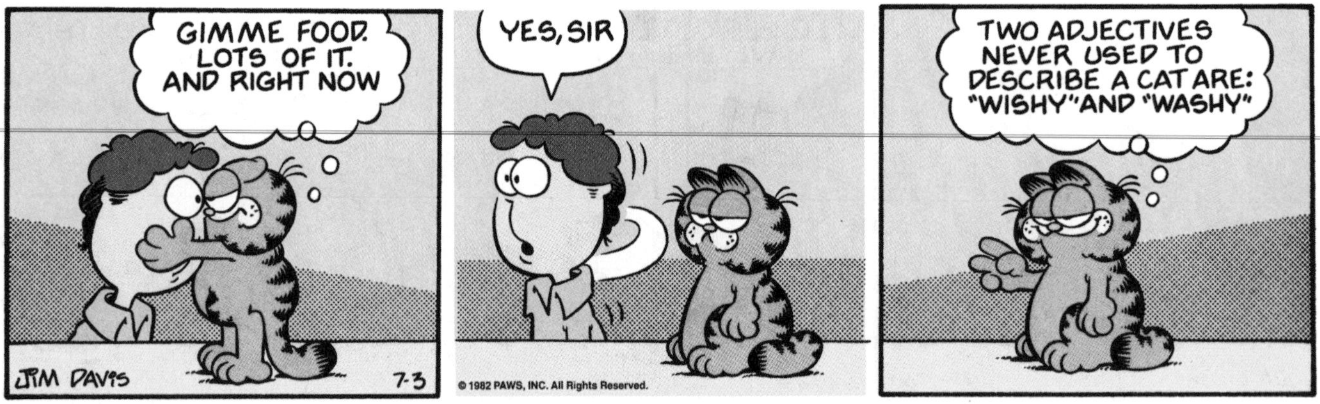
GIMME FOOD. LOTS OF IT. AND RIGHT NOW
JIM DAVIS 7-3
YES, SIR
© 1982 PAWS, INC. All Rights Reserved.
TWO ADJECTIVES NEVER USED TO DESCRIBE A CAT ARE: "WISHY" AND "WASHY"

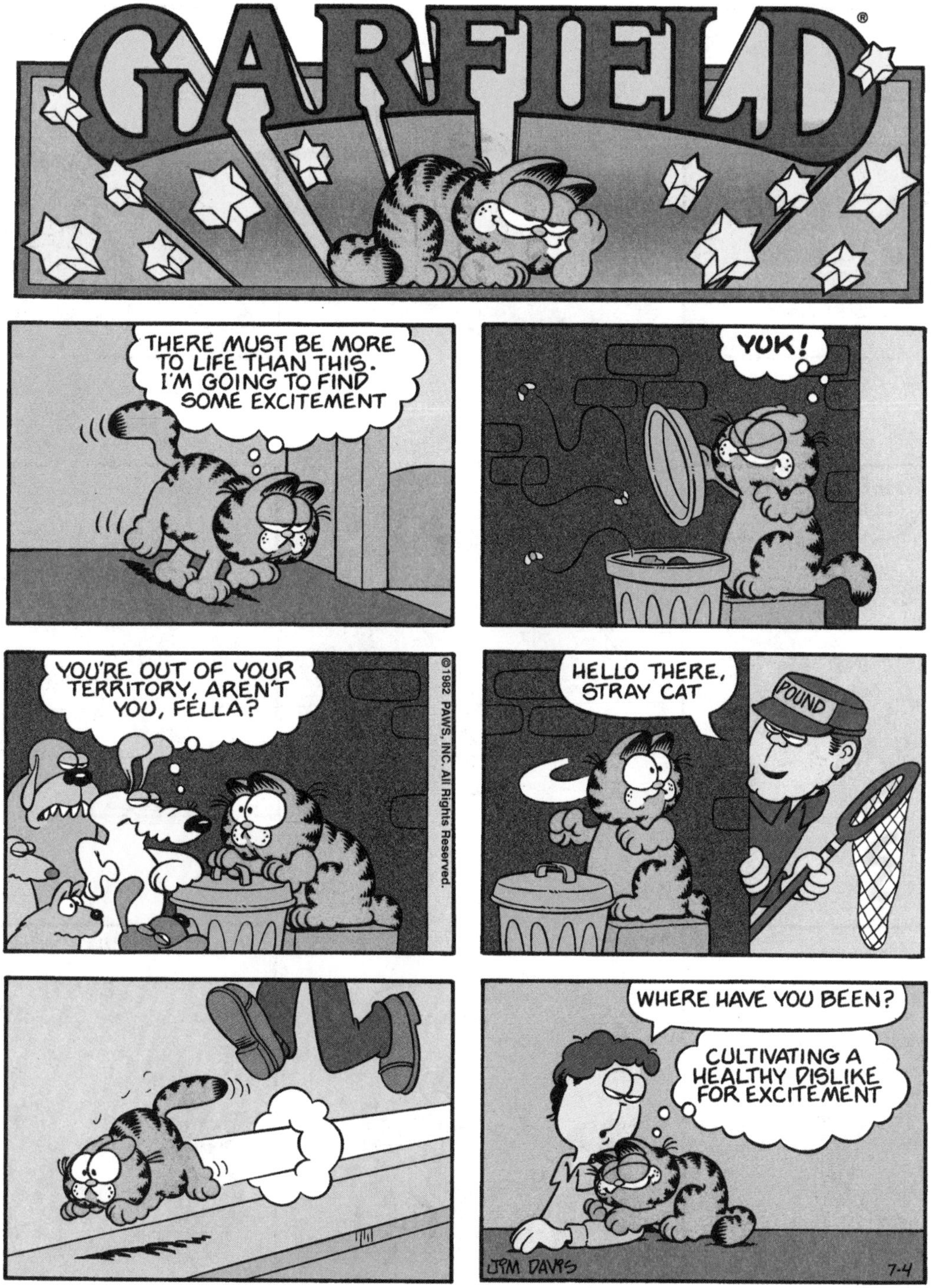
GARFIELD
THERE MUST BE MORE TO LIFE THAN THIS. I'M GOING TO FIND SOME EXCITEMENT
YUK!
YOU'RE OUT OF YOUR TERRITORY, AREN'T YOU, FELLA?
© 1982 PAWS, INC. All Rights Reserved.
HELLO THERE, STRAY CAT
POUND
WHERE HAVE YOU BEEN?
CULTIVATING A HEALTHY DISLIKE FOR EXCITEMENT
JIM DAVIS
7-4

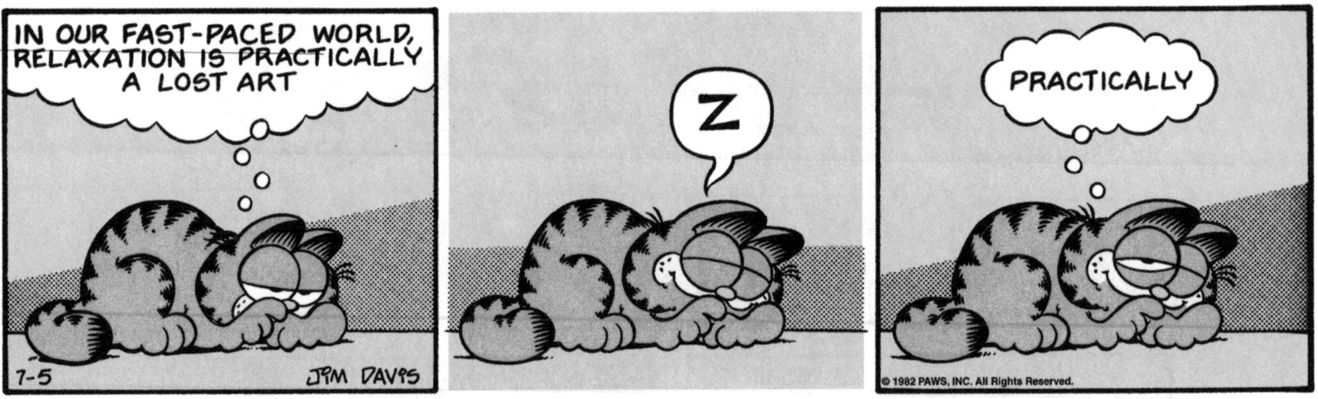
IN OUR FAST-PACED WORLD, RELAXATION IS PRACTICALLY A LOST ART
7-5
JIM DAVIS
Z
PRACTICALLY
© 1982 PAWS, INC. All Rights Reserved.

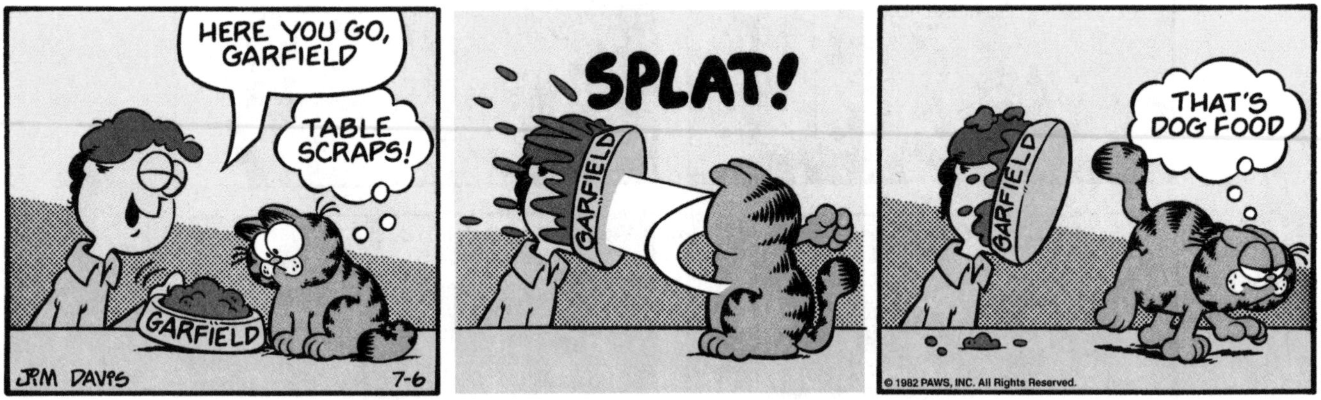
HERE YOU GO, GARFIELD
TABLE SCRAPS!
GARFIELD
JIM DAVIS
7-6
SPLAT!
GARFIELD
THAT'S DOG FOOD
GARFIELD
© 1982 PAWS, INC. All Rights Reserved.

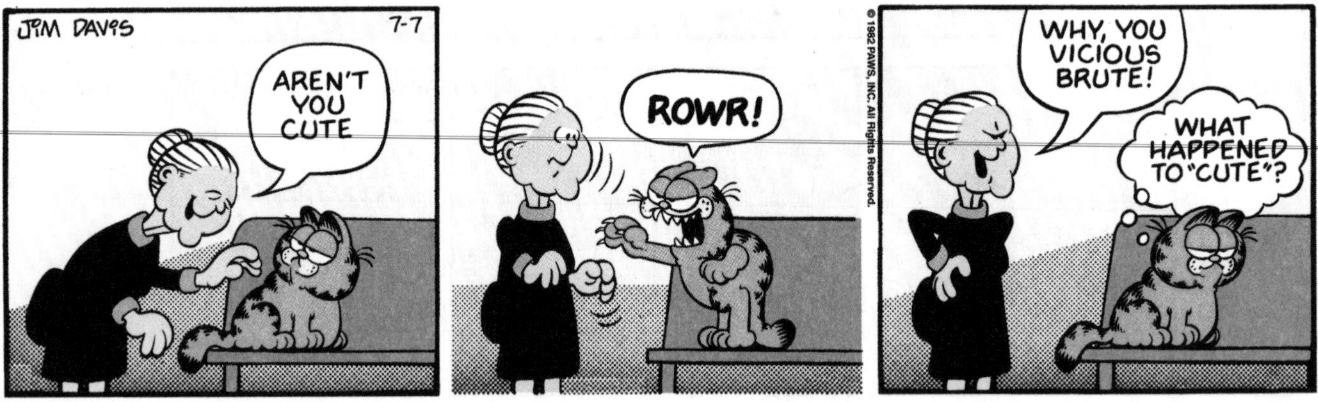
JIM DAVIS
7-7
AREN'T YOU CUTE
ROWR!
© 1982 PAWS, INC. All Rights Reserved.
WHY, YOU VICIOUS BRUTE!
WHAT HAPPENED TO "CUTE"?

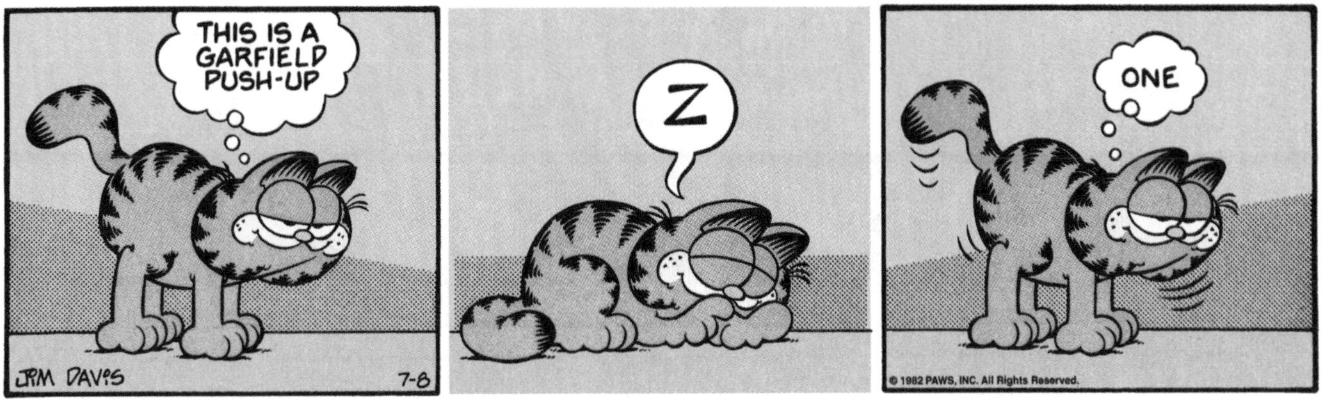
THIS IS A GARFIELD PUSH-UP
JIM DAVIS
7-8
Z
ONE
© 1982 PAWS, INC. All Rights Reserved.

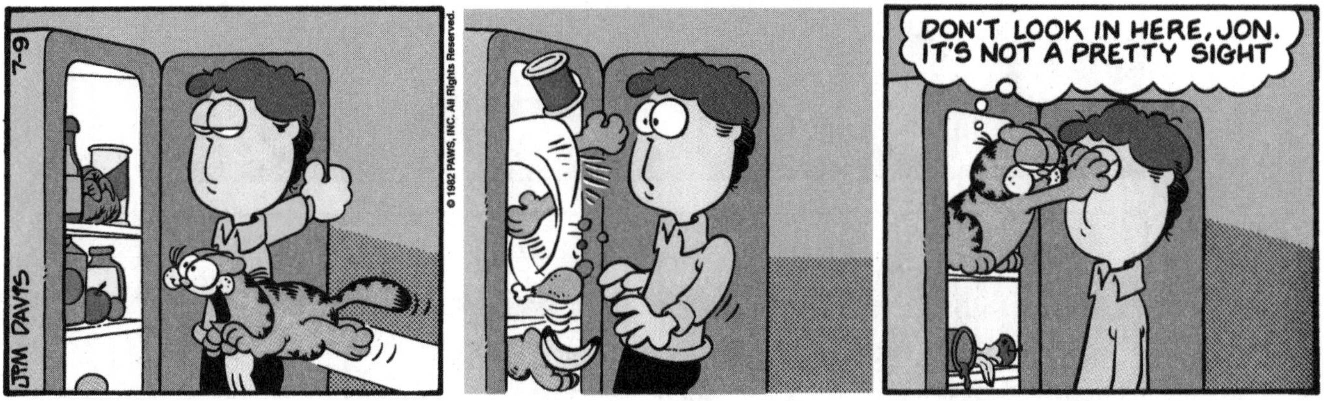
7-9
JIM DAVIS
© 1982 PAWS, INC. All Rights Reserved.
DON'T LOOK IN HERE, JON. IT'S NOT A PRETTY SIGHT

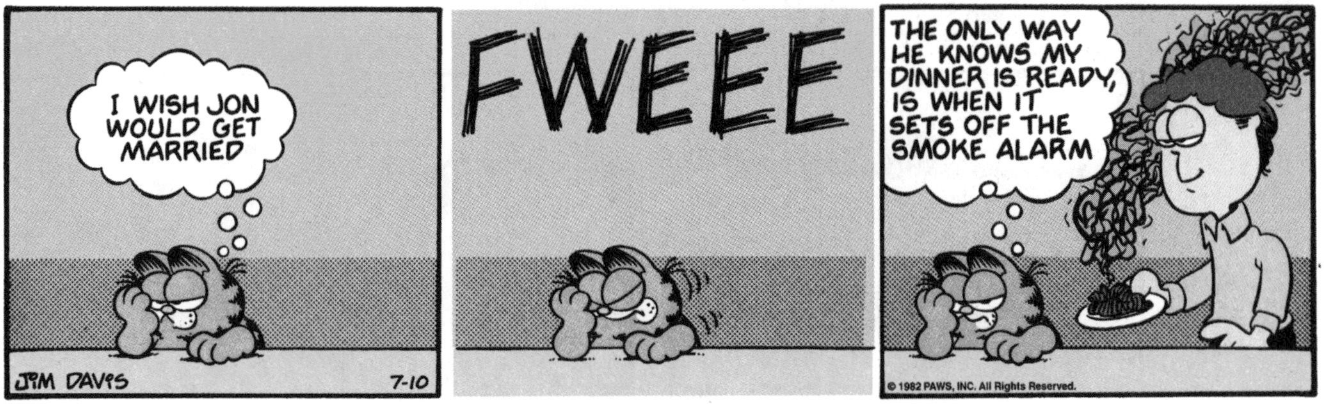
I WISH JON WOULD GET MARRIED
JIM DAVIS
7-10
FWEEE
THE ONLY WAY HE KNOWS MY DINNER IS READY, IS WHEN IT SETS OFF THE SMOKE ALARM
© 1982 PAWS, INC. All Rights Reserved.

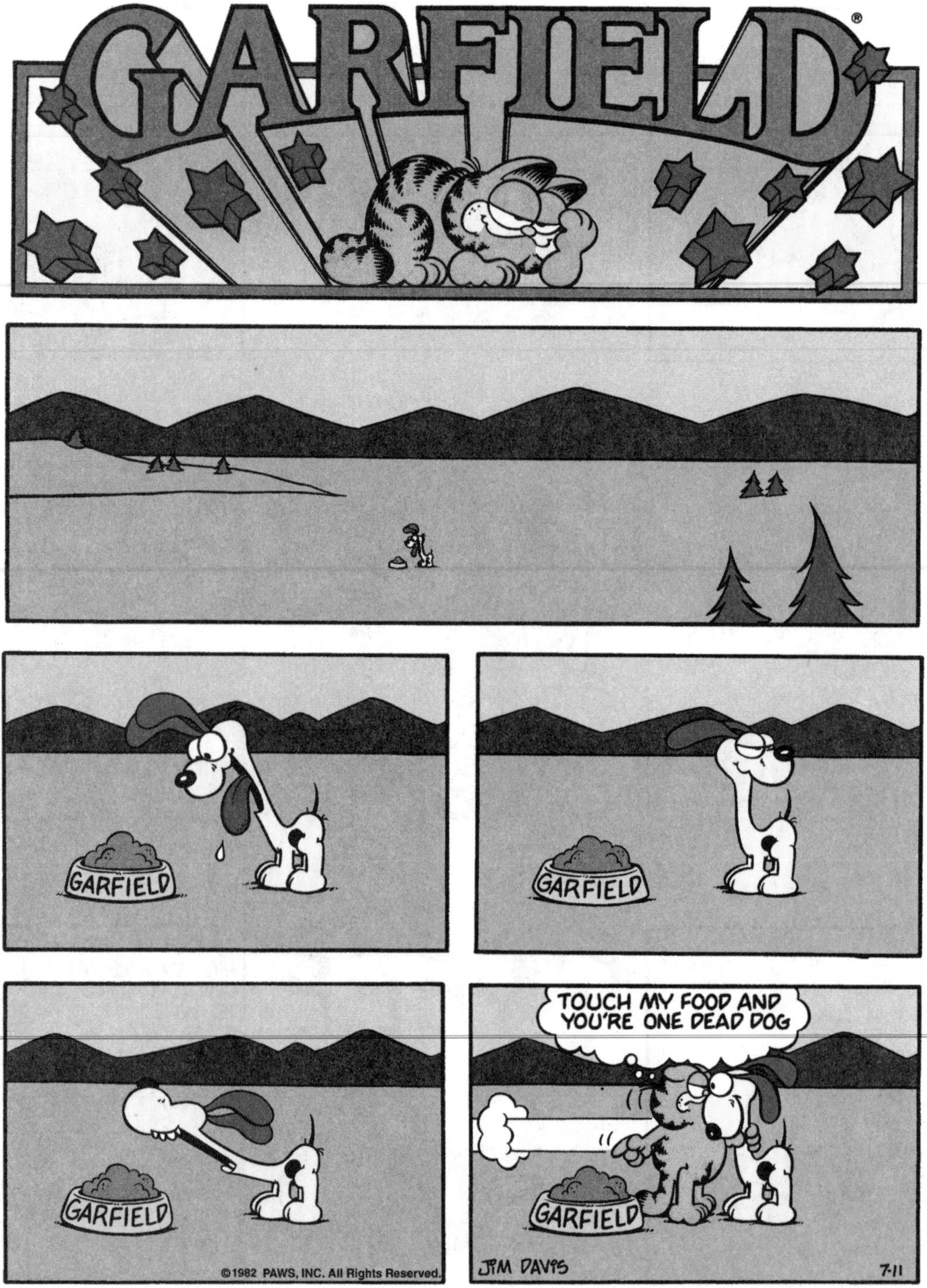
GARFIELD
GARFIELD
GARFIELD
GARFIELD
TOUCH MY FOOD AND YOU'RE ONE DEAD DOG
GARFIELD
©1982 PAWS, INC. All Rights Reserved.
JIM DAVIS
7-11

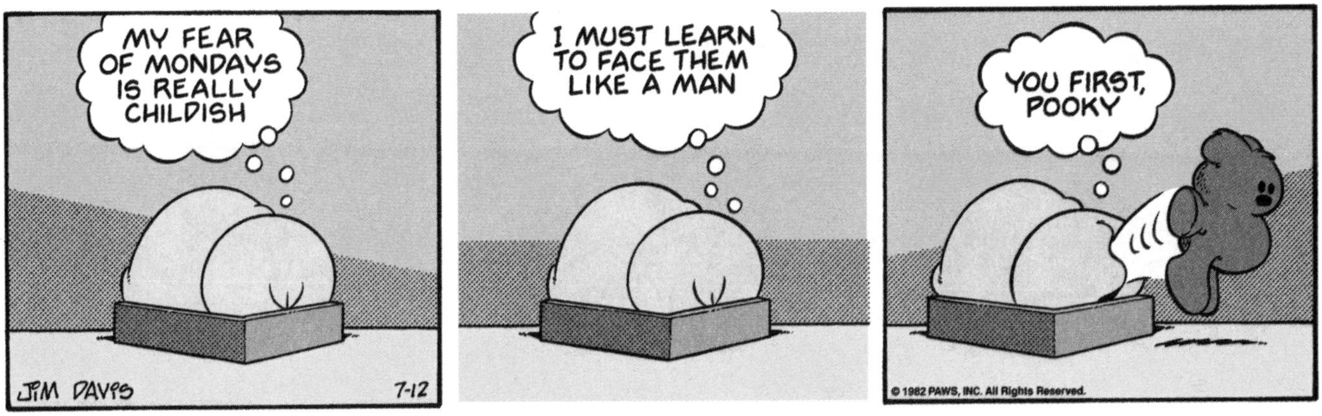
MY FEAR OF MONDAYS IS REALLY CHILDISH
JIM DAVIS 7-12
I MUST LEARN TO FACE THEM LIKE A MAN
YOU FIRST, POOKY
© 1982 PAWS, INC. All Rights Reserved.

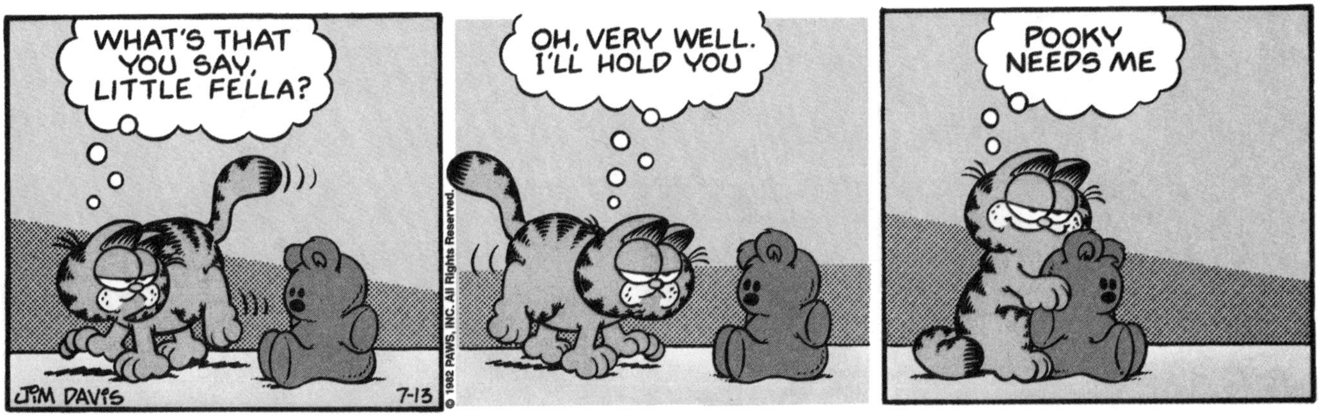
WHAT'S THAT YOU SAY, LITTLE FELLA?
JIM DAVIS 7-13
© 1982 PAWS, INC. All Rights Reserved.
OH, VERY WELL. I'LL HOLD YOU
POOKY NEEDS ME

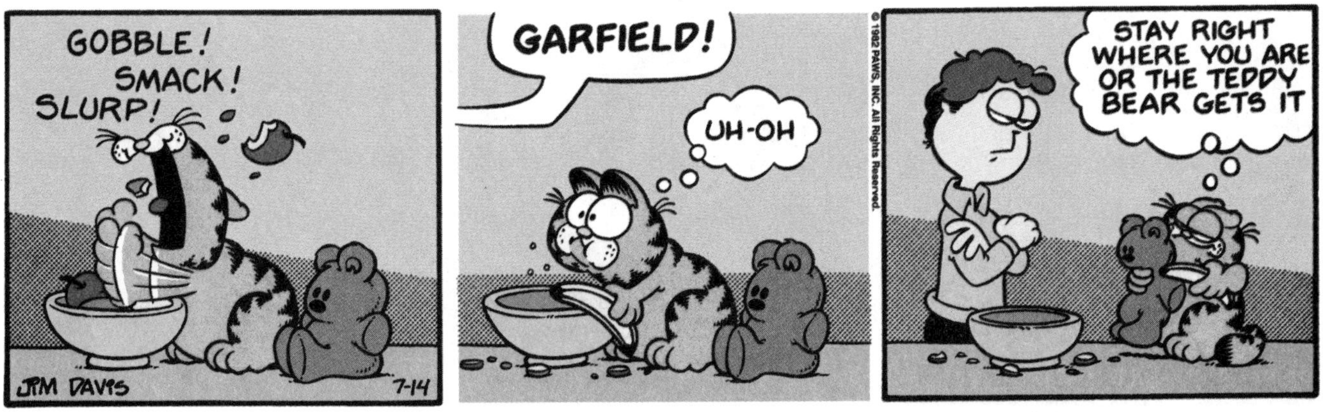
GOBBLE!
SMACK!
SLURP!
JIM DAVIS 7-14
GARFIELD!
UH-OH
© 1982 PAWS, INC. All Rights Reserved.
STAY RIGHT WHERE YOU ARE OR THE TEDDY BEAR GETS IT

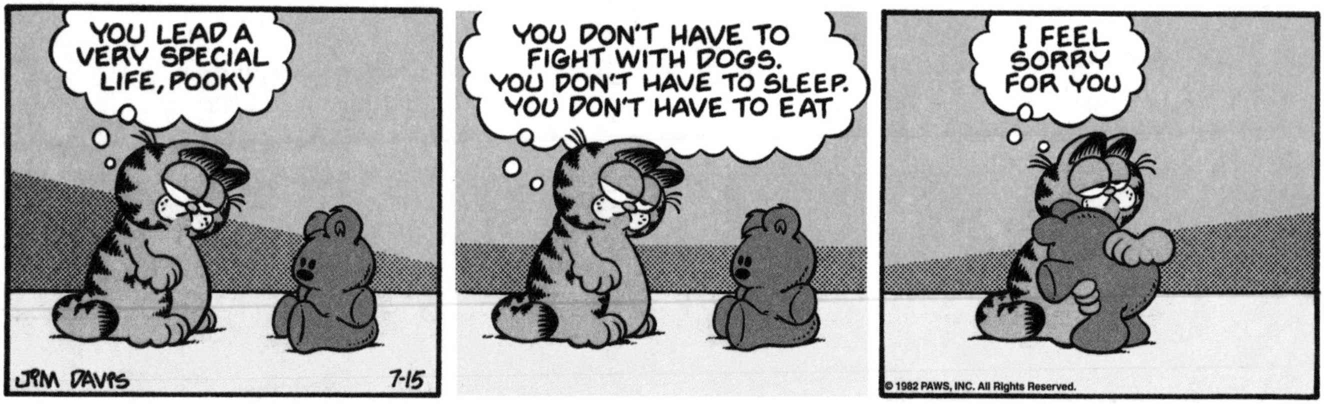
YOU LEAD A VERY SPECIAL LIFE, POOKY
JIM DAVIS
7-15
YOU DON'T HAVE TO FIGHT WITH DOGS. YOU DON'T HAVE TO SLEEP. YOU DON'T HAVE TO EAT
I FEEL SORRY FOR YOU
© 1982 PAWS, INC. All Rights Reserved.

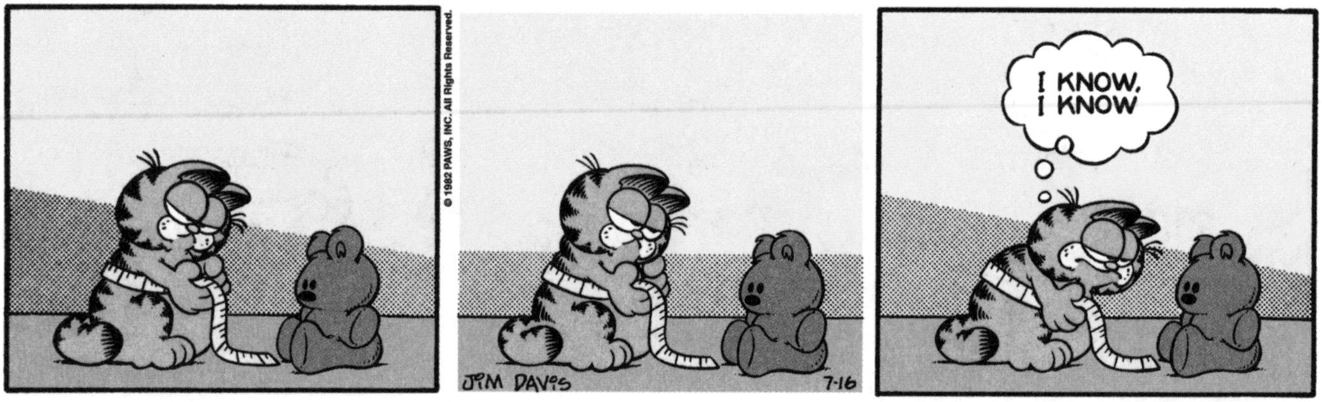
© 1982 PAWS, INC. All Rights Reserved.
JIM DAVIS
7-16
I KNOW, I KNOW

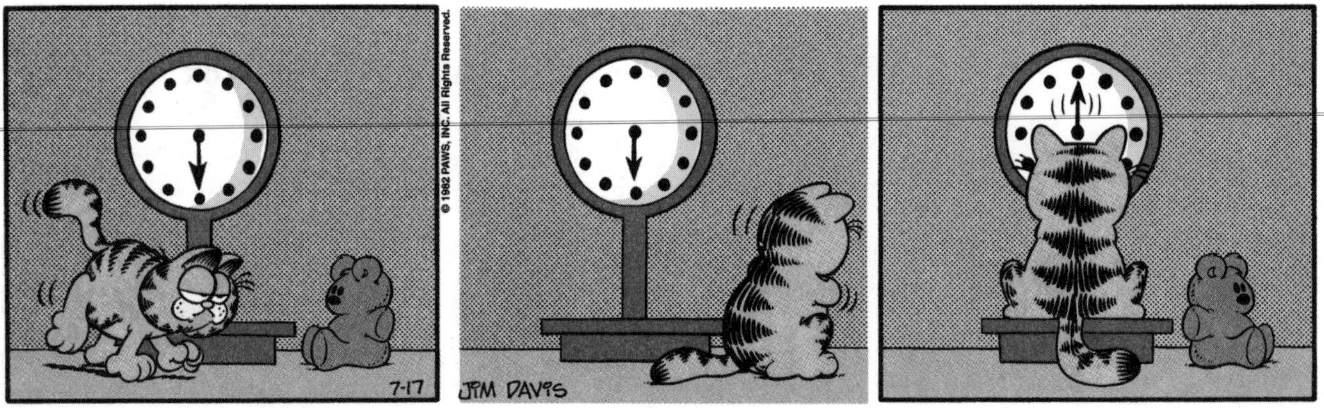
7-17
© 1982 PAWS, INC. All Rights Reserved.
JIM DAVIS

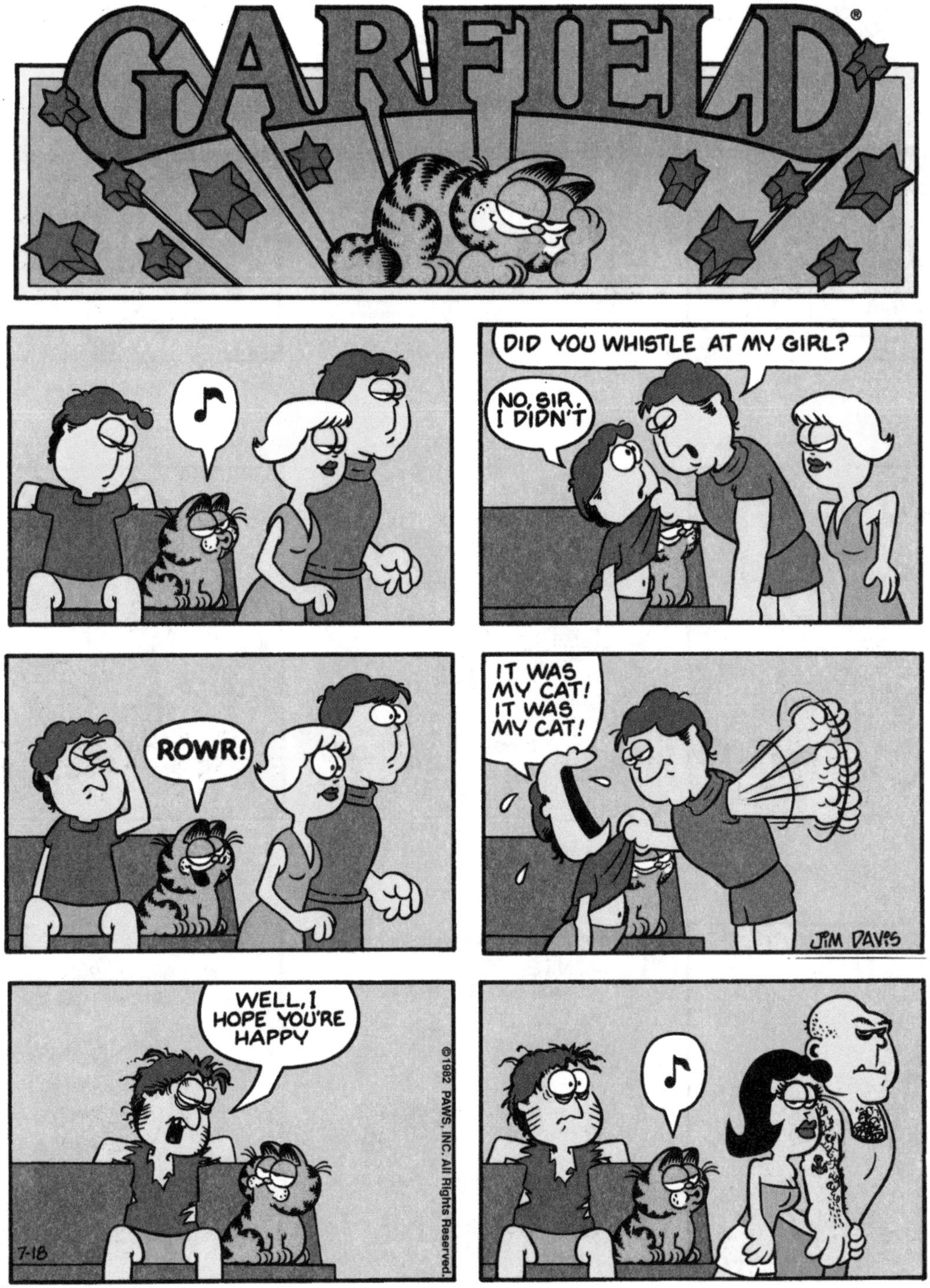
GARFIELD®
♪
DID YOU WHISTLE AT MY GIRL?
NO, SIR, I DIDN'T
ROWR!
IT WAS MY CAT! IT WAS MY CAT!
JIM DAVIS
WELL, I HOPE YOU'RE HAPPY
7-18
©1982 PAWS, INC. All Rights Reserved.
♪

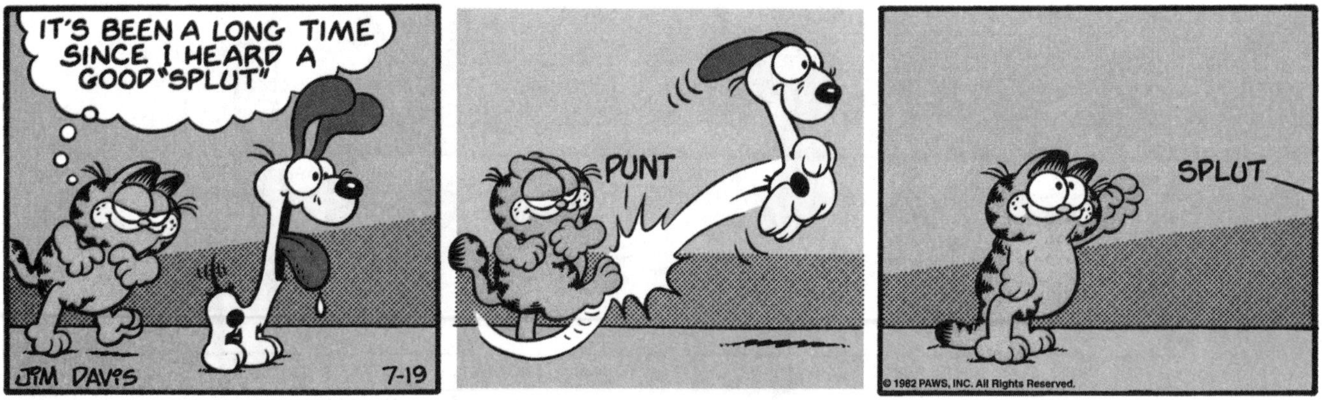
IT'S BEEN A LONG TIME SINCE I HEARD A GOOD "SPLUT"
JIM DAVIS
7-19
PUNT
SPLUT
© 1982 PAWS, INC. All Rights Reserved.

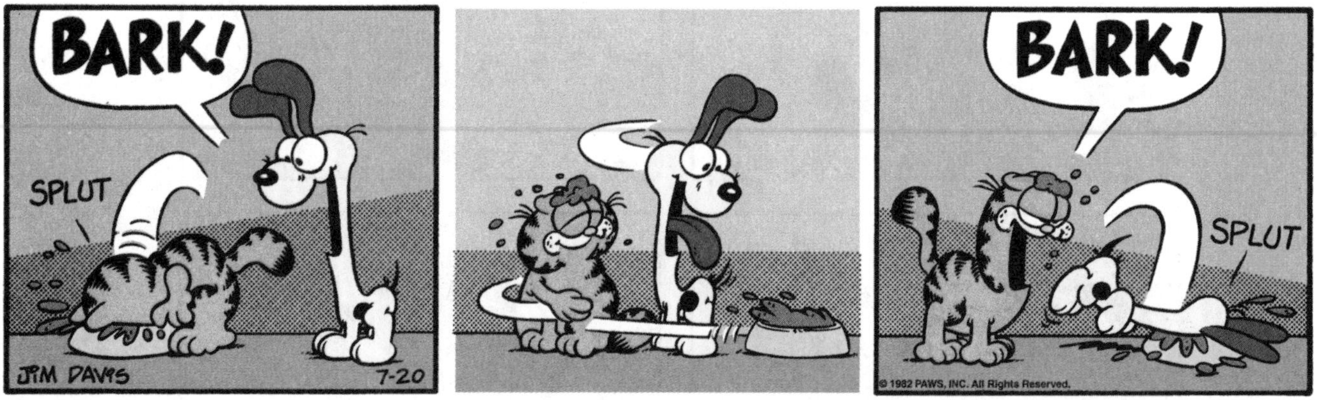
BARK!
SPLUT
JIM DAVIS
7-20
BARK!
SPLUT
© 1982 PAWS, INC. All Rights Reserved.

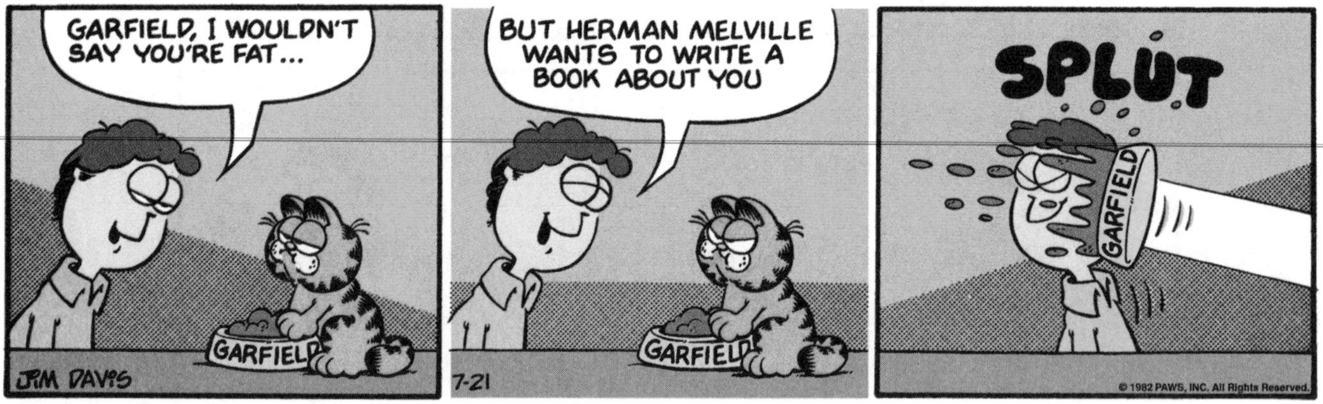
GARFIELD, I WOULDN'T SAY YOU'RE FAT...
GARFIELD
JIM DAVIS
BUT HERMAN MELVILLE WANTS TO WRITE A BOOK ABOUT YOU
GARFIELD
7-21
SPLUT
GARFIELD
© 1982 PAWS, INC. All Rights Reserved.

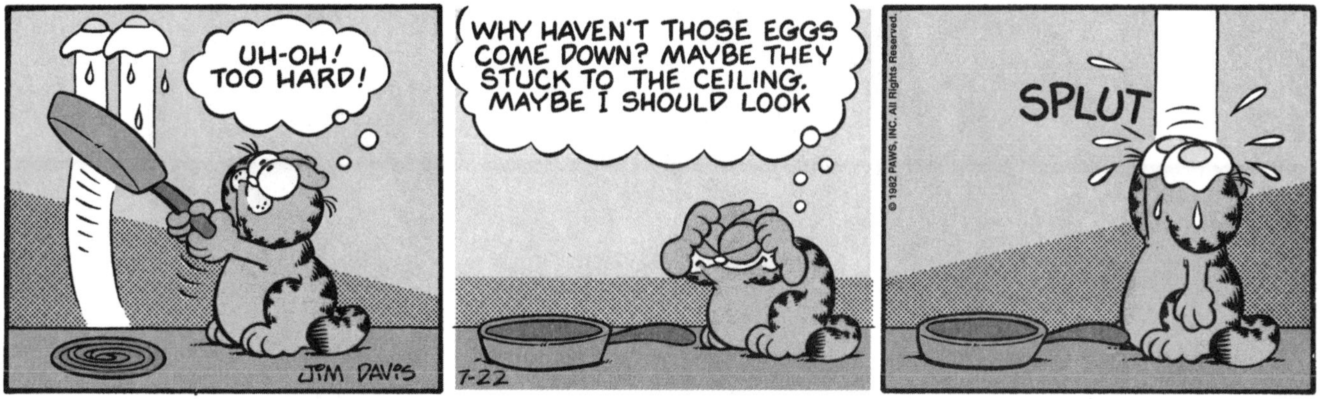
UH-OH! TOO HARD!
JIM DAVIS
WHY HAVEN'T THOSE EGGS COME DOWN? MAYBE THEY STUCK TO THE CEILING. MAYBE I SHOULD LOOK
7-22
© 1982 PAWS, INC. All Rights Reserved.
SPLUT

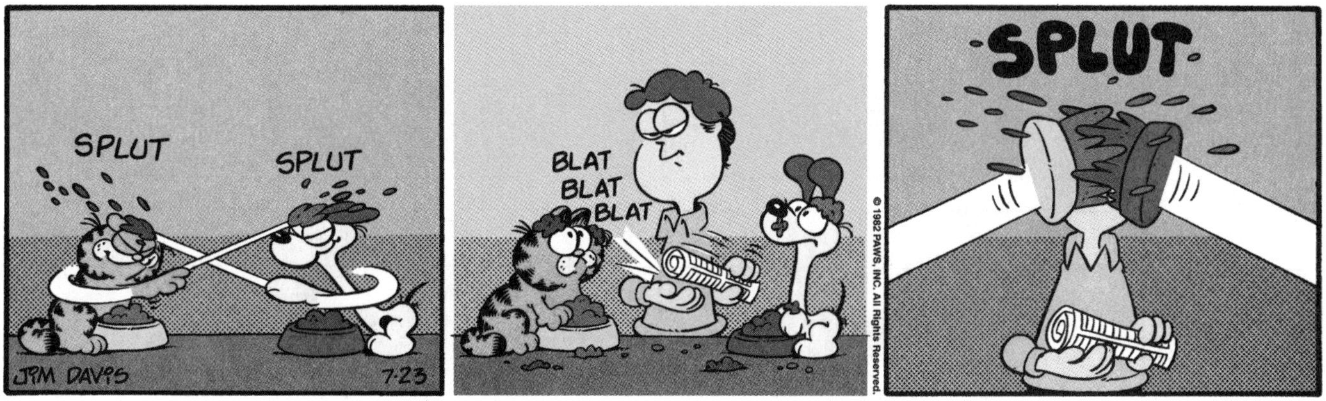
SPLUT
SPLUT
JIM DAVIS
7-23
BLAT
BLAT
BLAT
© 1982 PAWS, INC. All Rights Reserved.
SPLUT

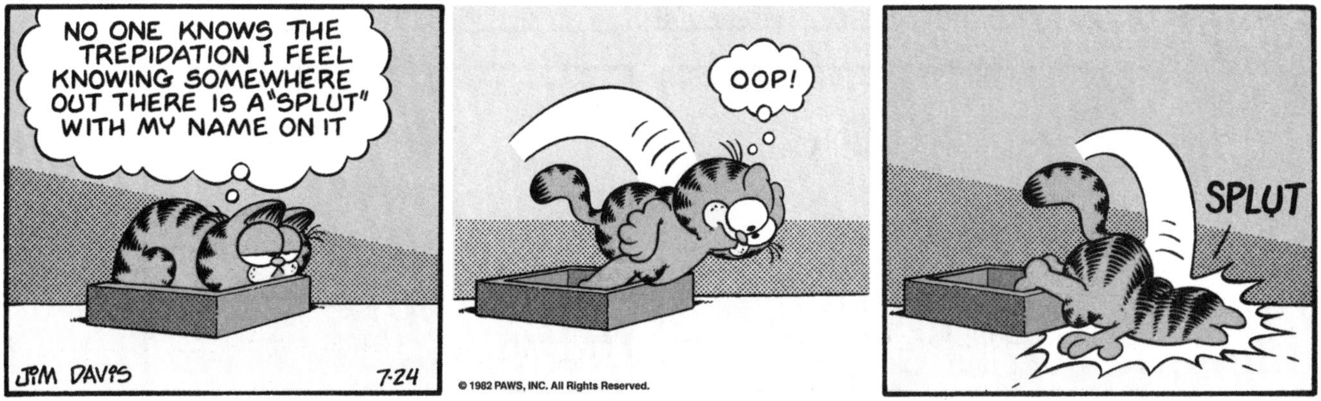
NO ONE KNOWS THE TREPIDATION I FEEL KNOWING SOMEWHERE OUT THERE IS A "SPLUT" WITH MY NAME ON IT
JIM DAVIS
7-24
OOP!
© 1982 PAWS, INC. All Rights Reserved.
SPLUT

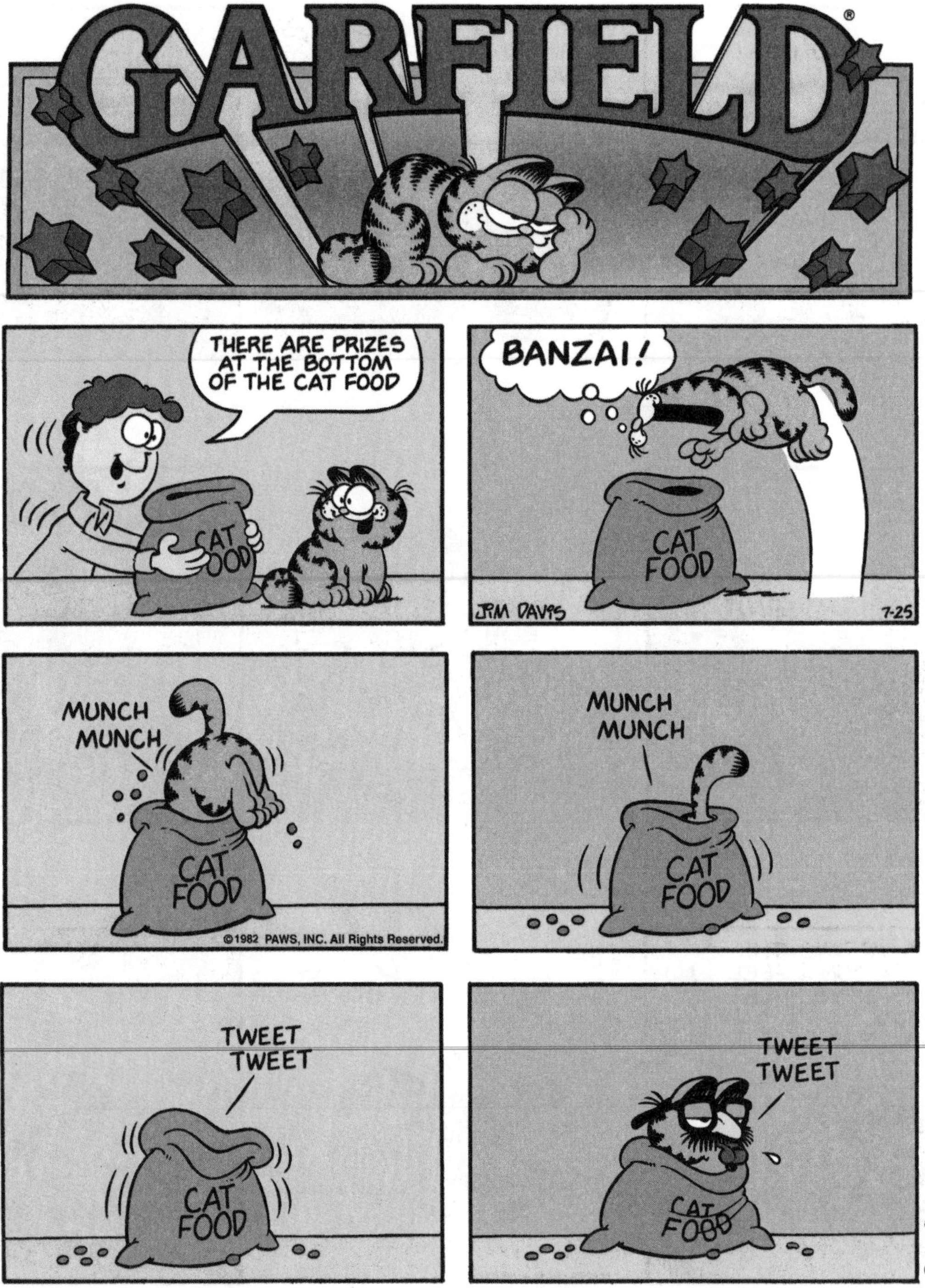
GARFIELD®
THERE ARE PRIZES AT THE BOTTOM OF THE CAT FOOD
CAT FOOD
BANZAI!
CAT FOOD
JIM DAVIS
7-25
MUNCH MUNCH
CAT FOOD
©1982 PAWS, INC. All Rights Reserved.
MUNCH MUNCH
CAT FOOD
TWEET TWEET
CAT FOOD
TWEET TWEET
CAT FOOD

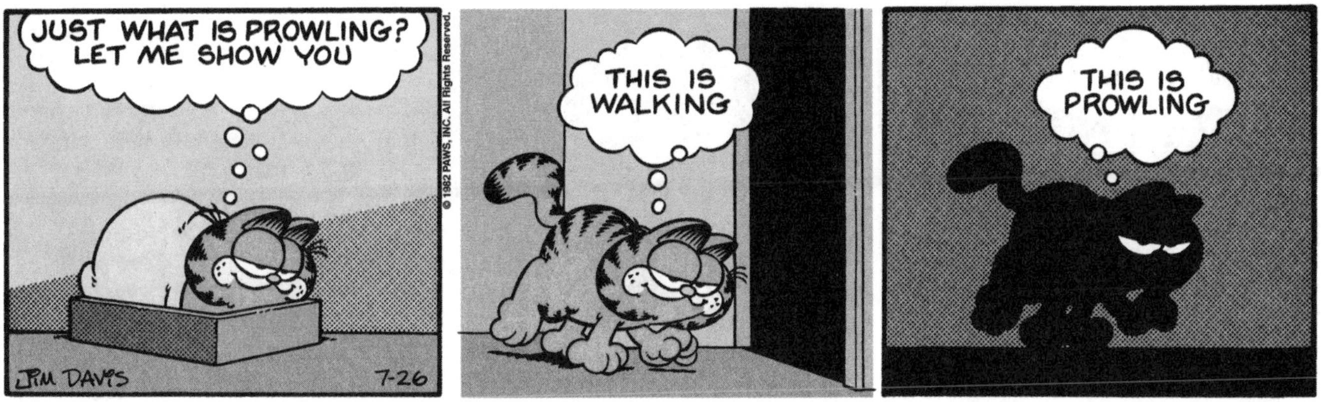
JUST WHAT IS PROWLING? LET ME SHOW YOU
JIM DAVIS
7-26
© 1982 PAWS, INC. All Rights Reserved.
THIS IS WALKING
THIS IS PROWLING

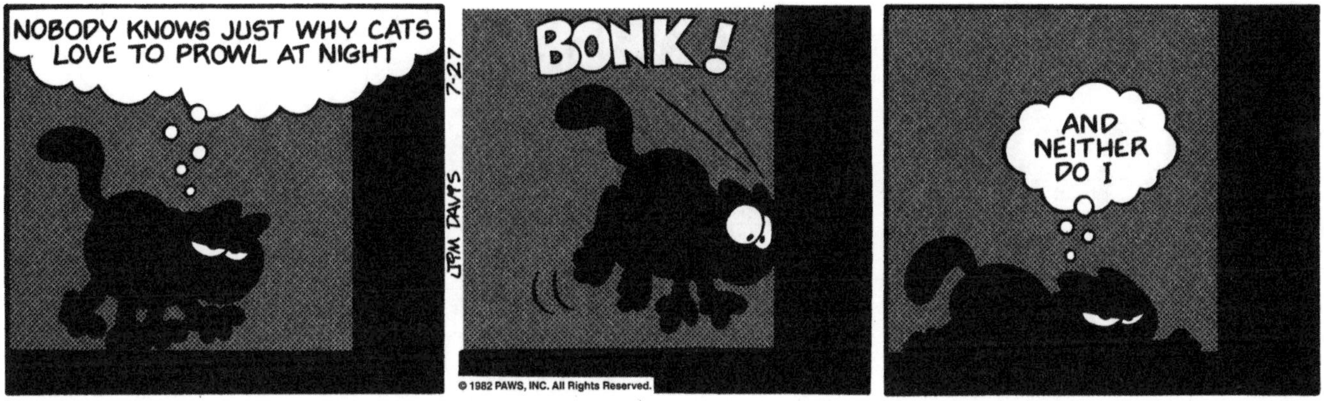
NOBODY KNOWS JUST WHY CATS LOVE TO PROWL AT NIGHT
7-27
JIM DAVIS
BONK!
© 1982 PAWS, INC. All Rights Reserved.
AND NEITHER DO I

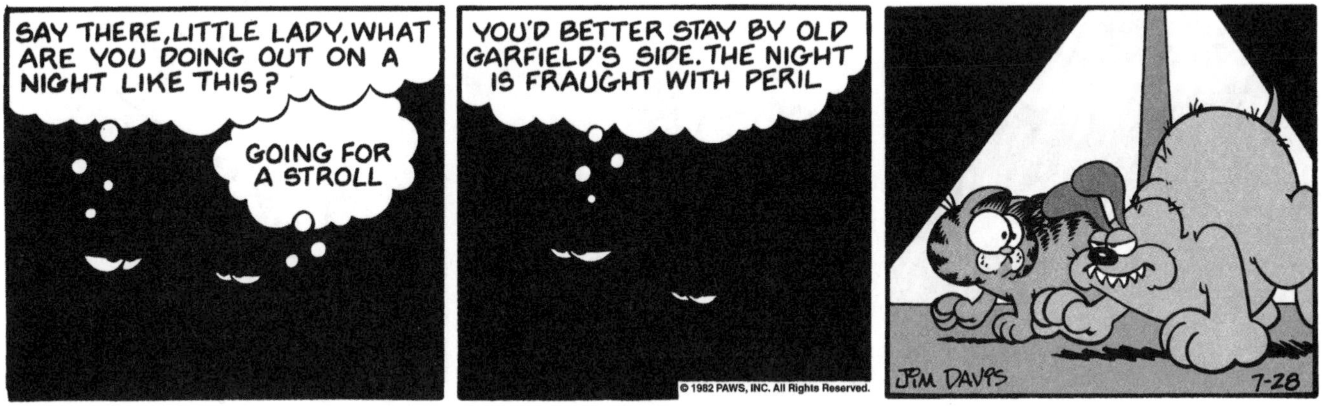
SAY THERE, LITTLE LADY, WHAT ARE YOU DOING OUT ON A NIGHT LIKE THIS?
GOING FOR A STROLL
YOU'D BETTER STAY BY OLD GARFIELD'S SIDE. THE NIGHT IS FRAUGHT WITH PERIL
© 1982 PAWS, INC. All Rights Reserved.
JIM DAVIS
7-28

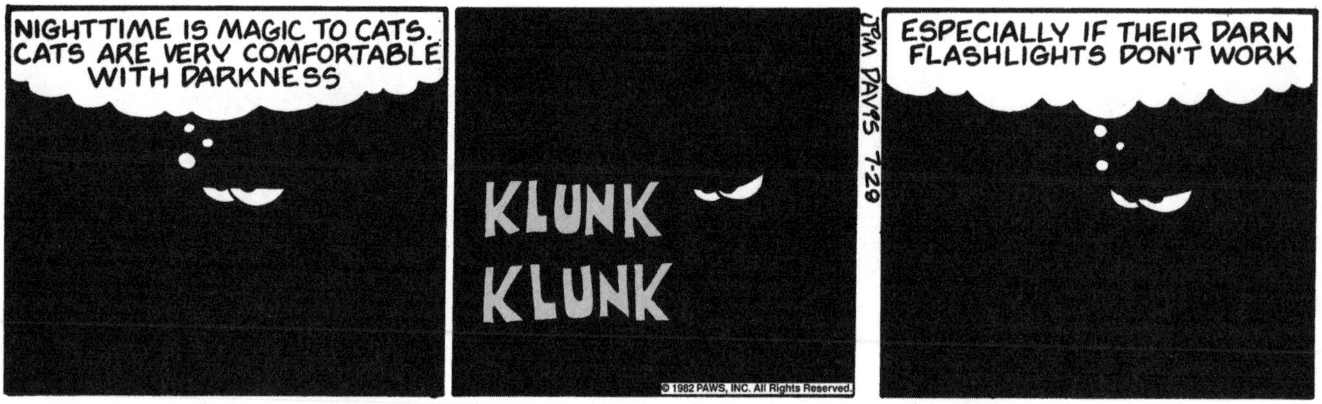
NIGHTTIME IS MAGIC TO CATS. CATS ARE VERY COMFORTABLE WITH DARKNESS
KLUNK KLUNK
JIM DAVIS 7-29
ESPECIALLY IF THEIR DARN FLASHLIGHTS DON'T WORK
© 1982 PAWS, INC. All Rights Reserved.

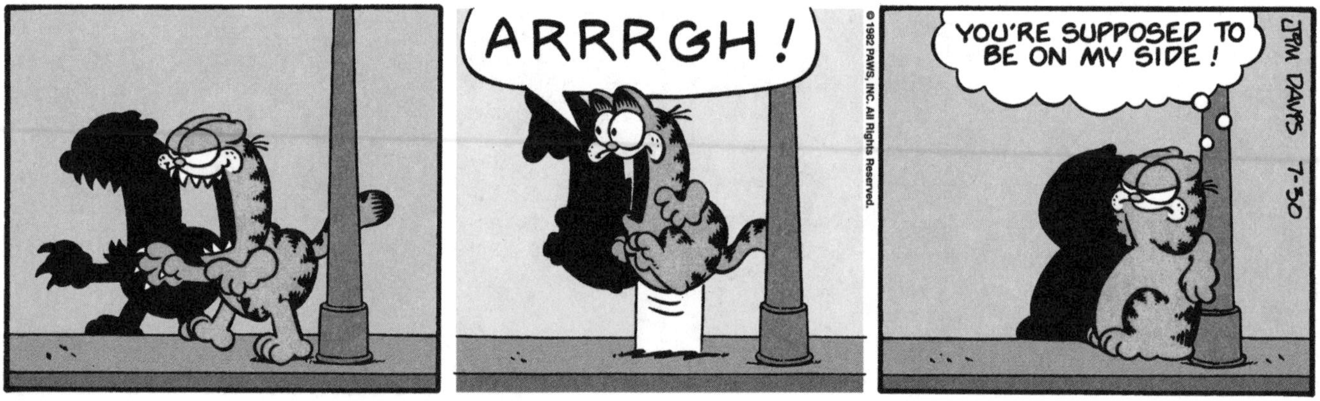
ARRRGH!
© 1982 PAWS, INC. All Rights Reserved.
YOU'RE SUPPOSED TO BE ON MY SIDE!
JIM DAVIS 7-30

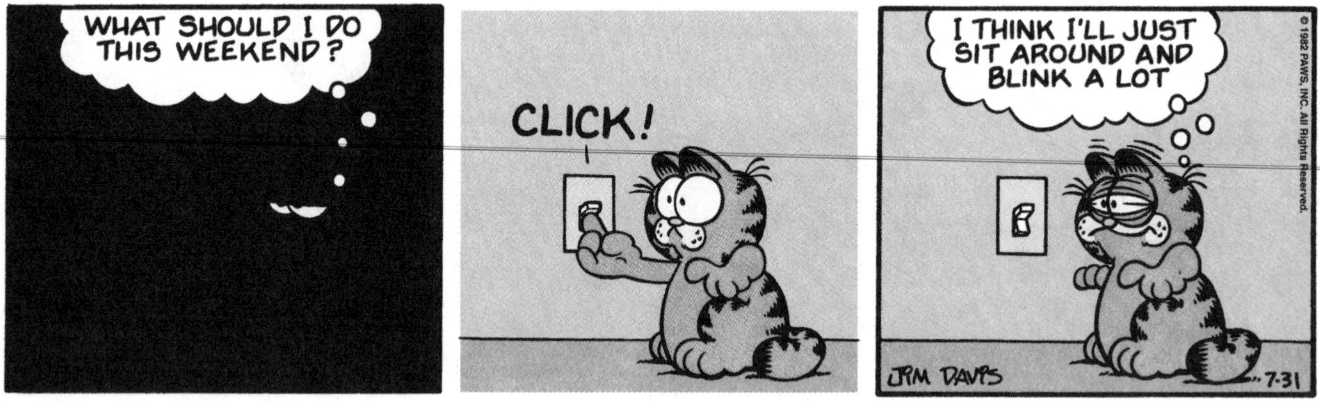
WHAT SHOULD I DO THIS WEEKEND?
CLICK!
I THINK I'LL JUST SIT AROUND AND BLINK A LOT
JIM DAVIS 7-31
© 1982 PAWS, INC. All Rights Reserved.

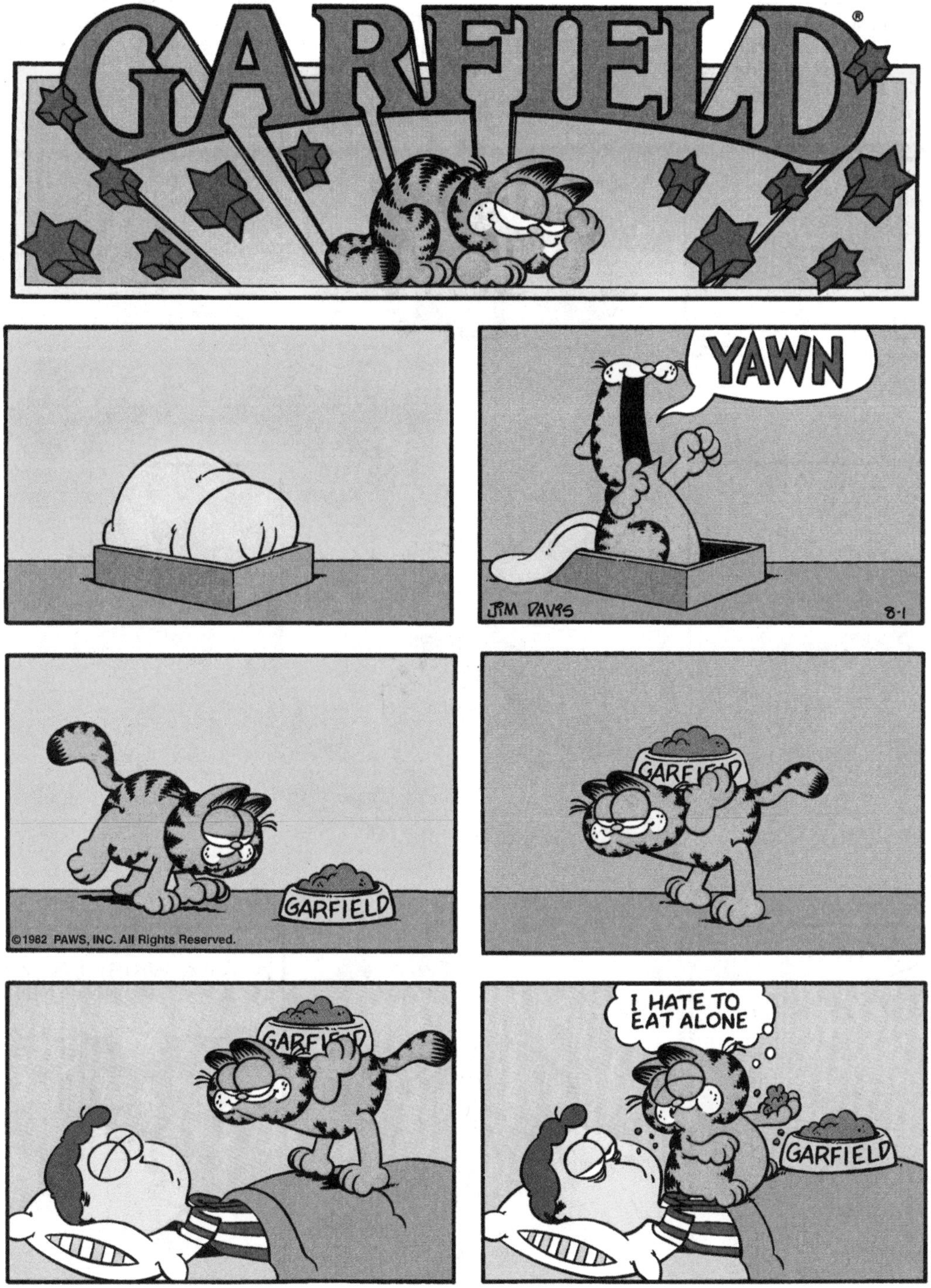
GARFIELD
YAWN
JIM DAVIS
8-1
GARFIELD
©1982 PAWS, INC. All Rights Reserved.
I HATE TO EAT ALONE
GARFIELD

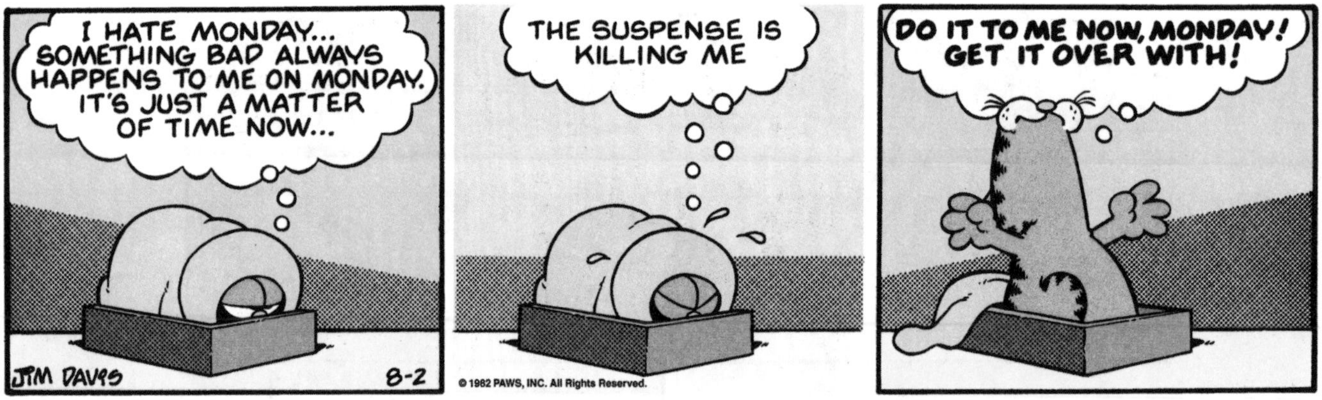
I HATE MONDAY... SOMETHING BAD ALWAYS HAPPENS TO ME ON MONDAY. IT'S JUST A MATTER OF TIME NOW...
JIM DAVIS 8-2
THE SUSPENSE IS KILLING ME
© 1982 PAWS, INC. All Rights Reserved.
DO IT TO ME NOW, MONDAY! GET IT OVER WITH!

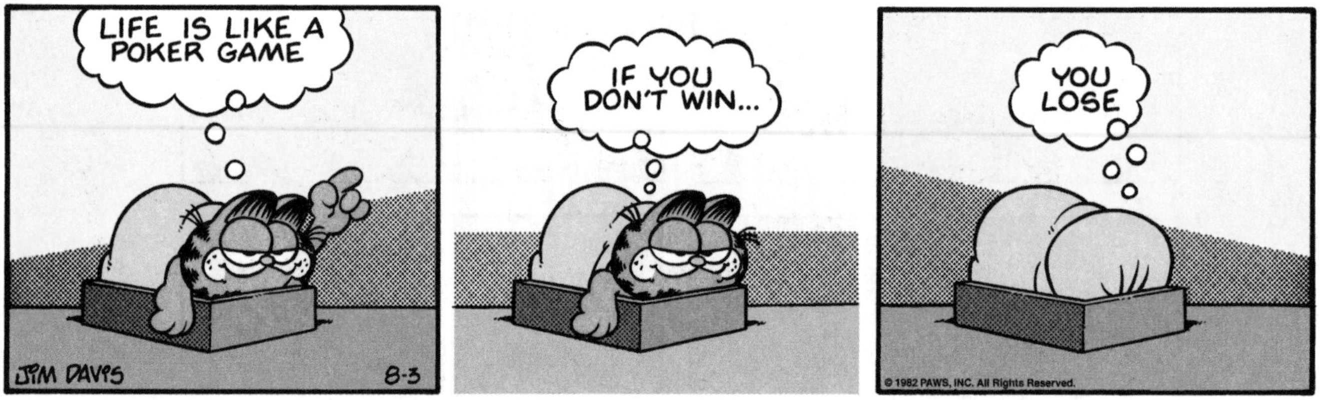
LIFE IS LIKE A POKER GAME
JIM DAVIS 8-3
IF YOU DON'T WIN...
YOU LOSE
© 1982 PAWS, INC. All Rights Reserved.

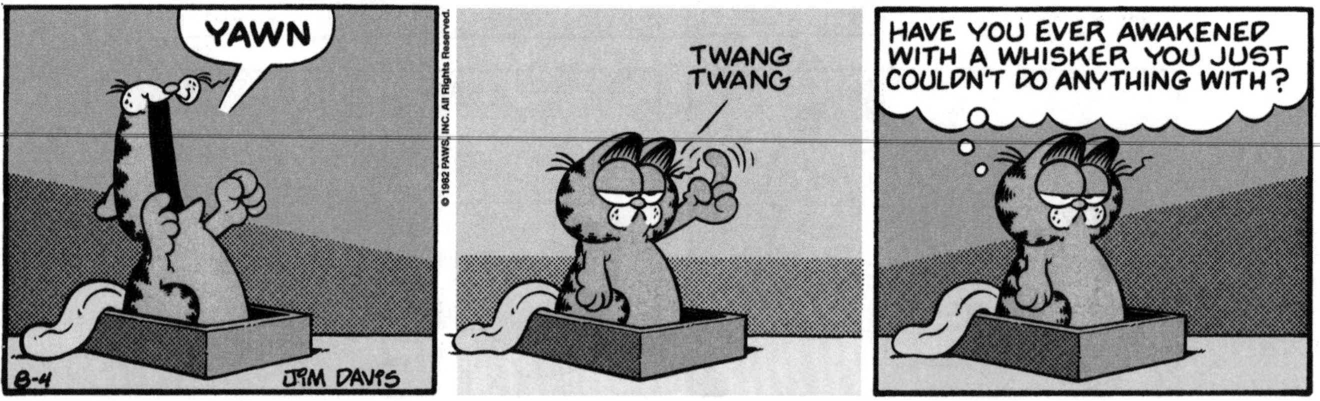
YAWN
8-4 JIM DAVIS
© 1982 PAWS, INC. All Rights Reserved.
TWANG TWANG
HAVE YOU EVER AWAKENED WITH A WHISKER YOU JUST COULDN'T DO ANYTHING WITH?

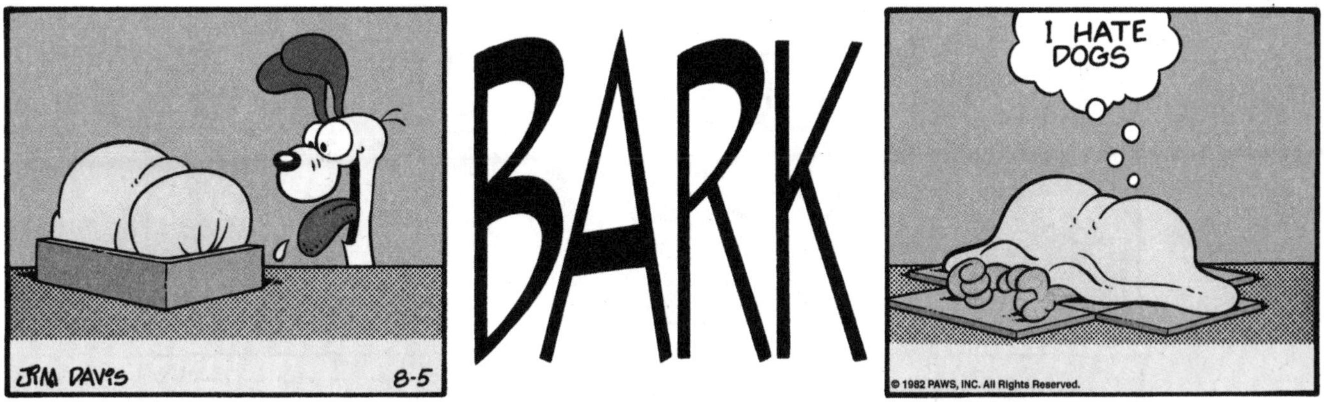
JIM DAVIS
8-5
BARK
I HATE DOGS
© 1982 PAWS, INC. All Rights Reserved.

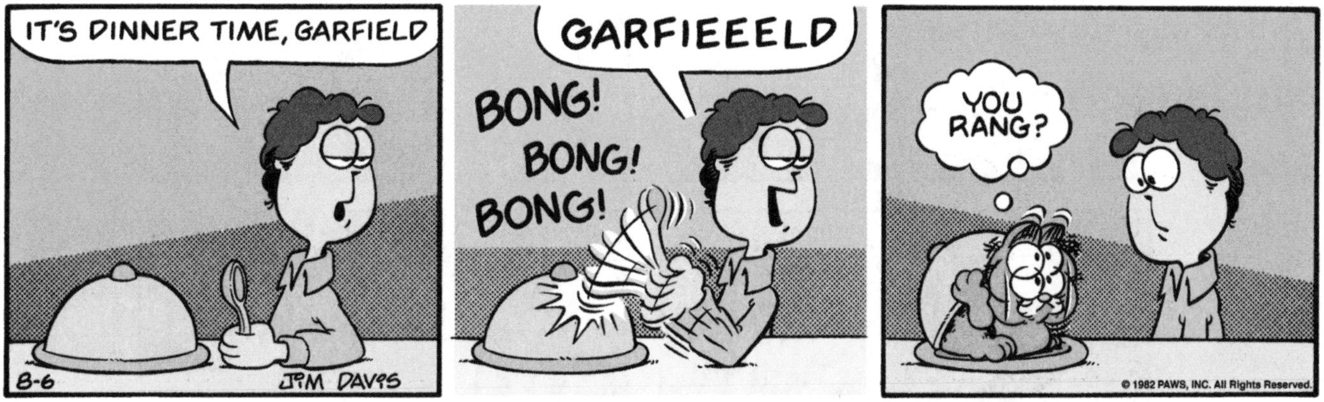
IT'S DINNER TIME, GARFIELD
8-6
JIM DAVIS
GARFIEEELD
BONG! BONG! BONG!
YOU RANG?
© 1982 PAWS, INC. All Rights Reserved.

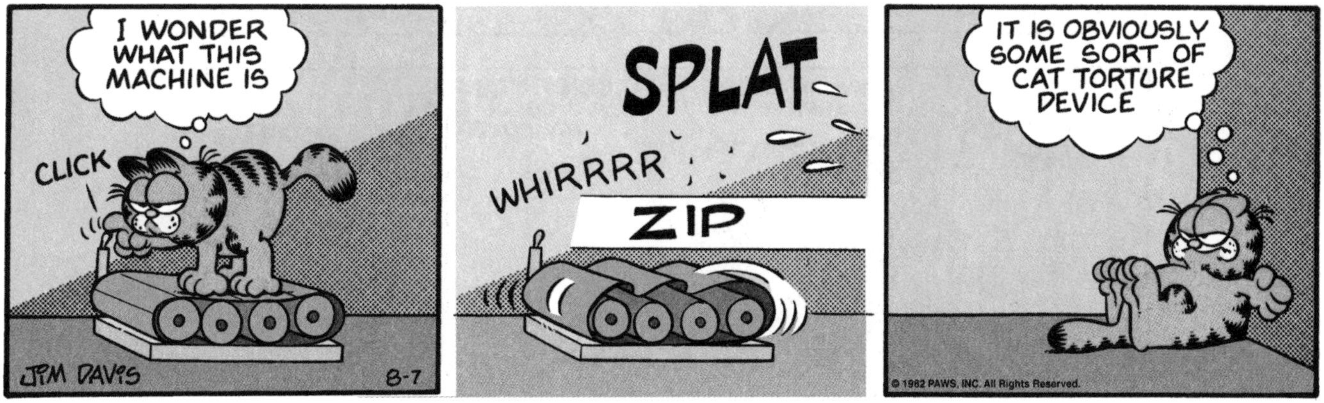
I WONDER WHAT THIS MACHINE IS
CLICK
JIM DAVIS
8-7
SPLAT
WHIRRRR
ZIP
IT IS OBVIOUSLY SOME SORT OF CAT TORTURE DEVICE
© 1982 PAWS, INC. All Rights Reserved.

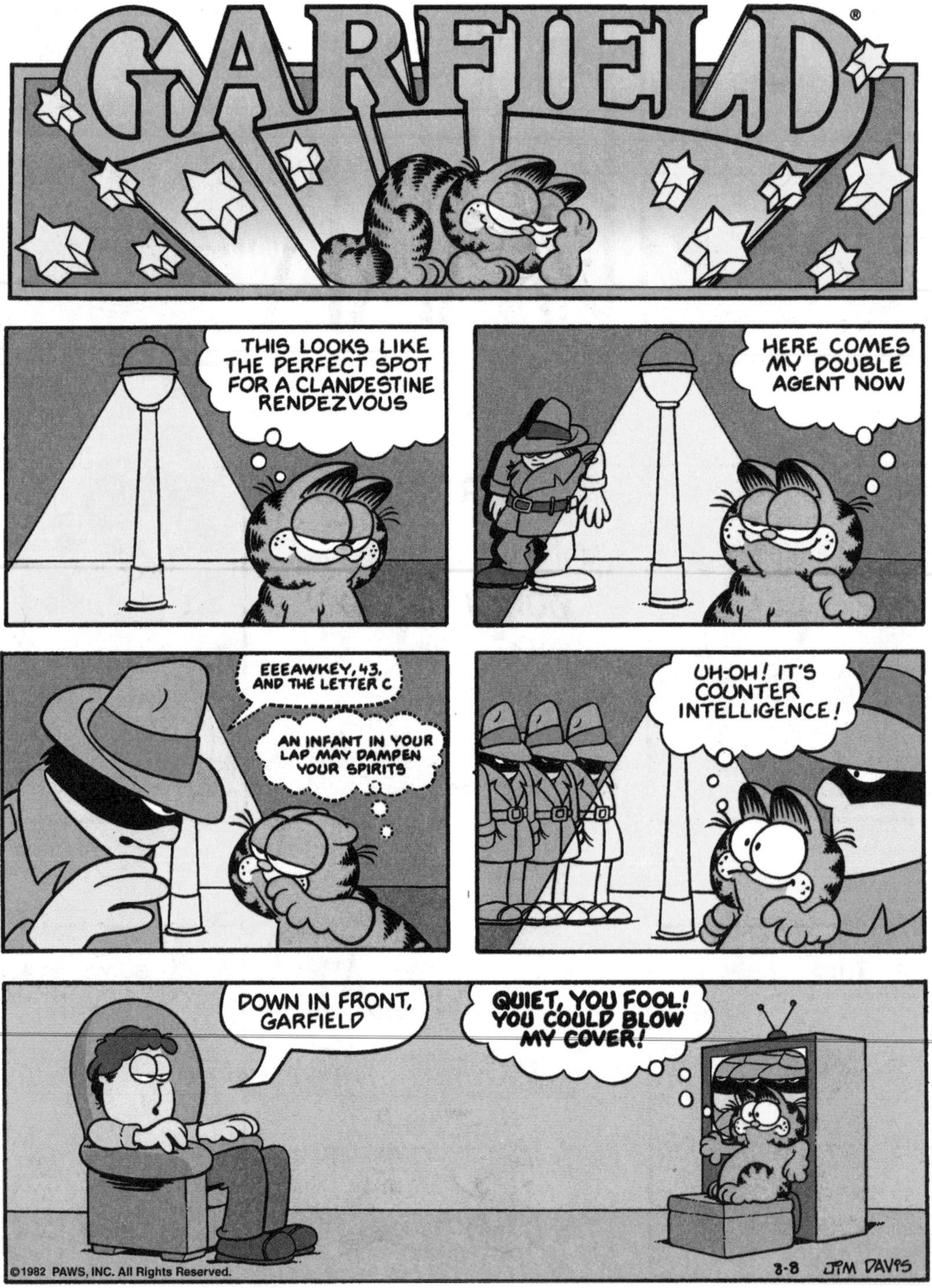
GARFIELD®
THIS LOOKS LIKE THE PERFECT SPOT FOR A CLANDESTINE RENDEZVOUS
HERE COMES MY DOUBLE AGENT NOW
EEEAWKEY, 43, AND THE LETTER C
AN INFANT IN YOUR LAP MAY DAMPEN YOUR SPIRITS
UH-OH! IT'S COUNTER INTELLIGENCE!
DOWN IN FRONT, GARFIELD
QUIET, YOU FOOL! YOU COULD BLOW MY COVER!
8-8 JIM DAVIS

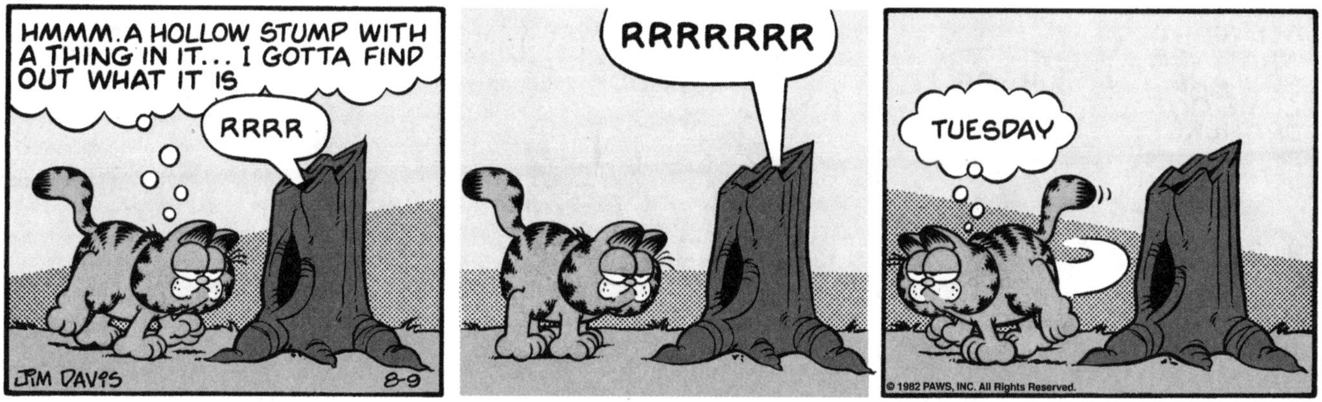
HMMM. A HOLLOW STUMP WITH A THING IN IT... I GOTTA FIND OUT WHAT IT IS
RRRR
JIM DAVIS
8-9
RRRRRRR
TUESDAY
© 1982 PAWS, INC. All Rights Reserved.

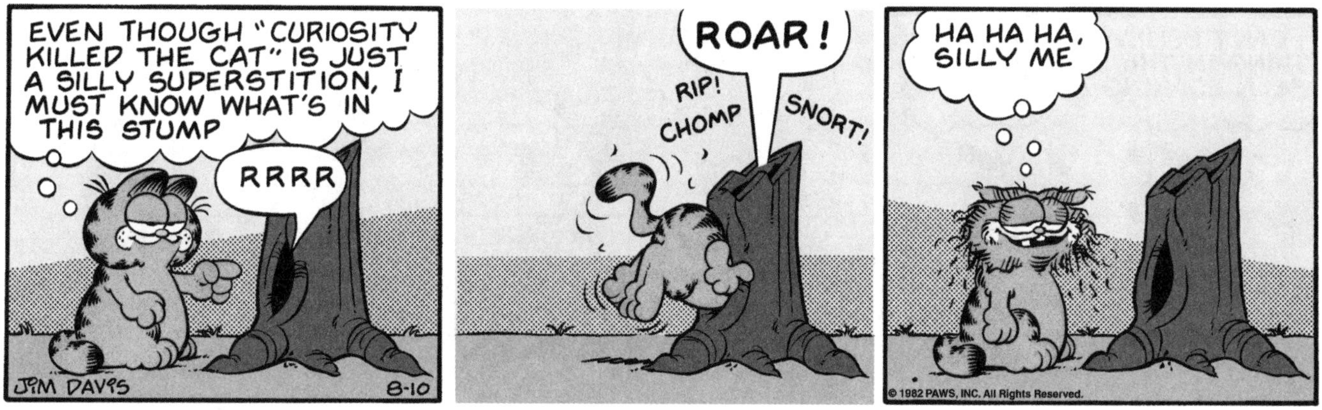
EVEN THOUGH "CURIOSITY KILLED THE CAT" IS JUST A SILLY SUPERSTITION, I MUST KNOW WHAT'S IN THIS STUMP
RRRR
JIM DAVIS
8-10
ROAR!
RIP!
CHOMP
SNORT!
HA HA HA, SILLY ME
© 1982 PAWS, INC. All Rights Reserved.

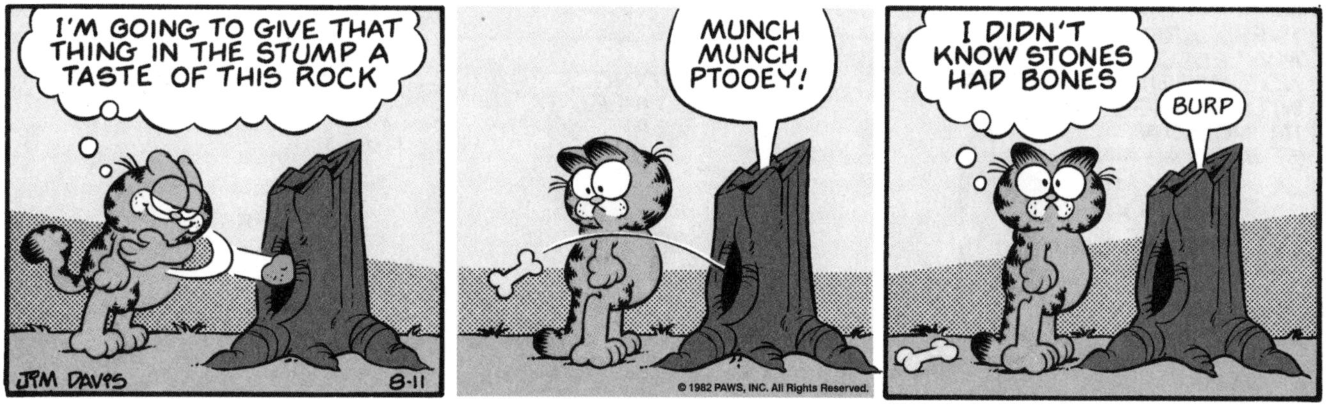
I'M GOING TO GIVE THAT THING IN THE STUMP A TASTE OF THIS ROCK
JIM DAVIS
8-11
MUNCH MUNCH PTOOEY!
© 1982 PAWS, INC. All Rights Reserved.
I DIDN'T KNOW STONES HAD BONES
BURP

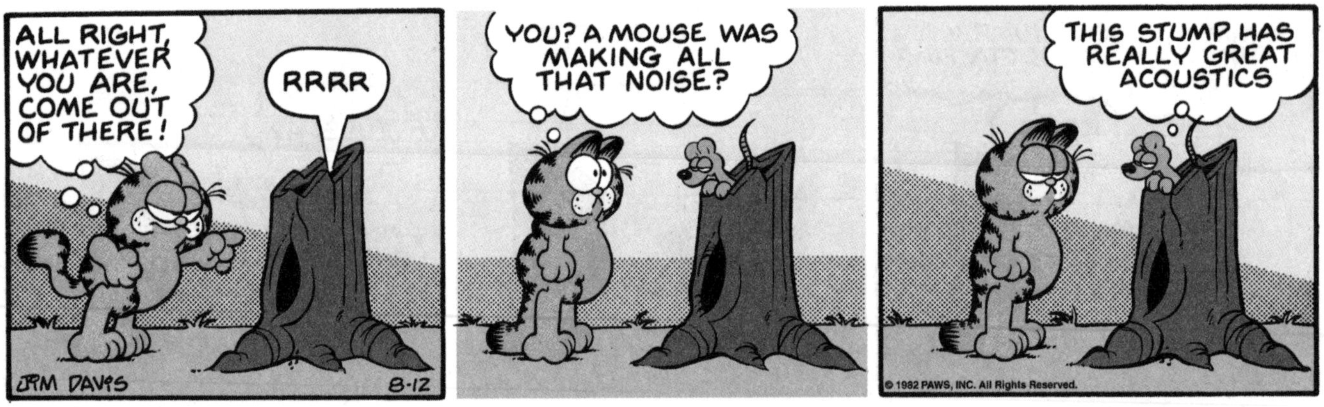
ALL RIGHT, WHATEVER YOU ARE, COME OUT OF THERE!
RRRR
JIM DAVIS
8-12
YOU? A MOUSE WAS MAKING ALL THAT NOISE?
THIS STUMP HAS REALLY GREAT ACOUSTICS
© 1982 PAWS, INC. All Rights Reserved.

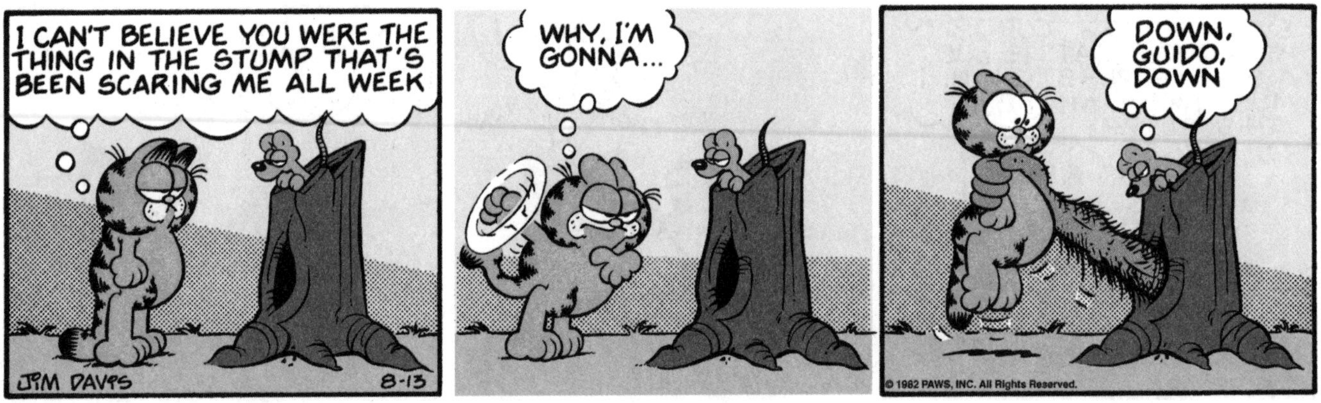
I CAN'T BELIEVE YOU WERE THE THING IN THE STUMP THAT'S BEEN SCARING ME ALL WEEK
JIM DAVIS
8-13
WHY, I'M GONNA...
DOWN, GUIDO, DOWN
© 1982 PAWS, INC. All Rights Reserved.

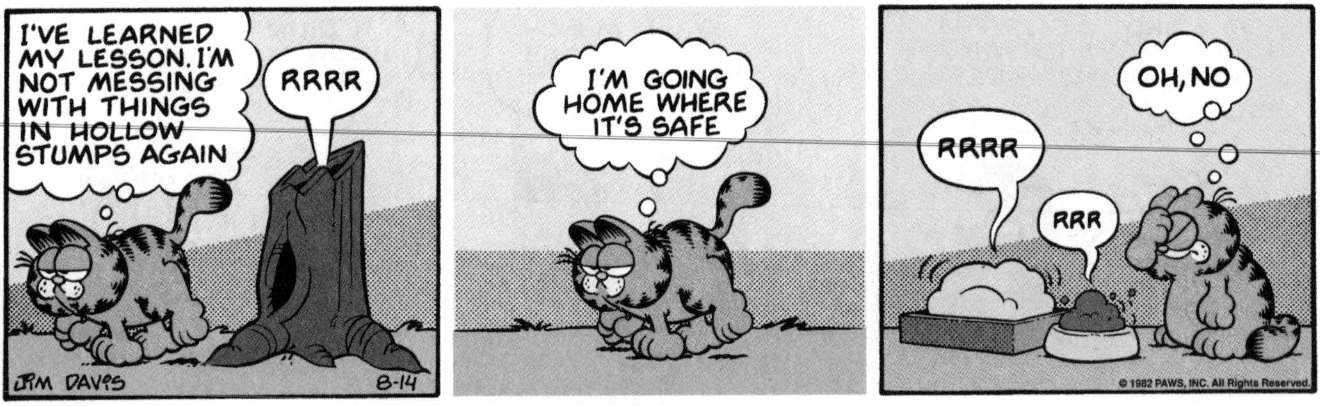
I'VE LEARNED MY LESSON. I'M NOT MESSING WITH THINGS IN HOLLOW STUMPS AGAIN
RRRR
JIM DAVIS
8-14
I'M GOING HOME WHERE IT'S SAFE
OH, NO
RRRR
RRR
© 1982 PAWS, INC. All Rights Reserved.

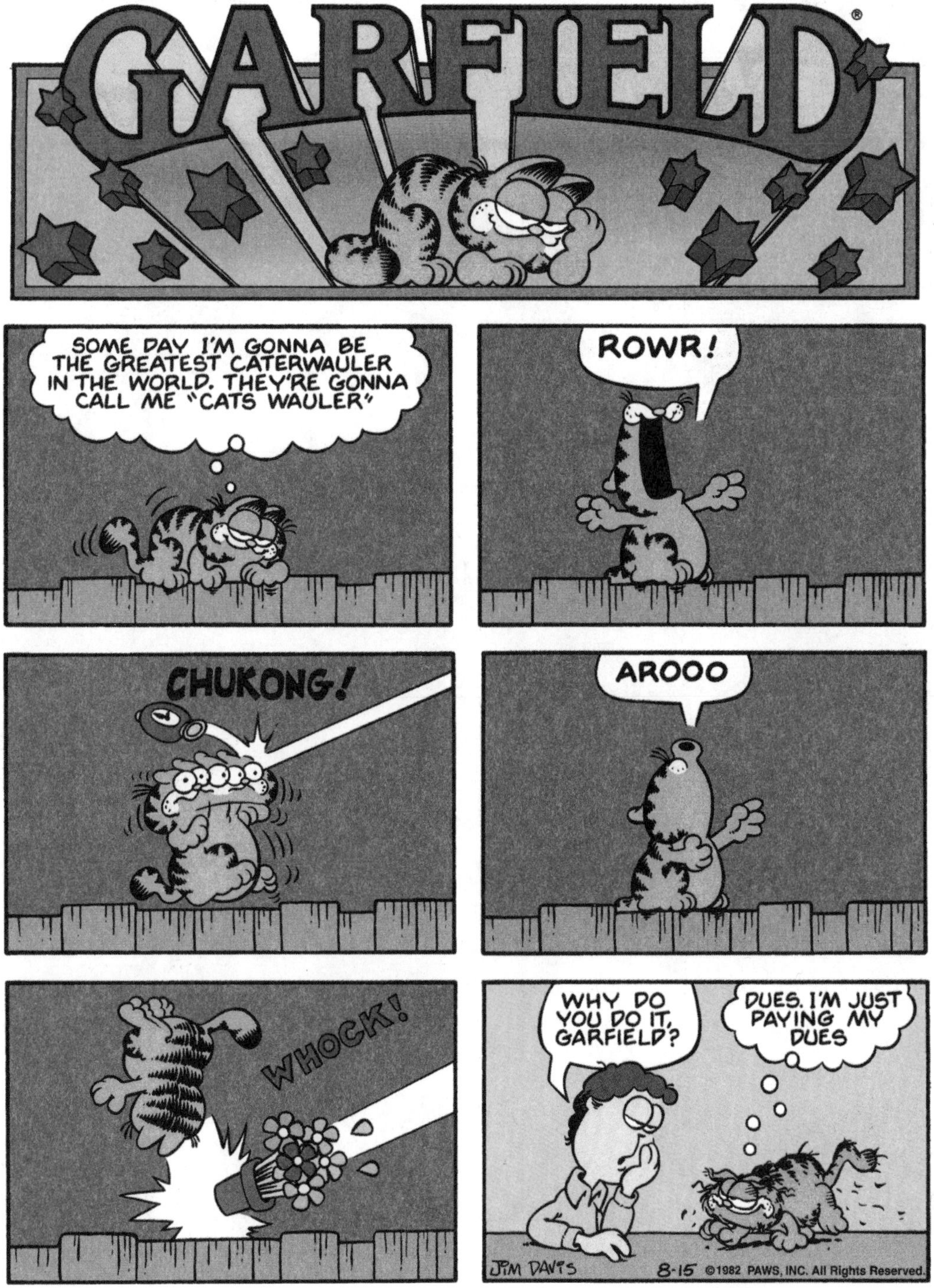

GARFIELD
SOME DAY I'M GONNA BE THE GREATEST CATERWAULER IN THE WORLD. THEY'RE GONNA CALL ME "CATS WAULER"
ROWR!
CHUKONG!
AROOO
WHOCK!
WHY DO YOU DO IT, GARFIELD?
DUES. I'M JUST PAYING MY DUES
JIM DAVIS
8-15 ©1982 PAWS, INC. All Rights Reserved.

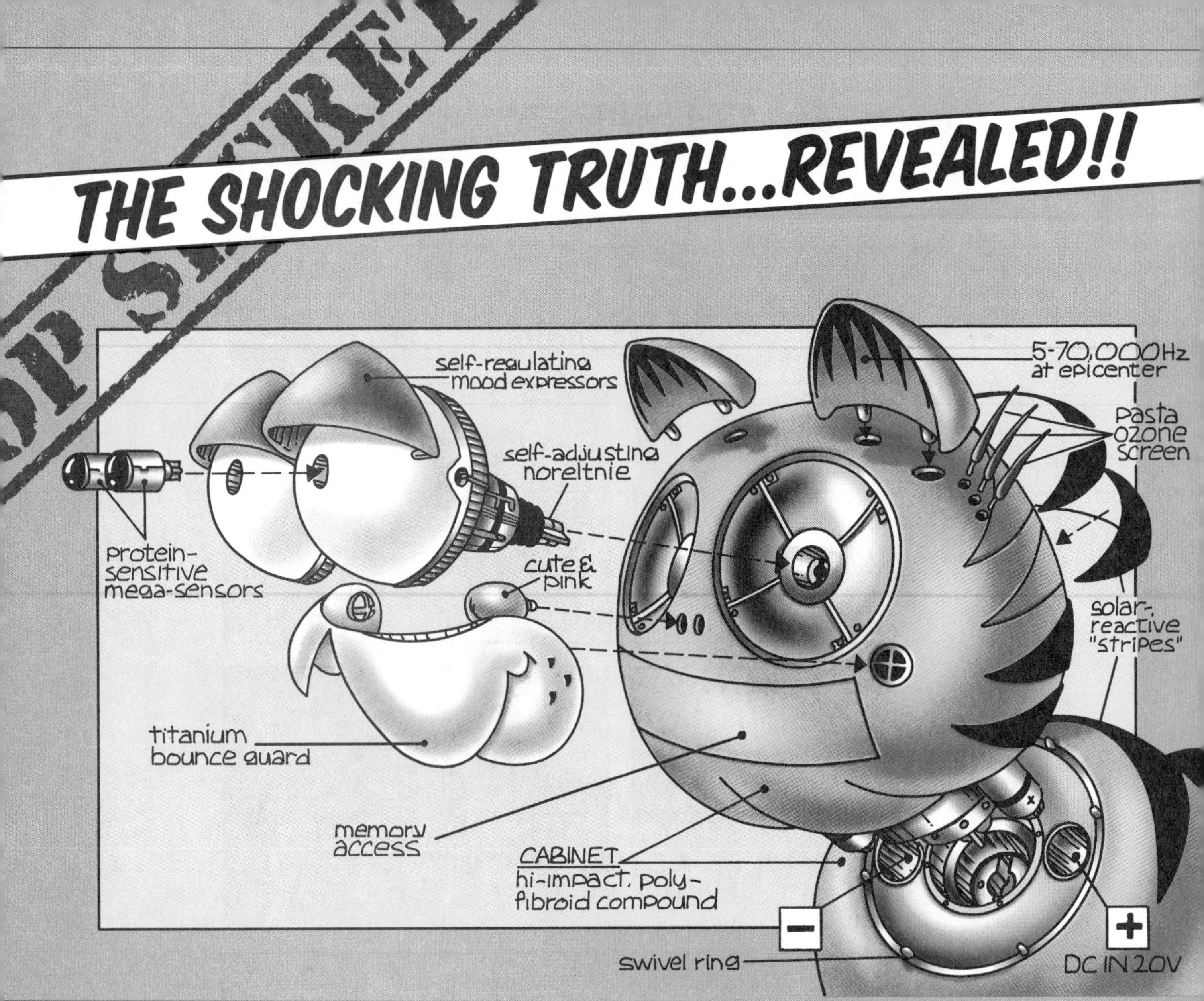
THE SHOCKING TRUTH...REVEALED!!
self-regulating mood expressors
self-adjusting noreltnie
protein-sensitive mega-sensors
cute & pink
titanium bounce guard
memory access
CABINET
hi-impact, poly-fibroid compound
swivel ring
5-70,000 Hz at epicenter
pasta ozone screen
solar-reactive "stripes"
DC IN 20V

MAJOR COMIC STRIP CHARACTER REPLACED BY A MACHINE!

Rumors are running rampant that Garfield the cat has retired to a South Sea island and has been replaced by a bionic duplicate. This schematic mysteriously ended up in the hands of the publisher. Fact . . . or fiction? Read this book and determine for yourself.

Garfield
tips the scales

BY JIM DAVIS

Ballantine Books • **New York**

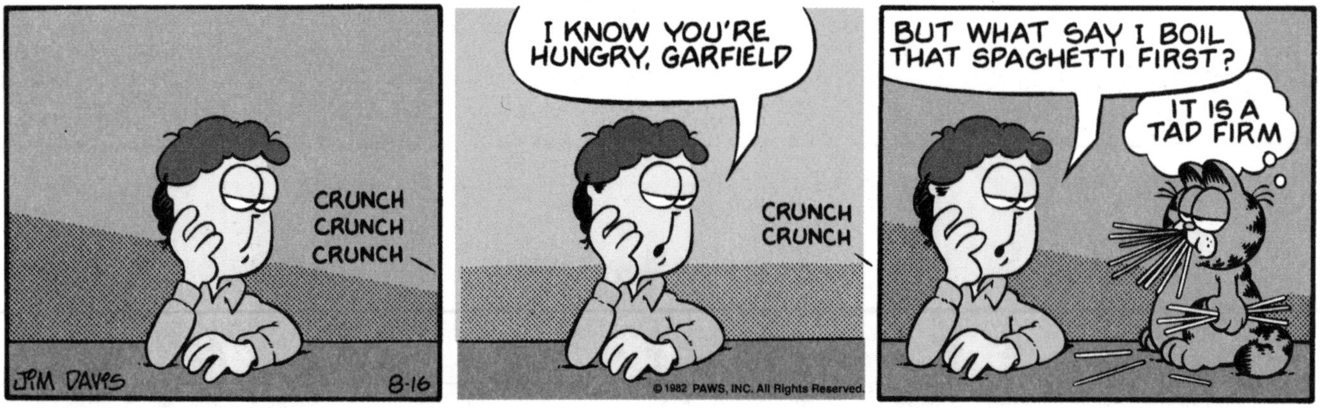
CRUNCH CRUNCH CRUNCH
JIM DAVIS
8-16
I KNOW YOU'RE HUNGRY, GARFIELD
CRUNCH CRUNCH
© 1982 PAWS, INC. All Rights Reserved.
BUT WHAT SAY I BOIL THAT SPAGHETTI FIRST?
IT IS A TAD FIRM

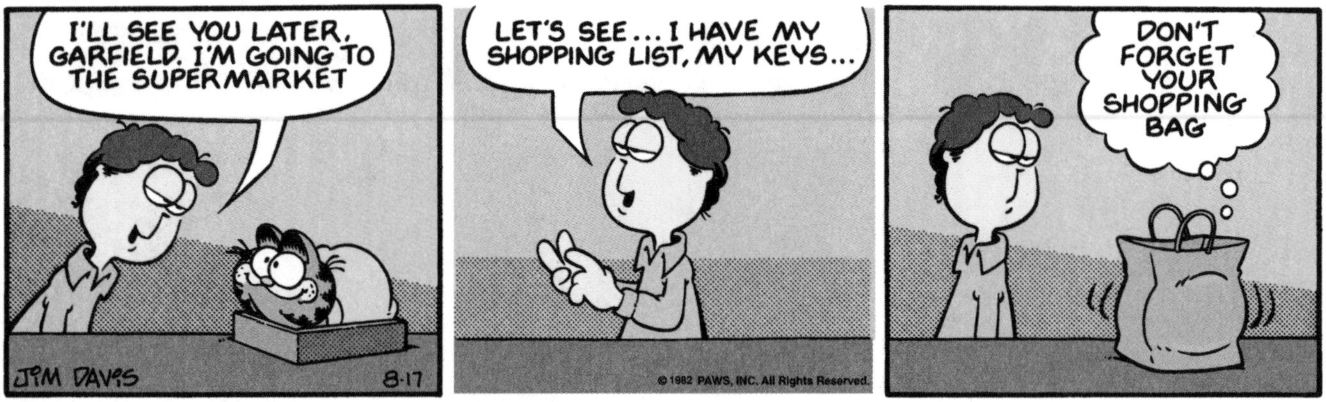
I'LL SEE YOU LATER, GARFIELD. I'M GOING TO THE SUPERMARKET
JIM DAVIS
8-17
LET'S SEE... I HAVE MY SHOPPING LIST, MY KEYS...
© 1982 PAWS, INC. All Rights Reserved.
DON'T FORGET YOUR SHOPPING BAG

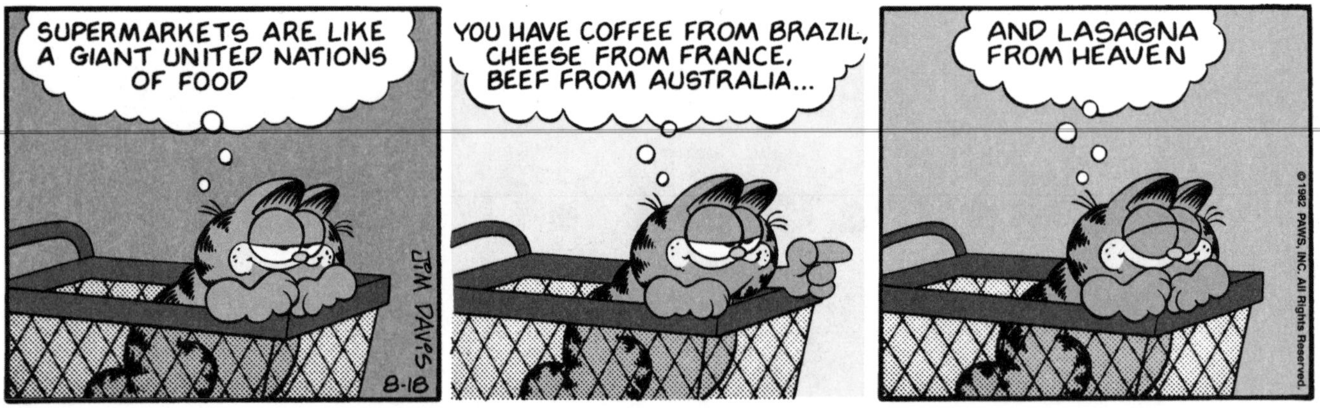
SUPERMARKETS ARE LIKE A GIANT UNITED NATIONS OF FOOD
JIM DAVIS
8-18
YOU HAVE COFFEE FROM BRAZIL, CHEESE FROM FRANCE, BEEF FROM AUSTRALIA...
AND LASAGNA FROM HEAVEN
© 1982 PAWS, INC. All Rights Reserved.

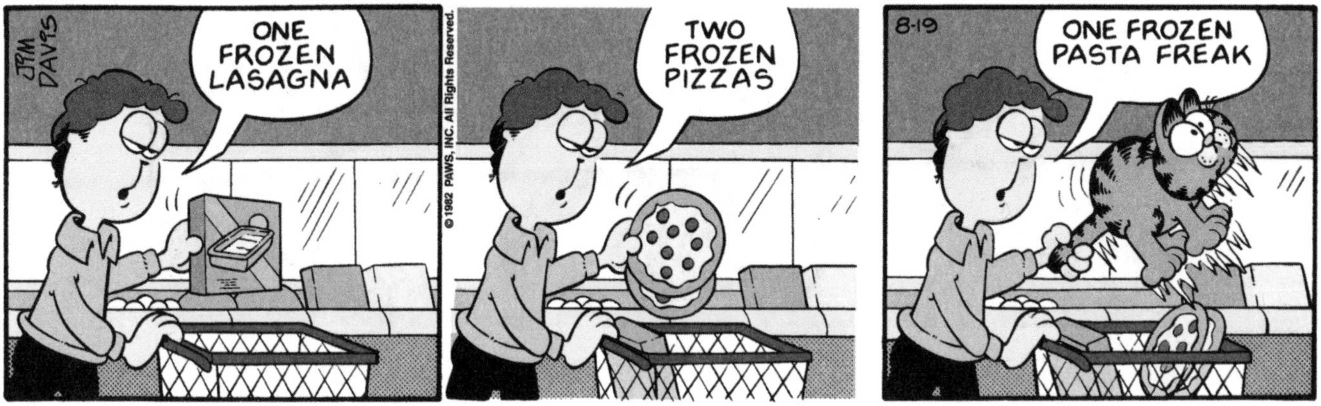
JIM DAVIS
ONE FROZEN LASAGNA
© 1982 PAWS, INC. All Rights Reserved.
TWO FROZEN PIZZAS
8-19
ONE FROZEN PASTA FREAK

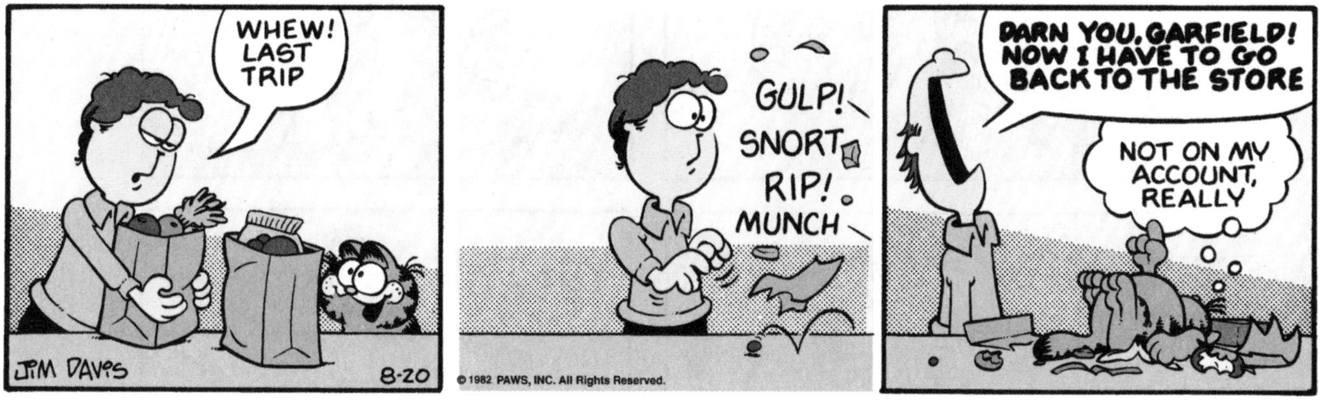
WHEW! LAST TRIP
JIM DAVIS
8-20
GULP! SNORT RIP! MUNCH
© 1982 PAWS, INC. All Rights Reserved.
DARN YOU, GARFIELD! NOW I HAVE TO GO BACK TO THE STORE
NOT ON MY ACCOUNT, REALLY

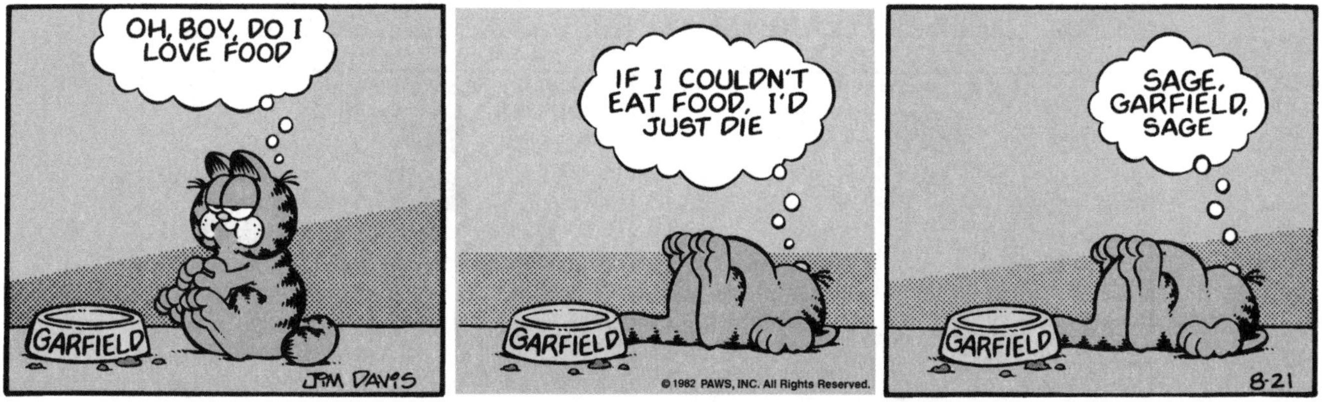
OH, BOY, DO I LOVE FOOD
GARFIELD
JIM DAVIS
IF I COULDN'T EAT FOOD, I'D JUST DIE
GARFIELD
© 1982 PAWS, INC. All Rights Reserved.
SAGE, GARFIELD, SAGE
GARFIELD
8-21

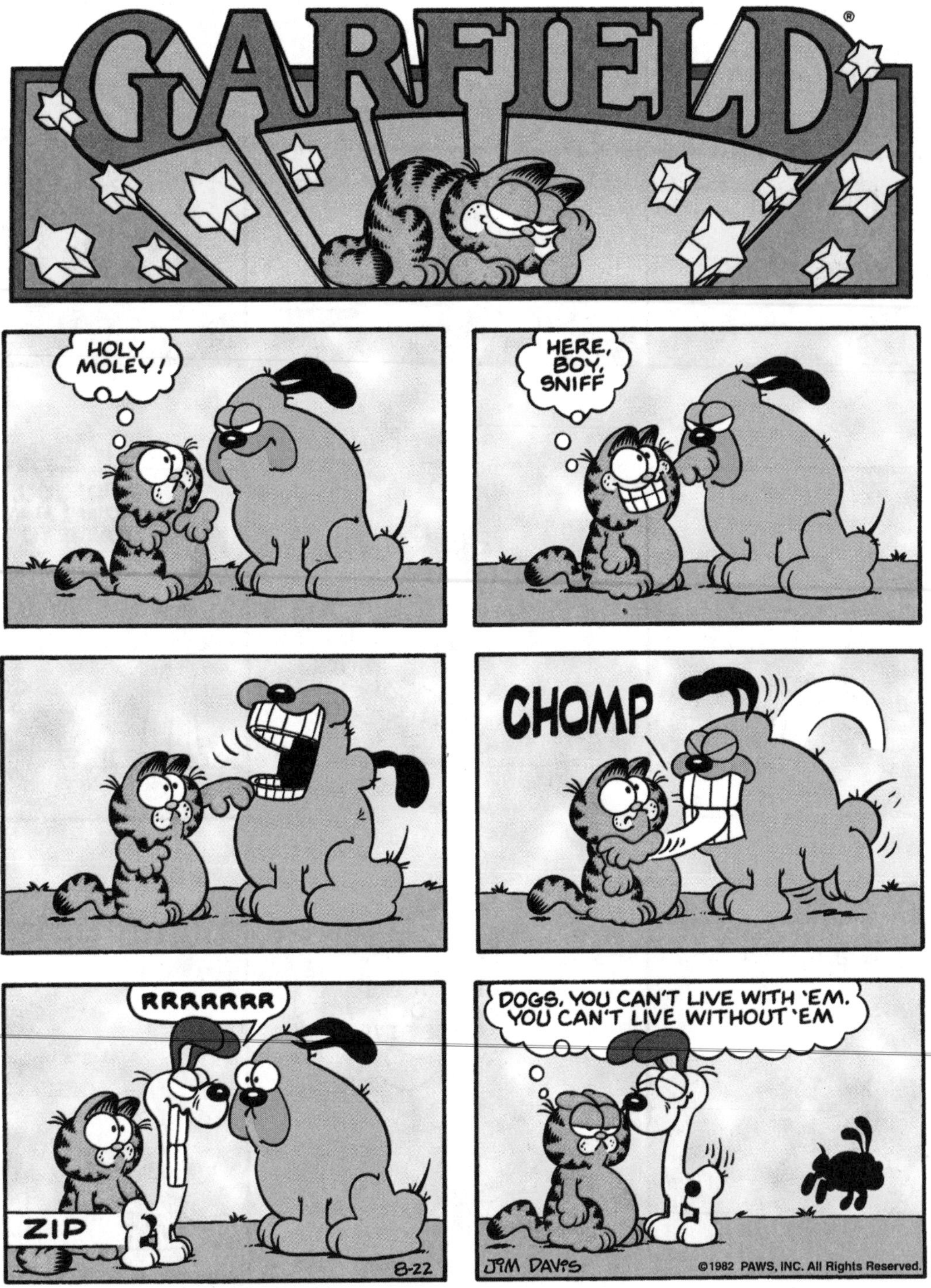
GARFIELD
HOLY MOLEY!
HERE, BOY, SNIFF
CHOMP
RRRRRRR
ZIP
8-22
DOGS, YOU CAN'T LIVE WITH 'EM. YOU CAN'T LIVE WITHOUT 'EM
JIM DAVIS
©1982 PAWS, INC. All Rights Reserved.

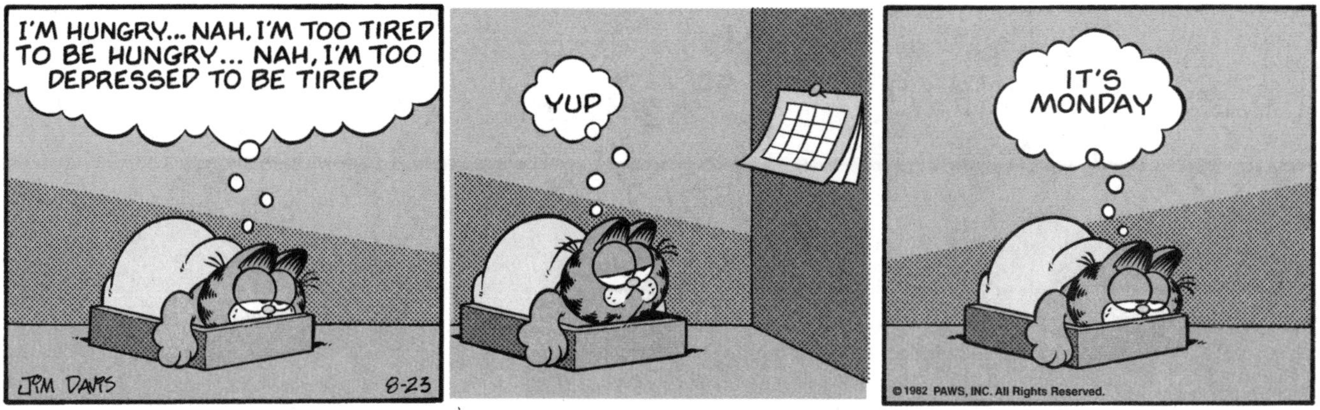
I'M HUNGRY... NAH, I'M TOO TIRED TO BE HUNGRY... NAH, I'M TOO DEPRESSED TO BE TIRED
JIM DAVIS
8-23
YUP
IT'S MONDAY
©1982 PAWS, INC. All Rights Reserved.

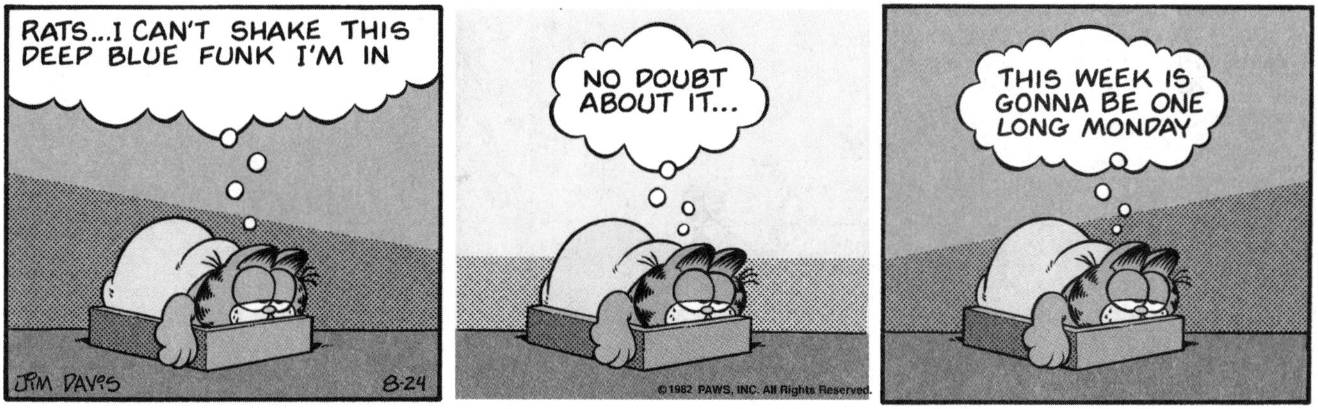
RATS...I CAN'T SHAKE THIS DEEP BLUE FUNK I'M IN
JIM DAVIS
8-24
NO DOUBT ABOUT IT...
©1982 PAWS, INC. All Rights Reserved.
THIS WEEK IS GONNA BE ONE LONG MONDAY

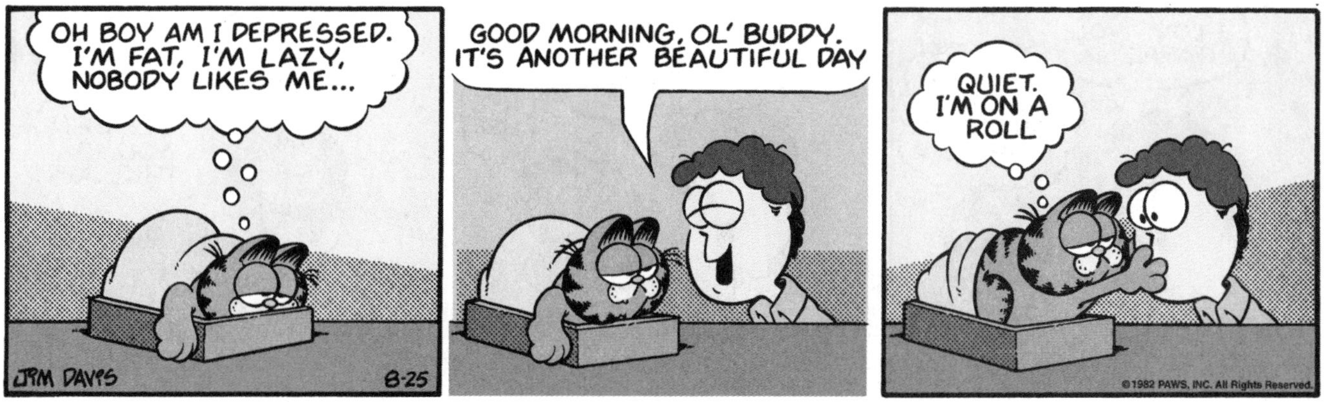
OH BOY AM I DEPRESSED. I'M FAT, I'M LAZY, NOBODY LIKES ME...
JIM DAVIS
8-25
GOOD MORNING, OL' BUDDY. IT'S ANOTHER BEAUTIFUL DAY
QUIET. I'M ON A ROLL
©1982 PAWS, INC. All Rights Reserved.

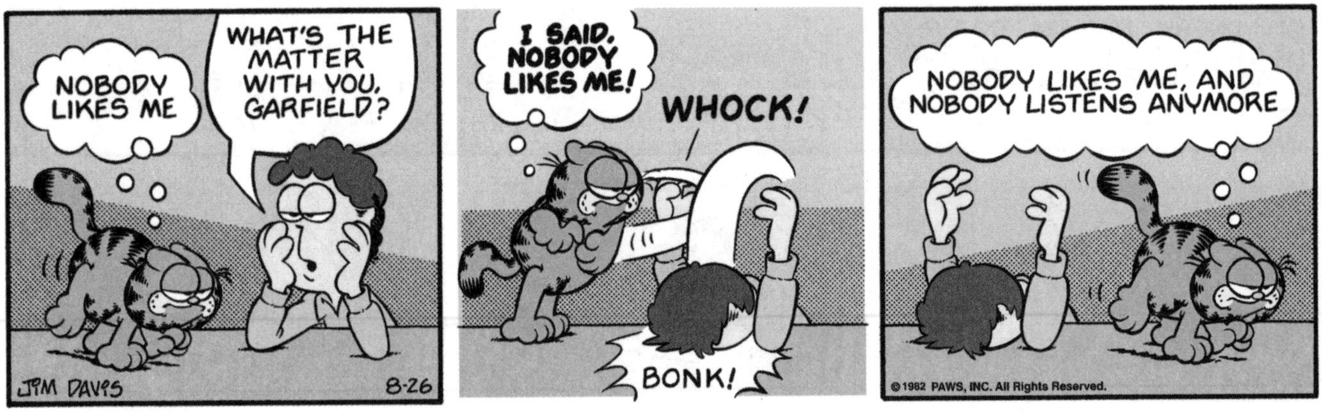
NOBODY LIKES ME
WHAT'S THE MATTER WITH YOU, GARFIELD?
JIM DAVIS
8-26
I SAID, NOBODY LIKES ME!
WHOCK!
BONK!
NOBODY LIKES ME, AND NOBODY LISTENS ANYMORE
© 1982 PAWS, INC. All Rights Reserved.

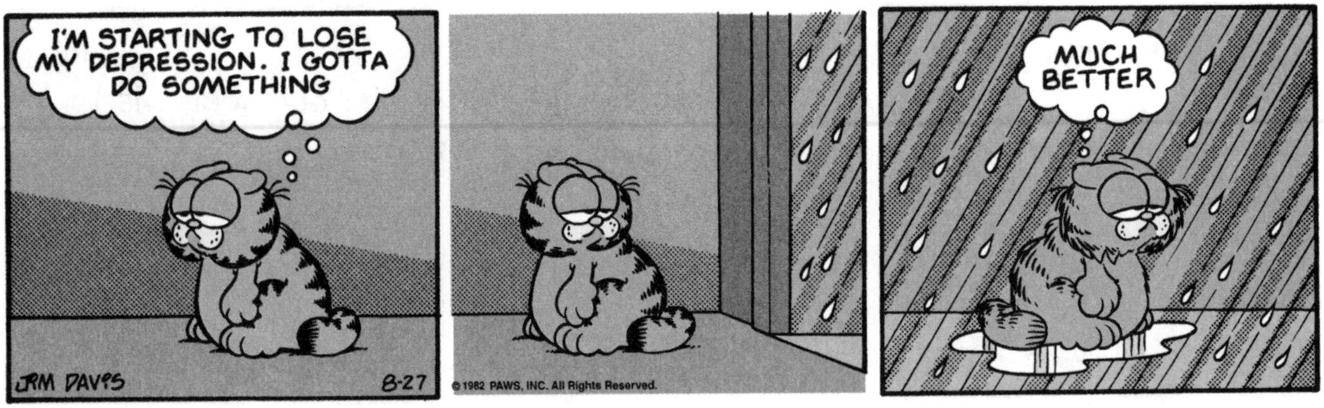
I'M STARTING TO LOSE MY DEPRESSION. I GOTTA DO SOMETHING
JIM DAVIS
8-27
© 1982 PAWS, INC. All Rights Reserved.
MUCH BETTER

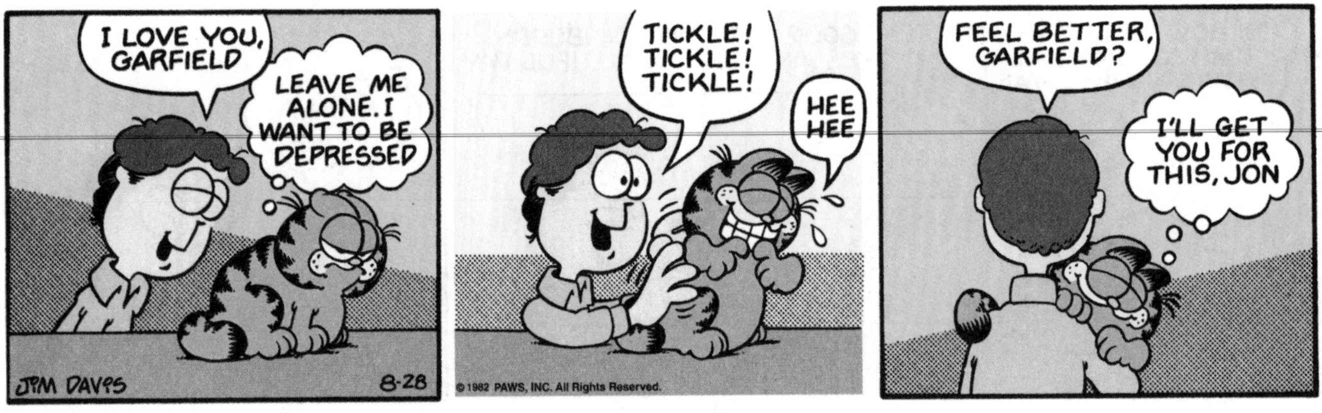
I LOVE YOU, GARFIELD
LEAVE ME ALONE. I WANT TO BE DEPRESSED
JIM DAVIS
8-28
TICKLE! TICKLE! TICKLE!
HEE HEE
© 1982 PAWS, INC. All Rights Reserved.
FEEL BETTER, GARFIELD?
I'LL GET YOU FOR THIS, JON

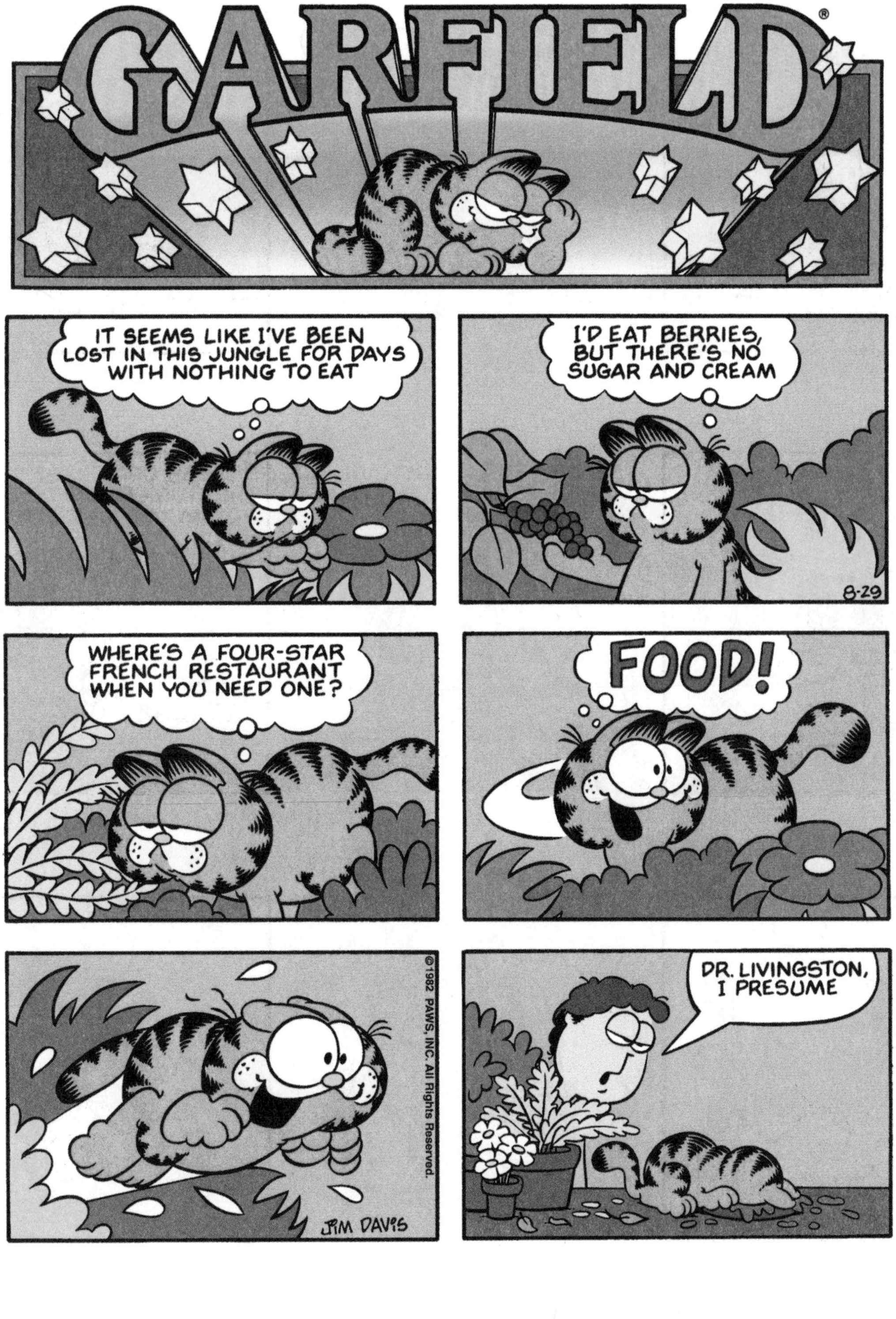
GARFIELD®
IT SEEMS LIKE I'VE BEEN LOST IN THIS JUNGLE FOR DAYS WITH NOTHING TO EAT
I'D EAT BERRIES, BUT THERE'S NO SUGAR AND CREAM
8-29
WHERE'S A FOUR-STAR FRENCH RESTAURANT WHEN YOU NEED ONE?
FOOD!
© 1982 PAWS, INC. All Rights Reserved.
JIM DAVIS
DR. LIVINGSTON, I PRESUME

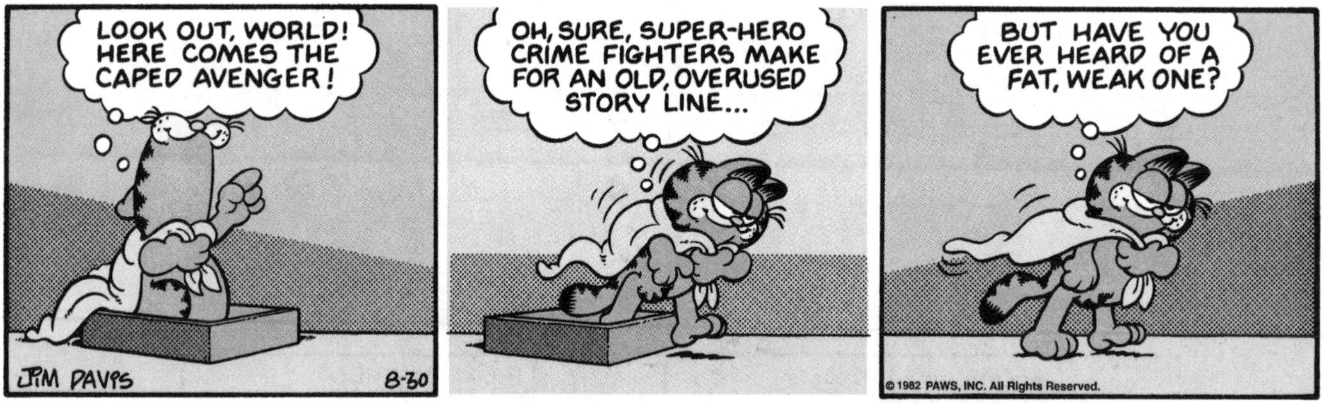
LOOK OUT, WORLD! HERE COMES THE CAPED AVENGER!
JIM DAVIS
8-30
OH, SURE, SUPER-HERO CRIME FIGHTERS MAKE FOR AN OLD, OVERUSED STORY LINE...
BUT HAVE YOU EVER HEARD OF A FAT, WEAK ONE?
© 1982 PAWS, INC. All Rights Reserved.

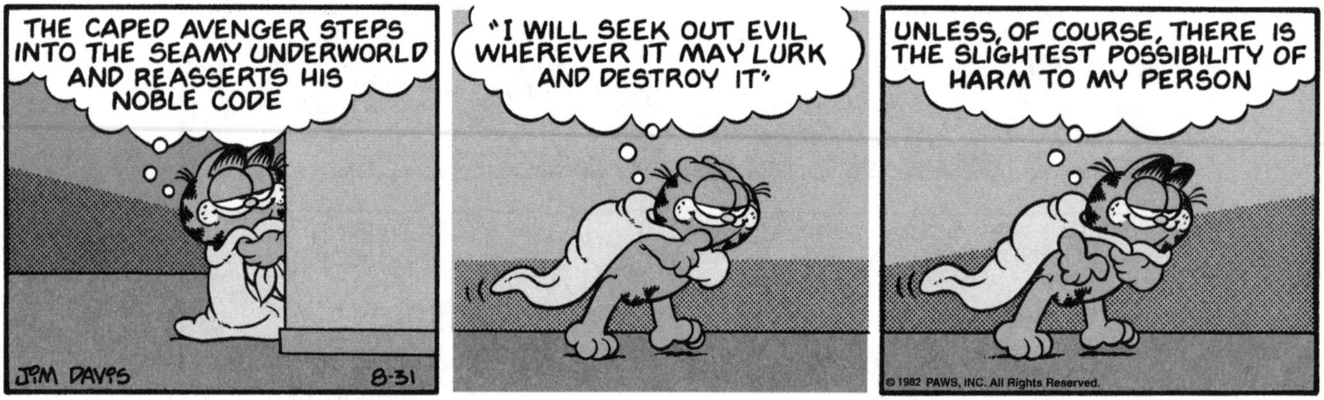
THE CAPED AVENGER STEPS INTO THE SEAMY UNDERWORLD AND REASSERTS HIS NOBLE CODE
JIM DAVIS
8-31
"I WILL SEEK OUT EVIL WHEREVER IT MAY LURK AND DESTROY IT"
UNLESS, OF COURSE, THERE IS THE SLIGHTEST POSSIBILITY OF HARM TO MY PERSON
© 1982 PAWS, INC. All Rights Reserved.

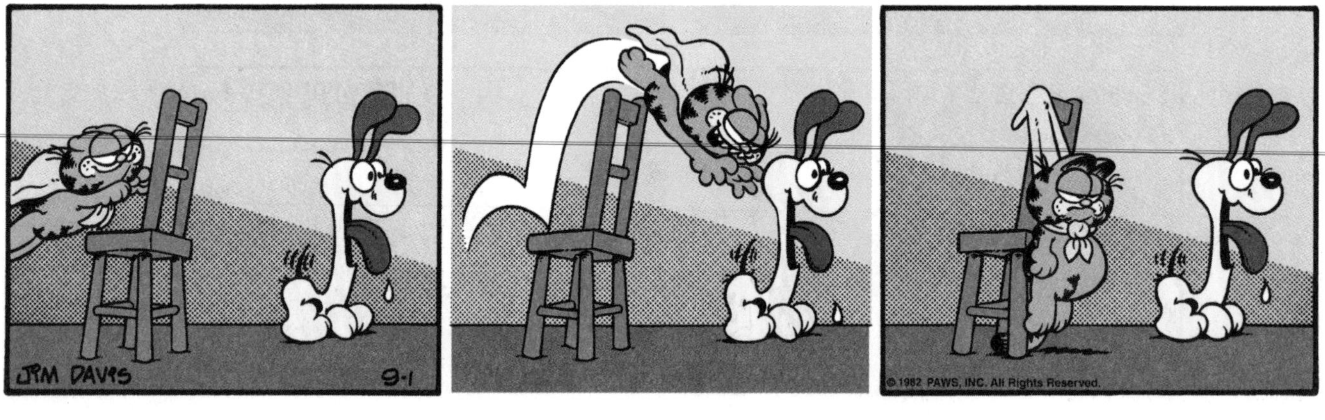
JIM DAVIS
9-1
© 1982 PAWS, INC. All Rights Reserved.

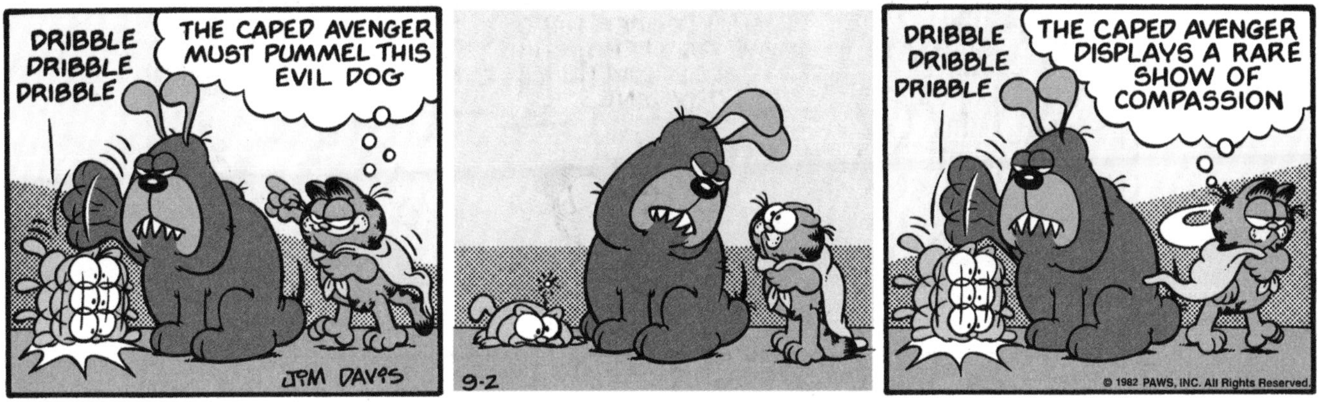
DRIBBLE DRIBBLE DRIBBLE
THE CAPED AVENGER MUST PUMMEL THIS EVIL DOG
JIM DAVIS
9-2
DRIBBLE DRIBBLE DRIBBLE
THE CAPED AVENGER DISPLAYS A RARE SHOW OF COMPASSION
© 1982 PAWS, INC. All Rights Reserved.

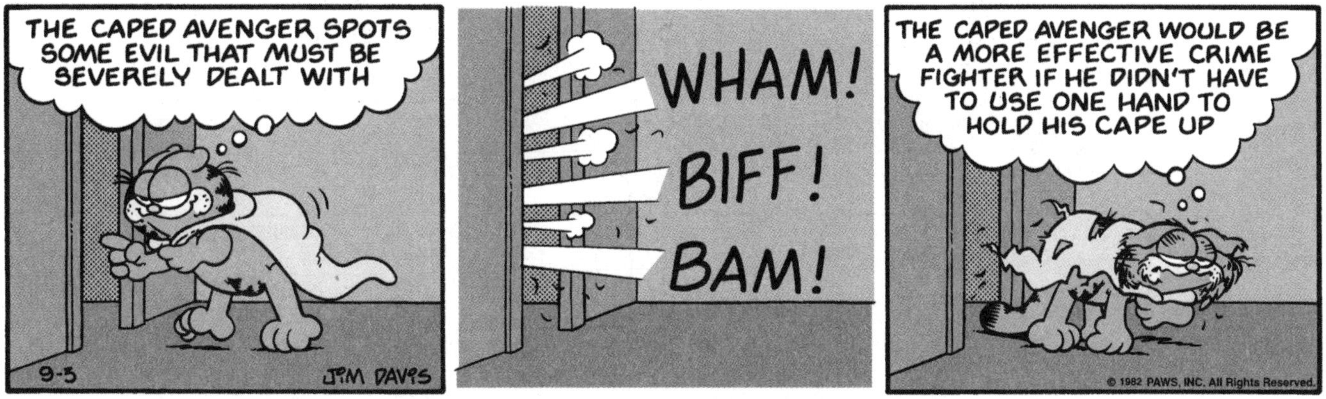
THE CAPED AVENGER SPOTS SOME EVIL THAT MUST BE SEVERELY DEALT WITH
9-3
JIM DAVIS
WHAM!
BIFF!
BAM!
THE CAPED AVENGER WOULD BE A MORE EFFECTIVE CRIME FIGHTER IF HE DIDN'T HAVE TO USE ONE HAND TO HOLD HIS CAPE UP
© 1982 PAWS, INC. All Rights Reserved.

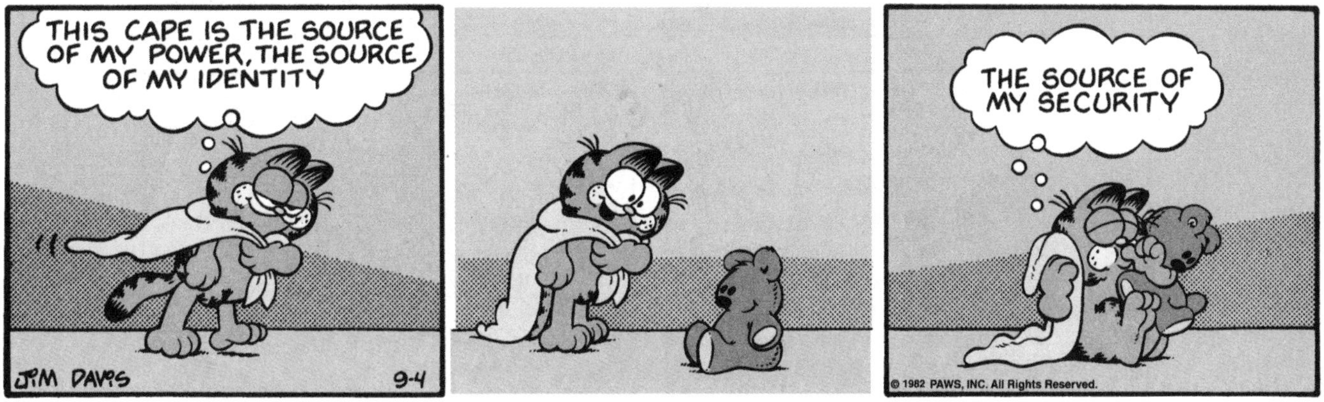
THIS CAPE IS THE SOURCE OF MY POWER, THE SOURCE OF MY IDENTITY
JIM DAVIS
9-4
THE SOURCE OF MY SECURITY
© 1982 PAWS, INC. All Rights Reserved.

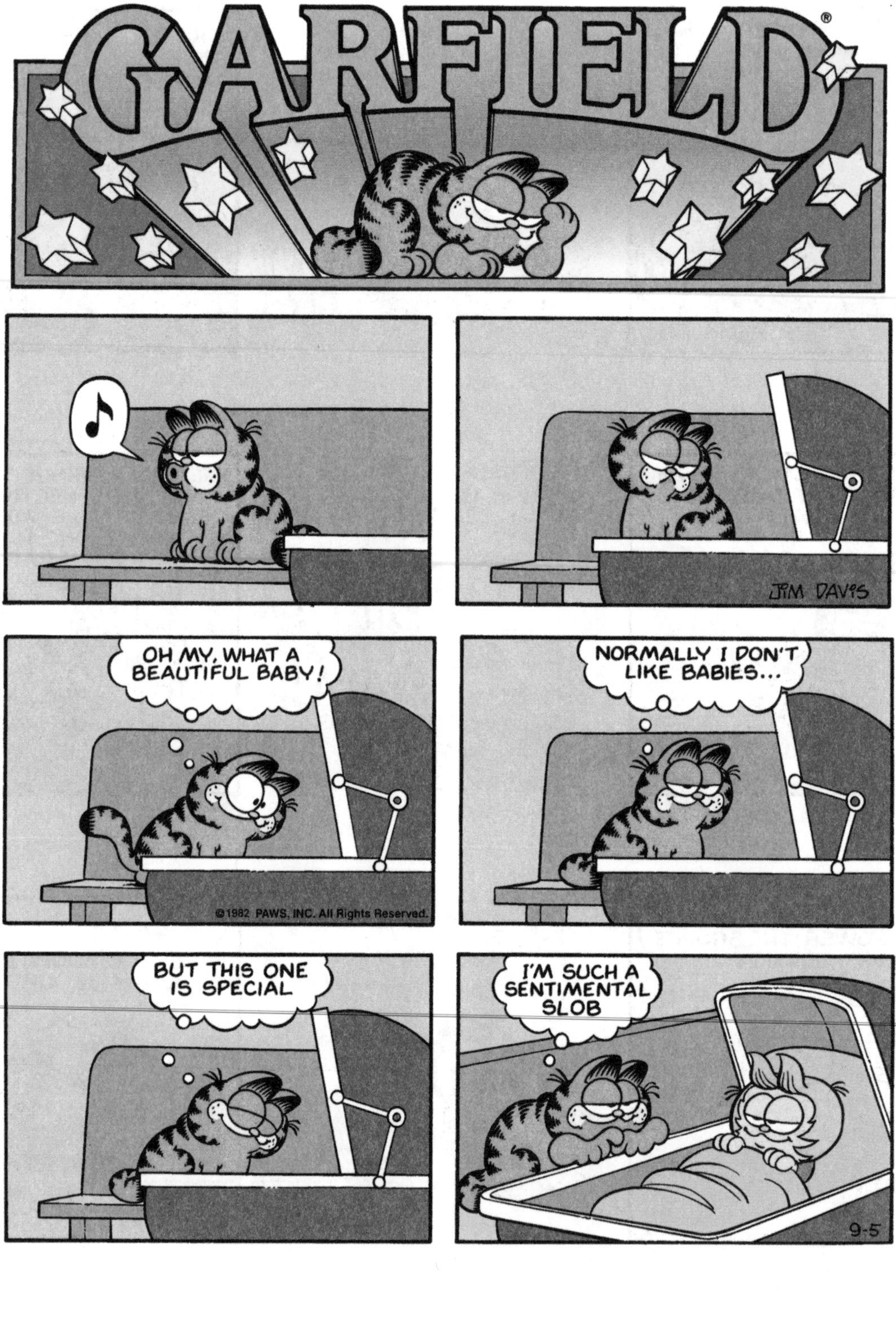
GARFIELD®
JIM DAVIS
OH MY, WHAT A BEAUTIFUL BABY!
©1982 PAWS, INC. All Rights Reserved.
NORMALLY I DON'T LIKE BABIES...
BUT THIS ONE IS SPECIAL
I'M SUCH A SENTIMENTAL SLOB
9-5

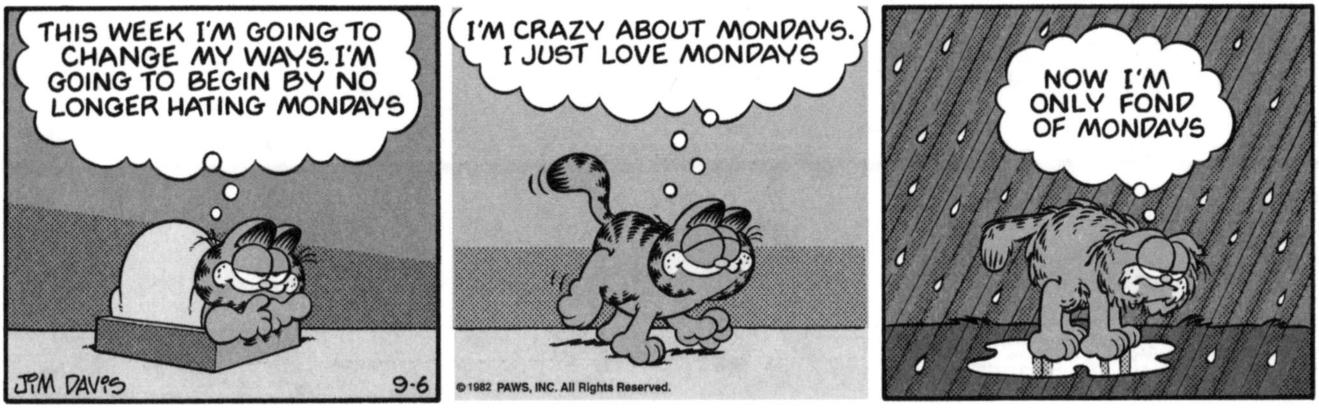
THIS WEEK I'M GOING TO CHANGE MY WAYS. I'M GOING TO BEGIN BY NO LONGER HATING MONDAYS
JIM DAVIS
9-6
I'M CRAZY ABOUT MONDAYS. I JUST LOVE MONDAYS
© 1982 PAWS, INC. All Rights Reserved.
NOW I'M ONLY FOND OF MONDAYS

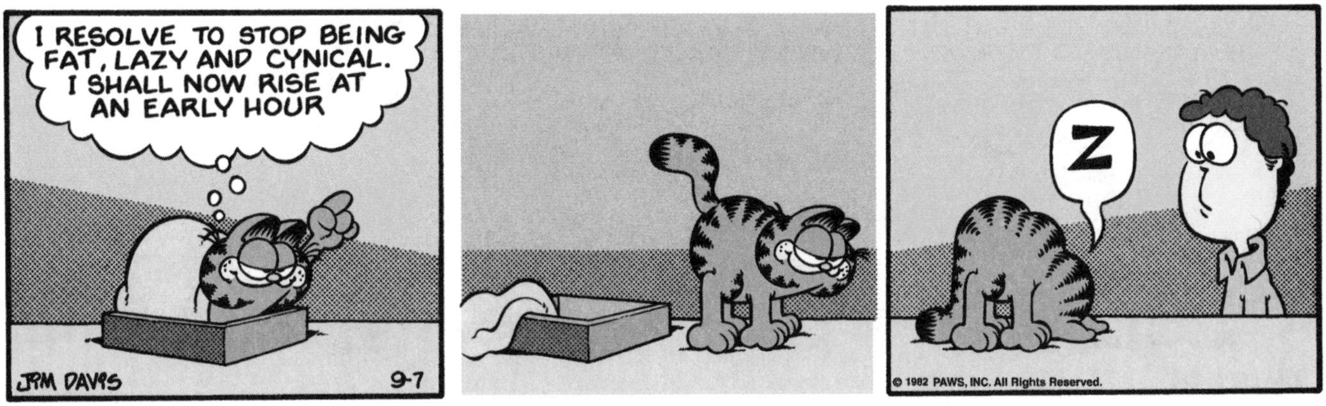
I RESOLVE TO STOP BEING FAT, LAZY AND CYNICAL. I SHALL NOW RISE AT AN EARLY HOUR
JIM DAVIS
9-7
Z
© 1982 PAWS, INC. All Rights Reserved.

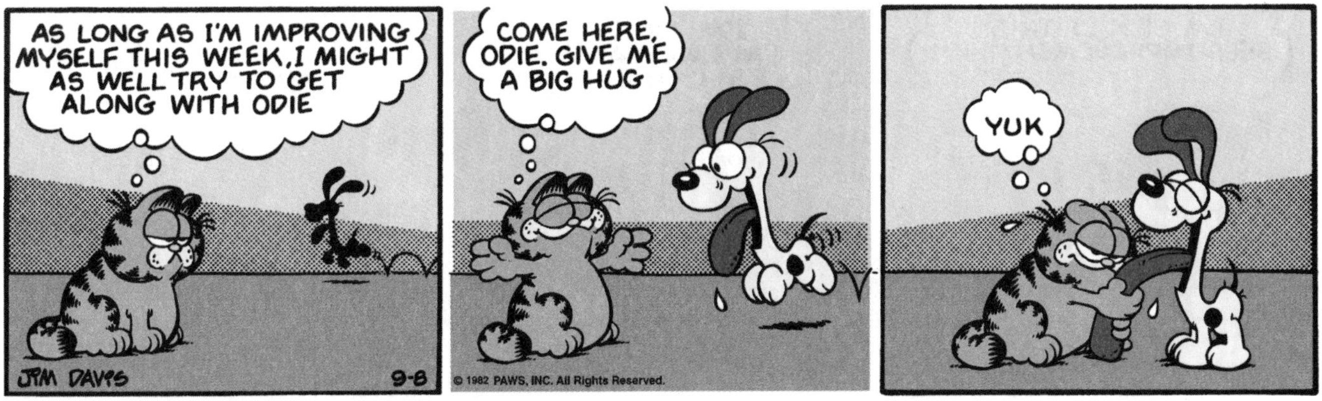
AS LONG AS I'M IMPROVING MYSELF THIS WEEK, I MIGHT AS WELL TRY TO GET ALONG WITH ODIE
JIM DAVIS
9-8
COME HERE, ODIE. GIVE ME A BIG HUG
© 1982 PAWS, INC. All Rights Reserved.
YUK

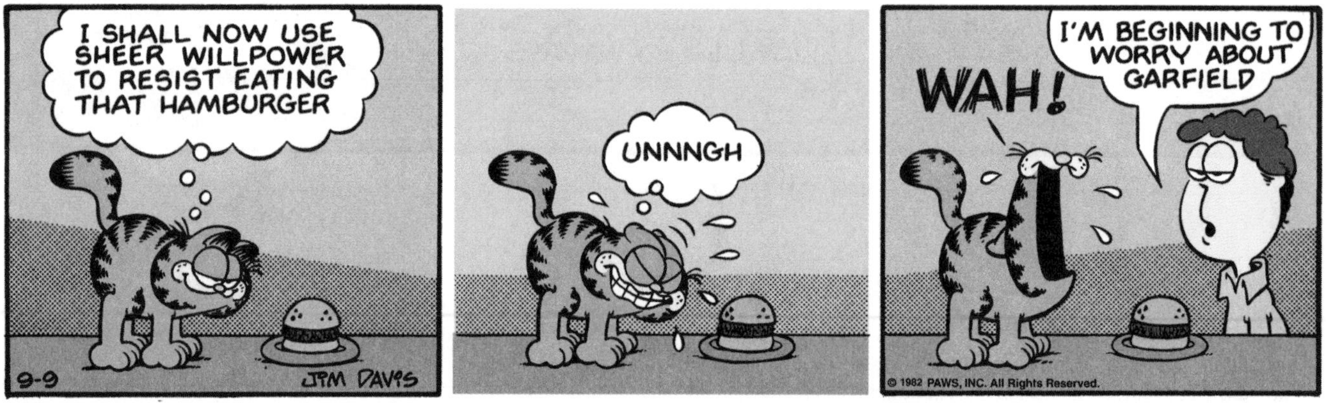
I SHALL NOW USE SHEER WILLPOWER TO RESIST EATING THAT HAMBURGER
9-9
JIM DAVIS
UNNNGH
WAH!
I'M BEGINNING TO WORRY ABOUT GARFIELD
© 1982 PAWS, INC. All Rights Reserved.

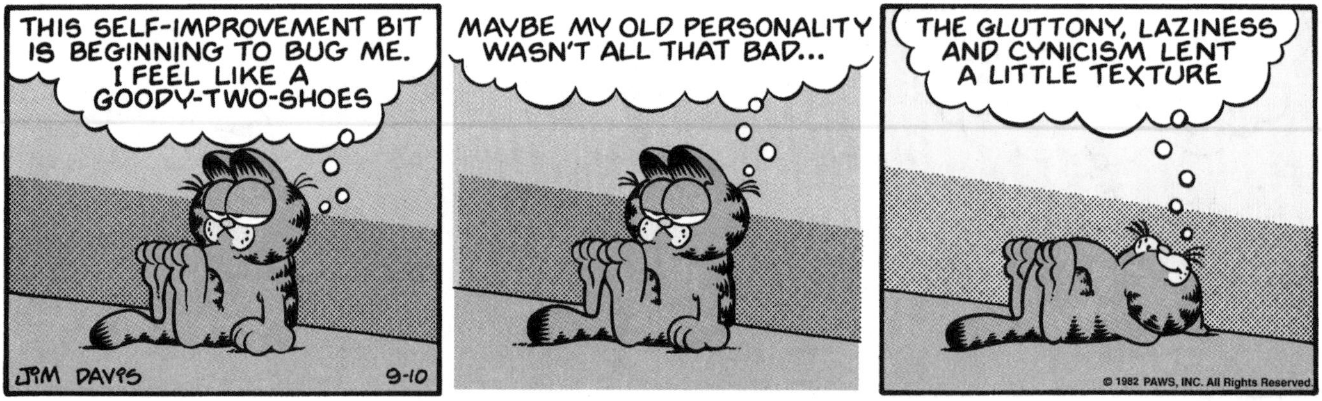
THIS SELF-IMPROVEMENT BIT IS BEGINNING TO BUG ME. I FEEL LIKE A GOODY-TWO-SHOES
JIM DAVIS
9-10
MAYBE MY OLD PERSONALITY WASN'T ALL THAT BAD...
THE GLUTTONY, LAZINESS AND CYNICISM LENT A LITTLE TEXTURE
© 1982 PAWS, INC. All Rights Reserved.

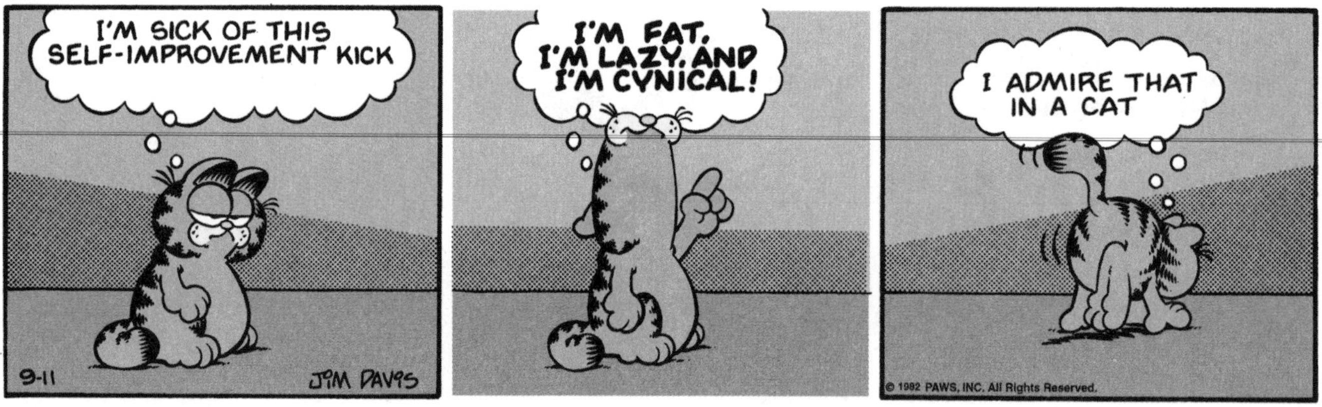
I'M SICK OF THIS SELF-IMPROVEMENT KICK
9-11
JIM DAVIS
I'M FAT, I'M LAZY, AND I'M CYNICAL!
I ADMIRE THAT IN A CAT
© 1982 PAWS, INC. All Rights Reserved.

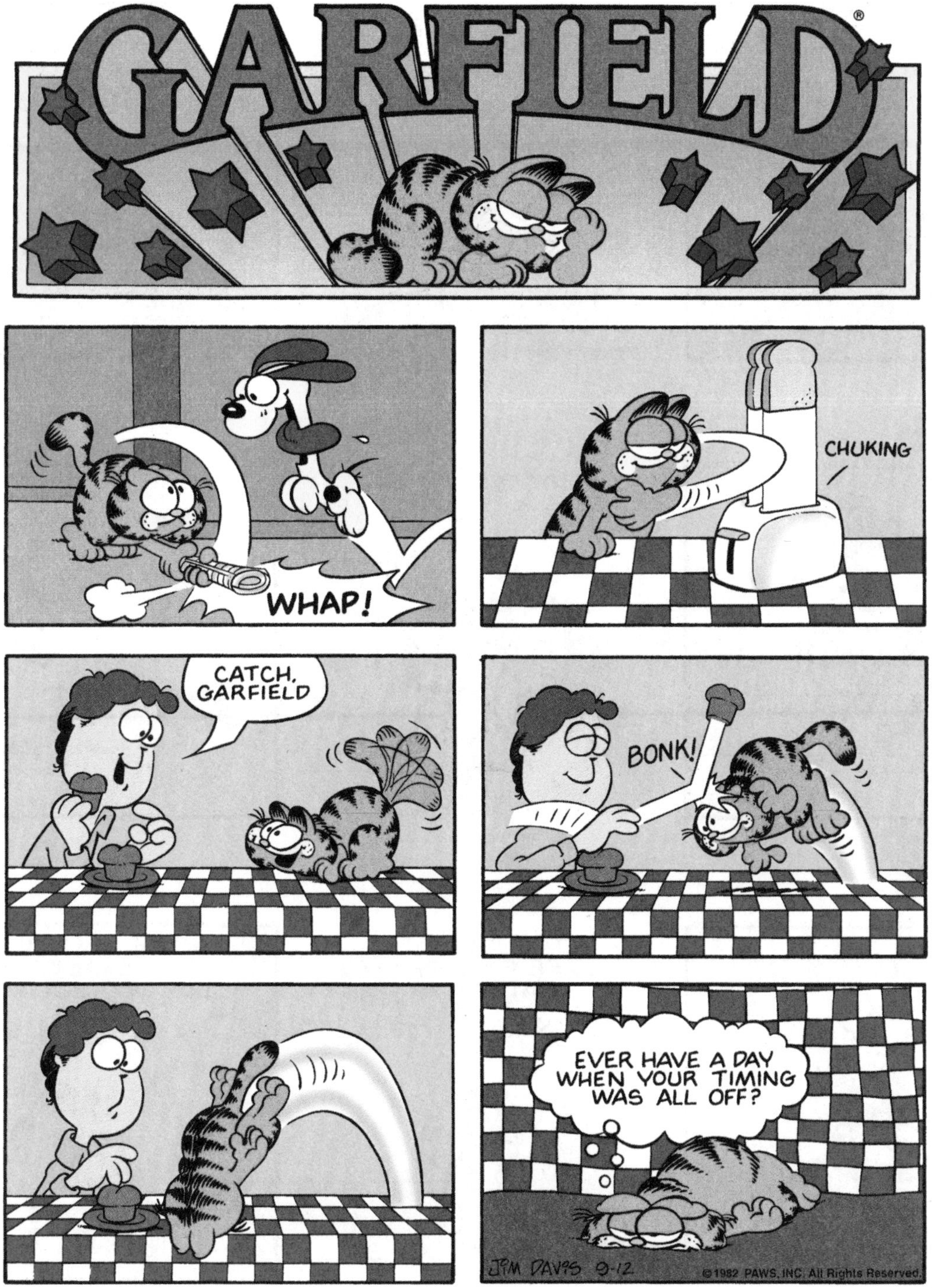
GARFIELD®
WHAP!
CHUKING
CATCH, GARFIELD
BONK!
EVER HAVE A DAY WHEN YOUR TIMING WAS ALL OFF?
JIM DAVIS 9-12
©1982 PAWS, INC. All Rights Reserved.

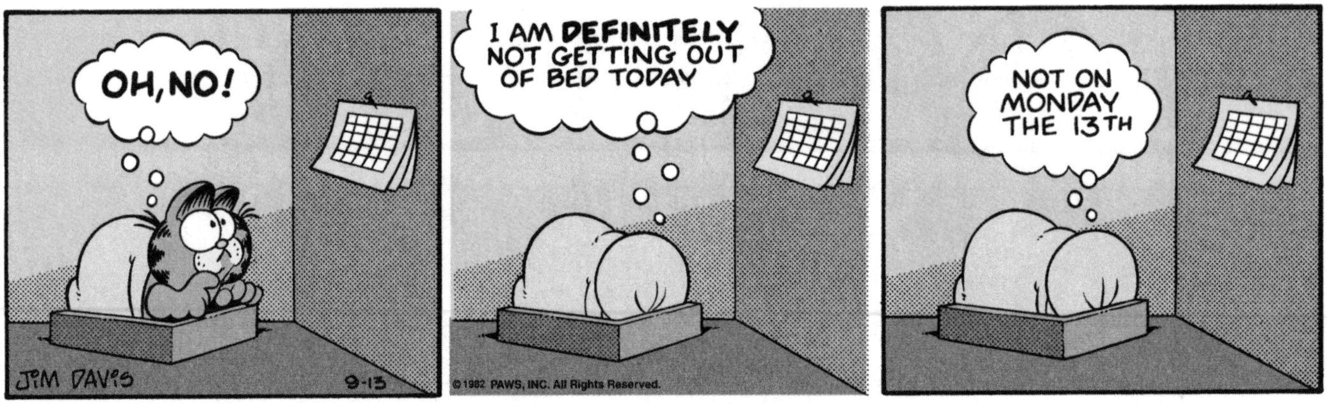
OH, NO!
JIM DAVIS
9-13
I AM **DEFINITELY** NOT GETTING OUT OF BED TODAY
© 1982 PAWS, INC. All Rights Reserved.
NOT ON MONDAY THE 13TH

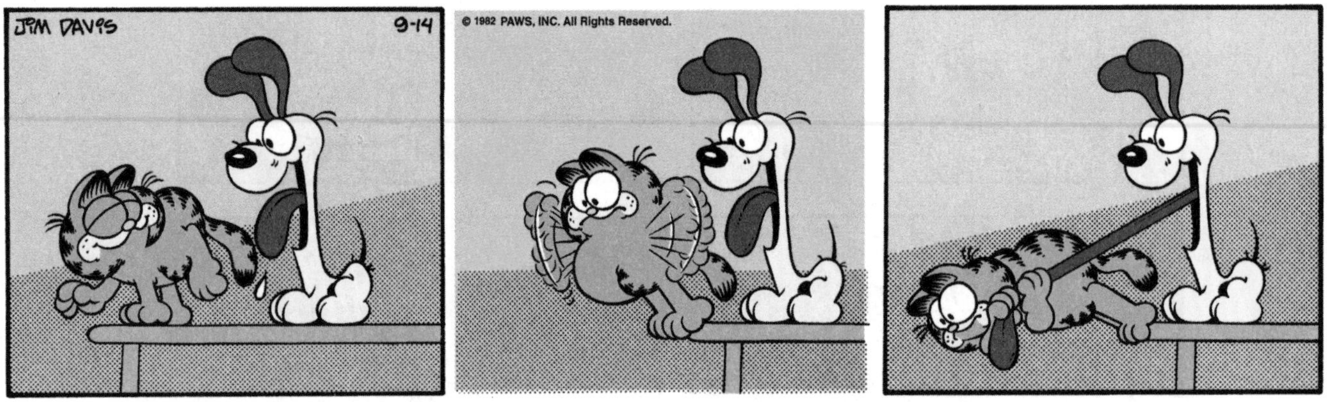
JIM DAVIS
9-14
© 1982 PAWS, INC. All Rights Reserved.

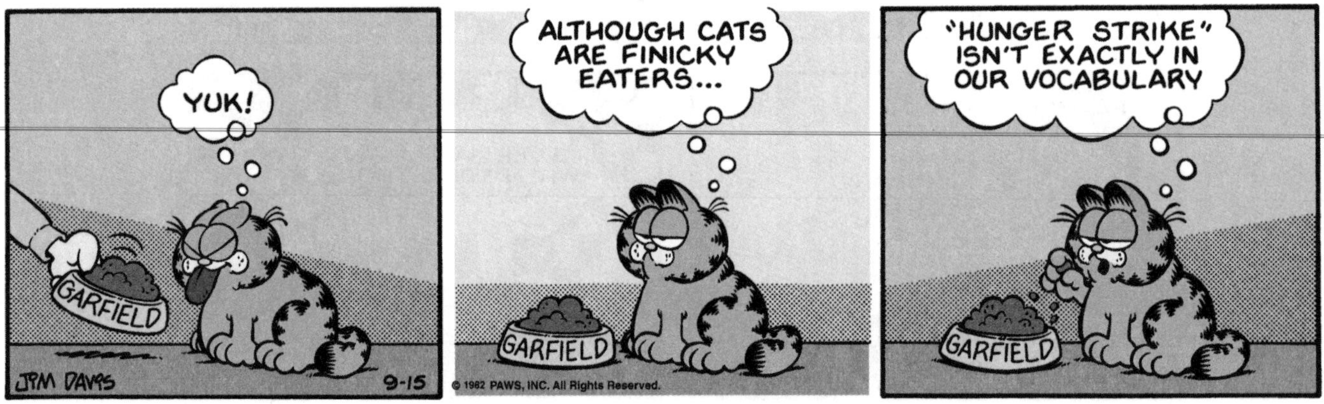
YUK!
GARFIELD
JIM DAVIS
9-15
ALTHOUGH CATS ARE FINICKY EATERS...
GARFIELD
© 1982 PAWS, INC. All Rights Reserved.
"HUNGER STRIKE" ISN'T EXACTLY IN OUR VOCABULARY
GARFIELD

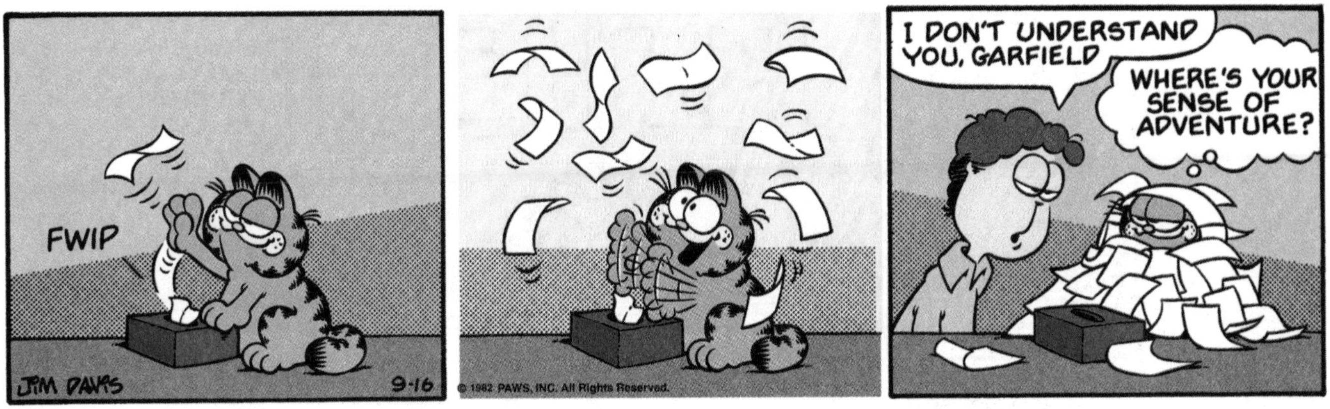
FWIP
JIM DAVIS
9-16
© 1982 PAWS, INC. All Rights Reserved.
I DON'T UNDERSTAND YOU, GARFIELD
WHERE'S YOUR SENSE OF ADVENTURE?

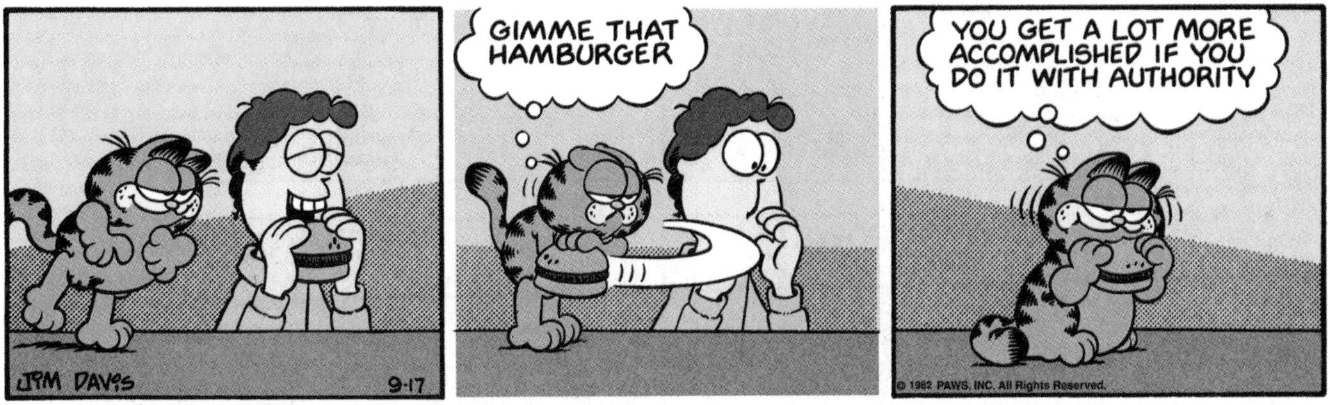
JIM DAVIS
9-17
GIMME THAT HAMBURGER
YOU GET A LOT MORE ACCOMPLISHED IF YOU DO IT WITH AUTHORITY
© 1982 PAWS, INC. All Rights Reserved.

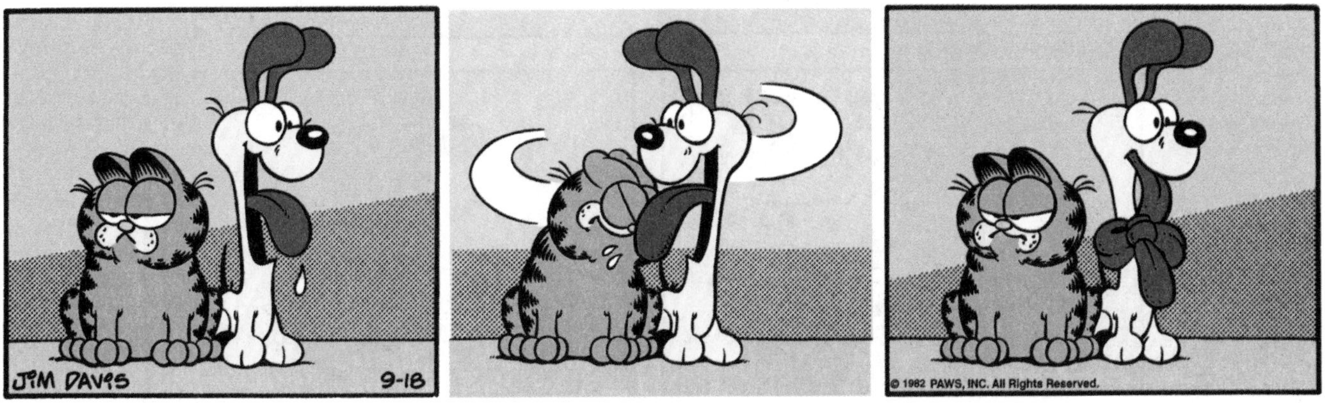
JIM DAVIS
9-18
© 1982 PAWS, INC. All Rights Reserved.

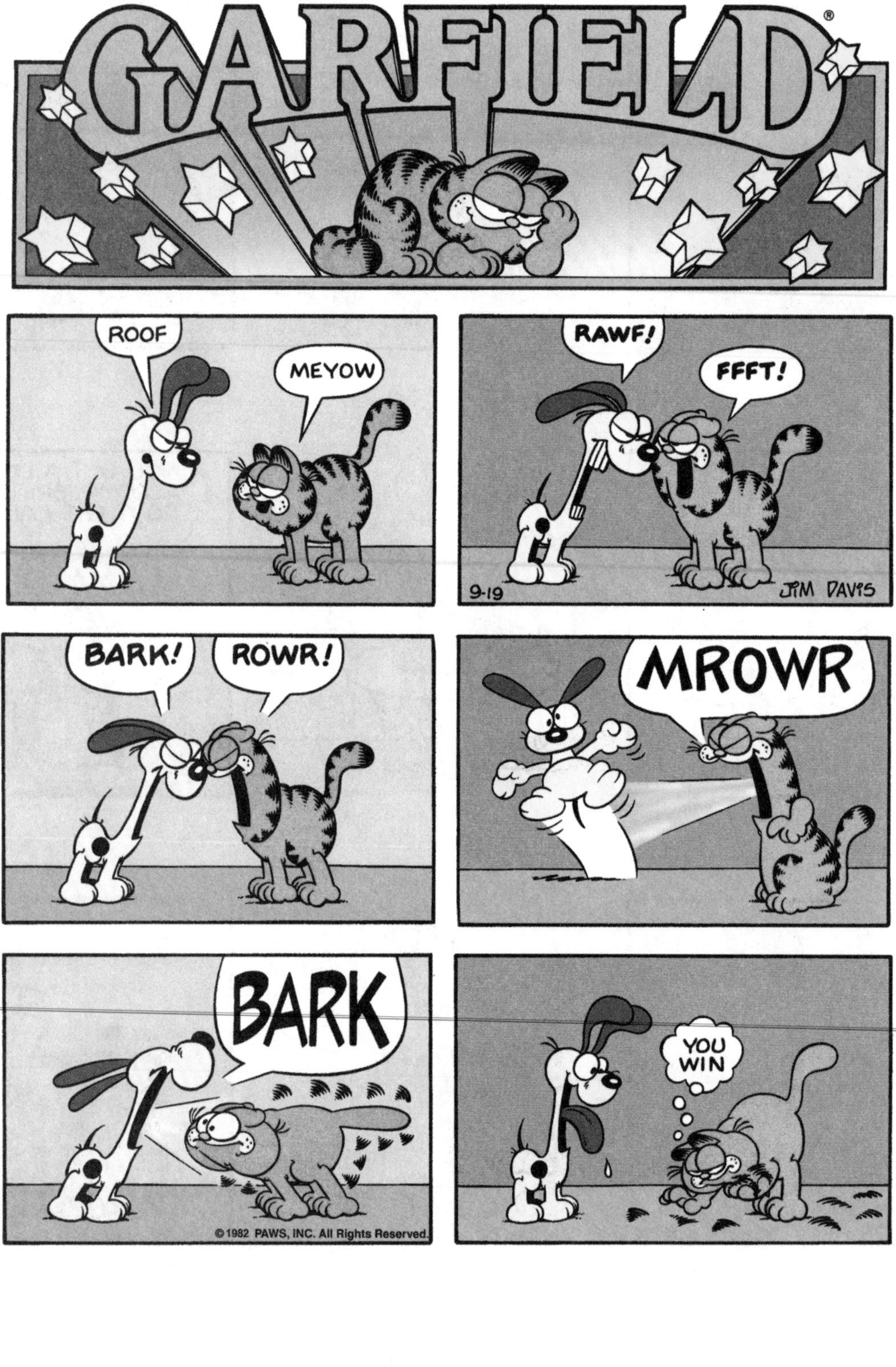

GARFIELD®
ROOF
MEYOW
RAWF!
FFFT!
9-19
JIM DAVIS
BARK!
ROWR!
MROWR
BARK
©1982 PAWS, INC. All Rights Reserved.
YOU WIN

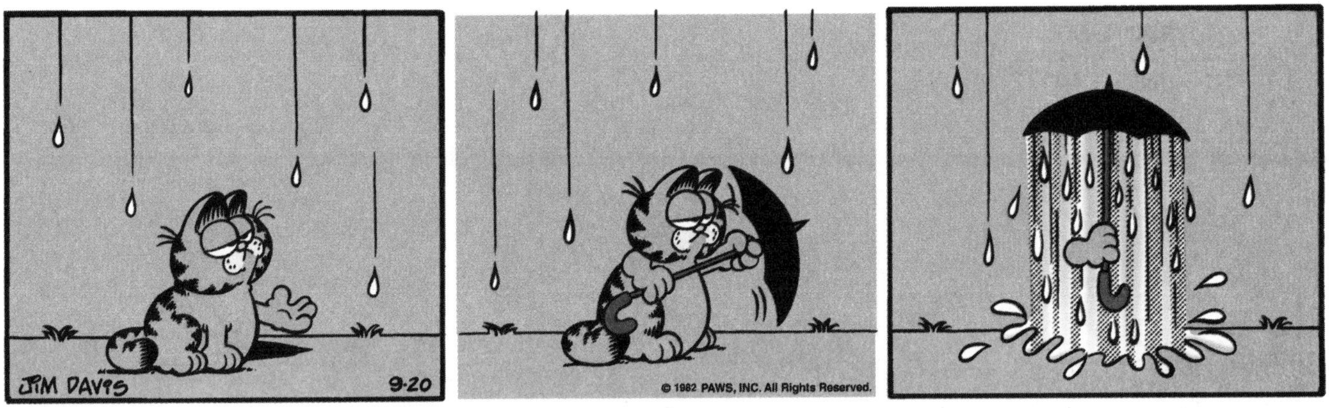
JIM DAVIS
9-20
© 1982 PAWS, INC. All Rights Reserved.

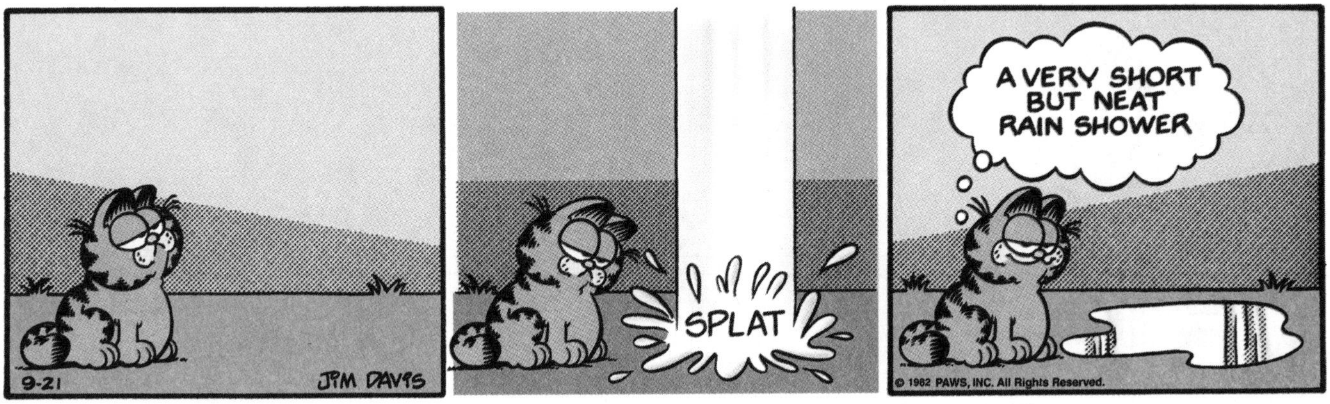
9-21
JIM DAVIS
SPLAT
A VERY SHORT BUT NEAT RAIN SHOWER
© 1982 PAWS, INC. All Rights Reserved.

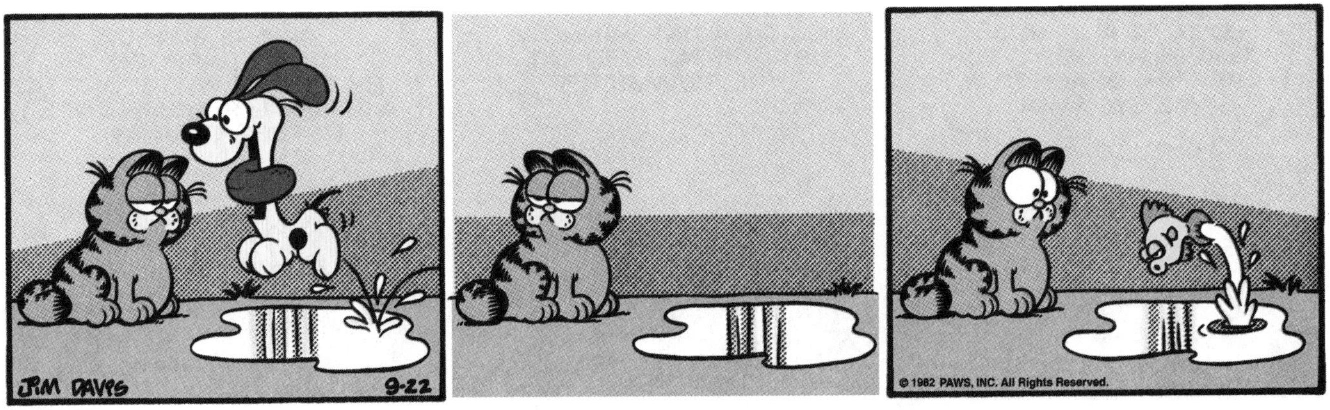
JIM DAVIS
9-22
© 1982 PAWS, INC. All Rights Reserved.

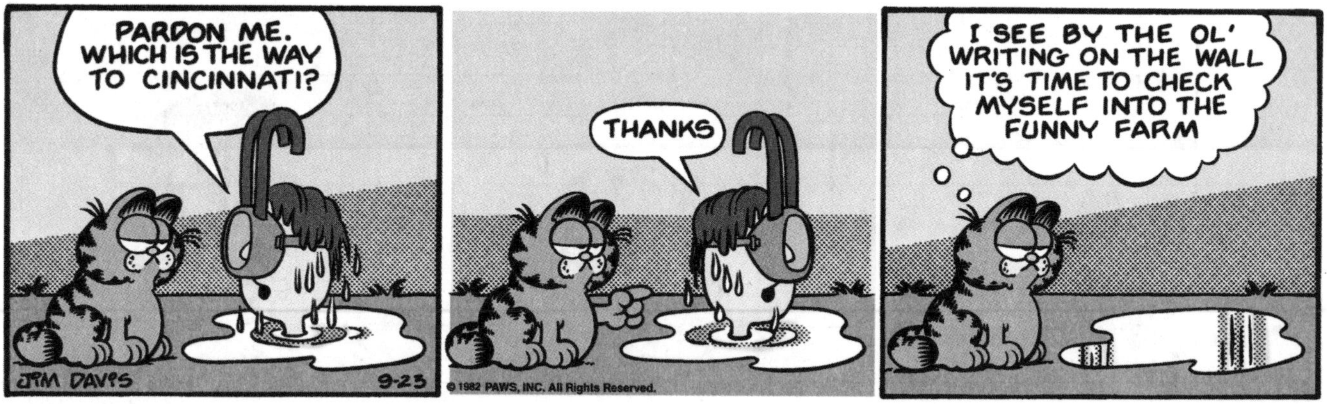
PARDON ME. WHICH IS THE WAY TO CINCINNATI?
JIM DAVIS
9-23
THANKS
© 1982 PAWS, INC. All Rights Reserved.
I SEE BY THE OL' WRITING ON THE WALL IT'S TIME TO CHECK MYSELF INTO THE FUNNY FARM

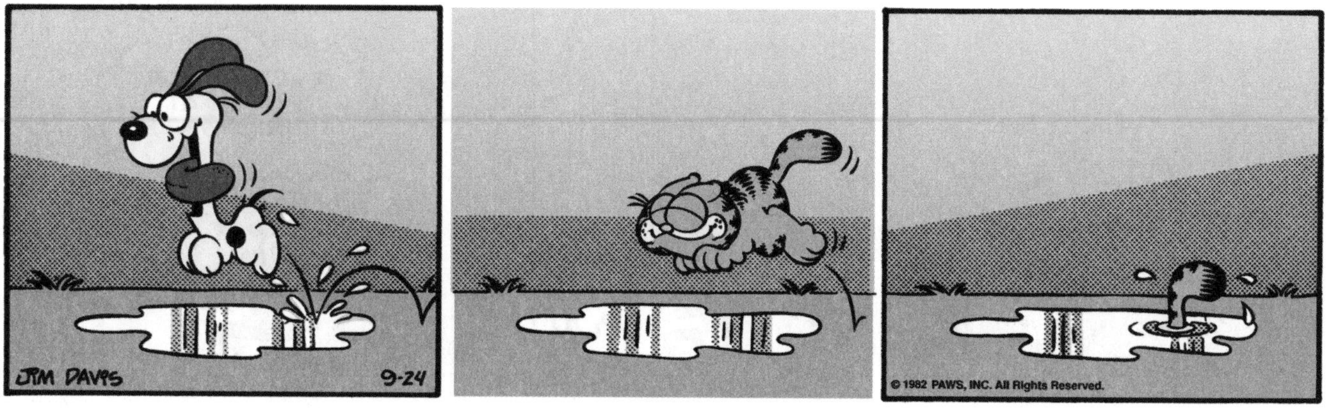
JIM DAVIS
9-24
© 1982 PAWS, INC. All Rights Reserved.

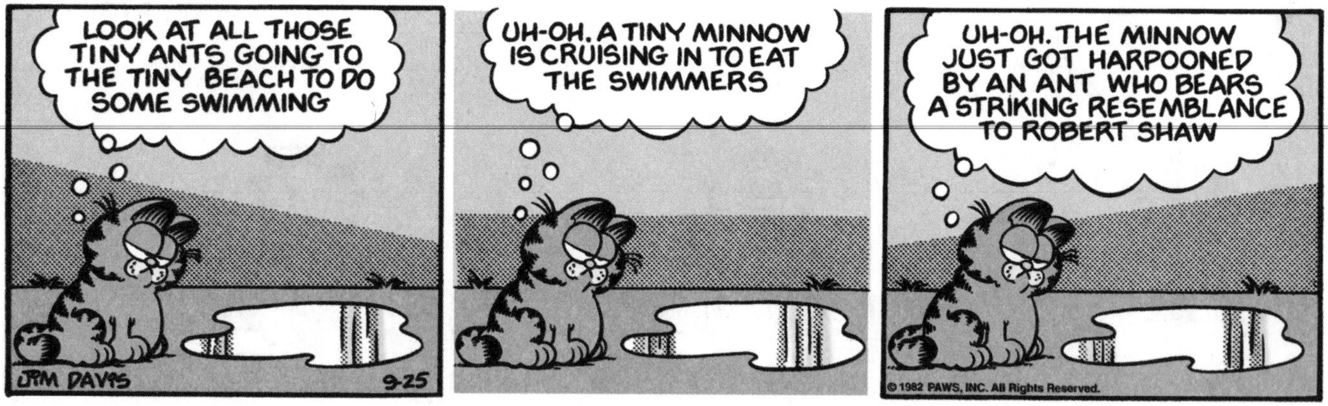
LOOK AT ALL THOSE TINY ANTS GOING TO THE TINY BEACH TO DO SOME SWIMMING
JIM DAVIS
9-25
UH-OH. A TINY MINNOW IS CRUISING IN TO EAT THE SWIMMERS
UH-OH. THE MINNOW JUST GOT HARPOONED BY AN ANT WHO BEARS A STRIKING RESEMBLANCE TO ROBERT SHAW
© 1982 PAWS, INC. All Rights Reserved.

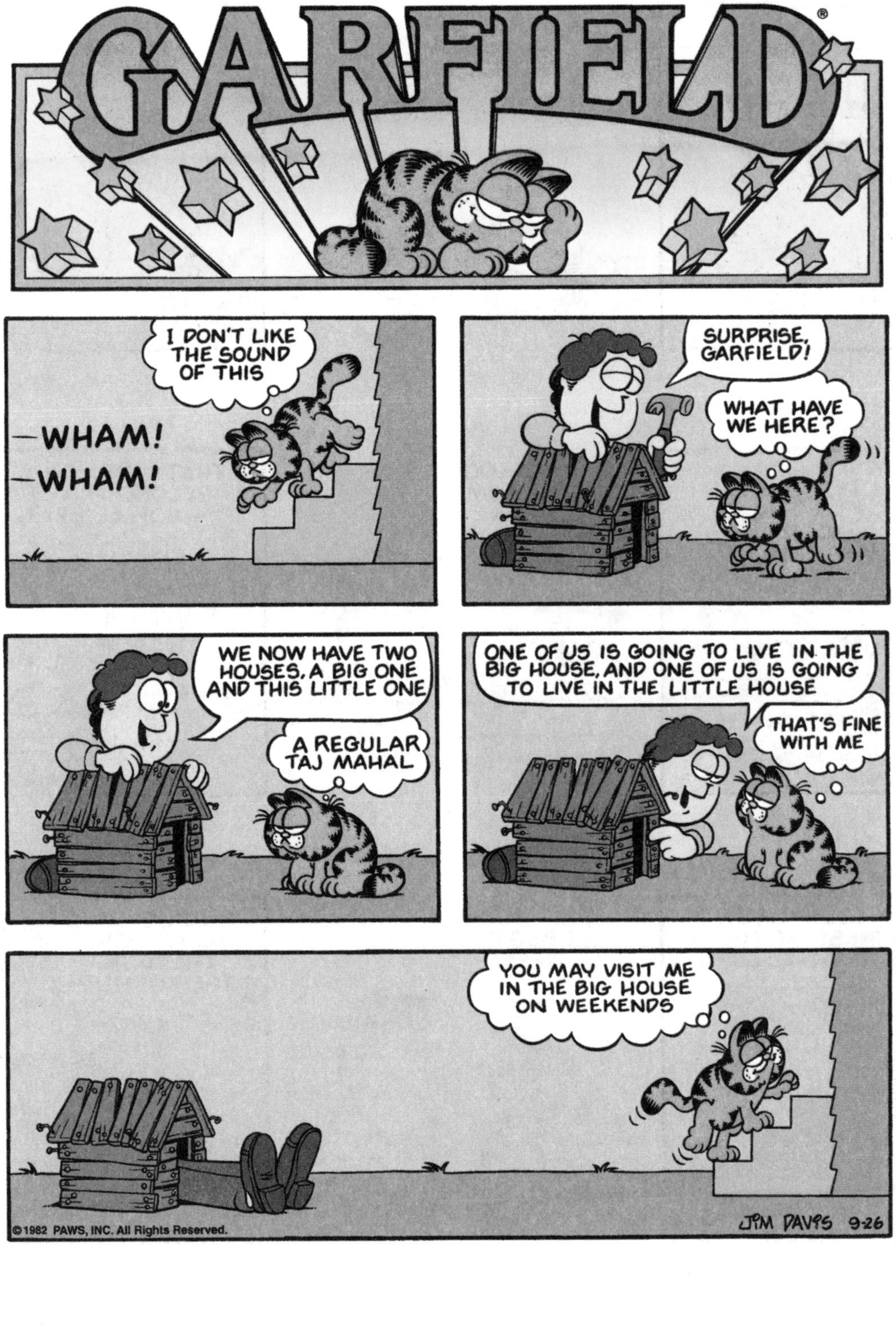
GARFIELD
I DON'T LIKE THE SOUND OF THIS
—WHAM!
—WHAM!
SURPRISE, GARFIELD!
WHAT HAVE WE HERE?
WE NOW HAVE TWO HOUSES, A BIG ONE AND THIS LITTLE ONE
A REGULAR TAJ MAHAL
ONE OF US IS GOING TO LIVE IN THE BIG HOUSE, AND ONE OF US IS GOING TO LIVE IN THE LITTLE HOUSE
THAT'S FINE WITH ME
YOU MAY VISIT ME IN THE BIG HOUSE ON WEEKENDS
© 1982 PAWS, INC. All Rights Reserved.
JIM DAVIS 9-26

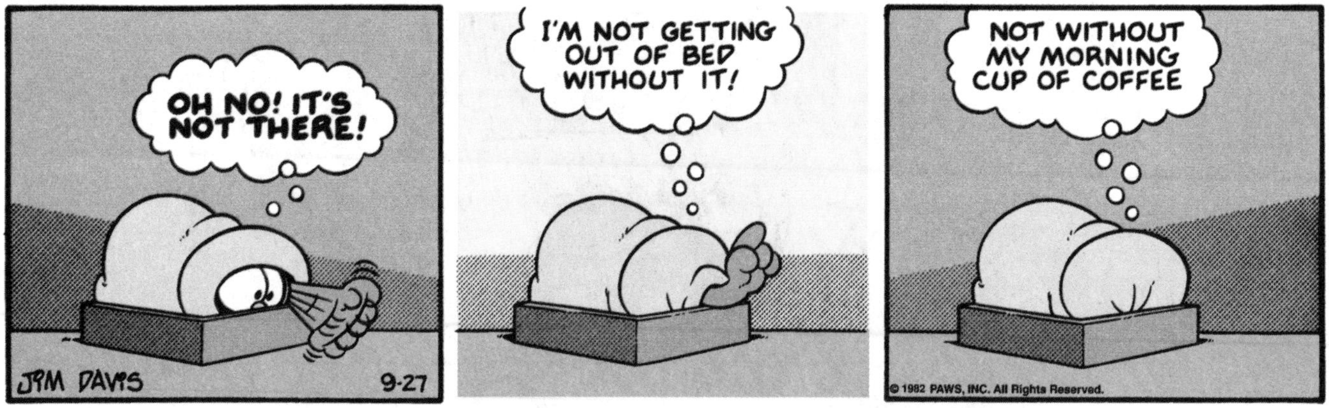
OH NO! IT'S NOT THERE!
JIM DAVIS
9-27
I'M NOT GETTING OUT OF BED WITHOUT IT!
NOT WITHOUT MY MORNING CUP OF COFFEE
© 1982 PAWS, INC. All Rights Reserved.

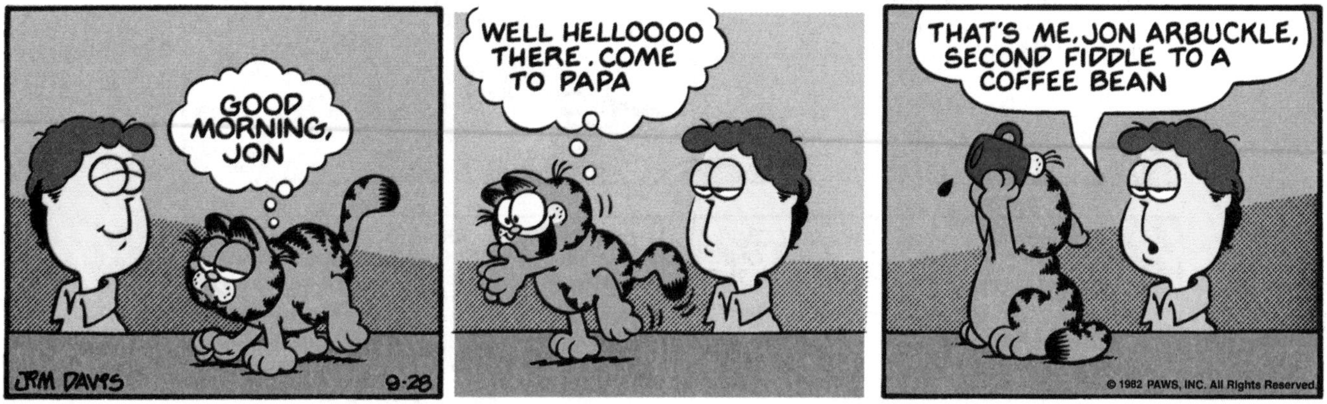
GOOD MORNING, JON
JIM DAVIS
9-28
WELL HELLOOOO THERE. COME TO PAPA
THAT'S ME, JON ARBUCKLE, SECOND FIDDLE TO A COFFEE BEAN
© 1982 PAWS, INC. All Rights Reserved.

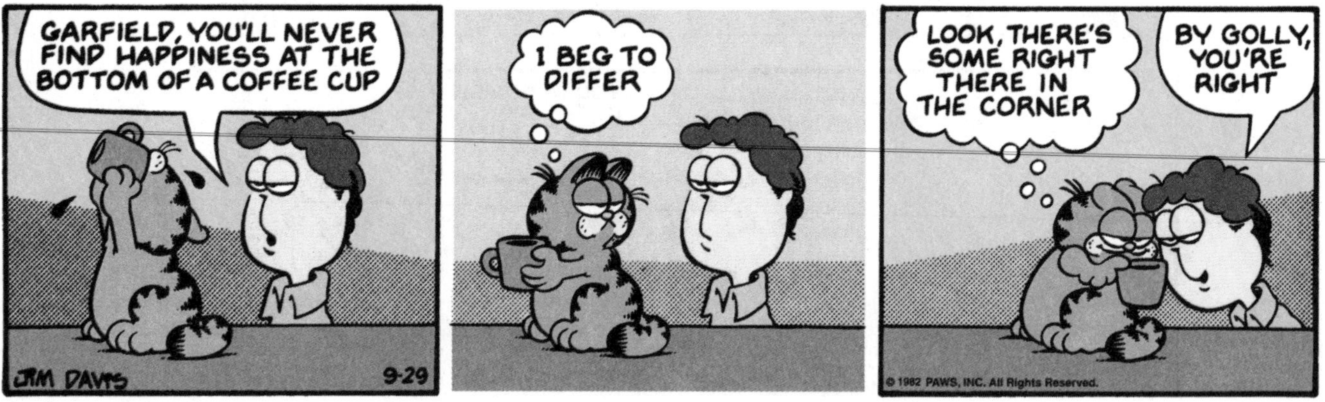
GARFIELD, YOU'LL NEVER FIND HAPPINESS AT THE BOTTOM OF A COFFEE CUP
JIM DAVIS
9-29
I BEG TO DIFFER
LOOK, THERE'S SOME RIGHT THERE IN THE CORNER
BY GOLLY, YOU'RE RIGHT
© 1982 PAWS, INC. All Rights Reserved.

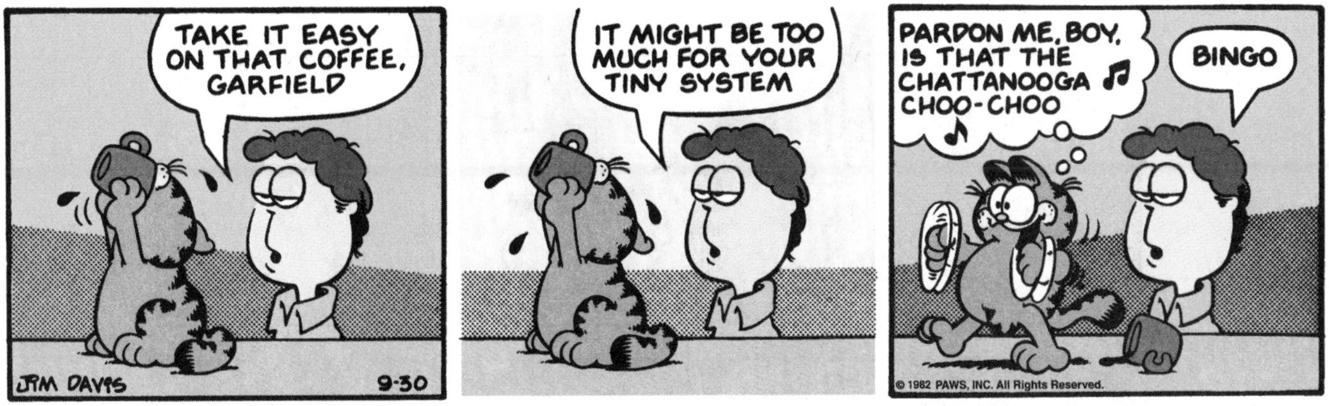
TAKE IT EASY ON THAT COFFEE, GARFIELD
JIM DAVIS
9-30
IT MIGHT BE TOO MUCH FOR YOUR TINY SYSTEM
PARDON ME, BOY, IS THAT THE CHATTANOOGA CHOO-CHOO
BINGO
© 1982 PAWS, INC. All Rights Reserved.

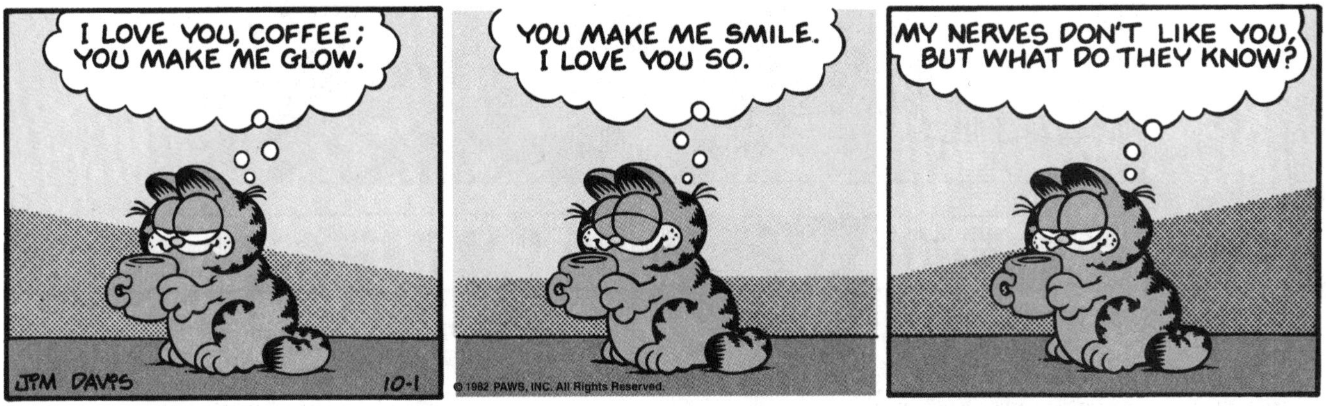
I LOVE YOU, COFFEE; YOU MAKE ME GLOW.
JIM DAVIS
10-1
YOU MAKE ME SMILE. I LOVE YOU SO.
© 1982 PAWS, INC. All Rights Reserved.
MY NERVES DON'T LIKE YOU, BUT WHAT DO THEY KNOW?

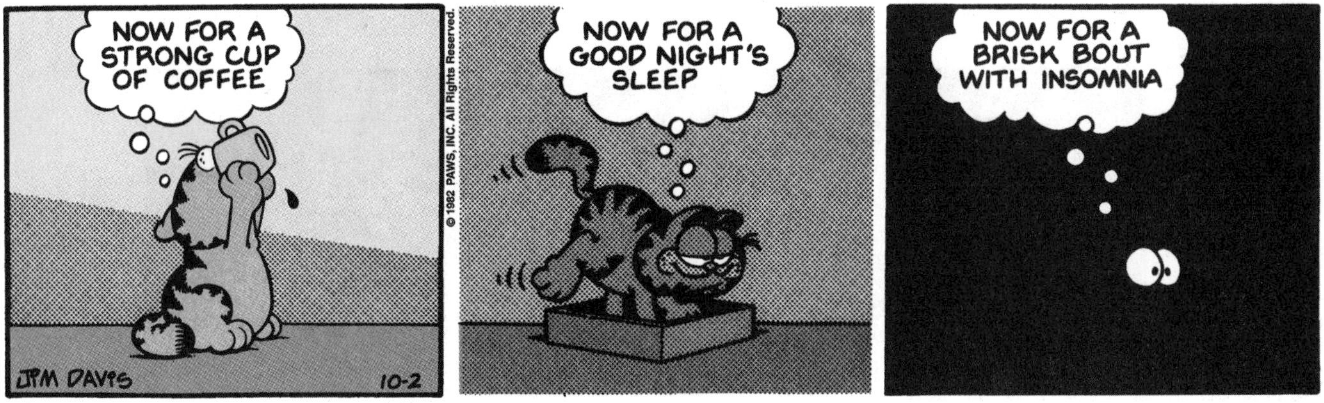
NOW FOR A STRONG CUP OF COFFEE
JIM DAVIS
10-2
© 1982 PAWS, INC. All Rights Reserved.
NOW FOR A GOOD NIGHT'S SLEEP
NOW FOR A BRISK BOUT WITH INSOMNIA

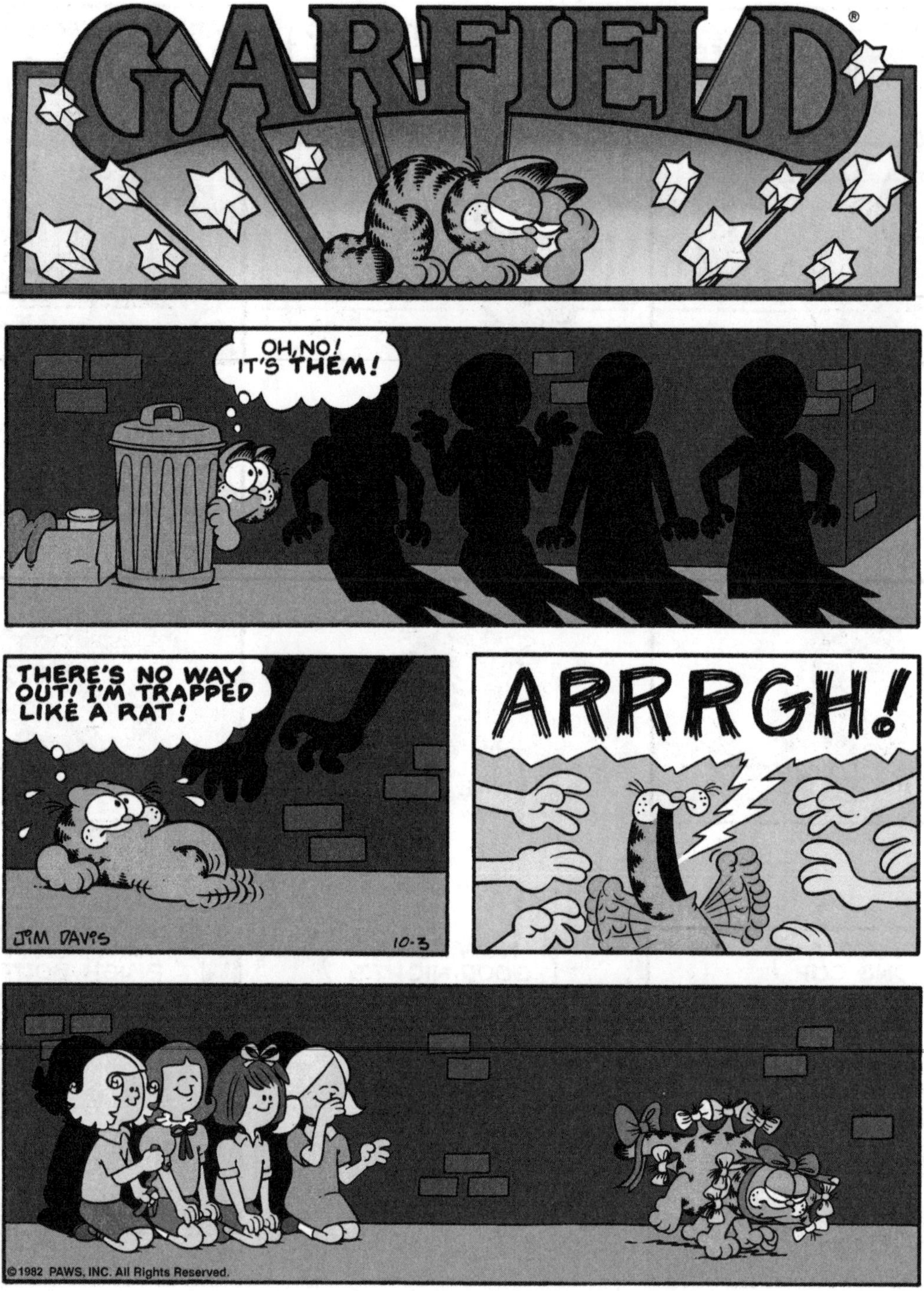
GARFIELD®
OH, NO! IT'S THEM!
THERE'S NO WAY OUT! I'M TRAPPED LIKE A RAT!
JIM DAVIS
10-3
ARRRGH!
©1982 PAWS, INC. All Rights Reserved.

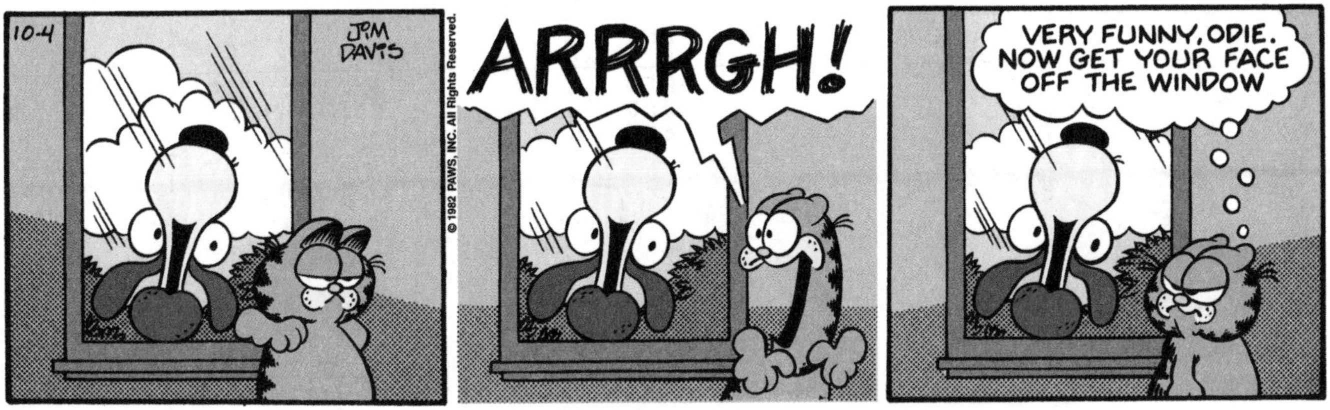
10-4
JIM DAVIS
© 1982 PAWS, INC. All Rights Reserved.
ARRRGH!
VERY FUNNY, ODIE. NOW GET YOUR FACE OFF THE WINDOW

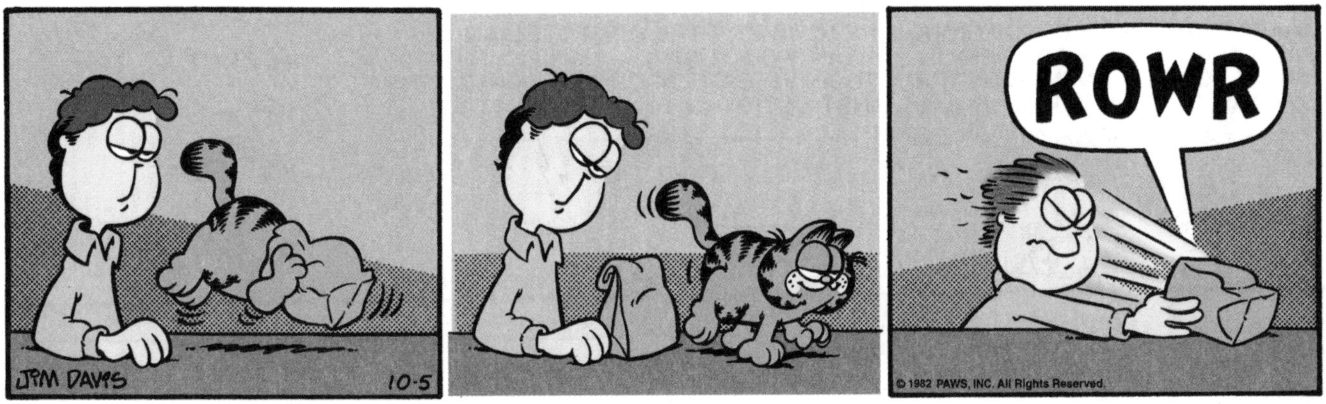
JIM DAVIS
10-5
ROWR
© 1982 PAWS, INC. All Rights Reserved.

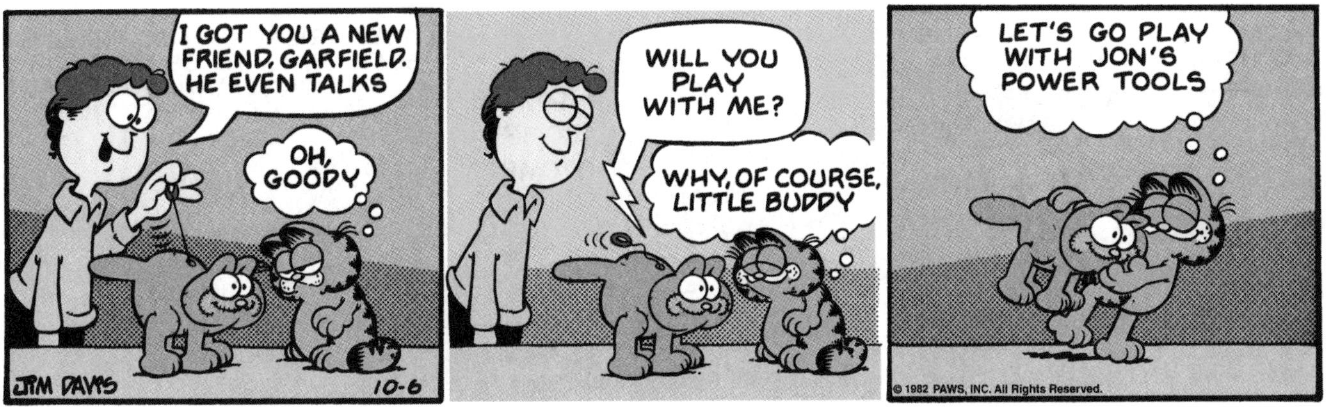
I GOT YOU A NEW FRIEND, GARFIELD. HE EVEN TALKS
OH, GOODY
JIM DAVIS
10-6
WILL YOU PLAY WITH ME?
WHY, OF COURSE, LITTLE BUDDY
LET'S GO PLAY WITH JON'S POWER TOOLS
© 1982 PAWS, INC. All Rights Reserved.

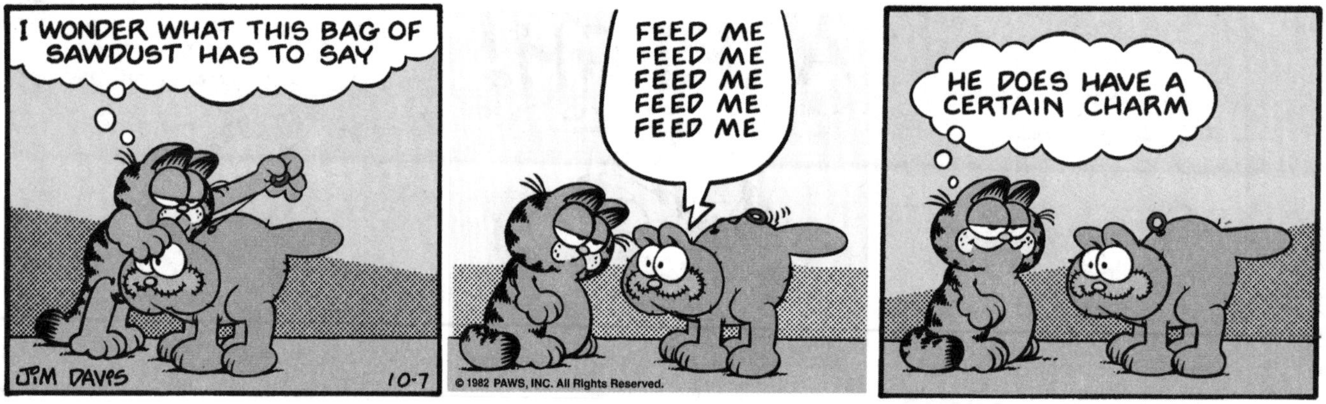
I WONDER WHAT THIS BAG OF SAWDUST HAS TO SAY
JIM DAVIS
10-7
FEED ME FEED ME FEED ME FEED ME FEED ME
© 1982 PAWS, INC. All Rights Reserved.
HE DOES HAVE A CERTAIN CHARM

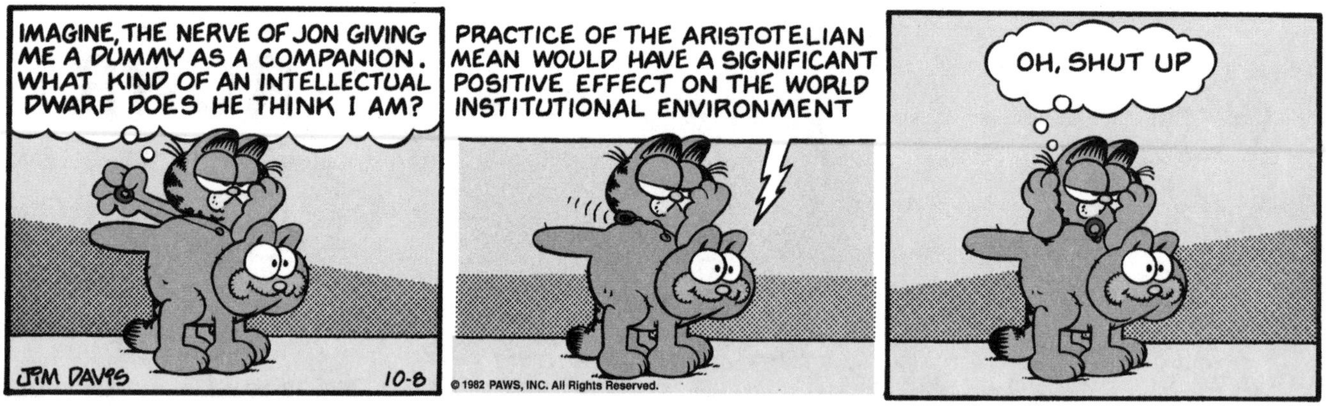
IMAGINE, THE NERVE OF JON GIVING ME A DUMMY AS A COMPANION. WHAT KIND OF AN INTELLECTUAL DWARF DOES HE THINK I AM?
JIM DAVIS
10-8
PRACTICE OF THE ARISTOTELIAN MEAN WOULD HAVE A SIGNIFICANT POSITIVE EFFECT ON THE WORLD INSTITUTIONAL ENVIRONMENT
© 1982 PAWS, INC. All Rights Reserved.
OH, SHUT UP

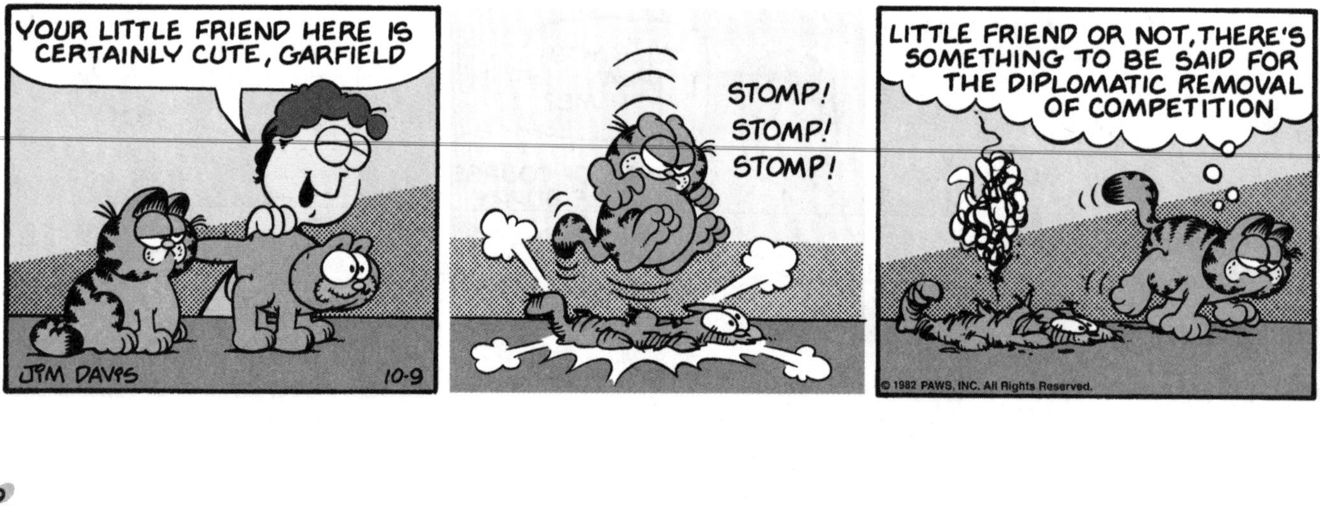
YOUR LITTLE FRIEND HERE IS CERTAINLY CUTE, GARFIELD
JIM DAVIS
10-9
STOMP! STOMP! STOMP!
LITTLE FRIEND OR NOT, THERE'S SOMETHING TO BE SAID FOR THE DIPLOMATIC REMOVAL OF COMPETITION
© 1982 PAWS, INC. All Rights Reserved.

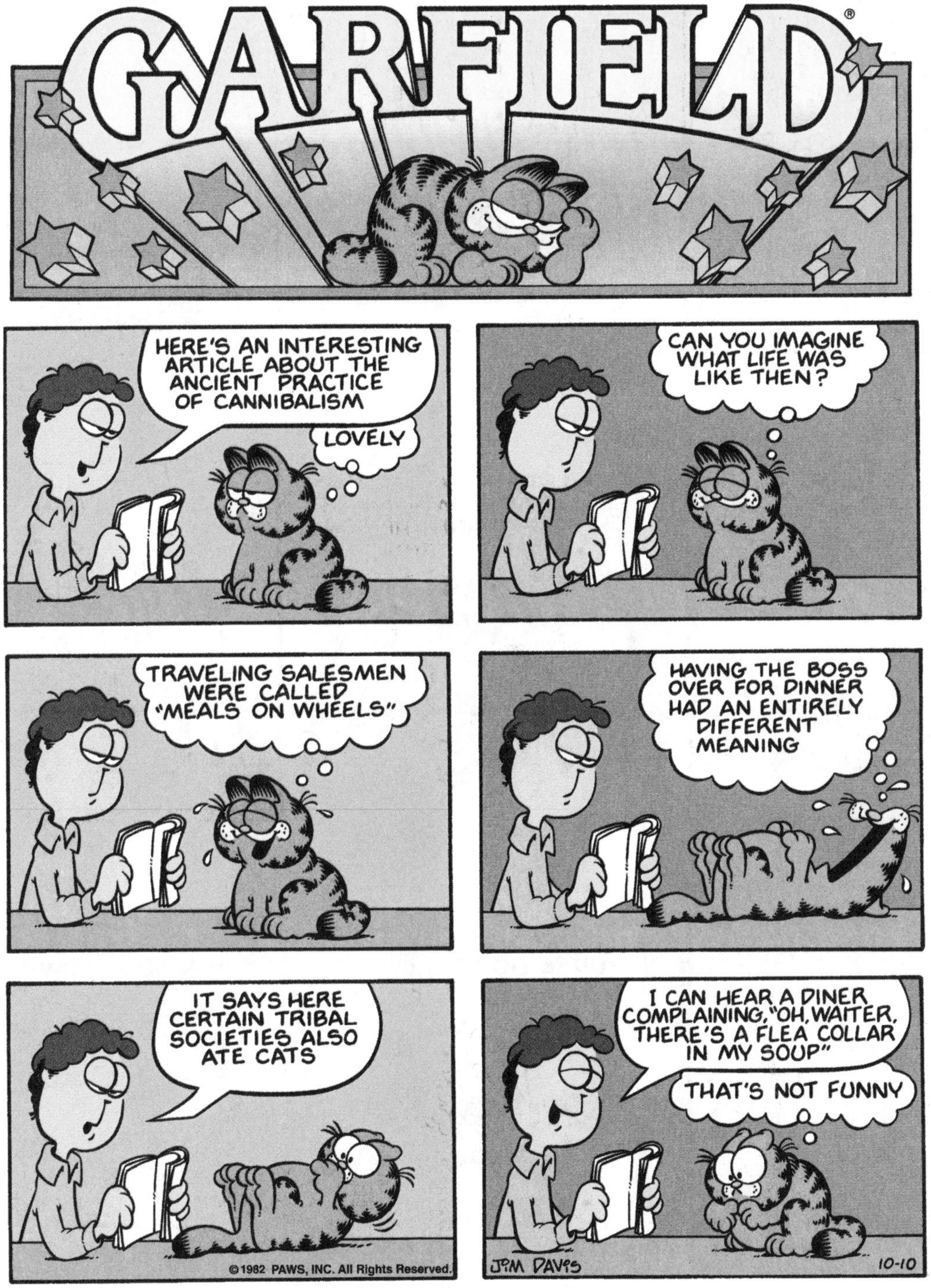
GARFIELD®
HERE'S AN INTERESTING ARTICLE ABOUT THE ANCIENT PRACTICE OF CANNIBALISM
LOVELY
CAN YOU IMAGINE WHAT LIFE WAS LIKE THEN?
TRAVELING SALESMEN WERE CALLED "MEALS ON WHEELS"
HAVING THE BOSS OVER FOR DINNER HAD AN ENTIRELY DIFFERENT MEANING
IT SAYS HERE CERTAIN TRIBAL SOCIETIES ALSO ATE CATS
I CAN HEAR A DINER COMPLAINING, "OH, WAITER, THERE'S A FLEA COLLAR IN MY SOUP"
THAT'S NOT FUNNY
©1982 PAWS, INC. All Rights Reserved.
JIM DAVIS
10-10

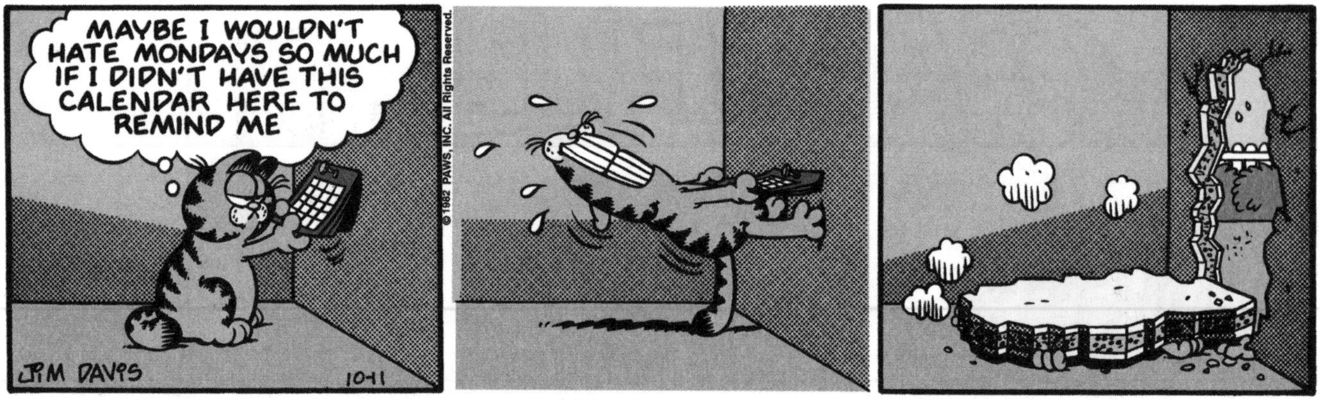
MAYBE I WOULDN'T HATE MONDAYS SO MUCH IF I DIDN'T HAVE THIS CALENDAR HERE TO REMIND ME
JIM DAVIS
10-11
© 1982 PAWS, INC. All Rights Reserved.

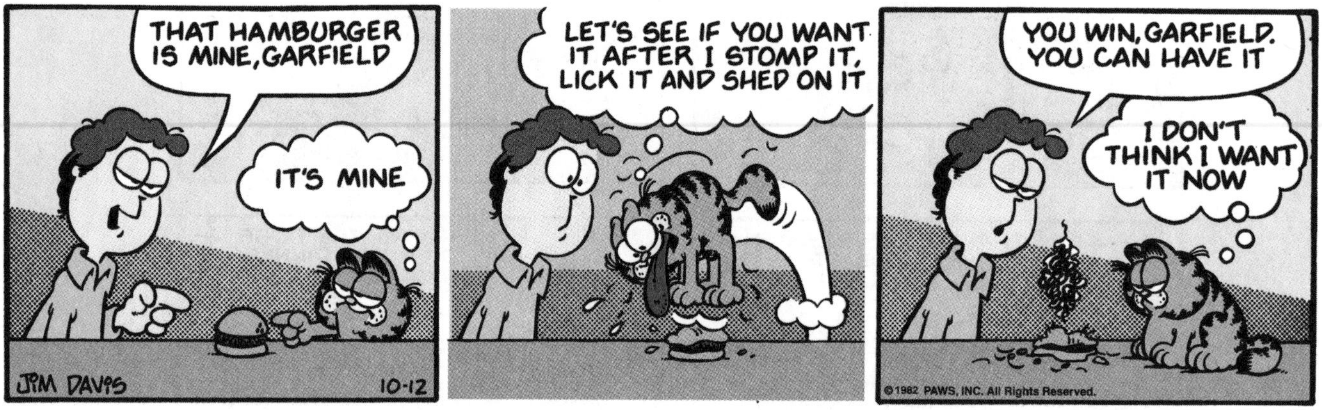
THAT HAMBURGER IS MINE, GARFIELD
IT'S MINE
JIM DAVIS
10-12
LET'S SEE IF YOU WANT IT AFTER I STOMP IT, LICK IT AND SHED ON IT
YOU WIN, GARFIELD. YOU CAN HAVE IT
I DON'T THINK I WANT IT NOW
© 1982 PAWS, INC. All Rights Reserved.

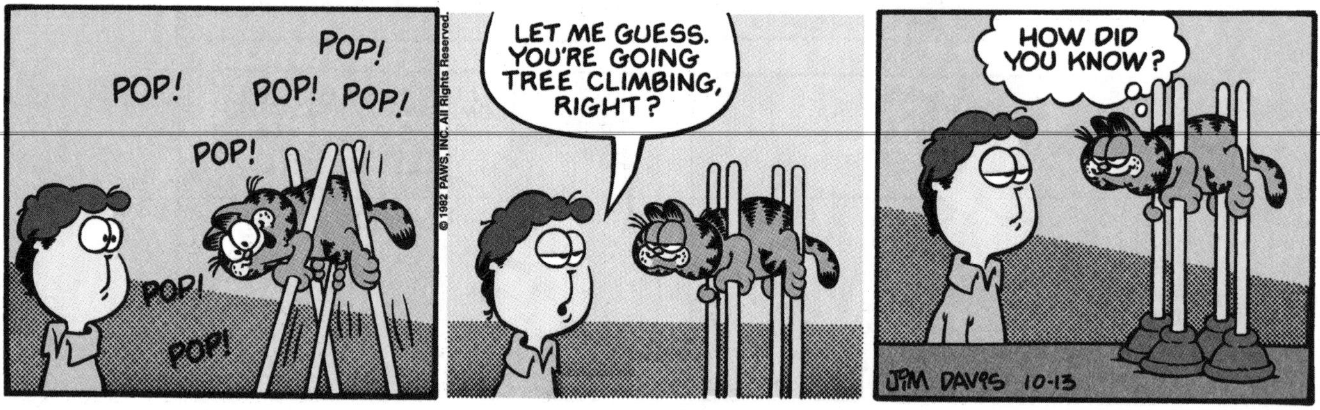
POP! POP! POP! POP! POP! POP! POP!
© 1982 PAWS, INC. All Rights Reserved.
LET ME GUESS. YOU'RE GOING TREE CLIMBING, RIGHT?
HOW DID YOU KNOW?
JIM DAVIS 10-13

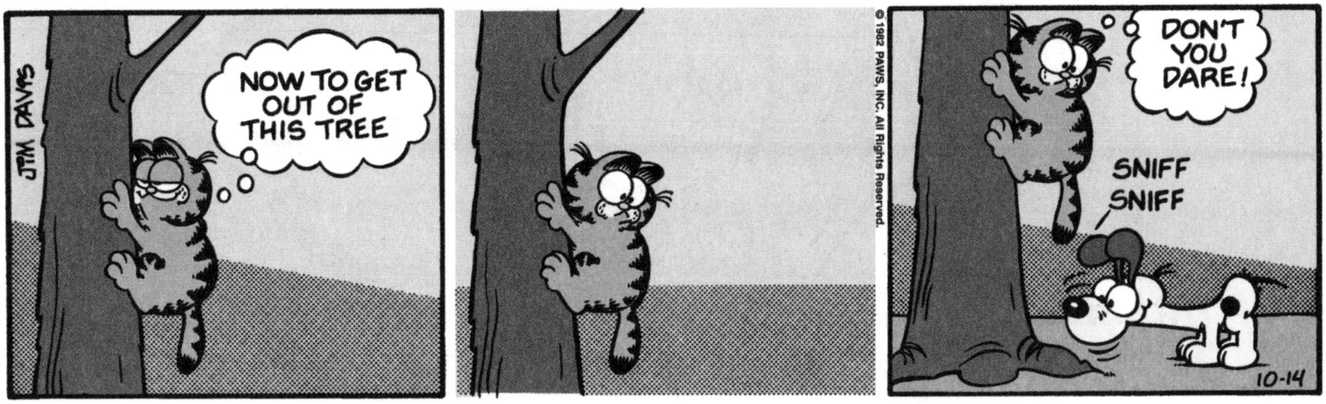
JIM DAVIS
NOW TO GET OUT OF THIS TREE
© 1982 PAWS, INC. All Rights Reserved.
DON'T YOU DARE!
SNIFF SNIFF
10-14

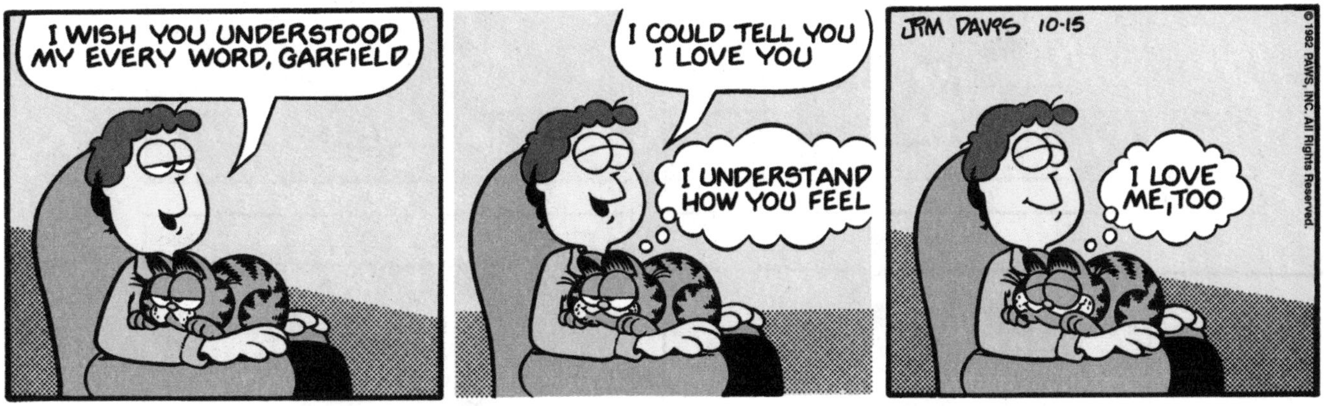
I WISH YOU UNDERSTOOD MY EVERY WORD, GARFIELD
I COULD TELL YOU I LOVE YOU
I UNDERSTAND HOW YOU FEEL
JIM DAVIS 10-15
I LOVE ME, TOO
© 1982 PAWS, INC. All Rights Reserved.

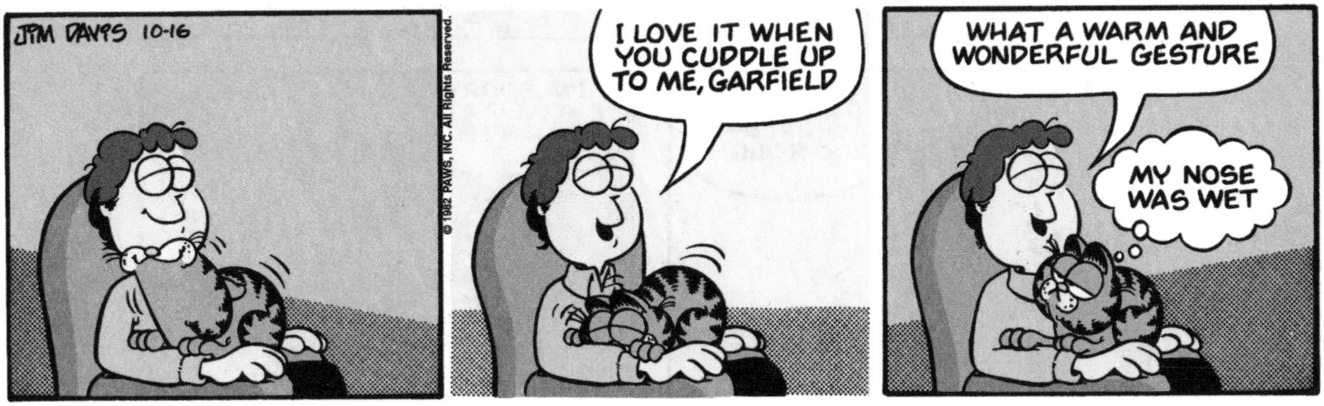
JIM DAVIS 10-16
© 1982 PAWS, INC. All Rights Reserved.
I LOVE IT WHEN YOU CUDDLE UP TO ME, GARFIELD
WHAT A WARM AND WONDERFUL GESTURE
MY NOSE WAS WET

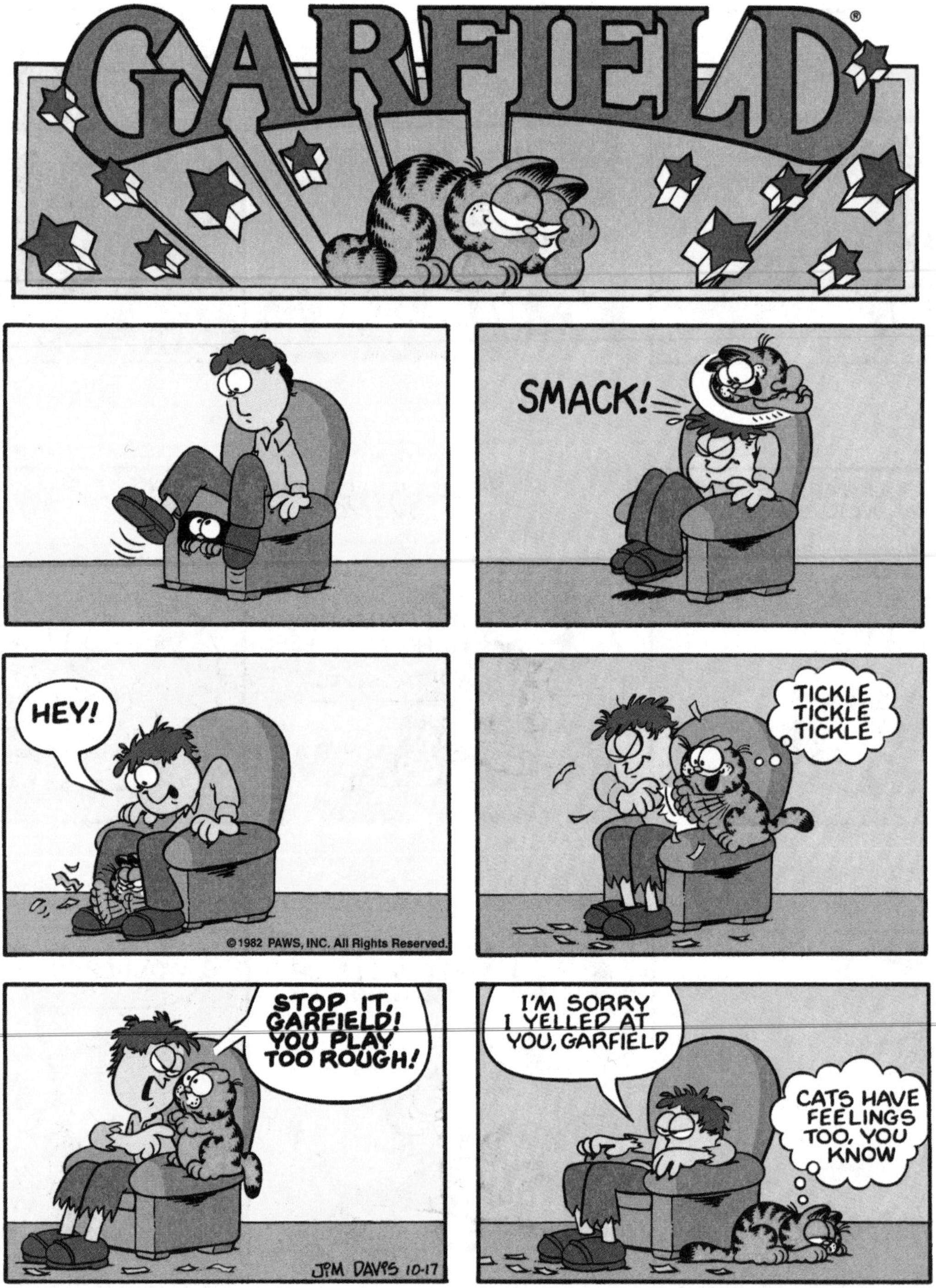
GARFIELD
SMACK!
HEY!
TICKLE TICKLE TICKLE
STOP IT, GARFIELD! YOU PLAY TOO ROUGH!
JIM DAVIS 10-17
I'M SORRY I YELLED AT YOU, GARFIELD
CATS HAVE FEELINGS TOO, YOU KNOW

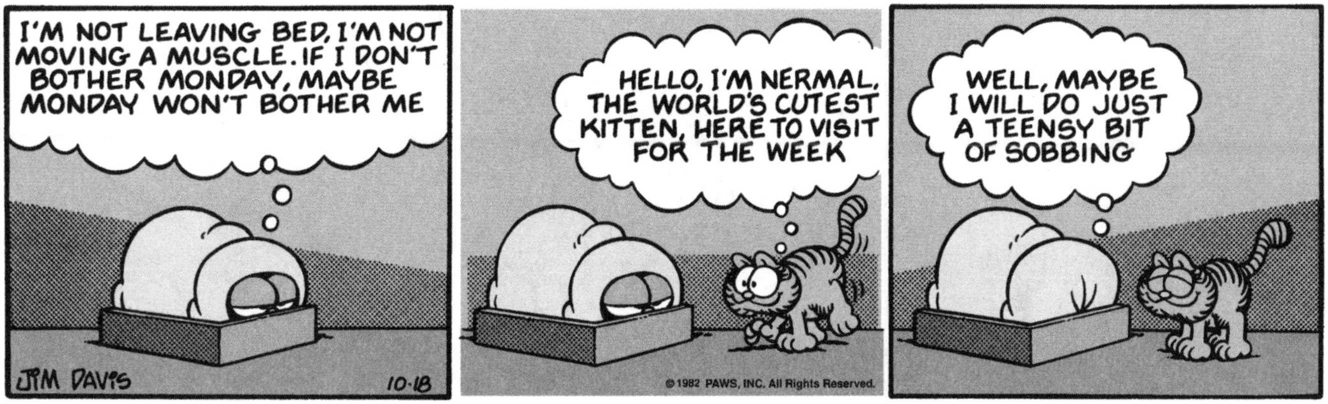
I'M NOT LEAVING BED, I'M NOT MOVING A MUSCLE. IF I DON'T BOTHER MONDAY, MAYBE MONDAY WON'T BOTHER ME
HELLO, I'M NERMAL, THE WORLD'S CUTEST KITTEN, HERE TO VISIT FOR THE WEEK
WELL, MAYBE I WILL DO JUST A TEENSY BIT OF SOBBING
JIM DAVIS
10·18
© 1982 PAWS, INC. All Rights Reserved.

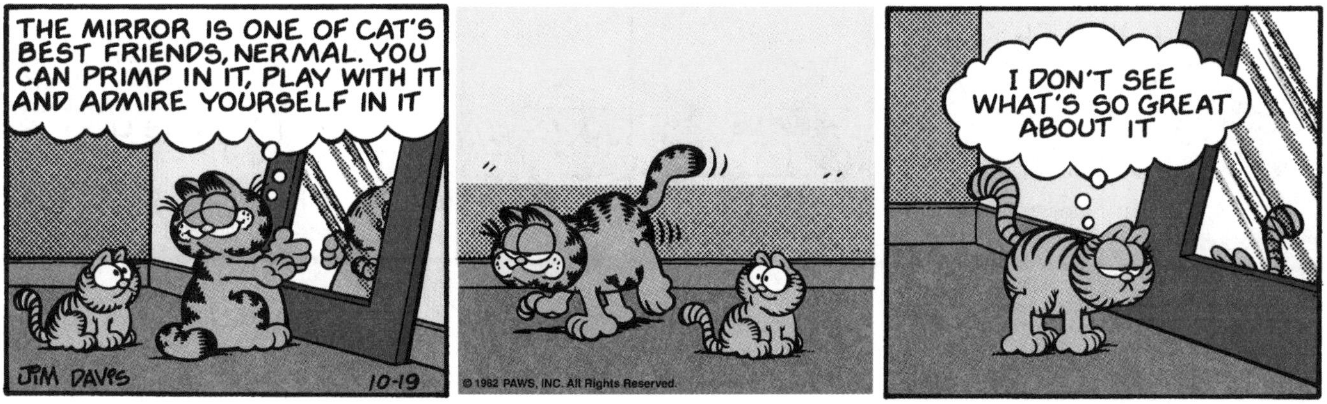
THE MIRROR IS ONE OF CAT'S BEST FRIENDS, NERMAL. YOU CAN PRIMP IN IT, PLAY WITH IT AND ADMIRE YOURSELF IN IT
JIM DAVIS
10-19
© 1982 PAWS, INC. All Rights Reserved.
I DON'T SEE WHAT'S SO GREAT ABOUT IT

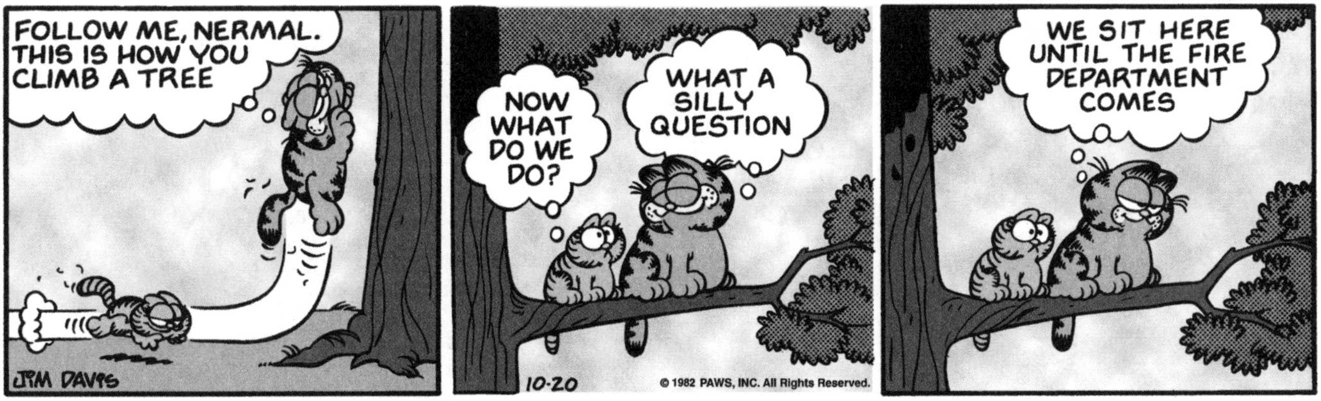
FOLLOW ME, NERMAL. THIS IS HOW YOU CLIMB A TREE
JIM DAVIS
NOW WHAT DO WE DO?
WHAT A SILLY QUESTION
10-20
© 1982 PAWS, INC. All Rights Reserved.
WE SIT HERE UNTIL THE FIRE DEPARTMENT COMES

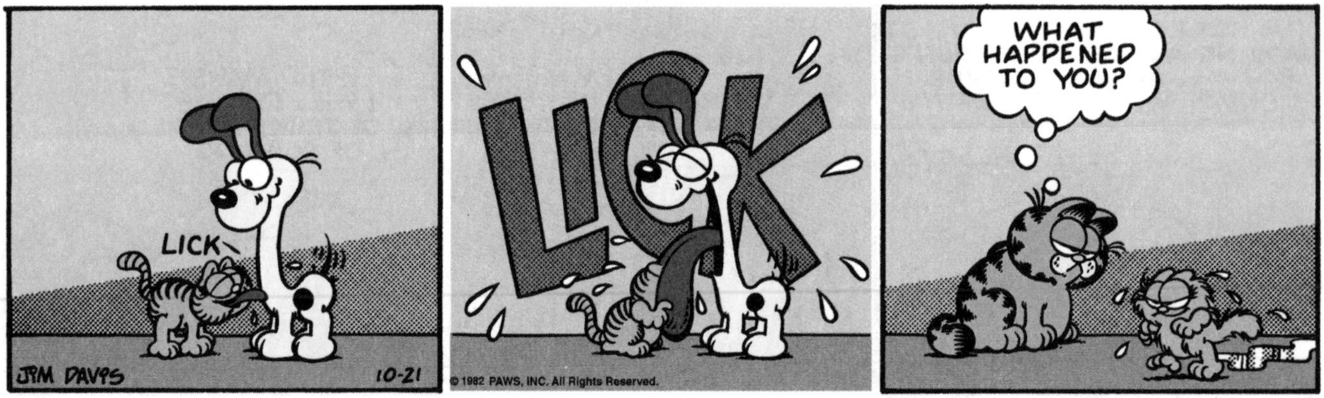
JIM DAVIS
10-21
LICK
LICK
© 1982 PAWS, INC. All Rights Reserved.
WHAT HAPPENED TO YOU?

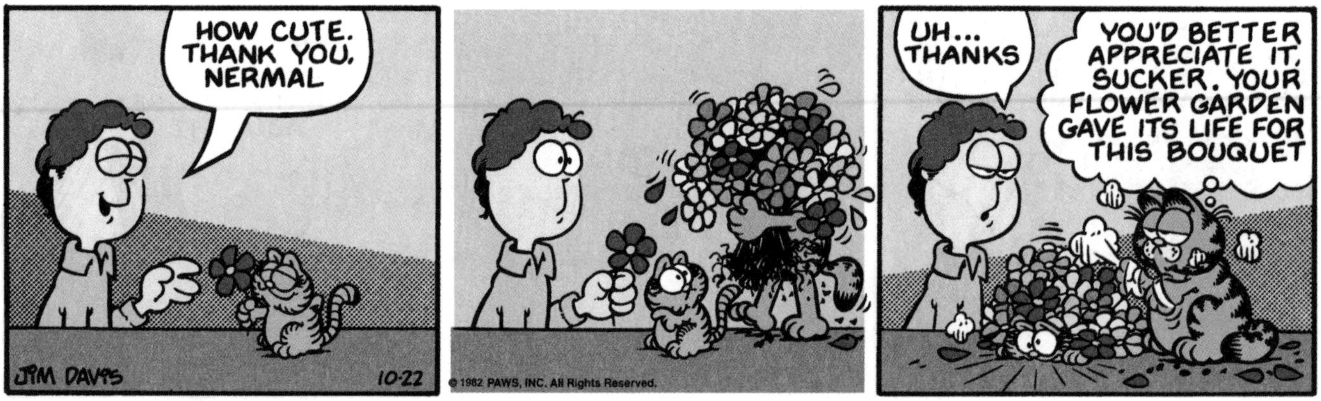
HOW CUTE. THANK YOU, NERMAL
JIM DAVIS
10-22
© 1982 PAWS, INC. All Rights Reserved.
UH... THANKS
YOU'D BETTER APPRECIATE IT, SUCKER. YOUR FLOWER GARDEN GAVE ITS LIFE FOR THIS BOUQUET

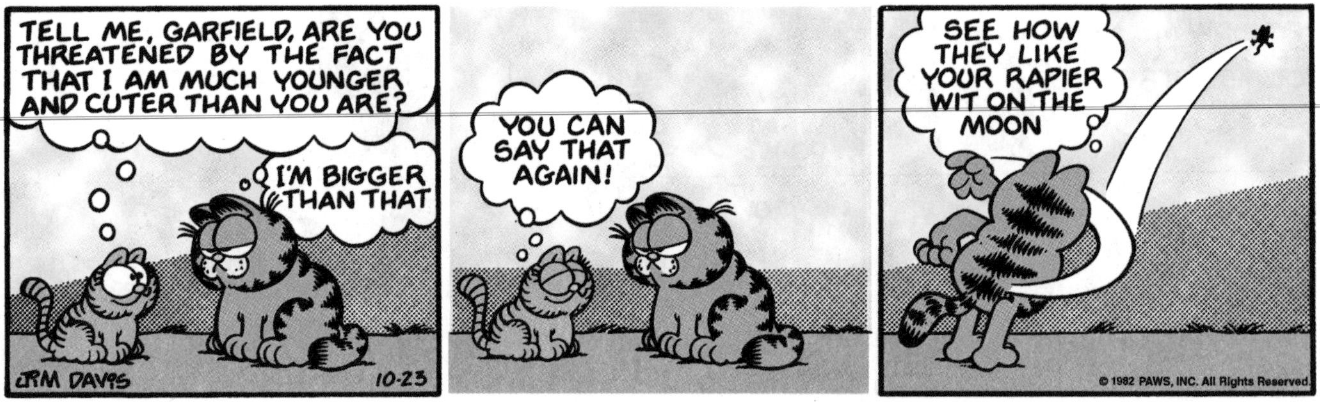
TELL ME, GARFIELD, ARE YOU THREATENED BY THE FACT THAT I AM MUCH YOUNGER AND CUTER THAN YOU ARE?
I'M BIGGER THAN THAT
JIM DAVIS
10-23
YOU CAN SAY THAT AGAIN!
SEE HOW THEY LIKE YOUR RAPIER WIT ON THE MOON
© 1982 PAWS, INC. All Rights Reserved.

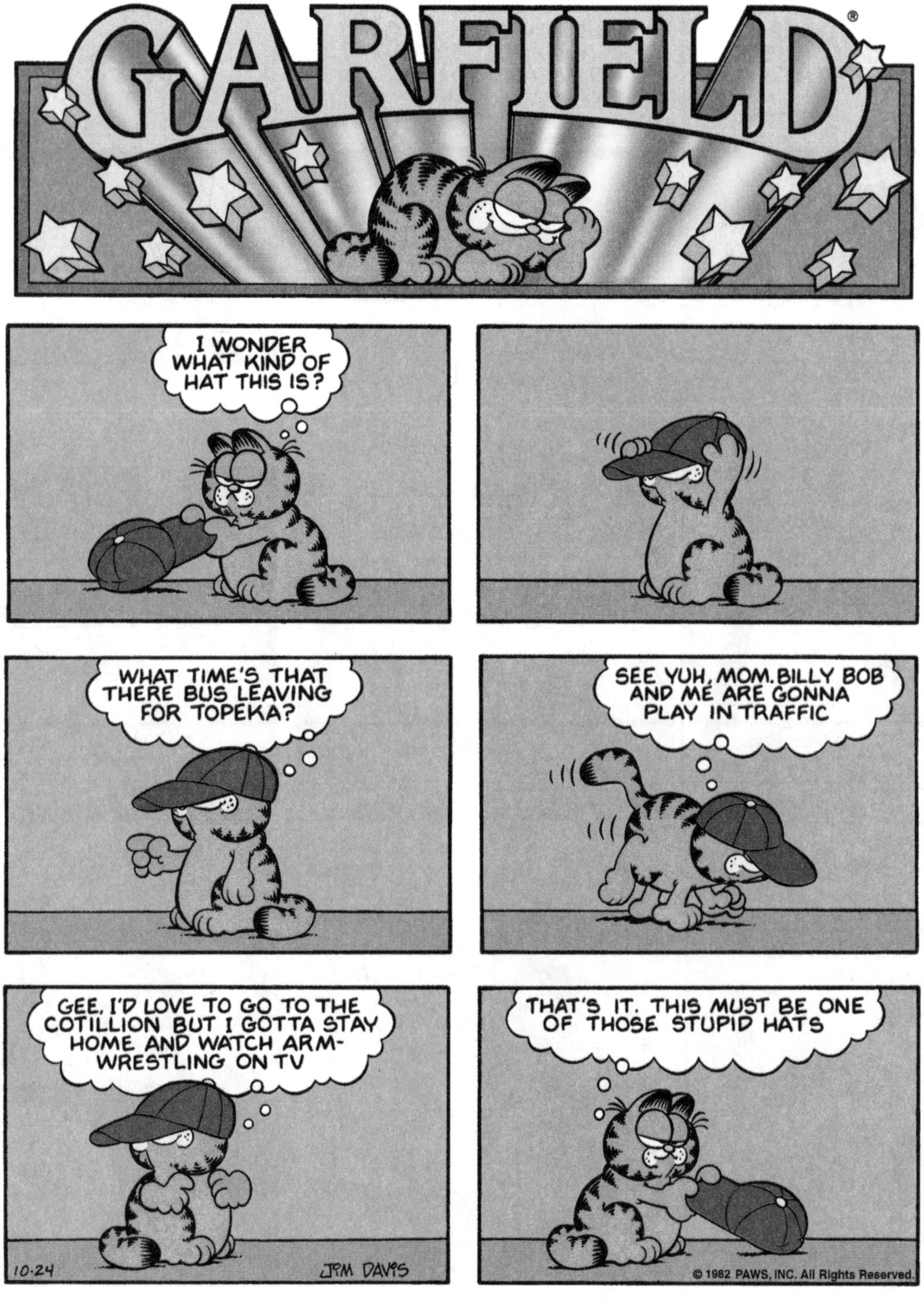

GARFIELD®
I WONDER WHAT KIND OF HAT THIS IS?
WHAT TIME'S THAT THERE BUS LEAVING FOR TOPEKA?
SEE YUH, MOM. BILLY BOB AND ME ARE GONNA PLAY IN TRAFFIC
GEE, I'D LOVE TO GO TO THE COTILLION BUT I GOTTA STAY HOME AND WATCH ARM-WRESTLING ON TV
10-24
JIM DAVIS
THAT'S IT. THIS MUST BE ONE OF THOSE STUPID HATS
© 1982 PAWS, INC. All Rights Reserved.

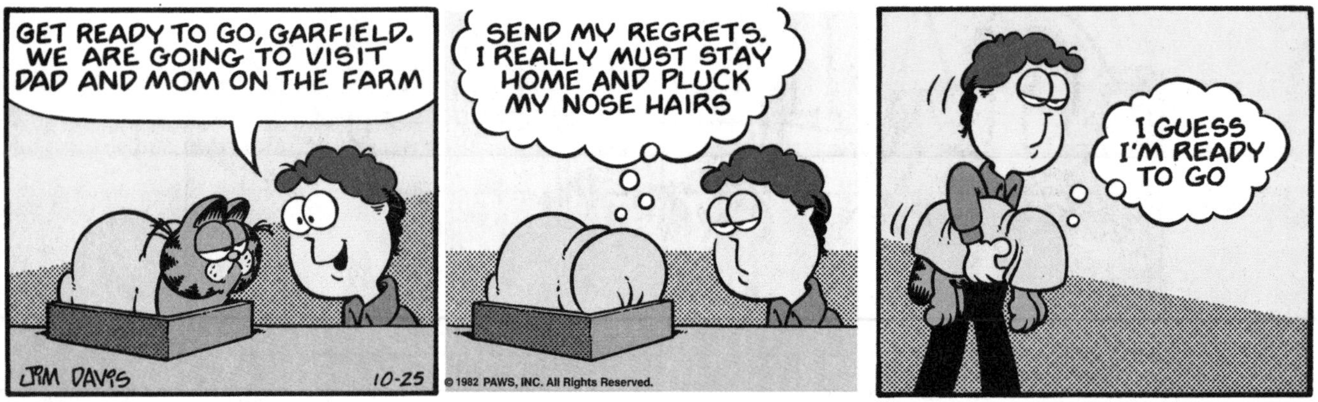
GET READY TO GO, GARFIELD. WE ARE GOING TO VISIT DAD AND MOM ON THE FARM
JIM DAVIS
10-25
SEND MY REGRETS. I REALLY MUST STAY HOME AND PLUCK MY NOSE HAIRS
© 1982 PAWS, INC. All Rights Reserved.
I GUESS I'M READY TO GO

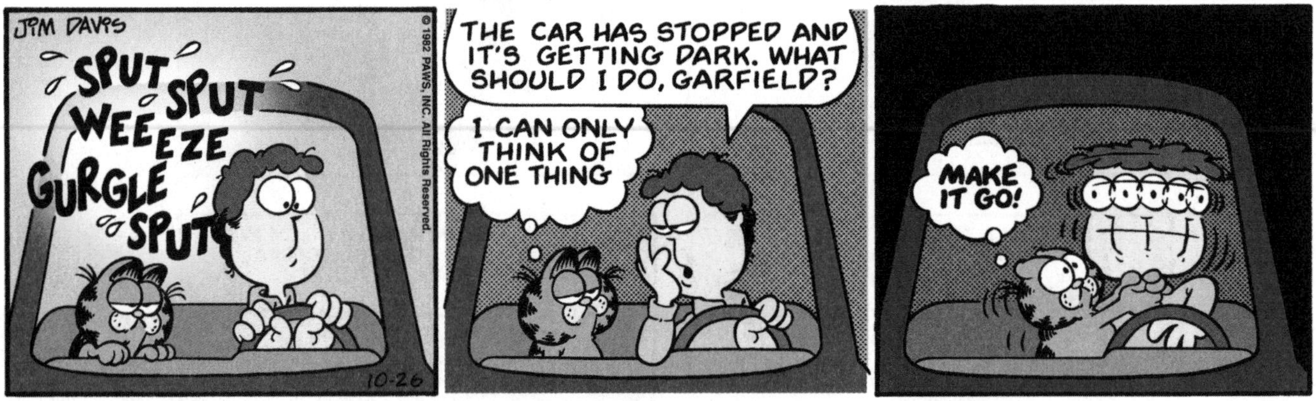
JIM DAVIS
SPUT SPUT WEEEZE GURGLE SPUT
© 1982 PAWS, INC. All Rights Reserved.
10-26
THE CAR HAS STOPPED AND IT'S GETTING DARK. WHAT SHOULD I DO, GARFIELD?
I CAN ONLY THINK OF ONE THING
MAKE IT GO!

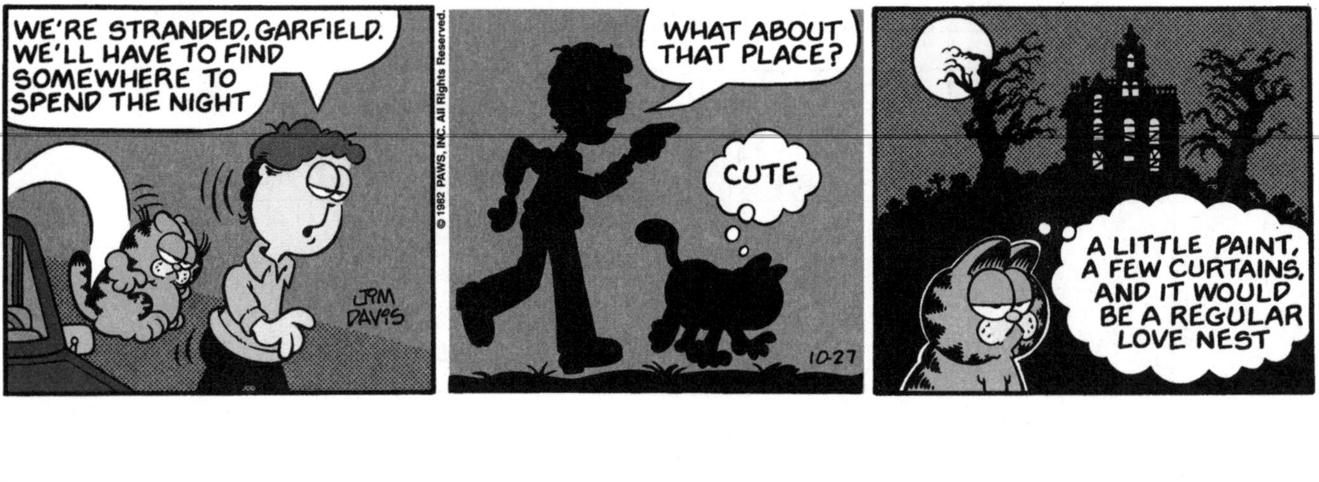
WE'RE STRANDED, GARFIELD. WE'LL HAVE TO FIND SOMEWHERE TO SPEND THE NIGHT
JIM DAVIS
© 1982 PAWS, INC. All Rights Reserved.
WHAT ABOUT THAT PLACE?
CUTE
10-27
A LITTLE PAINT, A FEW CURTAINS, AND IT WOULD BE A REGULAR LOVE NEST

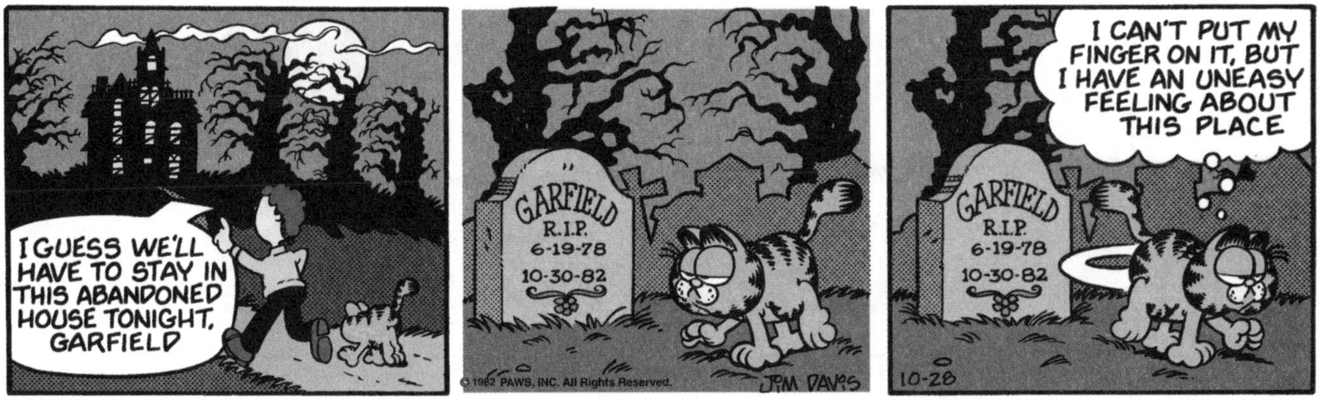
I GUESS WE'LL HAVE TO STAY IN THIS ABANDONED HOUSE TONIGHT, GARFIELD
GARFIELD R.I.P. 6-19-78 10-30-82
© 1982 PAWS, INC. All Rights Reserved.
JIM DAVIS
I CAN'T PUT MY FINGER ON IT, BUT I HAVE AN UNEASY FEELING ABOUT THIS PLACE
GARFIELD R.I.P. 6-19-78 10-30-82
10-28

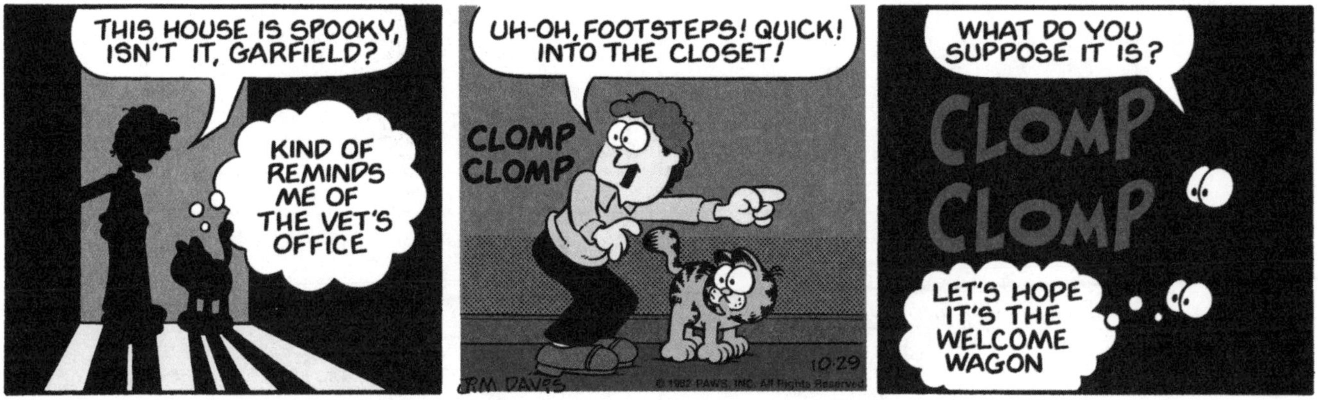
THIS HOUSE IS SPOOKY, ISN'T IT, GARFIELD?
KIND OF REMINDS ME OF THE VET'S OFFICE
UH-OH, FOOTSTEPS! QUICK! INTO THE CLOSET!
CLOMP CLOMP
JIM DAVIS
10-29
© 1982 PAWS, INC. All Rights Reserved.
WHAT DO YOU SUPPOSE IT IS?
CLOMP CLOMP
LET'S HOPE IT'S THE WELCOME WAGON

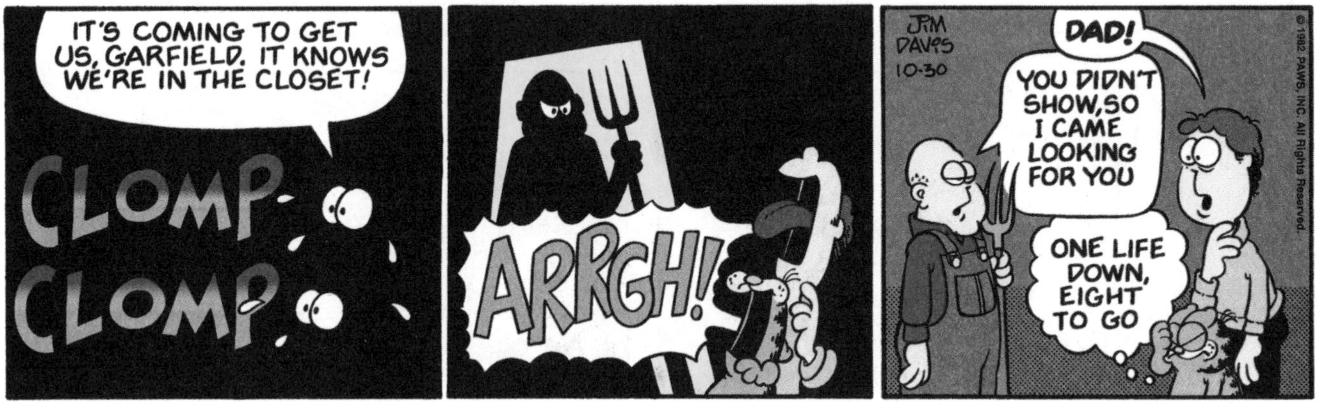
IT'S COMING TO GET US, GARFIELD. IT KNOWS WE'RE IN THE CLOSET!
CLOMP CLOMP
ARRGH!
JIM DAVIS
10-30
DAD!
YOU DIDN'T SHOW, SO I CAME LOOKING FOR YOU
ONE LIFE DOWN, EIGHT TO GO
© 1982 PAWS, INC. All Rights Reserved.

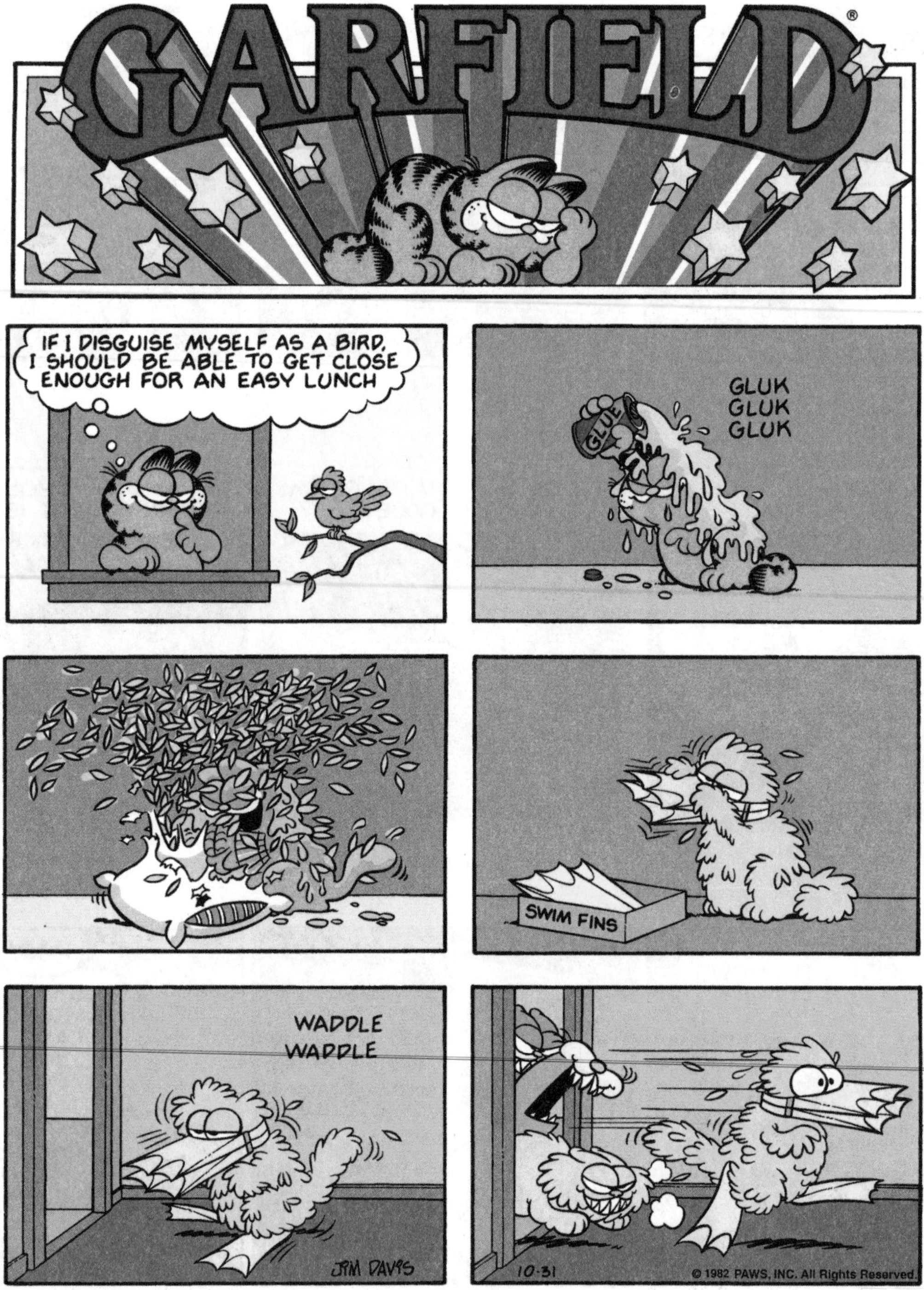

GARFIELD®
IF I DISGUISE MYSELF AS A BIRD, I SHOULD BE ABLE TO GET CLOSE ENOUGH FOR AN EASY LUNCH
GLUE
GLUK
GLUK
GLUK
SWIM FINS
WADDLE
WADDLE
JIM DAVIS
10-31
© 1982 PAWS, INC. All Rights Reserved.

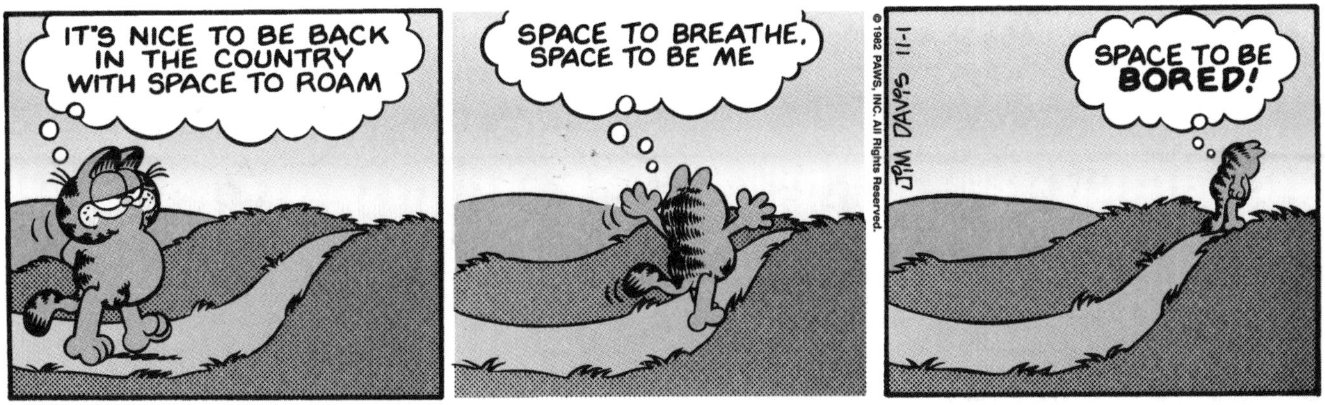
IT'S NICE TO BE BACK IN THE COUNTRY WITH SPACE TO ROAM
SPACE TO BREATHE, SPACE TO BE ME
© 1982 PAWS, INC. All Rights Reserved.
JIM DAVIS 11-1
SPACE TO BE **BORED!**

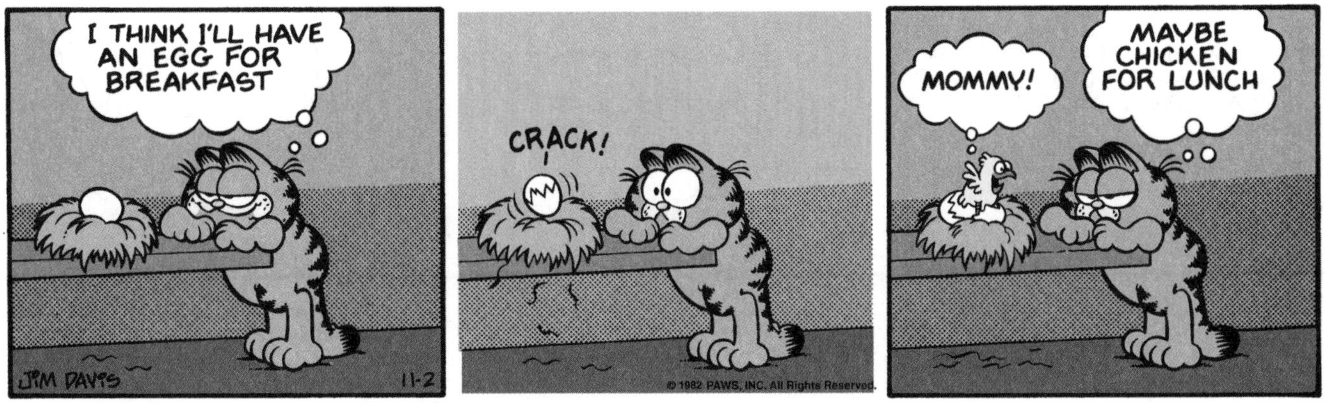
I THINK I'LL HAVE AN EGG FOR BREAKFAST
JIM DAVIS
11-2
CRACK!
© 1982 PAWS, INC. All Rights Reserved.
MOMMY!
MAYBE CHICKEN FOR LUNCH

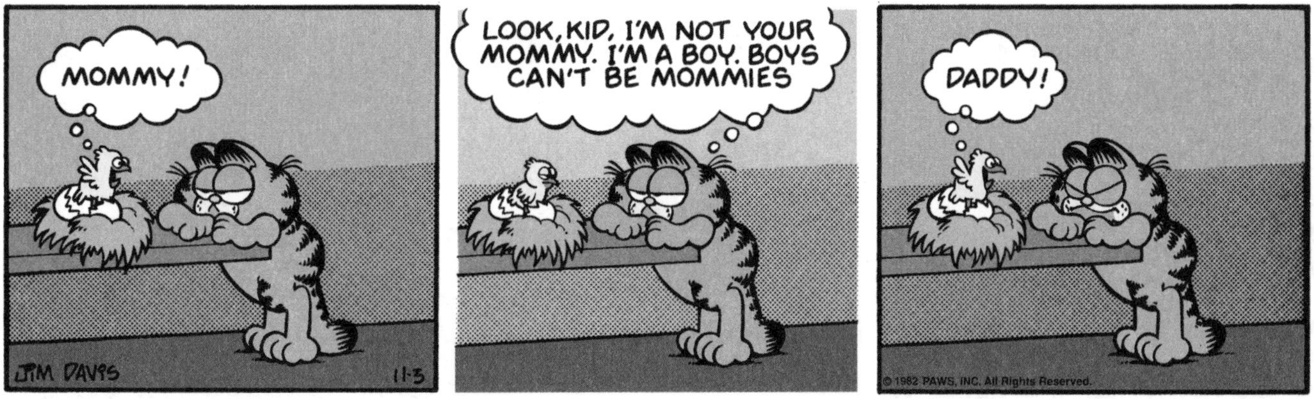
MOMMY!
JIM DAVIS
11-3
LOOK, KID, I'M NOT YOUR MOMMY. I'M A BOY. BOYS CAN'T BE MOMMIES
DADDY!
© 1982 PAWS, INC. All Rights Reserved.

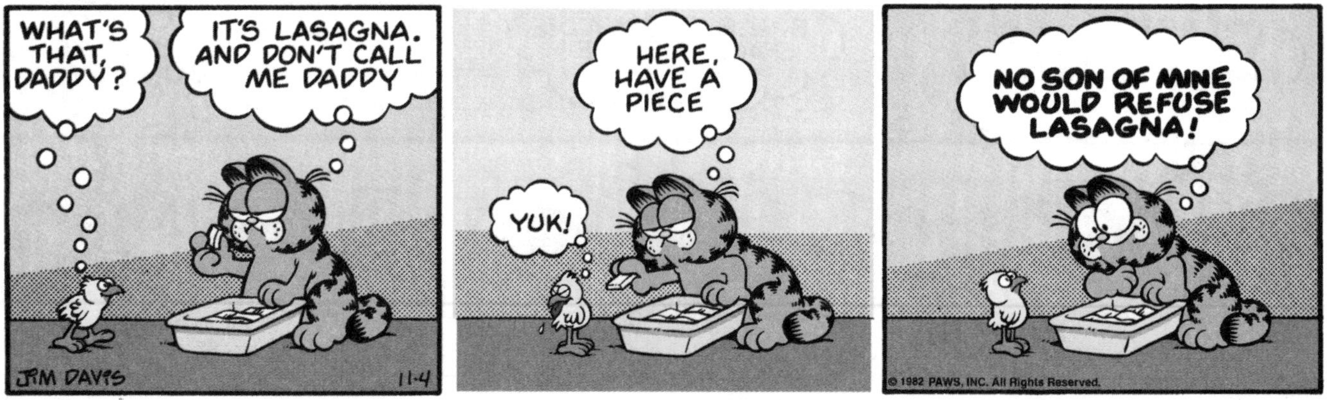
WHAT'S THAT, DADDY?
IT'S LASAGNA. AND DON'T CALL ME DADDY
JIM DAVIS
11-4
YUK!
HERE, HAVE A PIECE
NO SON OF MINE WOULD REFUSE LASAGNA!
© 1982 PAWS, INC. All Rights Reserved.

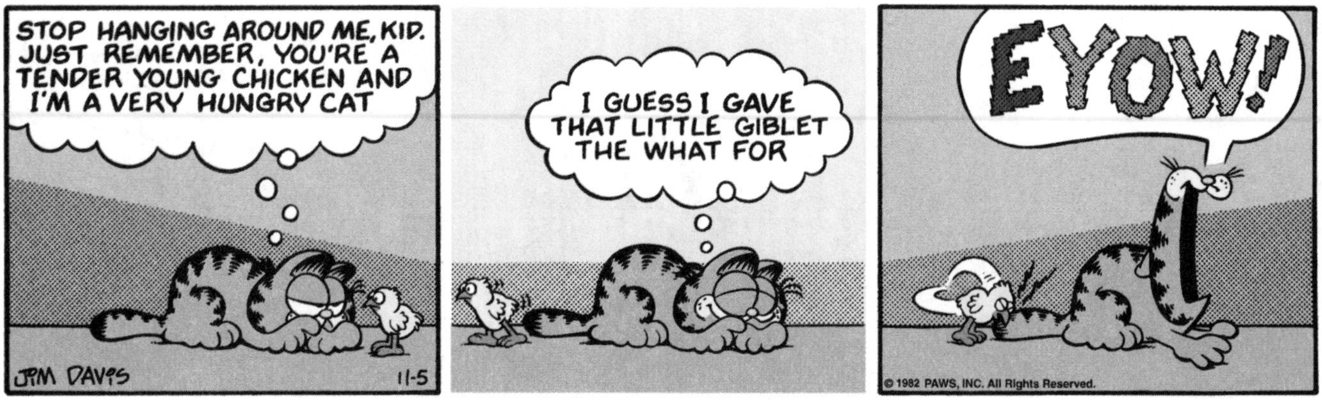
STOP HANGING AROUND ME, KID. JUST REMEMBER, YOU'RE A TENDER YOUNG CHICKEN AND I'M A VERY HUNGRY CAT
JIM DAVIS
11-5
I GUESS I GAVE THAT LITTLE GIBLET THE WHAT FOR
EYOW!
© 1982 PAWS, INC. All Rights Reserved.

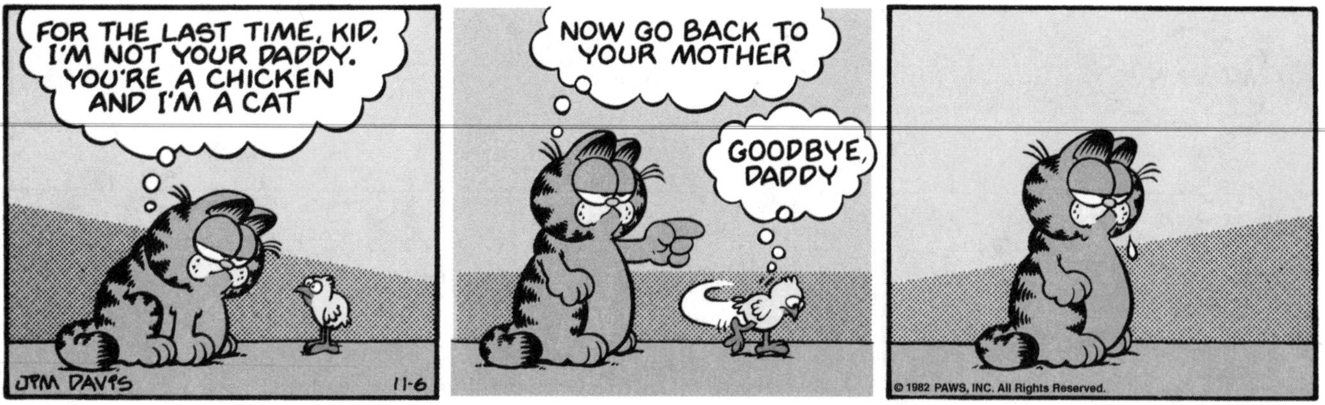
FOR THE LAST TIME, KID, I'M NOT YOUR DADDY. YOU'RE A CHICKEN AND I'M A CAT
JIM DAVIS
11-6
NOW GO BACK TO YOUR MOTHER
GOODBYE, DADDY
© 1982 PAWS, INC. All Rights Reserved.

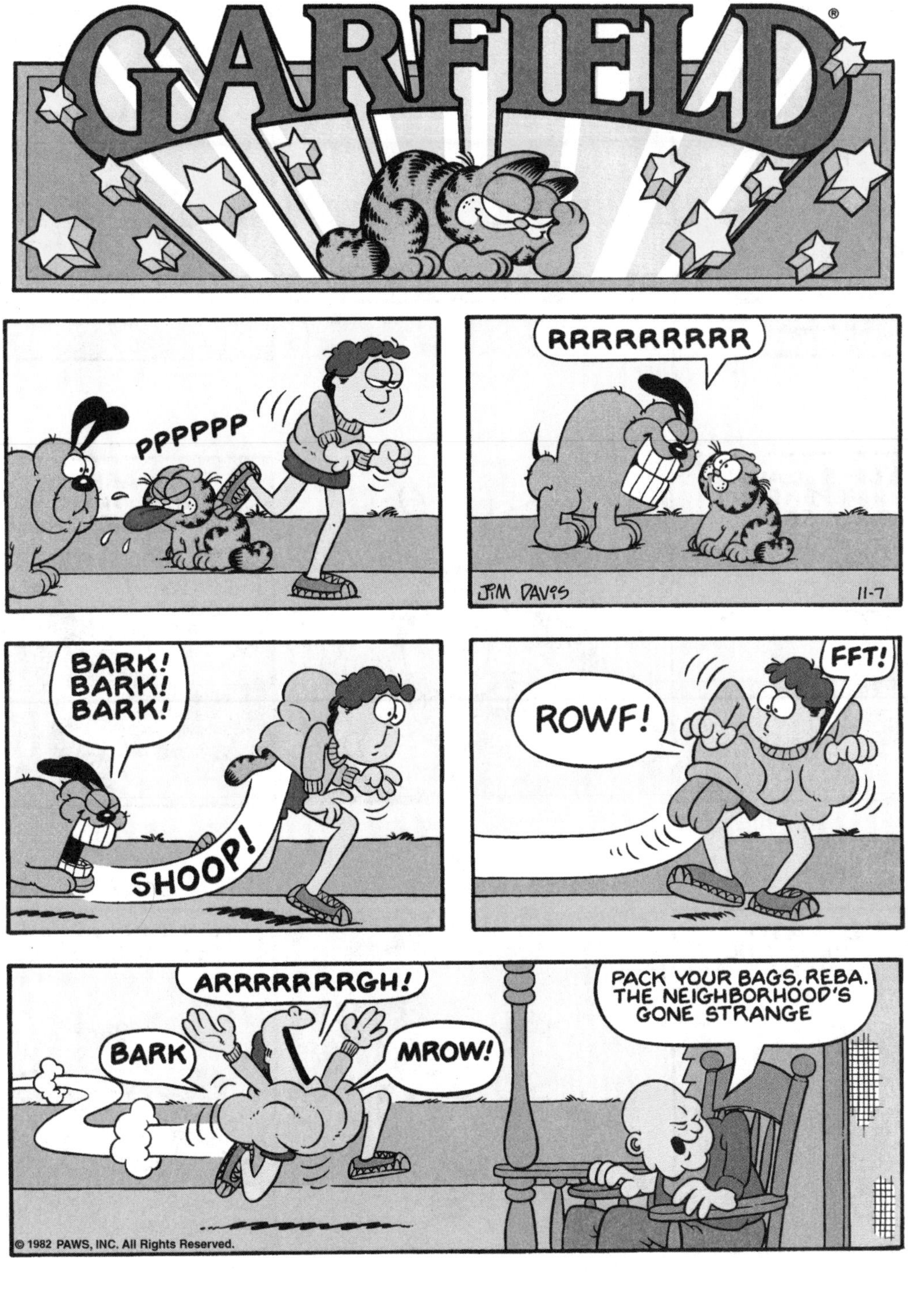
GARFIELD
PPPPPP
RRRRRRRRR
JIM DAVIS
11-7
BARK! BARK! BARK!
SHOOP!
ROWF!
FFT!
ARRRRRRRGH!
BARK
MROW!
PACK YOUR BAGS, REBA. THE NEIGHBORHOOD'S GONE STRANGE
© 1982 PAWS, INC. All Rights Reserved.

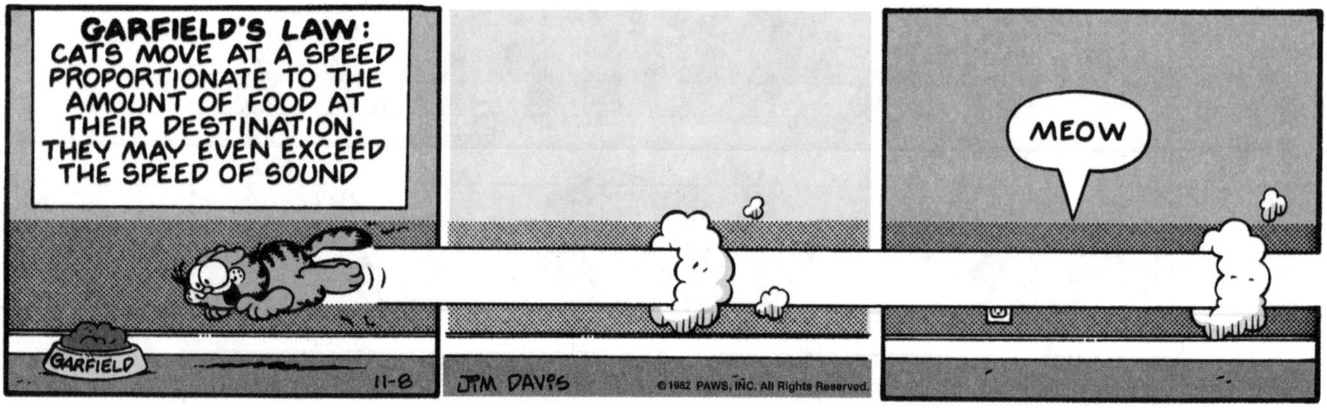
GARFIELD'S LAW:
CATS MOVE AT A SPEED PROPORTIONATE TO THE AMOUNT OF FOOD AT THEIR DESTINATION. THEY MAY EVEN EXCEED THE SPEED OF SOUND
GARFIELD
11-8
JIM DAVIS
© 1982 PAWS, INC. All Rights Reserved.
MEOW

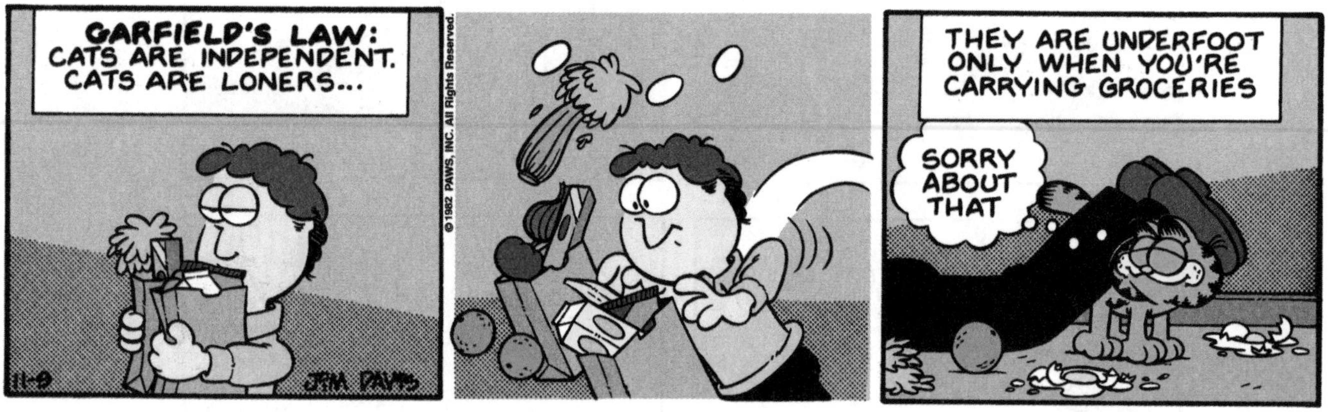
GARFIELD'S LAW:
CATS ARE INDEPENDENT. CATS ARE LONERS...
11-9
JIM DAVIS
© 1982 PAWS, INC. All Rights Reserved.
THEY ARE UNDERFOOT ONLY WHEN YOU'RE CARRYING GROCERIES
SORRY ABOUT THAT

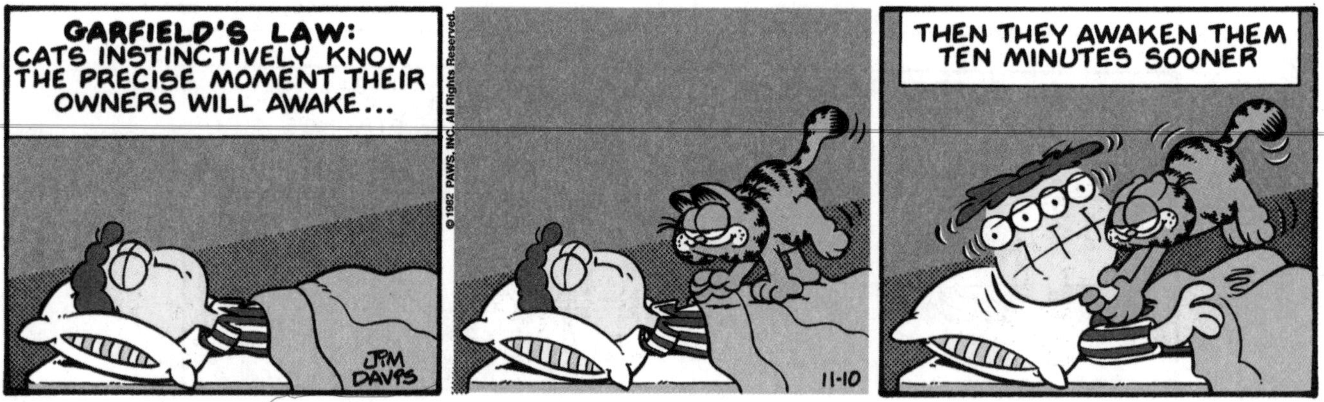
GARFIELD'S LAW:
CATS INSTINCTIVELY KNOW THE PRECISE MOMENT THEIR OWNERS WILL AWAKE...
JIM DAVIS
© 1982 PAWS, INC. All Rights Reserved.
11-10
THEN THEY AWAKEN THEM TEN MINUTES SOONER

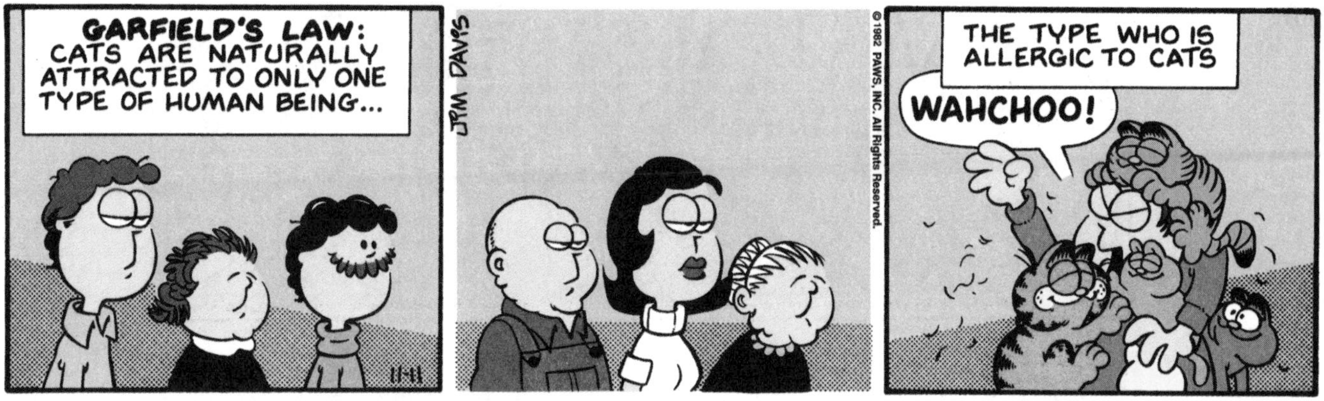
GARFIELD'S LAW: CATS ARE NATURALLY ATTRACTED TO ONLY ONE TYPE OF HUMAN BEING...
11-11
JIM DAVIS
© 1982 PAWS, INC. All Rights Reserved.
THE TYPE WHO IS ALLERGIC TO CATS
WAHCHOO!

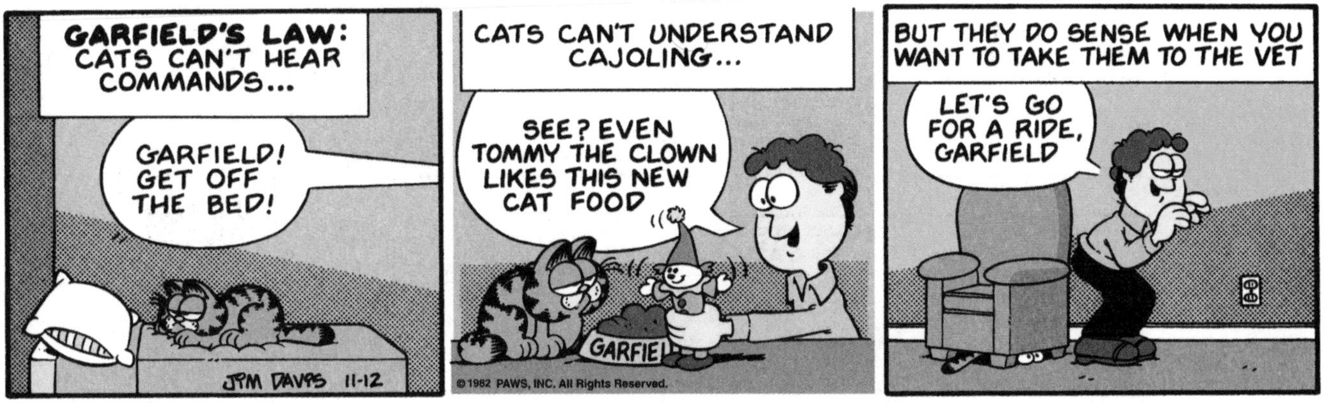
GARFIELD'S LAW: CATS CAN'T HEAR COMMANDS...
GARFIELD! GET OFF THE BED!
JIM DAVIS 11-12
CATS CAN'T UNDERSTAND CAJOLING...
SEE? EVEN TOMMY THE CLOWN LIKES THIS NEW CAT FOOD
GARFIE
© 1982 PAWS, INC. All Rights Reserved.
BUT THEY DO SENSE WHEN YOU WANT TO TAKE THEM TO THE VET
LET'S GO FOR A RIDE, GARFIELD

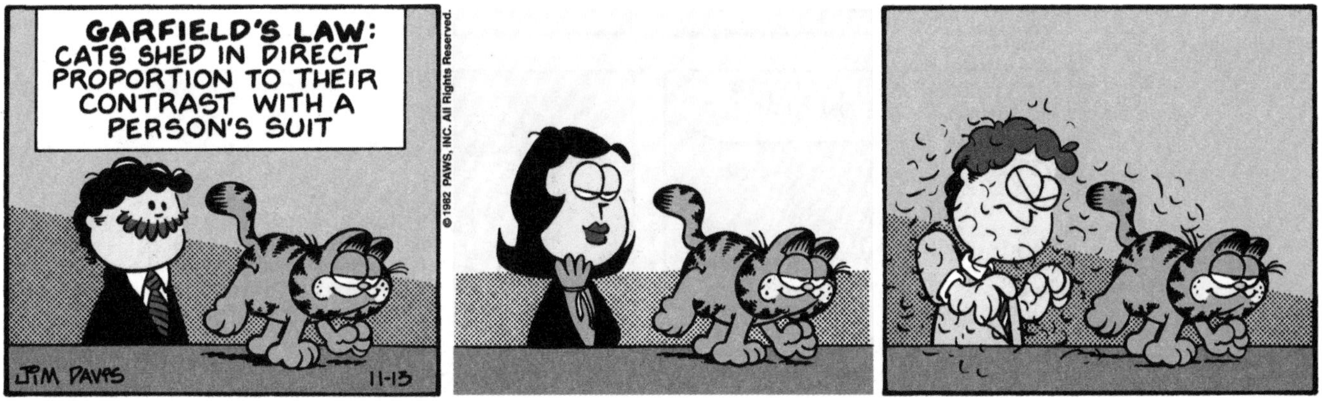
GARFIELD'S LAW: CATS SHED IN DIRECT PROPORTION TO THEIR CONTRAST WITH A PERSON'S SUIT
JIM DAVIS
11-13
© 1982 PAWS, INC. All Rights Reserved.

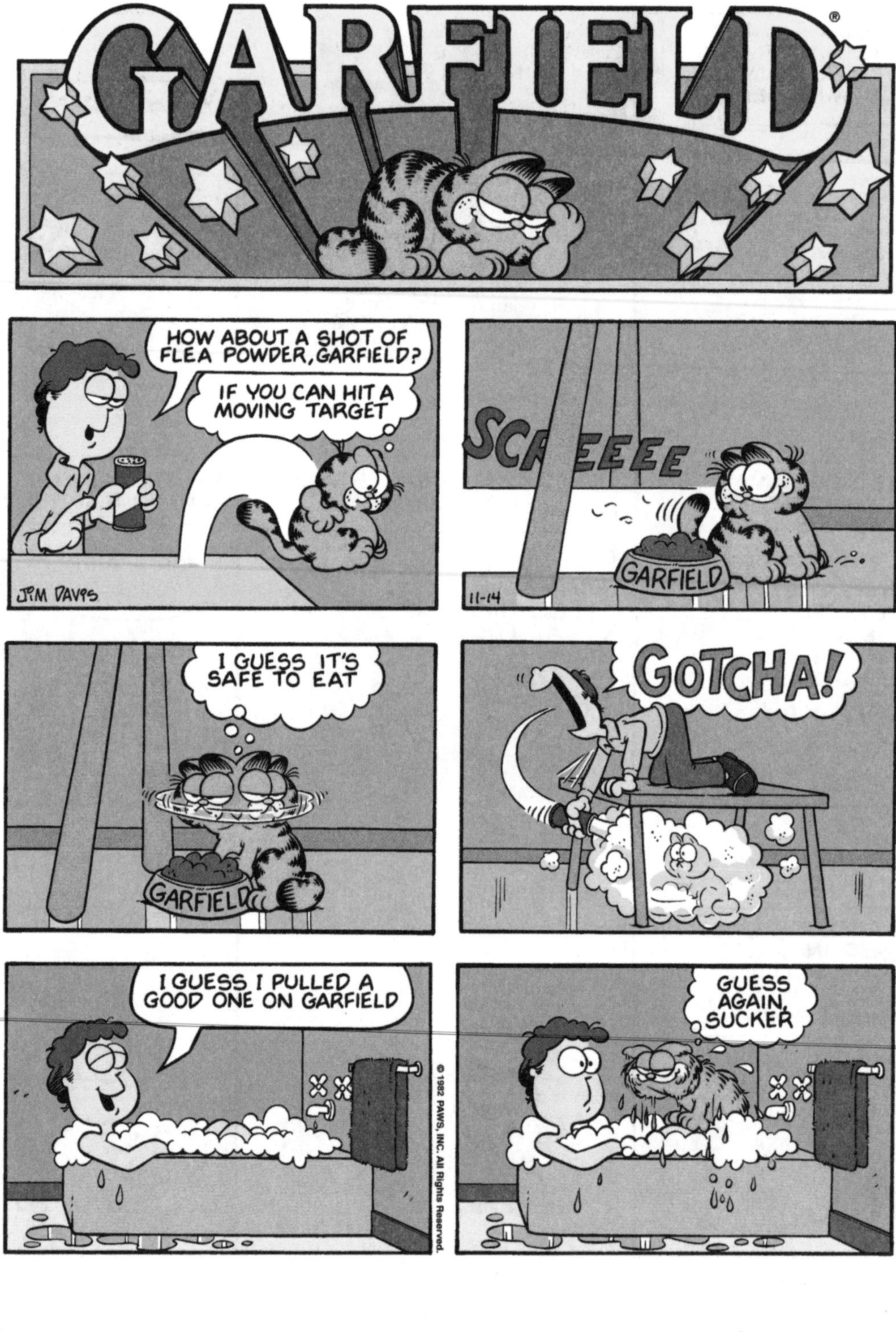
GARFIELD®
HOW ABOUT A SHOT OF FLEA POWDER, GARFIELD?
IF YOU CAN HIT A MOVING TARGET
JIM DAVIS
SCREEEEE
GARFIELD
11-14
I GUESS IT'S SAFE TO EAT
GARFIELD
GOTCHA!
I GUESS I PULLED A GOOD ONE ON GARFIELD
GUESS AGAIN, SUCKER

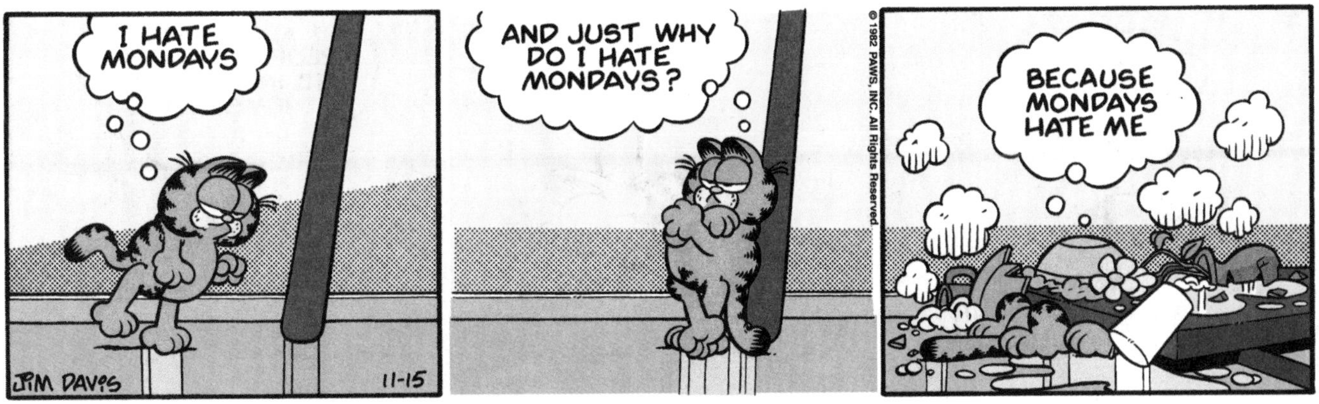
I HATE MONDAYS
JIM DAVIS
11-15
AND JUST WHY DO I HATE MONDAYS?
© 1982 PAWS, INC. All Rights Reserved.
BECAUSE MONDAYS HATE ME

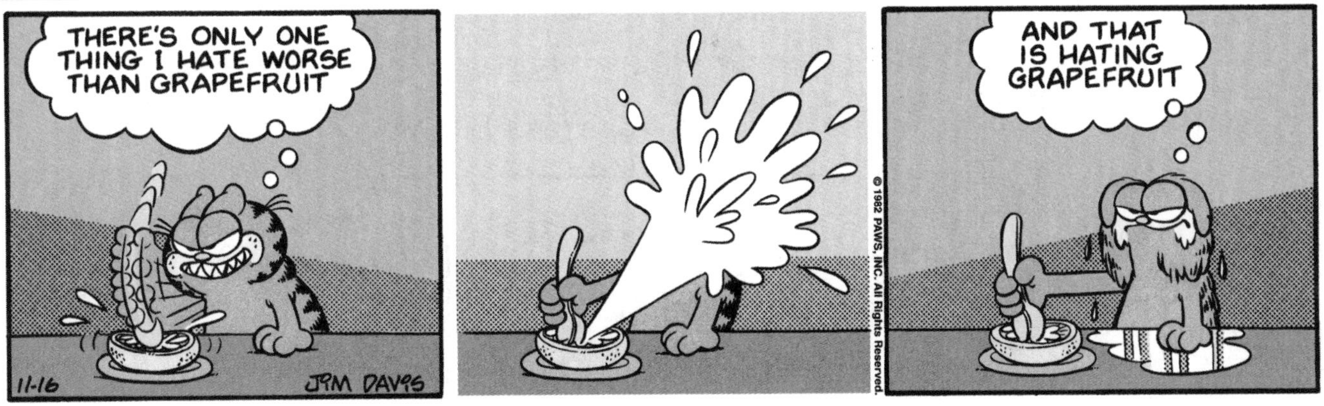
THERE'S ONLY ONE THING I HATE WORSE THAN GRAPEFRUIT
11-16
JIM DAVIS
© 1982 PAWS, INC. All Rights Reserved.
AND THAT IS HATING GRAPEFRUIT

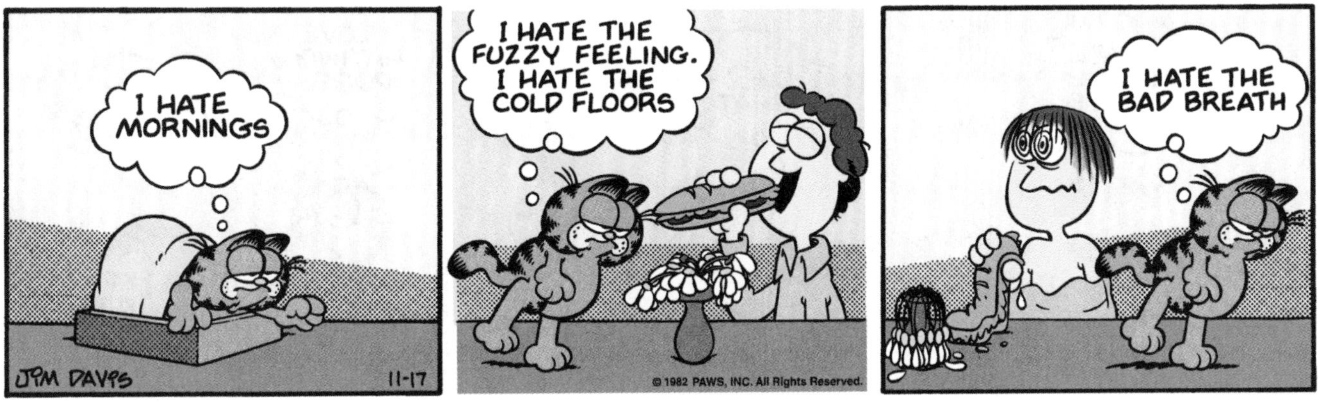
I HATE MORNINGS
JIM DAVIS
11-17
I HATE THE FUZZY FEELING. I HATE THE COLD FLOORS
© 1982 PAWS, INC. All Rights Reserved.
I HATE THE BAD BREATH

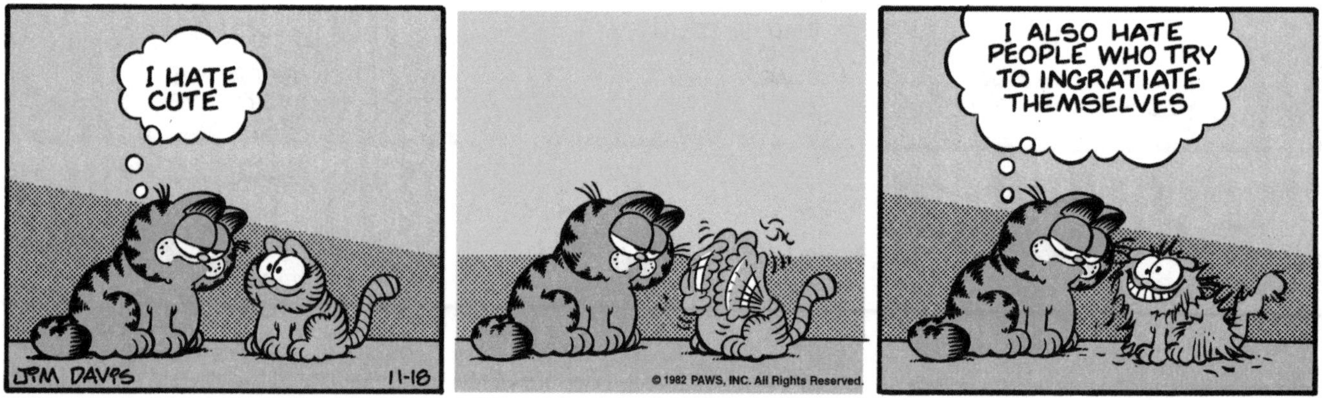
I HATE CUTE
JIM DAVIS
11-18
© 1982 PAWS, INC. All Rights Reserved.
I ALSO HATE PEOPLE WHO TRY TO INGRATIATE THEMSELVES

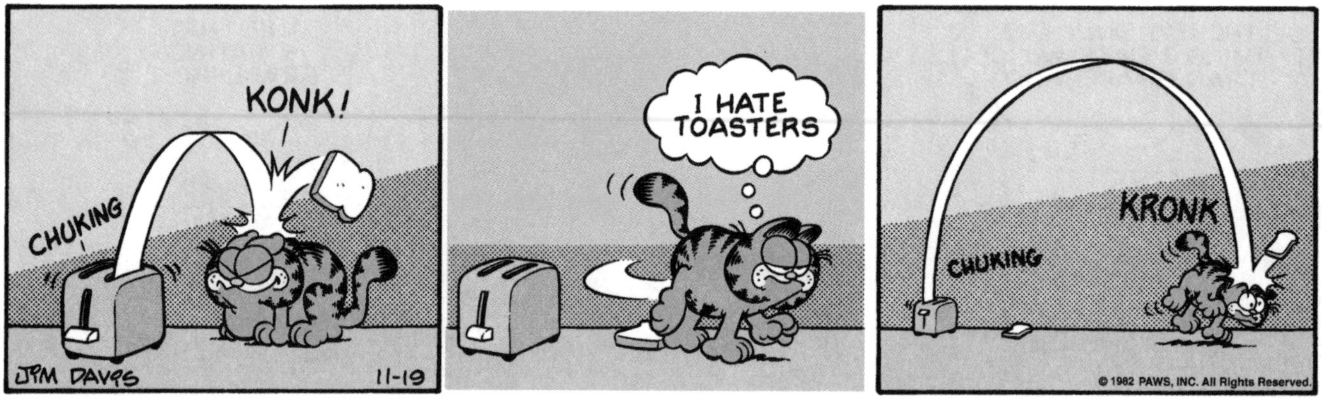
KONK!
CHUKING
JIM DAVIS
11-19
I HATE TOASTERS
CHUKING
KRONK
© 1982 PAWS, INC. All Rights Reserved.

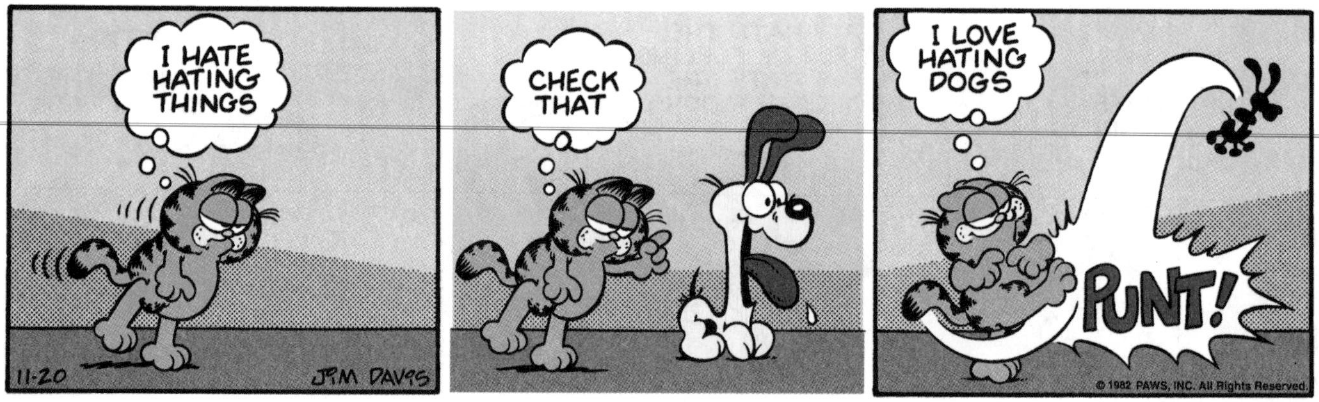
I HATE HATING THINGS
11-20
JIM DAVIS
CHECK THAT
I LOVE HATING DOGS
PUNT!
© 1982 PAWS, INC. All Rights Reserved.

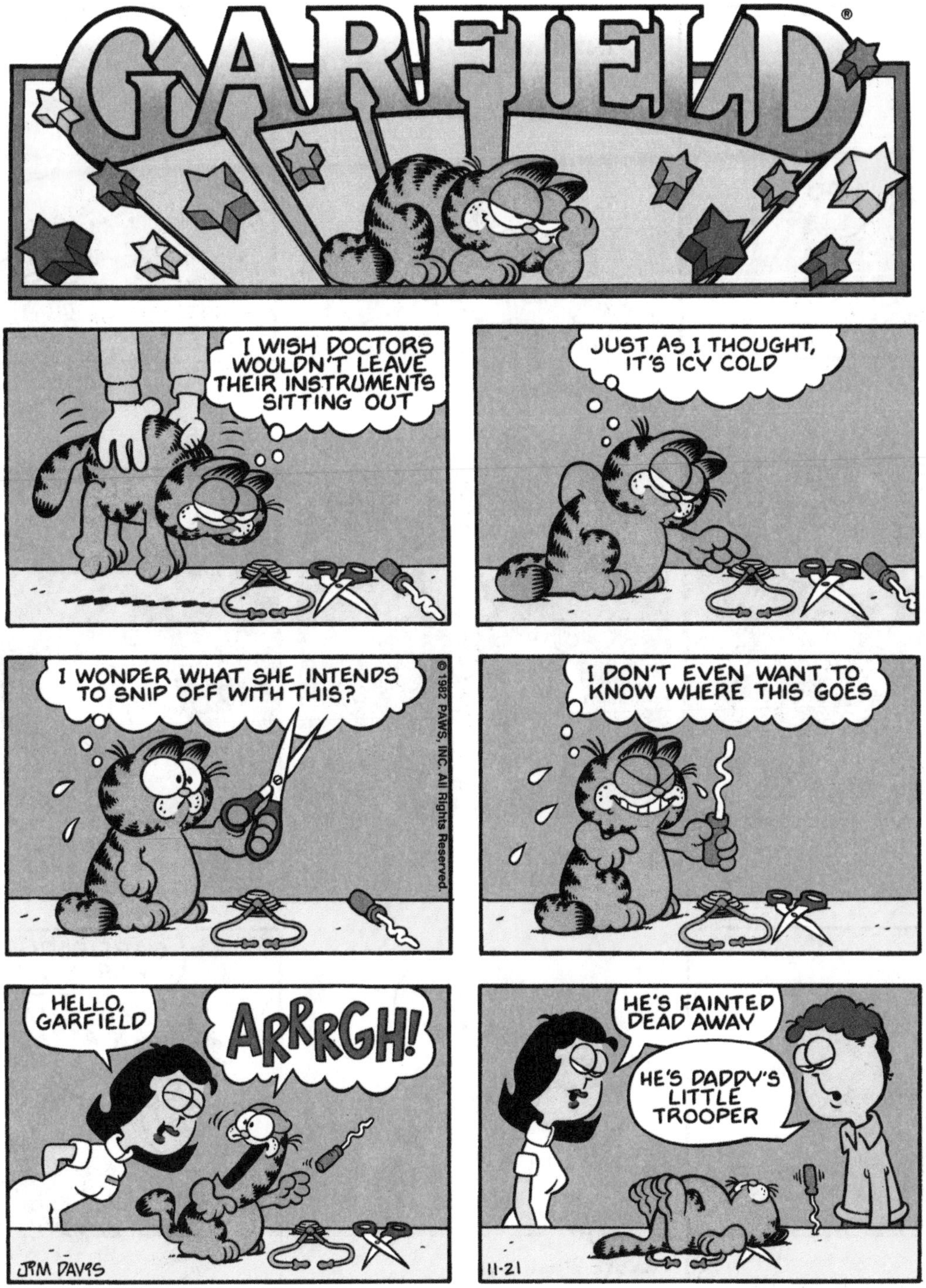
GARFIELD®
I WISH DOCTORS WOULDN'T LEAVE THEIR INSTRUMENTS SITTING OUT
JUST AS I THOUGHT, IT'S ICY COLD
I WONDER WHAT SHE INTENDS TO SNIP OFF WITH THIS?
© 1982 PAWS, INC. All Rights Reserved.
I DON'T EVEN WANT TO KNOW WHERE THIS GOES
HELLO, GARFIELD
ARRRGH!
JIM DAVIS
11-21
HE'S FAINTED DEAD AWAY
HE'S DADDY'S LITTLE TROOPER

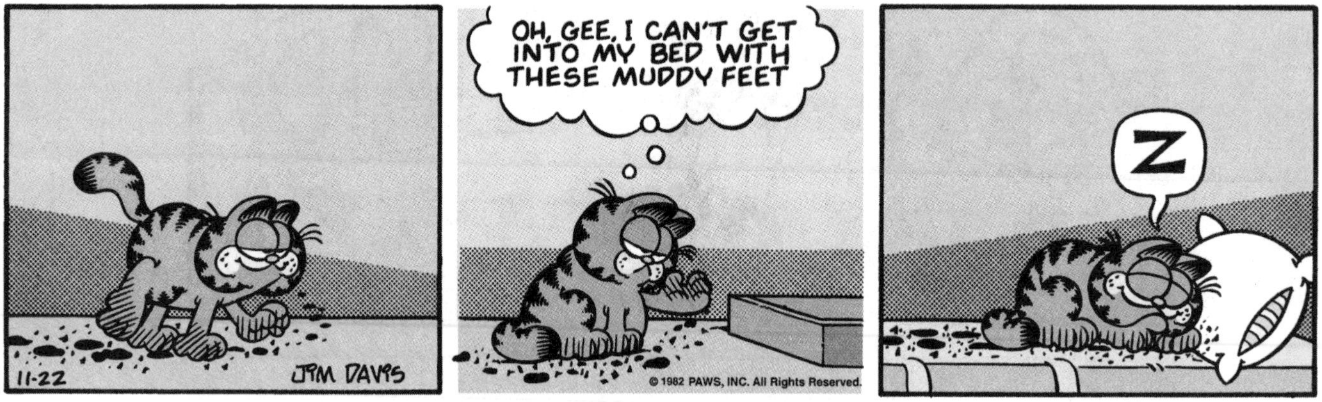
11-22
JIM DAVIS
OH, GEE, I CAN'T GET INTO MY BED WITH THESE MUDDY FEET
© 1982 PAWS, INC. All Rights Reserved.
Z

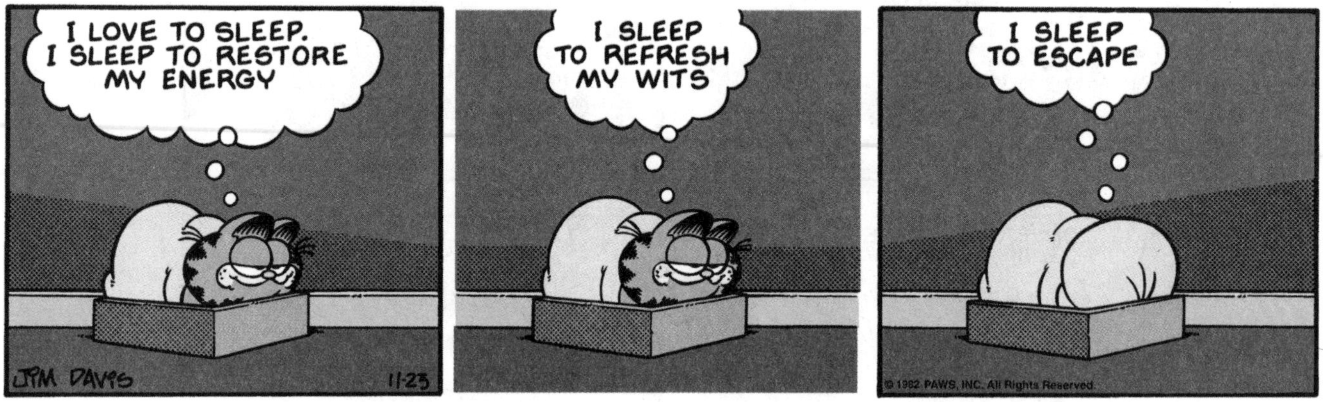
I LOVE TO SLEEP. I SLEEP TO RESTORE MY ENERGY
JIM DAVIS
11-23
I SLEEP TO REFRESH MY WITS
I SLEEP TO ESCAPE
© 1982 PAWS, INC. All Rights Reserved.

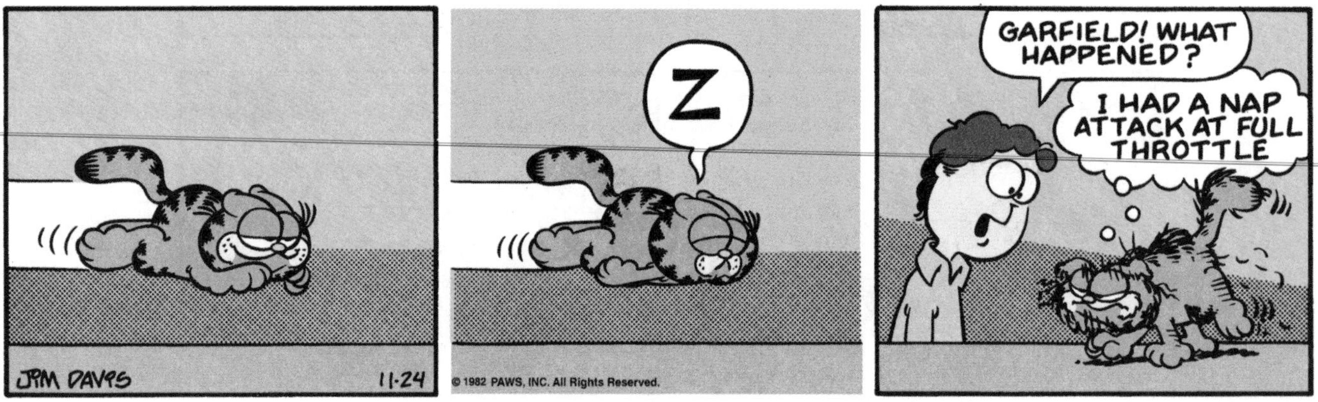
JIM DAVIS
11-24
Z
© 1982 PAWS, INC. All Rights Reserved.
GARFIELD! WHAT HAPPENED?
I HAD A NAP ATTACK AT FULL THROTTLE

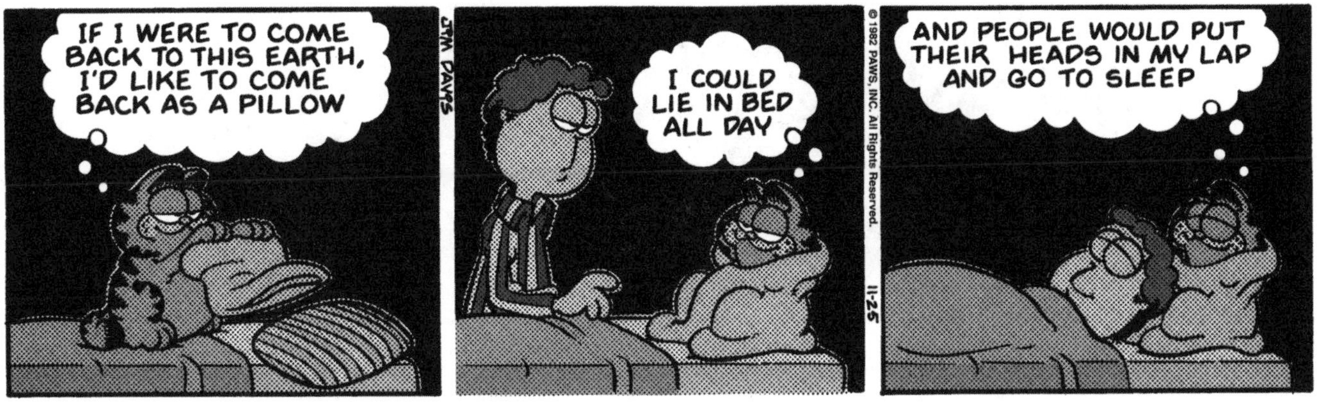
IF I WERE TO COME BACK TO THIS EARTH, I'D LIKE TO COME BACK AS A PILLOW
I COULD LIE IN BED ALL DAY
AND PEOPLE WOULD PUT THEIR HEADS IN MY LAP AND GO TO SLEEP
JIM DAVIS
11-25
© 1982 PAWS, INC. All Rights Reserved.

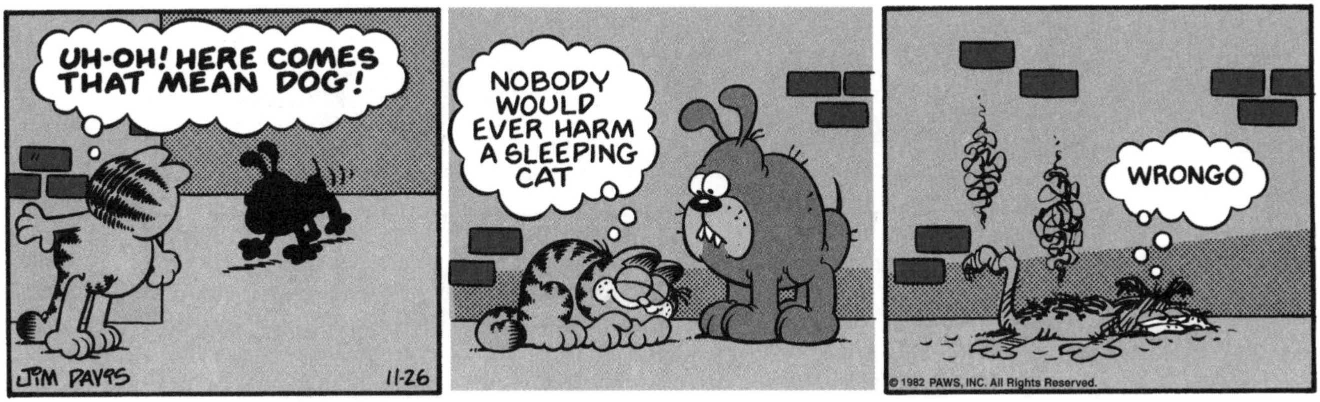
UH-OH! HERE COMES THAT MEAN DOG!
JIM DAVIS
11-26
NOBODY WOULD EVER HARM A SLEEPING CAT
WRONGO
© 1982 PAWS, INC. All Rights Reserved.

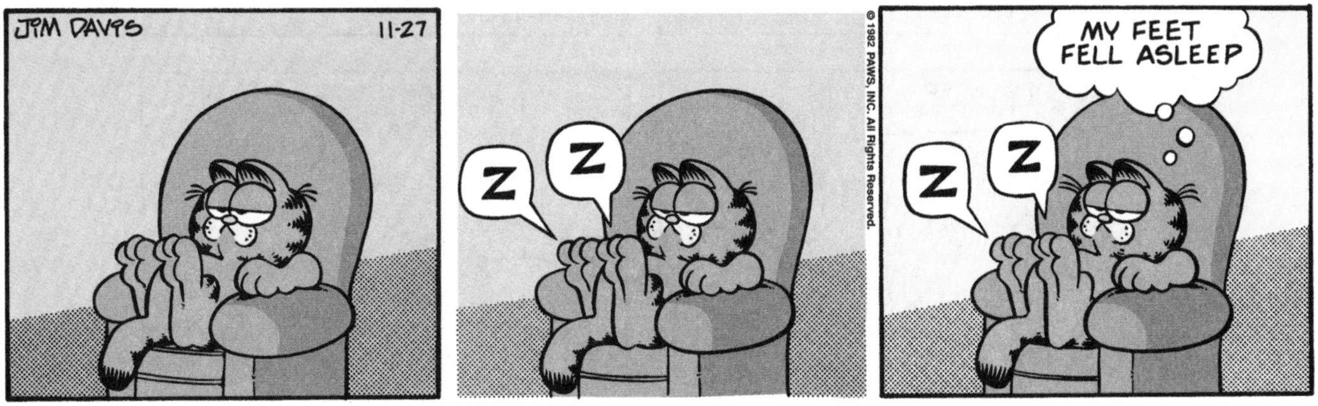
JIM DAVIS
11-27
Z
Z
© 1982 PAWS, INC. All Rights Reserved.
Z
Z
MY FEET FELL ASLEEP

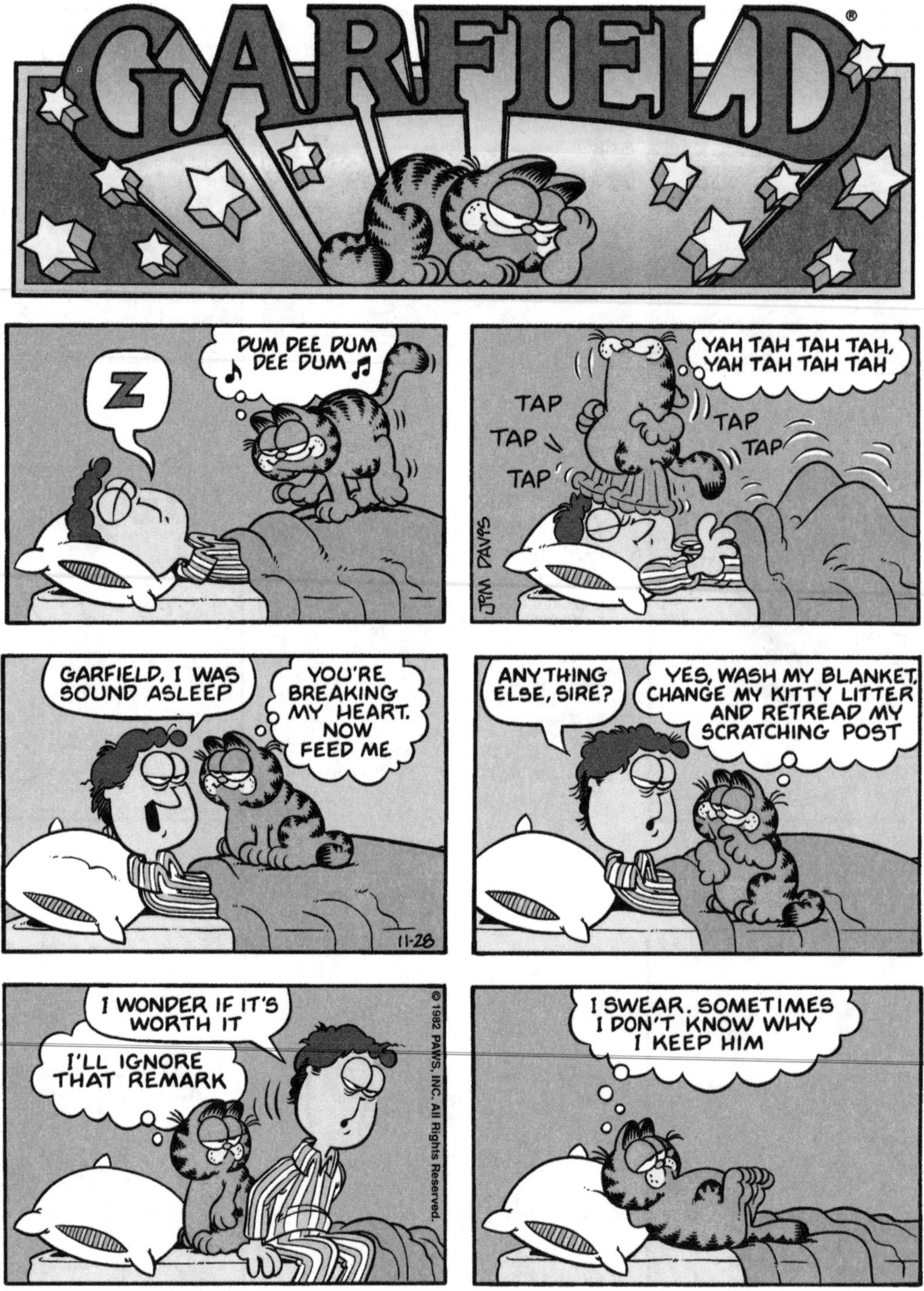
GARFIELD®
Z
DUM DEE DUM DEE DUM
TAP
TAP
TAP
TAP
TAP
TAP
YAH TAH TAH TAH, YAH TAH TAH TAH
JIM DAVIS
GARFIELD, I WAS SOUND ASLEEP
YOU'RE BREAKING MY HEART. NOW FEED ME
11-28
ANYTHING ELSE, SIRE?
YES, WASH MY BLANKET, CHANGE MY KITTY LITTER AND RETREAD MY SCRATCHING POST
I WONDER IF IT'S WORTH IT
I'LL IGNORE THAT REMARK
© 1982 PAWS, INC. All Rights Reserved.
I SWEAR. SOMETIMES I DON'T KNOW WHY I KEEP HIM

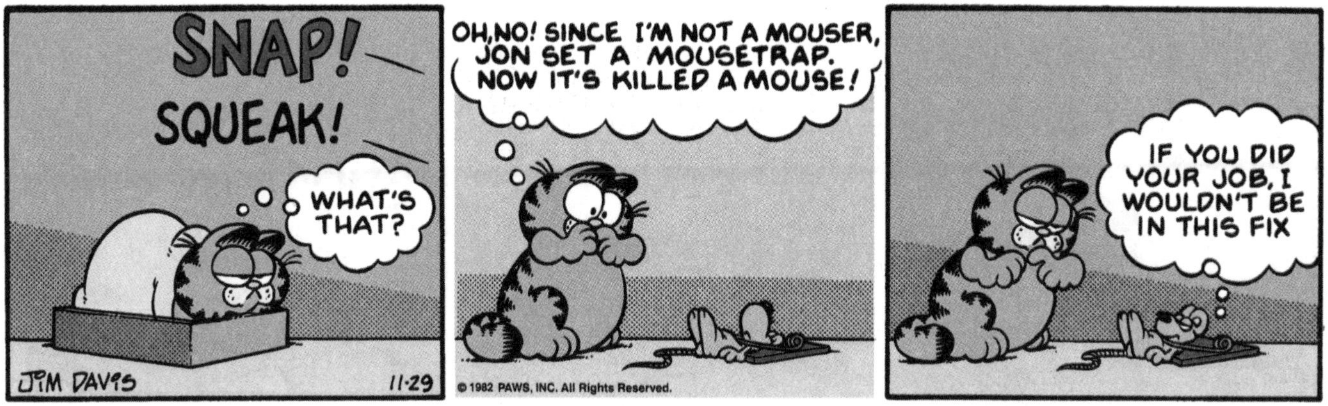
SNAP!
SQUEAK!
WHAT'S THAT?
JIM DAVIS 11-29
OH, NO! SINCE I'M NOT A MOUSER, JON SET A MOUSETRAP. NOW IT'S KILLED A MOUSE!
© 1982 PAWS, INC. All Rights Reserved.
IF YOU DID YOUR JOB, I WOULDN'T BE IN THIS FIX

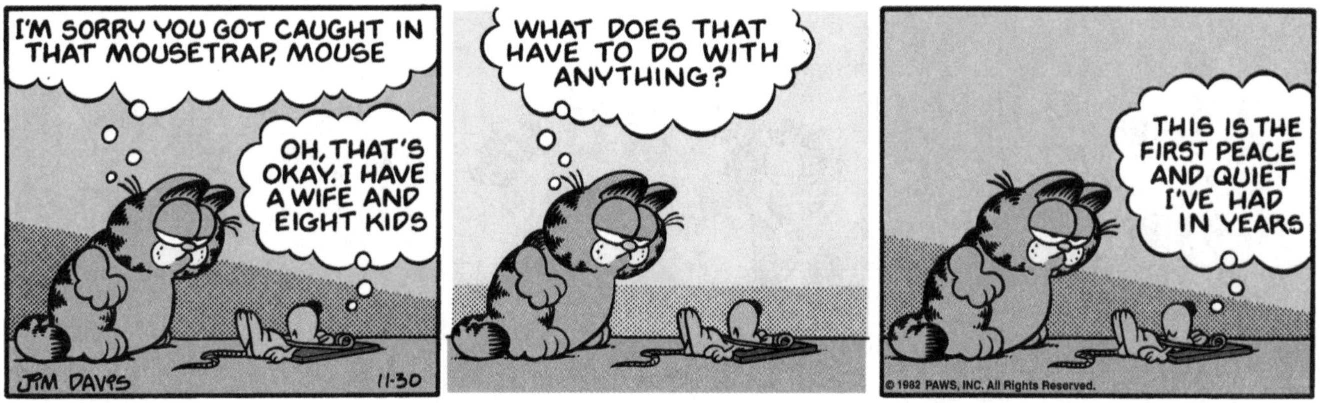
I'M SORRY YOU GOT CAUGHT IN THAT MOUSETRAP, MOUSE
OH, THAT'S OKAY. I HAVE A WIFE AND EIGHT KIDS
JIM DAVIS 11-30
WHAT DOES THAT HAVE TO DO WITH ANYTHING?
THIS IS THE FIRST PEACE AND QUIET I'VE HAD IN YEARS
© 1982 PAWS, INC. All Rights Reserved.

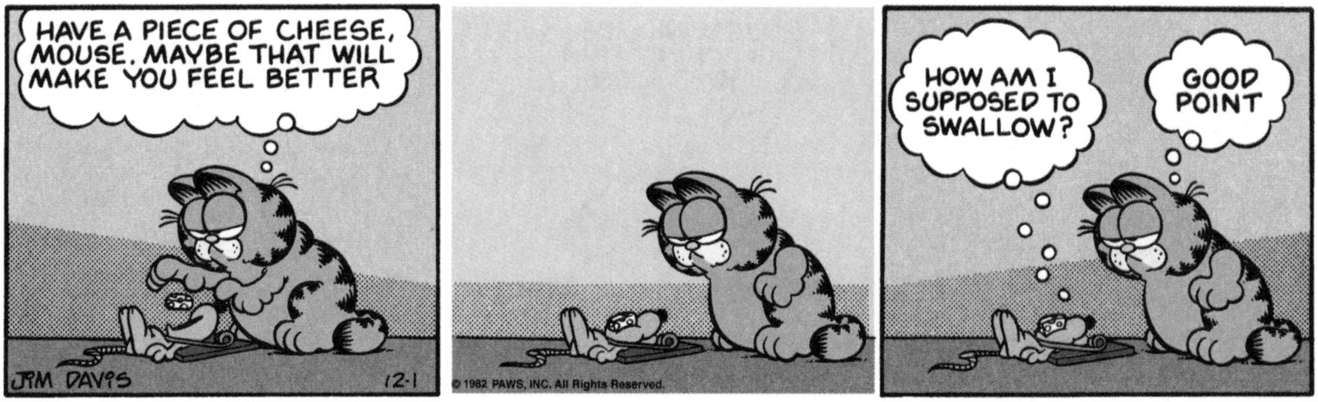
HAVE A PIECE OF CHEESE, MOUSE. MAYBE THAT WILL MAKE YOU FEEL BETTER
JIM DAVIS 12-1
© 1982 PAWS, INC. All Rights Reserved.
HOW AM I SUPPOSED TO SWALLOW?
GOOD POINT

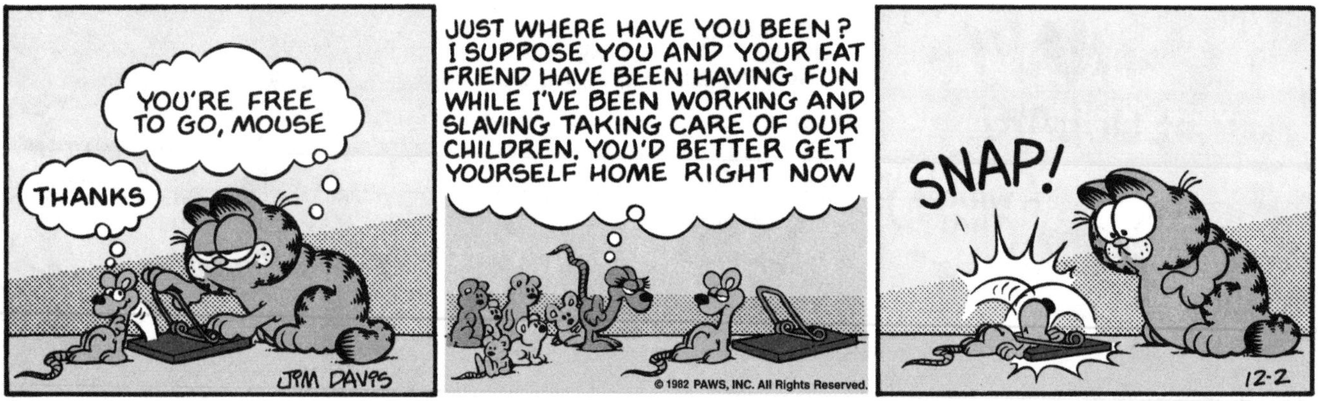
YOU'RE FREE TO GO, MOUSE
THANKS
JIM DAVIS
JUST WHERE HAVE YOU BEEN? I SUPPOSE YOU AND YOUR FAT FRIEND HAVE BEEN HAVING FUN WHILE I'VE BEEN WORKING AND SLAVING TAKING CARE OF OUR CHILDREN. YOU'D BETTER GET YOURSELF HOME RIGHT NOW
© 1982 PAWS, INC. All Rights Reserved.
SNAP!
12-2

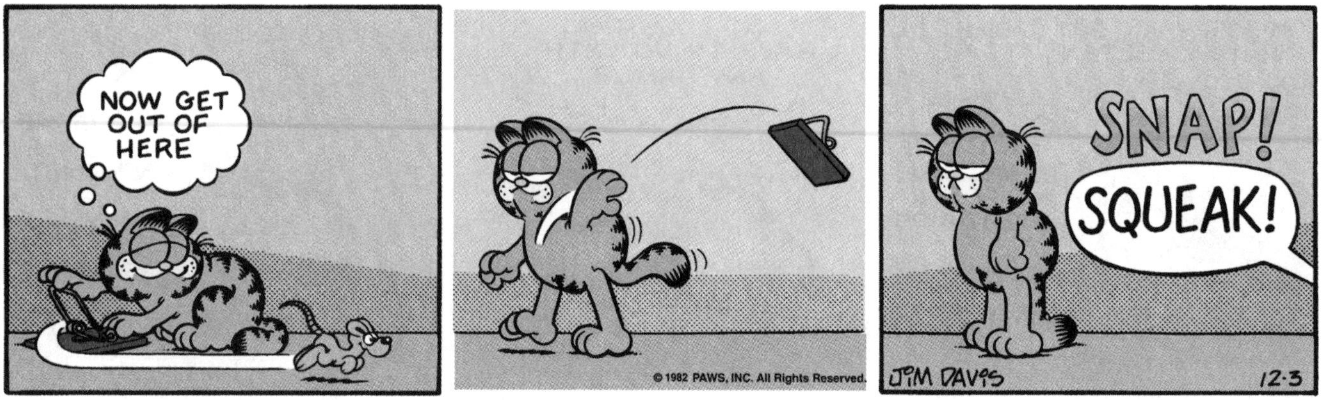
NOW GET OUT OF HERE
© 1982 PAWS, INC. All Rights Reserved.
SNAP!
SQUEAK!
JIM DAVIS
12-3

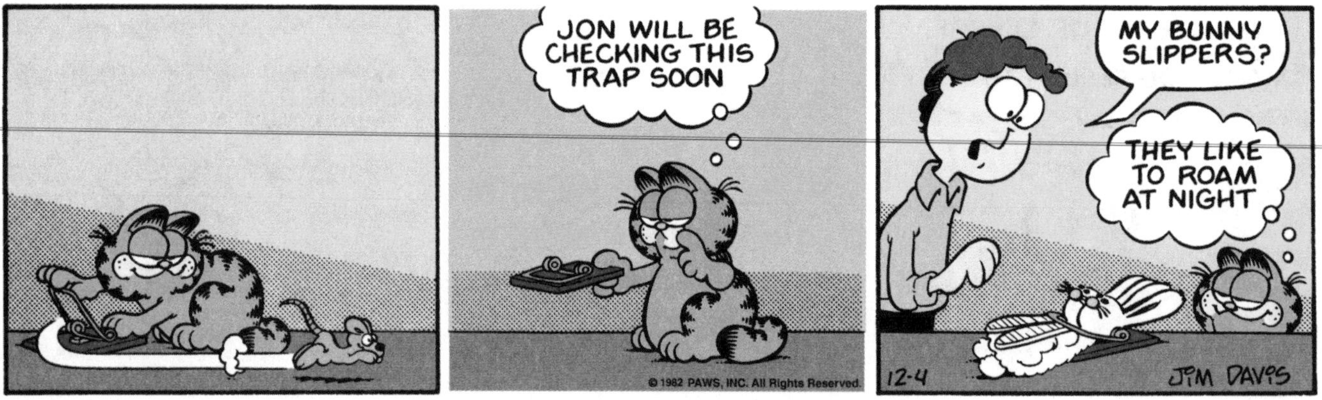
JON WILL BE CHECKING THIS TRAP SOON
© 1982 PAWS, INC. All Rights Reserved.
MY BUNNY SLIPPERS?
THEY LIKE TO ROAM AT NIGHT
12-4
JIM DAVIS

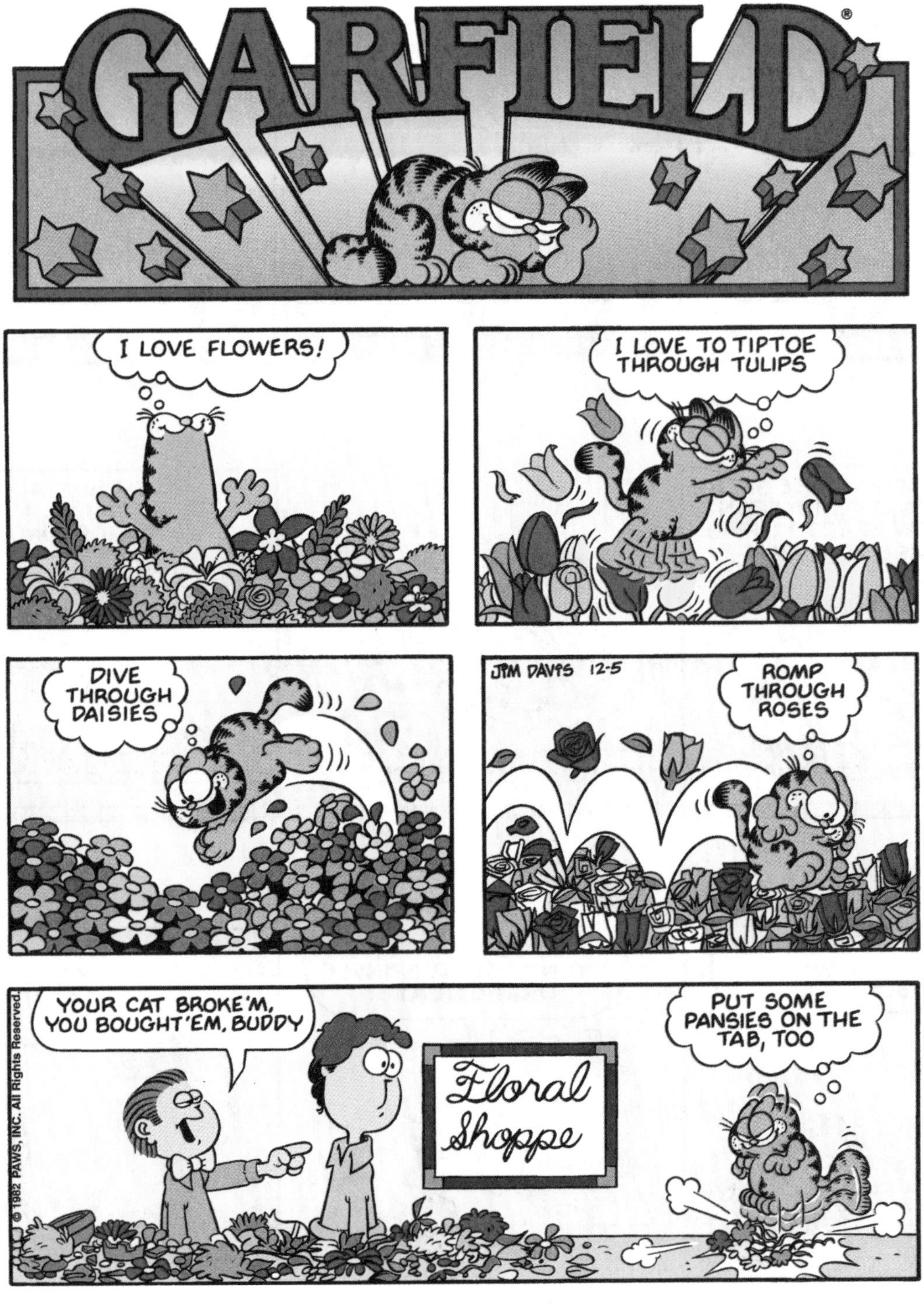
GARFIELD
I LOVE FLOWERS!
I LOVE TO TIPTOE THROUGH TULIPS
DIVE THROUGH DAISIES
JIM DAVIS 12-5
ROMP THROUGH ROSES
YOUR CAT BROKE'M, YOU BOUGHT'EM, BUDDY
Floral Shoppe
PUT SOME PANSIES ON THE TAB, TOO
© 1982 PAWS, INC. All Rights Reserved.

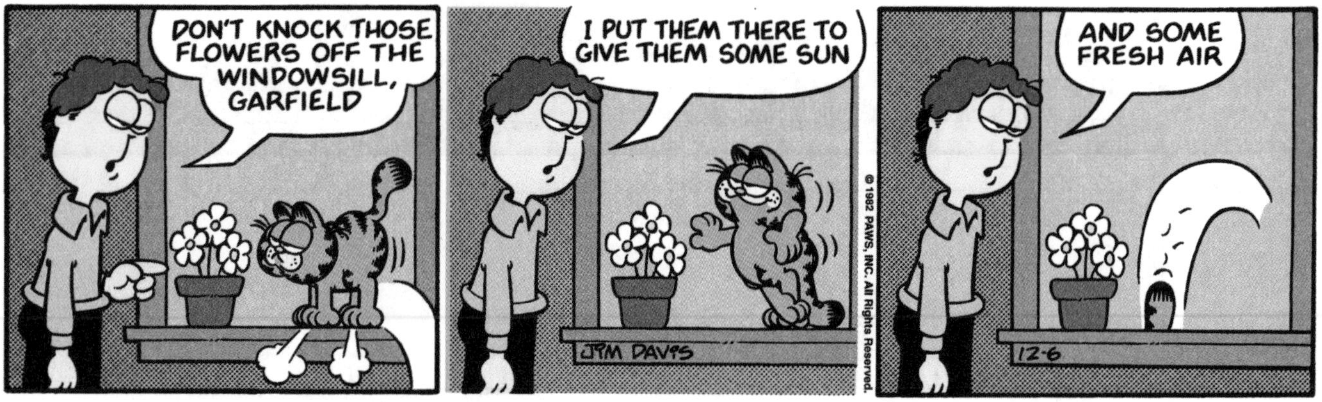
DON'T KNOCK THOSE FLOWERS OFF THE WINDOWSILL, GARFIELD
I PUT THEM THERE TO GIVE THEM SOME SUN
AND SOME FRESH AIR
JIM DAVIS
12-6
© 1982 PAWS, INC. All Rights Reserved.

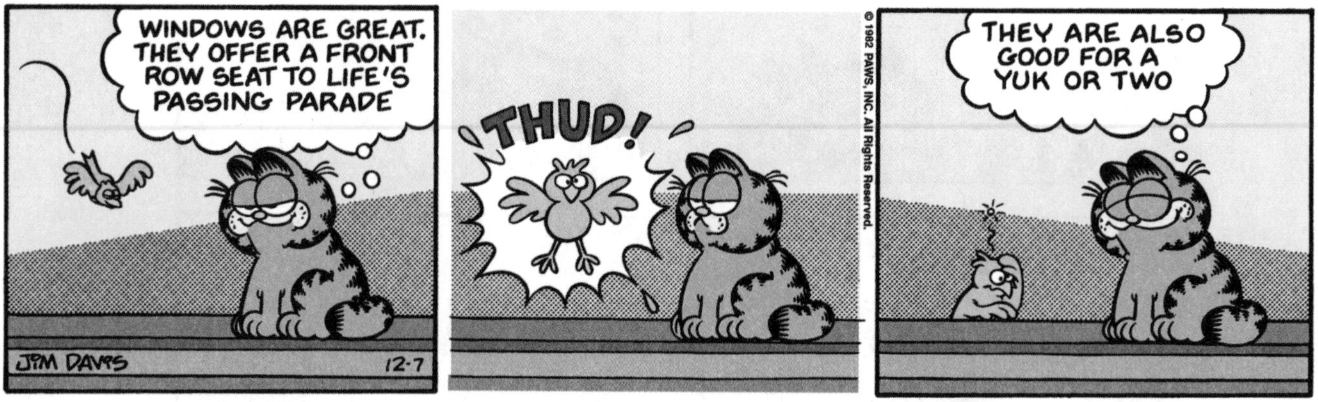
WINDOWS ARE GREAT. THEY OFFER A FRONT ROW SEAT TO LIFE'S PASSING PARADE
JIM DAVIS
12-7
THUD!
THEY ARE ALSO GOOD FOR A YUK OR TWO
© 1982 PAWS, INC. All Rights Reserved.

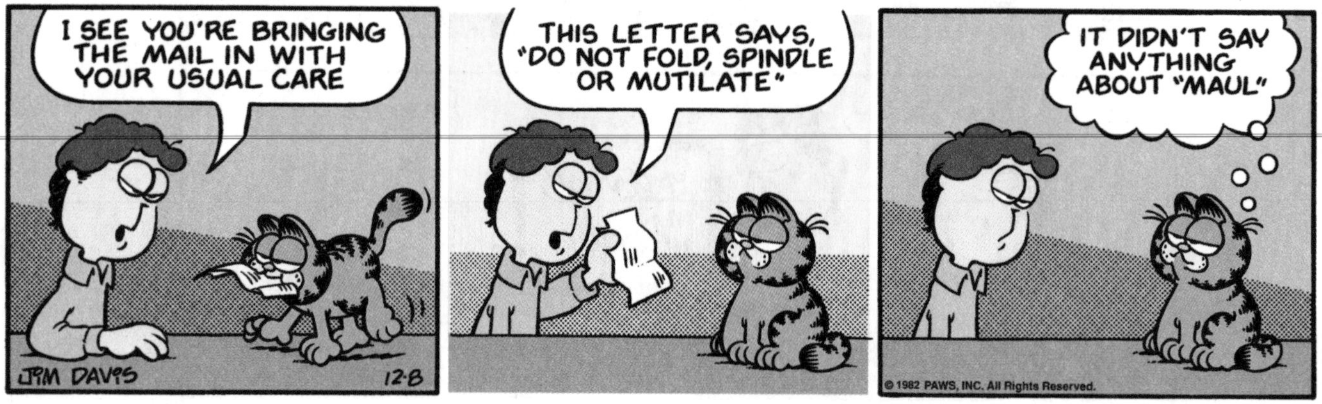
I SEE YOU'RE BRINGING THE MAIL IN WITH YOUR USUAL CARE
JIM DAVIS
12-8
THIS LETTER SAYS, "DO NOT FOLD, SPINDLE OR MUTILATE"
IT DIDN'T SAY ANYTHING ABOUT "MAUL"
© 1982 PAWS, INC. All Rights Reserved.

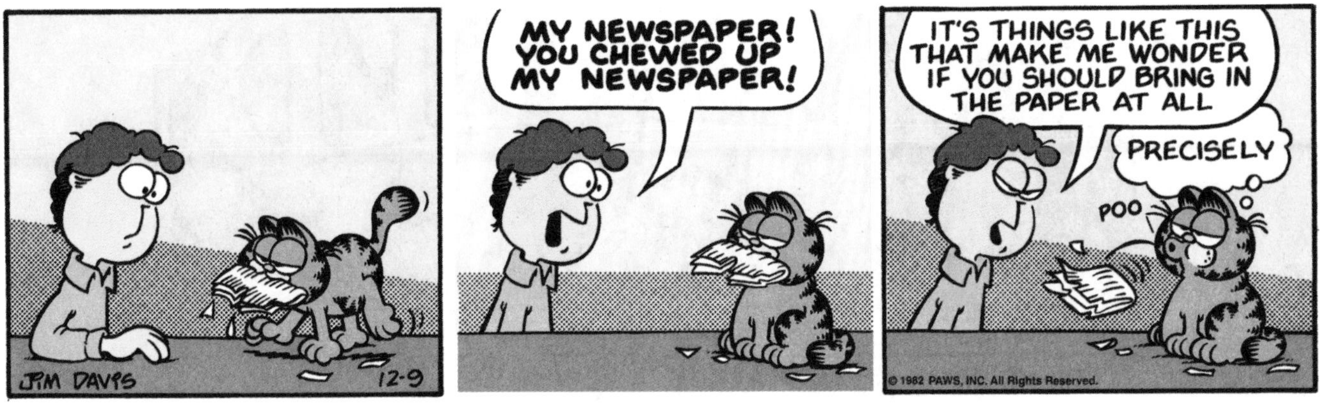
JIM DAVIS
12-9
MY NEWSPAPER! YOU CHEWED UP MY NEWSPAPER!
IT'S THINGS LIKE THIS THAT MAKE ME WONDER IF YOU SHOULD BRING IN THE PAPER AT ALL
PRECISELY
POO
© 1982 PAWS, INC. All Rights Reserved.

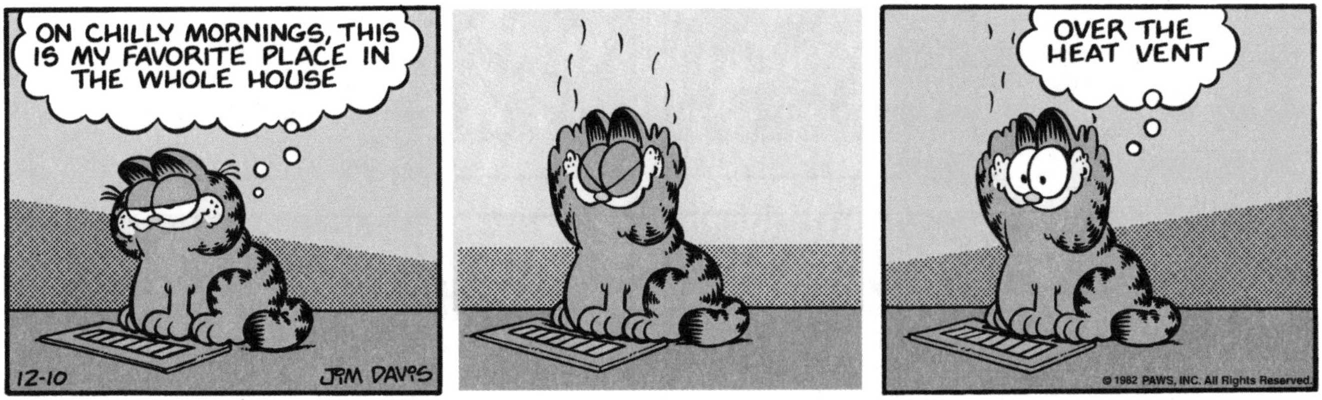
ON CHILLY MORNINGS, THIS IS MY FAVORITE PLACE IN THE WHOLE HOUSE
12-10
JIM DAVIS
OVER THE HEAT VENT
© 1982 PAWS, INC. All Rights Reserved.

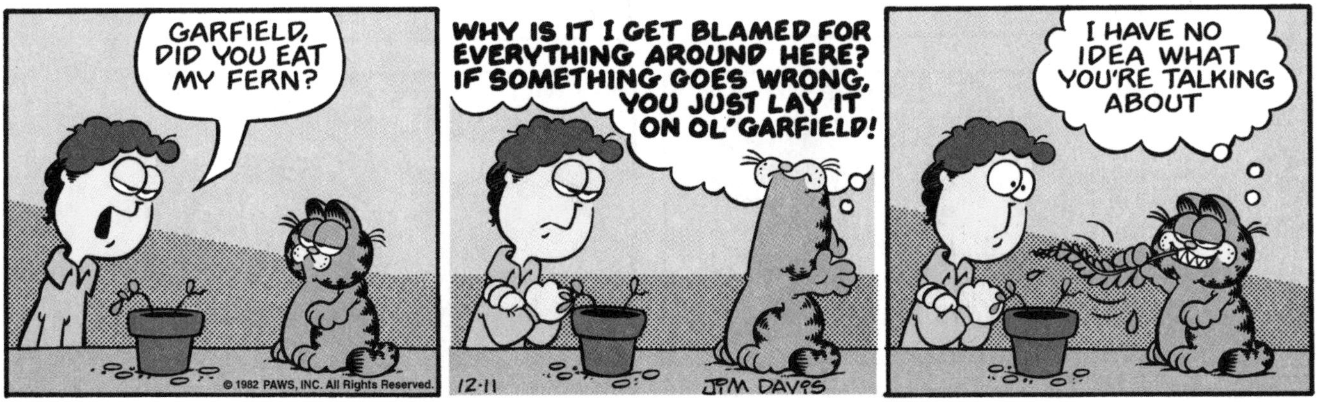
GARFIELD, DID YOU EAT MY FERN?
© 1982 PAWS, INC. All Rights Reserved.
WHY IS IT I GET BLAMED FOR EVERYTHING AROUND HERE? IF SOMETHING GOES WRONG, YOU JUST LAY IT ON OL' GARFIELD!
12-11
JIM DAVIS
I HAVE NO IDEA WHAT YOU'RE TALKING ABOUT

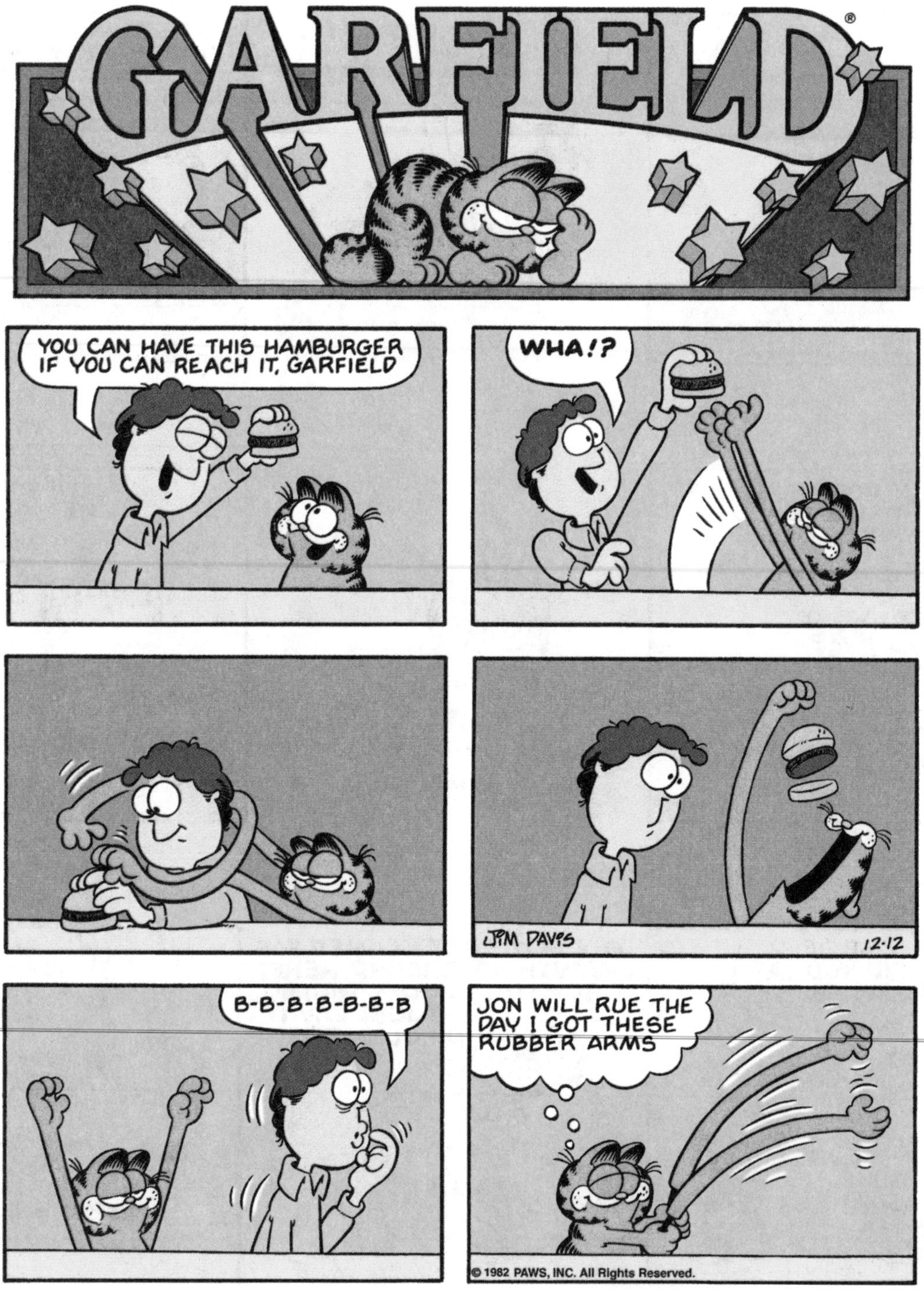
GARFIELD®
YOU CAN HAVE THIS HAMBURGER IF YOU CAN REACH IT, GARFIELD
WHA!?
JIM DAVIS
12-12
B-B-B-B-B-B-B
JON WILL RUE THE DAY I GOT THESE RUBBER ARMS
© 1982 PAWS, INC. All Rights Reserved.

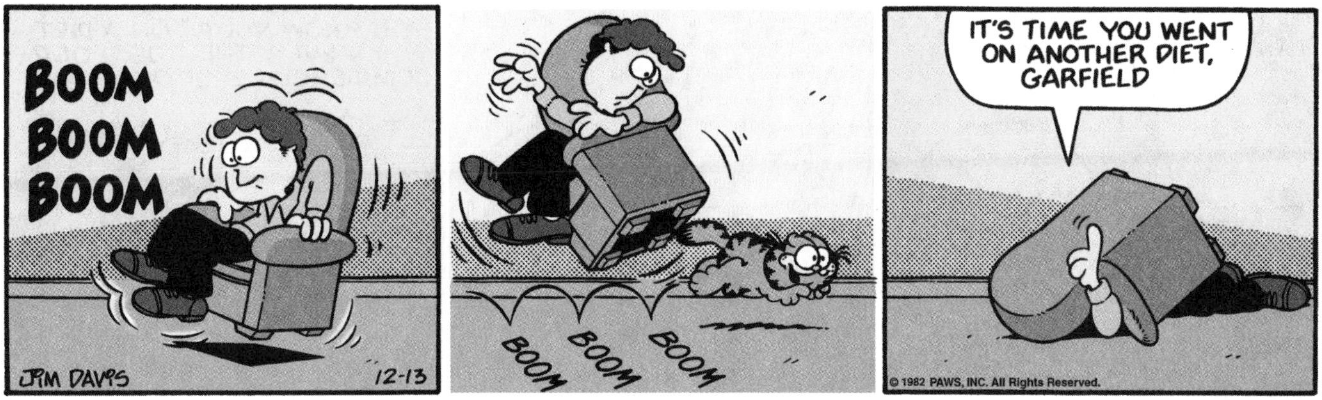
BOOM
BOOM
BOOM
JIM DAVIS
12-13
BOOM BOOM BOOM
IT'S TIME YOU WENT ON ANOTHER DIET, GARFIELD
© 1982 PAWS, INC. All Rights Reserved.

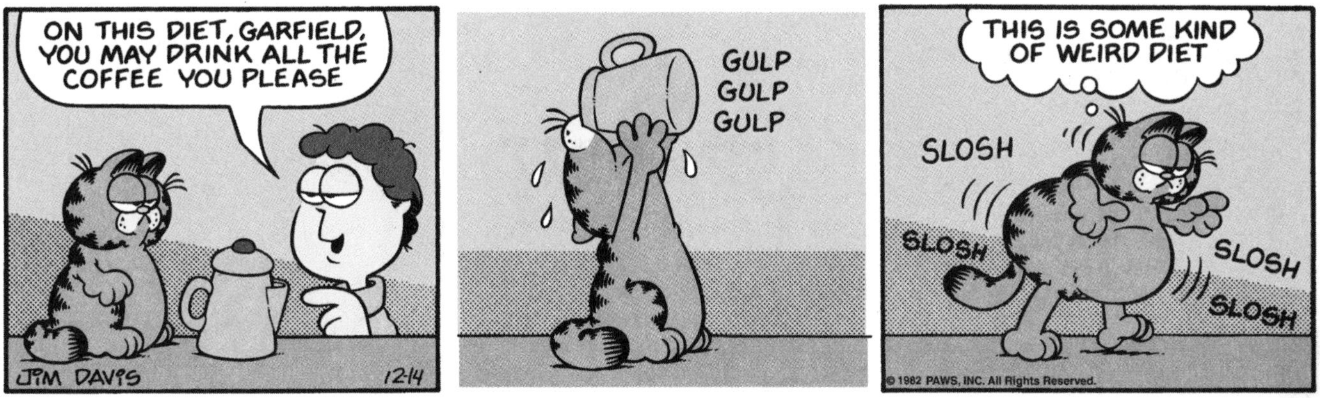
ON THIS DIET, GARFIELD, YOU MAY DRINK ALL THE COFFEE YOU PLEASE
JIM DAVIS
12-14
GULP
GULP
GULP
THIS IS SOME KIND OF WEIRD DIET
SLOSH
SLOSH
SLOSH
SLOSH
© 1982 PAWS, INC. All Rights Reserved.

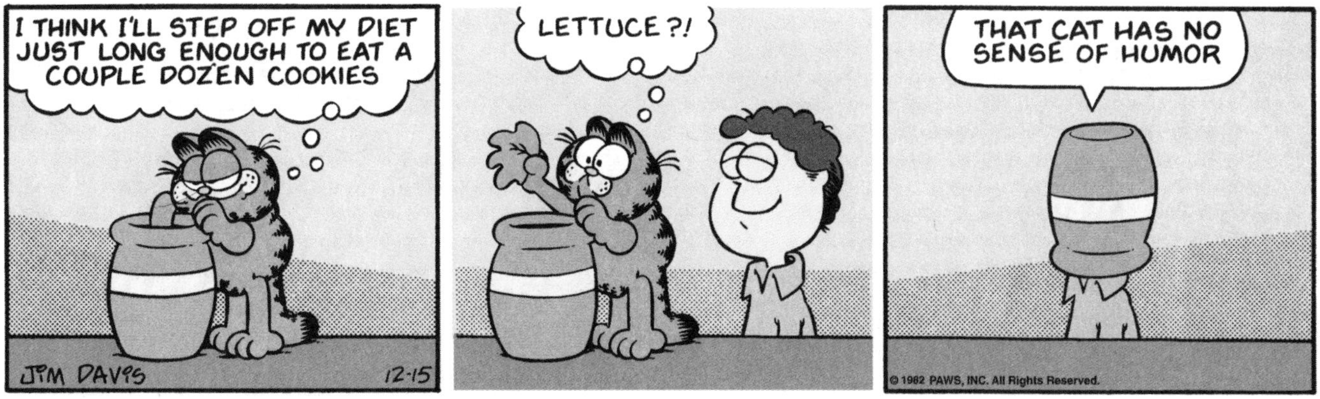
I THINK I'LL STEP OFF MY DIET JUST LONG ENOUGH TO EAT A COUPLE DOZEN COOKIES
JIM DAVIS
12-15
LETTUCE?!
THAT CAT HAS NO SENSE OF HUMOR
© 1982 PAWS, INC. All Rights Reserved.

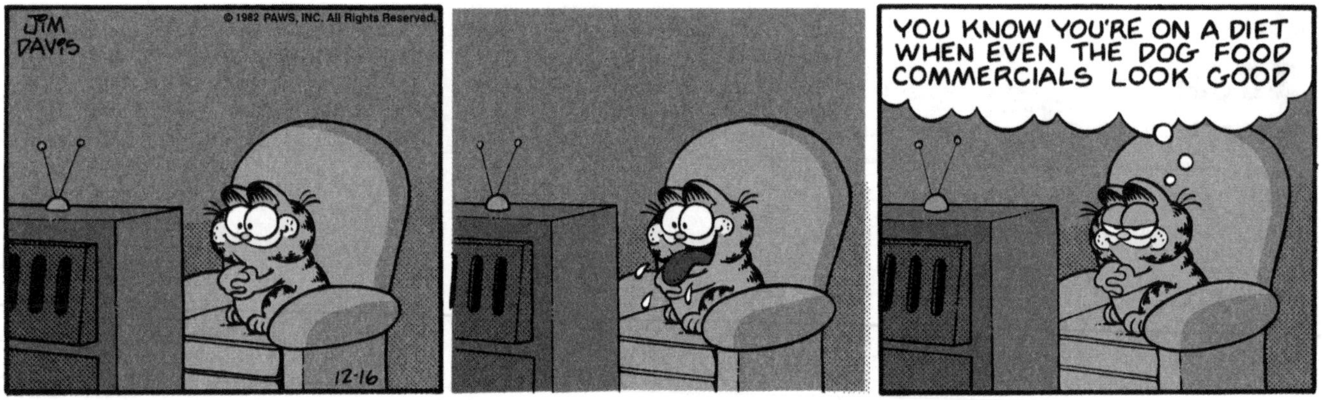
JIM DAVIS
© 1982 PAWS, INC. All Rights Reserved.
12-16
YOU KNOW YOU'RE ON A DIET WHEN EVEN THE DOG FOOD COMMERCIALS LOOK GOOD

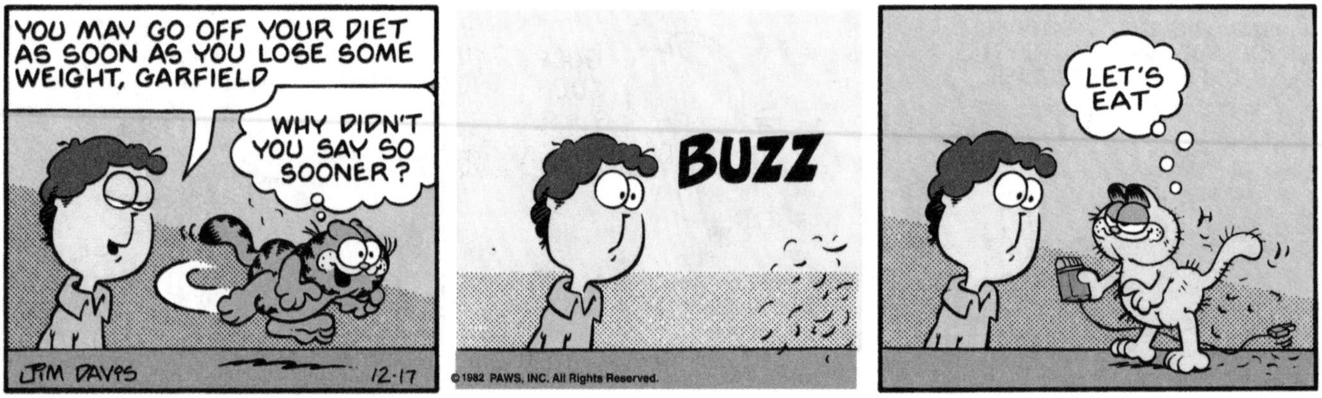
YOU MAY GO OFF YOUR DIET AS SOON AS YOU LOSE SOME WEIGHT, GARFIELD
WHY DIDN'T YOU SAY SO SOONER?
JIM DAVIS
12-17
BUZZ
© 1982 PAWS, INC. All Rights Reserved.
LET'S EAT

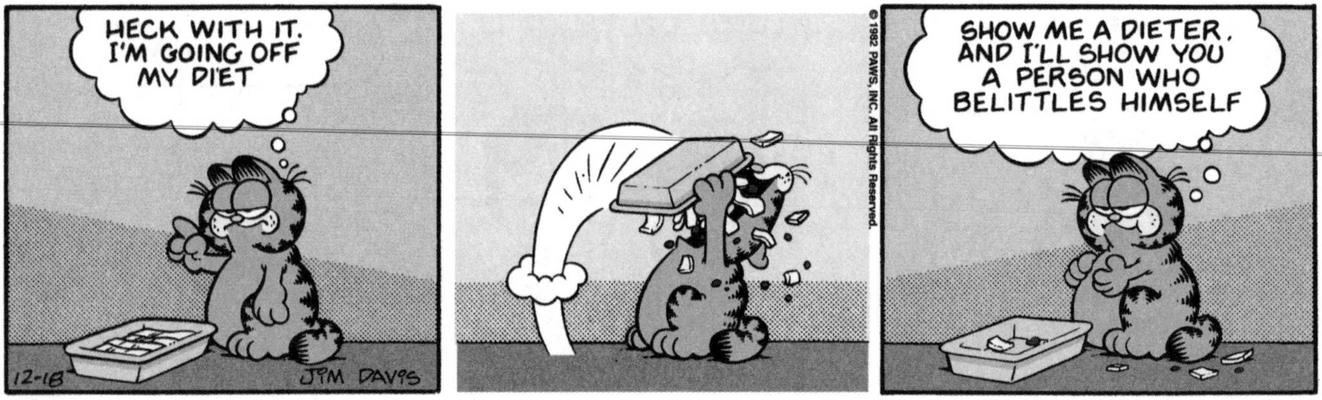
HECK WITH IT. I'M GOING OFF MY DIET
12-18
JIM DAVIS
© 1982 PAWS, INC. All Rights Reserved.
SHOW ME A DIETER, AND I'LL SHOW YOU A PERSON WHO BELITTLES HIMSELF

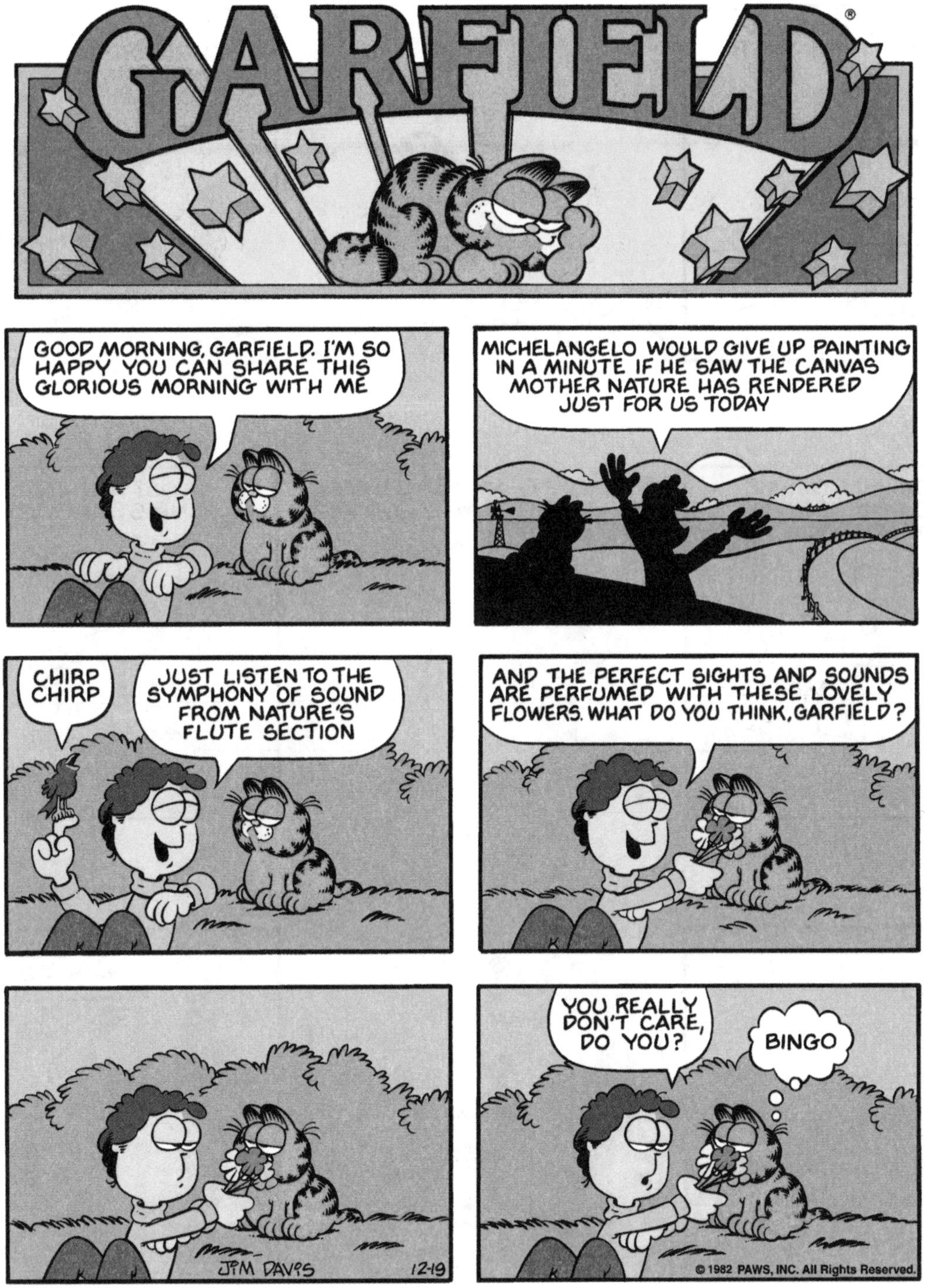
GARFIELD
GOOD MORNING, GARFIELD. I'M SO HAPPY YOU CAN SHARE THIS GLORIOUS MORNING WITH ME
MICHELANGELO WOULD GIVE UP PAINTING IN A MINUTE IF HE SAW THE CANVAS MOTHER NATURE HAS RENDERED JUST FOR US TODAY
CHIRP CHIRP
JUST LISTEN TO THE SYMPHONY OF SOUND FROM NATURE'S FLUTE SECTION
AND THE PERFECT SIGHTS AND SOUNDS ARE PERFUMED WITH THESE LOVELY FLOWERS. WHAT DO YOU THINK, GARFIELD?
JIM DAVIS 12-19
YOU REALLY DON'T CARE, DO YOU?
BINGO
© 1982 PAWS, INC. All Rights Reserved.

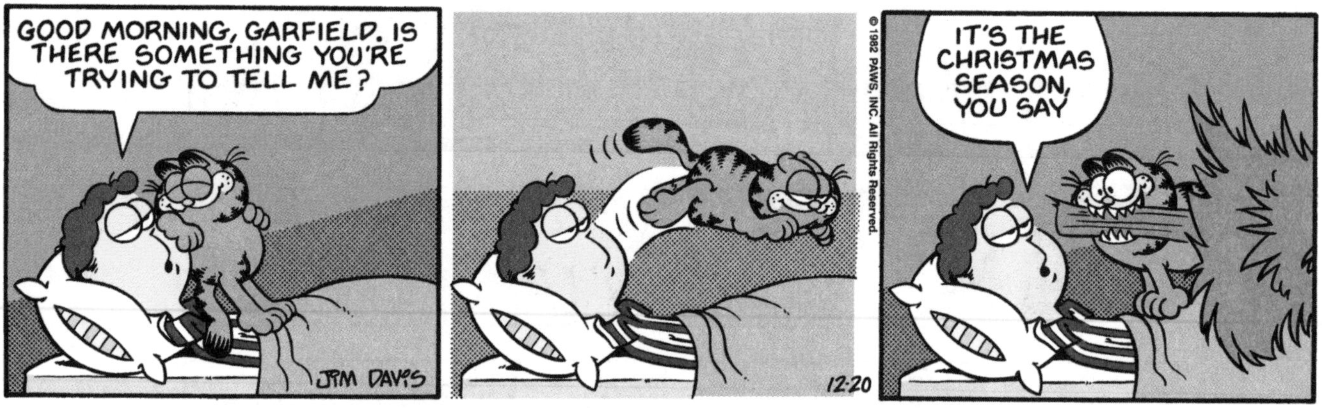
GOOD MORNING, GARFIELD. IS THERE SOMETHING YOU'RE TRYING TO TELL ME?
JIM DAVIS
12·20
© 1982 PAWS, INC. All Rights Reserved.
IT'S THE CHRISTMAS SEASON, YOU SAY

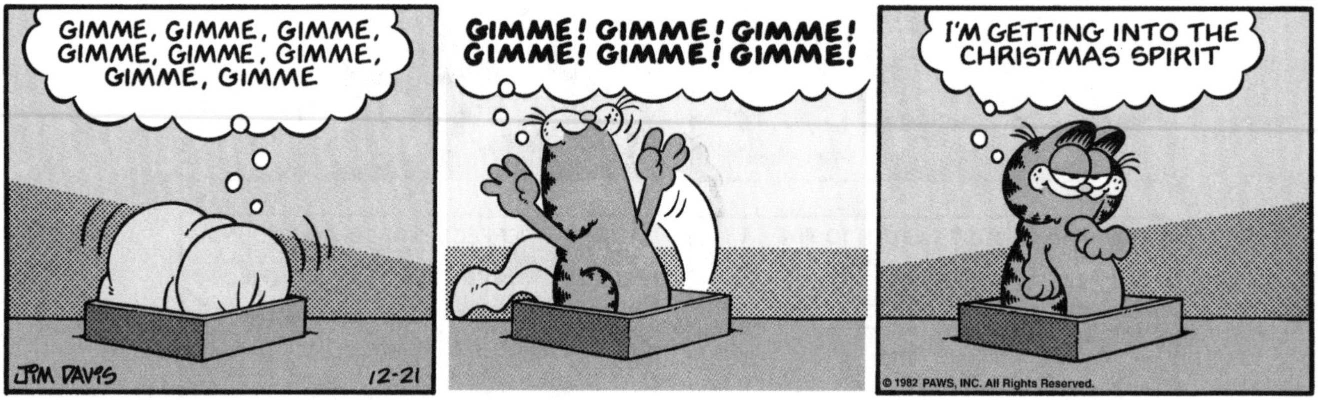
GIMME, GIMME, GIMME, GIMME, GIMME, GIMME, GIMME, GIMME
JIM DAVIS
12-21
GIMME! GIMME! GIMME! GIMME! GIMME! GIMME!
I'M GETTING INTO THE CHRISTMAS SPIRIT
© 1982 PAWS, INC. All Rights Reserved.

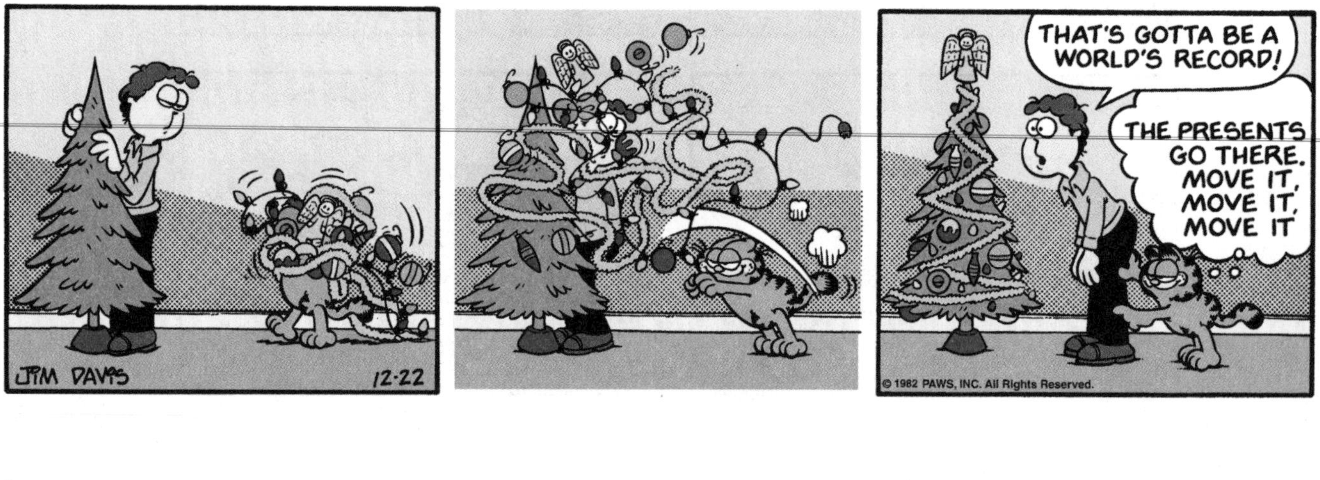
JIM DAVIS
12-22
THAT'S GOTTA BE A WORLD'S RECORD!
THE PRESENTS GO THERE. MOVE IT, MOVE IT, MOVE IT
© 1982 PAWS, INC. All Rights Reserved.

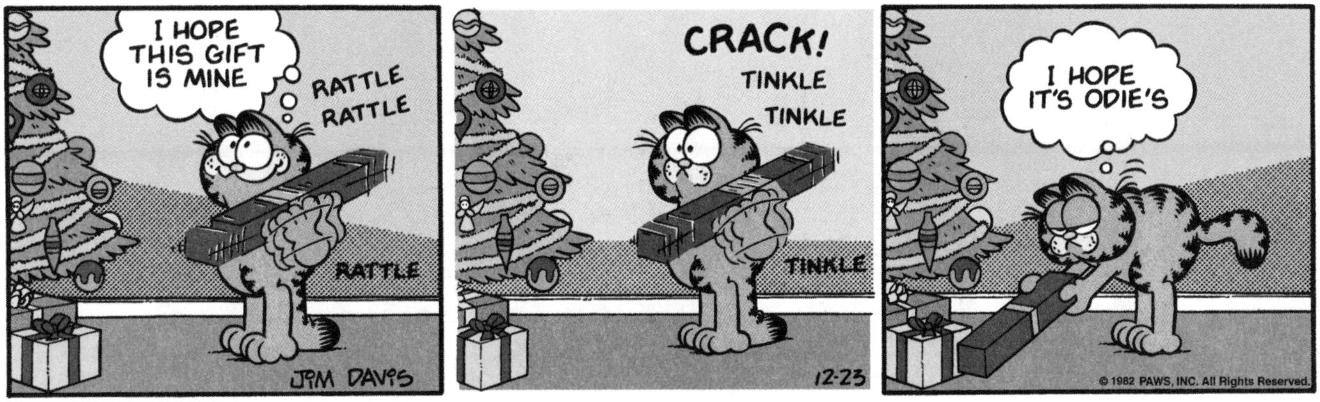
I HOPE THIS GIFT IS MINE
RATTLE RATTLE
RATTLE
JIM DAVIS
CRACK!
TINKLE
TINKLE
TINKLE
12-23
I HOPE IT'S ODIE'S
© 1982 PAWS, INC. All Rights Reserved.

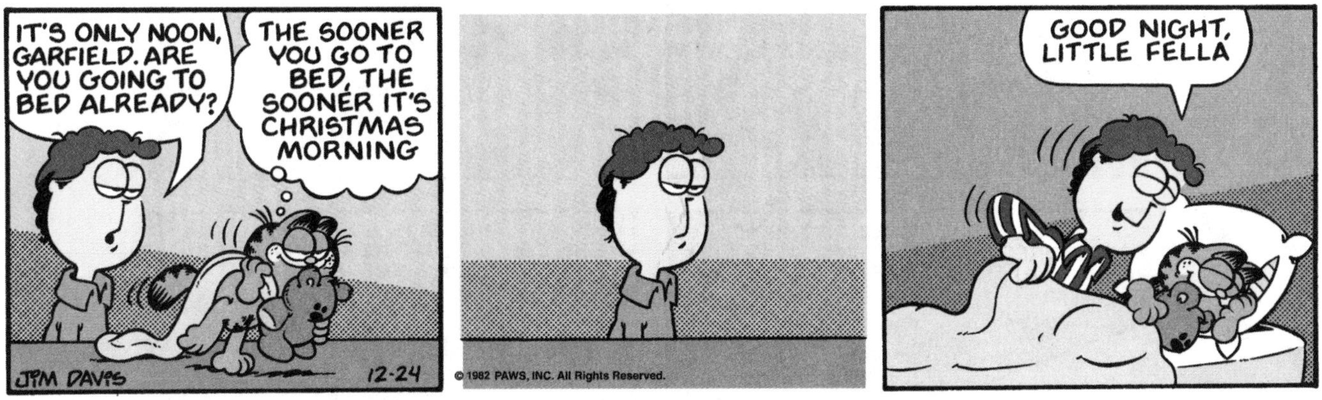
IT'S ONLY NOON, GARFIELD. ARE YOU GOING TO BED ALREADY?
THE SOONER YOU GO TO BED, THE SOONER IT'S CHRISTMAS MORNING
JIM DAVIS
12-24
© 1982 PAWS, INC. All Rights Reserved.
GOOD NIGHT, LITTLE FELLA

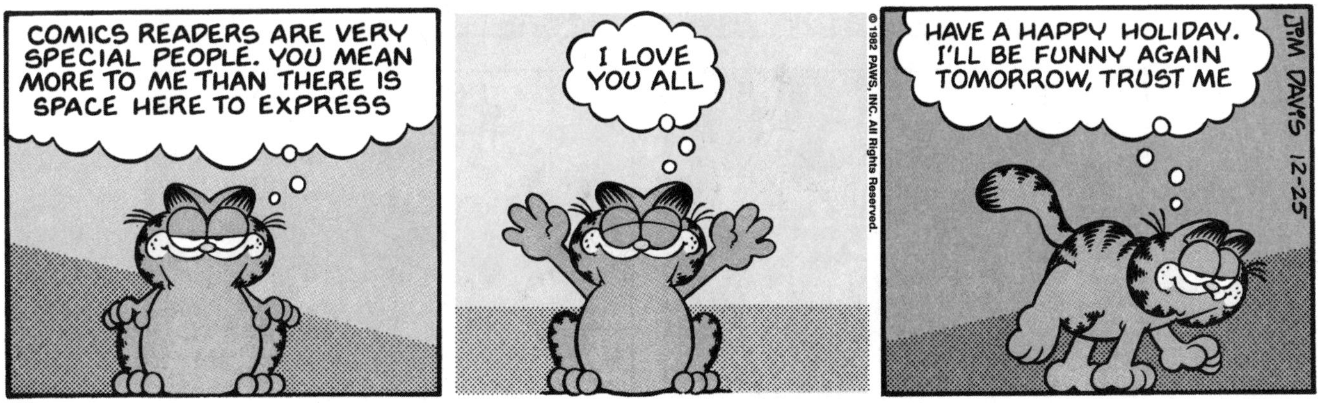
COMICS READERS ARE VERY SPECIAL PEOPLE. YOU MEAN MORE TO ME THAN THERE IS SPACE HERE TO EXPRESS
I LOVE YOU ALL
© 1982 PAWS, INC. All Rights Reserved.
HAVE A HAPPY HOLIDAY. I'LL BE FUNNY AGAIN TOMORROW, TRUST ME
JIM DAVIS 12-25

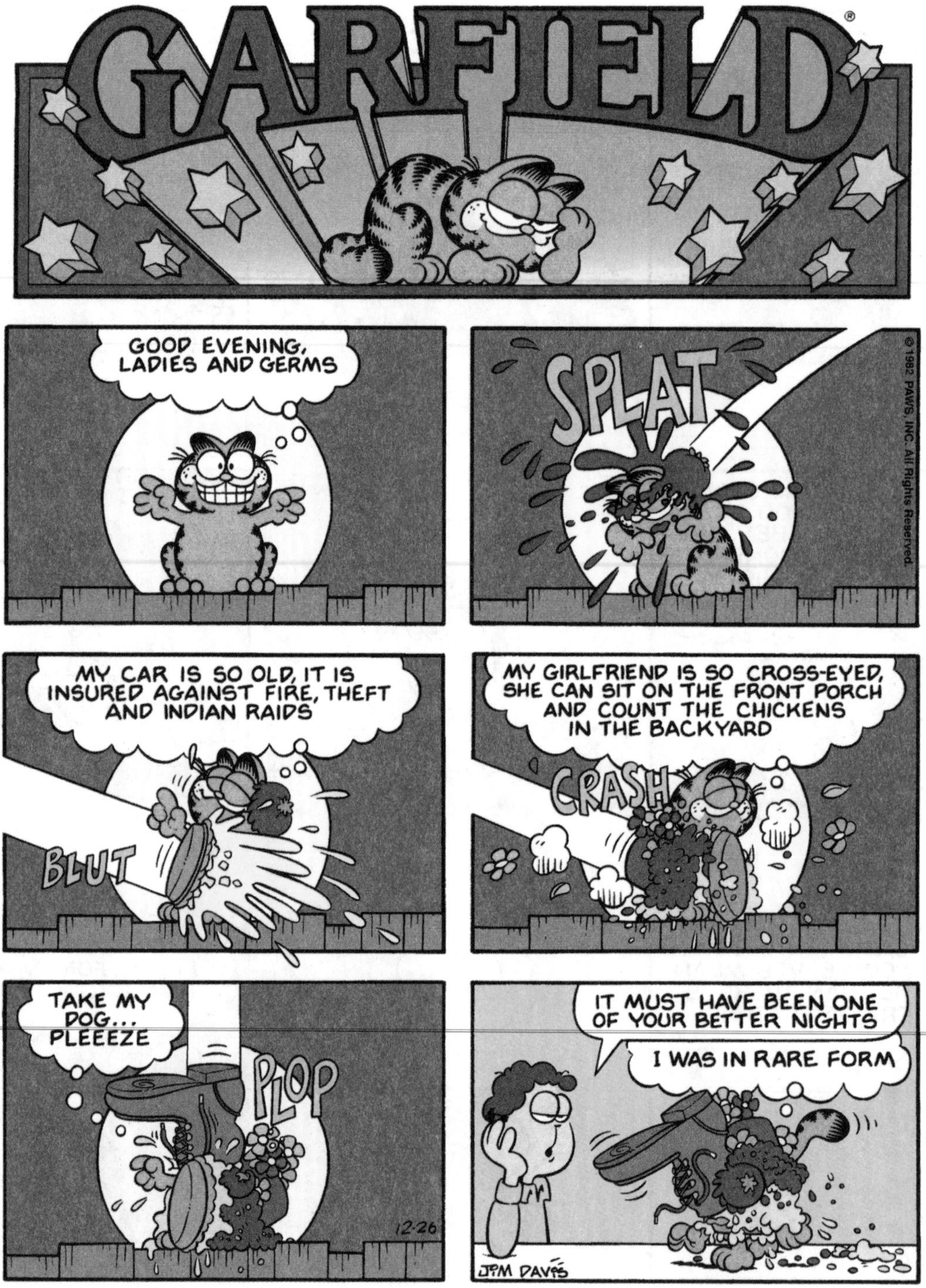
GARFIELD
GOOD EVENING, LADIES AND GERMS
SPLAT
© 1982 PAWS, INC. All Rights Reserved.
MY CAR IS SO OLD, IT IS INSURED AGAINST FIRE, THEFT AND INDIAN RAIDS
BLUT
MY GIRLFRIEND IS SO CROSS-EYED, SHE CAN SIT ON THE FRONT PORCH AND COUNT THE CHICKENS IN THE BACKYARD
CRASH
TAKE MY DOG... PLEEEZE
PLOP
12-26
IT MUST HAVE BEEN ONE OF YOUR BETTER NIGHTS
I WAS IN RARE FORM
JIM DAVIS

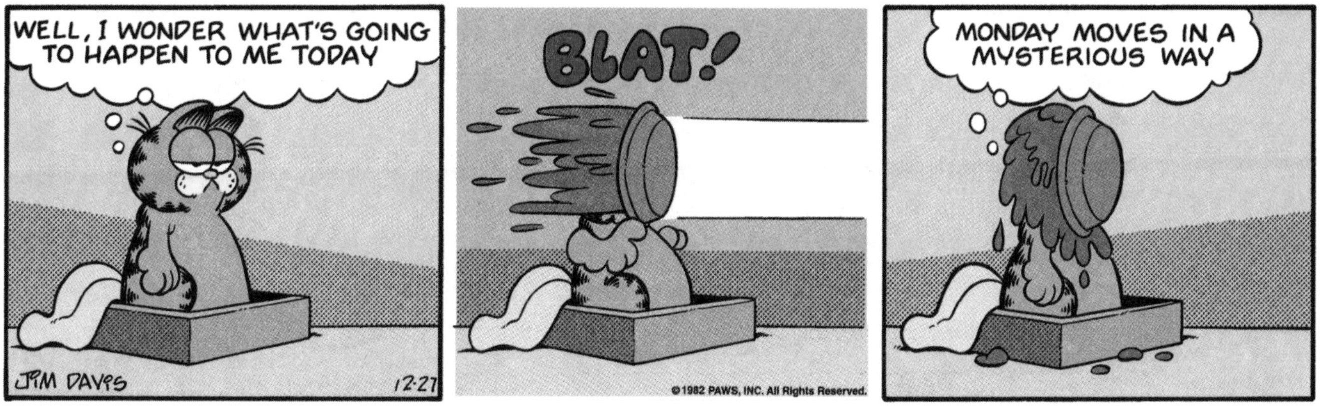
WELL, I WONDER WHAT'S GOING TO HAPPEN TO ME TODAY
JIM DAVIS
12-27
BLAT!
© 1982 PAWS, INC. All Rights Reserved.
MONDAY MOVES IN A MYSTERIOUS WAY

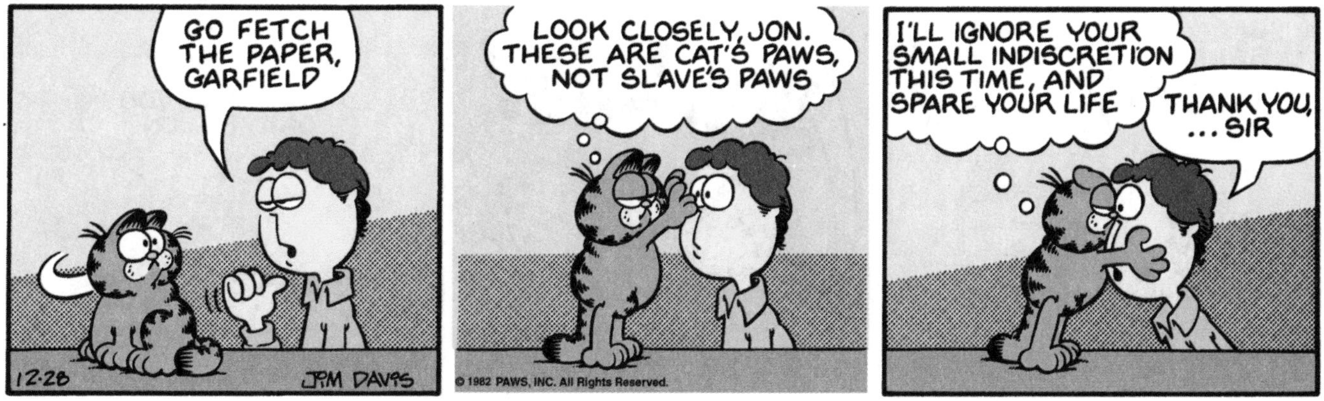
GO FETCH THE PAPER, GARFIELD
12-28
JIM DAVIS
LOOK CLOSELY, JON. THESE ARE CAT'S PAWS, NOT SLAVE'S PAWS
© 1982 PAWS, INC. All Rights Reserved.
I'LL IGNORE YOUR SMALL INDISCRETION THIS TIME, AND SPARE YOUR LIFE
THANK YOU, ... SIR

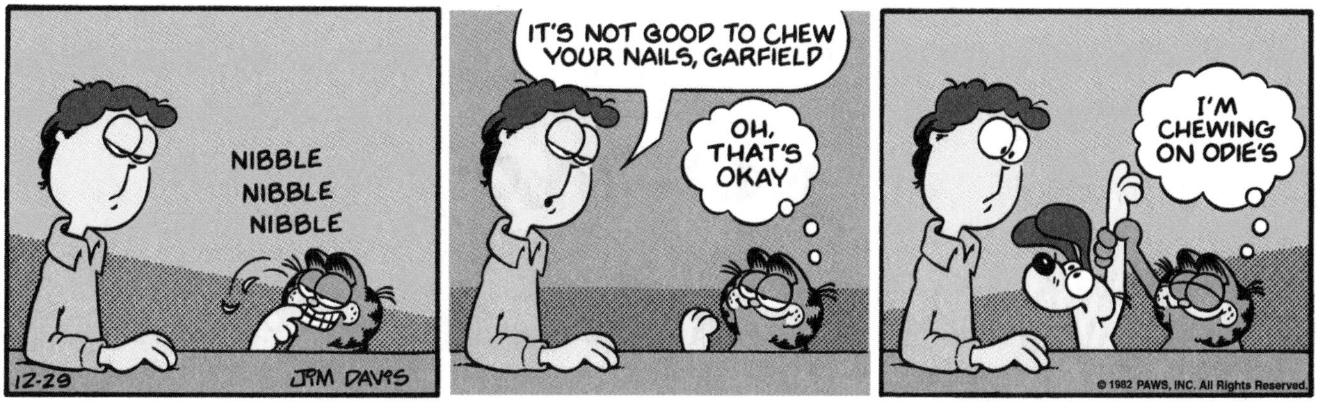
NIBBLE
NIBBLE
NIBBLE
12-29
JIM DAVIS
IT'S NOT GOOD TO CHEW YOUR NAILS, GARFIELD
OH, THAT'S OKAY
I'M CHEWING ON ODIE'S
© 1982 PAWS, INC. All Rights Reserved.

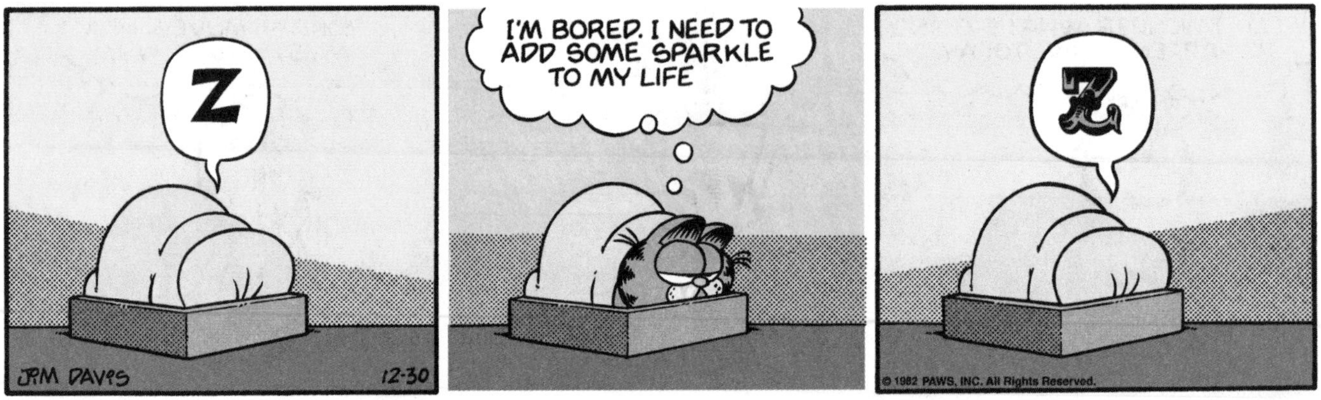
Z
I'M BORED. I NEED TO ADD SOME SPARKLE TO MY LIFE
Z
JIM DAVIS
12-30
© 1982 PAWS, INC. All Rights Reserved.

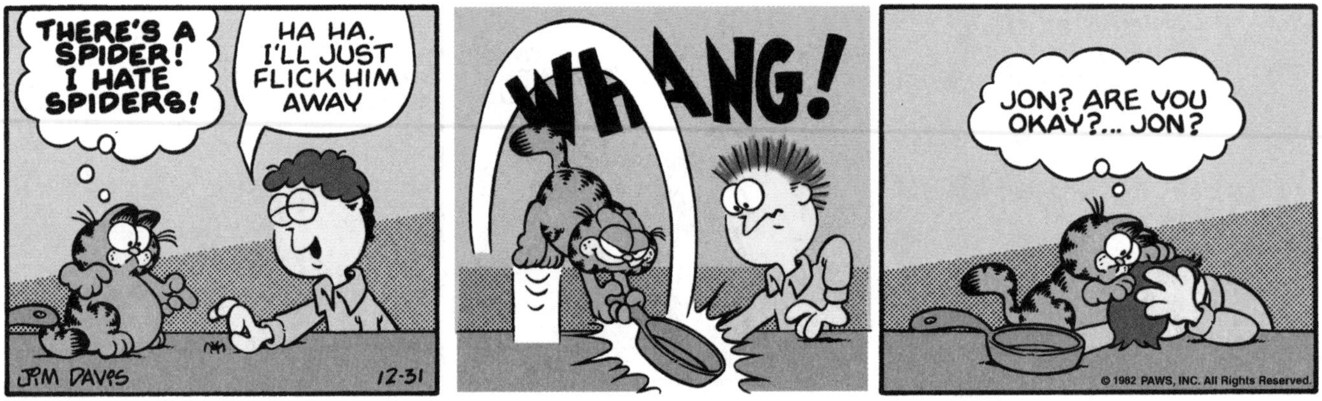
THERE'S A SPIDER! I HATE SPIDERS!
HA HA. I'LL JUST FLICK HIM AWAY
WHANG!
JON? ARE YOU OKAY?... JON?
JIM DAVIS
12-31
© 1982 PAWS, INC. All Rights Reserved.

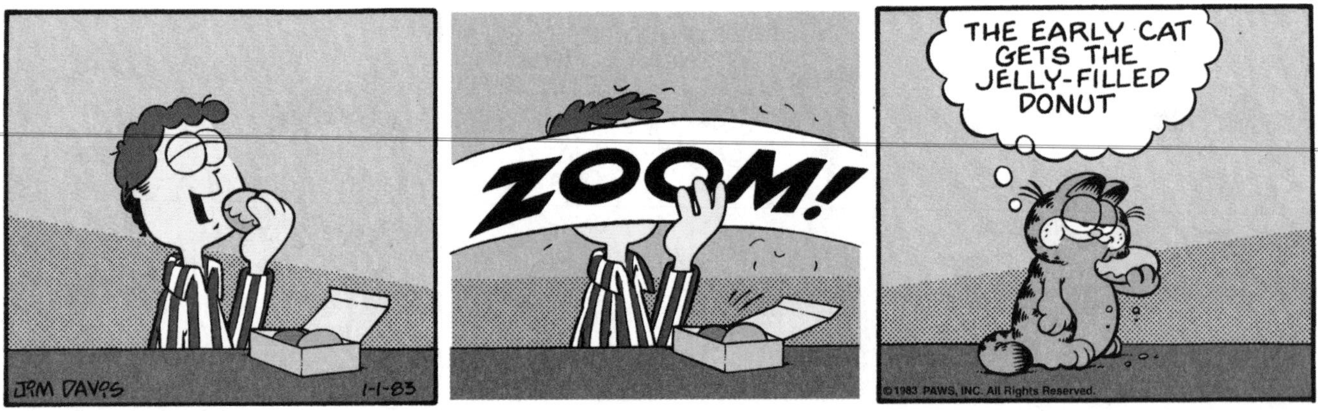
ZOOM!
THE EARLY CAT GETS THE JELLY-FILLED DONUT
JIM DAVIS
1-1-83
©1983 PAWS, INC. All Rights Reserved.

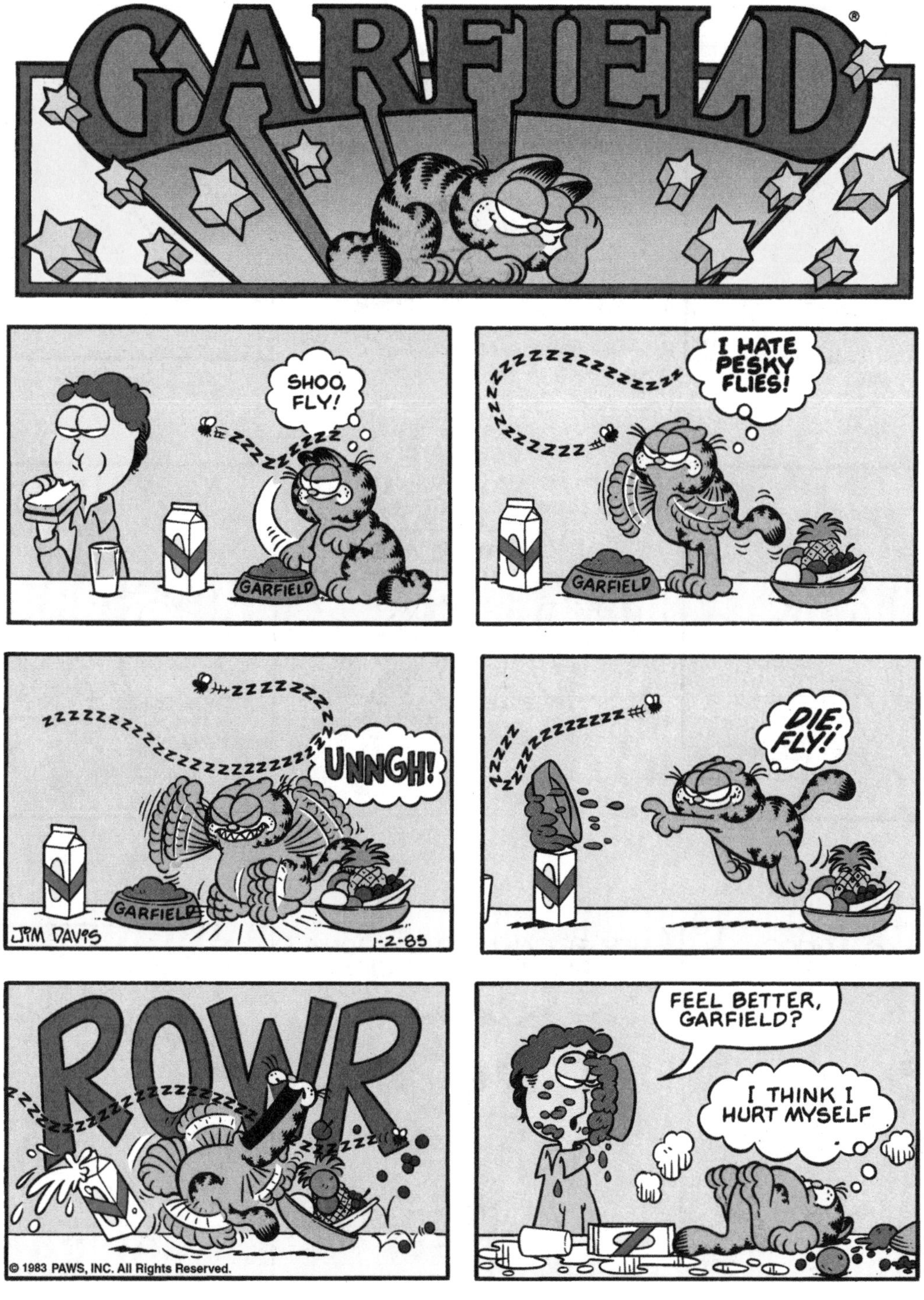
GARFIELD®
SHOO, FLY!
GARFIELD
I HATE PESKY FLIES!
GARFIELD
UNNGH!
GARFIELD
JIM DAVIS
1-2-85
DIE, FLY!
ROWR
© 1983 PAWS, INC. All Rights Reserved.
FEEL BETTER, GARFIELD?
I THINK I HURT MYSELF

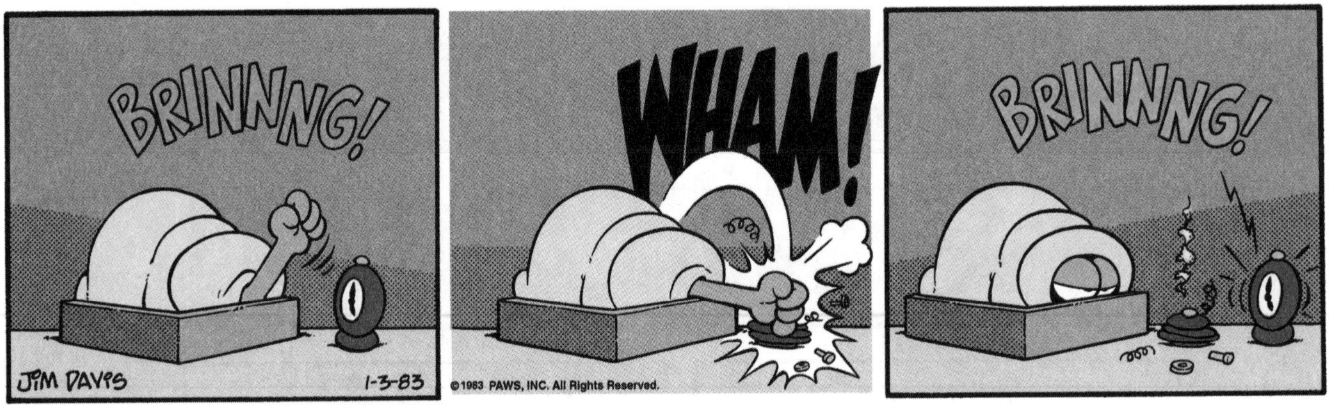
BRINNNG!
JIM DAVIS
1-3-83
WHAM!
©1983 PAWS, INC. All Rights Reserved.
BRINNNG!

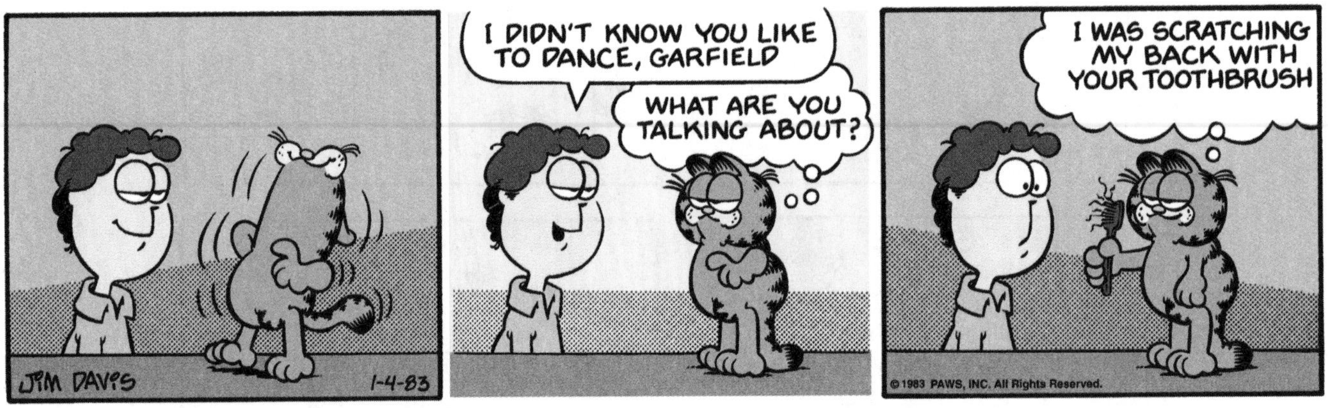
JIM DAVIS
1-4-83
I DIDN'T KNOW YOU LIKE TO DANCE, GARFIELD
WHAT ARE YOU TALKING ABOUT?
I WAS SCRATCHING MY BACK WITH YOUR TOOTHBRUSH
©1983 PAWS, INC. All Rights Reserved.

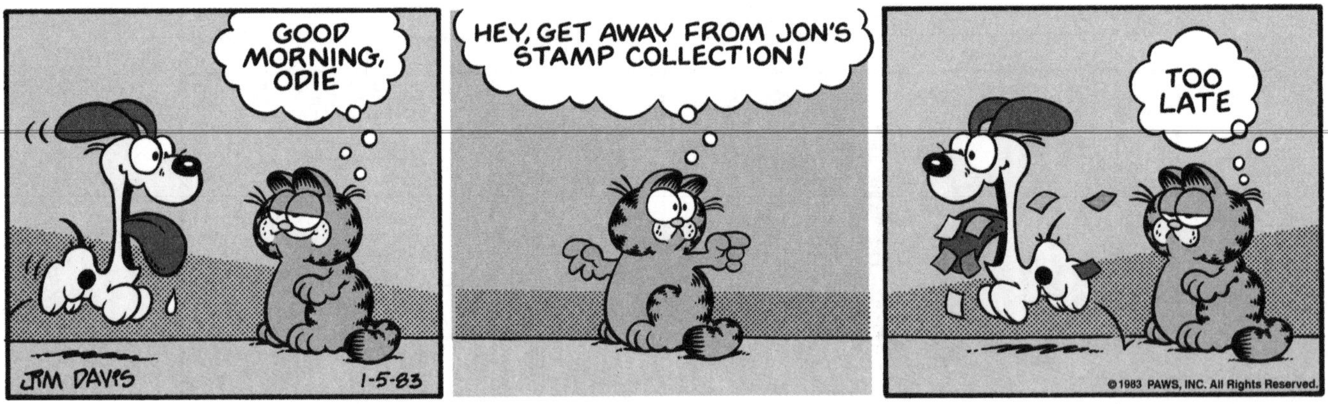
GOOD MORNING, ODIE
JIM DAVIS
1-5-83
HEY, GET AWAY FROM JON'S STAMP COLLECTION!
TOO LATE
©1983 PAWS, INC. All Rights Reserved.

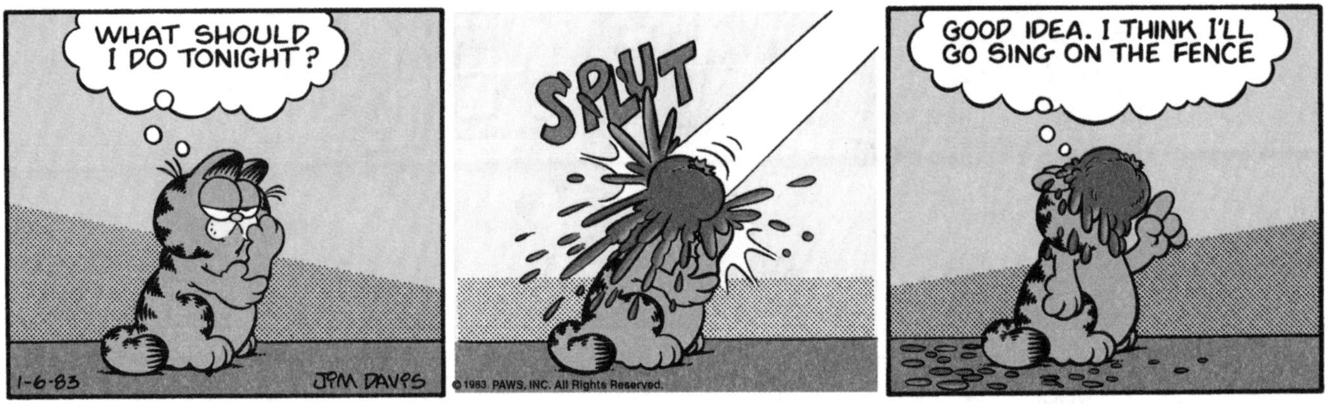
WHAT SHOULD I DO TONIGHT?
1-6-83
JIM DAVIS
SPLUT
© 1983 PAWS, INC. All Rights Reserved.
GOOD IDEA. I THINK I'LL GO SING ON THE FENCE

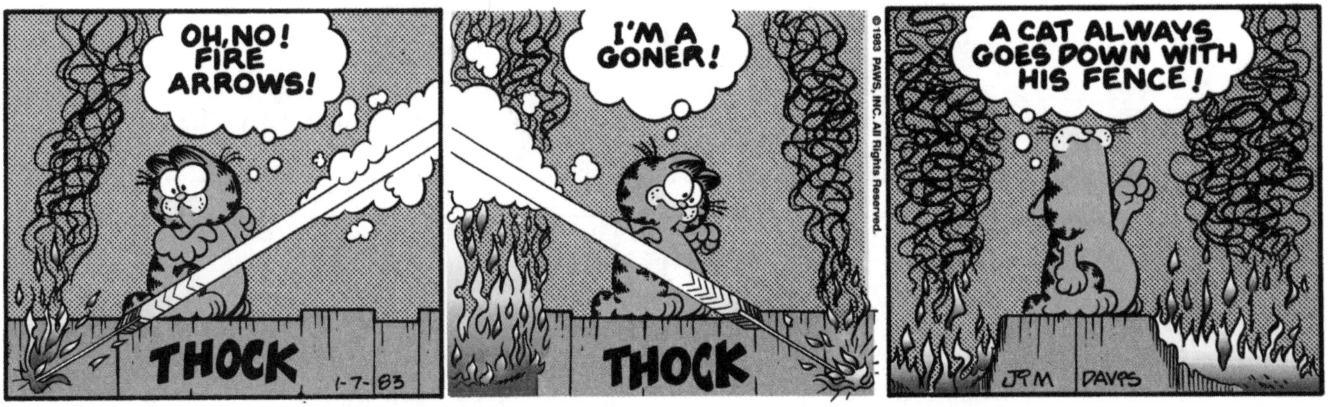
OH, NO! FIRE ARROWS!
THOCK
1-7-83
I'M A GONER!
THOCK
© 1983 PAWS, INC. All Rights Reserved.
A CAT ALWAYS GOES DOWN WITH HIS FENCE!
JIM DAVIS

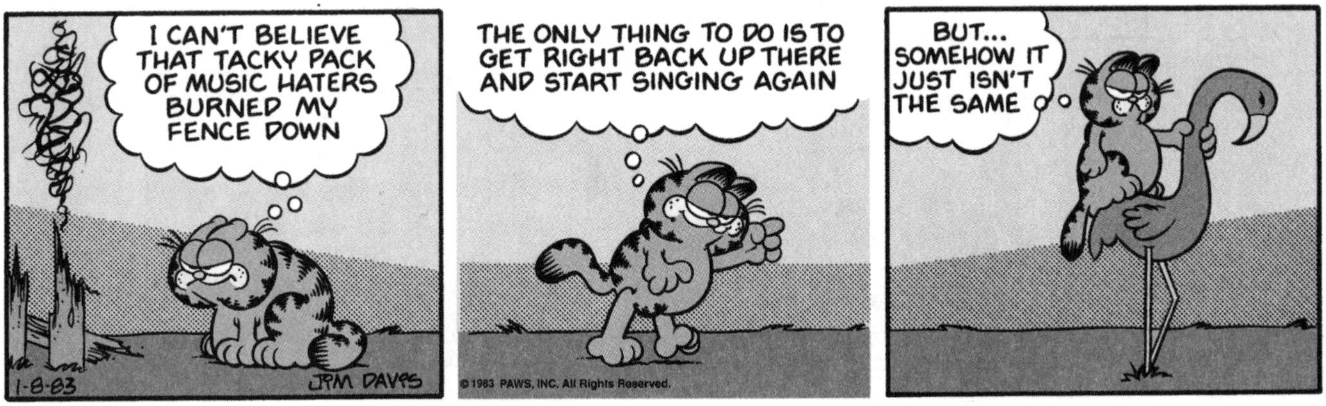
I CAN'T BELIEVE THAT TACKY PACK OF MUSIC HATERS BURNED MY FENCE DOWN
1-8-83
JIM DAVIS
THE ONLY THING TO DO IS TO GET RIGHT BACK UP THERE AND START SINGING AGAIN
© 1983 PAWS, INC. All Rights Reserved.
BUT... SOMEHOW IT JUST ISN'T THE SAME

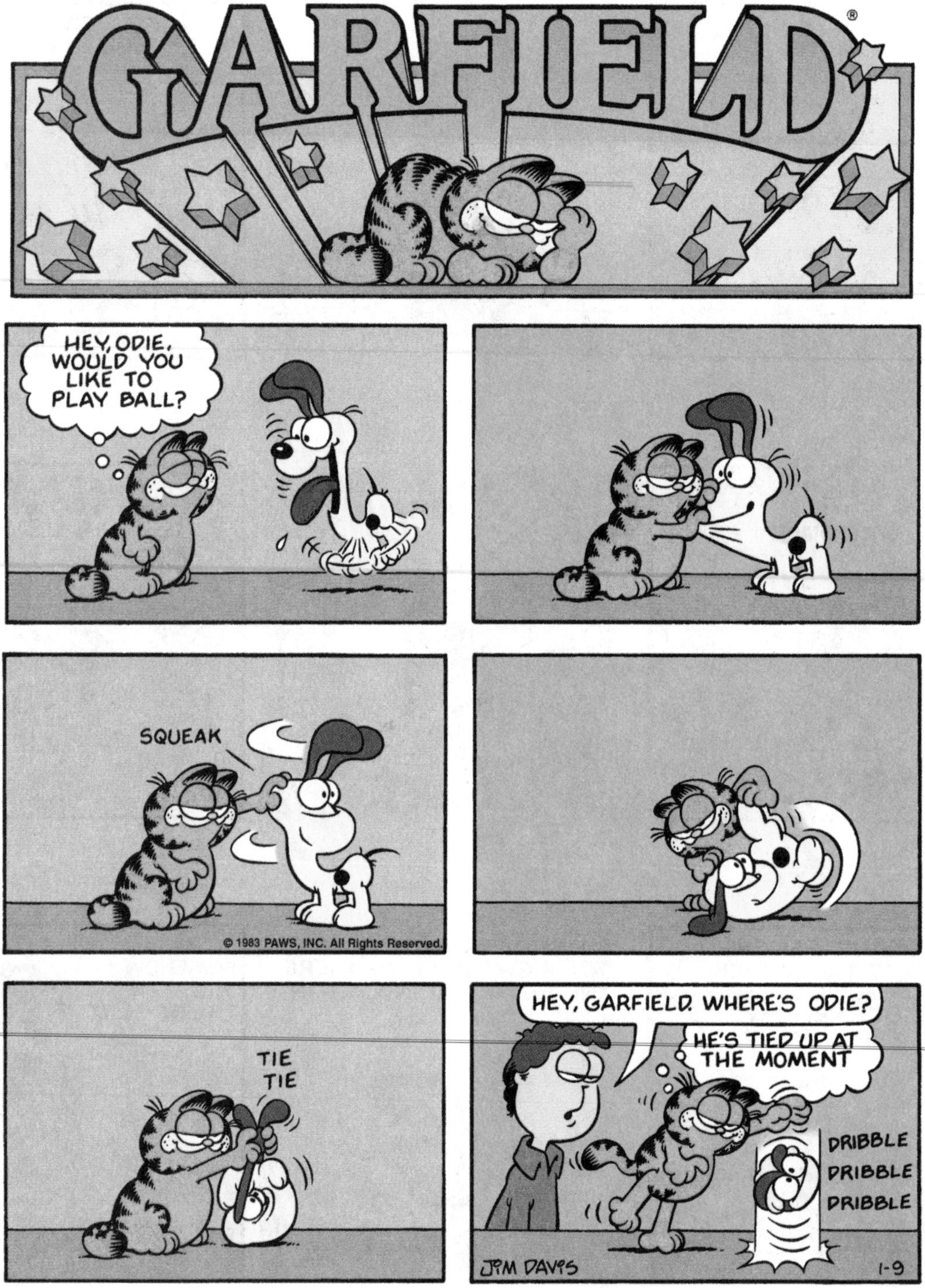
GARFIELD®
HEY, ODIE, WOULD YOU LIKE TO PLAY BALL?
SQUEAK
© 1983 PAWS, INC. All Rights Reserved.
TIE
TIE
HEY, GARFIELD. WHERE'S ODIE?
HE'S TIED UP AT THE MOMENT
DRIBBLE
DRIBBLE
DRIBBLE
JIM DAVIS
1-9

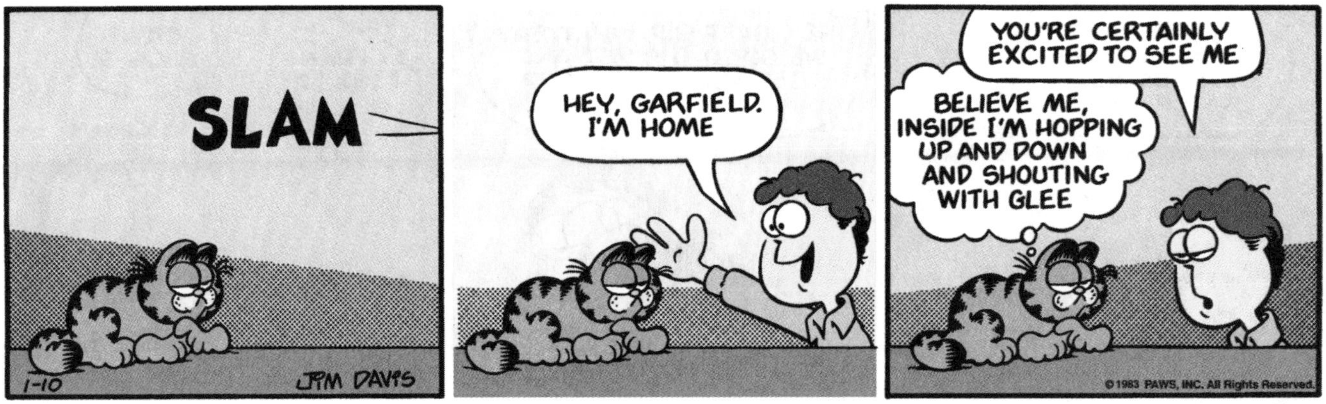
SLAM
HEY, GARFIELD. I'M HOME
YOU'RE CERTAINLY EXCITED TO SEE ME
BELIEVE ME, INSIDE I'M HOPPING UP AND DOWN AND SHOUTING WITH GLEE
1-10
JIM DAVIS
© 1983 PAWS, INC. All Rights Reserved.

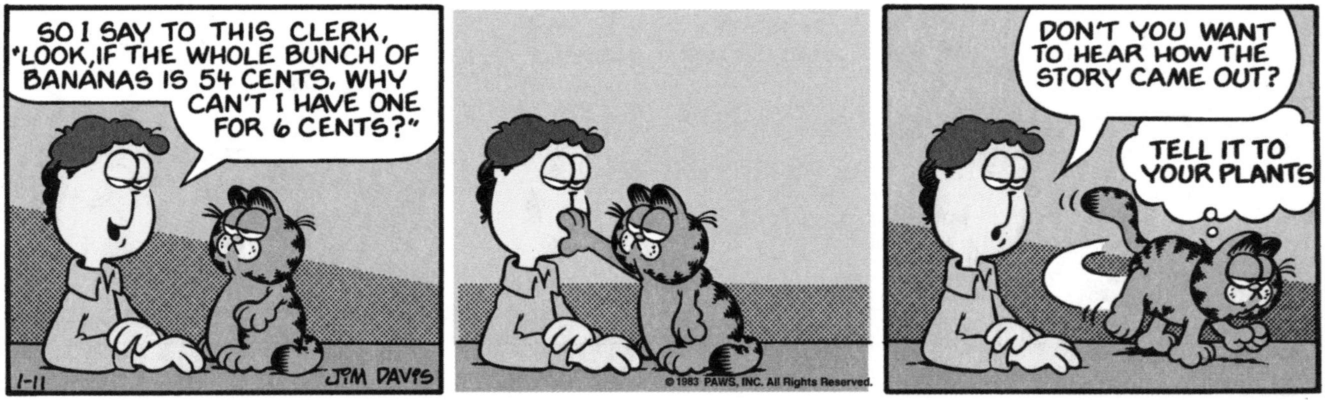
SO I SAY TO THIS CLERK, "LOOK, IF THE WHOLE BUNCH OF BANANAS IS 54 CENTS, WHY CAN'T I HAVE ONE FOR 6 CENTS?"
1-11
JIM DAVIS
© 1983 PAWS, INC. All Rights Reserved.
DON'T YOU WANT TO HEAR HOW THE STORY CAME OUT?
TELL IT TO YOUR PLANTS

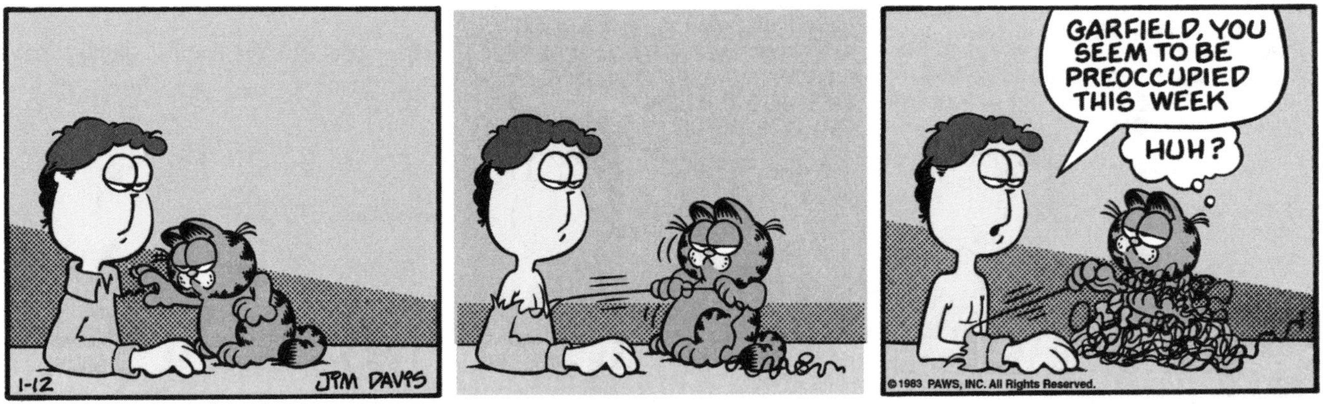
1-12
JIM DAVIS
GARFIELD, YOU SEEM TO BE PREOCCUPIED THIS WEEK
HUH?
© 1983 PAWS, INC. All Rights Reserved.

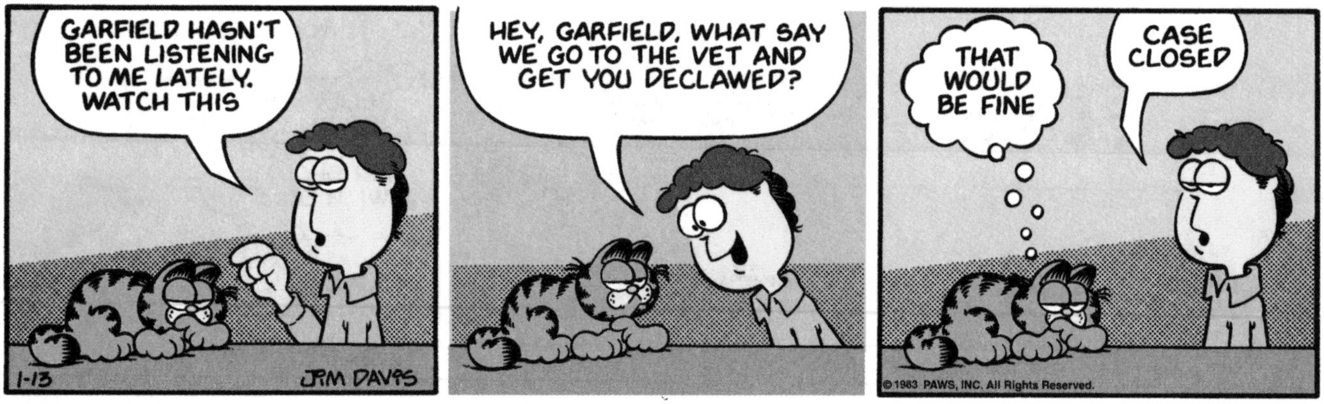
GARFIELD HASN'T BEEN LISTENING TO ME LATELY. WATCH THIS
1-13
JIM DAVIS
HEY, GARFIELD, WHAT SAY WE GO TO THE VET AND GET YOU DECLAWED?
THAT WOULD BE FINE
CASE CLOSED
©1983 PAWS, INC. All Rights Reserved.

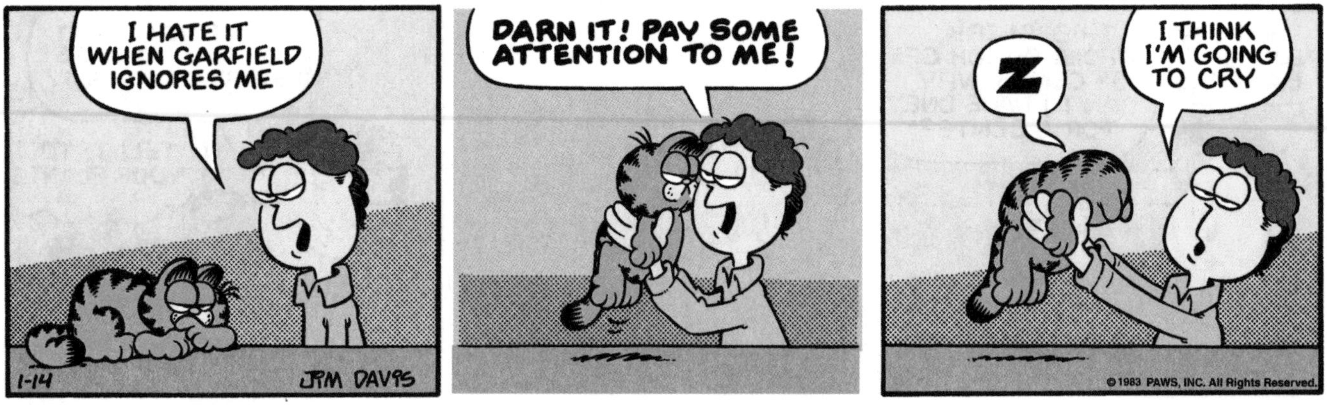
I HATE IT WHEN GARFIELD IGNORES ME
1-14
JIM DAVIS
DARN IT! PAY SOME ATTENTION TO ME!
Z
I THINK I'M GOING TO CRY
©1983 PAWS, INC. All Rights Reserved.

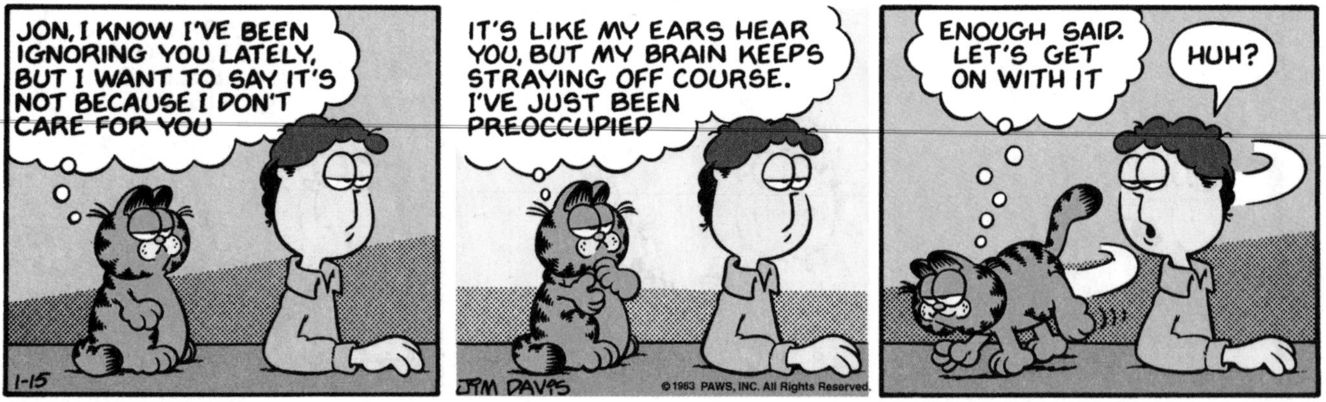
JON, I KNOW I'VE BEEN IGNORING YOU LATELY, BUT I WANT TO SAY IT'S NOT BECAUSE I DON'T CARE FOR YOU
1-15
IT'S LIKE MY EARS HEAR YOU, BUT MY BRAIN KEEPS STRAYING OFF COURSE. I'VE JUST BEEN PREOCCUPIED
JIM DAVIS
©1983 PAWS, INC. All Rights Reserved.
ENOUGH SAID. LET'S GET ON WITH IT
HUH?

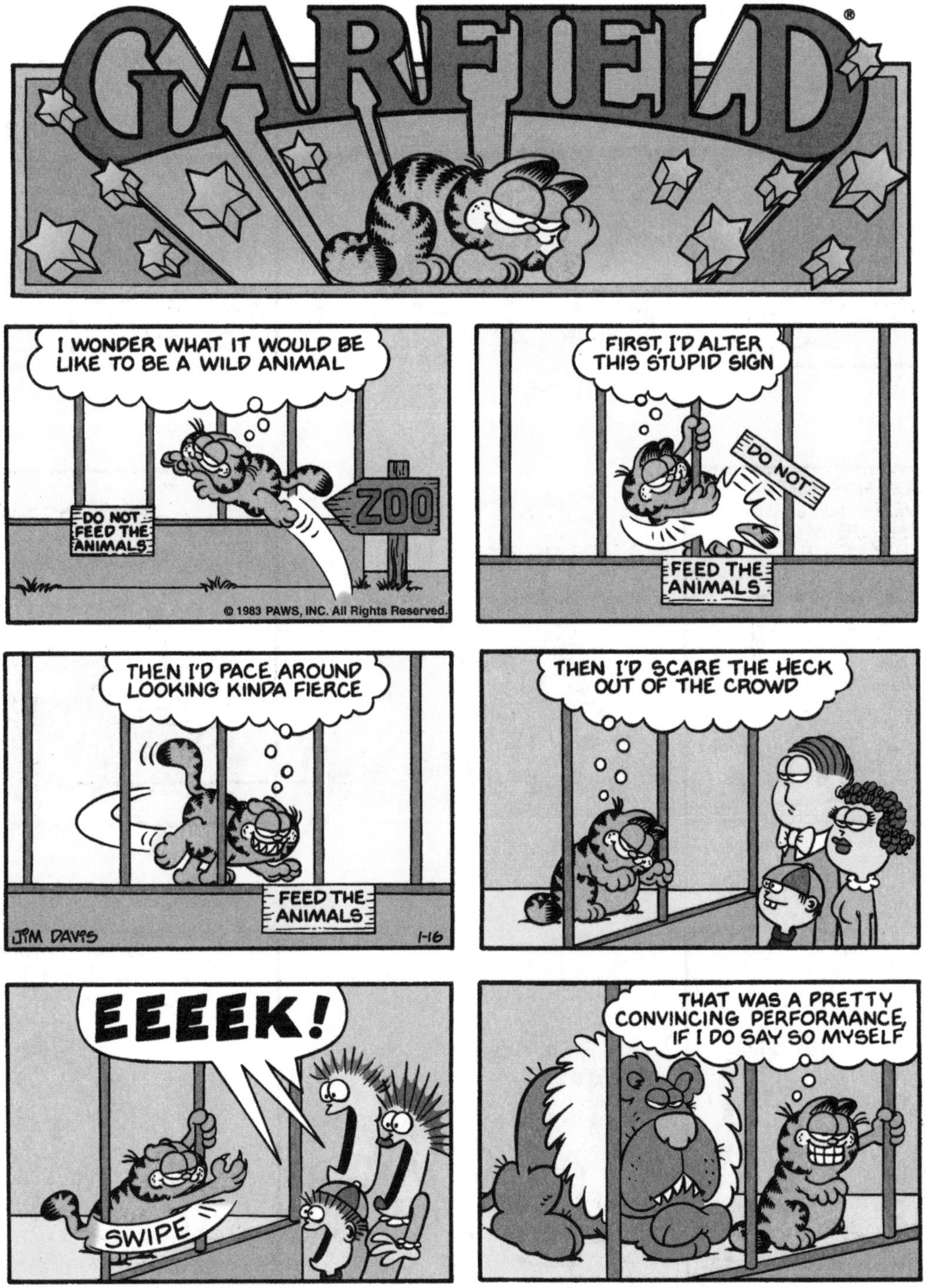
GARFIELD®
I WONDER WHAT IT WOULD BE LIKE TO BE A WILD ANIMAL
DO NOT FEED THE ANIMALS
ZOO
© 1983 PAWS, INC. All Rights Reserved.
FIRST, I'D ALTER THIS STUPID SIGN
DO NOT
FEED THE ANIMALS
THEN I'D PACE AROUND LOOKING KINDA FIERCE
FEED THE ANIMALS
JIM DAVIS
1-16
THEN I'D SCARE THE HECK OUT OF THE CROWD
EEEEK!
SWIPE
THAT WAS A PRETTY CONVINCING PERFORMANCE, IF I DO SAY SO MYSELF

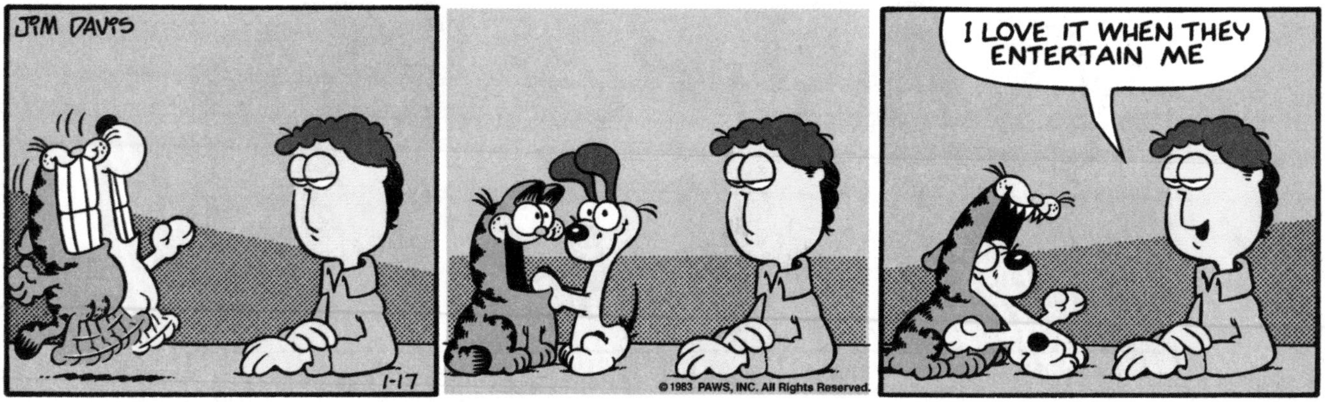
JIM DAVIS
1-17
© 1983 PAWS, INC. All Rights Reserved.
I LOVE IT WHEN THEY ENTERTAIN ME

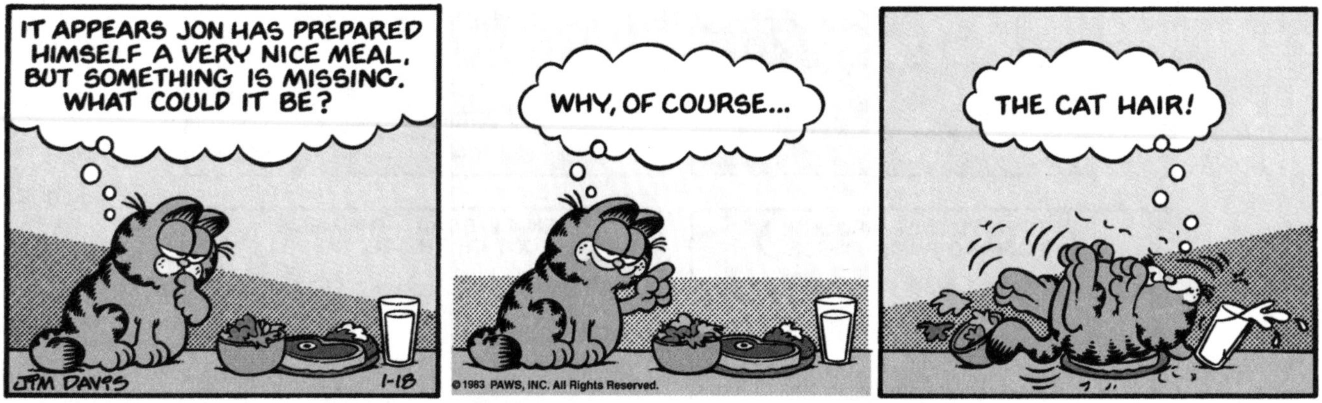
IT APPEARS JON HAS PREPARED HIMSELF A VERY NICE MEAL, BUT SOMETHING IS MISSING. WHAT COULD IT BE?
JIM DAVIS
1-18
WHY, OF COURSE...
© 1983 PAWS, INC. All Rights Reserved.
THE CAT HAIR!

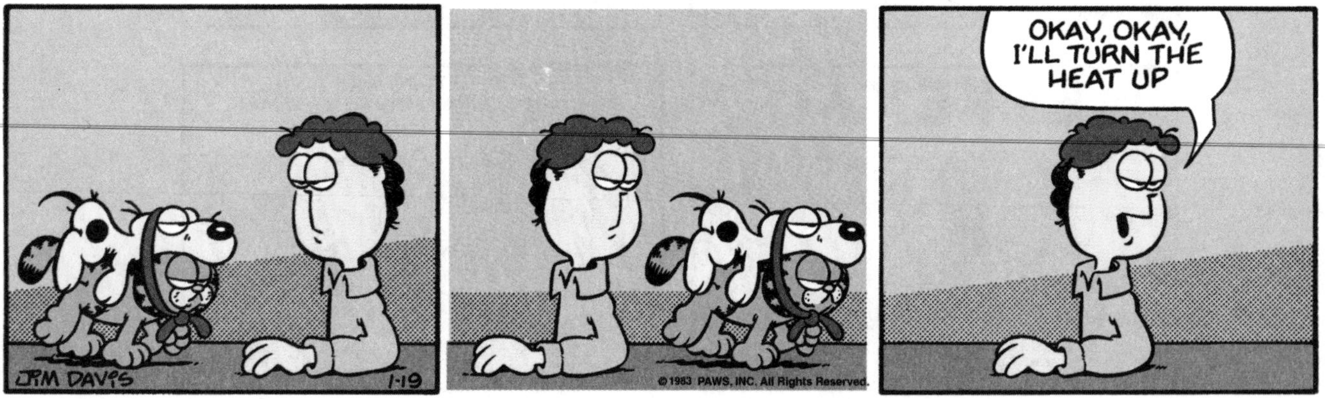
JIM DAVIS
1-19
© 1983 PAWS, INC. All Rights Reserved.
OKAY, OKAY, I'LL TURN THE HEAT UP

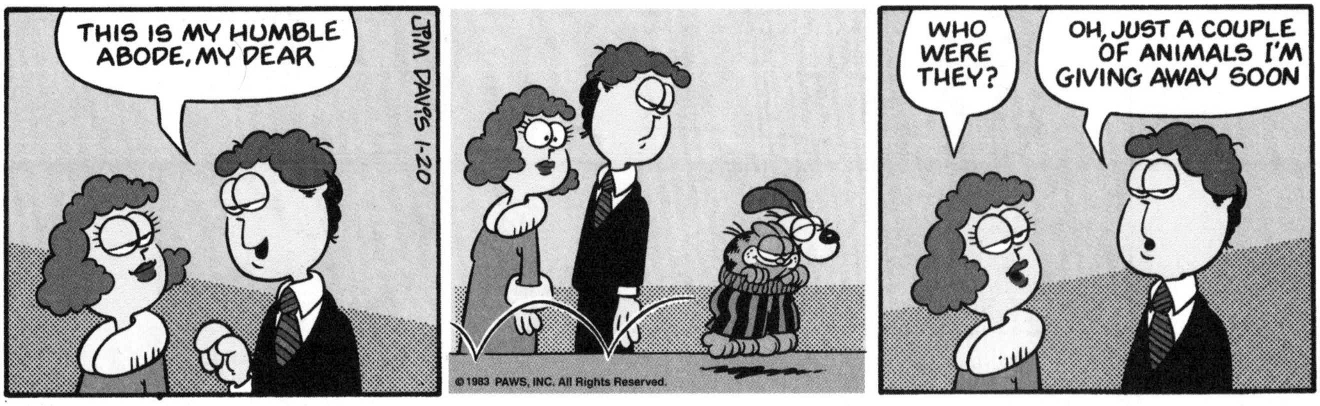
THIS IS MY HUMBLE ABODE, MY DEAR
JIM DAVIS 1-20
© 1983 PAWS, INC. All Rights Reserved.
WHO WERE THEY?
OH, JUST A COUPLE OF ANIMALS I'M GIVING AWAY SOON

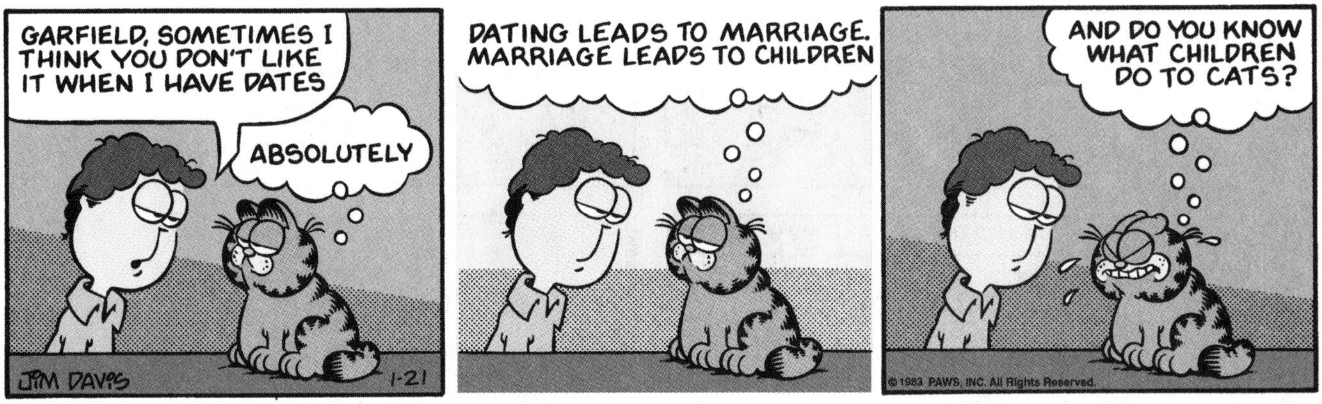
GARFIELD, SOMETIMES I THINK YOU DON'T LIKE IT WHEN I HAVE DATES
ABSOLUTELY
JIM DAVIS
1-21
DATING LEADS TO MARRIAGE. MARRIAGE LEADS TO CHILDREN
AND DO YOU KNOW WHAT CHILDREN DO TO CATS?
© 1983 PAWS, INC. All Rights Reserved.

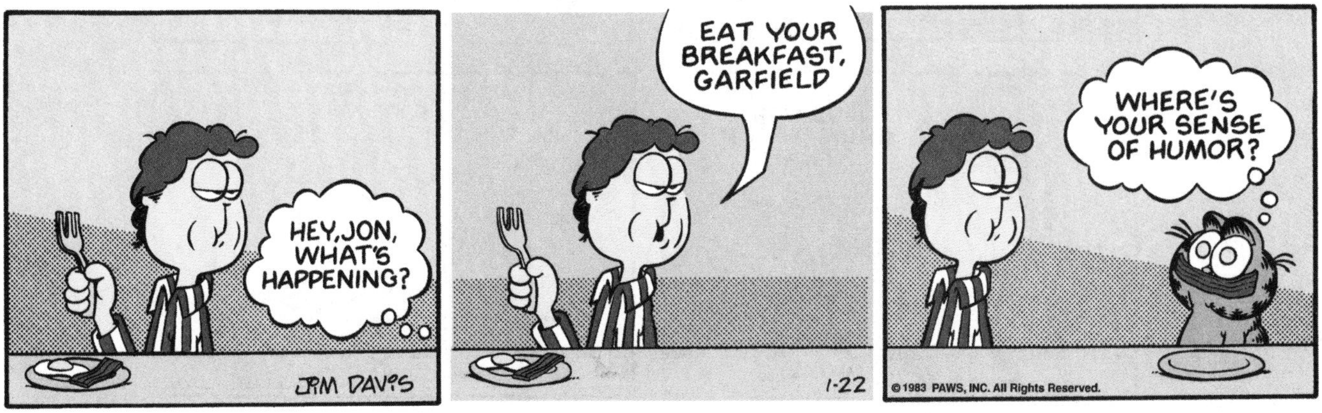
HEY, JON, WHAT'S HAPPENING?
JIM DAVIS
EAT YOUR BREAKFAST, GARFIELD
1-22
WHERE'S YOUR SENSE OF HUMOR?
© 1983 PAWS, INC. All Rights Reserved.

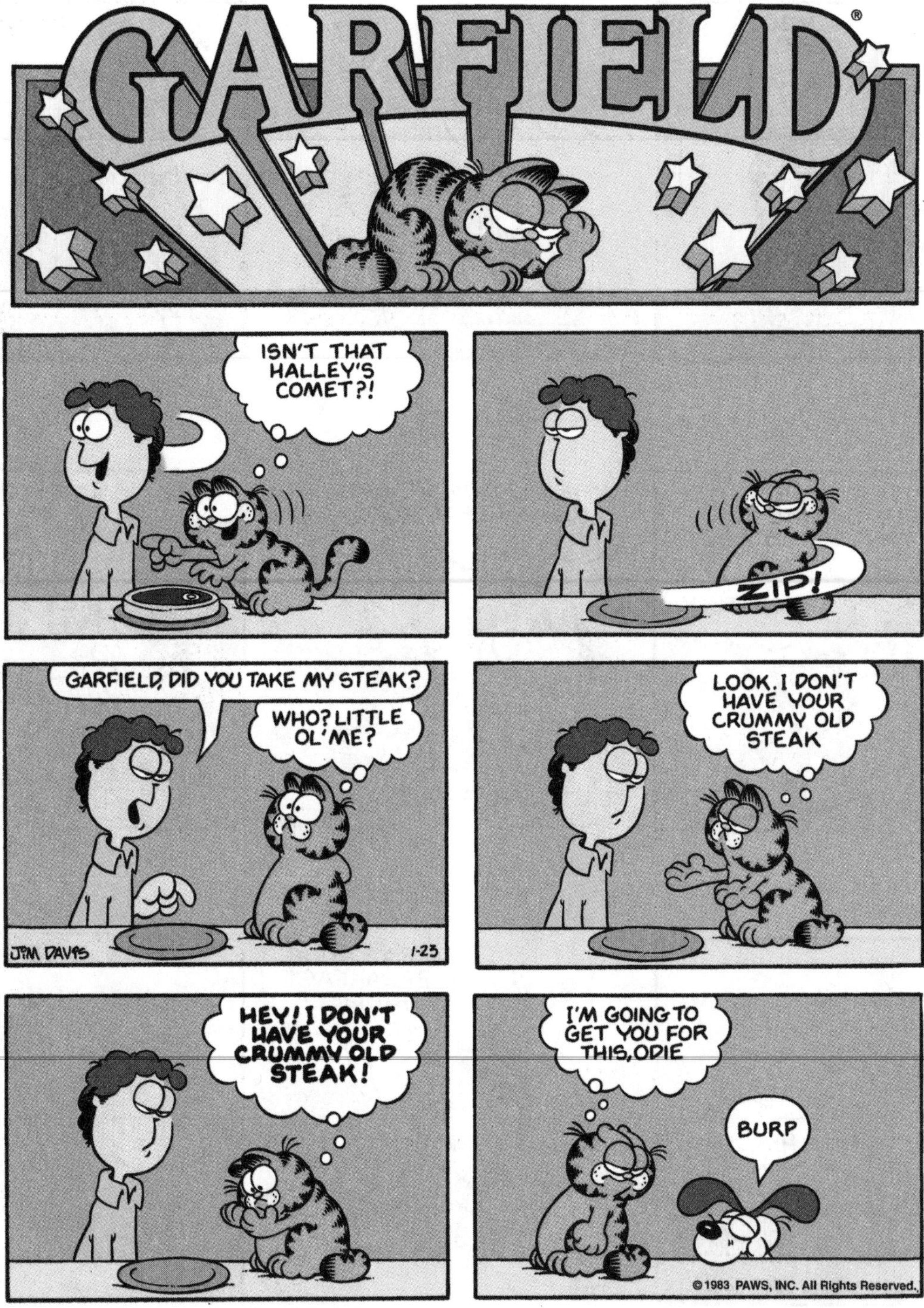
GARFIELD
ISN'T THAT HALLEY'S COMET?!
ZIP!
GARFIELD, DID YOU TAKE MY STEAK?
WHO? LITTLE OL' ME?
JIM DAVIS
1-23
LOOK. I DON'T HAVE YOUR CRUMMY OLD STEAK
HEY! I DON'T HAVE YOUR CRUMMY OLD STEAK!
I'M GOING TO GET YOU FOR THIS, ODIE
BURP
© 1983 PAWS, INC. All Rights Reserved.

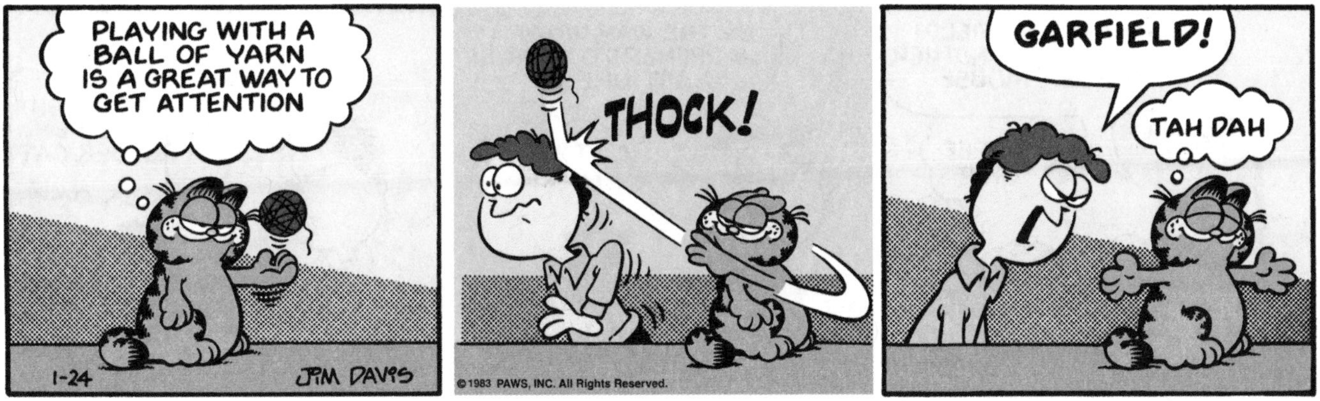
PLAYING WITH A BALL OF YARN IS A GREAT WAY TO GET ATTENTION
1-24
JIM DAVIS
THOCK!
© 1983 PAWS, INC. All Rights Reserved.
GARFIELD!
TAH DAH

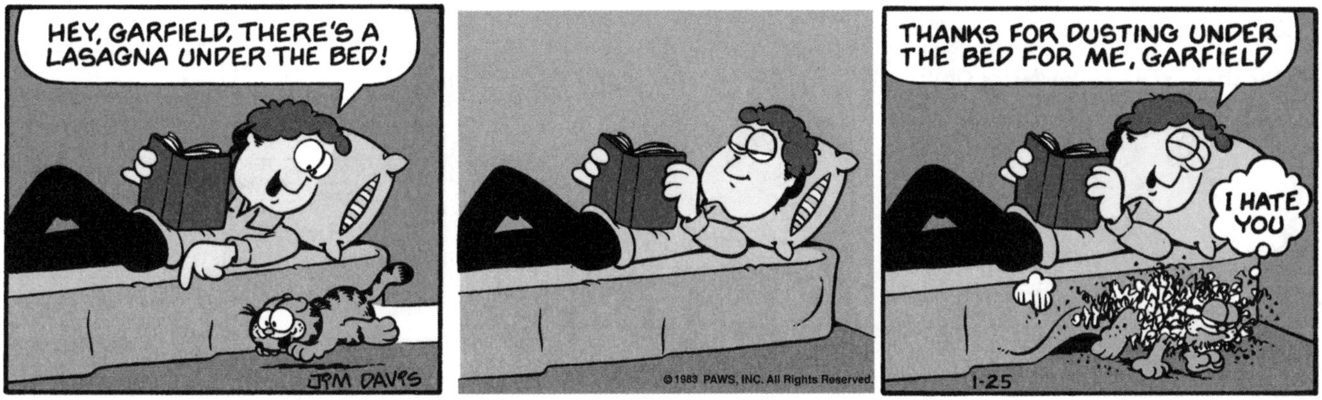
HEY, GARFIELD, THERE'S A LASAGNA UNDER THE BED!
JIM DAVIS
© 1983 PAWS, INC. All Rights Reserved.
THANKS FOR DUSTING UNDER THE BED FOR ME, GARFIELD
I HATE YOU
1-25

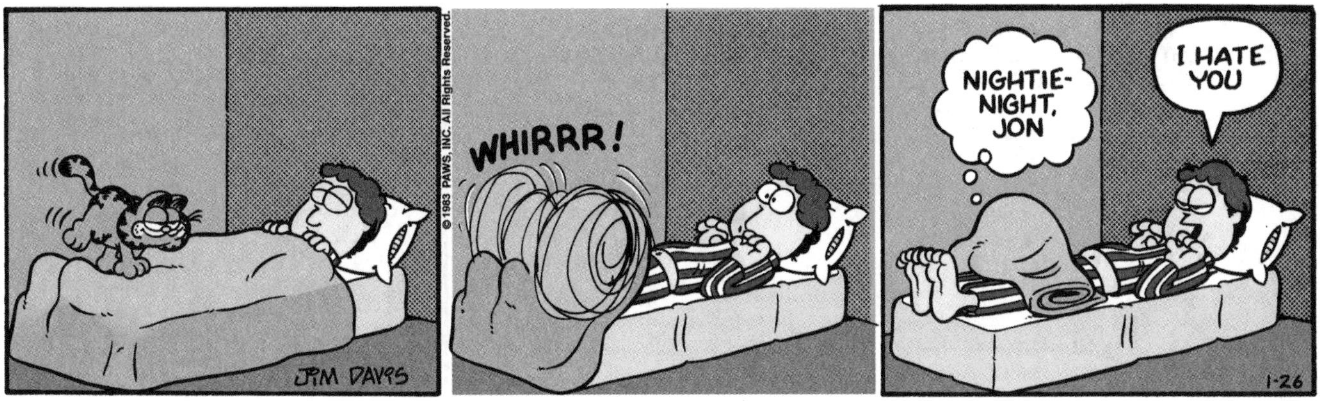
JIM DAVIS
© 1983 PAWS, INC. All Rights Reserved.
WHIRRR!
NIGHTIE-NIGHT, JON
I HATE YOU
1-26

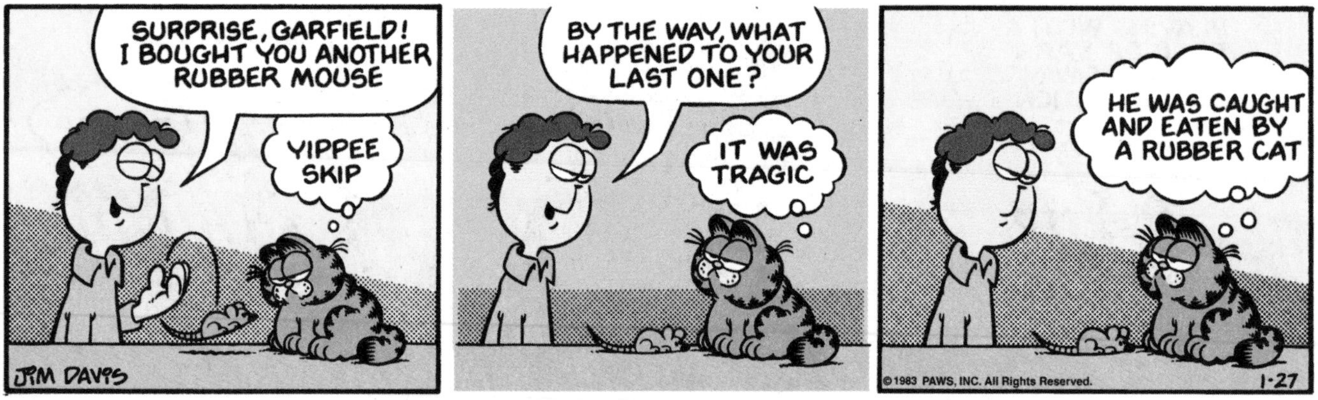
SURPRISE, GARFIELD! I BOUGHT YOU ANOTHER RUBBER MOUSE
YIPPEE SKIP
BY THE WAY, WHAT HAPPENED TO YOUR LAST ONE?
IT WAS TRAGIC
HE WAS CAUGHT AND EATEN BY A RUBBER CAT
JIM DAVIS
© 1983 PAWS, INC. All Rights Reserved.
1-27

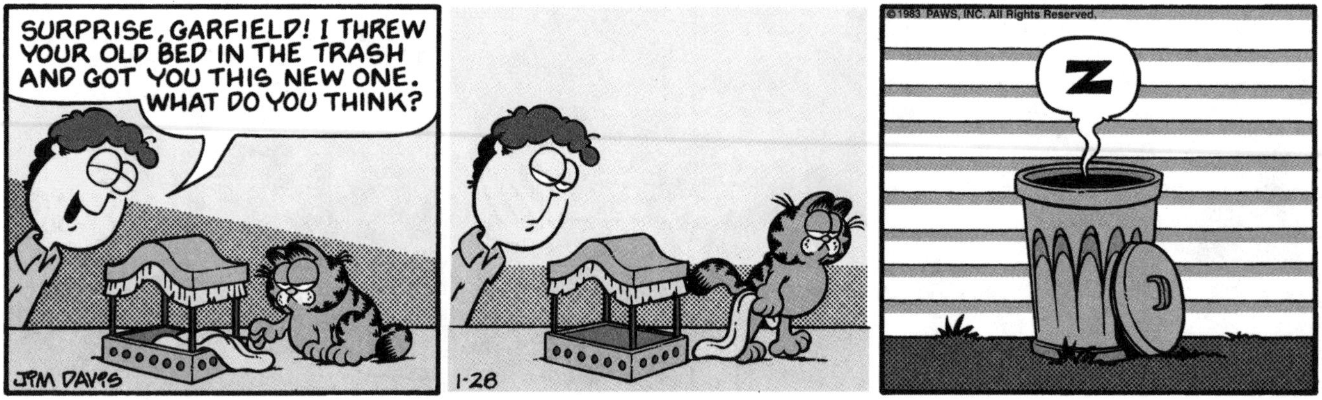
SURPRISE, GARFIELD! I THREW YOUR OLD BED IN THE TRASH AND GOT YOU THIS NEW ONE. WHAT DO YOU THINK?
JIM DAVIS
1-28
© 1983 PAWS, INC. All Rights Reserved.
Z

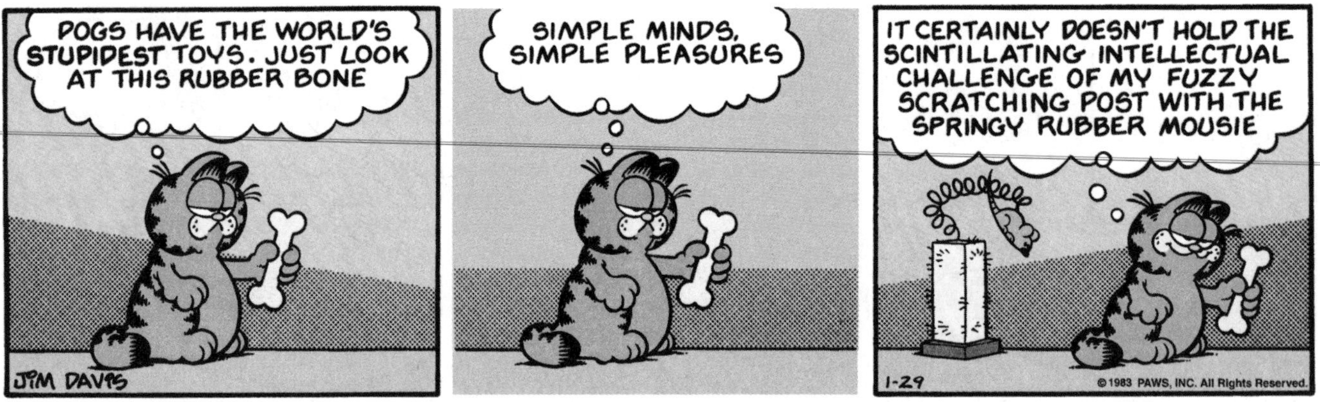
DOGS HAVE THE WORLD'S STUPIDEST TOYS. JUST LOOK AT THIS RUBBER BONE
SIMPLE MINDS, SIMPLE PLEASURES
IT CERTAINLY DOESN'T HOLD THE SCINTILLATING INTELLECTUAL CHALLENGE OF MY FUZZY SCRATCHING POST WITH THE SPRINGY RUBBER MOUSIE
JIM DAVIS
1-29
© 1983 PAWS, INC. All Rights Reserved.

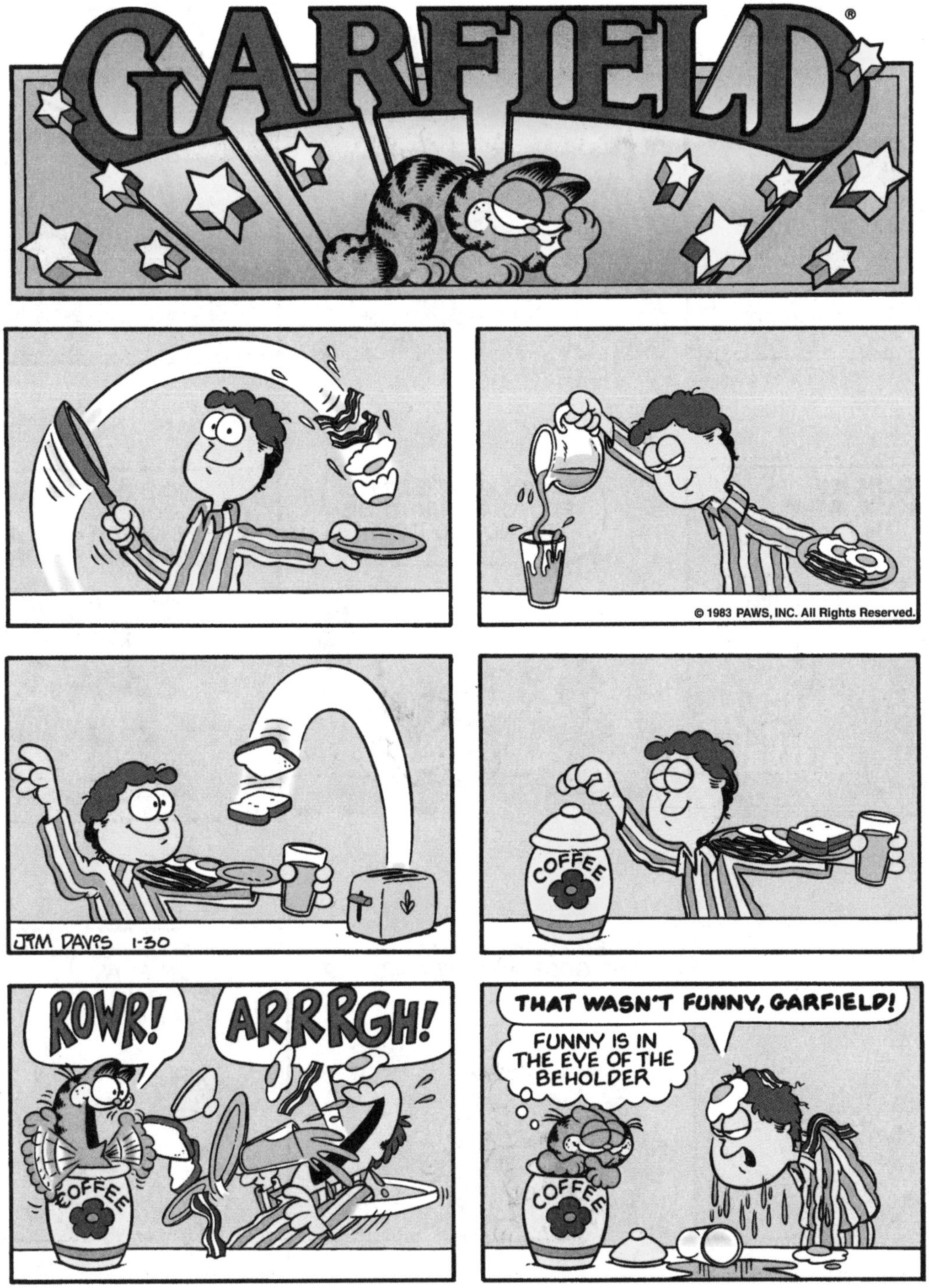
GARFIELD®
© 1983 PAWS, INC. All Rights Reserved.
JIM DAVIS 1-30
ROWR!
ARRRGH!
THAT WASN'T FUNNY, GARFIELD!
FUNNY IS IN THE EYE OF THE BEHOLDER
COFFEE

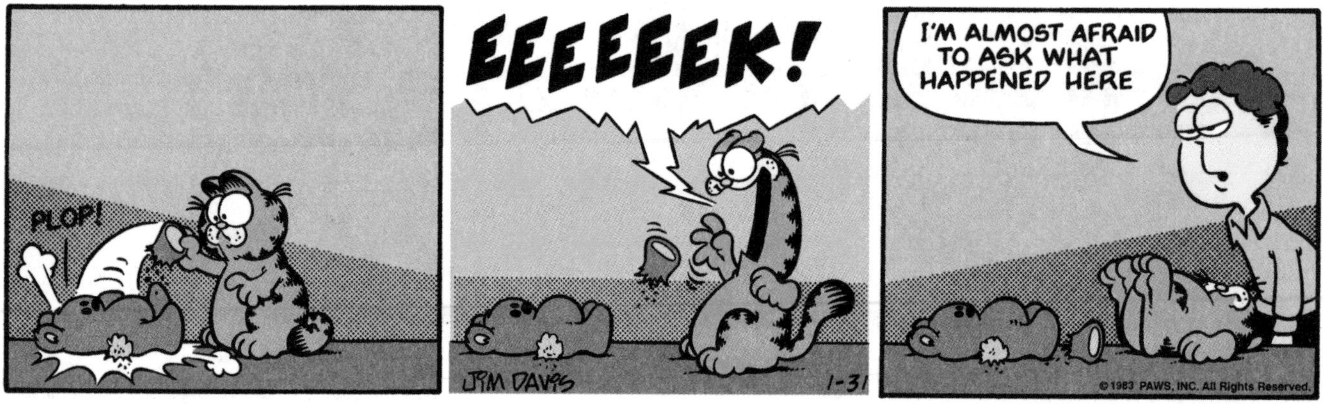
PLOP!
EEEEEEK!
JIM DAVIS
1-31
I'M ALMOST AFRAID TO ASK WHAT HAPPENED HERE
© 1983 PAWS, INC. All Rights Reserved.

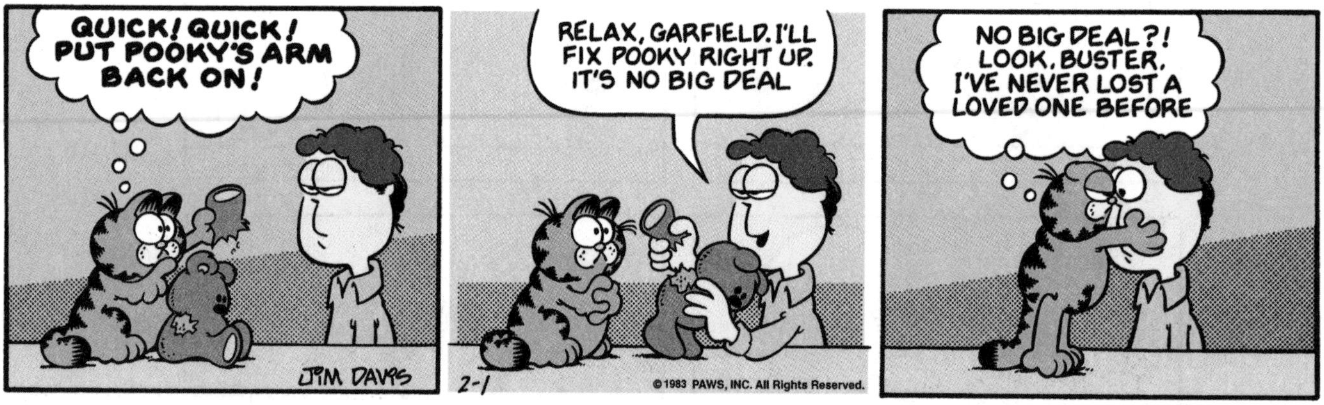
QUICK! QUICK! PUT POOKY'S ARM BACK ON!
JIM DAVIS
RELAX, GARFIELD. I'LL FIX POOKY RIGHT UP. IT'S NO BIG DEAL
2-1
© 1983 PAWS, INC. All Rights Reserved.
NO BIG DEAL?! LOOK, BUSTER, I'VE NEVER LOST A LOVED ONE BEFORE

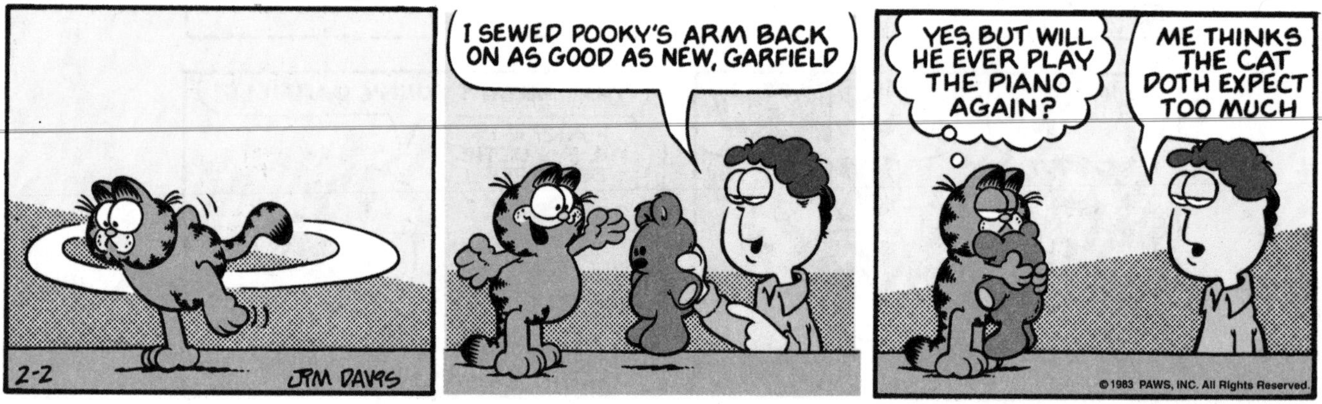
2-2
JIM DAVIS
I SEWED POOKY'S ARM BACK ON AS GOOD AS NEW, GARFIELD
YES, BUT WILL HE EVER PLAY THE PIANO AGAIN?
ME THINKS THE CAT DOTH EXPECT TOO MUCH
© 1983 PAWS, INC. All Rights Reserved.

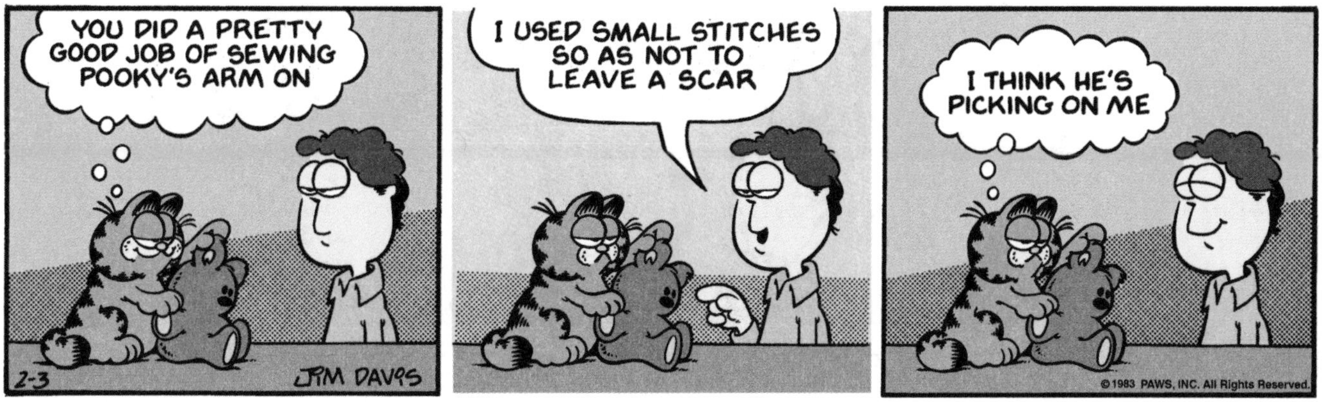
2-3
YOU DID A PRETTY GOOD JOB OF SEWING POOKY'S ARM ON
JIM DAVIS
I USED SMALL STITCHES SO AS NOT TO LEAVE A SCAR
I THINK HE'S PICKING ON ME
© 1983 PAWS, INC. All Rights Reserved.

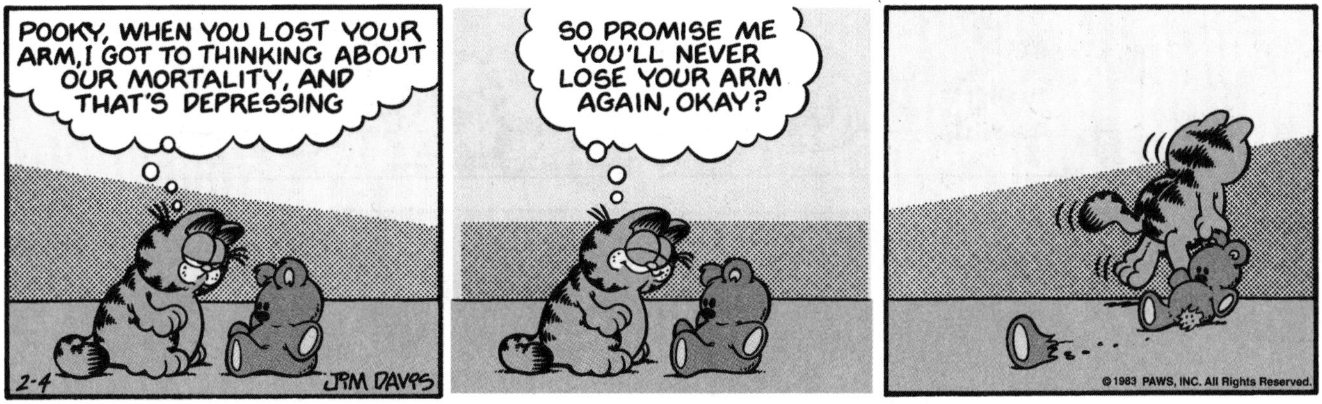
2-4
POOKY, WHEN YOU LOST YOUR ARM, I GOT TO THINKING ABOUT OUR MORTALITY, AND THAT'S DEPRESSING
JIM DAVIS
SO PROMISE ME YOU'LL NEVER LOSE YOUR ARM AGAIN, OKAY?
© 1983 PAWS, INC. All Rights Reserved.

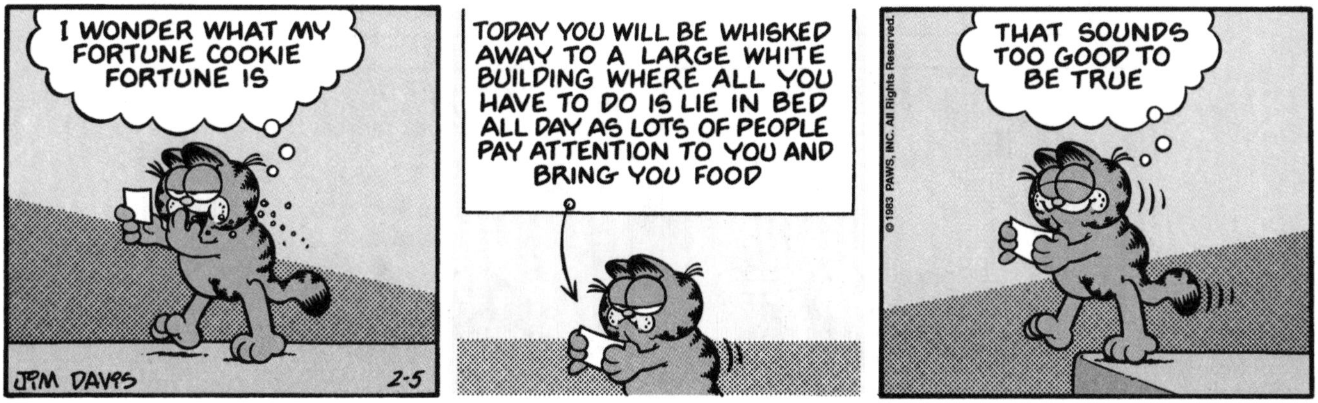
I WONDER WHAT MY FORTUNE COOKIE FORTUNE IS
JIM DAVIS
2-5
TODAY YOU WILL BE WHISKED AWAY TO A LARGE WHITE BUILDING WHERE ALL YOU HAVE TO DO IS LIE IN BED ALL DAY AS LOTS OF PEOPLE PAY ATTENTION TO YOU AND BRING YOU FOOD
© 1983 PAWS, INC. All Rights Reserved.
THAT SOUNDS TOO GOOD TO BE TRUE

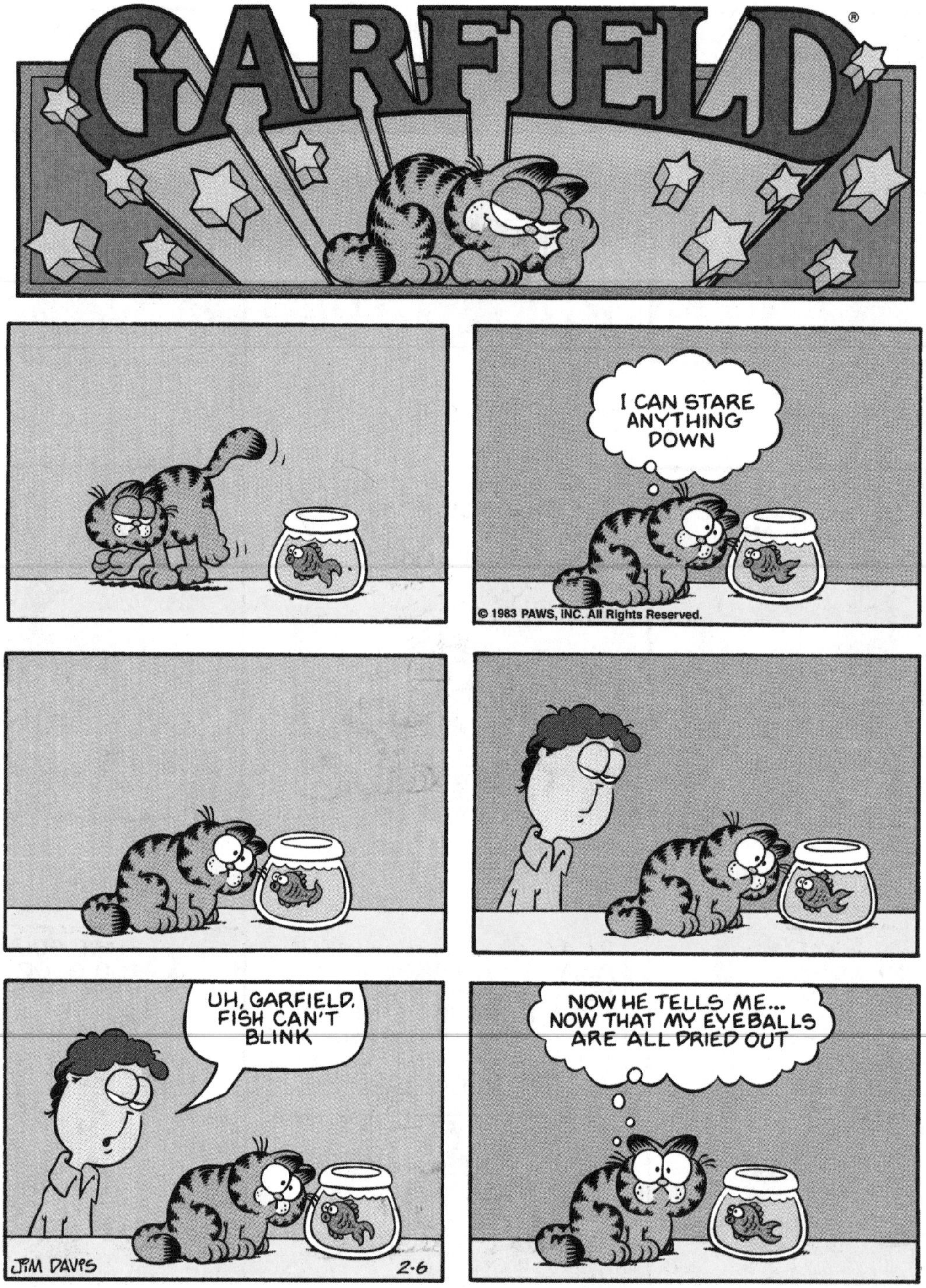
GARFIELD
I CAN STARE ANYTHING DOWN
© 1983 PAWS, INC. All Rights Reserved.
UH, GARFIELD, FISH CAN'T BLINK
JIM DAVIS
2-6
NOW HE TELLS ME... NOW THAT MY EYEBALLS ARE ALL DRIED OUT

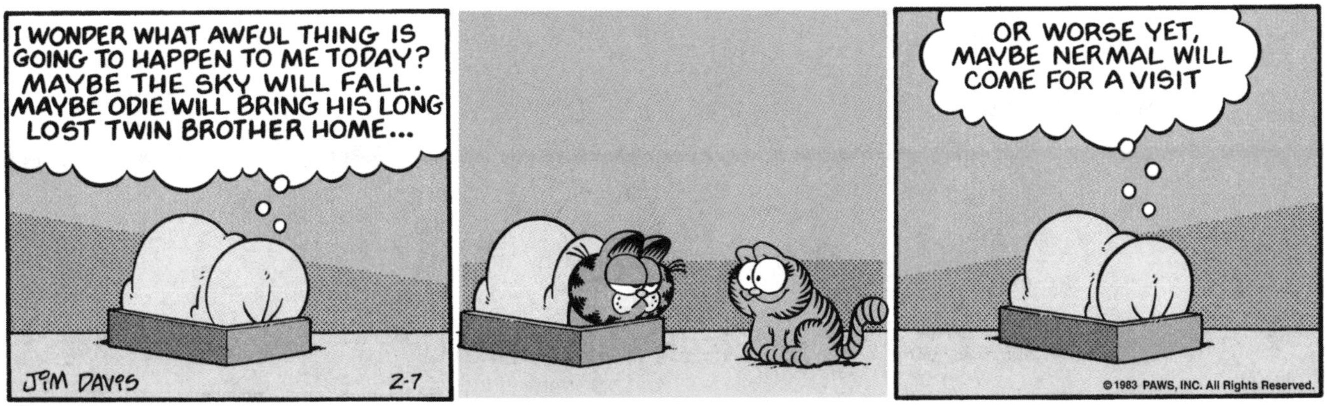
I WONDER WHAT AWFUL THING IS GOING TO HAPPEN TO ME TODAY? MAYBE THE SKY WILL FALL. MAYBE ODIE WILL BRING HIS LONG LOST TWIN BROTHER HOME...
JIM DAVIS
2-7
OR WORSE YET, MAYBE NERMAL WILL COME FOR A VISIT
© 1983 PAWS, INC. All Rights Reserved.

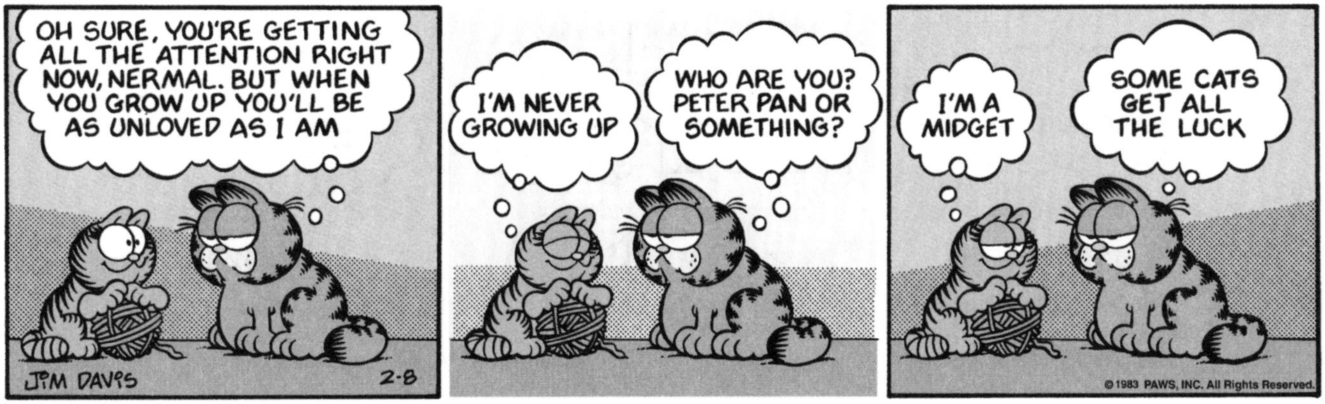
OH SURE, YOU'RE GETTING ALL THE ATTENTION RIGHT NOW, NERMAL. BUT WHEN YOU GROW UP YOU'LL BE AS UNLOVED AS I AM
JIM DAVIS
2-8
I'M NEVER GROWING UP
WHO ARE YOU? PETER PAN OR SOMETHING?
I'M A MIDGET
SOME CATS GET ALL THE LUCK
© 1983 PAWS, INC. All Rights Reserved.

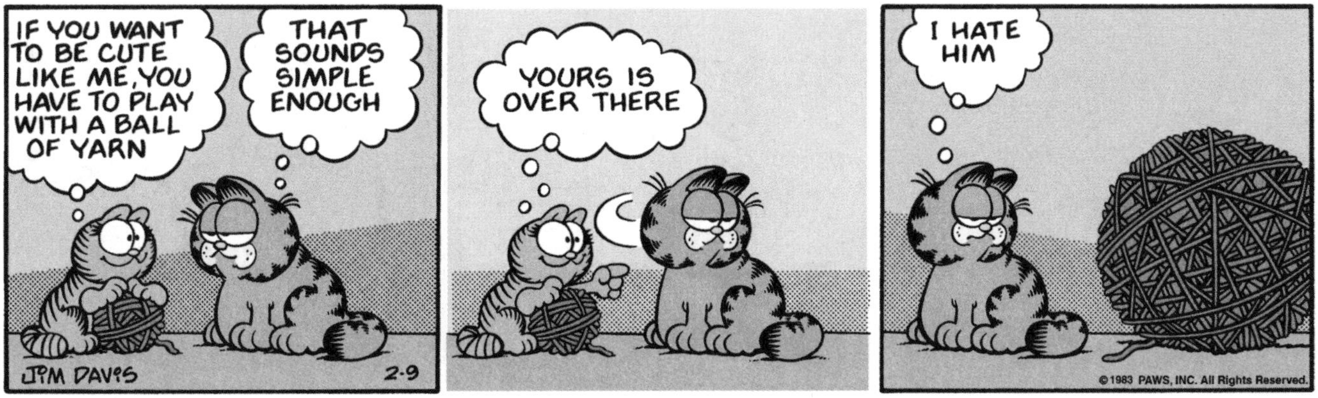
IF YOU WANT TO BE CUTE LIKE ME, YOU HAVE TO PLAY WITH A BALL OF YARN
THAT SOUNDS SIMPLE ENOUGH
JIM DAVIS
2-9
YOURS IS OVER THERE
I HATE HIM
© 1983 PAWS, INC. All Rights Reserved.

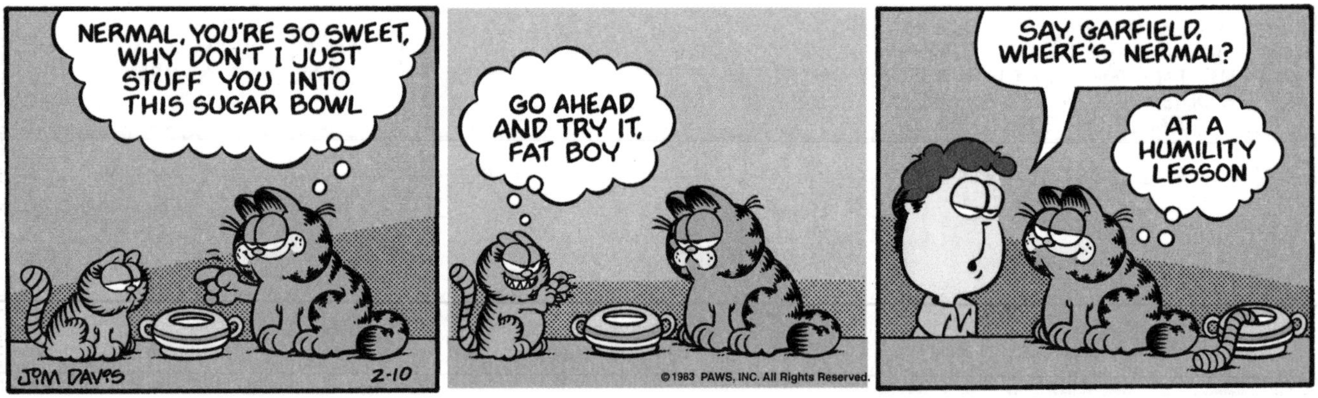
NERMAL, YOU'RE SO SWEET, WHY DON'T I JUST STUFF YOU INTO THIS SUGAR BOWL
GO AHEAD AND TRY IT, FAT BOY
SAY, GARFIELD, WHERE'S NERMAL?
AT A HUMILITY LESSON
JIM DAVIS
2-10
©1983 PAWS, INC. All Rights Reserved.

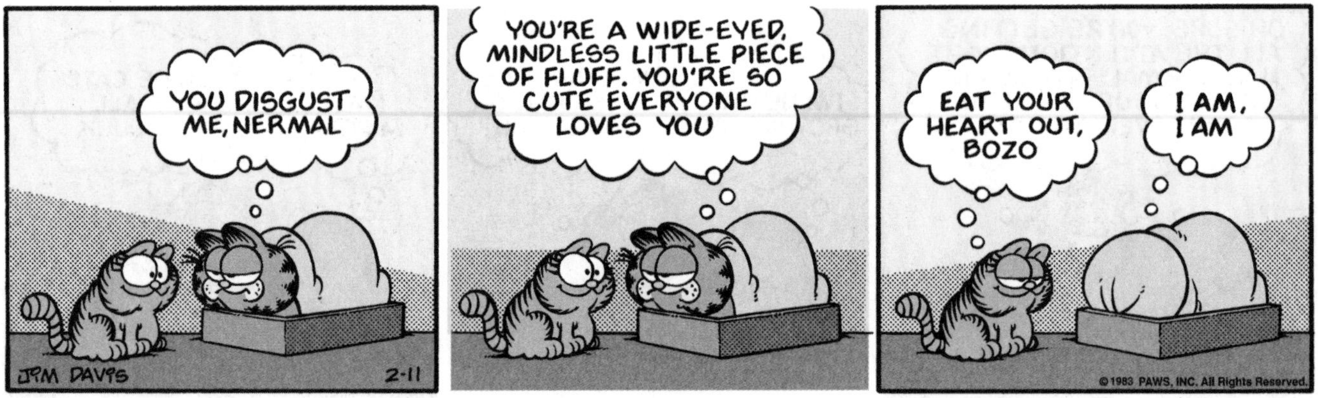
YOU DISGUST ME, NERMAL
YOU'RE A WIDE-EYED, MINDLESS LITTLE PIECE OF FLUFF. YOU'RE SO CUTE EVERYONE LOVES YOU
EAT YOUR HEART OUT, BOZO
I AM, I AM
JIM DAVIS
2-11
©1983 PAWS, INC. All Rights Reserved.

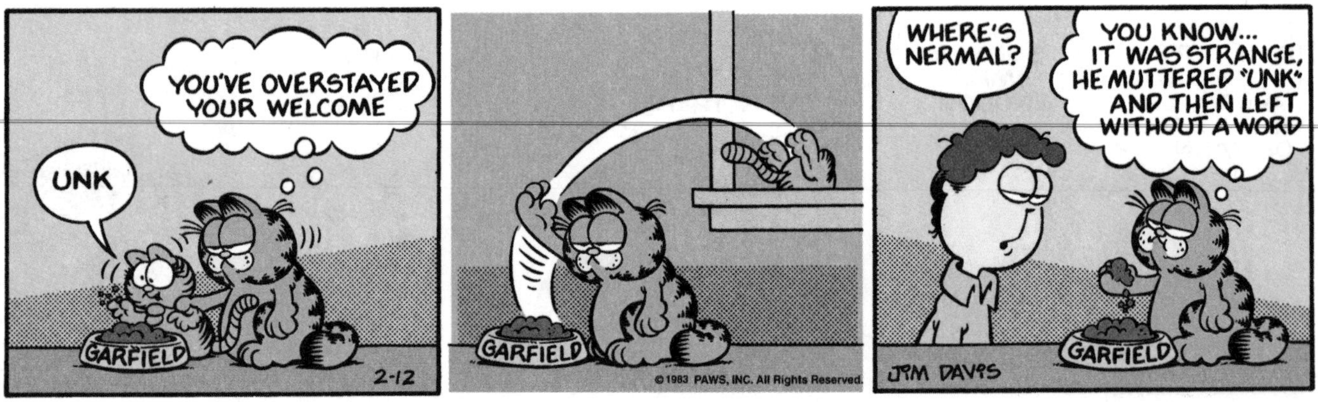
YOU'VE OVERSTAYED YOUR WELCOME
UNK
GARFIELD
GARFIELD
WHERE'S NERMAL?
YOU KNOW... IT WAS STRANGE, HE MUTTERED "UNK" AND THEN LEFT WITHOUT A WORD
GARFIELD
JIM DAVIS
2-12
©1983 PAWS, INC. All Rights Reserved.

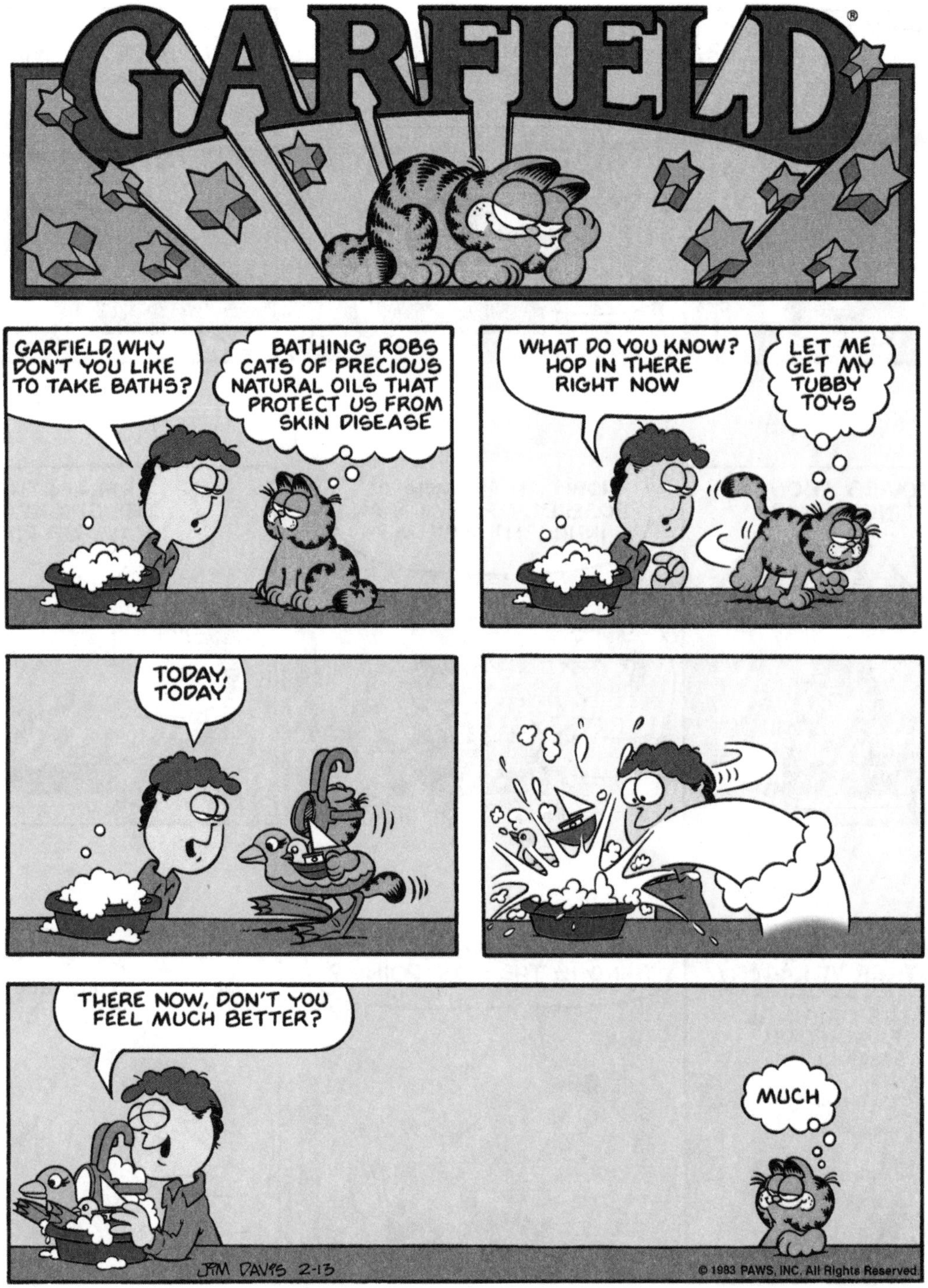
GARFIELD®
GARFIELD, WHY DON'T YOU LIKE TO TAKE BATHS?
BATHING ROBS CATS OF PRECIOUS NATURAL OILS THAT PROTECT US FROM SKIN DISEASE
WHAT DO YOU KNOW? HOP IN THERE RIGHT NOW
LET ME GET MY TUBBY TOYS
TODAY, TODAY
THERE NOW, DON'T YOU FEEL MUCH BETTER?
MUCH
JIM DAVIS 2-13
© 1983 PAWS, INC. All Rights Reserved.

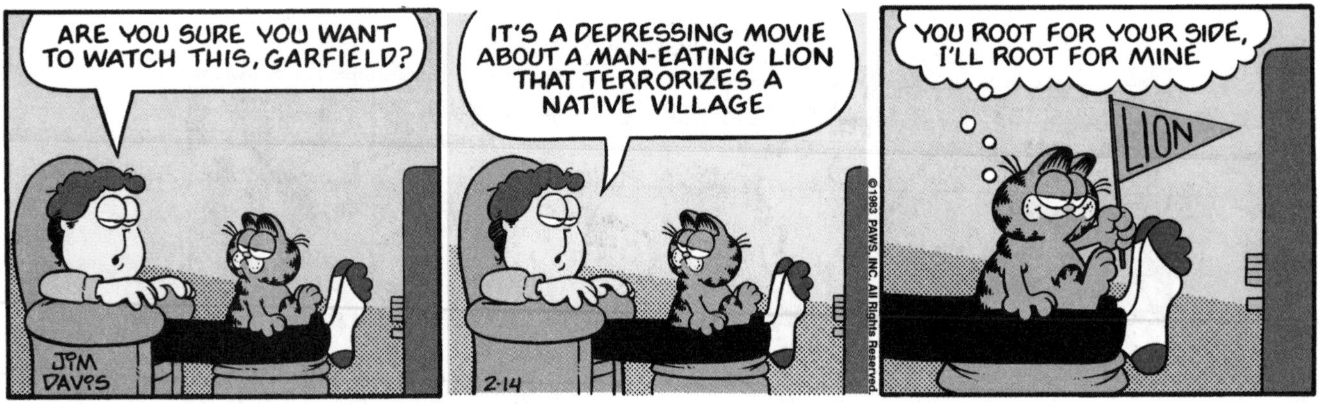
ARE YOU SURE YOU WANT TO WATCH THIS, GARFIELD?
JIM DAVIS
IT'S A DEPRESSING MOVIE ABOUT A MAN-EATING LION THAT TERRORIZES A NATIVE VILLAGE
2-14
© 1983 PAWS, INC. All Rights Reserved.
YOU ROOT FOR YOUR SIDE, I'LL ROOT FOR MINE
LION

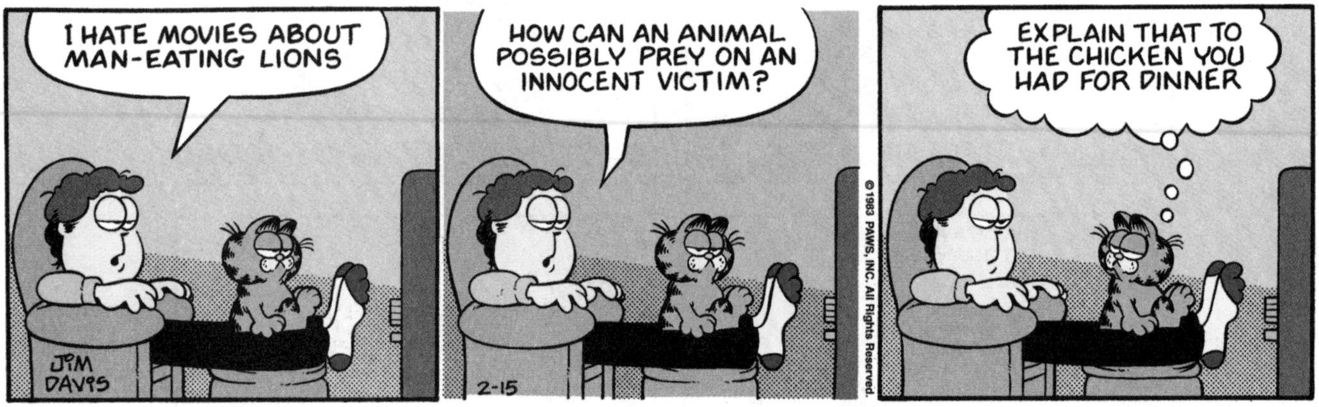
I HATE MOVIES ABOUT MAN-EATING LIONS
JIM DAVIS
HOW CAN AN ANIMAL POSSIBLY PREY ON AN INNOCENT VICTIM?
2-15
© 1983 PAWS, INC. All Rights Reserved.
EXPLAIN THAT TO THE CHICKEN YOU HAD FOR DINNER

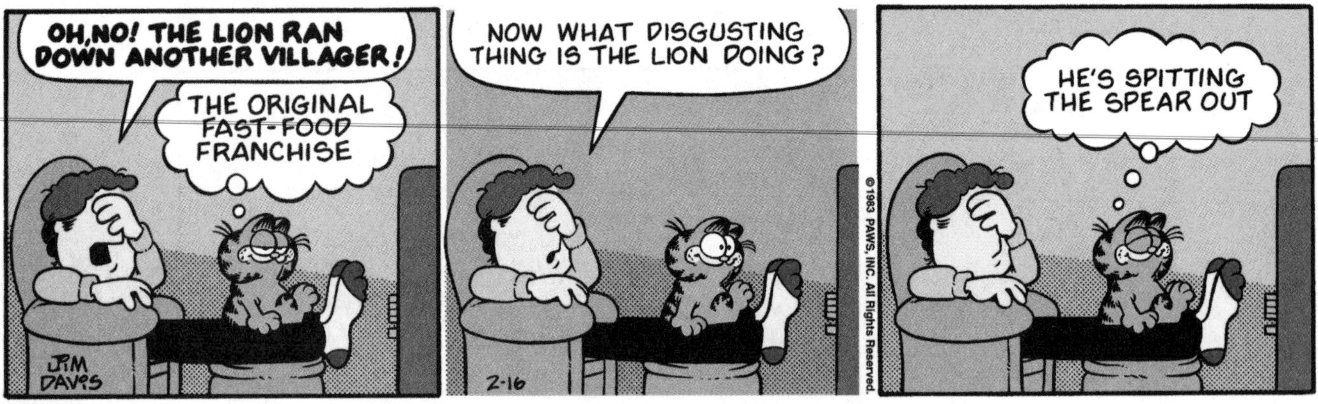
OH, NO! THE LION RAN DOWN ANOTHER VILLAGER!
THE ORIGINAL FAST-FOOD FRANCHISE
JIM DAVIS
NOW WHAT DISGUSTING THING IS THE LION DOING?
2-16
© 1983 PAWS, INC. All Rights Reserved.
HE'S SPITTING THE SPEAR OUT

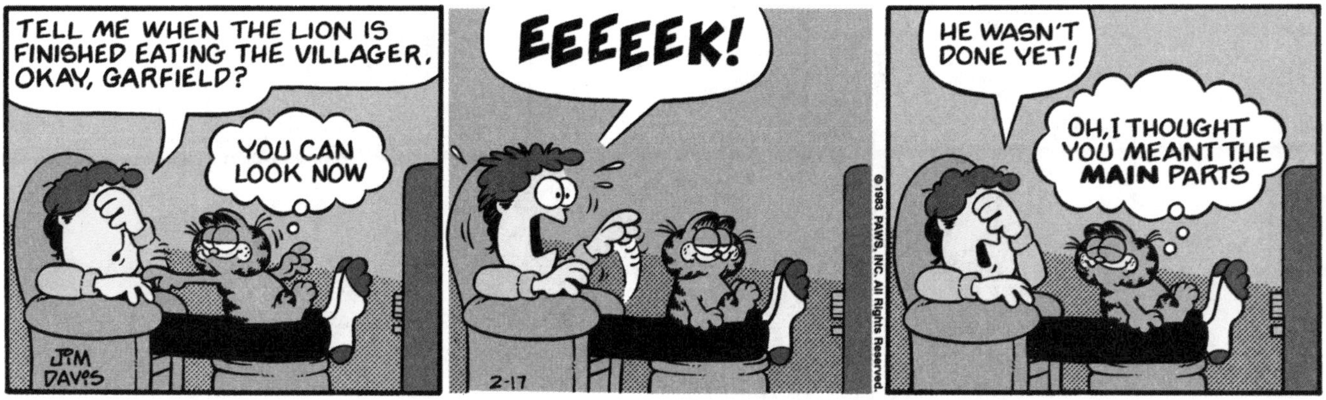
TELL ME WHEN THE LION IS FINISHED EATING THE VILLAGER, OKAY, GARFIELD?
YOU CAN LOOK NOW
JIM DAVIS
EEEEEK!
2-17
© 1983 PAWS, INC. All Rights Reserved.
HE WASN'T DONE YET!
OH, I THOUGHT YOU MEANT THE MAIN PARTS

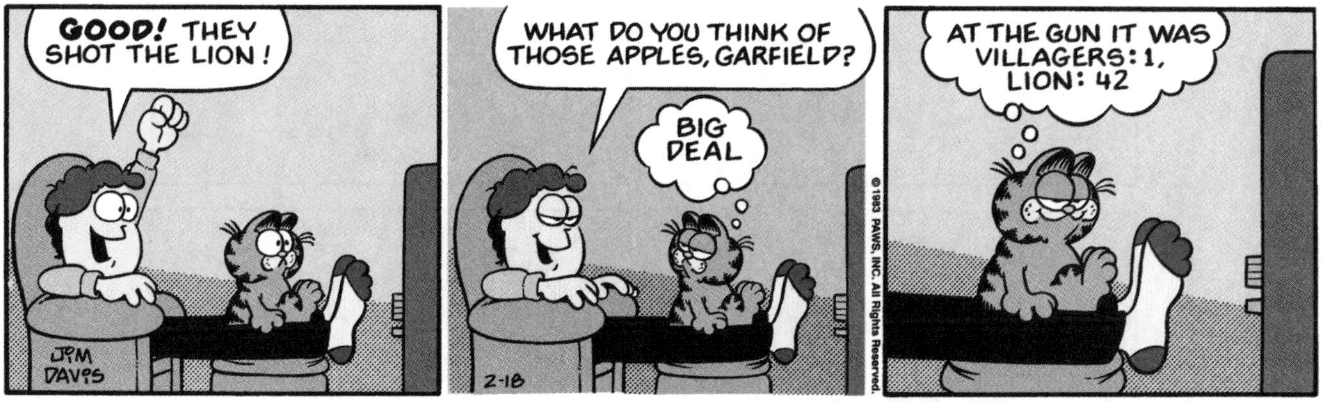
GOOD! THEY SHOT THE LION!
JIM DAVIS
WHAT DO YOU THINK OF THOSE APPLES, GARFIELD?
BIG DEAL
2-18
© 1983 PAWS, INC. All Rights Reserved.
AT THE GUN IT WAS VILLAGERS: 1, LION: 42

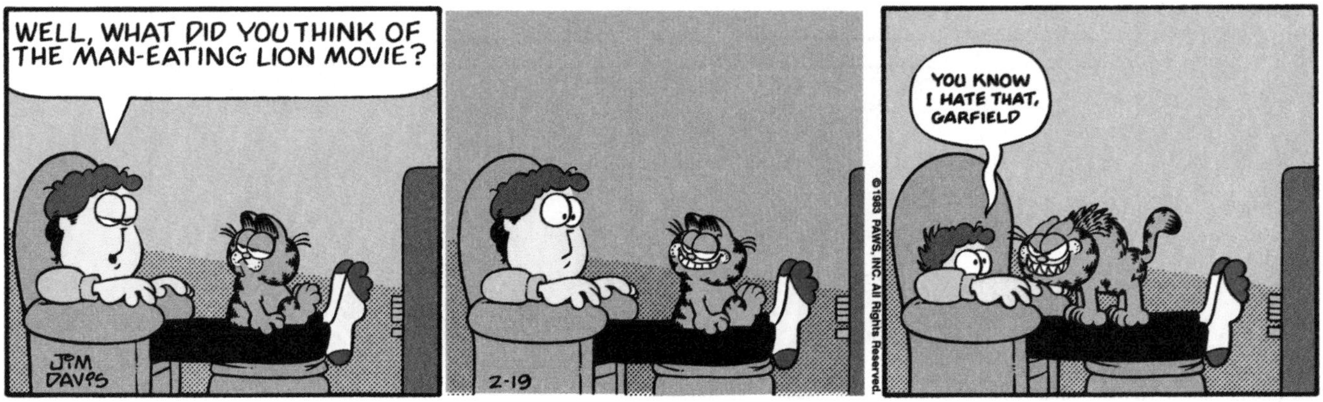
WELL, WHAT DID YOU THINK OF THE MAN-EATING LION MOVIE?
JIM DAVIS
2-19
© 1983 PAWS, INC. All Rights Reserved.
YOU KNOW I HATE THAT, GARFIELD

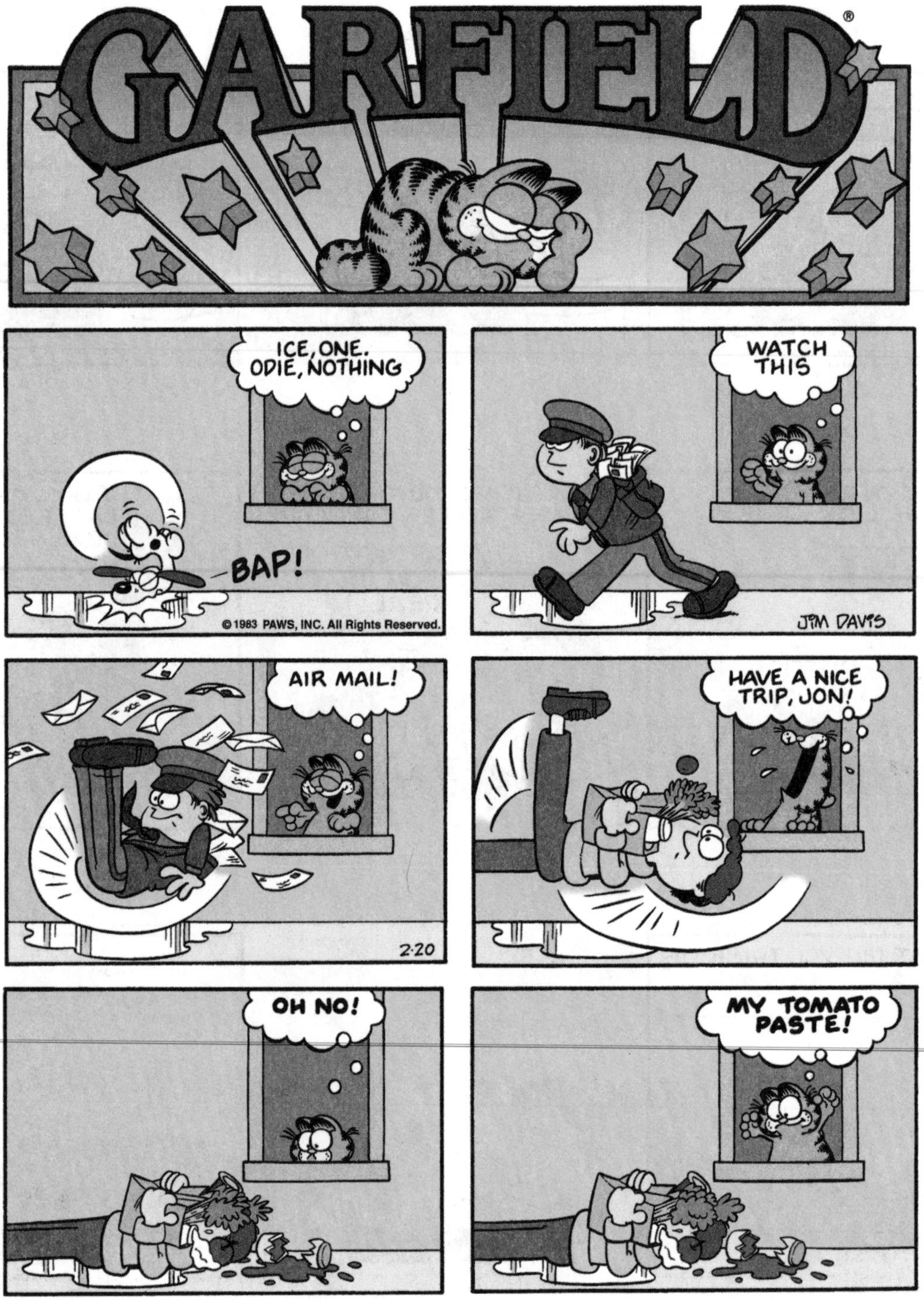
GARFIELD®
ICE, ONE. ODIE, NOTHING
BAP!
© 1983 PAWS, INC. All Rights Reserved.
WATCH THIS
JIM DAVIS
AIR MAIL!
2-20
HAVE A NICE TRIP, JON!
OH NO!
MY TOMATO PASTE!

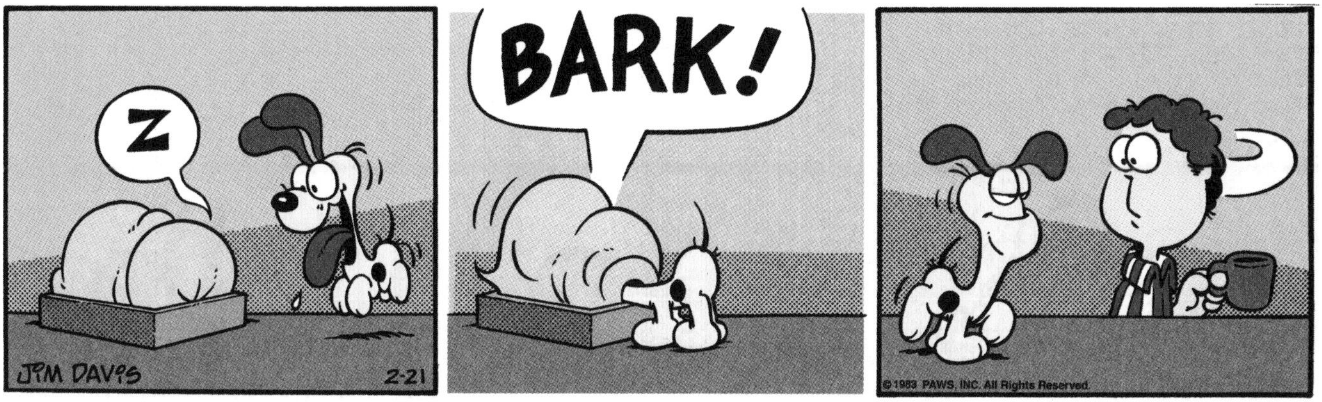
Z
JIM DAVIS
2-21
BARK!
© 1983 PAWS, INC. All Rights Reserved.

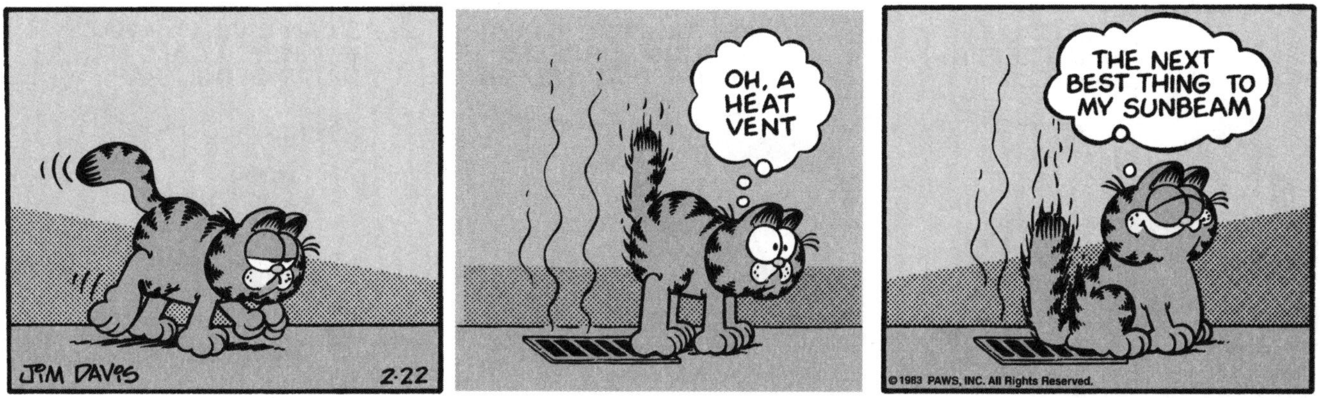
JIM DAVIS
2-22
OH, A HEAT VENT
THE NEXT BEST THING TO MY SUNBEAM
© 1983 PAWS, INC. All Rights Reserved.

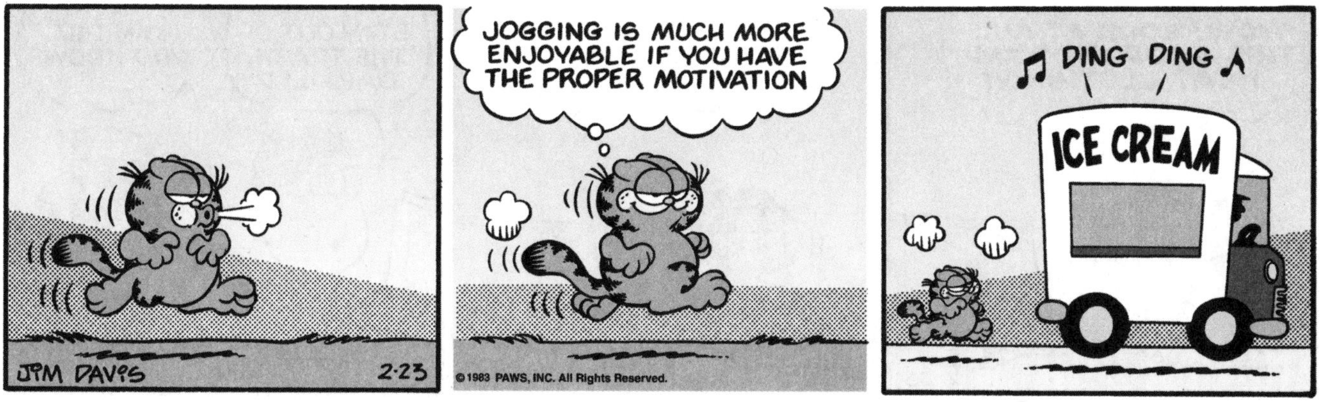
JIM DAVIS
2-23
JOGGING IS MUCH MORE ENJOYABLE IF YOU HAVE THE PROPER MOTIVATION
© 1983 PAWS, INC. All Rights Reserved.
DING DING
ICE CREAM

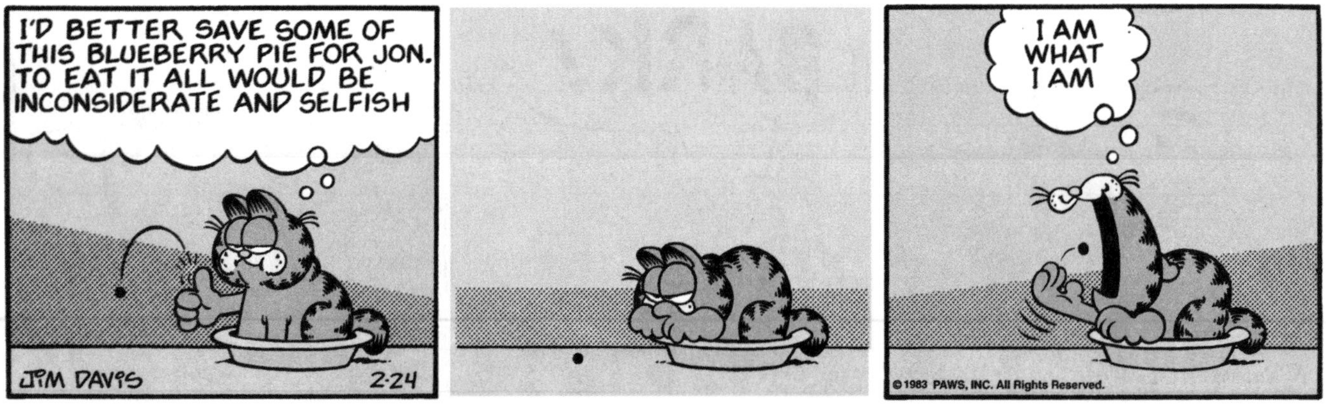
I'D BETTER SAVE SOME OF THIS BLUEBERRY PIE FOR JON. TO EAT IT ALL WOULD BE INCONSIDERATE AND SELFISH
JIM DAVIS
2-24
I AM WHAT I AM
© 1983 PAWS, INC. All Rights Reserved.

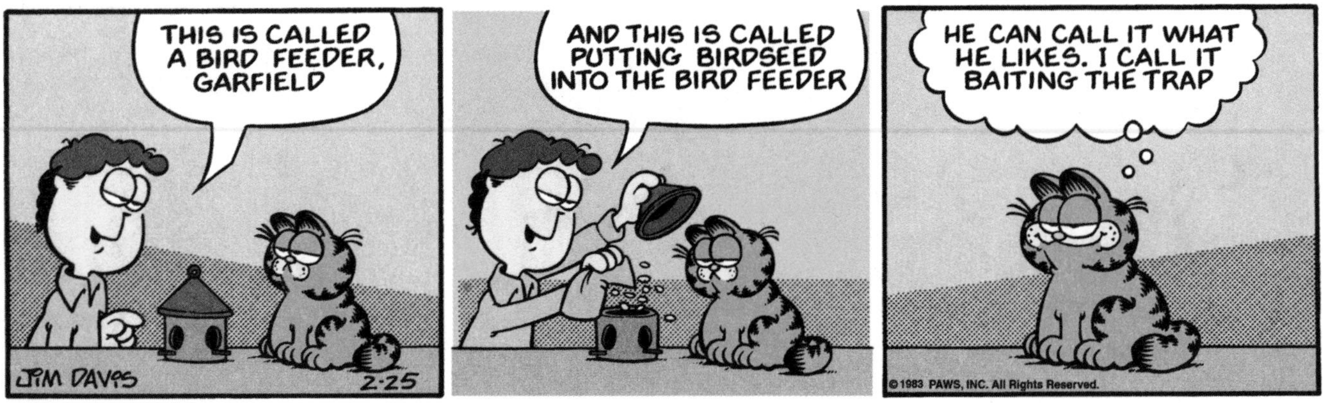
THIS IS CALLED A BIRD FEEDER, GARFIELD
JIM DAVIS
2-25
AND THIS IS CALLED PUTTING BIRDSEED INTO THE BIRD FEEDER
HE CAN CALL IT WHAT HE LIKES. I CALL IT BAITING THE TRAP
© 1983 PAWS, INC. All Rights Reserved.

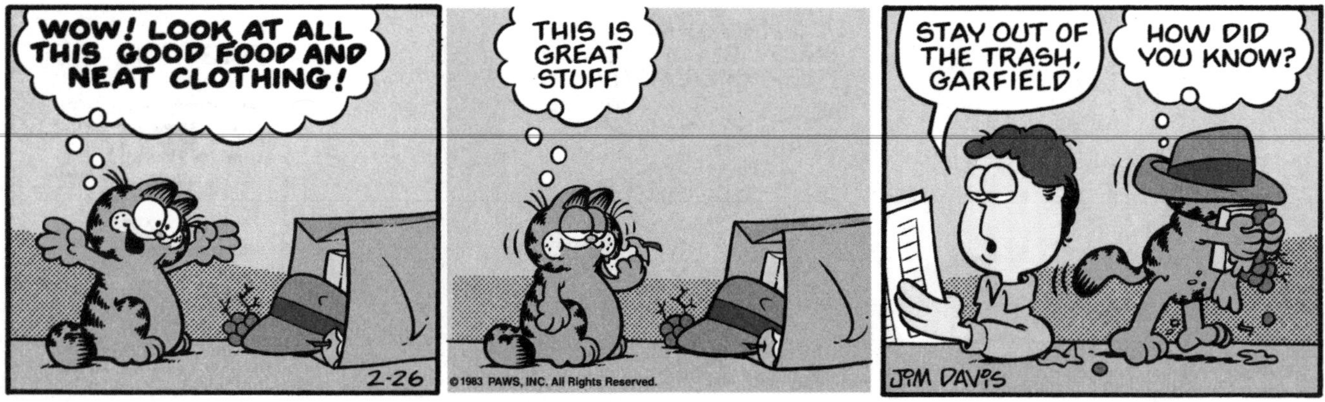
WOW! LOOK AT ALL THIS GOOD FOOD AND NEAT CLOTHING!
2-26
THIS IS GREAT STUFF
© 1983 PAWS, INC. All Rights Reserved.
STAY OUT OF THE TRASH, GARFIELD
HOW DID YOU KNOW?
JIM DAVIS

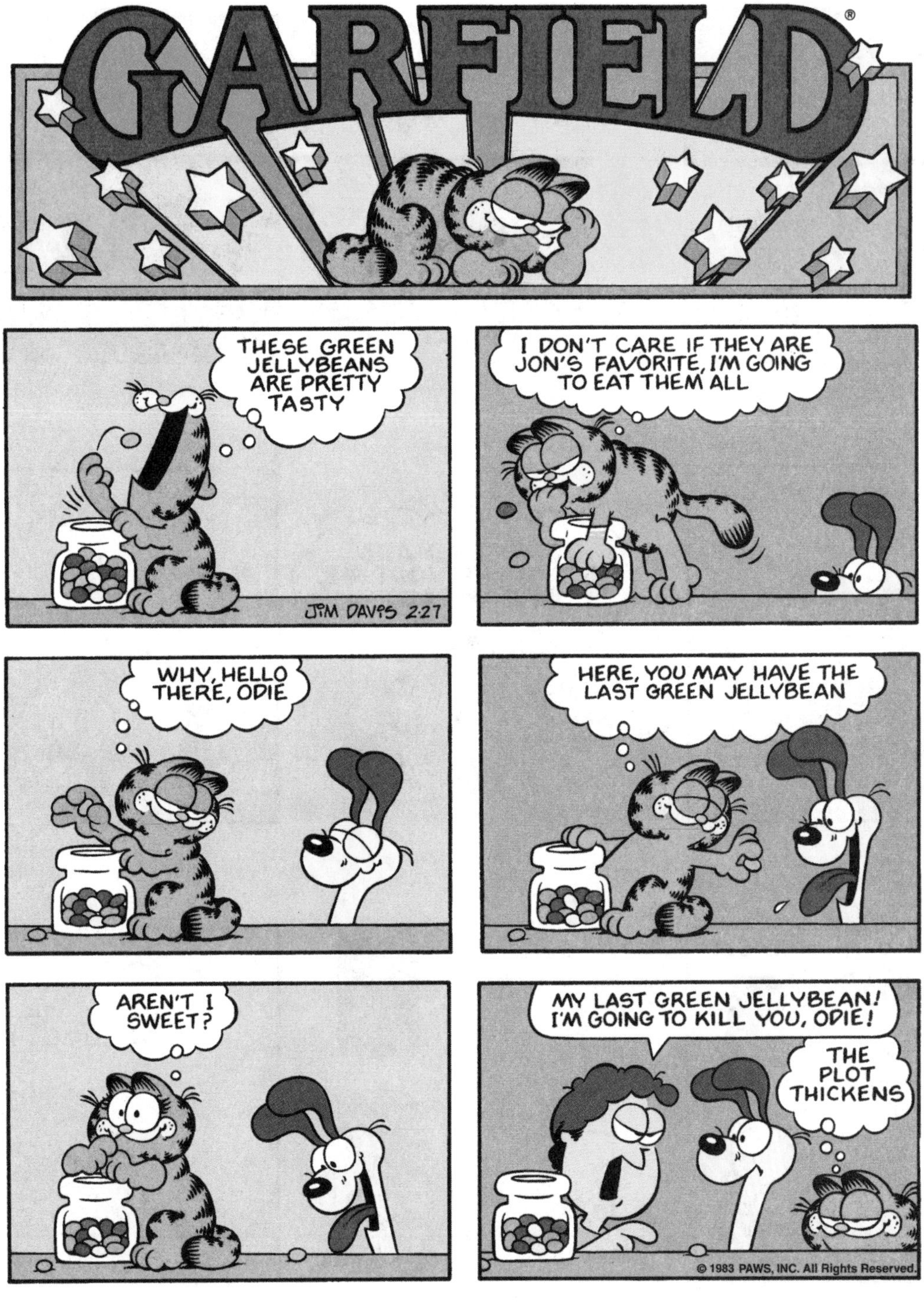
GARFIELD®
THESE GREEN JELLYBEANS ARE PRETTY TASTY
JIM DAVIS 2·27
I DON'T CARE IF THEY ARE JON'S FAVORITE, I'M GOING TO EAT THEM ALL
WHY, HELLO THERE, ODIE
HERE, YOU MAY HAVE THE LAST GREEN JELLYBEAN
AREN'T I SWEET?
MY LAST GREEN JELLYBEAN! I'M GOING TO KILL YOU, ODIE!
THE PLOT THICKENS
© 1983 PAWS, INC. All Rights Reserved.

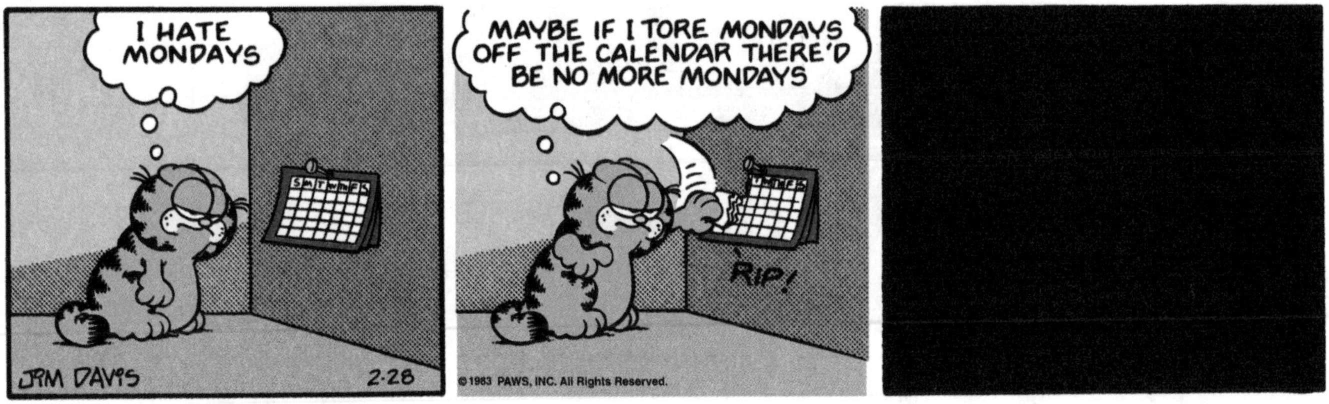
I HATE MONDAYS
JIM DAVIS
2-28
MAYBE IF I TORE MONDAYS OFF THE CALENDAR THERE'D BE NO MORE MONDAYS
RIP!
©1983 PAWS, INC. All Rights Reserved.
[redacted]

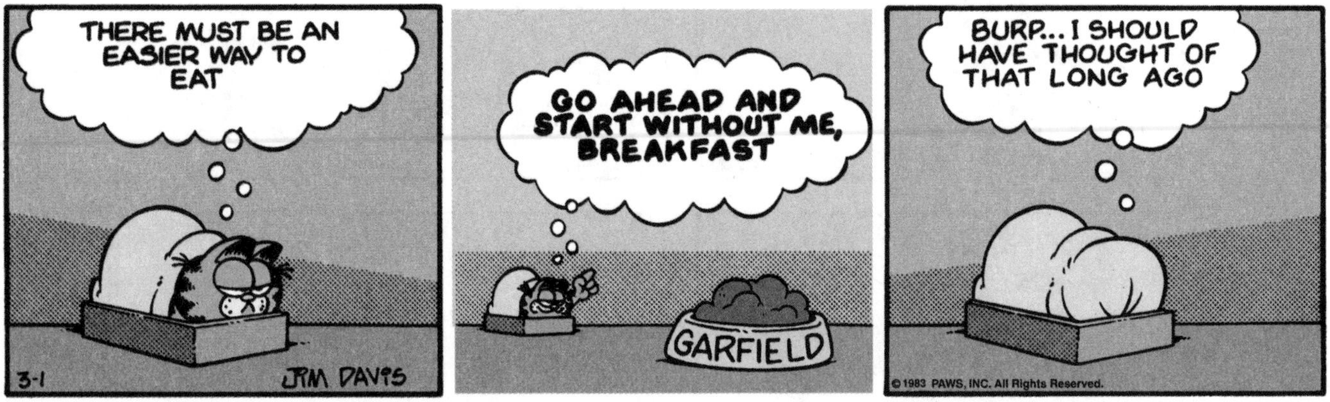
THERE MUST BE AN EASIER WAY TO EAT
3-1
JIM DAVIS
GO AHEAD AND START WITHOUT ME, BREAKFAST
GARFIELD
BURP... I SHOULD HAVE THOUGHT OF THAT LONG AGO
©1983 PAWS, INC. All Rights Reserved.

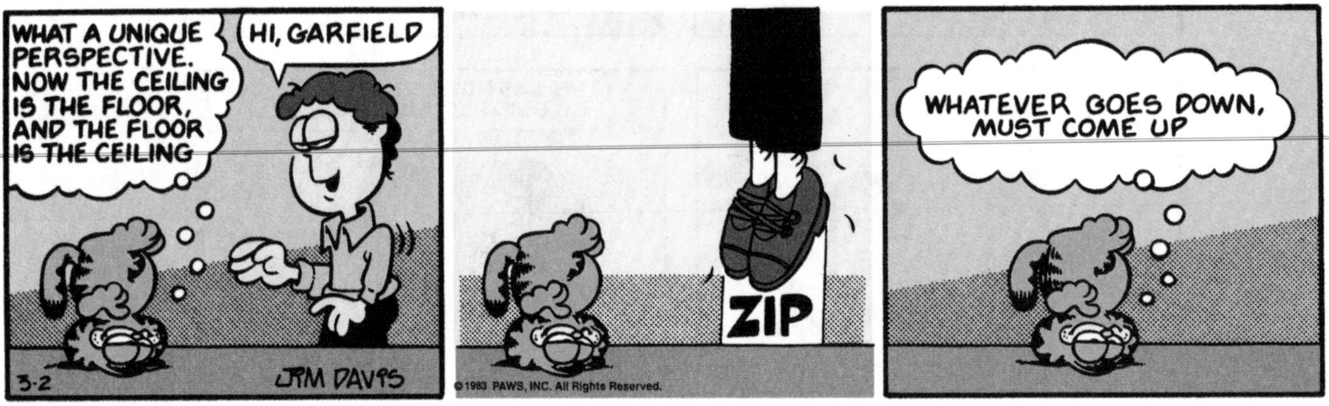
WHAT A UNIQUE PERSPECTIVE. NOW THE CEILING IS THE FLOOR, AND THE FLOOR IS THE CEILING
HI, GARFIELD
3-2
JIM DAVIS
ZIP
©1983 PAWS, INC. All Rights Reserved.
WHATEVER GOES DOWN, MUST COME UP

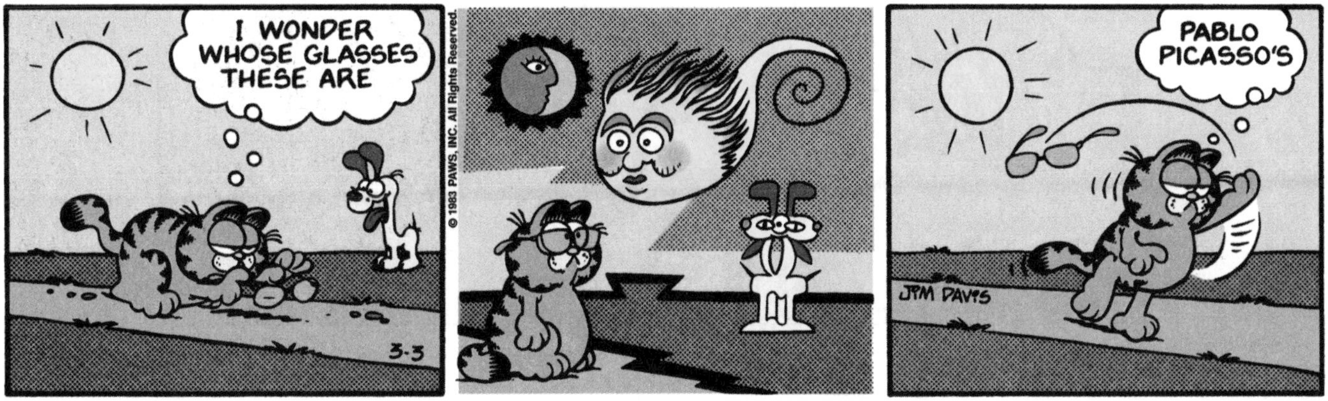
I WONDER WHOSE GLASSES THESE ARE
3-3
© 1983 PAWS, INC. All Rights Reserved.
PABLO PICASSO'S
JIM DAVIS

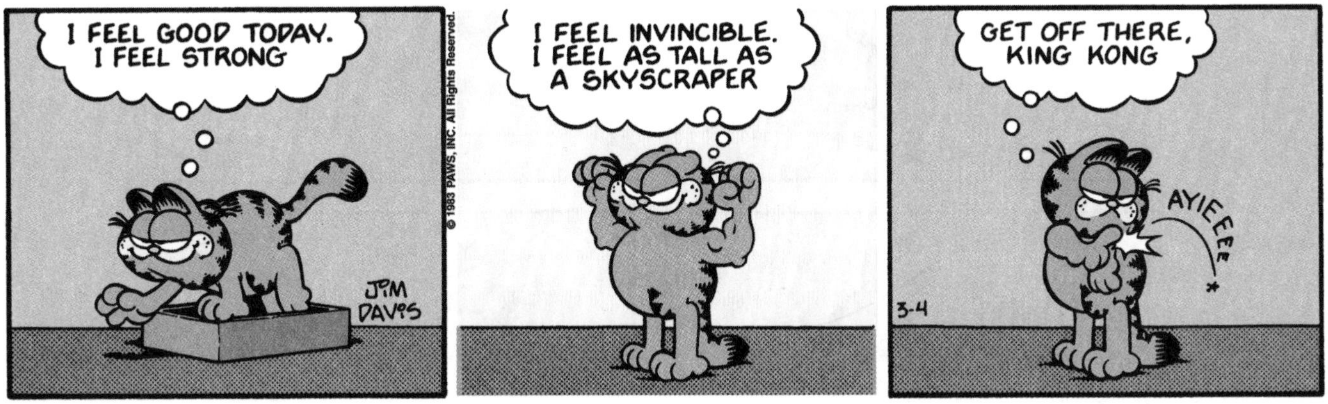
I FEEL GOOD TODAY. I FEEL STRONG
JIM DAVIS
© 1983 PAWS, INC. All Rights Reserved.
I FEEL INVINCIBLE. I FEEL AS TALL AS A SKYSCRAPER
GET OFF THERE, KING KONG
AYIEEEE
3-4

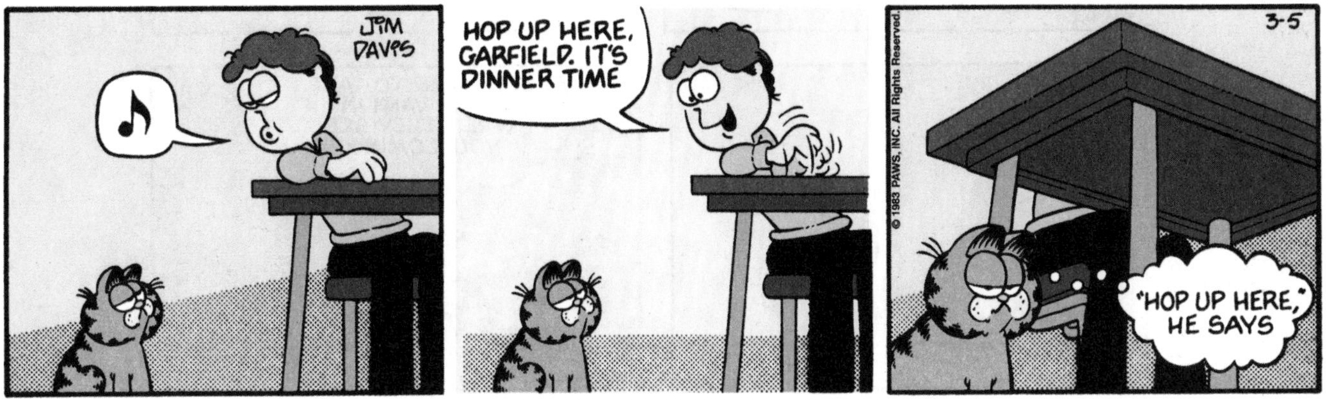
JIM DAVIS
♪
HOP UP HERE, GARFIELD. IT'S DINNER TIME
© 1983 PAWS, INC. All Rights Reserved.
3-5
"HOP UP HERE," HE SAYS

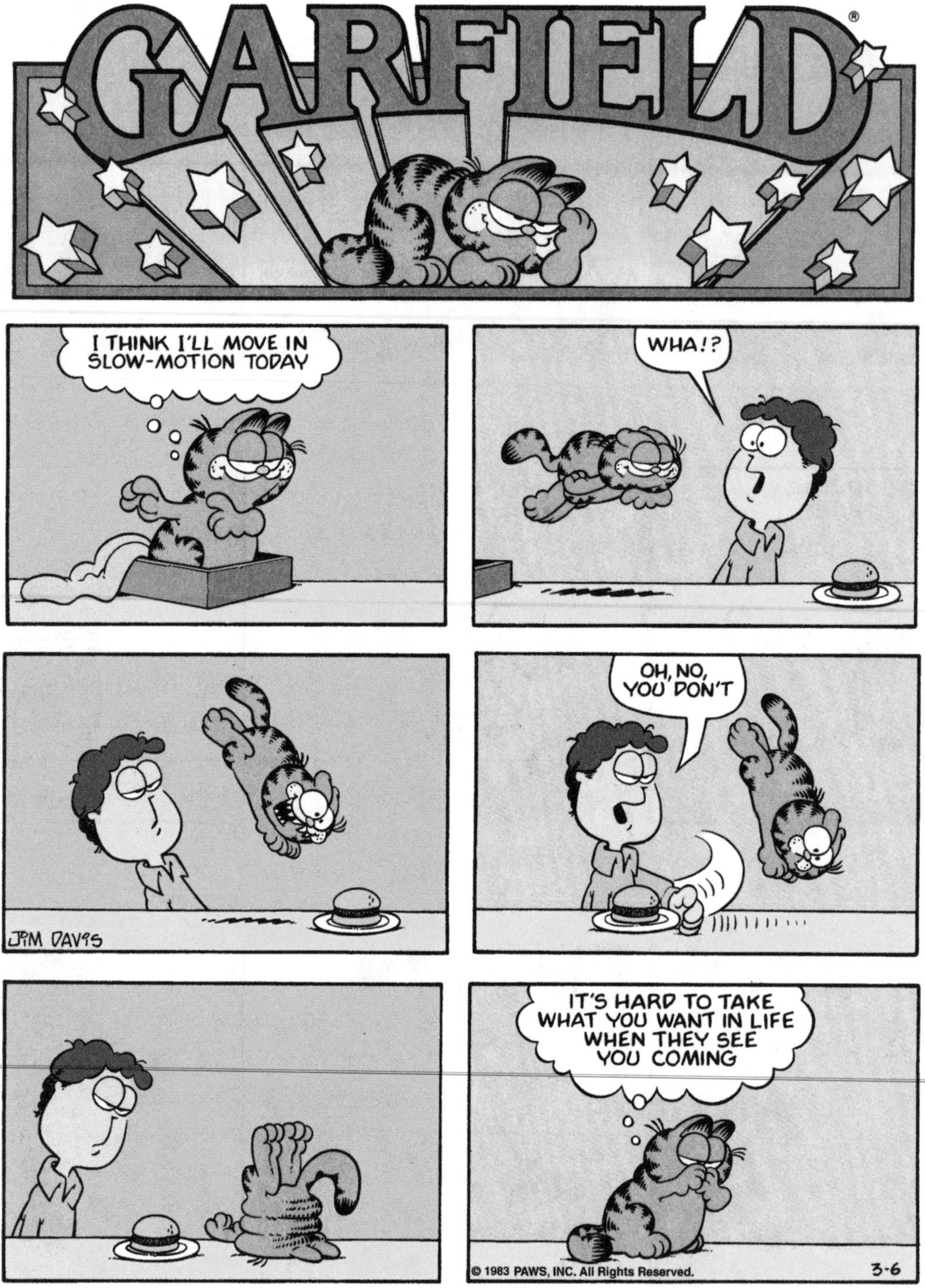
GARFIELD
I THINK I'LL MOVE IN SLOW-MOTION TODAY
WHA!?
OH, NO, YOU DON'T
JIM DAVIS
IT'S HARD TO TAKE WHAT YOU WANT IN LIFE WHEN THEY SEE YOU COMING
© 1983 PAWS, INC. All Rights Reserved.
3-6

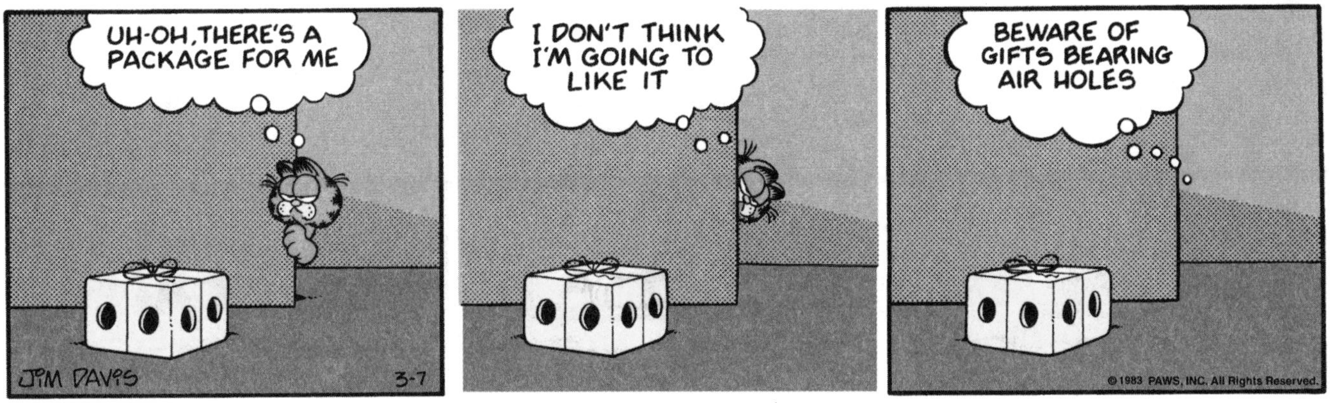
UH-OH, THERE'S A PACKAGE FOR ME
JIM DAVIS
3-7
I DON'T THINK I'M GOING TO LIKE IT
BEWARE OF GIFTS BEARING AIR HOLES
© 1983 PAWS, INC. All Rights Reserved.

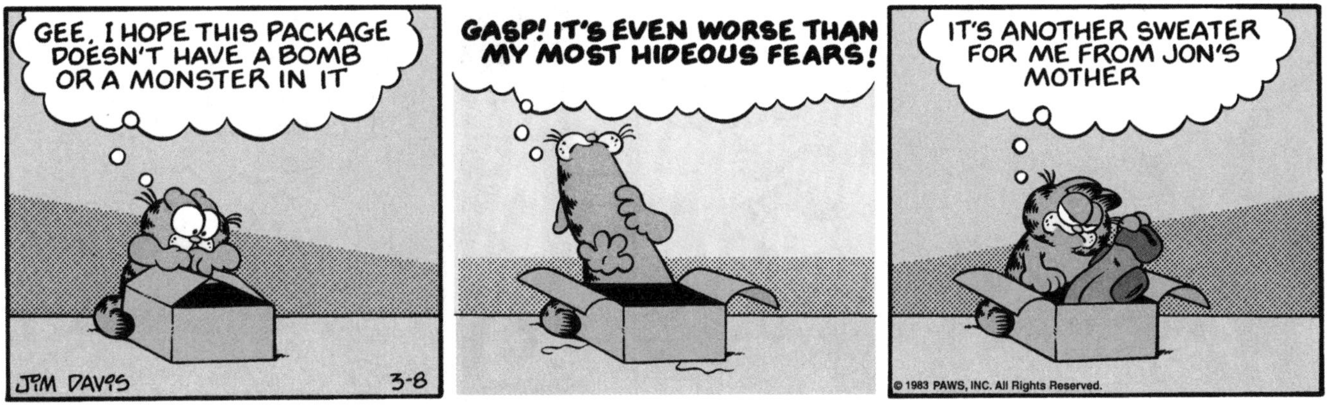
GEE, I HOPE THIS PACKAGE DOESN'T HAVE A BOMB OR A MONSTER IN IT
JIM DAVIS
3-8
GASP! IT'S EVEN WORSE THAN MY MOST HIDEOUS FEARS!
IT'S ANOTHER SWEATER FOR ME FROM JON'S MOTHER
© 1983 PAWS, INC. All Rights Reserved.

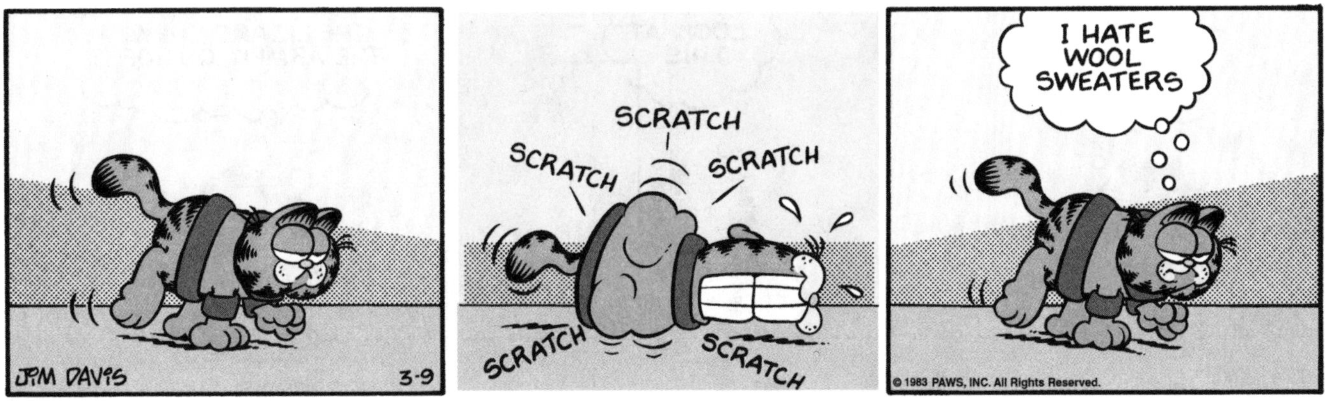
JIM DAVIS
3-9
SCRATCH
SCRATCH
SCRATCH
SCRATCH
SCRATCH
I HATE WOOL SWEATERS
© 1983 PAWS, INC. All Rights Reserved.

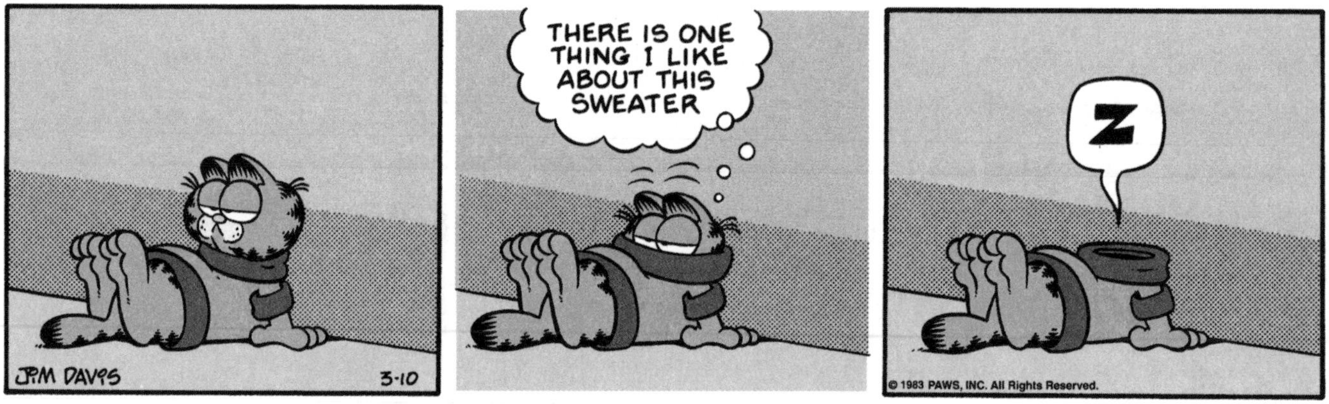
JIM DAVIS
3-10
THERE IS ONE THING I LIKE ABOUT THIS SWEATER
Z
© 1983 PAWS, INC. All Rights Reserved.

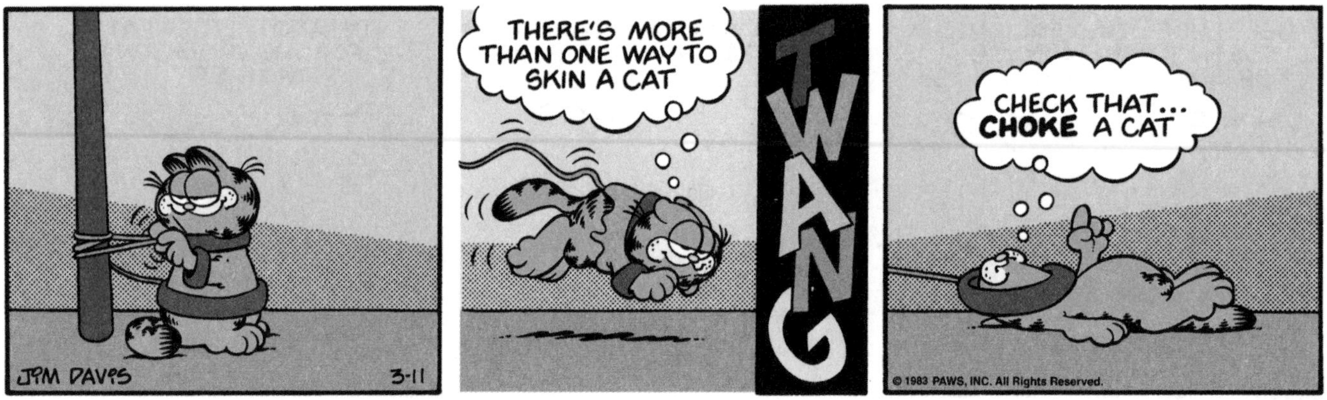
JIM DAVIS
3-11
THERE'S MORE THAN ONE WAY TO SKIN A CAT
TWANG
CHECK THAT... **CHOKE** A CAT
© 1983 PAWS, INC. All Rights Reserved.

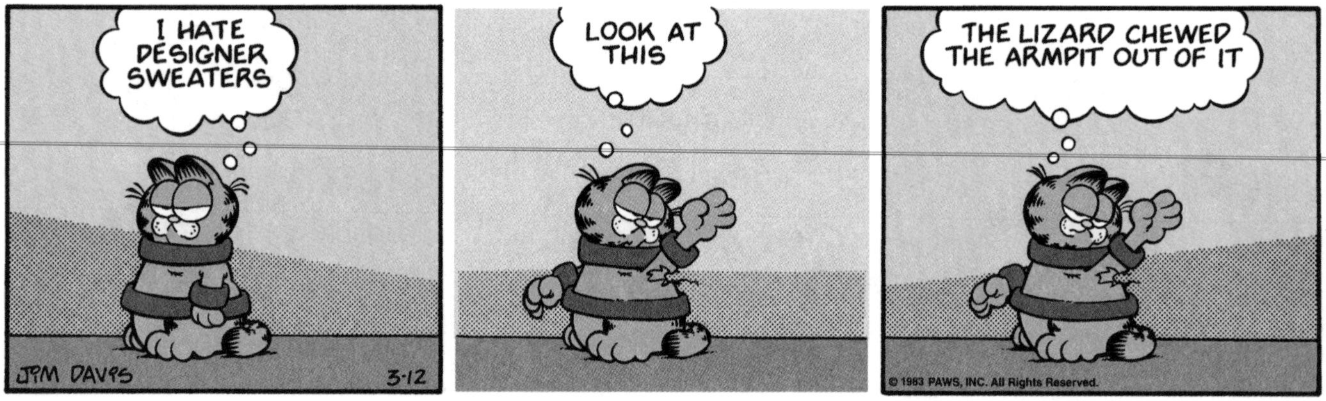
I HATE DESIGNER SWEATERS
JIM DAVIS
3-12
LOOK AT THIS
THE LIZARD CHEWED THE ARMPIT OUT OF IT
© 1983 PAWS, INC. All Rights Reserved.

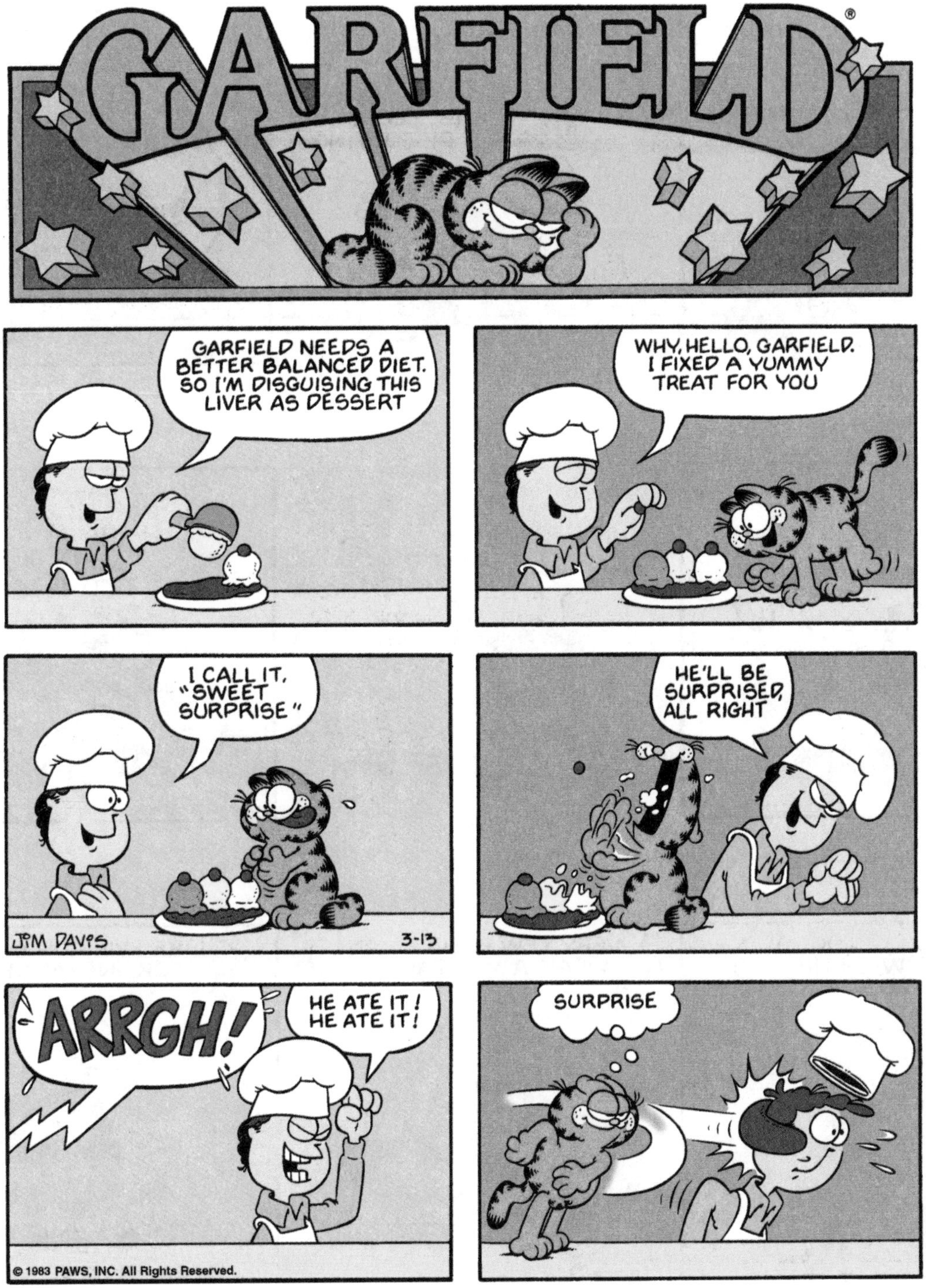
GARFIELD®
GARFIELD NEEDS A BETTER BALANCED DIET. SO I'M DISGUISING THIS LIVER AS DESSERT
WHY, HELLO, GARFIELD. I FIXED A YUMMY TREAT FOR YOU
I CALL IT, "SWEET SURPRISE"
HE'LL BE SURPRISED, ALL RIGHT
JIM DAVIS 3-13
ARRGH!
HE ATE IT! HE ATE IT!
SURPRISE

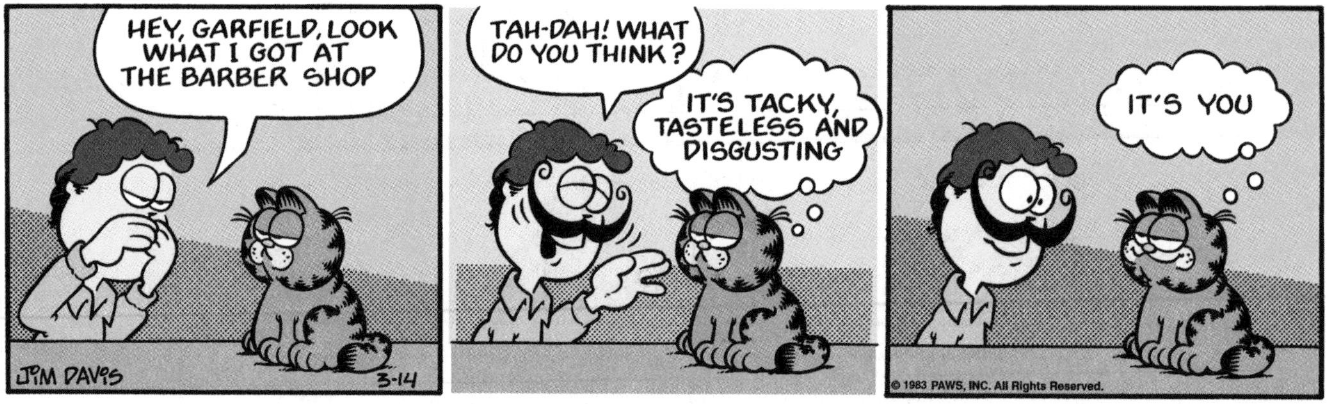
HEY, GARFIELD, LOOK WHAT I GOT AT THE BARBER SHOP
JIM DAVIS
3-14
TAH-DAH! WHAT DO YOU THINK?
IT'S TACKY, TASTELESS AND DISGUSTING
IT'S YOU
© 1983 PAWS, INC. All Rights Reserved.

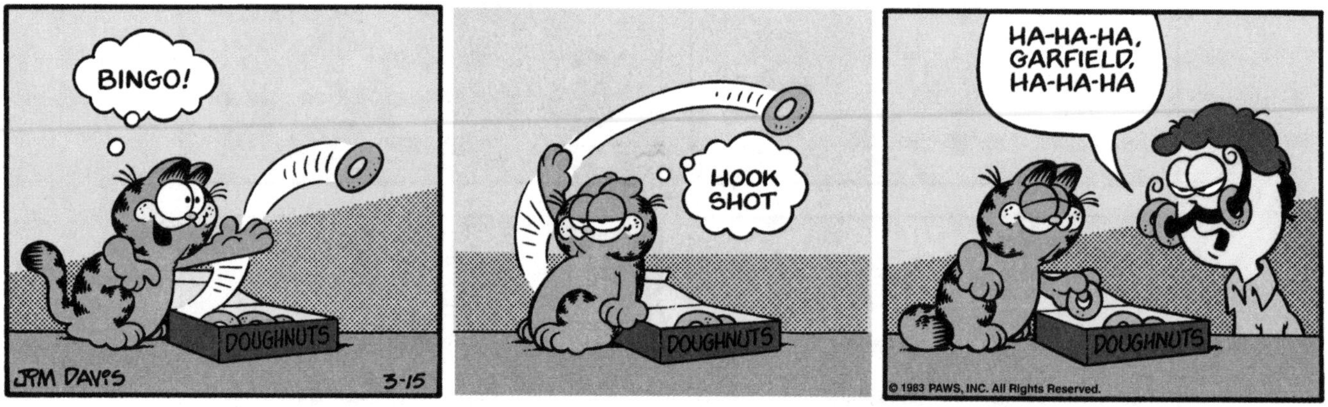
BINGO!
DOUGHNUTS
JIM DAVIS
3-15
HOOK SHOT
DOUGHNUTS
HA-HA-HA, GARFIELD, HA-HA-HA
DOUGHNUTS
© 1983 PAWS, INC. All Rights Reserved.

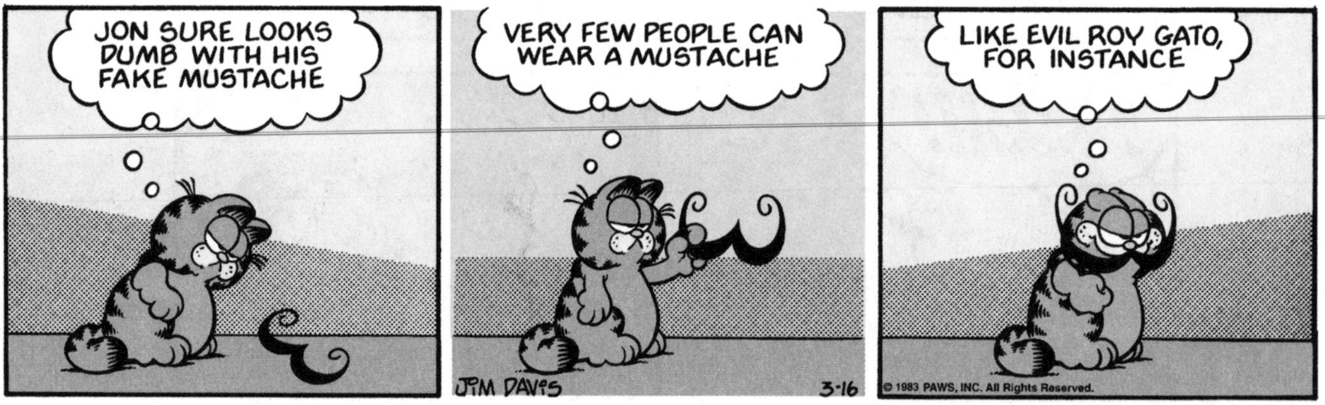
JON SURE LOOKS DUMB WITH HIS FAKE MUSTACHE
VERY FEW PEOPLE CAN WEAR A MUSTACHE
JIM DAVIS
3-16
LIKE EVIL ROY GATO, FOR INSTANCE
© 1983 PAWS, INC. All Rights Reserved.

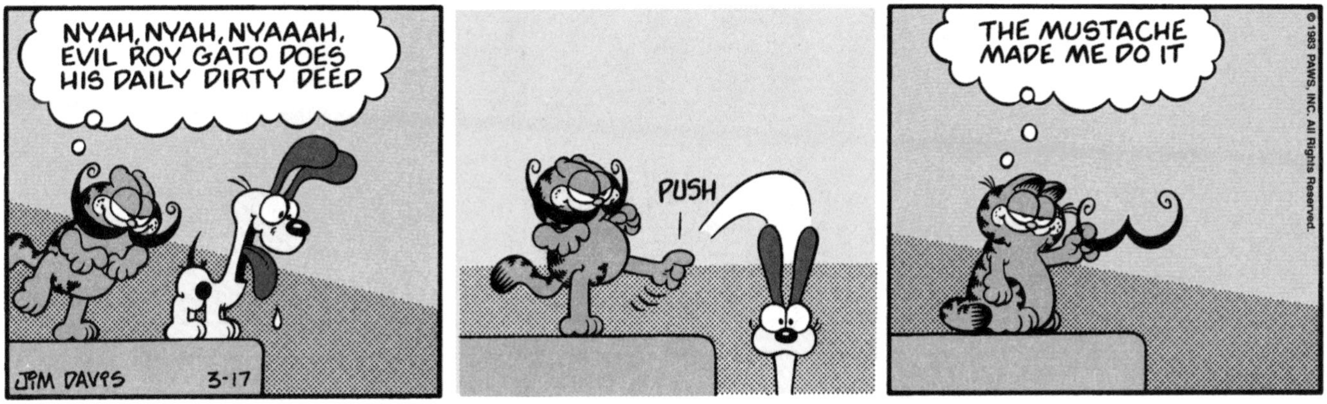
NYAH, NYAH, NYAAAH. EVIL ROY GATO DOES HIS DAILY DIRTY DEED
JIM DAVIS 3-17
PUSH
THE MUSTACHE MADE ME DO IT
© 1983 PAWS, INC. All Rights Reserved.

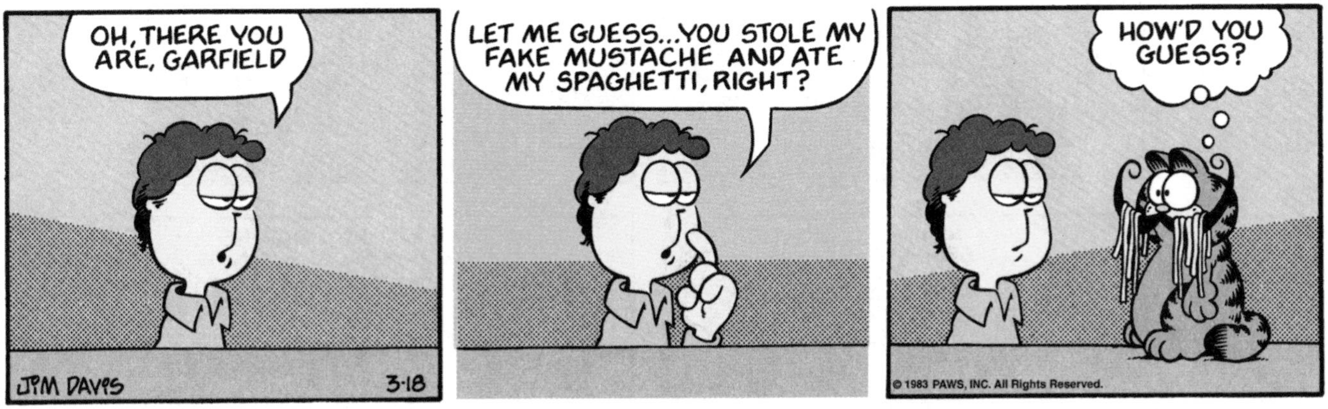
OH, THERE YOU ARE, GARFIELD
JIM DAVIS 3-18
LET ME GUESS... YOU STOLE MY FAKE MUSTACHE AND ATE MY SPAGHETTI, RIGHT?
HOW'D YOU GUESS?
© 1983 PAWS, INC. All Rights Reserved.

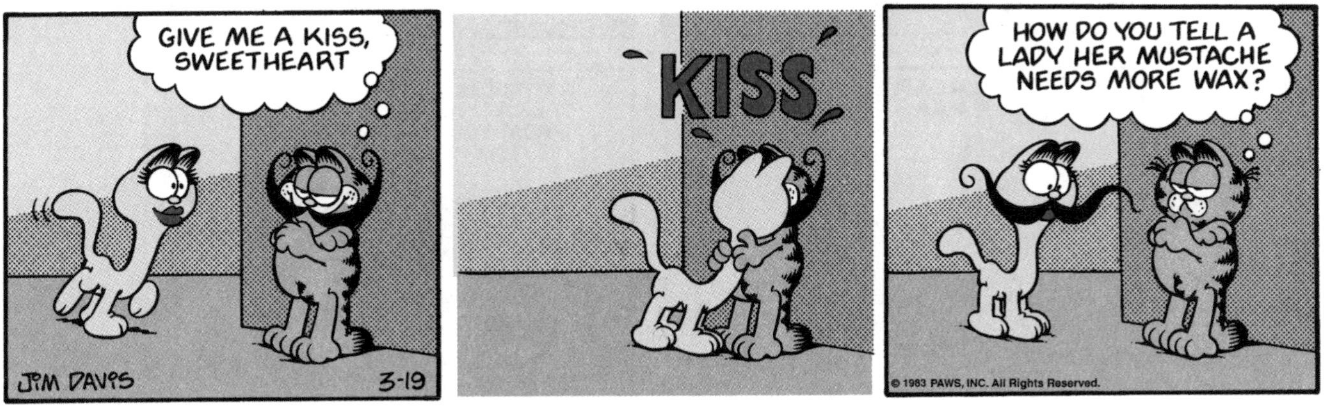
GIVE ME A KISS, SWEETHEART
JIM DAVIS 3-19
KISS
HOW DO YOU TELL A LADY HER MUSTACHE NEEDS MORE WAX?
© 1983 PAWS, INC. All Rights Reserved.

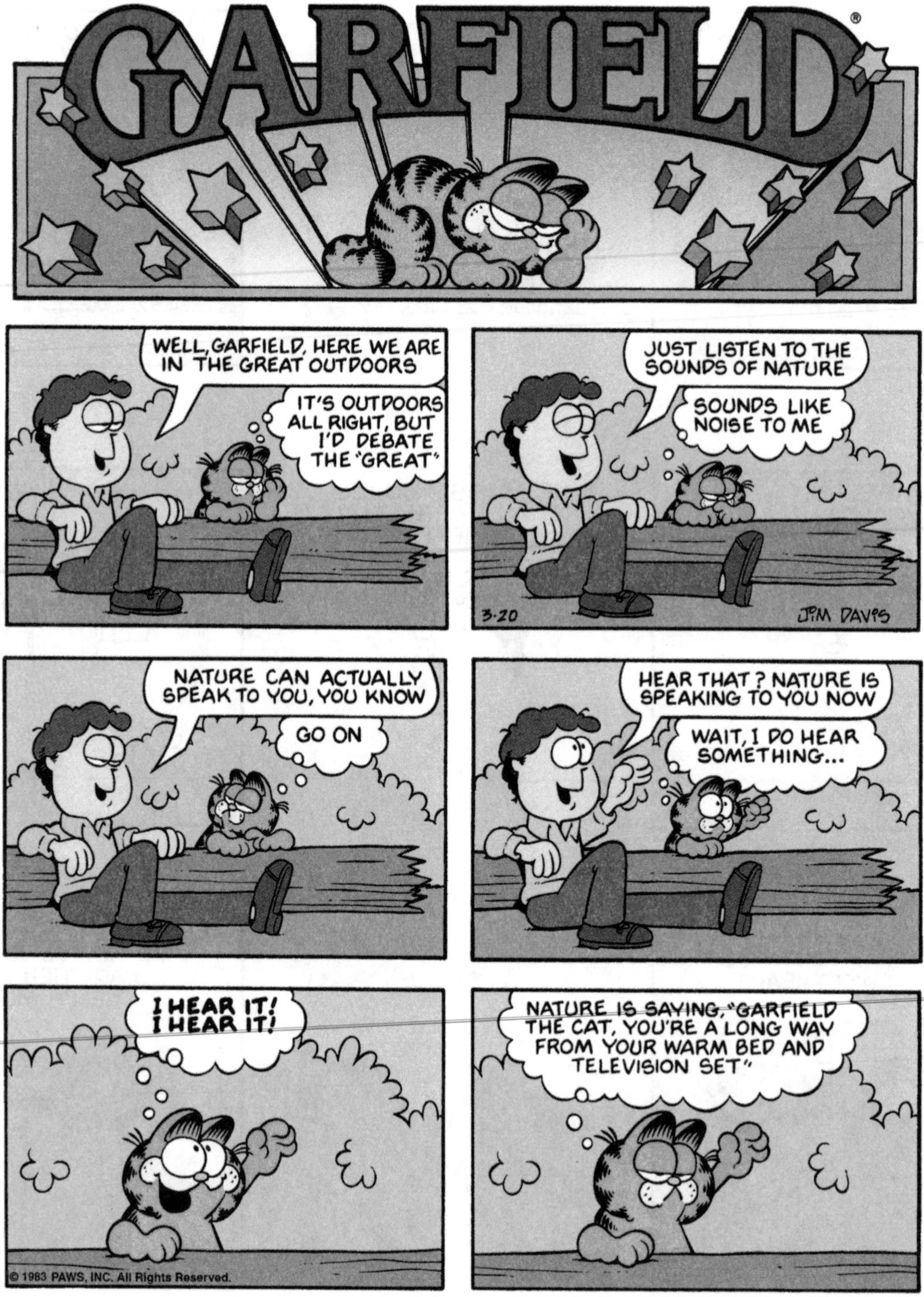
GARFIELD®
WELL, GARFIELD, HERE WE ARE IN THE GREAT OUTDOORS
IT'S OUTDOORS ALL RIGHT, BUT I'D DEBATE THE "GREAT"
JUST LISTEN TO THE SOUNDS OF NATURE
SOUNDS LIKE NOISE TO ME
3-20
JIM DAVIS
NATURE CAN ACTUALLY SPEAK TO YOU, YOU KNOW
GO ON
HEAR THAT? NATURE IS SPEAKING TO YOU NOW
WAIT, I DO HEAR SOMETHING...
I HEAR IT! I HEAR IT!
NATURE IS SAYING, "GARFIELD THE CAT, YOU'RE A LONG WAY FROM YOUR WARM BED AND TELEVISION SET"

Garfield loses his feet

BY JIM DAVIS

Ballantine Books ● **New York**

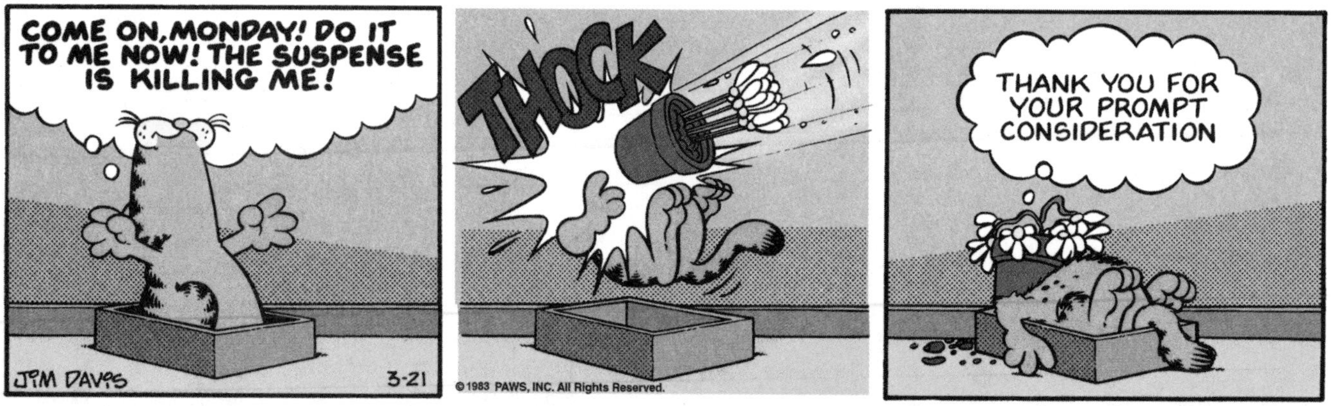
COME ON, MONDAY! DO IT TO ME NOW! THE SUSPENSE IS KILLING ME!
JIM DAVIS
3-21
THOCK
© 1983 PAWS, INC. All Rights Reserved.
THANK YOU FOR YOUR PROMPT CONSIDERATION

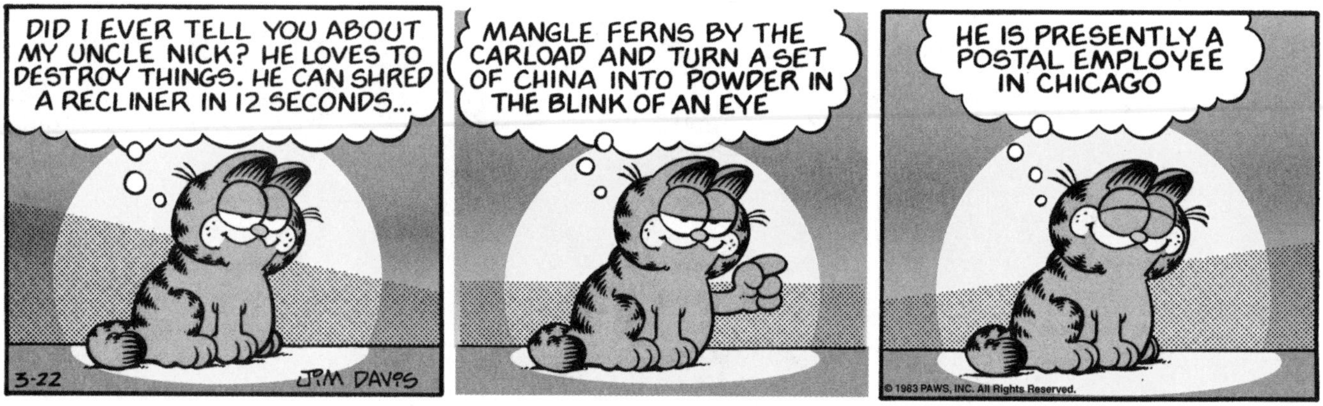
DID I EVER TELL YOU ABOUT MY UNCLE NICK? HE LOVES TO DESTROY THINGS. HE CAN SHRED A RECLINER IN 12 SECONDS...
3-22
JIM DAVIS
MANGLE FERNS BY THE CARLOAD AND TURN A SET OF CHINA INTO POWDER IN THE BLINK OF AN EYE
HE IS PRESENTLY A POSTAL EMPLOYEE IN CHICAGO
© 1983 PAWS, INC. All Rights Reserved.

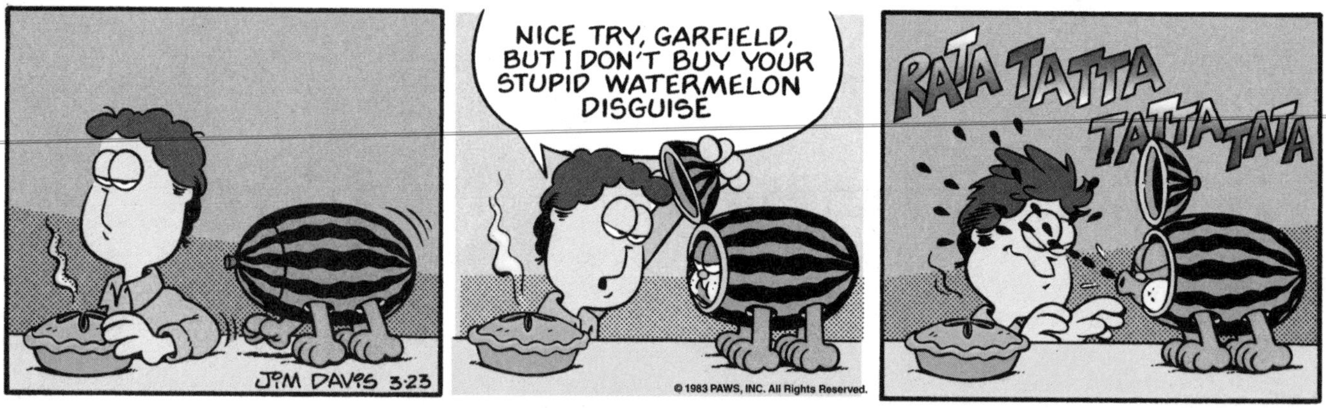
JIM DAVIS 3-23
NICE TRY, GARFIELD, BUT I DON'T BUY YOUR STUPID WATERMELON DISGUISE
© 1983 PAWS, INC. All Rights Reserved.
RATA TATTA TATTA TATA

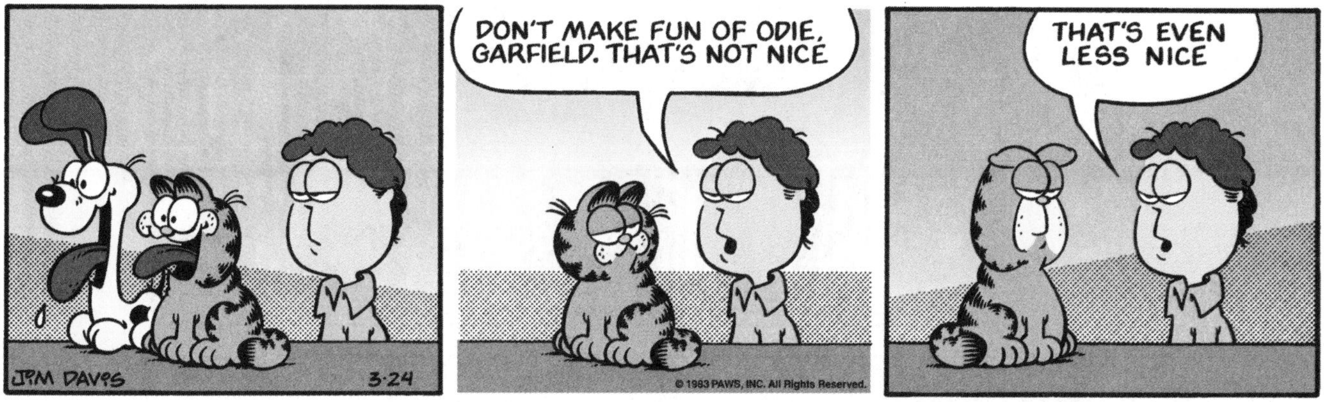
JIM DAVIS
3-24
DON'T MAKE FUN OF ODIE, GARFIELD. THAT'S NOT NICE
© 1983 PAWS, INC. All Rights Reserved.
THAT'S EVEN LESS NICE

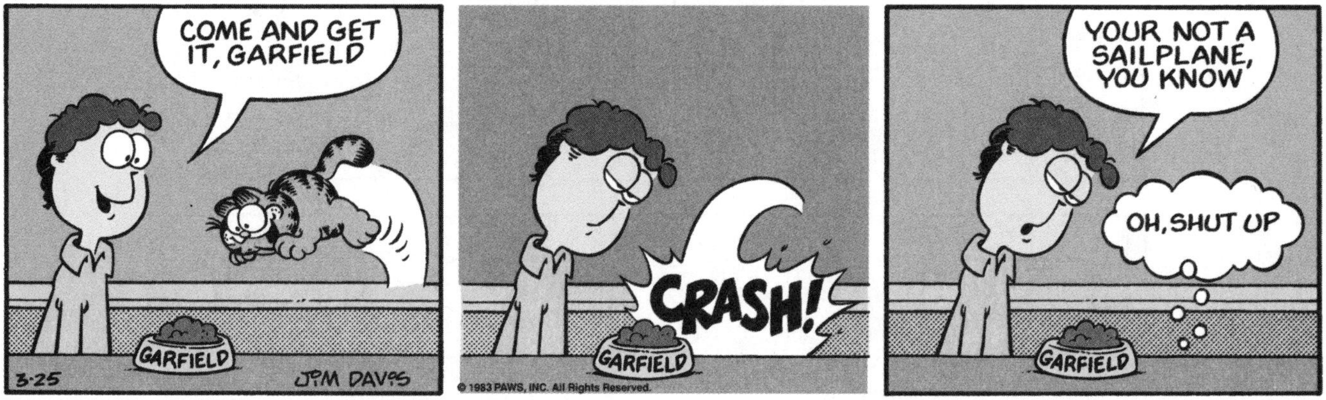
COME AND GET IT, GARFIELD
GARFIELD
3-25
JIM DAVIS
CRASH!
GARFIELD
© 1983 PAWS, INC. All Rights Reserved.
YOUR NOT A SAILPLANE, YOU KNOW
OH, SHUT UP
GARFIELD

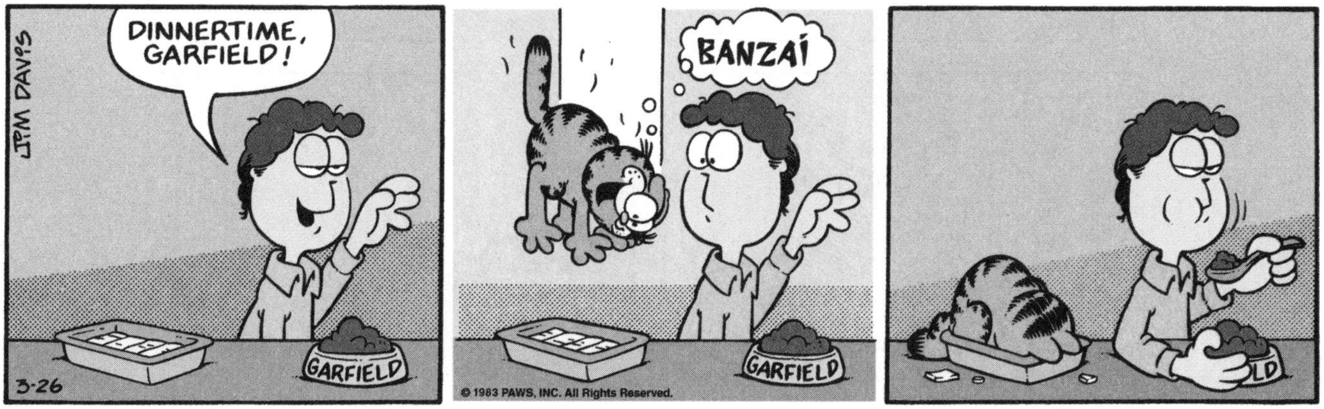
JIM DAVIS
DINNERTIME, GARFIELD!
GARFIELD
3-26
BANZAI
GARFIELD
© 1983 PAWS, INC. All Rights Reserved.

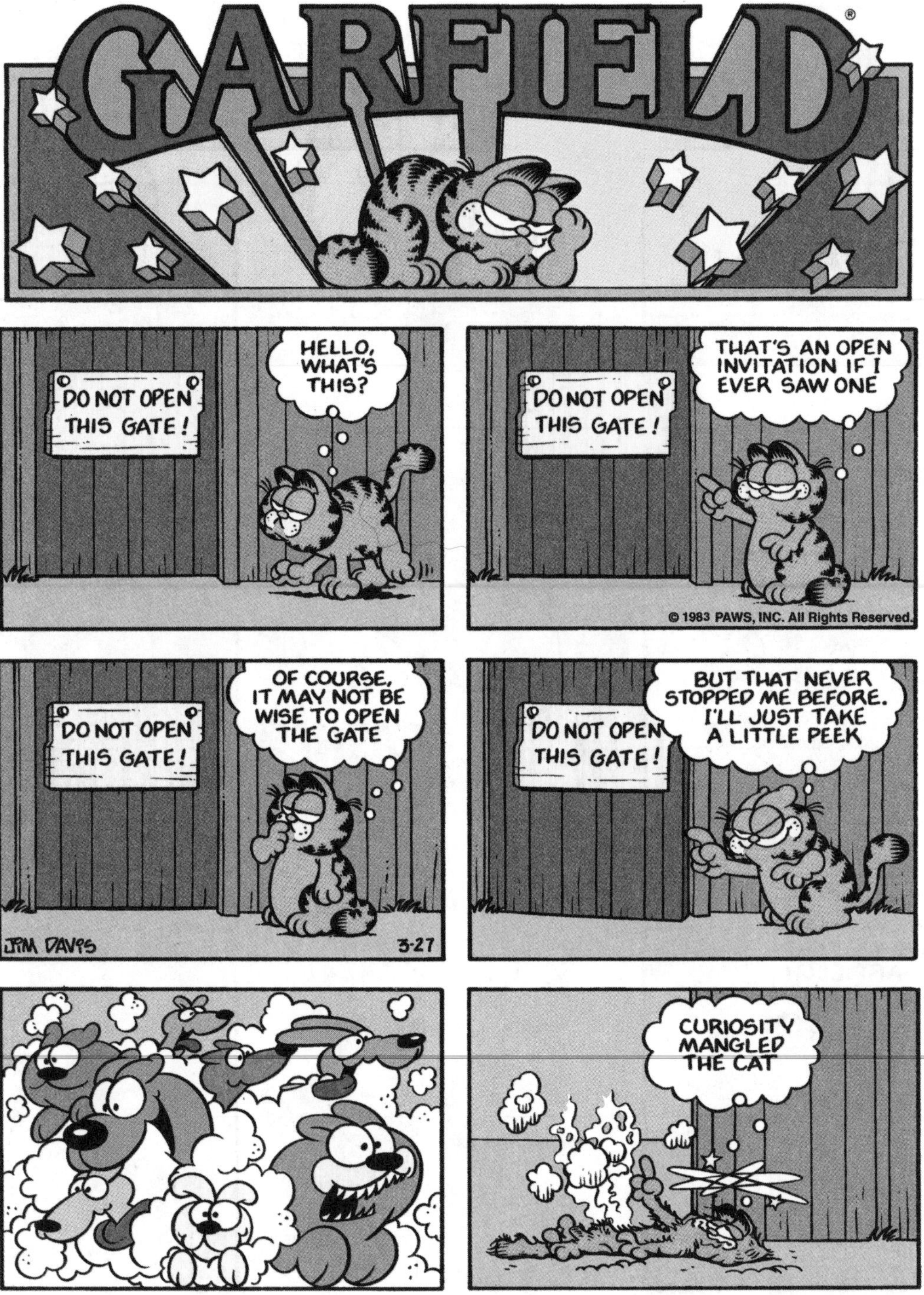
GARFIELD®
DO NOT OPEN THIS GATE!
HELLO, WHAT'S THIS?
DO NOT OPEN THIS GATE!
THAT'S AN OPEN INVITATION IF I EVER SAW ONE
© 1983 PAWS, INC. All Rights Reserved.
DO NOT OPEN THIS GATE!
OF COURSE, IT MAY NOT BE WISE TO OPEN THE GATE
JIM DAVIS
3-27
DO NOT OPEN THIS GATE!
BUT THAT NEVER STOPPED ME BEFORE. I'LL JUST TAKE A LITTLE PEEK
CURIOSITY MANGLED THE CAT

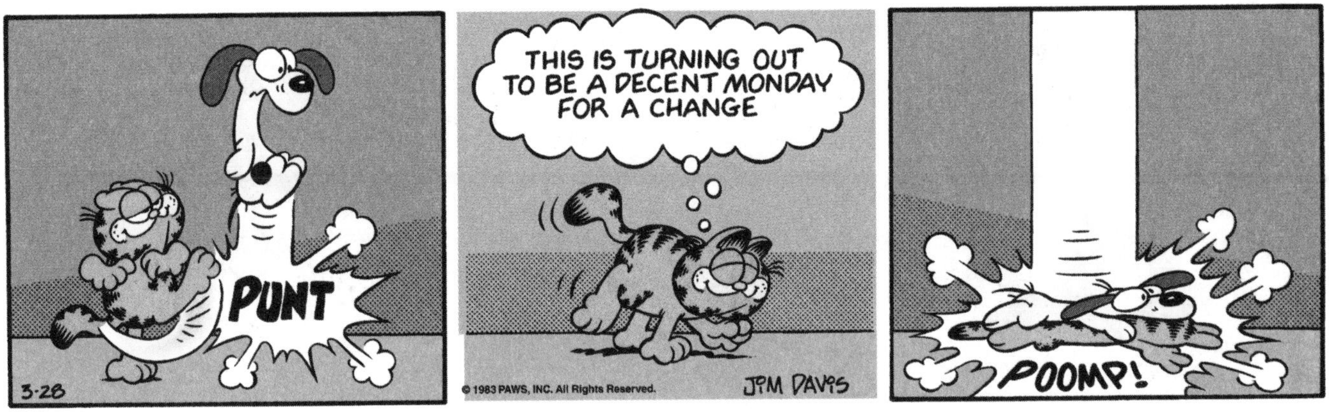
PUNT
3-28
THIS IS TURNING OUT TO BE A DECENT MONDAY FOR A CHANGE
© 1983 PAWS, INC. All Rights Reserved.
JIM DAVIS
POOMP!

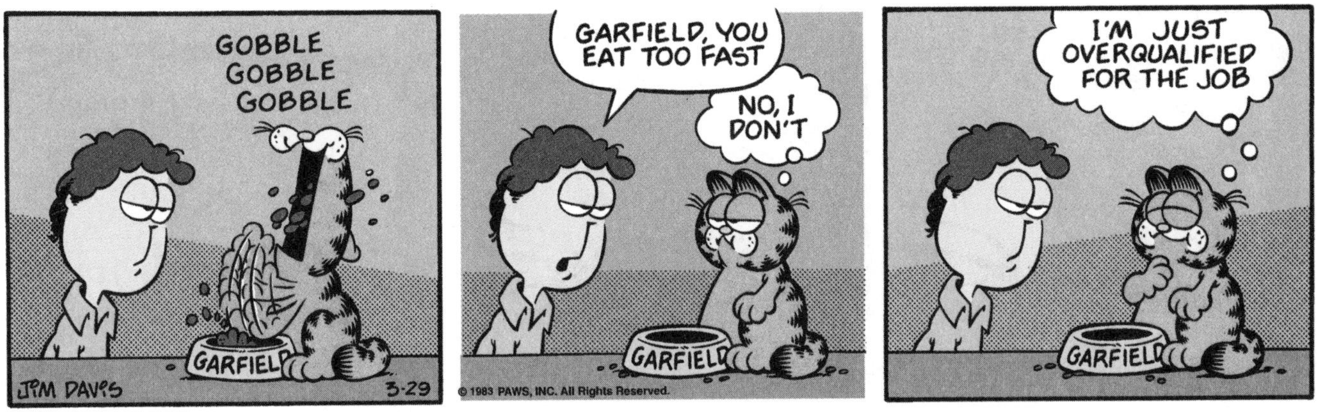
GOBBLE GOBBLE GOBBLE
GARFIELD
JIM DAVIS
3-29
GARFIELD, YOU EAT TOO FAST
NO, I DON'T
GARFIELD
© 1983 PAWS, INC. All Rights Reserved.
I'M JUST OVERQUALIFIED FOR THE JOB
GARFIELD

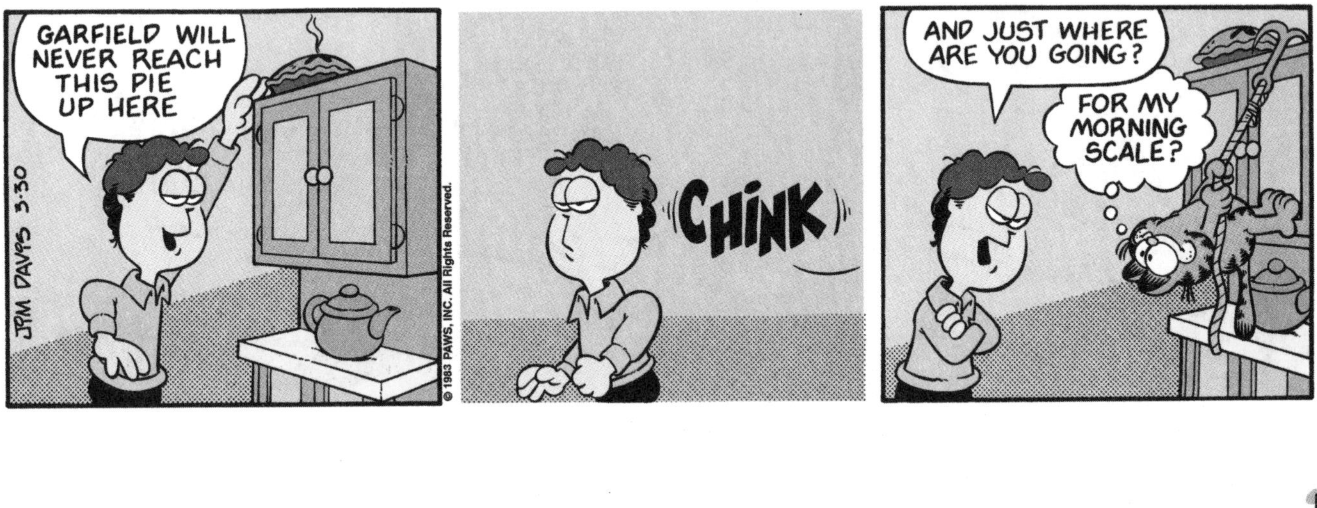
GARFIELD WILL NEVER REACH THIS PIE UP HERE
JIM DAVIS 3-30
© 1983 PAWS, INC. All Rights Reserved.
CHINK
AND JUST WHERE ARE YOU GOING?
FOR MY MORNING SCALE?

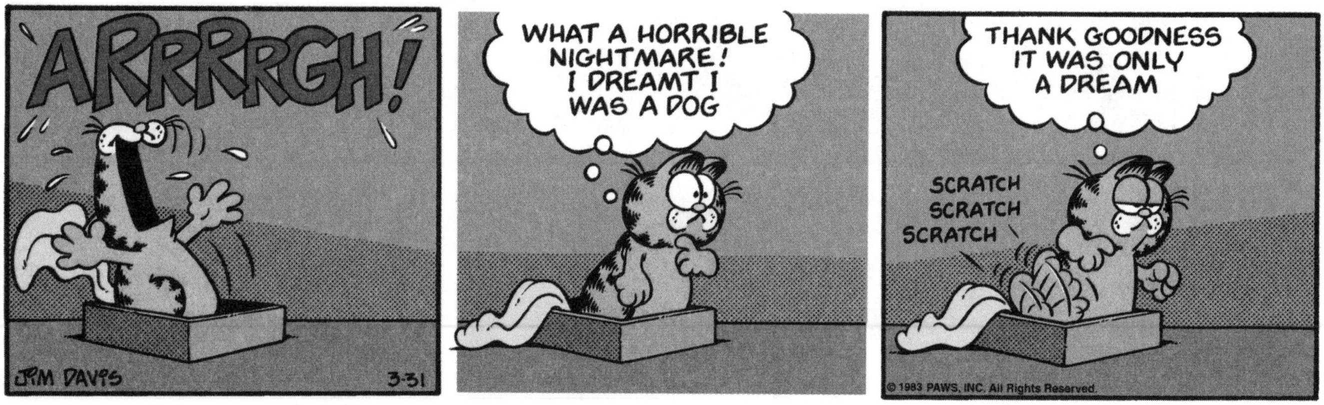
ARRRRGH!
JIM DAVIS
3-31
WHAT A HORRIBLE NIGHTMARE! I DREAMT I WAS A DOG
THANK GOODNESS IT WAS ONLY A DREAM
SCRATCH SCRATCH SCRATCH
© 1983 PAWS, INC. All Rights Reserved.

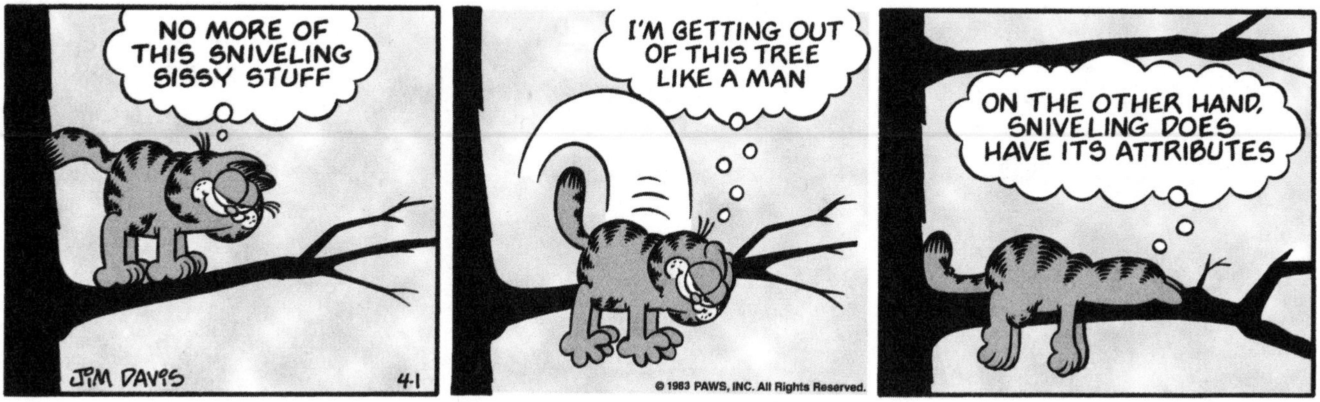
NO MORE OF THIS SNIVELING SISSY STUFF
JIM DAVIS
4-1
I'M GETTING OUT OF THIS TREE LIKE A MAN
© 1983 PAWS, INC. All Rights Reserved.
ON THE OTHER HAND, SNIVELING DOES HAVE ITS ATTRIBUTES

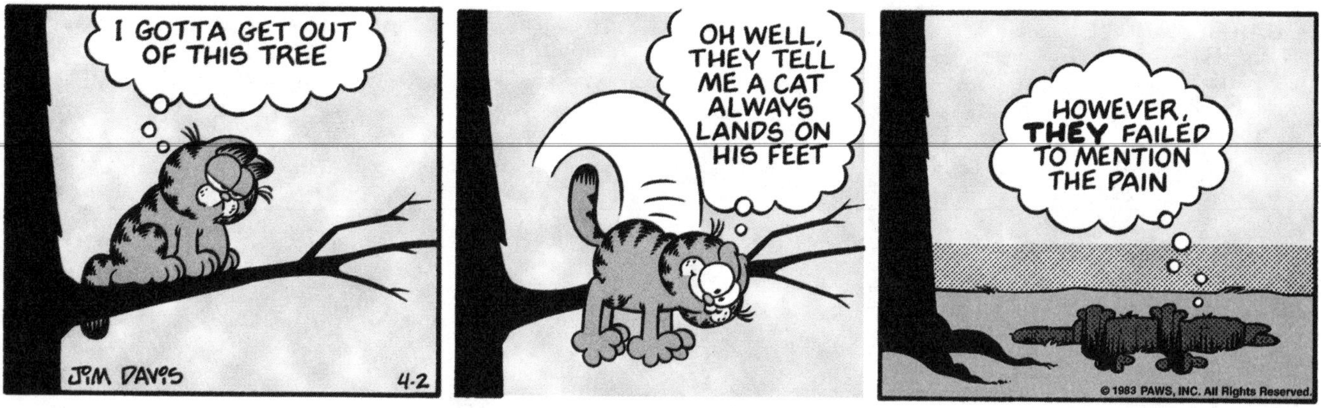
I GOTTA GET OUT OF THIS TREE
JIM DAVIS
4-2
OH WELL, THEY TELL ME A CAT ALWAYS LANDS ON HIS FEET
HOWEVER, **THEY** FAILED TO MENTION THE PAIN
© 1983 PAWS, INC. All Rights Reserved.

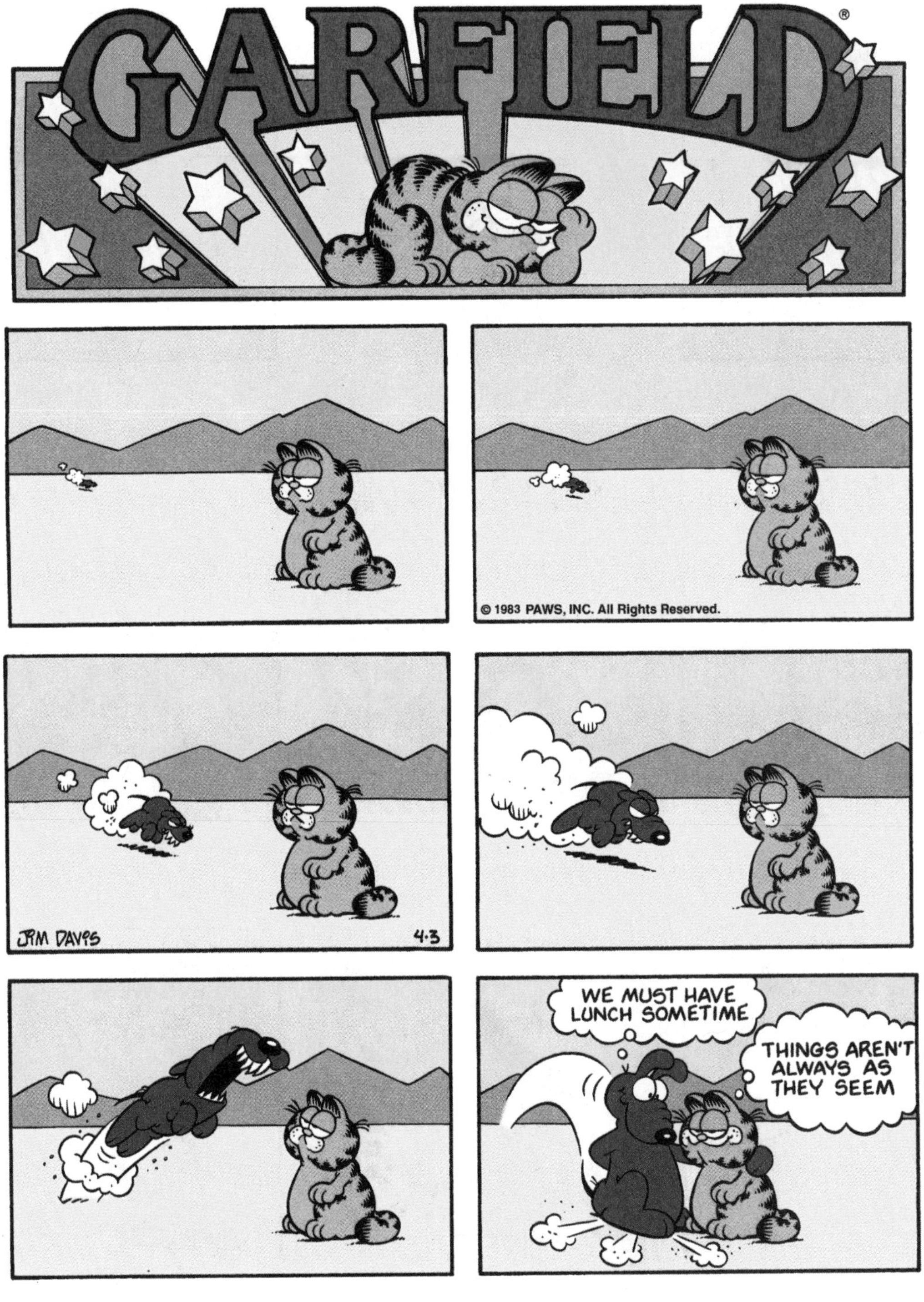
GARFIELD®
© 1983 PAWS, INC. All Rights Reserved.
JIM DAVIS
4·3
WE MUST HAVE LUNCH SOMETIME
THINGS AREN'T ALWAYS AS THEY SEEM

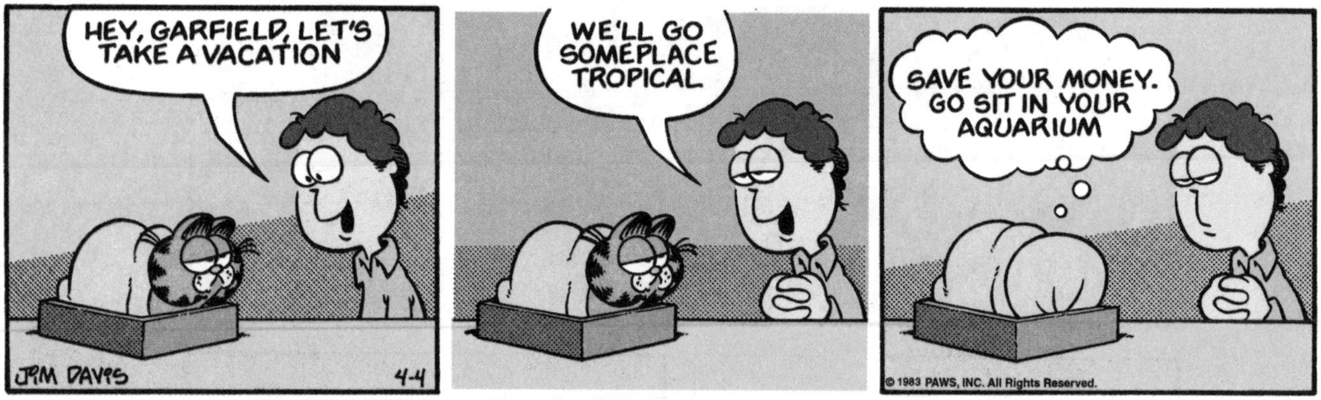
HEY, GARFIELD, LET'S TAKE A VACATION
JIM DAVIS
4-4
WE'LL GO SOMEPLACE TROPICAL
SAVE YOUR MONEY. GO SIT IN YOUR AQUARIUM
© 1983 PAWS, INC. All Rights Reserved.

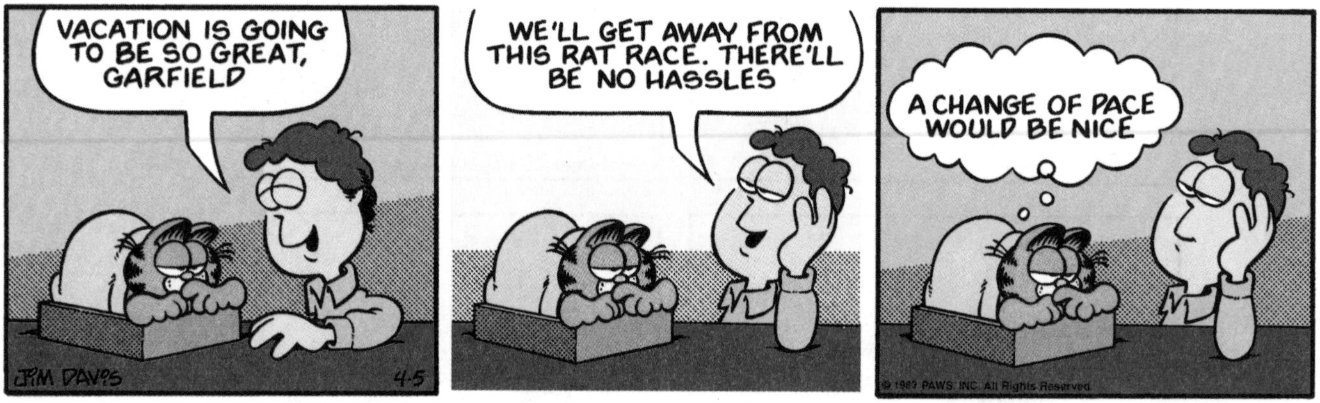
VACATION IS GOING TO BE SO GREAT, GARFIELD
JIM DAVIS
4-5
WE'LL GET AWAY FROM THIS RAT RACE. THERE'LL BE NO HASSLES
A CHANGE OF PACE WOULD BE NICE
© 1983 PAWS, INC. All Rights Reserved.

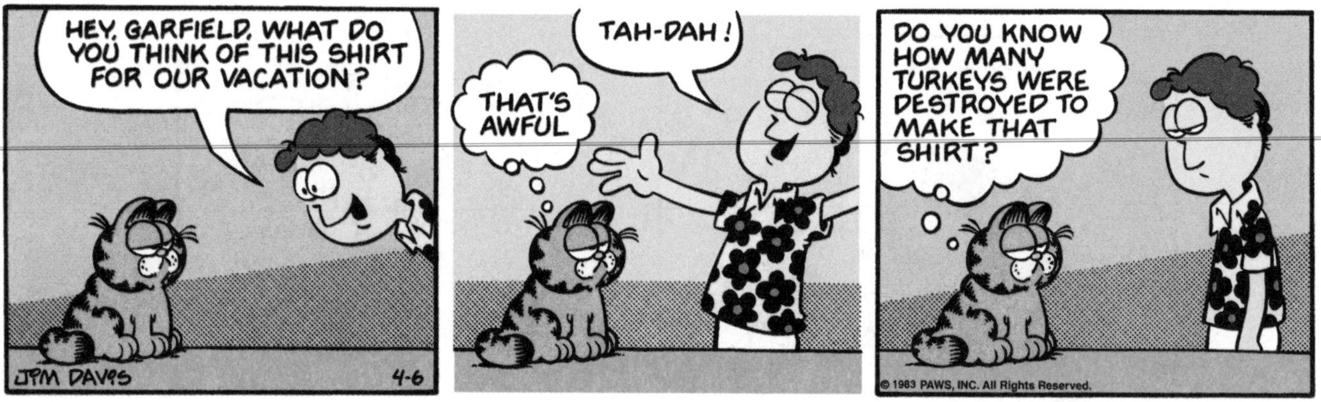
HEY, GARFIELD, WHAT DO YOU THINK OF THIS SHIRT FOR OUR VACATION?
JIM DAVIS
4-6
TAH-DAH!
THAT'S AWFUL
DO YOU KNOW HOW MANY TURKEYS WERE DESTROYED TO MAKE THAT SHIRT?
© 1983 PAWS, INC. All Rights Reserved.

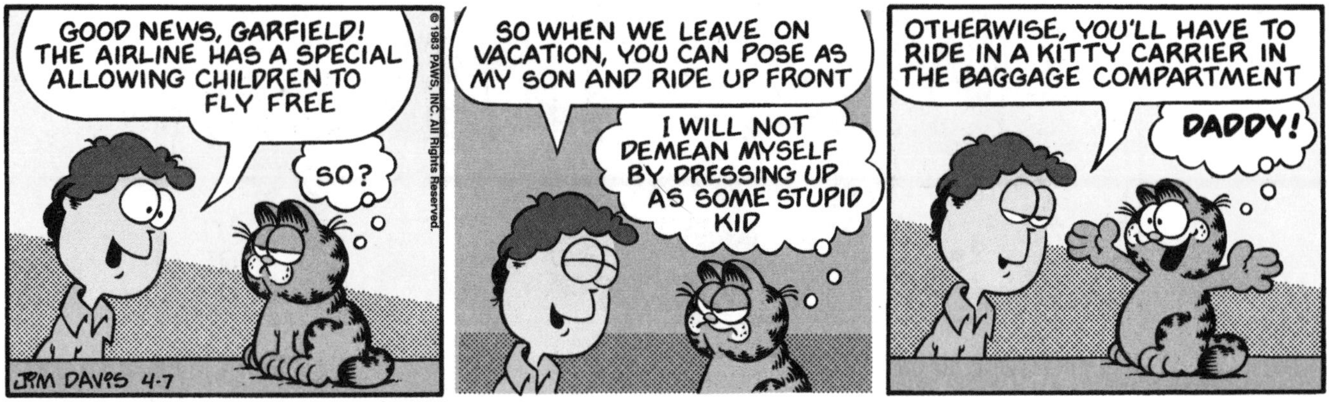
GOOD NEWS, GARFIELD! THE AIRLINE HAS A SPECIAL ALLOWING CHILDREN TO FLY FREE
SO?
JIM DAVIS 4-7
© 1983 PAWS, INC. All Rights Reserved.
SO WHEN WE LEAVE ON VACATION, YOU CAN POSE AS MY SON AND RIDE UP FRONT
I WILL NOT DEMEAN MYSELF BY DRESSING UP AS SOME STUPID KID
OTHERWISE, YOU'LL HAVE TO RIDE IN A KITTY CARRIER IN THE BAGGAGE COMPARTMENT
DADDY!

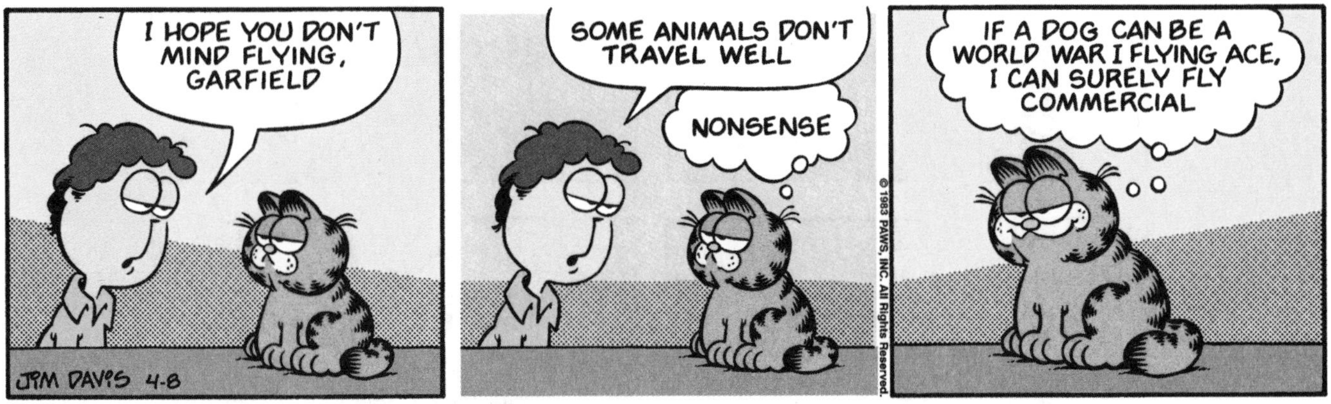
I HOPE YOU DON'T MIND FLYING, GARFIELD
JIM DAVIS 4-8
SOME ANIMALS DON'T TRAVEL WELL
NONSENSE
© 1983 PAWS, INC. All Rights Reserved.
IF A DOG CAN BE A WORLD WAR I FLYING ACE, I CAN SURELY FLY COMMERCIAL

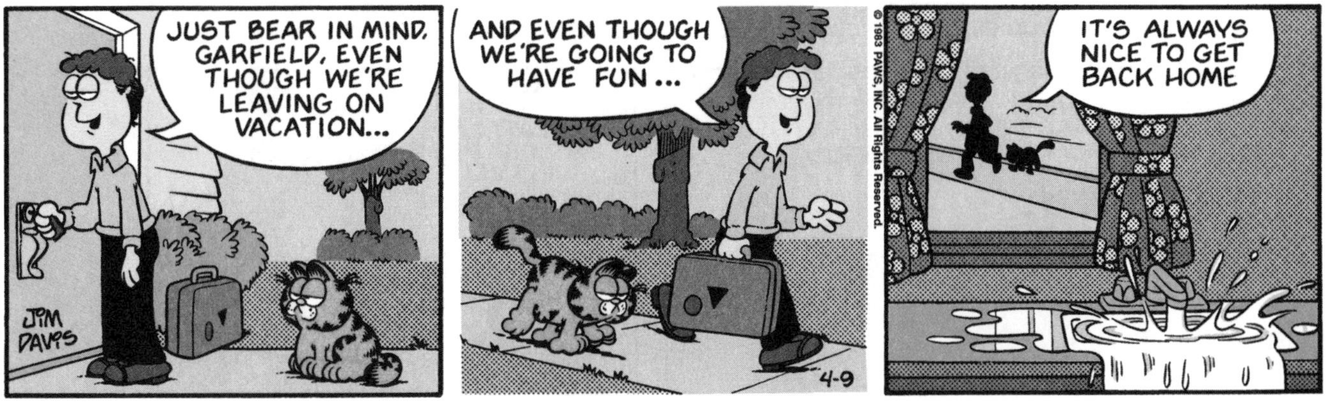
JUST BEAR IN MIND, GARFIELD, EVEN THOUGH WE'RE LEAVING ON VACATION...
JIM DAVIS
AND EVEN THOUGH WE'RE GOING TO HAVE FUN...
4-9
© 1983 PAWS, INC. All Rights Reserved.
IT'S ALWAYS NICE TO GET BACK HOME

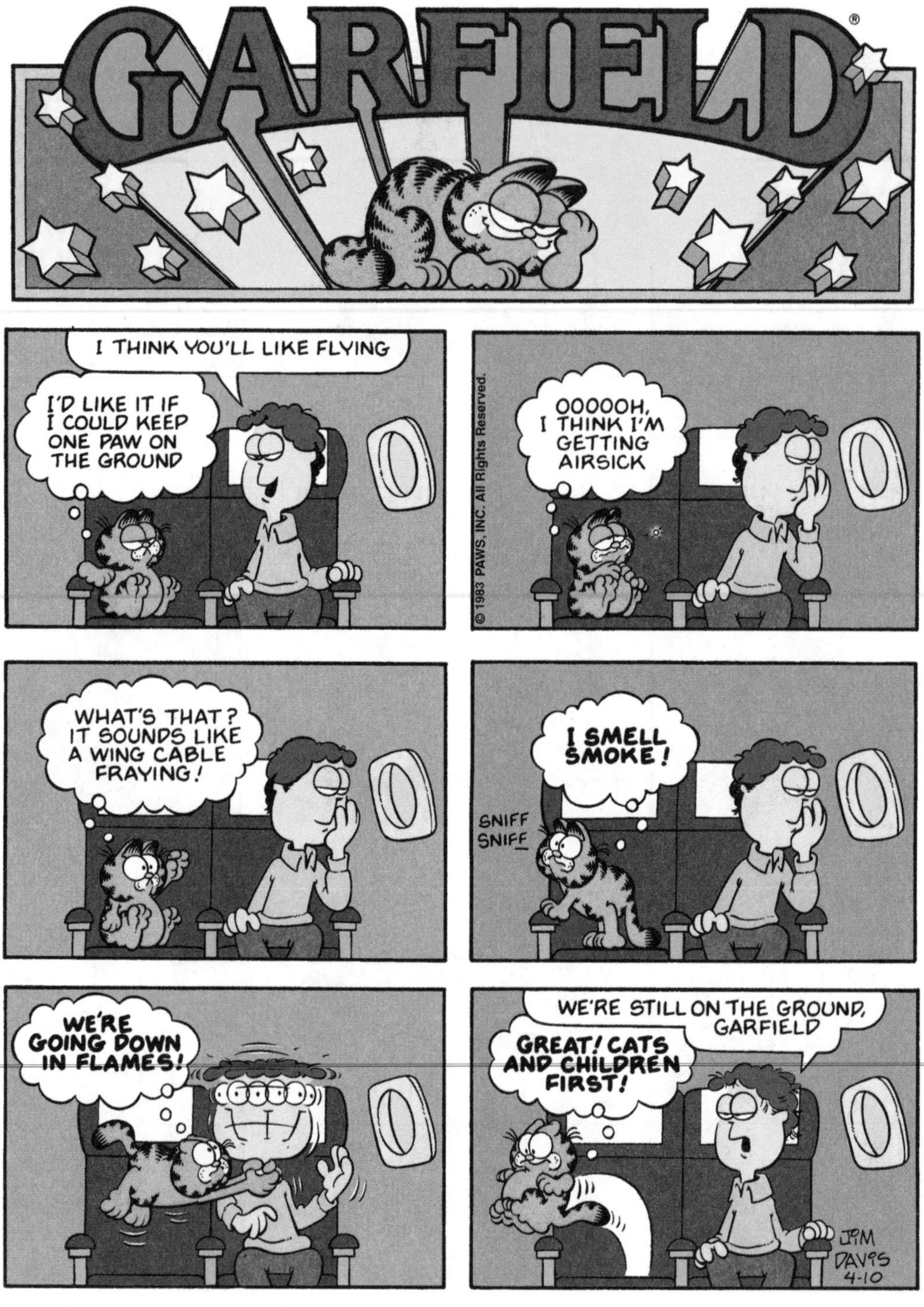
GARFIELD®
I THINK YOU'LL LIKE FLYING
I'D LIKE IT IF I COULD KEEP ONE PAW ON THE GROUND
© 1983 PAWS, INC. All Rights Reserved.
OOOOOH, I THINK I'M GETTING AIRSICK
WHAT'S THAT? IT SOUNDS LIKE A WING CABLE FRAYING!
I SMELL SMOKE!
SNIFF SNIFF
WE'RE GOING DOWN IN FLAMES!
WE'RE STILL ON THE GROUND, GARFIELD
GREAT! CATS AND CHILDREN FIRST!
JIM DAVIS 4-10

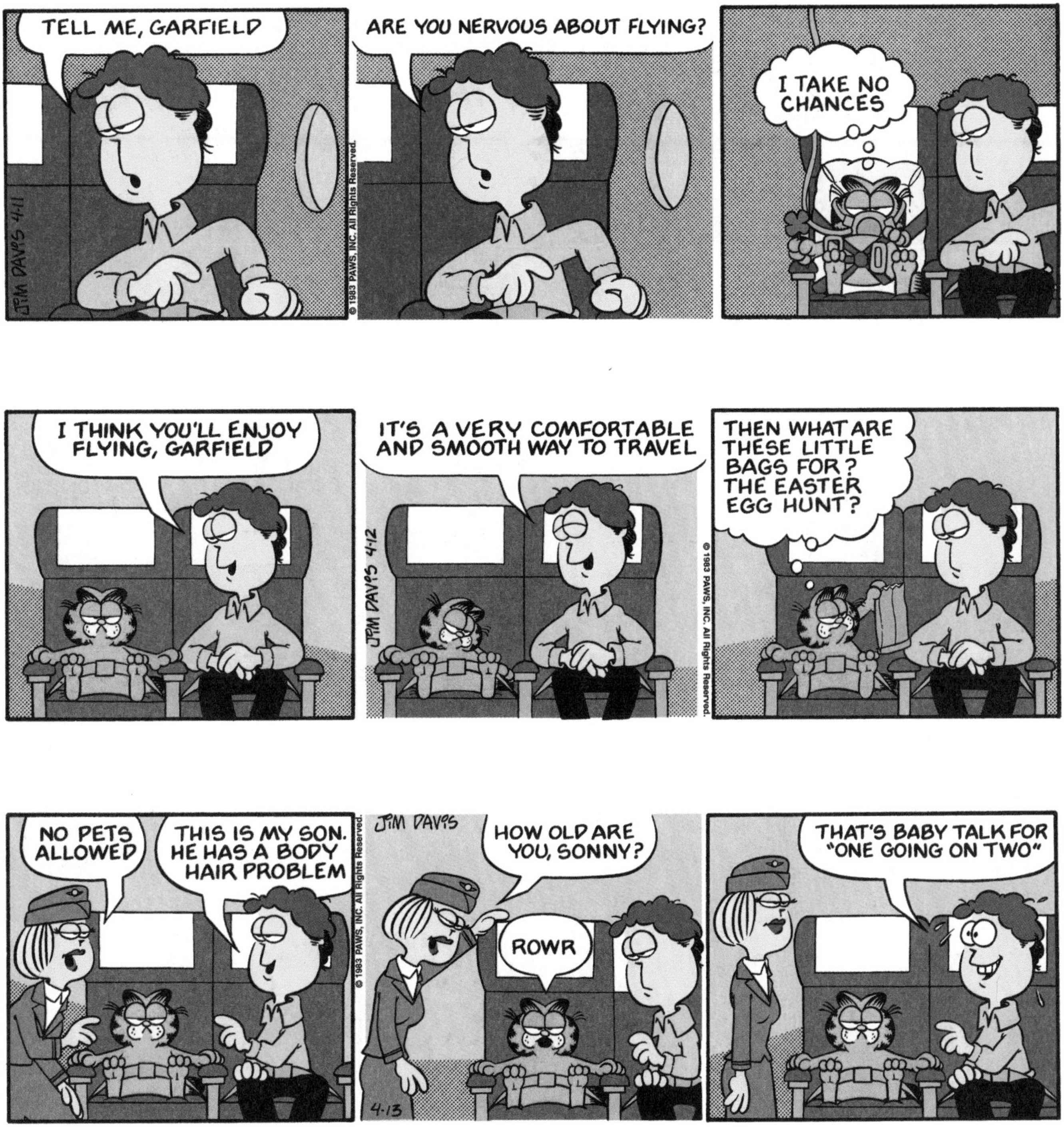
TELL ME, GARFIELD
JIM DAVIS 4-11
© 1983 PAWS, INC. All Rights Reserved.
ARE YOU NERVOUS ABOUT FLYING?
I TAKE NO CHANCES
I THINK YOU'LL ENJOY FLYING, GARFIELD
JIM DAVIS 4-12
IT'S A VERY COMFORTABLE AND SMOOTH WAY TO TRAVEL
© 1983 PAWS, INC. All Rights Reserved.
THEN WHAT ARE THESE LITTLE BAGS FOR? THE EASTER EGG HUNT?
NO PETS ALLOWED
THIS IS MY SON. HE HAS A BODY HAIR PROBLEM
© 1983 PAWS, INC. All Rights Reserved.
JIM DAVIS
HOW OLD ARE YOU, SONNY?
ROWR
4-13
THAT'S BABY TALK FOR "ONE GOING ON TWO"

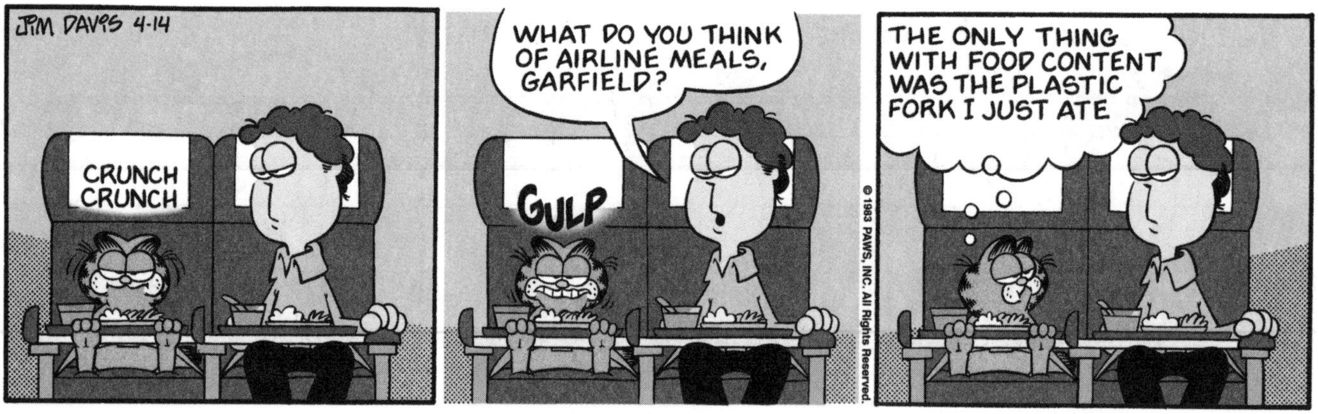
JIM DAVIS 4-14
CRUNCH CRUNCH
WHAT DO YOU THINK OF AIRLINE MEALS, GARFIELD?
GULP
© 1983 PAWS, INC. All Rights Reserved.
THE ONLY THING WITH FOOD CONTENT WAS THE PLASTIC FORK I JUST ATE

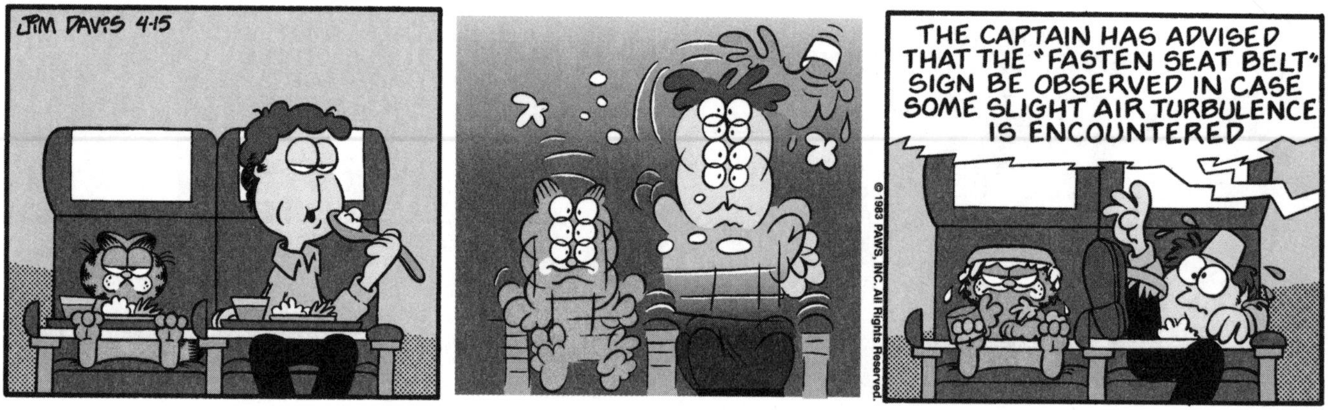
JIM DAVIS 4-15
© 1983 PAWS, INC. All Rights Reserved.
THE CAPTAIN HAS ADVISED THAT THE "FASTEN SEAT BELT" SIGN BE OBSERVED IN CASE SOME SLIGHT AIR TURBULENCE IS ENCOUNTERED

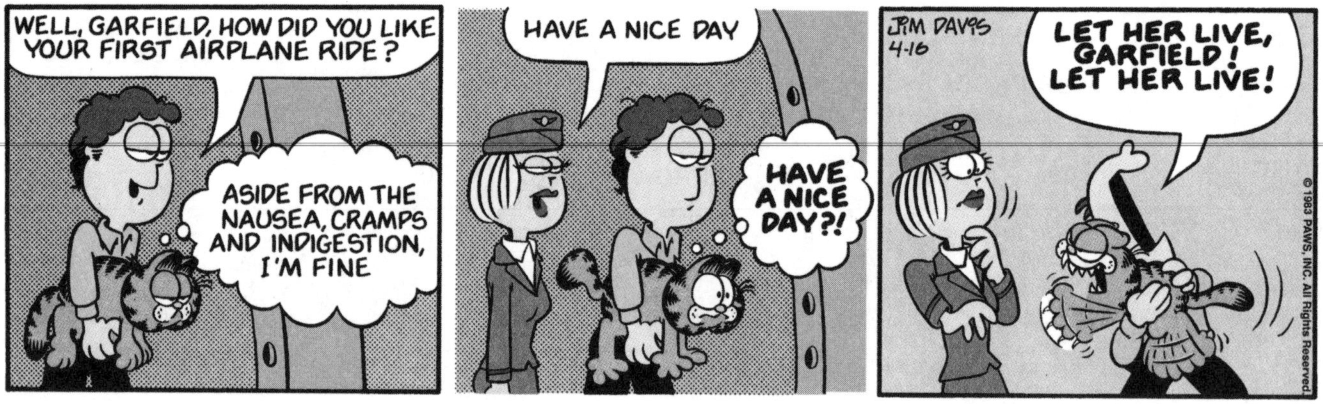
WELL, GARFIELD, HOW DID YOU LIKE YOUR FIRST AIRPLANE RIDE?
ASIDE FROM THE NAUSEA, CRAMPS AND INDIGESTION, I'M FINE
HAVE A NICE DAY
HAVE A NICE DAY?!
JIM DAVIS 4-16
LET HER LIVE, GARFIELD! LET HER LIVE!
© 1983 PAWS, INC. All Rights Reserved.

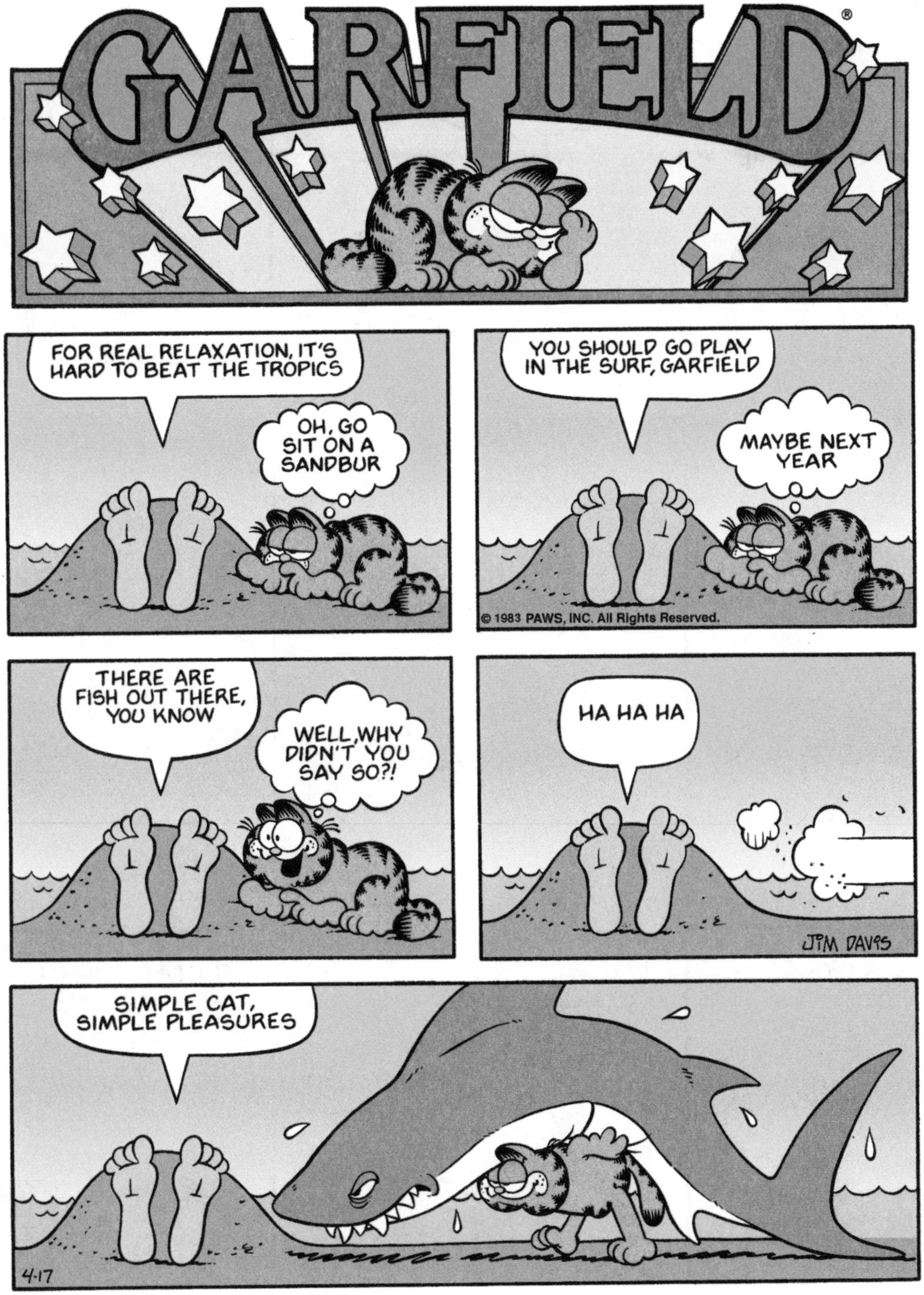
GARFIELD®
FOR REAL RELAXATION, IT'S HARD TO BEAT THE TROPICS
OH, GO SIT ON A SANDBUR
YOU SHOULD GO PLAY IN THE SURF, GARFIELD
MAYBE NEXT YEAR
© 1983 PAWS, INC. All Rights Reserved.
THERE ARE FISH OUT THERE, YOU KNOW
WELL, WHY DIDN'T YOU SAY SO?!
HA HA HA
JIM DAVIS
SIMPLE CAT, SIMPLE PLEASURES
4-17

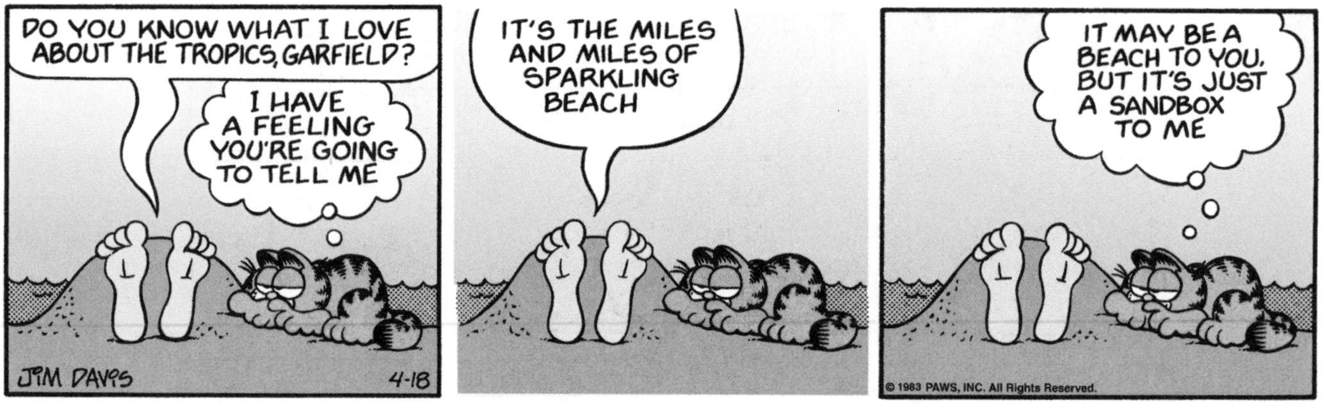
DO YOU KNOW WHAT I LOVE ABOUT THE TROPICS, GARFIELD?
I HAVE A FEELING YOU'RE GOING TO TELL ME
JIM DAVIS 4-18
IT'S THE MILES AND MILES OF SPARKLING BEACH
IT MAY BE A BEACH TO YOU, BUT IT'S JUST A SANDBOX TO ME
© 1983 PAWS, INC. All Rights Reserved.

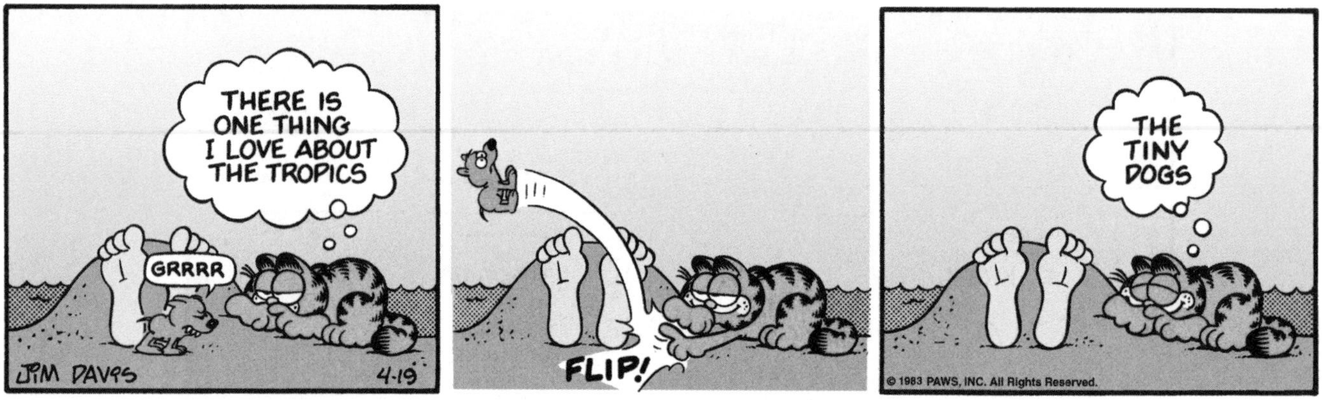
THERE IS ONE THING I LOVE ABOUT THE TROPICS
GRRRR
JIM DAVIS 4-19
FLIP!
THE TINY DOGS
© 1983 PAWS, INC. All Rights Reserved.

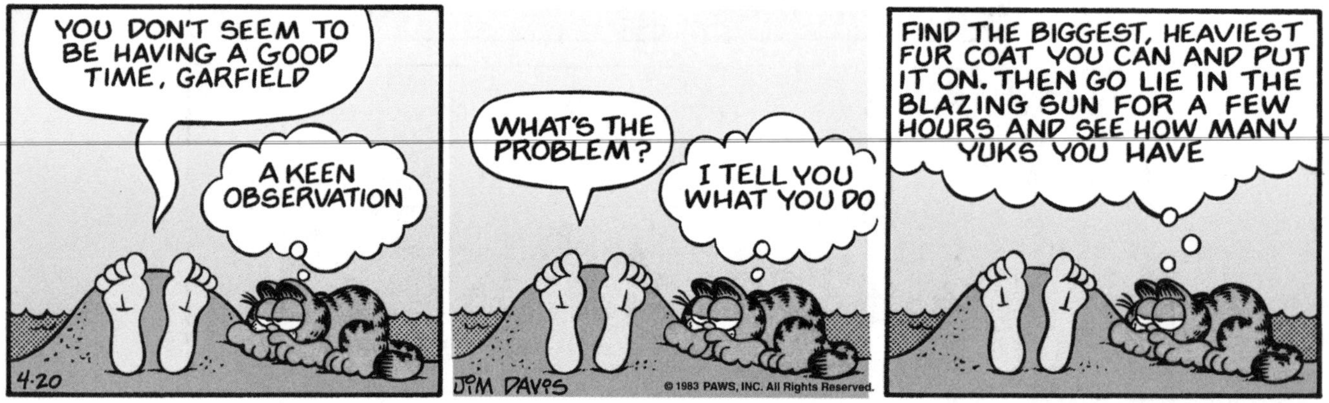
YOU DON'T SEEM TO BE HAVING A GOOD TIME, GARFIELD
A KEEN OBSERVATION
4-20
WHAT'S THE PROBLEM?
I TELL YOU WHAT YOU DO
JIM DAVIS
© 1983 PAWS, INC. All Rights Reserved.
FIND THE BIGGEST, HEAVIEST FUR COAT YOU CAN AND PUT IT ON. THEN GO LIE IN THE BLAZING SUN FOR A FEW HOURS AND SEE HOW MANY YUKS YOU HAVE

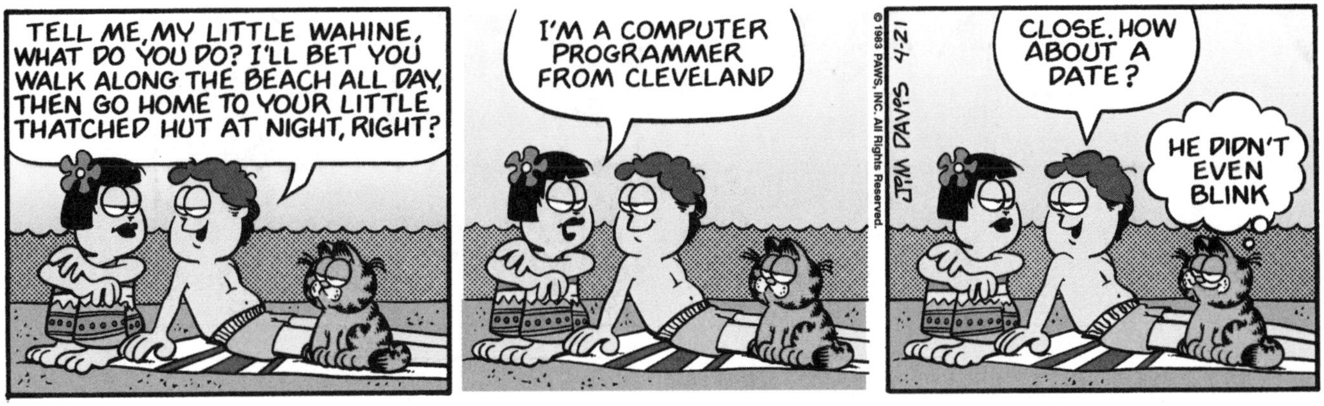
TELL ME, MY LITTLE WAHINE, WHAT DO YOU DO? I'LL BET YOU WALK ALONG THE BEACH ALL DAY, THEN GO HOME TO YOUR LITTLE THATCHED HUT AT NIGHT, RIGHT?
I'M A COMPUTER PROGRAMMER FROM CLEVELAND
© 1983 PAWS, INC. All Rights Reserved.
JIM DAVIS 4-21
CLOSE. HOW ABOUT A DATE?
HE DIDN'T EVEN BLINK

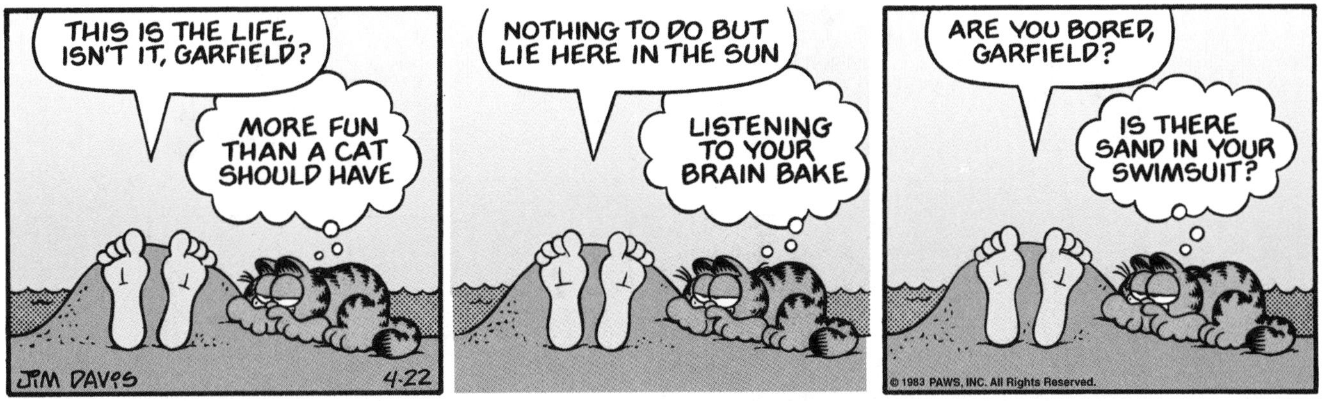
THIS IS THE LIFE, ISN'T IT, GARFIELD?
MORE FUN THAN A CAT SHOULD HAVE
JIM DAVIS
4-22
NOTHING TO DO BUT LIE HERE IN THE SUN
LISTENING TO YOUR BRAIN BAKE
ARE YOU BORED, GARFIELD?
IS THERE SAND IN YOUR SWIMSUIT?
© 1983 PAWS, INC. All Rights Reserved.

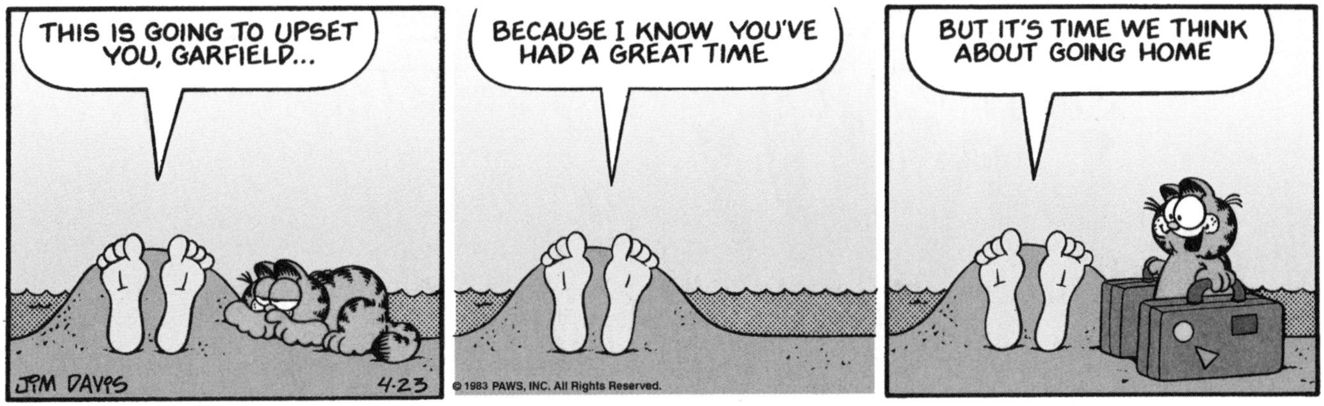
THIS IS GOING TO UPSET YOU, GARFIELD...
JIM DAVIS
4-23
BECAUSE I KNOW YOU'VE HAD A GREAT TIME
© 1983 PAWS, INC. All Rights Reserved.
BUT IT'S TIME WE THINK ABOUT GOING HOME

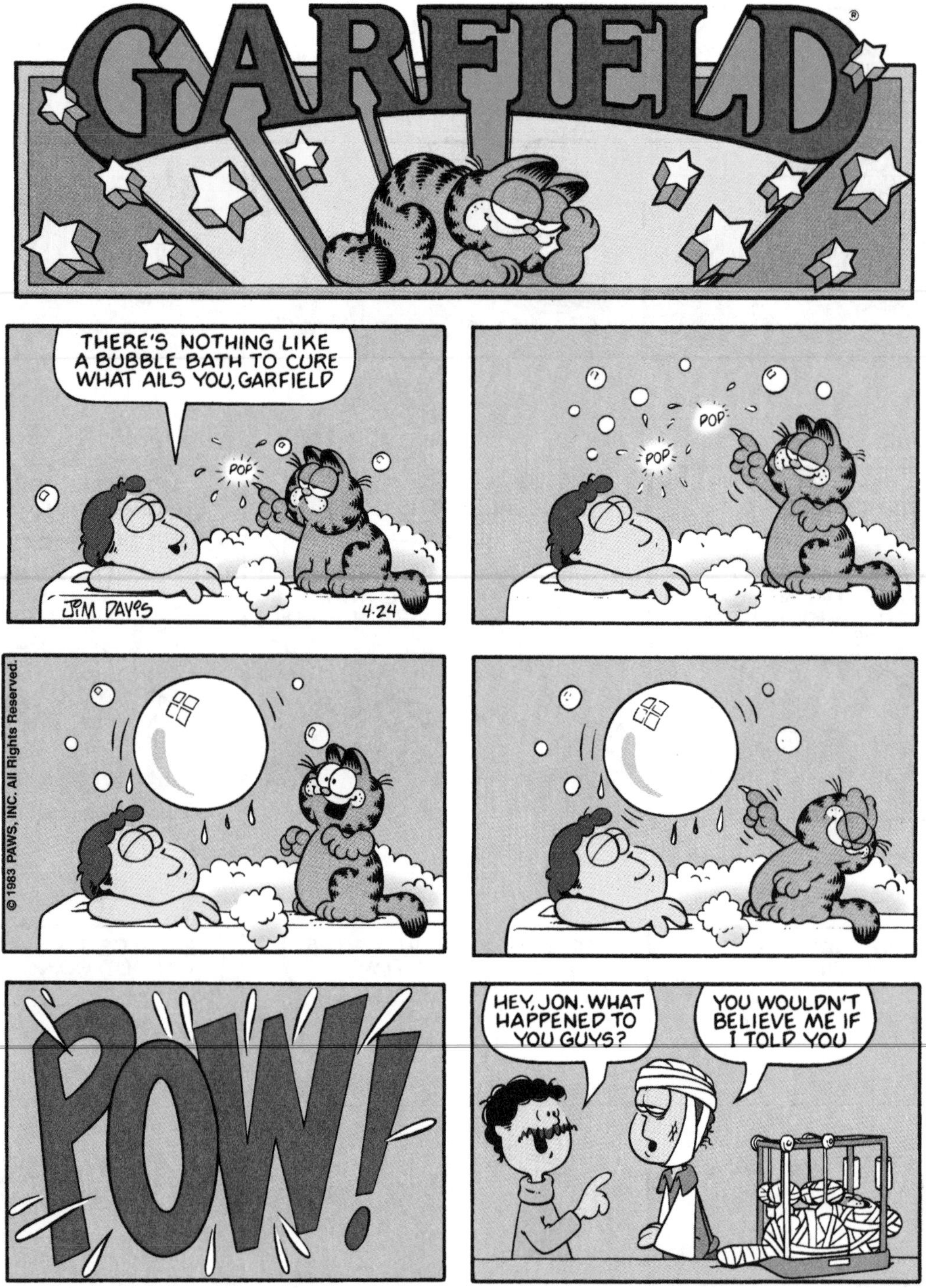
GARFIELD®
THERE'S NOTHING LIKE A BUBBLE BATH TO CURE WHAT AILS YOU, GARFIELD
POP
JIM DAVIS
4-24
POP
POP
© 1983 PAWS, INC. All Rights Reserved.
POW!
HEY, JON. WHAT HAPPENED TO YOU GUYS?
YOU WOULDN'T BELIEVE ME IF I TOLD YOU

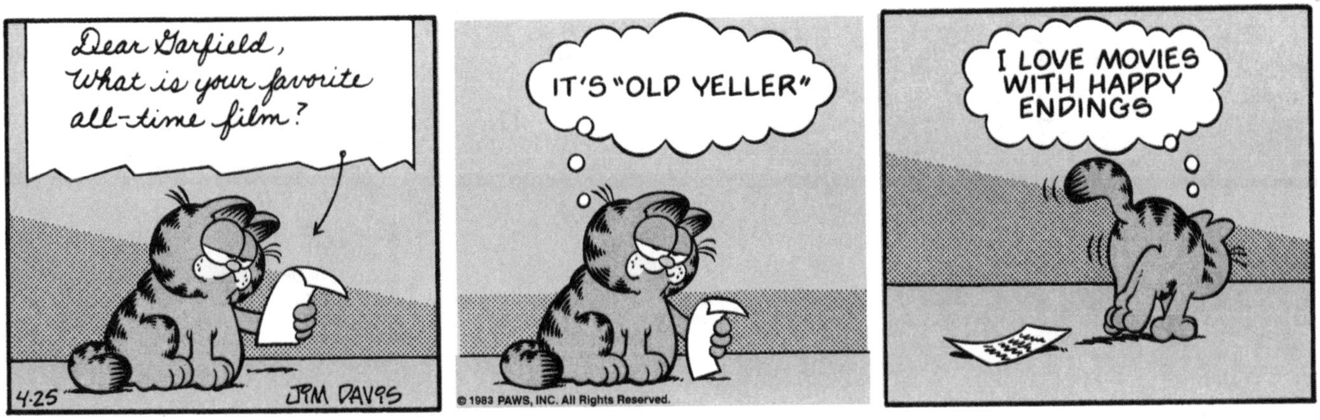
Dear Garfield,
What is your favorite all-time film?
4-25
JIM DAVIS
IT'S "OLD YELLER"
© 1983 PAWS, INC. All Rights Reserved.
I LOVE MOVIES WITH HAPPY ENDINGS

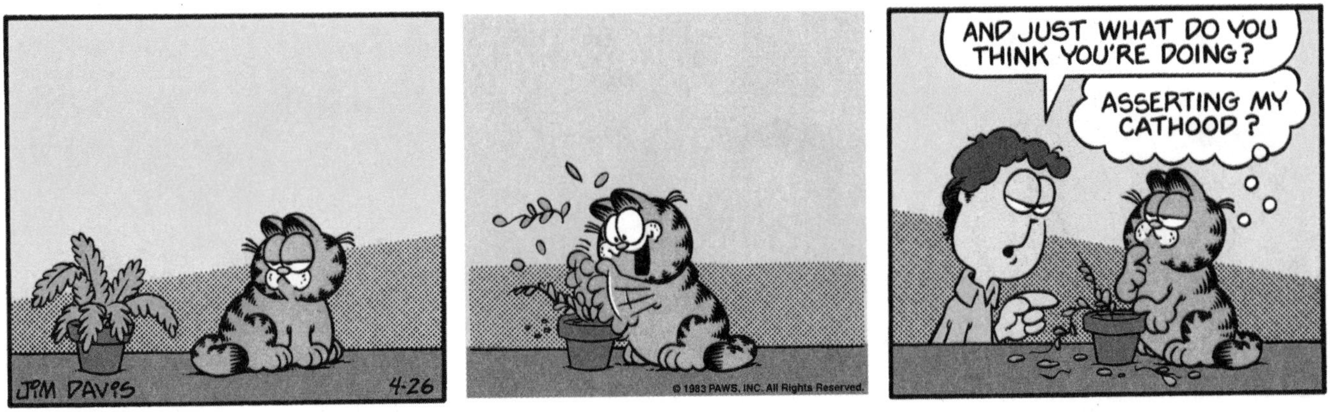
JIM DAVIS
4-26
© 1983 PAWS, INC. All Rights Reserved.
AND JUST WHAT DO YOU THINK YOU'RE DOING?
ASSERTING MY CATHOOD?

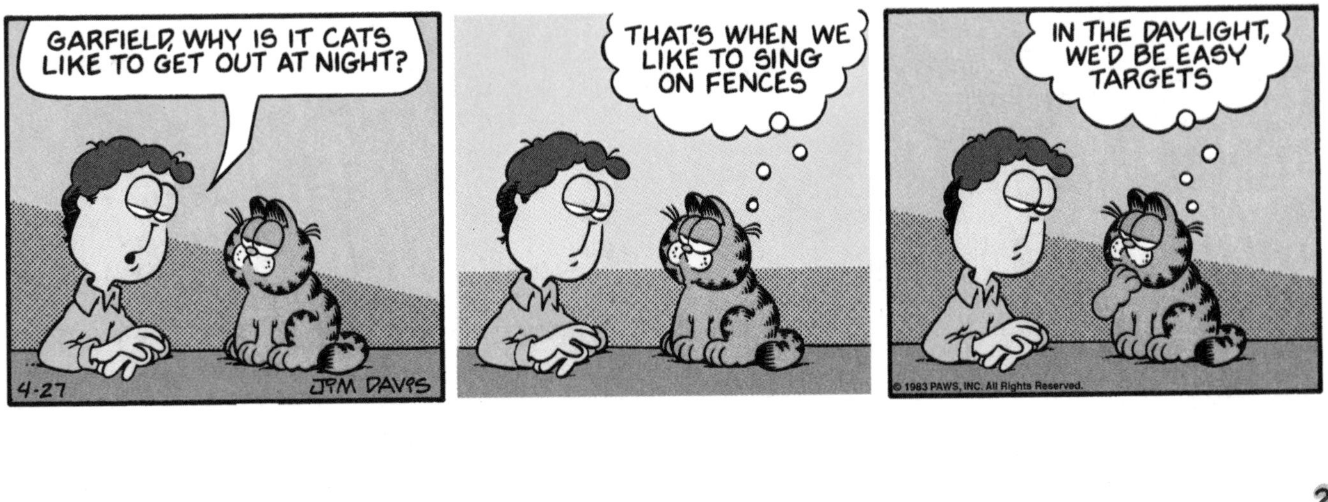
GARFIELD, WHY IS IT CATS LIKE TO GET OUT AT NIGHT?
4-27
JIM DAVIS
THAT'S WHEN WE LIKE TO SING ON FENCES
IN THE DAYLIGHT, WE'D BE EASY TARGETS
© 1983 PAWS, INC. All Rights Reserved.

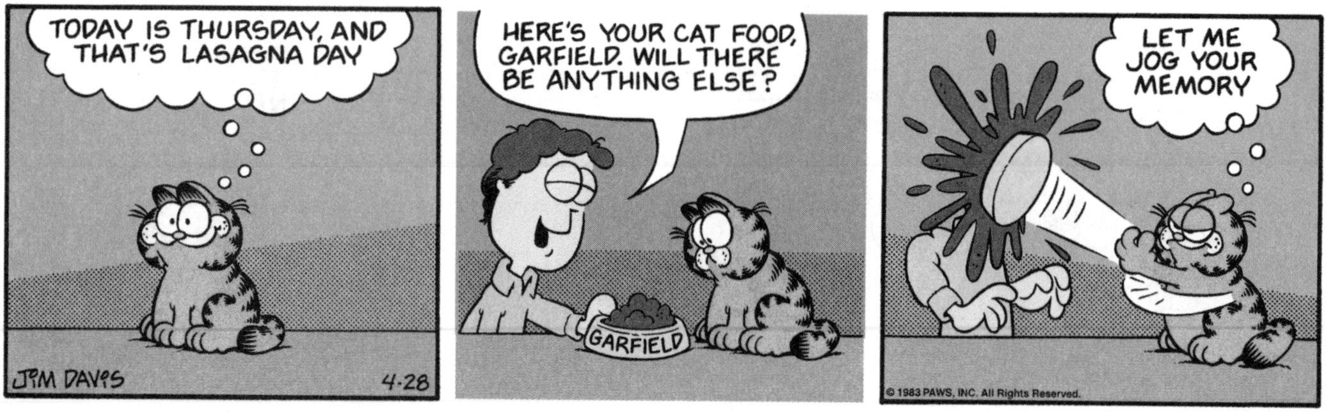
TODAY IS THURSDAY, AND THAT'S LASAGNA DAY
JIM DAVIS
4-28
HERE'S YOUR CAT FOOD, GARFIELD. WILL THERE BE ANYTHING ELSE?
GARFIELD
LET ME JOG YOUR MEMORY
© 1983 PAWS, INC. All Rights Reserved.

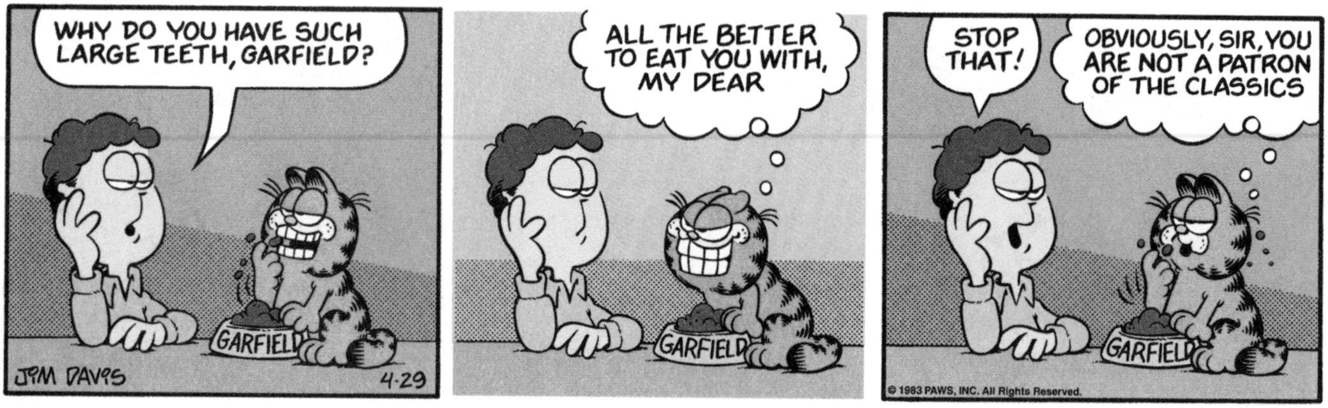
WHY DO YOU HAVE SUCH LARGE TEETH, GARFIELD?
GARFIELD
JIM DAVIS
4-29
ALL THE BETTER TO EAT YOU WITH, MY DEAR
GARFIELD
STOP THAT!
OBVIOUSLY, SIR, YOU ARE NOT A PATRON OF THE CLASSICS
GARFIELD
© 1983 PAWS, INC. All Rights Reserved.

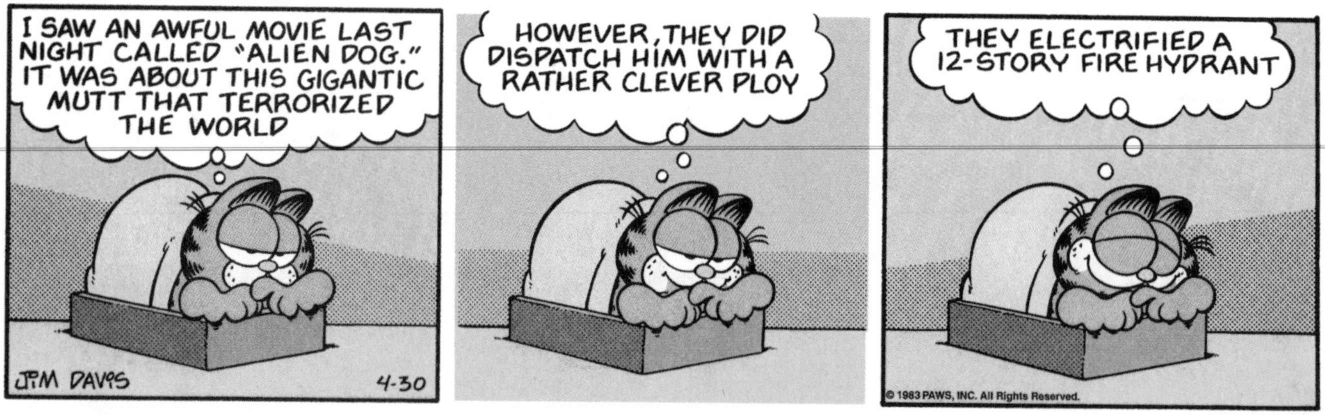
I SAW AN AWFUL MOVIE LAST NIGHT CALLED "ALIEN DOG." IT WAS ABOUT THIS GIGANTIC MUTT THAT TERRORIZED THE WORLD
JIM DAVIS
4-30
HOWEVER, THEY DID DISPATCH HIM WITH A RATHER CLEVER PLOY
THEY ELECTRIFIED A 12-STORY FIRE HYDRANT
© 1983 PAWS, INC. All Rights Reserved.

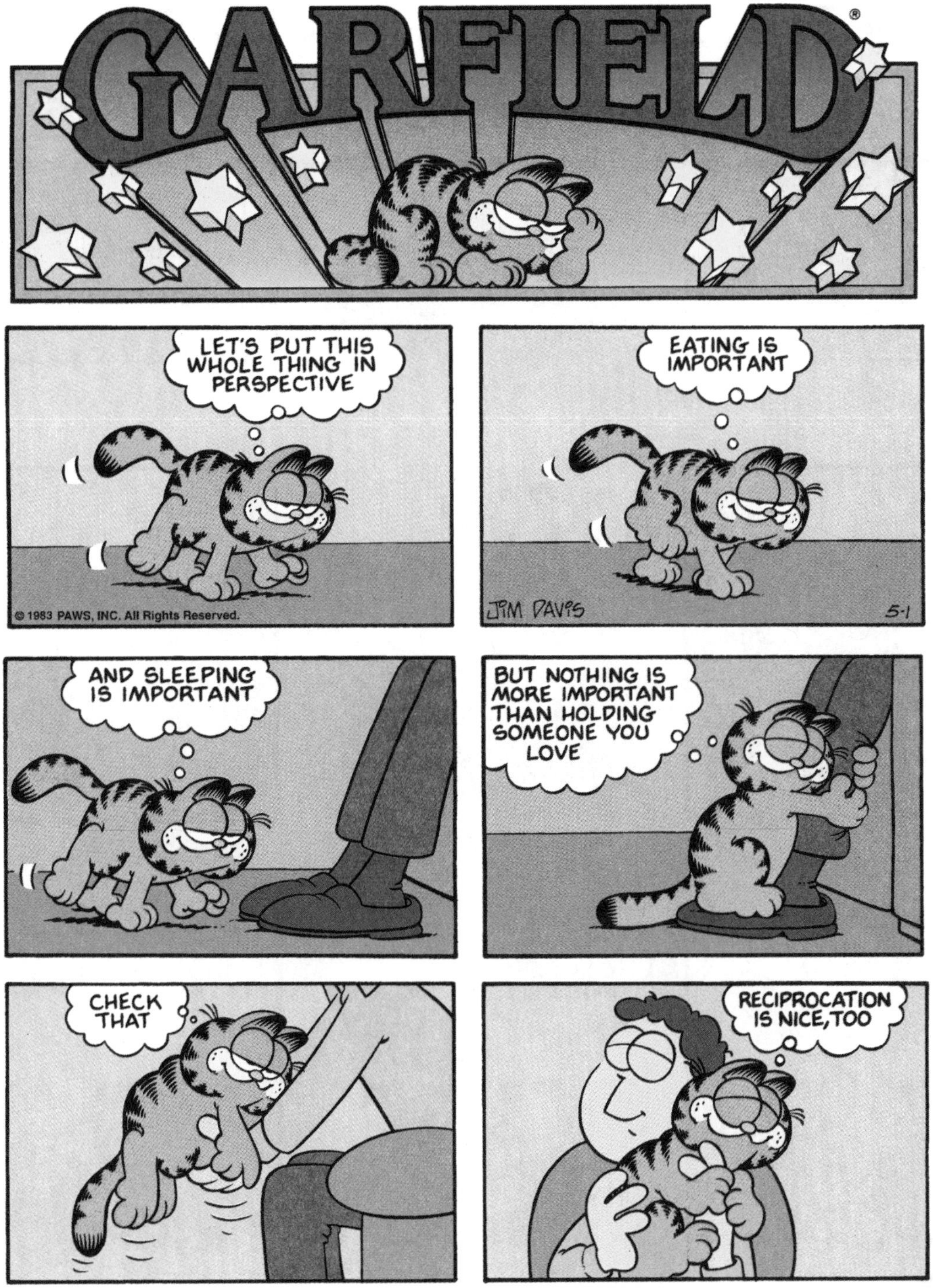
GARFIELD®
LET'S PUT THIS WHOLE THING IN PERSPECTIVE
© 1983 PAWS, INC. All Rights Reserved.
EATING IS IMPORTANT
JIM DAVIS
5-1
AND SLEEPING IS IMPORTANT
BUT NOTHING IS MORE IMPORTANT THAN HOLDING SOMEONE YOU LOVE
CHECK THAT
RECIPROCATION IS NICE, TOO

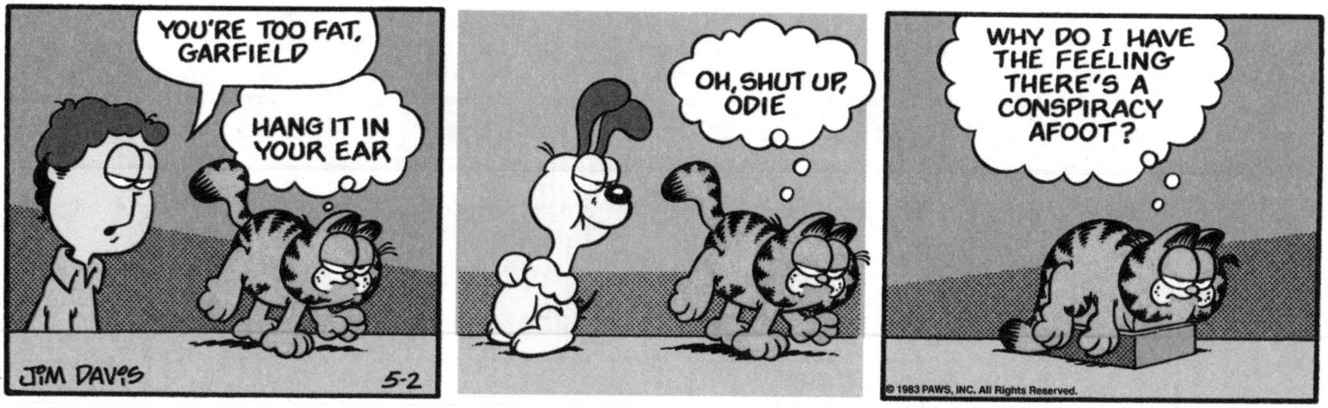
YOU'RE TOO FAT, GARFIELD
HANG IT IN YOUR EAR
JIM DAVIS
5-2
OH, SHUT UP, ODIE
WHY DO I HAVE THE FEELING THERE'S A CONSPIRACY AFOOT?
© 1983 PAWS, INC. All Rights Reserved.

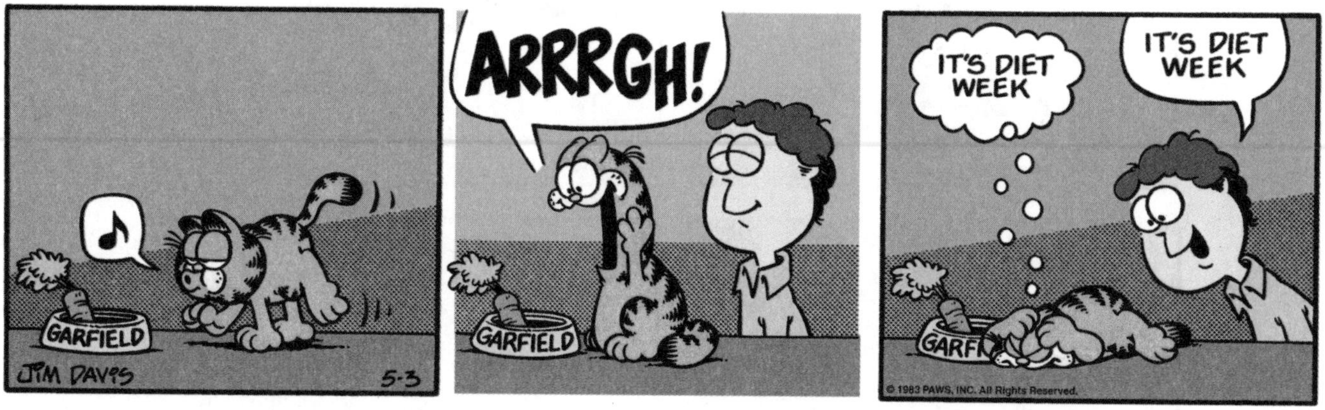
♪
GARFIELD
JIM DAVIS
5-3
ARRRGH!
GARFIELD
IT'S DIET WEEK
IT'S DIET WEEK
GARFI
© 1983 PAWS, INC. All Rights Reserved.

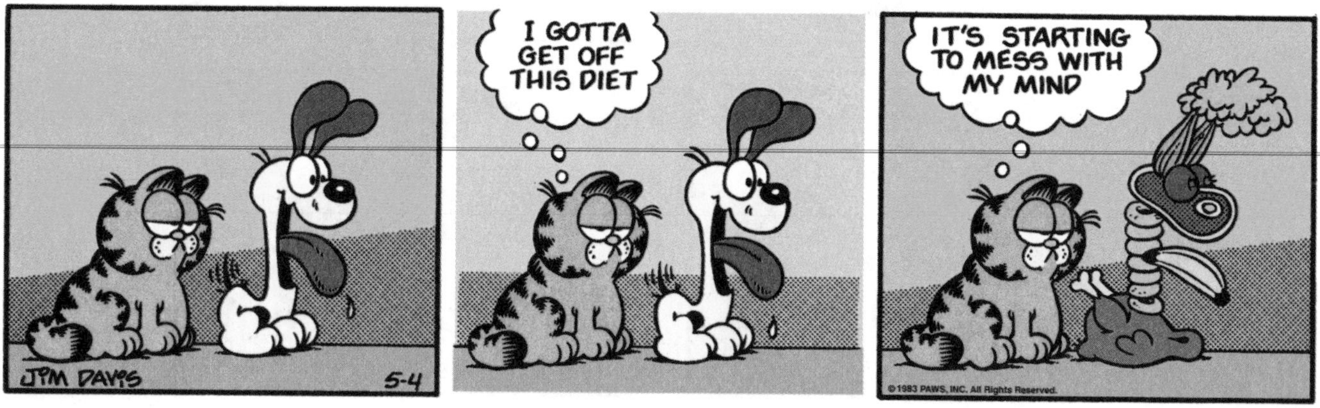
JIM DAVIS
5-4
I GOTTA GET OFF THIS DIET
IT'S STARTING TO MESS WITH MY MIND
© 1983 PAWS, INC. All Rights Reserved.

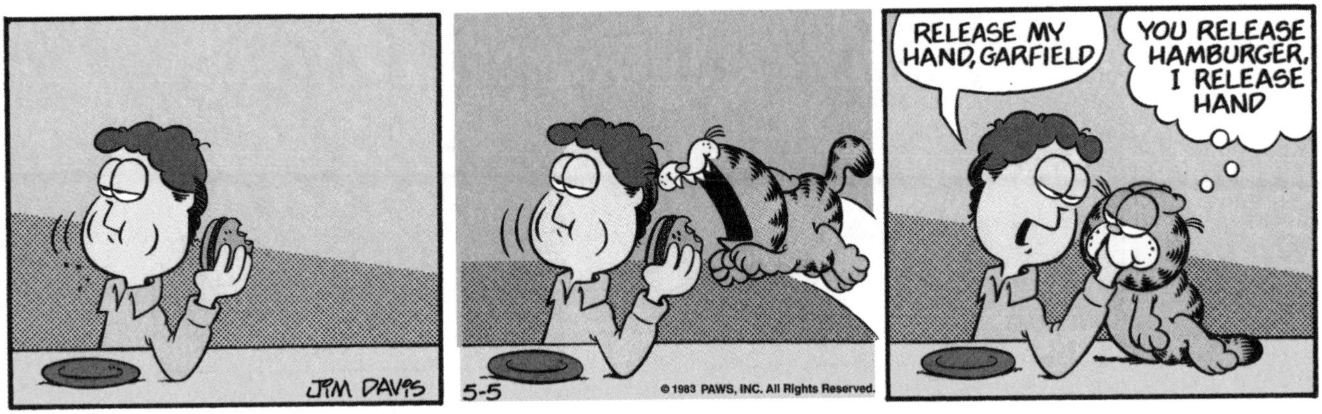
JIM DAVIS
5-5
© 1983 PAWS, INC. All Rights Reserved.
RELEASE MY HAND, GARFIELD
YOU RELEASE HAMBURGER, I RELEASE HAND

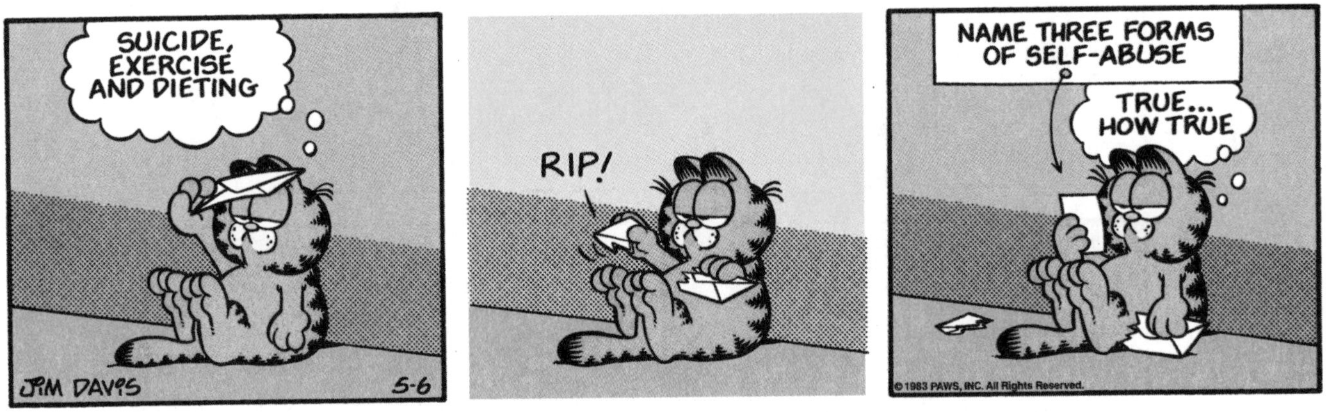
SUICIDE, EXERCISE AND DIETING
JIM DAVIS
5-6
RIP!
NAME THREE FORMS OF SELF-ABUSE
TRUE... HOW TRUE
© 1983 PAWS, INC. All Rights Reserved.

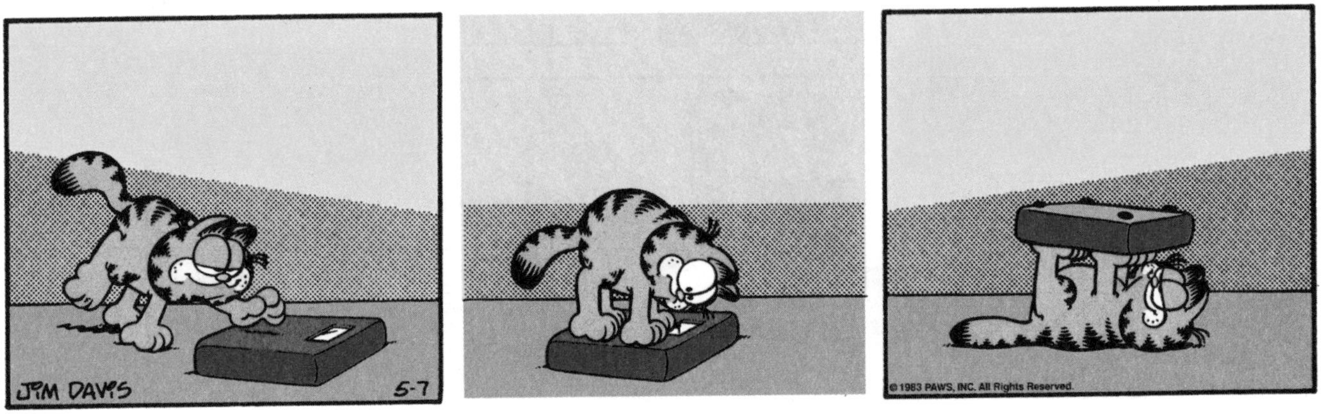
JIM DAVIS
5-7
© 1983 PAWS, INC. All Rights Reserved.

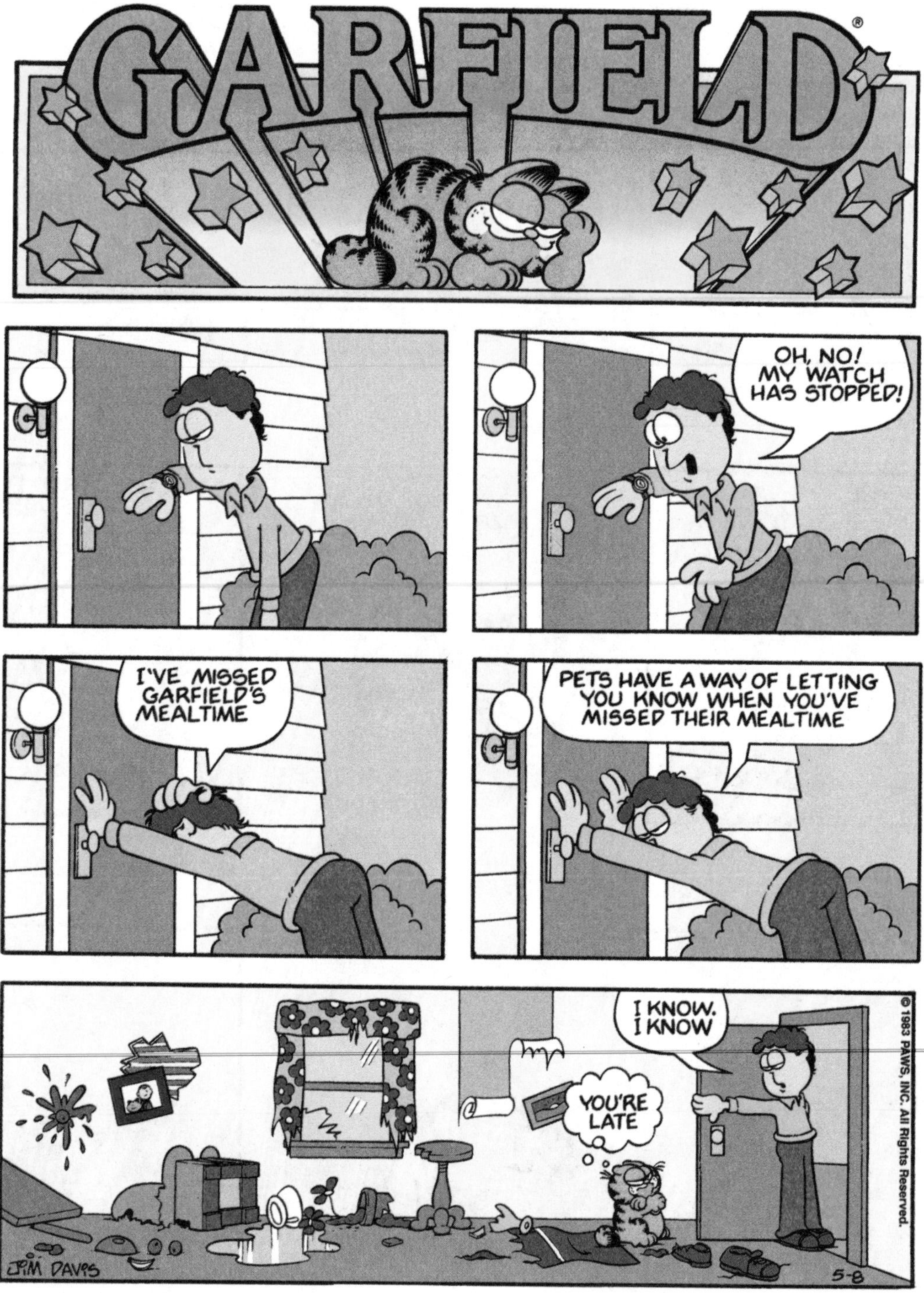
GARFIELD®
OH, NO! MY WATCH HAS STOPPED!
I'VE MISSED GARFIELD'S MEALTIME
PETS HAVE A WAY OF LETTING YOU KNOW WHEN YOU'VE MISSED THEIR MEALTIME
I KNOW. I KNOW
YOU'RE LATE
© 1983 PAWS, INC. All Rights Reserved.
JIM DAVIS
5-8

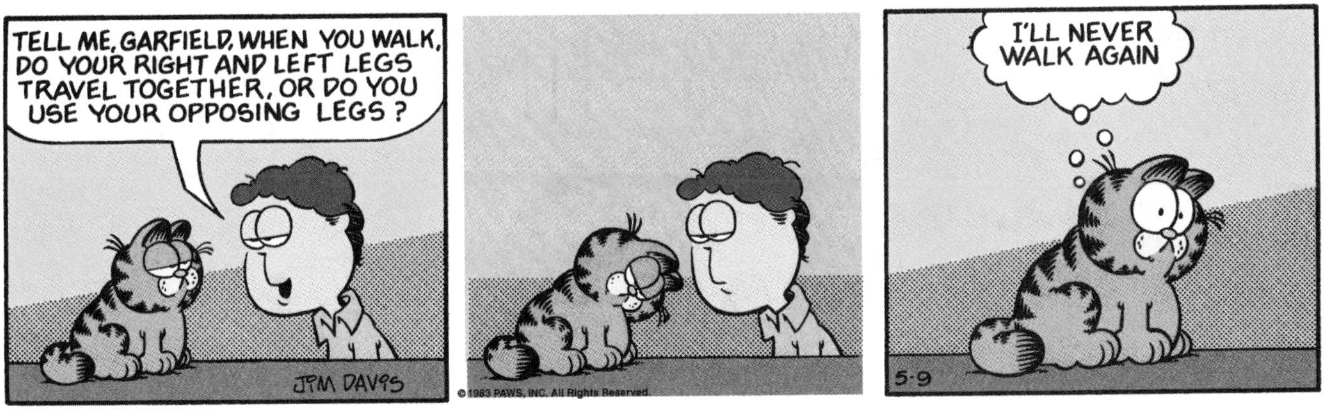
TELL ME, GARFIELD, WHEN YOU WALK, DO YOUR RIGHT AND LEFT LEGS TRAVEL TOGETHER, OR DO YOU USE YOUR OPPOSING LEGS ?
JIM DAVIS
© 1983 PAWS, INC. All Rights Reserved.
I'LL NEVER WALK AGAIN
5-9

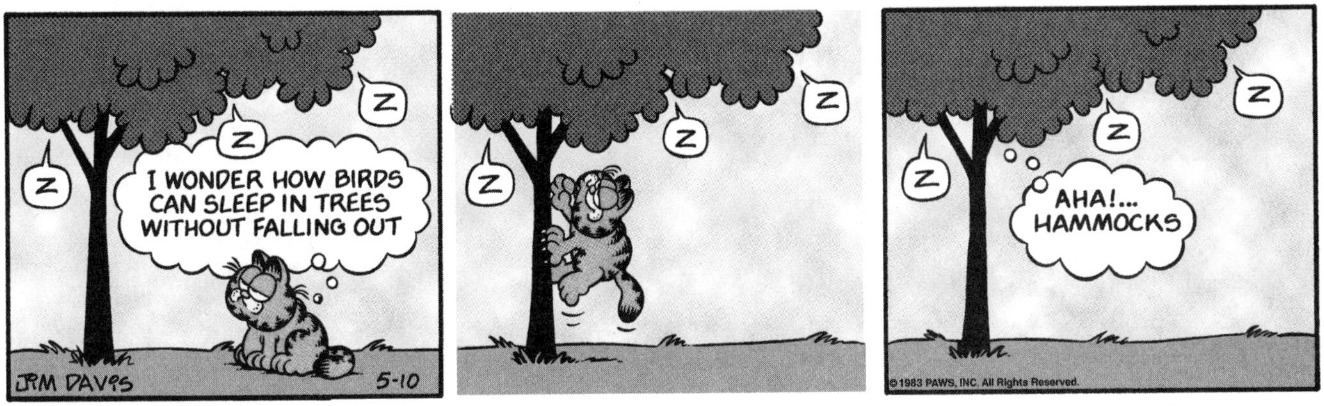
Z
Z
Z
I WONDER HOW BIRDS CAN SLEEP IN TREES WITHOUT FALLING OUT
JIM DAVIS
5-10
Z
Z
Z
Z
Z
Z
AHA!... HAMMOCKS
© 1983 PAWS, INC. All Rights Reserved.

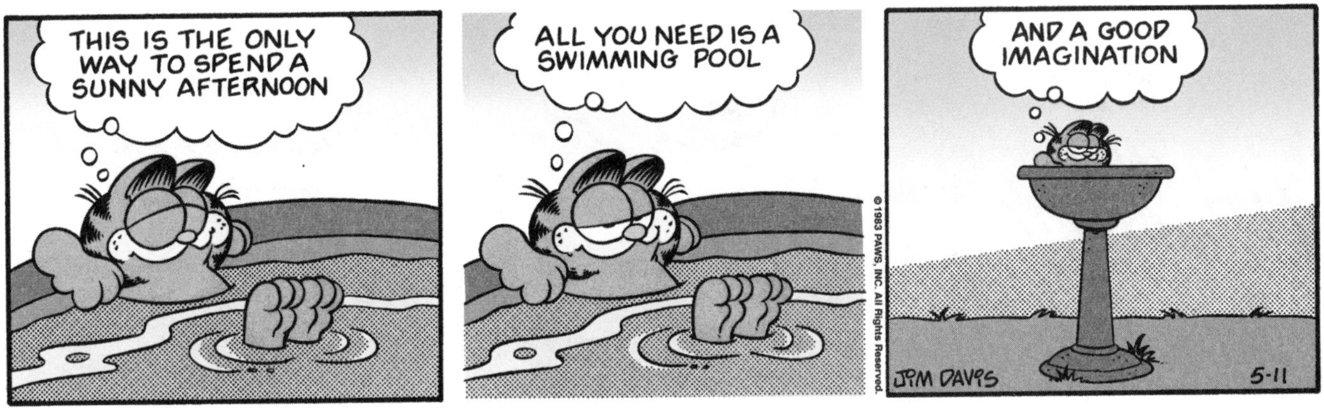
THIS IS THE ONLY WAY TO SPEND A SUNNY AFTERNOON
ALL YOU NEED IS A SWIMMING POOL
© 1983 PAWS, INC. All Rights Reserved.
AND A GOOD IMAGINATION
JIM DAVIS
5-11

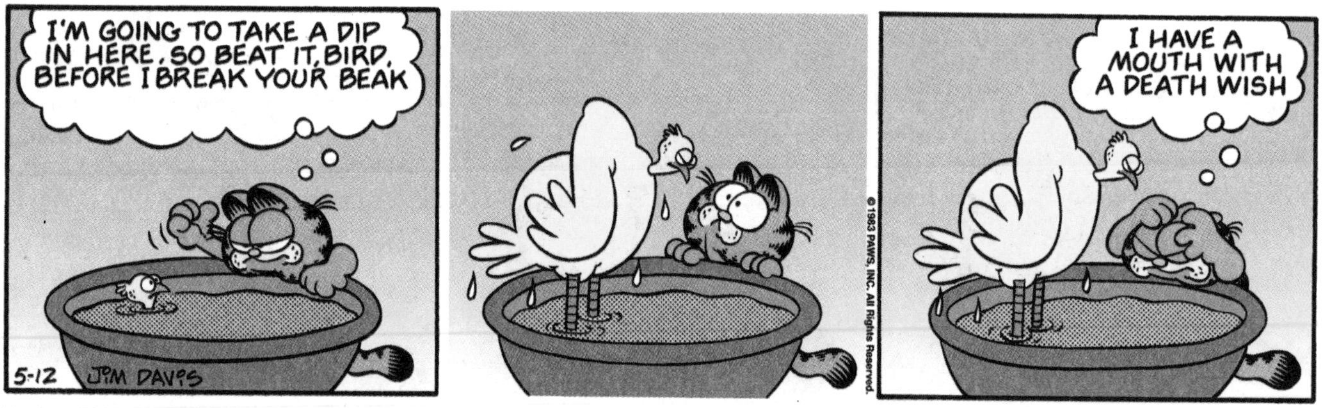
I'M GOING TO TAKE A DIP IN HERE, SO BEAT IT, BIRD, BEFORE I BREAK YOUR BEAK
5-12 JIM DAVIS
© 1983 PAWS, INC. All Rights Reserved.
I HAVE A MOUTH WITH A DEATH WISH

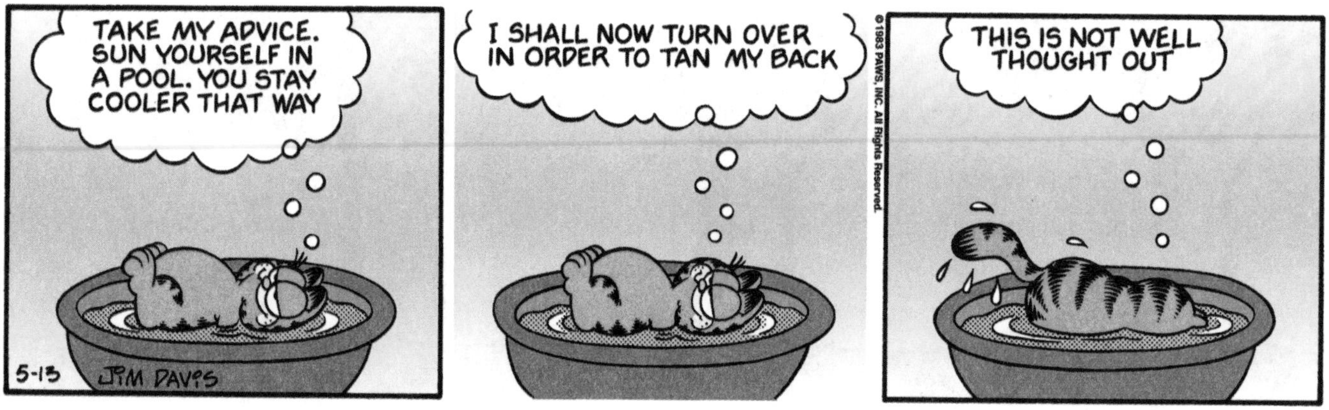
TAKE MY ADVICE. SUN YOURSELF IN A POOL. YOU STAY COOLER THAT WAY
5-13 JIM DAVIS
I SHALL NOW TURN OVER IN ORDER TO TAN MY BACK
© 1983 PAWS, INC. All Rights Reserved.
THIS IS NOT WELL THOUGHT OUT

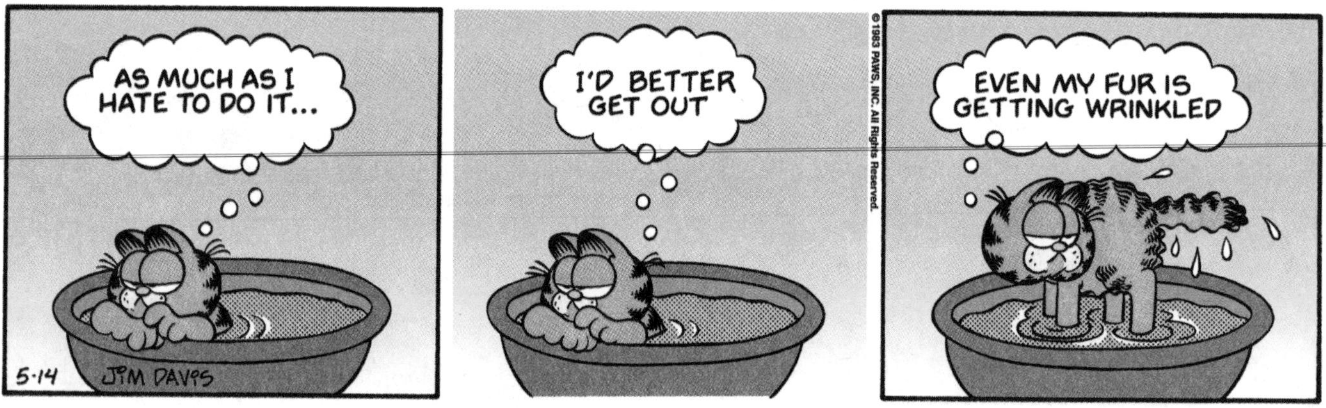
AS MUCH AS I HATE TO DO IT...
5-14 JIM DAVIS
I'D BETTER GET OUT
© 1983 PAWS, INC. All Rights Reserved.
EVEN MY FUR IS GETTING WRINKLED

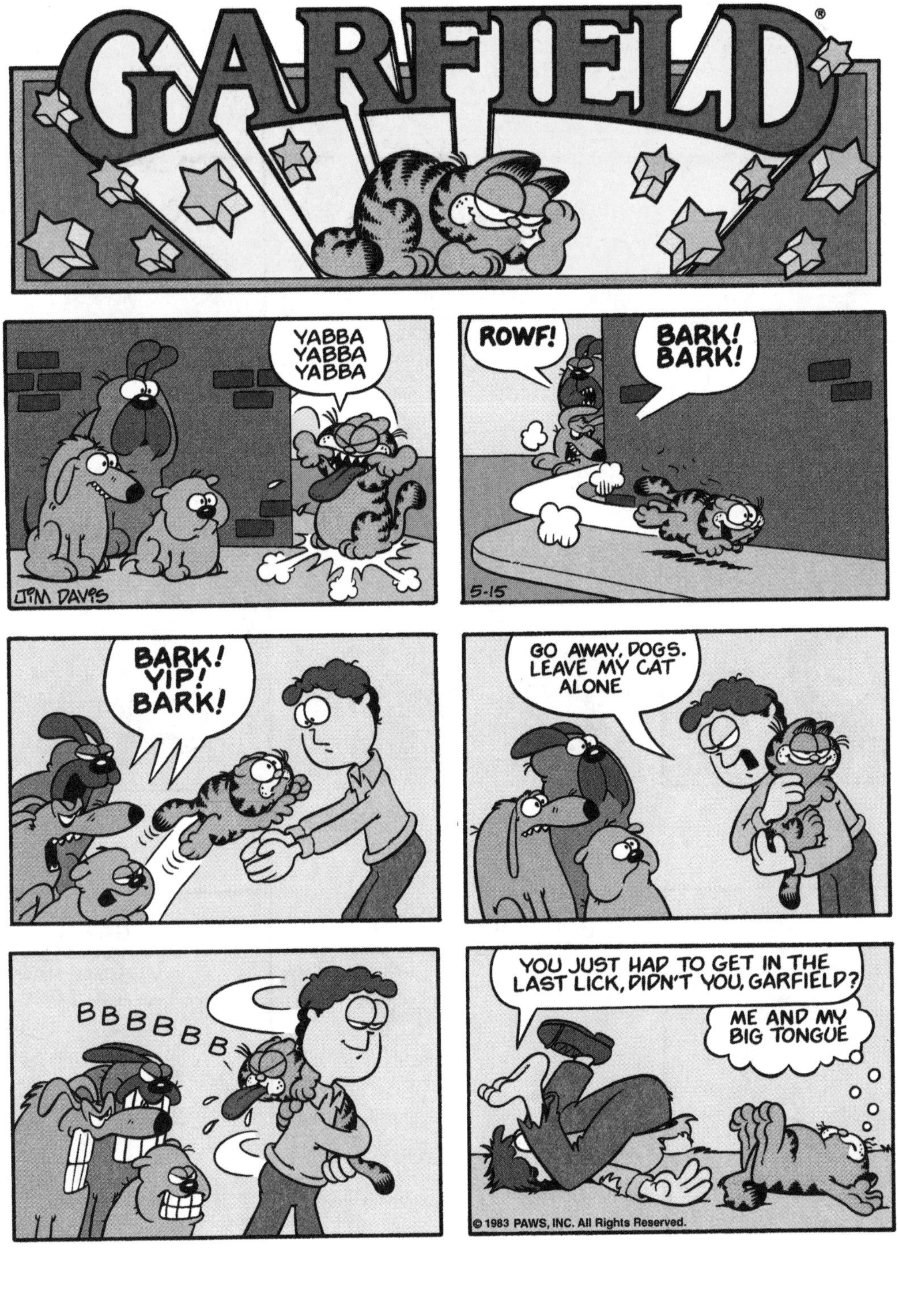
GARFIELD®
YABBA YABBA YABBA
JIM DAVIS
ROWF!
BARK! BARK!
5-15
BARK! YIP! BARK!
GO AWAY, DOGS. LEAVE MY CAT ALONE
BBBBBBB
YOU JUST HAD TO GET IN THE LAST LICK, DIDN'T YOU, GARFIELD?
ME AND MY BIG TONGUE
© 1983 PAWS, INC. All Rights Reserved.

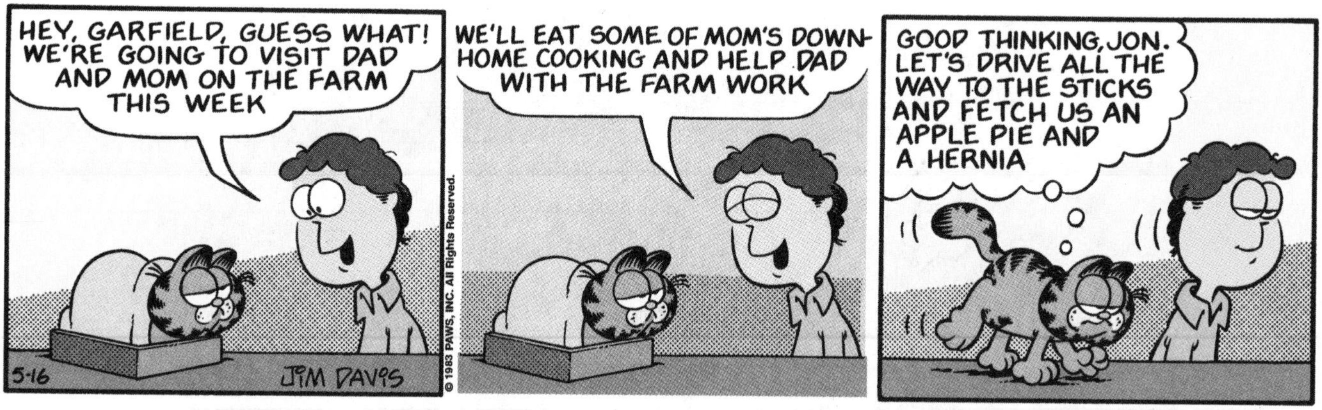
HEY, GARFIELD, GUESS WHAT! WE'RE GOING TO VISIT DAD AND MOM ON THE FARM THIS WEEK
5-16
JIM DAVIS
WE'LL EAT SOME OF MOM'S DOWN-HOME COOKING AND HELP DAD WITH THE FARM WORK
© 1983 PAWS, INC. All Rights Reserved.
GOOD THINKING, JON. LET'S DRIVE ALL THE WAY TO THE STICKS AND FETCH US AN APPLE PIE AND A HERNIA

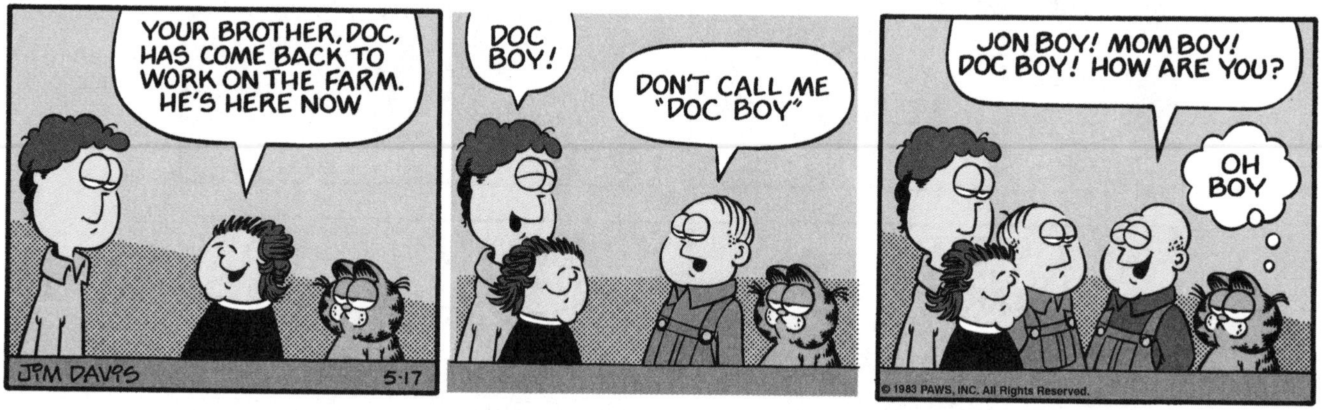
YOUR BROTHER, DOC, HAS COME BACK TO WORK ON THE FARM. HE'S HERE NOW
JIM DAVIS
5-17
DOC BOY!
DON'T CALL ME "DOC BOY"
JON BOY! MOM BOY! DOC BOY! HOW ARE YOU?
OH BOY
© 1983 PAWS, INC. All Rights Reserved.

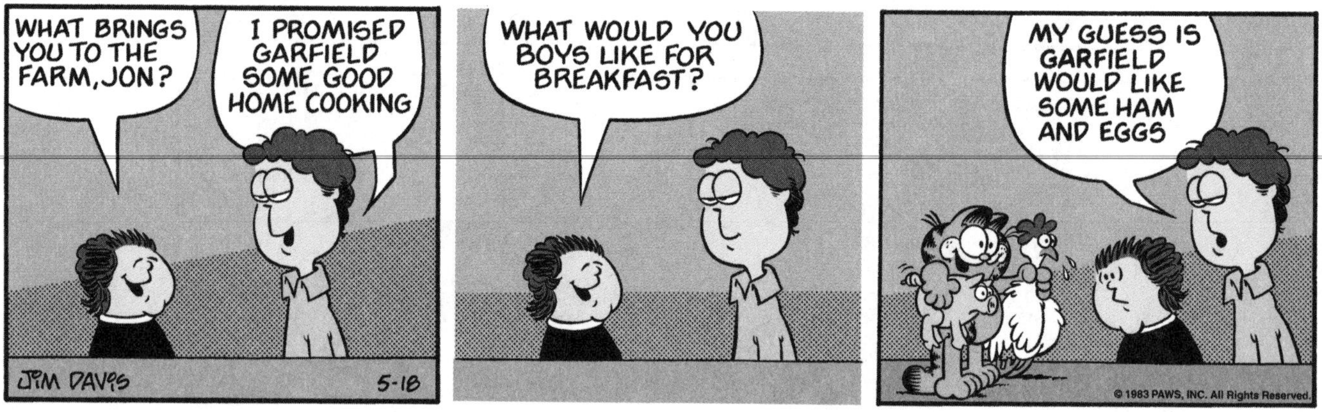
WHAT BRINGS YOU TO THE FARM, JON?
I PROMISED GARFIELD SOME GOOD HOME COOKING
JIM DAVIS
5-18
WHAT WOULD YOU BOYS LIKE FOR BREAKFAST?
MY GUESS IS GARFIELD WOULD LIKE SOME HAM AND EGGS
© 1983 PAWS, INC. All Rights Reserved.

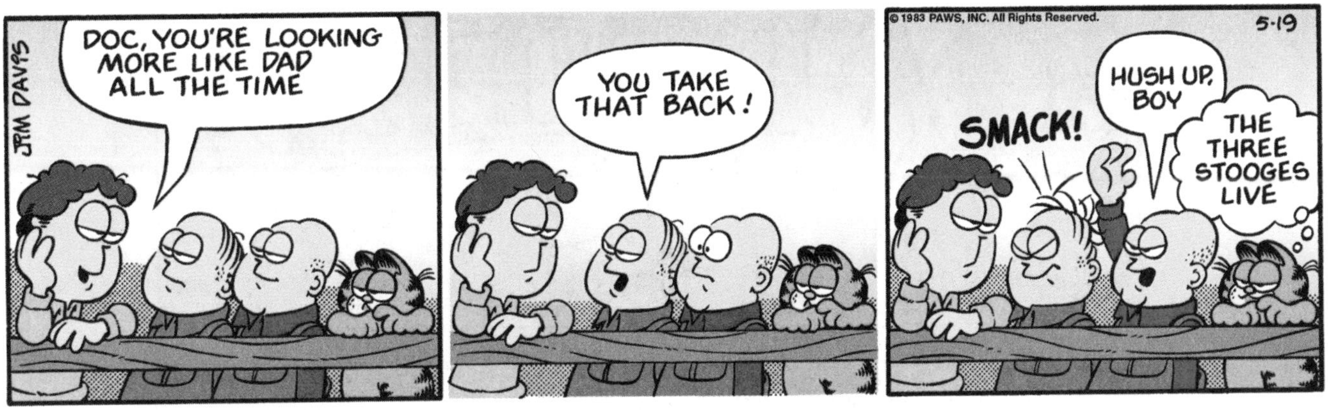
JIM DAVIS
© 1983 PAWS, INC. All Rights Reserved.
5-19
DOC, YOU'RE LOOKING MORE LIKE DAD ALL THE TIME
YOU TAKE THAT BACK!
SMACK!
HUSH UP, BOY
THE THREE STOOGES LIVE

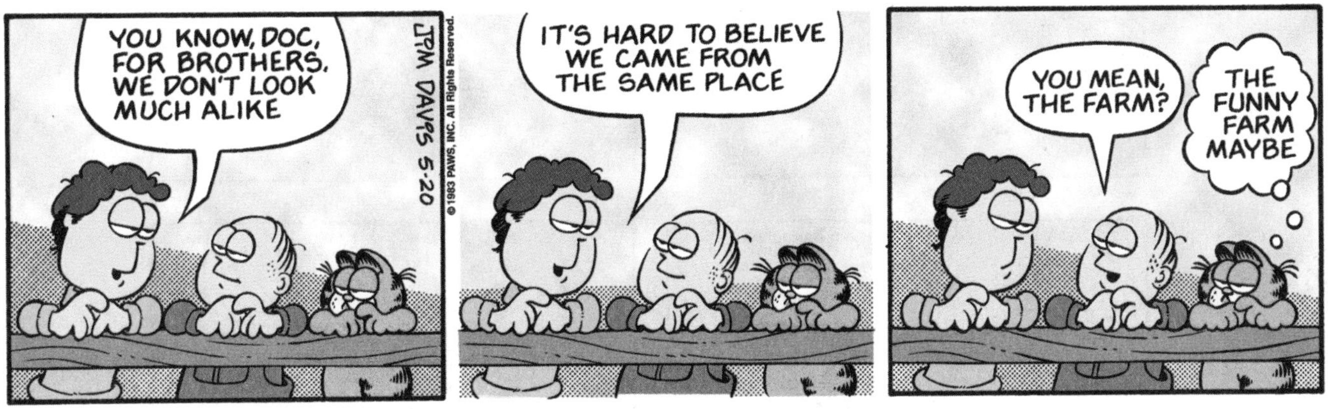
YOU KNOW, DOC, FOR BROTHERS, WE DON'T LOOK MUCH ALIKE
JIM DAVIS 5-20
© 1983 PAWS, INC. All Rights Reserved.
IT'S HARD TO BELIEVE WE CAME FROM THE SAME PLACE
YOU MEAN, THE FARM?
THE FUNNY FARM MAYBE

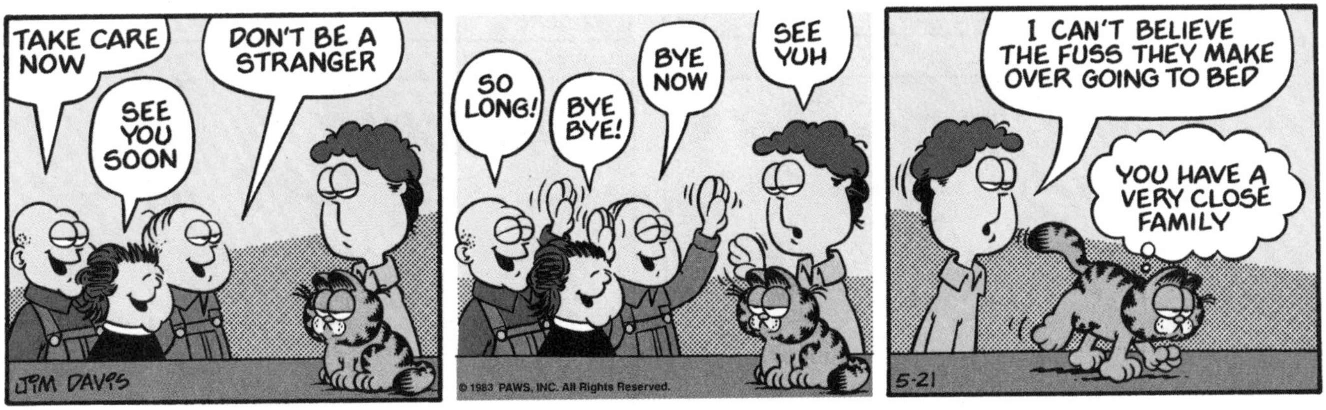
TAKE CARE NOW
SEE YOU SOON
DON'T BE A STRANGER
JIM DAVIS
SO LONG!
BYE BYE!
BYE NOW
SEE YUH
© 1983 PAWS, INC. All Rights Reserved.
I CAN'T BELIEVE THE FUSS THEY MAKE OVER GOING TO BED
YOU HAVE A VERY CLOSE FAMILY
5-21

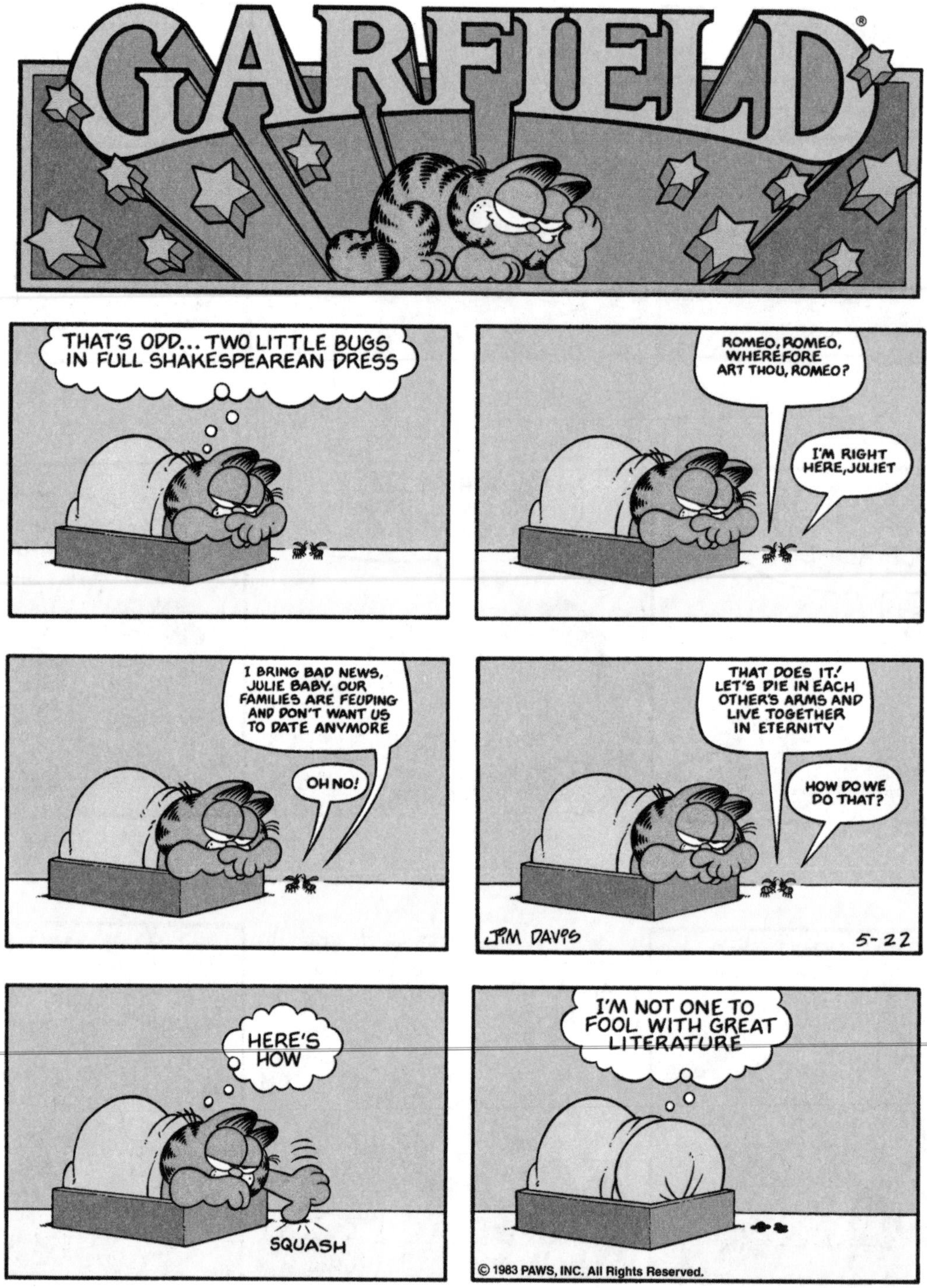
GARFIELD®
THAT'S ODD... TWO LITTLE BUGS IN FULL SHAKESPEAREAN DRESS
ROMEO, ROMEO, WHEREFORE ART THOU, ROMEO?
I'M RIGHT HERE, JULIET
I BRING BAD NEWS, JULIE BABY. OUR FAMILIES ARE FEUDING AND DON'T WANT US TO DATE ANYMORE
OH NO!
THAT DOES IT! LET'S DIE IN EACH OTHER'S ARMS AND LIVE TOGETHER IN ETERNITY
HOW DO WE DO THAT?
JIM DAVIS
5-22
HERE'S HOW
SQUASH
I'M NOT ONE TO FOOL WITH GREAT LITERATURE
© 1983 PAWS, INC. All Rights Reserved.

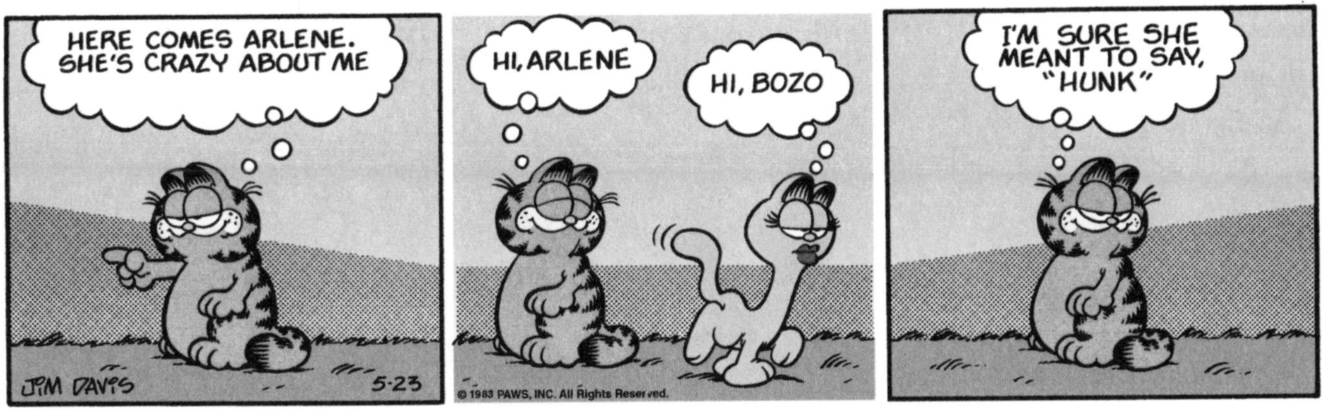
HERE COMES ARLENE. SHE'S CRAZY ABOUT ME
JIM DAVIS
5-23
HI, ARLENE
HI, BOZO
© 1983 PAWS, INC. All Rights Reserved.
I'M SURE SHE MEANT TO SAY, "HUNK"

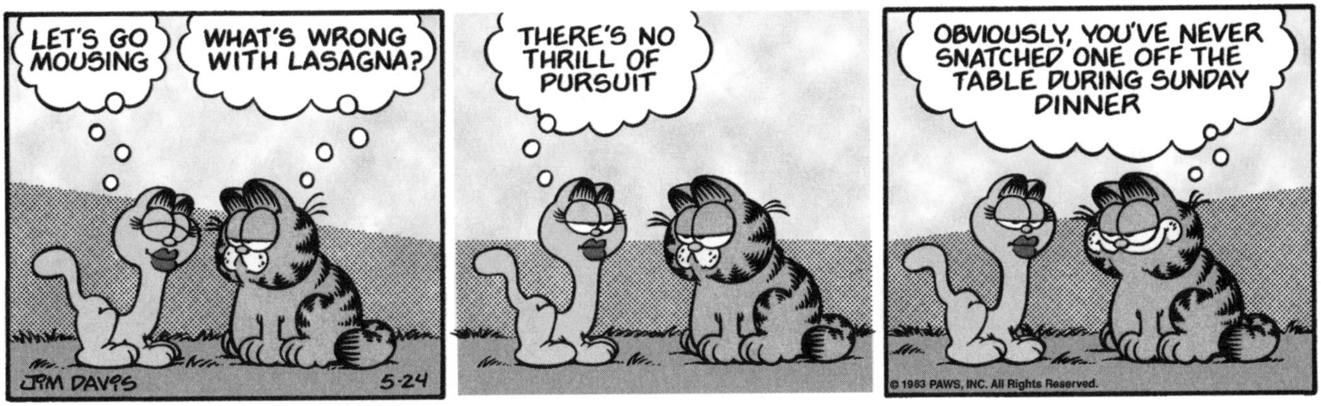
LET'S GO MOUSING
WHAT'S WRONG WITH LASAGNA?
JIM DAVIS
5-24
THERE'S NO THRILL OF PURSUIT
OBVIOUSLY, YOU'VE NEVER SNATCHED ONE OFF THE TABLE DURING SUNDAY DINNER
© 1983 PAWS, INC. All Rights Reserved.

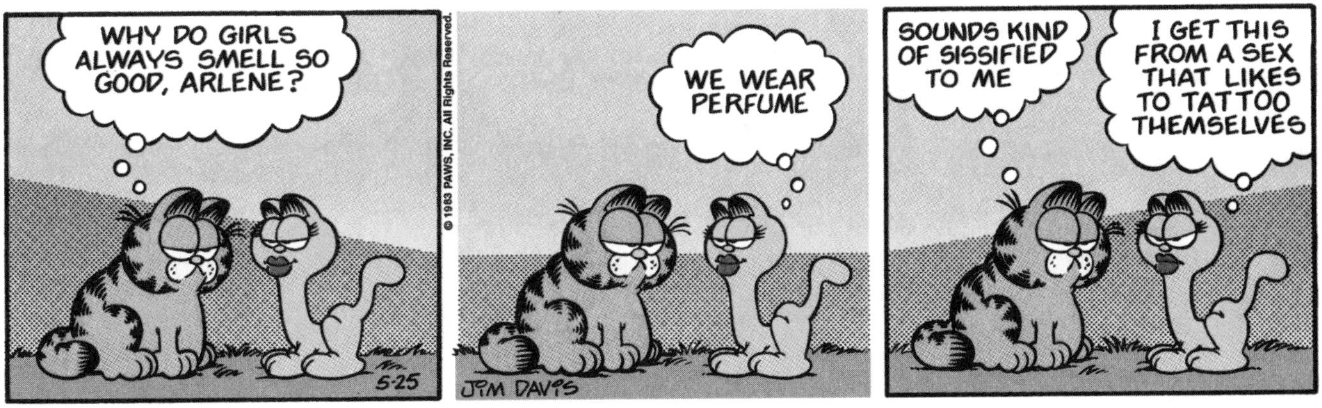
WHY DO GIRLS ALWAYS SMELL SO GOOD, ARLENE?
5-25
© 1983 PAWS, INC. All Rights Reserved.
WE WEAR PERFUME
JIM DAVIS
SOUNDS KIND OF SISSIFIED TO ME
I GET THIS FROM A SEX THAT LIKES TO TATTOO THEMSELVES

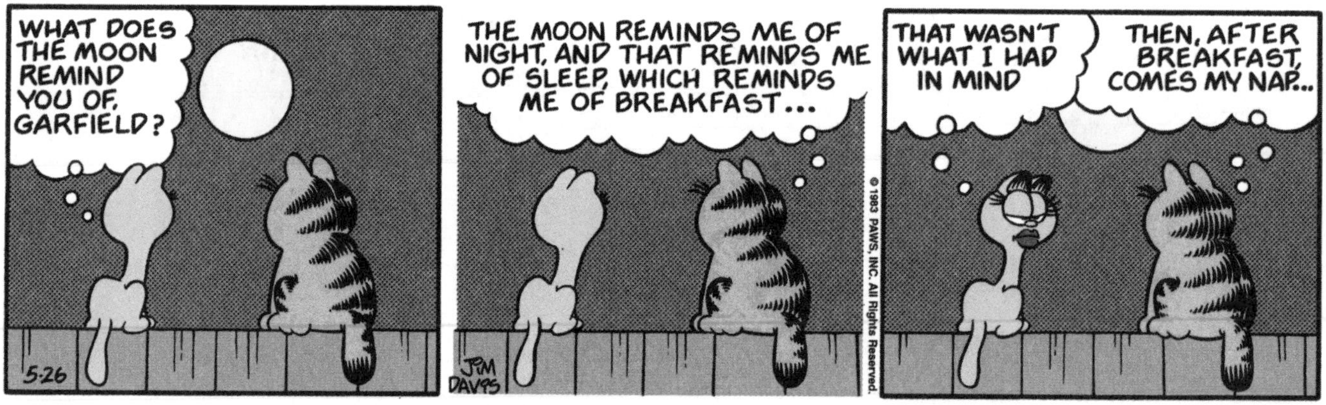
WHAT DOES THE MOON REMIND YOU OF, GARFIELD?
5-26
THE MOON REMINDS ME OF NIGHT, AND THAT REMINDS ME OF SLEEP, WHICH REMINDS ME OF BREAKFAST...
JIM DAVIS
© 1983 PAWS, INC. All Rights Reserved.
THAT WASN'T WHAT I HAD IN MIND
THEN, AFTER BREAKFAST, COMES MY NAP...

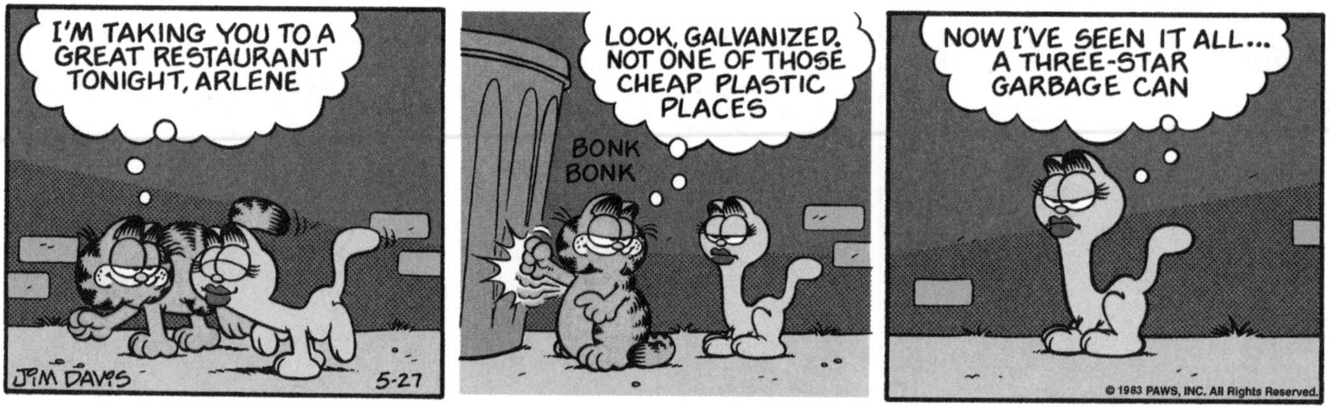
I'M TAKING YOU TO A GREAT RESTAURANT TONIGHT, ARLENE
JIM DAVIS
5-27
LOOK, GALVANIZED. NOT ONE OF THOSE CHEAP PLASTIC PLACES
BONK BONK
NOW I'VE SEEN IT ALL... A THREE-STAR GARBAGE CAN
© 1983 PAWS, INC. All Rights Reserved.

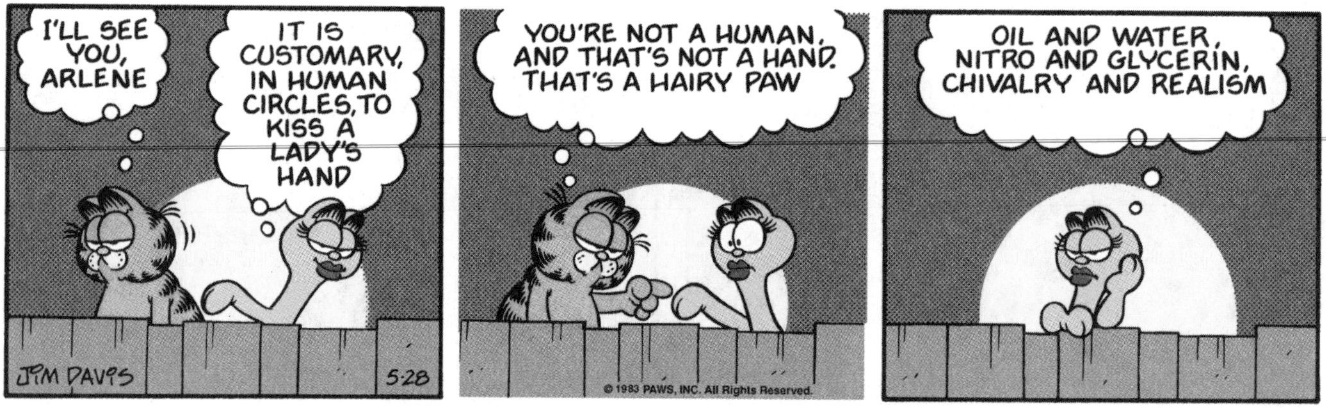
I'LL SEE YOU, ARLENE
IT IS CUSTOMARY, IN HUMAN CIRCLES, TO KISS A LADY'S HAND
JIM DAVIS
5-28
YOU'RE NOT A HUMAN, AND THAT'S NOT A HAND. THAT'S A HAIRY PAW
© 1983 PAWS, INC. All Rights Reserved.
OIL AND WATER, NITRO AND GLYCERIN, CHIVALRY AND REALISM

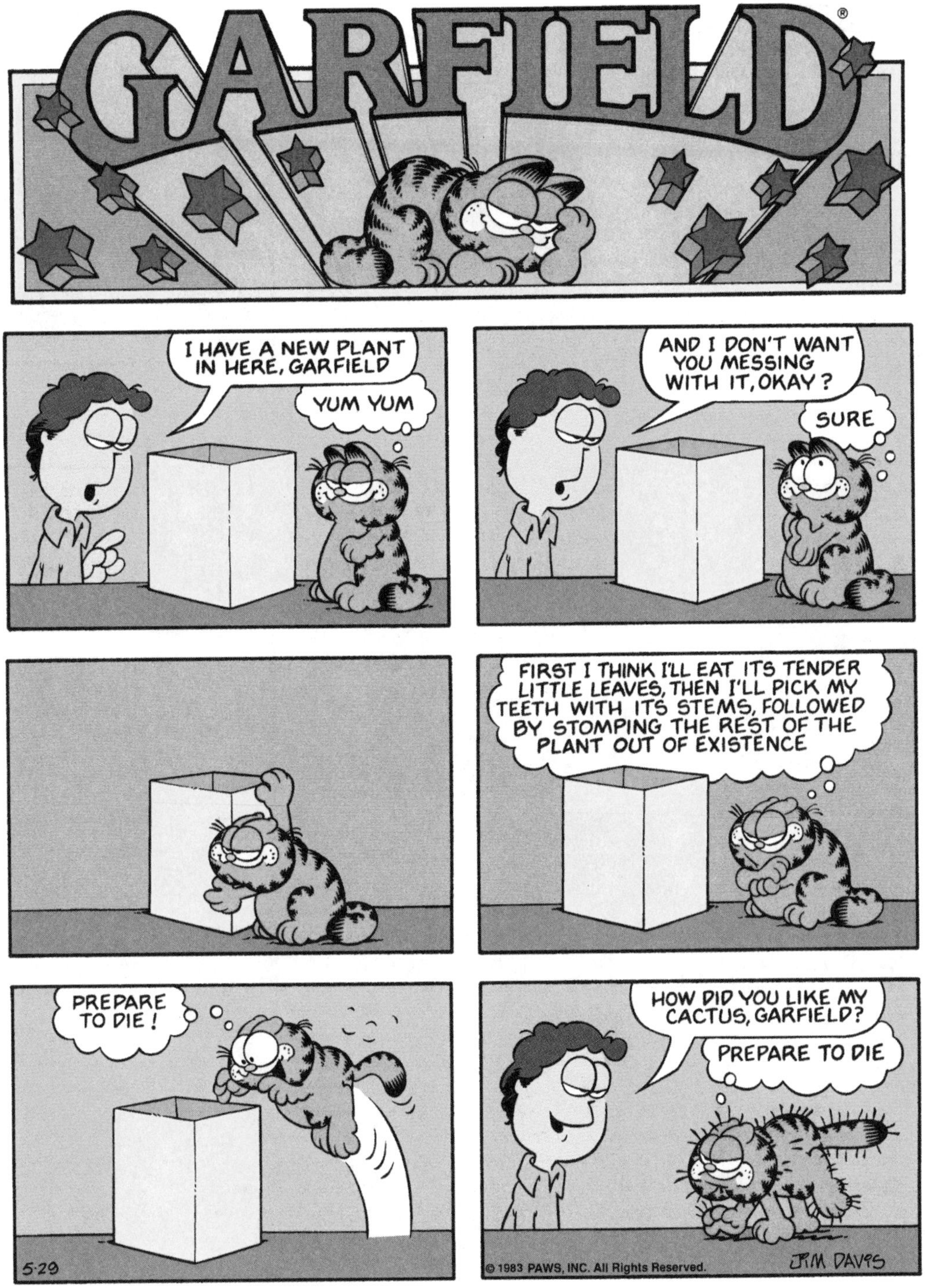
GARFIELD®
I HAVE A NEW PLANT IN HERE, GARFIELD
YUM YUM
AND I DON'T WANT YOU MESSING WITH IT, OKAY?
SURE
FIRST I THINK I'LL EAT ITS TENDER LITTLE LEAVES, THEN I'LL PICK MY TEETH WITH ITS STEMS, FOLLOWED BY STOMPING THE REST OF THE PLANT OUT OF EXISTENCE
PREPARE TO DIE!
5·29
HOW DID YOU LIKE MY CACTUS, GARFIELD?
PREPARE TO DIE
© 1983 PAWS, INC. All Rights Reserved.
JIM DAVIS

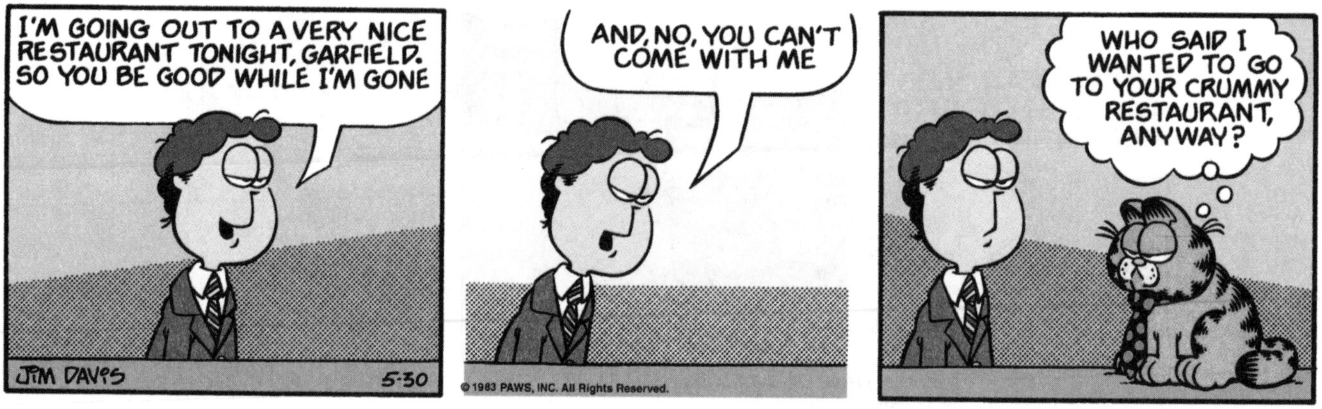
I'M GOING OUT TO A VERY NICE RESTAURANT TONIGHT, GARFIELD. SO YOU BE GOOD WHILE I'M GONE
JIM DAVIS
5-30
AND, NO, YOU CAN'T COME WITH ME
© 1983 PAWS, INC. All Rights Reserved.
WHO SAID I WANTED TO GO TO YOUR CRUMMY RESTAURANT, ANYWAY?

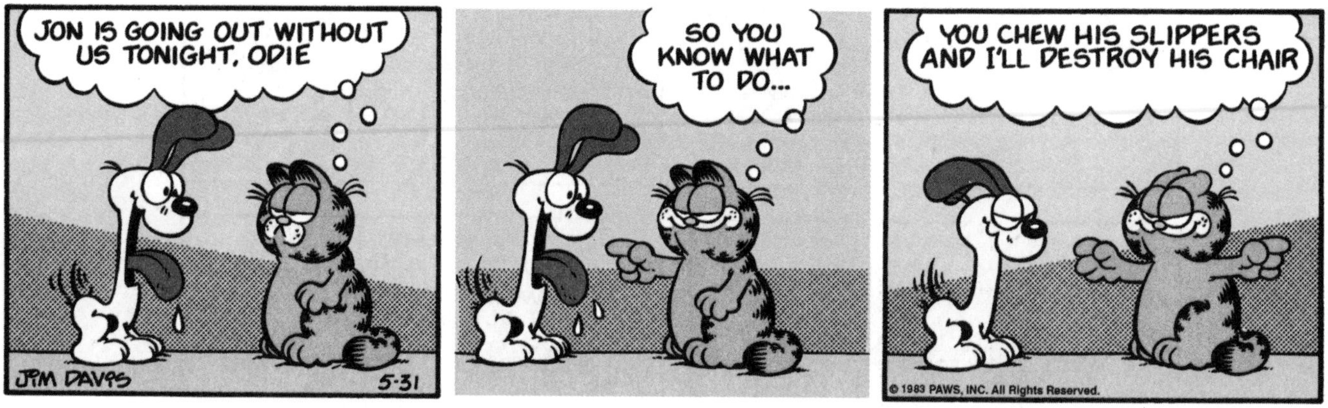
JON IS GOING OUT WITHOUT US TONIGHT, ODIE
JIM DAVIS
5-31
SO YOU KNOW WHAT TO DO...
YOU CHEW HIS SLIPPERS AND I'LL DESTROY HIS CHAIR
© 1983 PAWS, INC. All Rights Reserved.

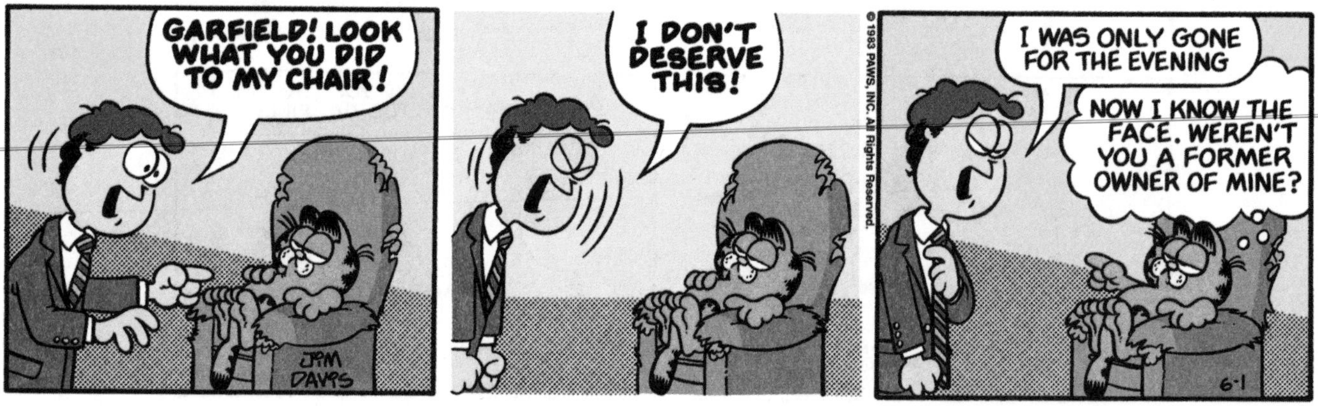
GARFIELD! LOOK WHAT YOU DID TO MY CHAIR!
JIM DAVIS
I DON'T DESERVE THIS!
© 1983 PAWS, INC. All Rights Reserved.
I WAS ONLY GONE FOR THE EVENING
NOW I KNOW THE FACE. WEREN'T YOU A FORMER OWNER OF MINE?
6-1

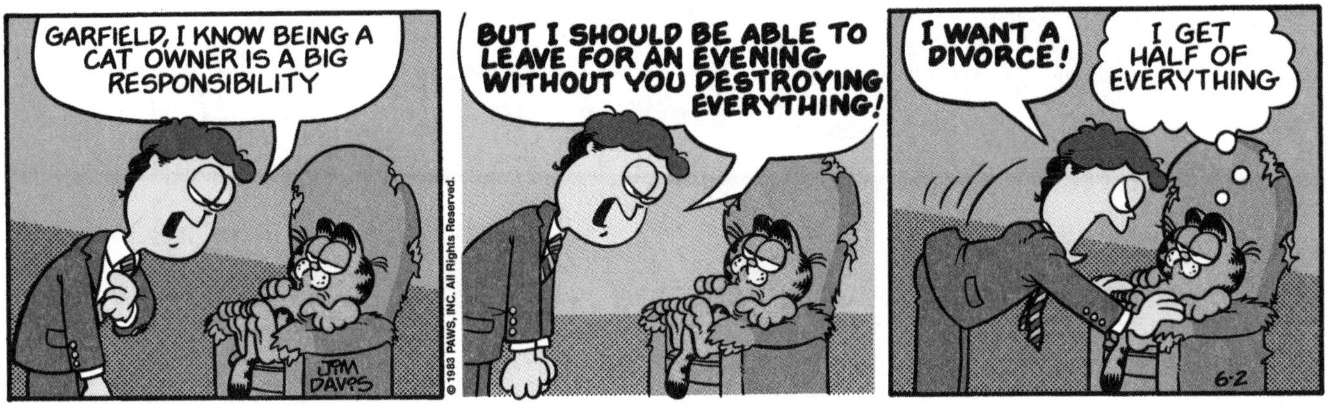
GARFIELD, I KNOW BEING A CAT OWNER IS A BIG RESPONSIBILITY
JIM DAVIS
© 1983 PAWS, INC. All Rights Reserved.
BUT I SHOULD BE ABLE TO LEAVE FOR AN EVENING WITHOUT YOU DESTROYING EVERYTHING!
I WANT A DIVORCE!
I GET HALF OF EVERYTHING
6-2

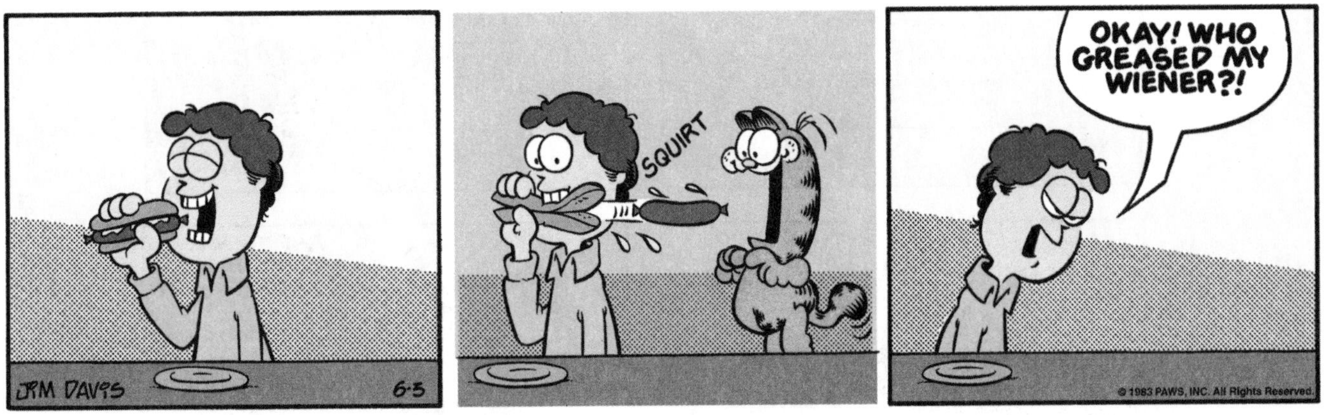
JIM DAVIS
6-3
SQUIRT
OKAY! WHO GREASED MY WIENER?!
© 1983 PAWS, INC. All Rights Reserved.

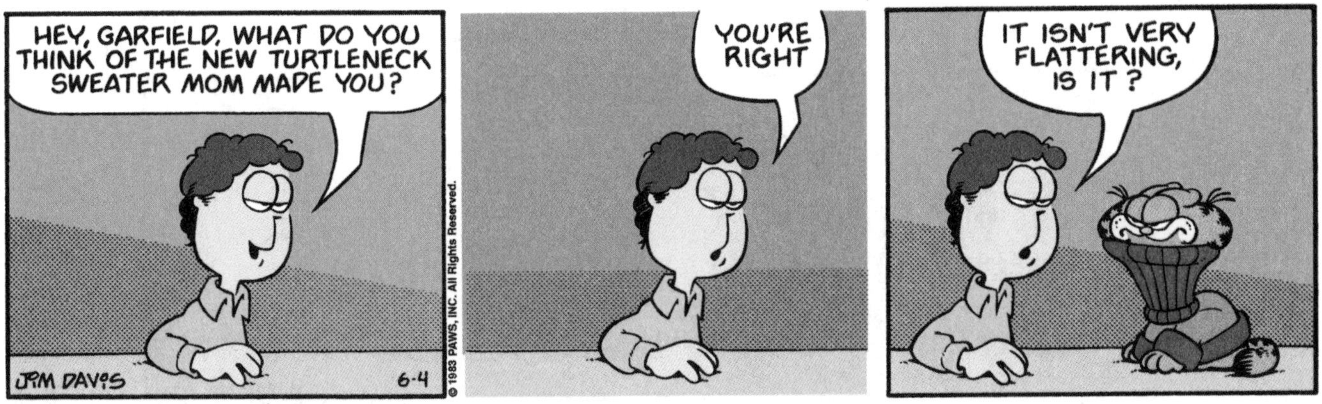
HEY, GARFIELD, WHAT DO YOU THINK OF THE NEW TURTLENECK SWEATER MOM MADE YOU?
JIM DAVIS
6-4
© 1983 PAWS, INC. All Rights Reserved.
YOU'RE RIGHT
IT ISN'T VERY FLATTERING, IS IT?

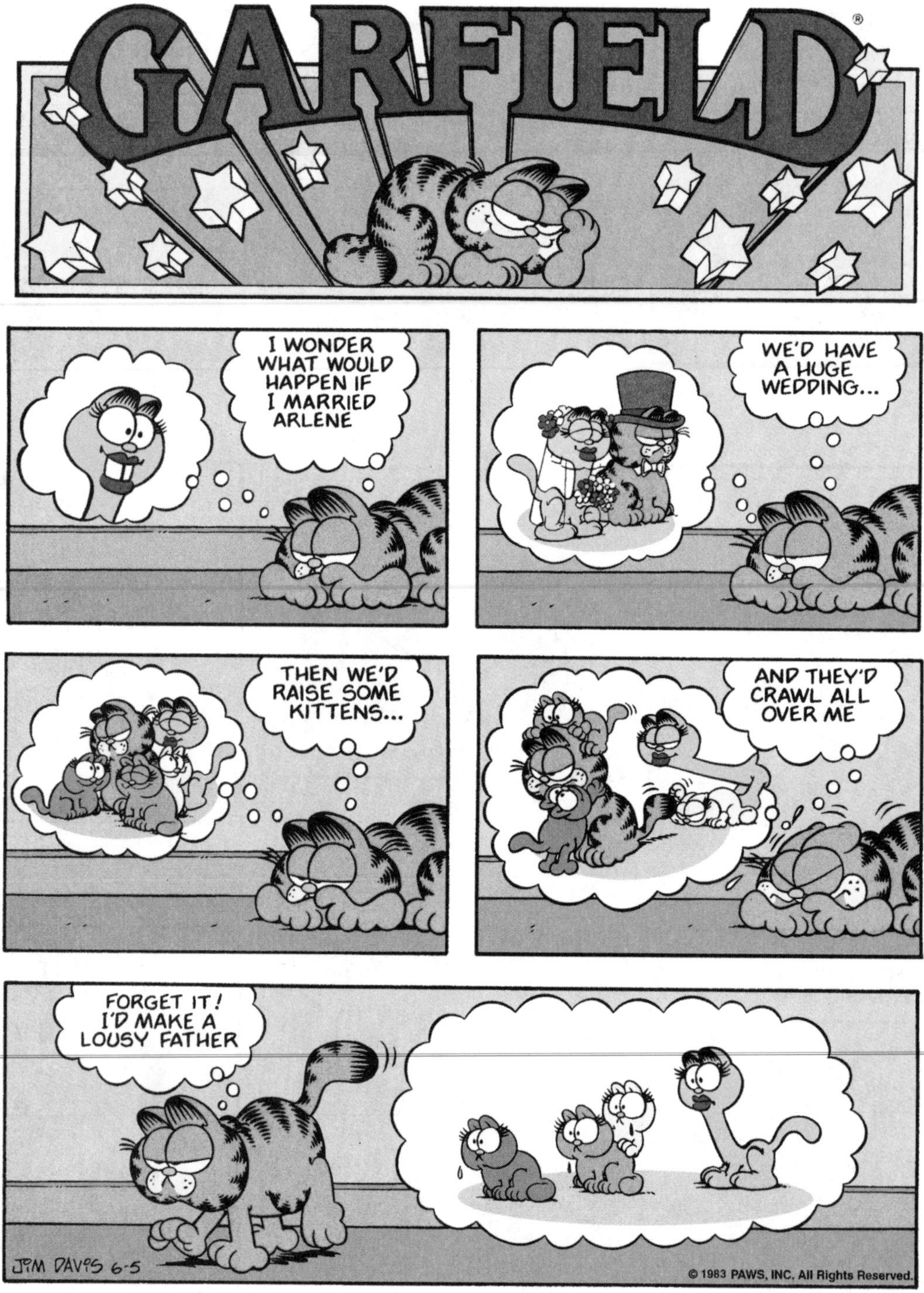
GARFIELD®
I WONDER WHAT WOULD HAPPEN IF I MARRIED ARLENE
WE'D HAVE A HUGE WEDDING...
THEN WE'D RAISE SOME KITTENS...
AND THEY'D CRAWL ALL OVER ME
FORGET IT! I'D MAKE A LOUSY FATHER
JIM DAVIS 6-5
© 1983 PAWS, INC. All Rights Reserved.

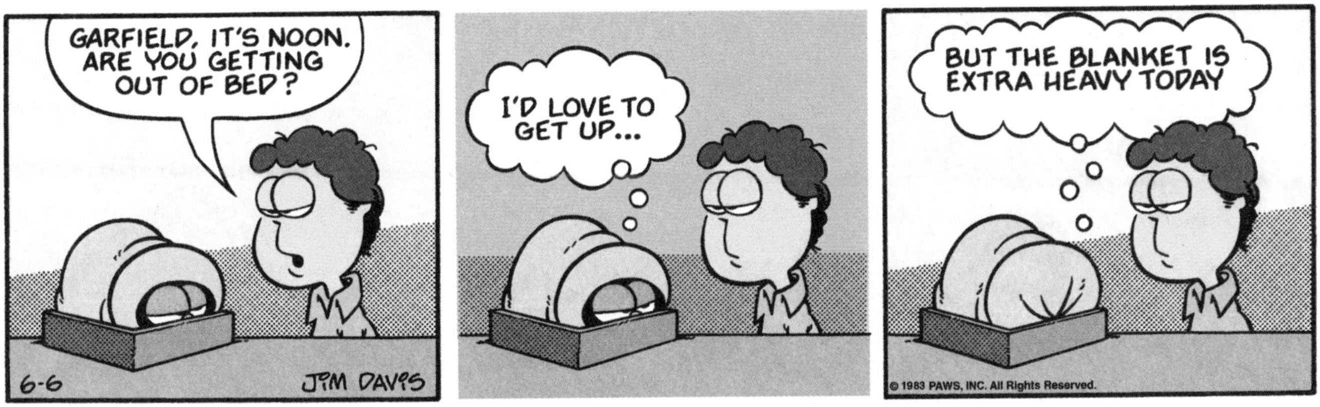
GARFIELD, IT'S NOON. ARE YOU GETTING OUT OF BED?
6-6
JIM DAVIS
I'D LOVE TO GET UP...
BUT THE BLANKET IS EXTRA HEAVY TODAY
© 1983 PAWS, INC. All Rights Reserved.

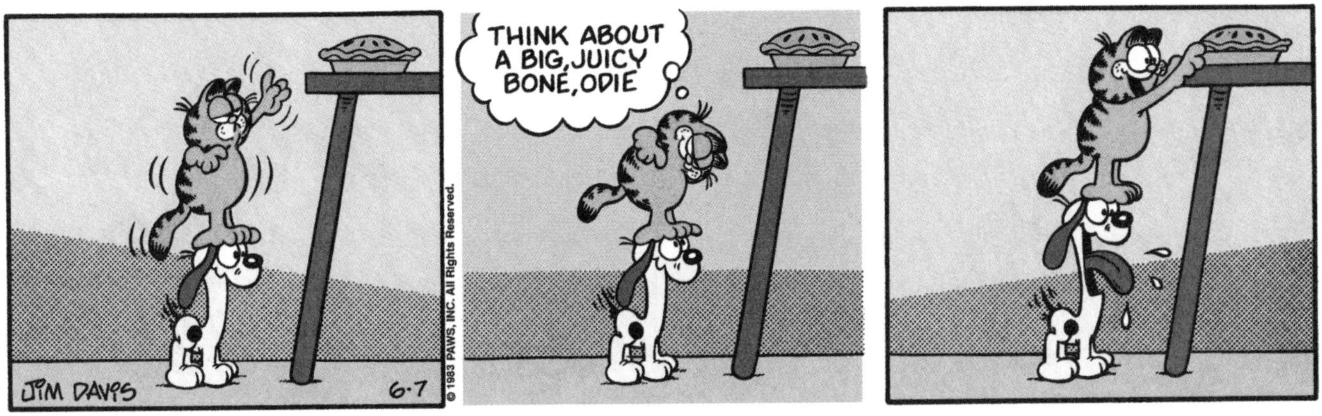
JIM DAVIS
6-7
© 1983 PAWS, INC. All Rights Reserved.
THINK ABOUT A BIG, JUICY BONE, ODIE

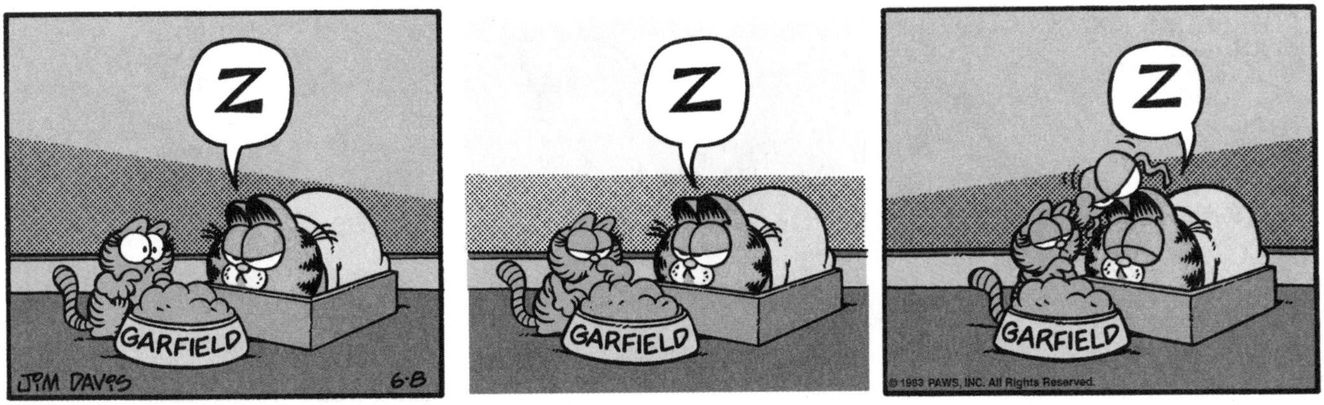
Z
GARFIELD
JIM DAVIS
6-8
Z
GARFIELD
Z
GARFIELD
© 1983 PAWS, INC. All Rights Reserved.

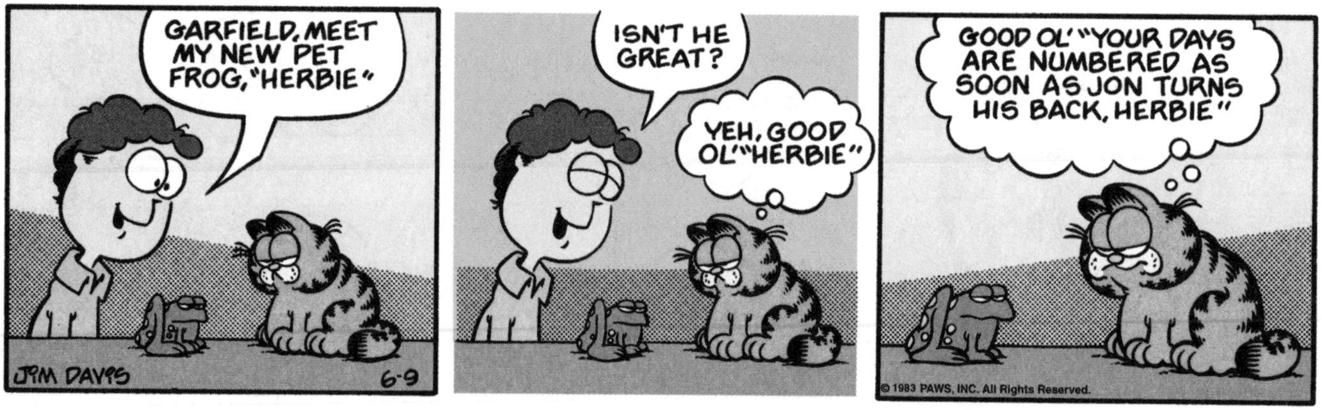
GARFIELD, MEET MY NEW PET FROG, "HERBIE"
JIM DAVIS
6-9
ISN'T HE GREAT?
YEH, GOOD OL' "HERBIE"
GOOD OL' "YOUR DAYS ARE NUMBERED AS SOON AS JON TURNS HIS BACK, HERBIE"
© 1983 PAWS, INC. All Rights Reserved.

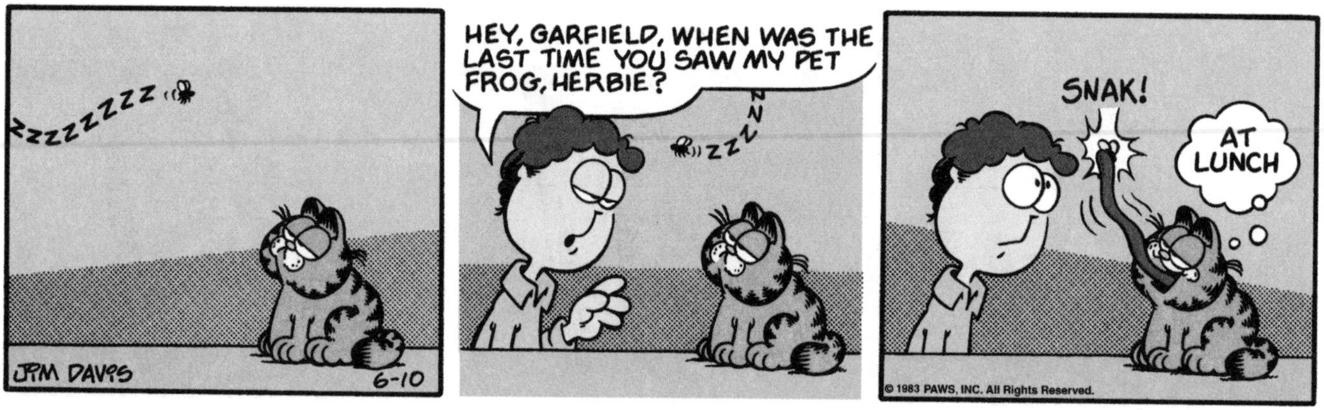
ZZZZZZZZ
JIM DAVIS
6-10
HEY, GARFIELD, WHEN WAS THE LAST TIME YOU SAW MY PET FROG, HERBIE?
ZZZZ
SNAK!
AT LUNCH
© 1983 PAWS, INC. All Rights Reserved.

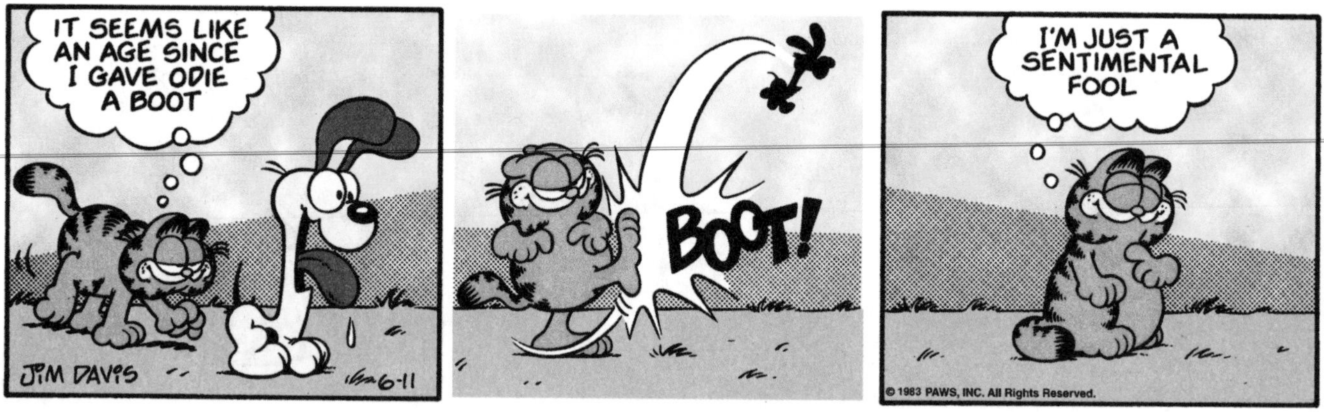
IT SEEMS LIKE AN AGE SINCE I GAVE ODIE A BOOT
JIM DAVIS
6-11
BOOT!
I'M JUST A SENTIMENTAL FOOL
© 1983 PAWS, INC. All Rights Reserved.

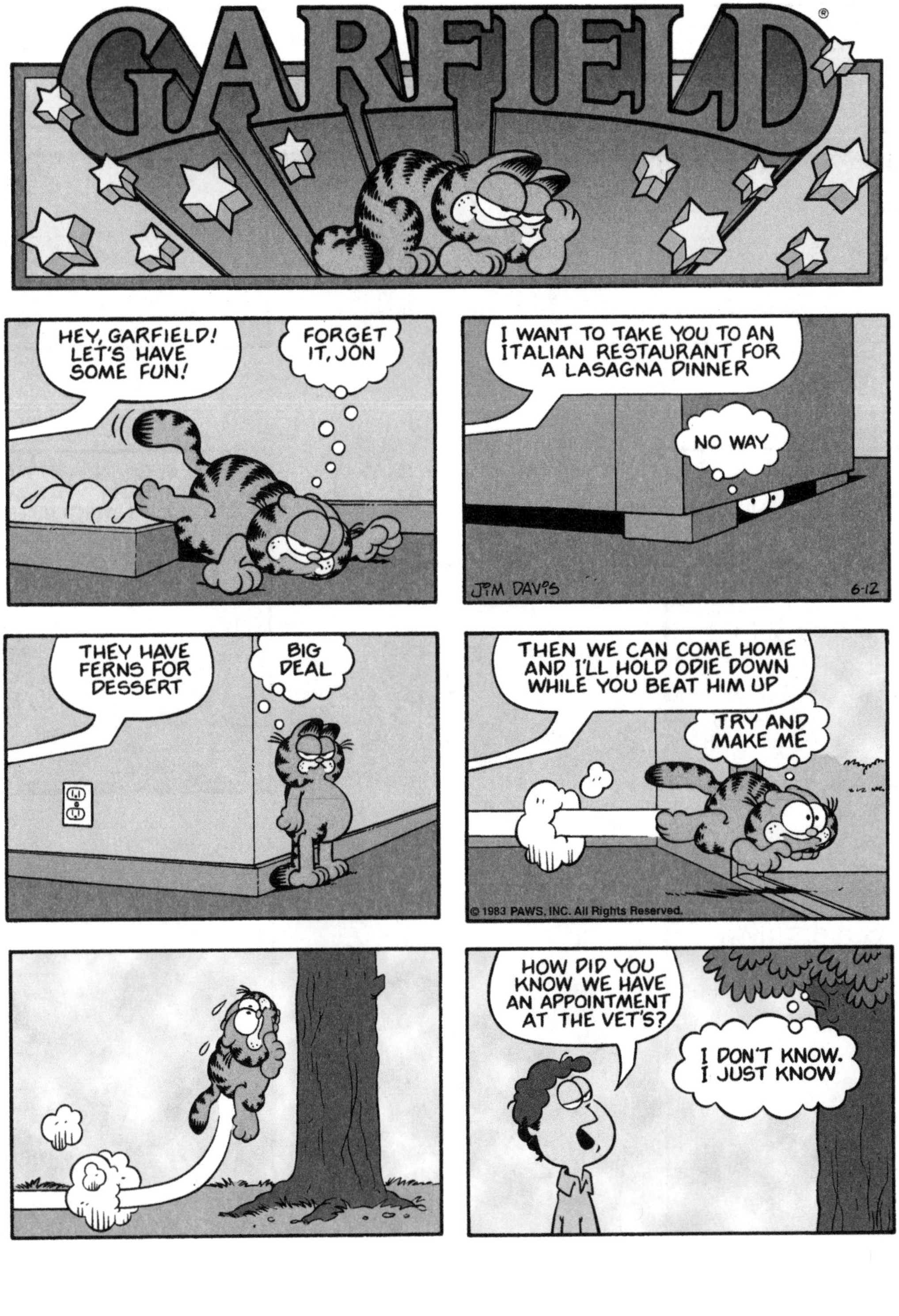
GARFIELD
HEY, GARFIELD! LET'S HAVE SOME FUN!
FORGET IT, JON
I WANT TO TAKE YOU TO AN ITALIAN RESTAURANT FOR A LASAGNA DINNER
NO WAY
JIM DAVIS
6-12
THEY HAVE FERNS FOR DESSERT
BIG DEAL
THEN WE CAN COME HOME AND I'LL HOLD ODIE DOWN WHILE YOU BEAT HIM UP
TRY AND MAKE ME
© 1983 PAWS, INC. All Rights Reserved.
HOW DID YOU KNOW WE HAVE AN APPOINTMENT AT THE VET'S?
I DON'T KNOW. I JUST KNOW

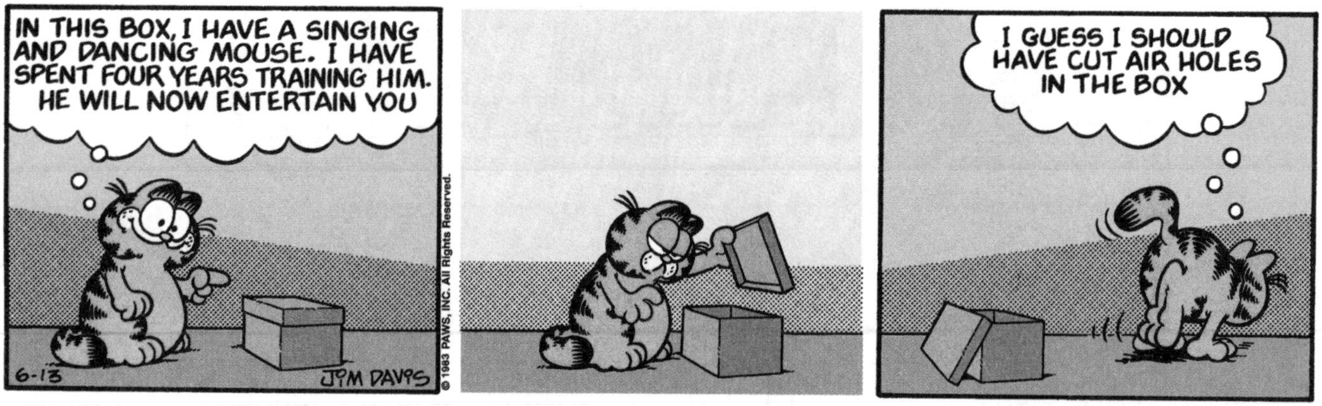
IN THIS BOX, I HAVE A SINGING AND DANCING MOUSE. I HAVE SPENT FOUR YEARS TRAINING HIM. HE WILL NOW ENTERTAIN YOU
6-13
JIM DAVIS
© 1983 PAWS, INC. All Rights Reserved.
I GUESS I SHOULD HAVE CUT AIR HOLES IN THE BOX

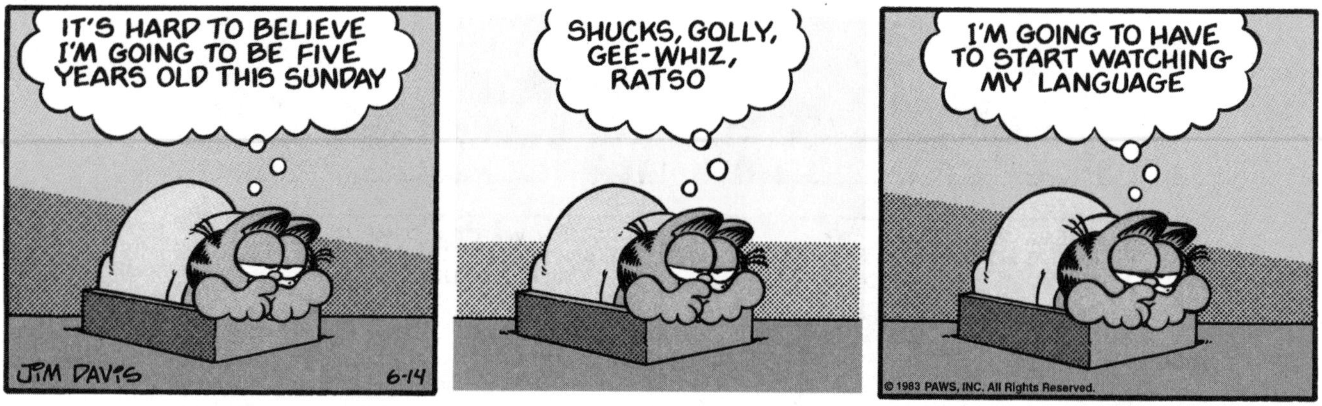
IT'S HARD TO BELIEVE I'M GOING TO BE FIVE YEARS OLD THIS SUNDAY
JIM DAVIS
6-14
SHUCKS, GOLLY, GEE-WHIZ, RATSO
I'M GOING TO HAVE TO START WATCHING MY LANGUAGE
© 1983 PAWS, INC. All Rights Reserved.

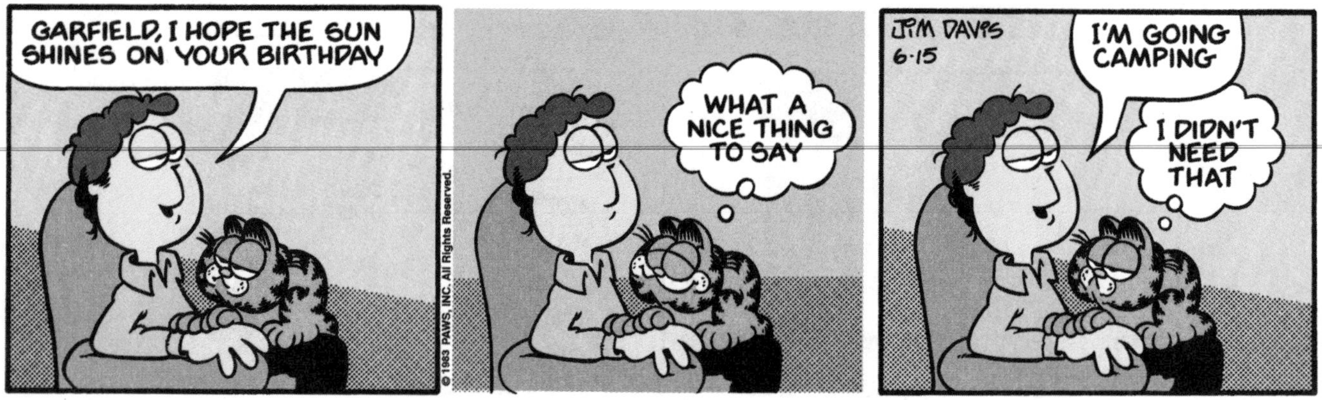
GARFIELD, I HOPE THE SUN SHINES ON YOUR BIRTHDAY
© 1983 PAWS, INC. All Rights Reserved.
WHAT A NICE THING TO SAY
JIM DAVIS
6-15
I'M GOING CAMPING
I DIDN'T NEED THAT

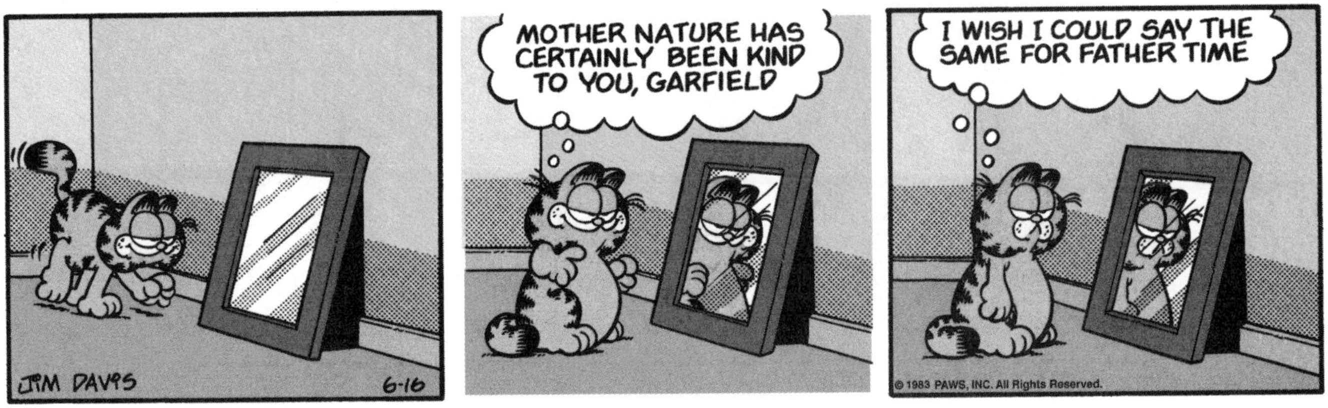
JIM DAVIS
6-16
MOTHER NATURE HAS CERTAINLY BEEN KIND TO YOU, GARFIELD
I WISH I COULD SAY THE SAME FOR FATHER TIME
© 1983 PAWS, INC. All Rights Reserved.

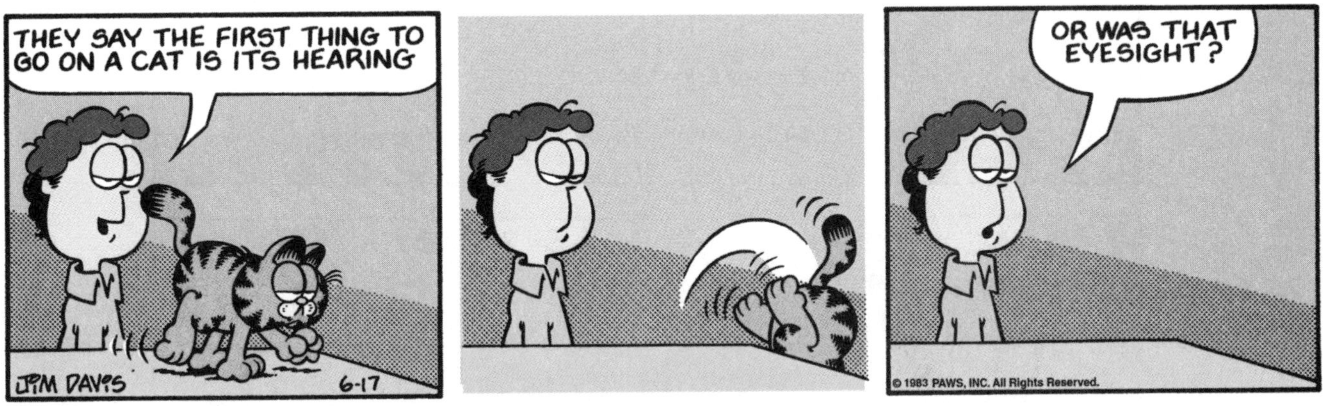
THEY SAY THE FIRST THING TO GO ON A CAT IS ITS HEARING
JIM DAVIS
6-17
OR WAS THAT EYESIGHT?
© 1983 PAWS, INC. All Rights Reserved.

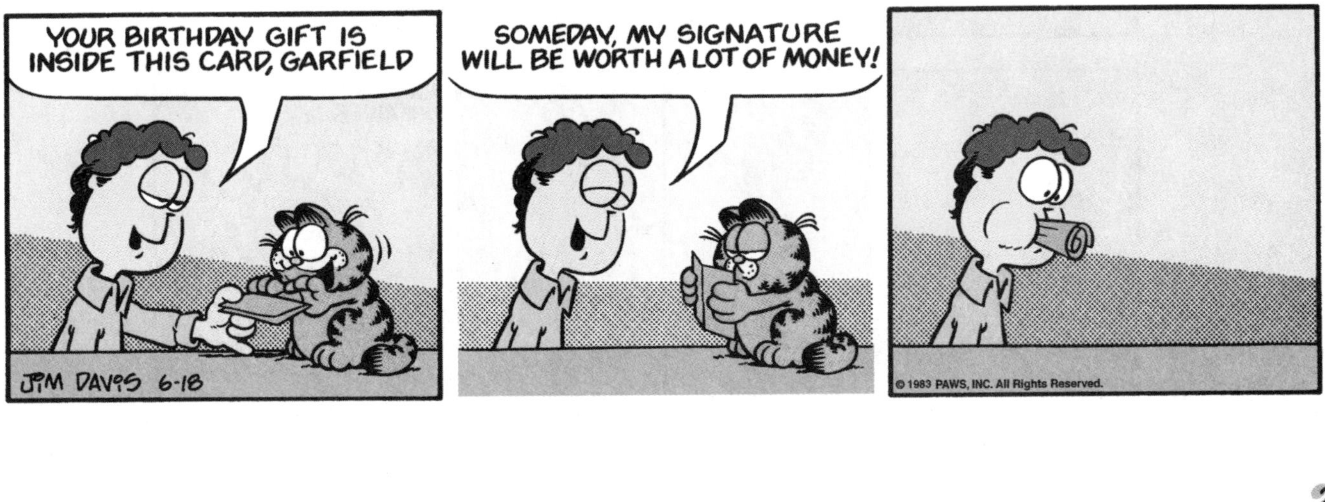
YOUR BIRTHDAY GIFT IS INSIDE THIS CARD, GARFIELD
JIM DAVIS 6-18
SOMEDAY, MY SIGNATURE WILL BE WORTH A LOT OF MONEY!
© 1983 PAWS, INC. All Rights Reserved.

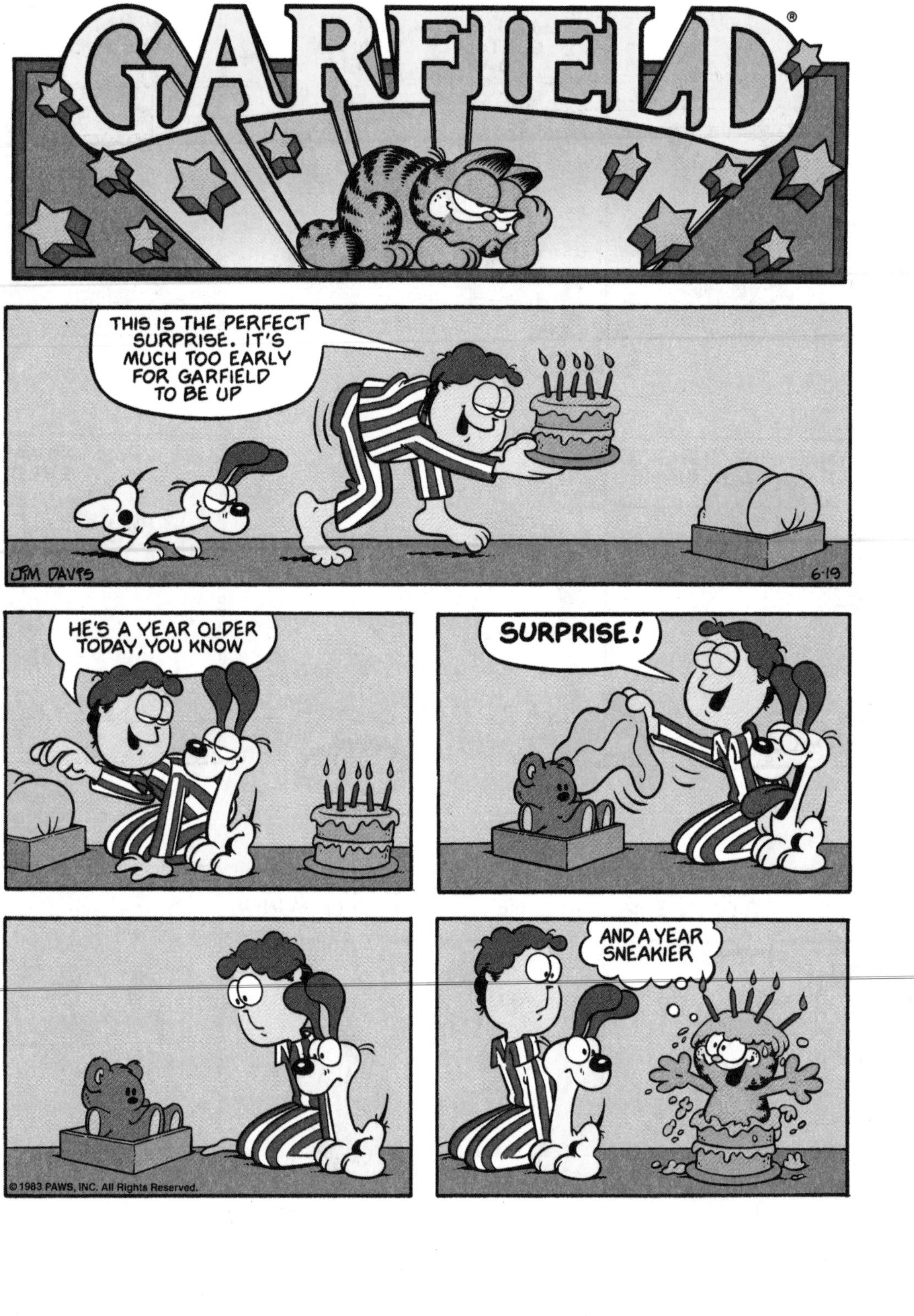
GARFIELD®
THIS IS THE PERFECT SURPRISE. IT'S MUCH TOO EARLY FOR GARFIELD TO BE UP
JIM DAVIS
6-19
HE'S A YEAR OLDER TODAY, YOU KNOW
SURPRISE!
AND A YEAR SNEAKIER
© 1983 PAWS, INC. All Rights Reserved.

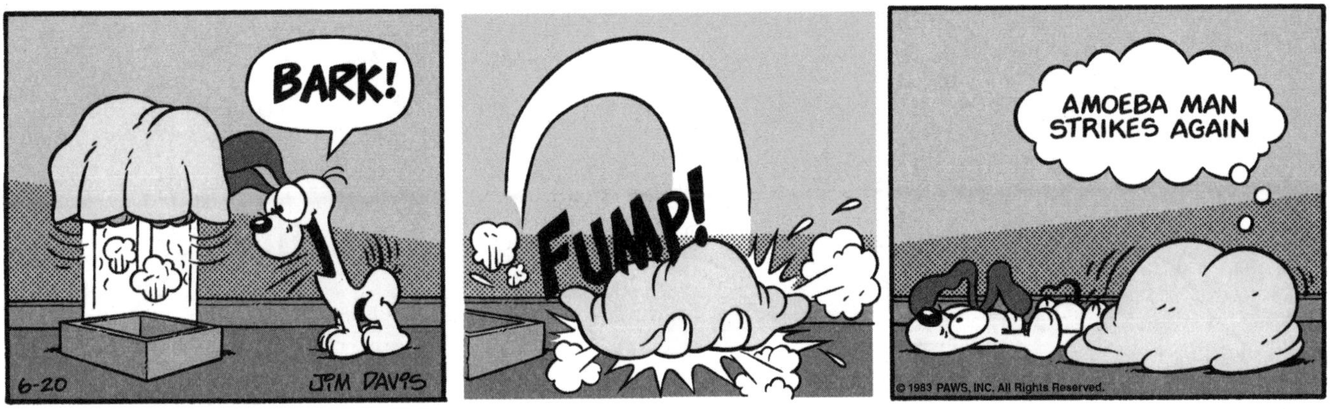
BARK!
6-20
JIM DAVIS
FUMP!
AMOEBA MAN STRIKES AGAIN
© 1983 PAWS, INC. All Rights Reserved.

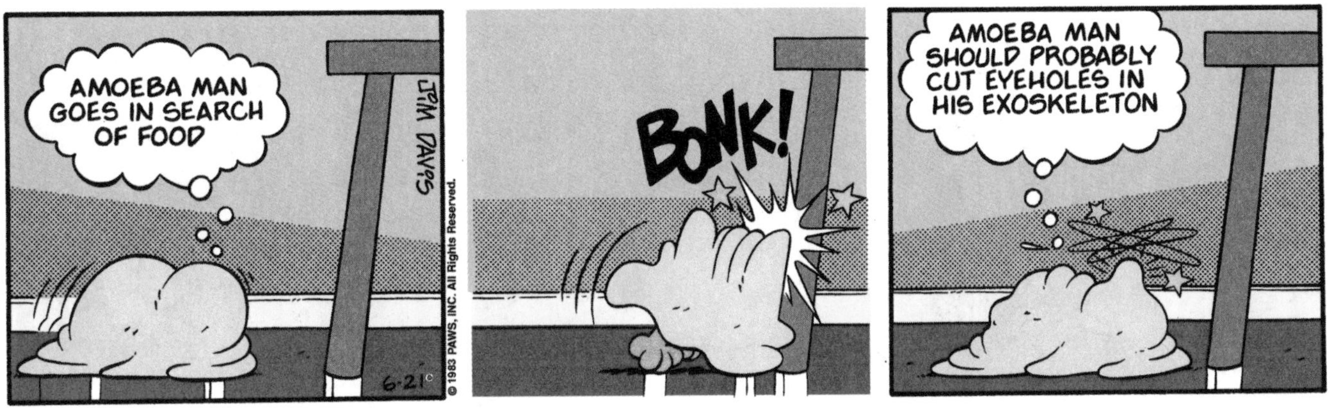
AMOEBA MAN GOES IN SEARCH OF FOOD
JIM DAVIS
6-21
© 1983 PAWS, INC. All Rights Reserved.
BONK!
AMOEBA MAN SHOULD PROBABLY CUT EYEHOLES IN HIS EXOSKELETON

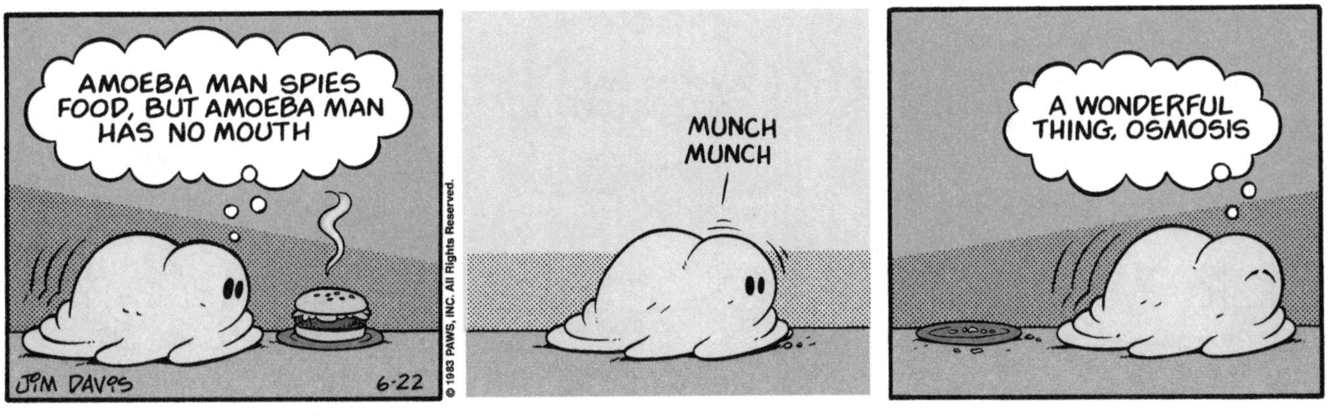
AMOEBA MAN SPIES FOOD, BUT AMOEBA MAN HAS NO MOUTH
JIM DAVIS
6-22
© 1983 PAWS, INC. All Rights Reserved.
MUNCH MUNCH
A WONDERFUL THING, OSMOSIS

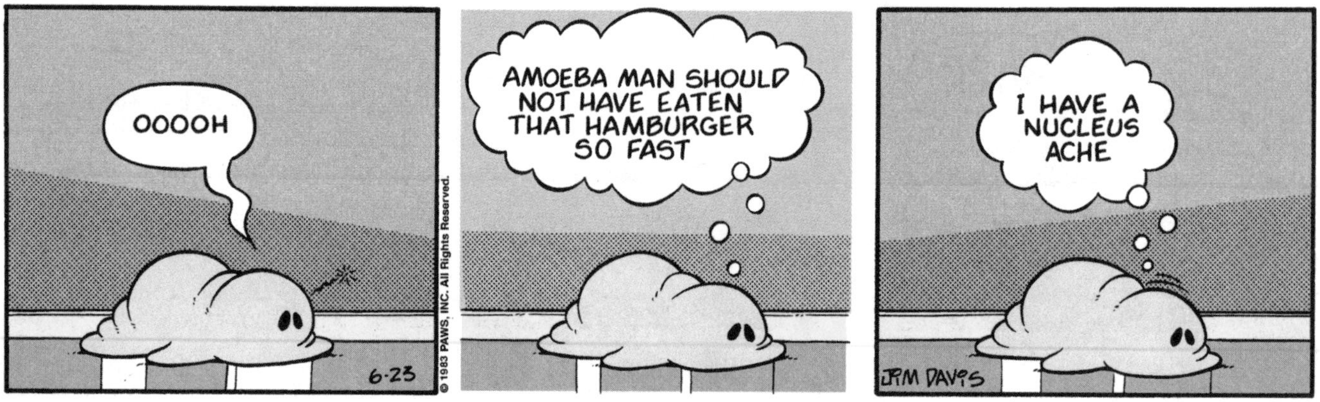
OOOOH
© 1983 PAWS, INC. All Rights Reserved.
6-23
AMOEBA MAN SHOULD NOT HAVE EATEN THAT HAMBURGER SO FAST
I HAVE A NUCLEUS ACHE
JIM DAVIS

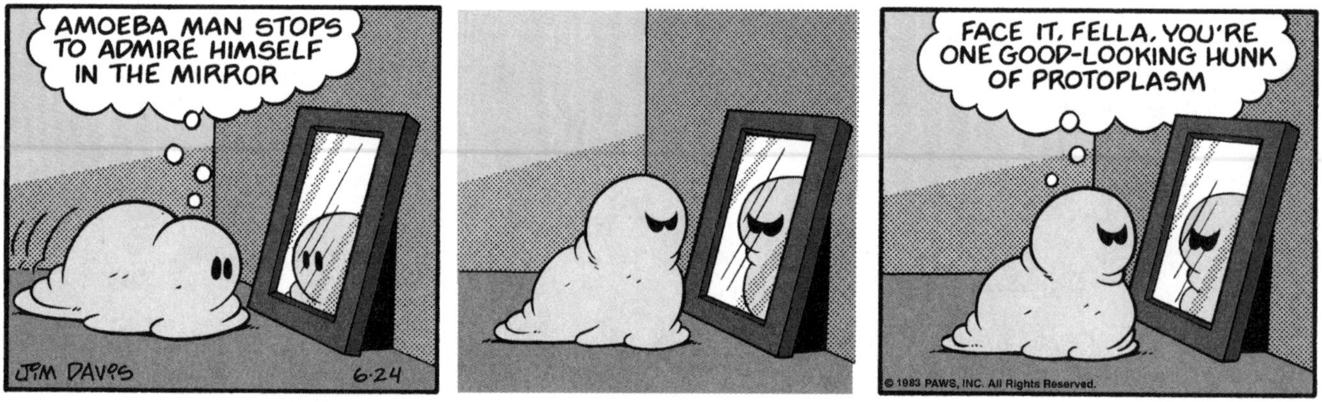
AMOEBA MAN STOPS TO ADMIRE HIMSELF IN THE MIRROR
JIM DAVIS
6-24
FACE IT, FELLA, YOU'RE ONE GOOD-LOOKING HUNK OF PROTOPLASM
© 1983 PAWS, INC. All Rights Reserved.

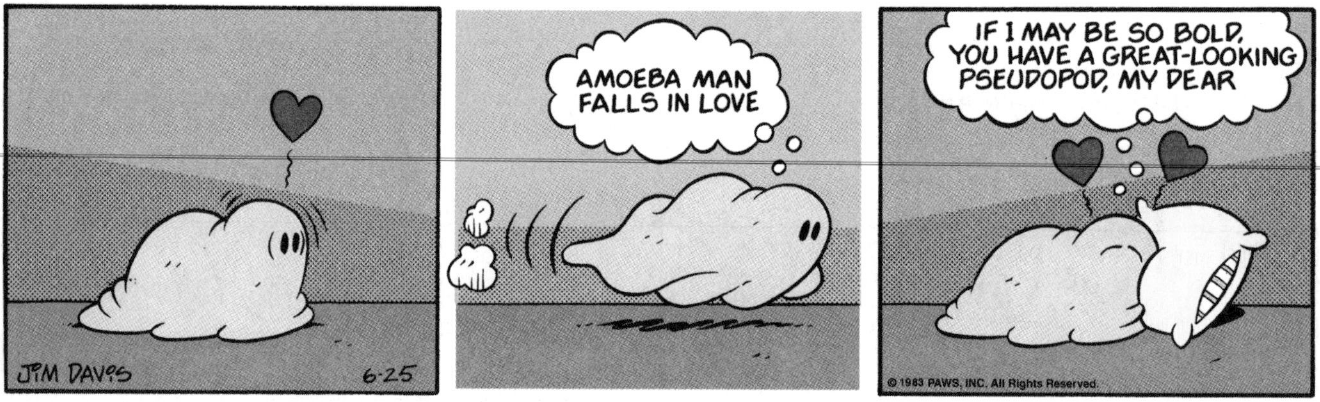
JIM DAVIS
6-25
AMOEBA MAN FALLS IN LOVE
IF I MAY BE SO BOLD, YOU HAVE A GREAT-LOOKING PSEUDOPOD, MY DEAR
© 1983 PAWS, INC. All Rights Reserved.

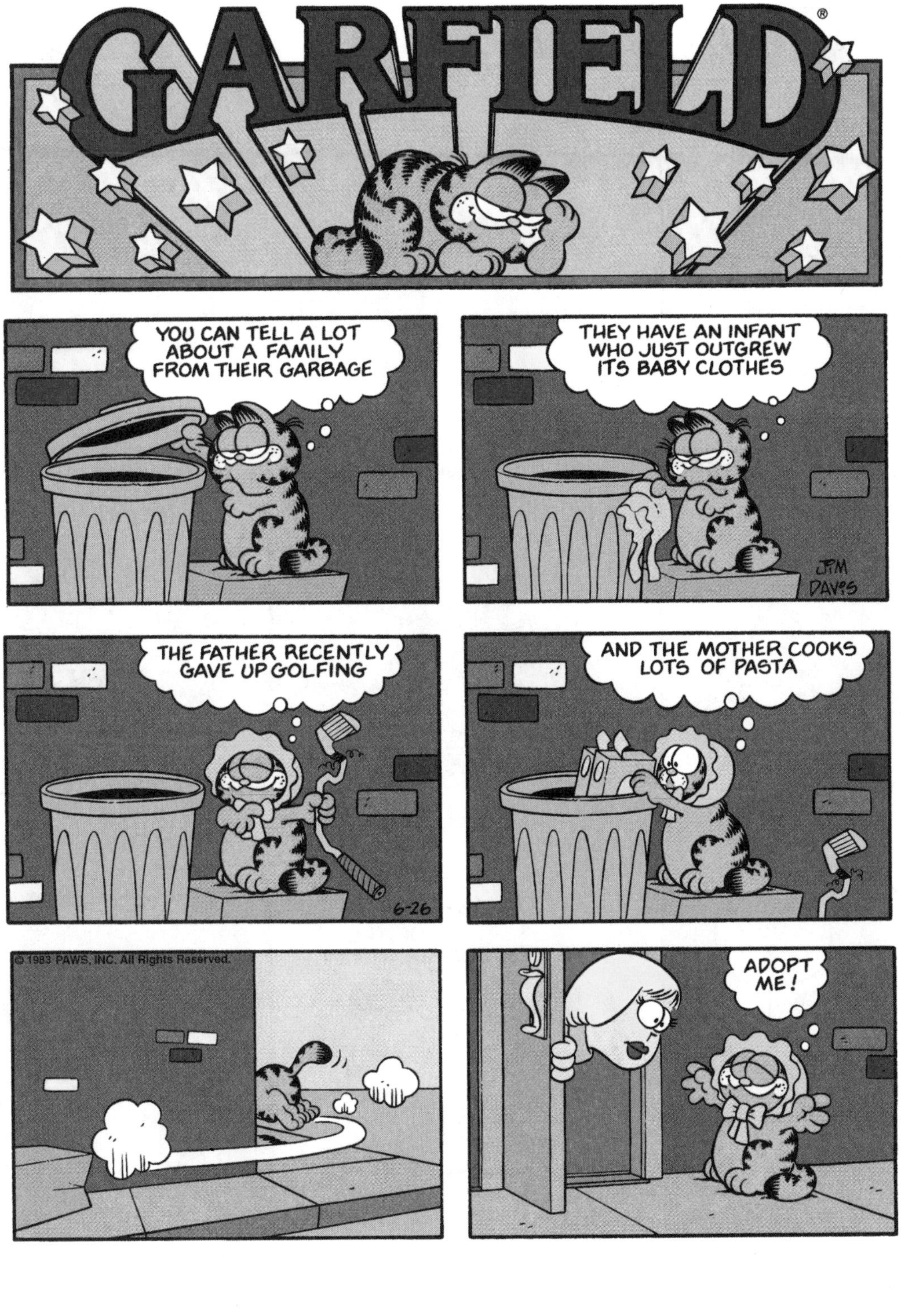
GARFIELD®
YOU CAN TELL A LOT ABOUT A FAMILY FROM THEIR GARBAGE
THEY HAVE AN INFANT WHO JUST OUTGREW ITS BABY CLOTHES
JIM DAVIS
THE FATHER RECENTLY GAVE UP GOLFING
6-26
AND THE MOTHER COOKS LOTS OF PASTA
© 1983 PAWS, INC. All Rights Reserved.
ADOPT ME!

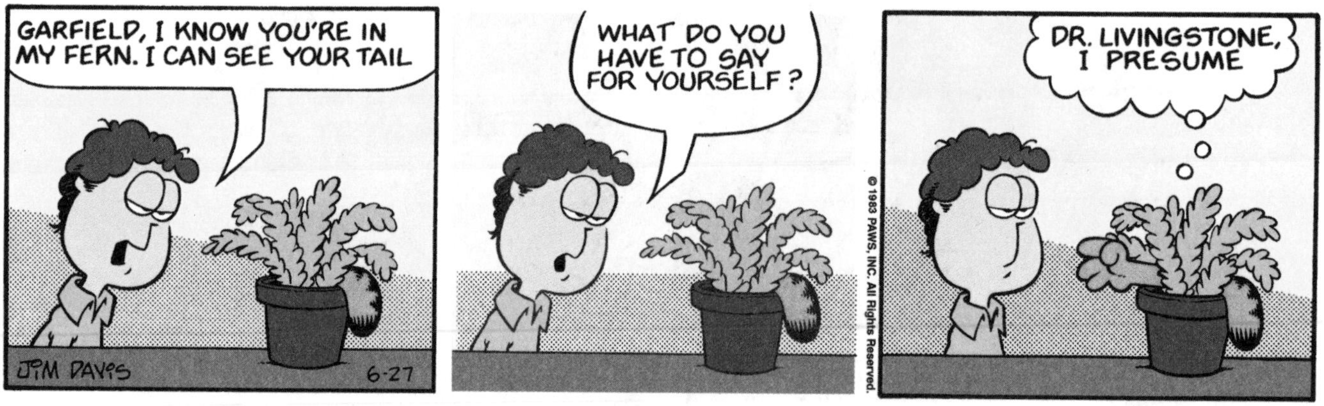
GARFIELD, I KNOW YOU'RE IN MY FERN. I CAN SEE YOUR TAIL
JIM DAVIS
6-27
WHAT DO YOU HAVE TO SAY FOR YOURSELF?
© 1983 PAWS, INC. All Rights Reserved.
DR. LIVINGSTONE, I PRESUME

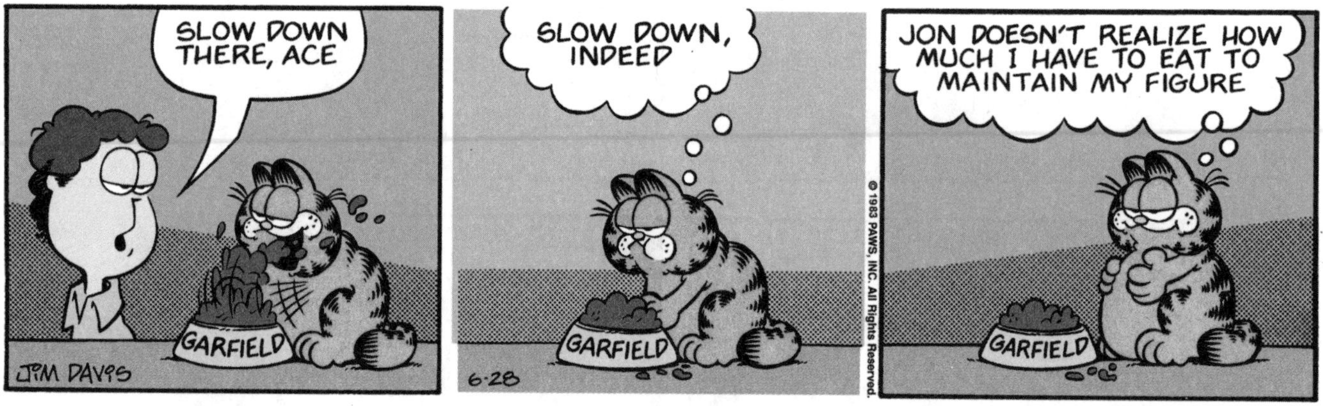
SLOW DOWN THERE, ACE
GARFIELD
JIM DAVIS
SLOW DOWN, INDEED
GARFIELD
6-28
© 1983 PAWS, INC. All Rights Reserved.
JON DOESN'T REALIZE HOW MUCH I HAVE TO EAT TO MAINTAIN MY FIGURE
GARFIELD

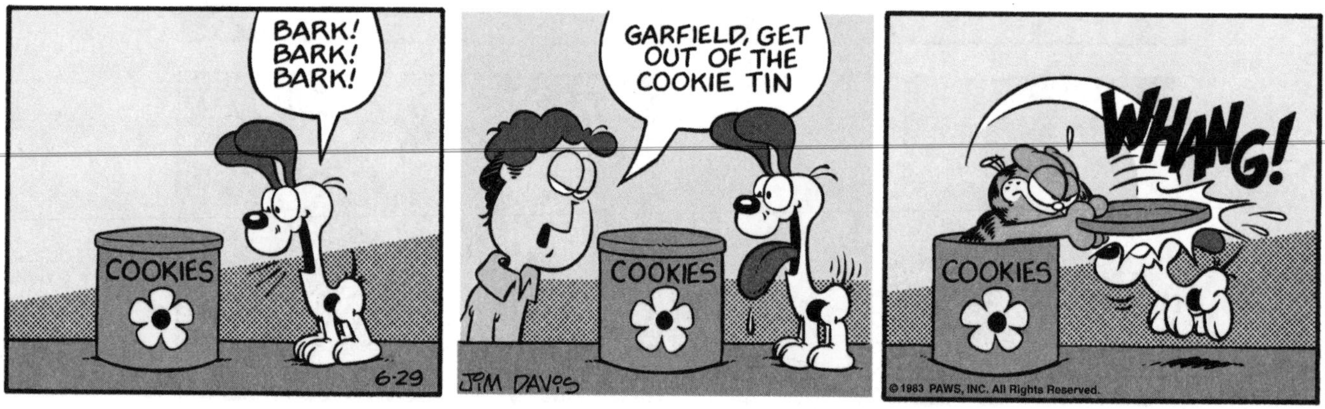
BARK! BARK! BARK!
COOKIES
6-29
GARFIELD, GET OUT OF THE COOKIE TIN
COOKIES
JIM DAVIS
WHANG!
COOKIES
© 1983 PAWS, INC. All Rights Reserved.

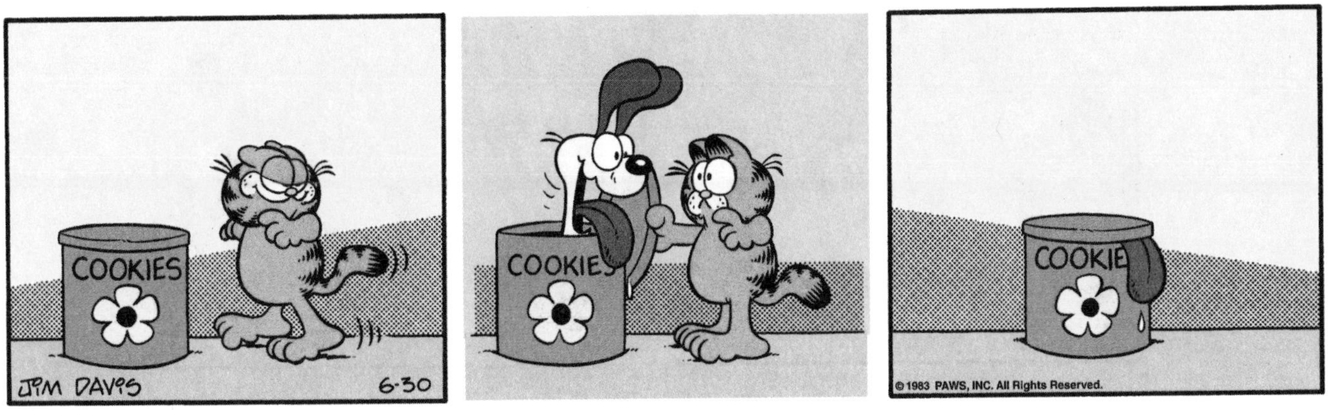
COOKIES
JIM DAVIS
6-30
COOKIES
COOKIE
© 1983 PAWS, INC. All Rights Reserved.

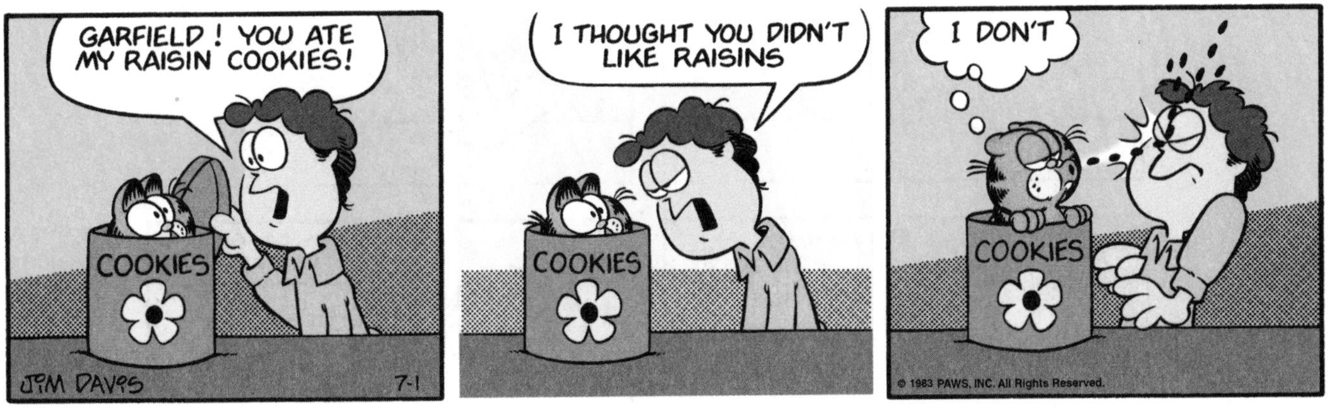
GARFIELD! YOU ATE MY RAISIN COOKIES!
COOKIES
JIM DAVIS
7-1
I THOUGHT YOU DIDN'T LIKE RAISINS
COOKIES
I DON'T
COOKIES
© 1983 PAWS, INC. All Rights Reserved.

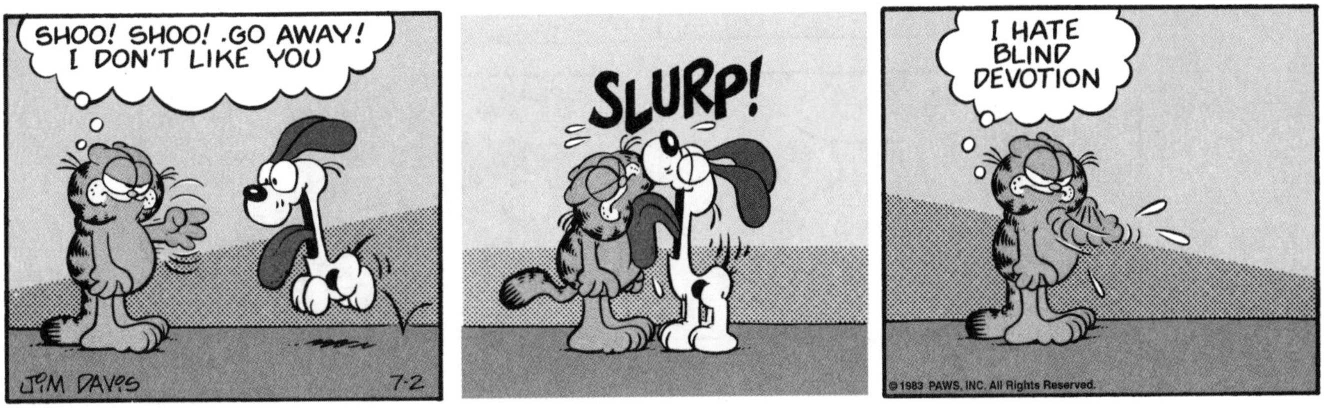
SHOO! SHOO! .GO AWAY! I DON'T LIKE YOU
JIM DAVIS
7-2
SLURP!
I HATE BLIND DEVOTION
© 1983 PAWS, INC. All Rights Reserved.

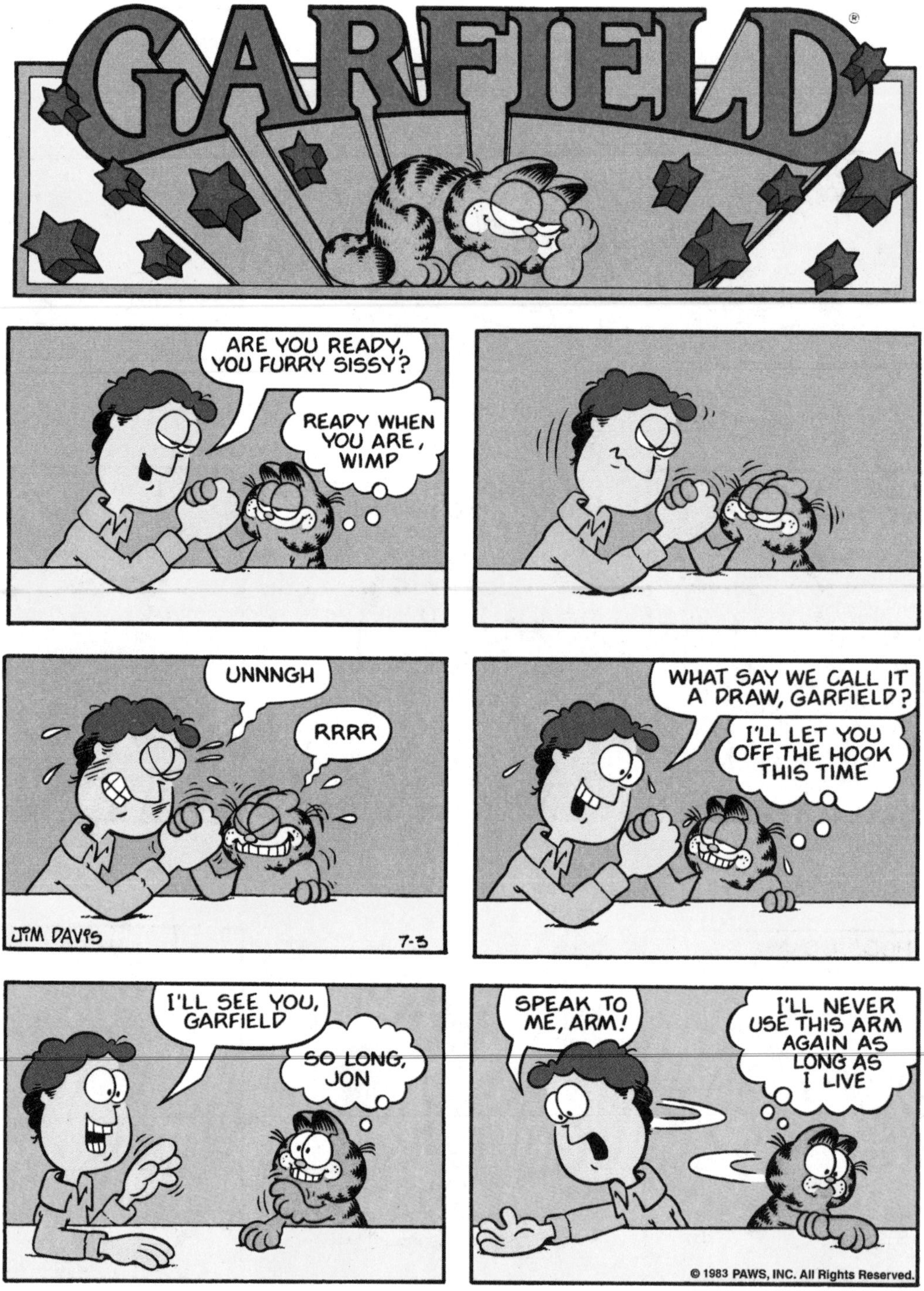
GARFIELD®
ARE YOU READY, YOU FURRY SISSY?
READY WHEN YOU ARE, WIMP
UNNNGH
RRRR
WHAT SAY WE CALL IT A DRAW, GARFIELD?
I'LL LET YOU OFF THE HOOK THIS TIME
JIM DAVIS
7-3
I'LL SEE YOU, GARFIELD
SO LONG, JON
SPEAK TO ME, ARM!
I'LL NEVER USE THIS ARM AGAIN AS LONG AS I LIVE
© 1983 PAWS, INC. All Rights Reserved.

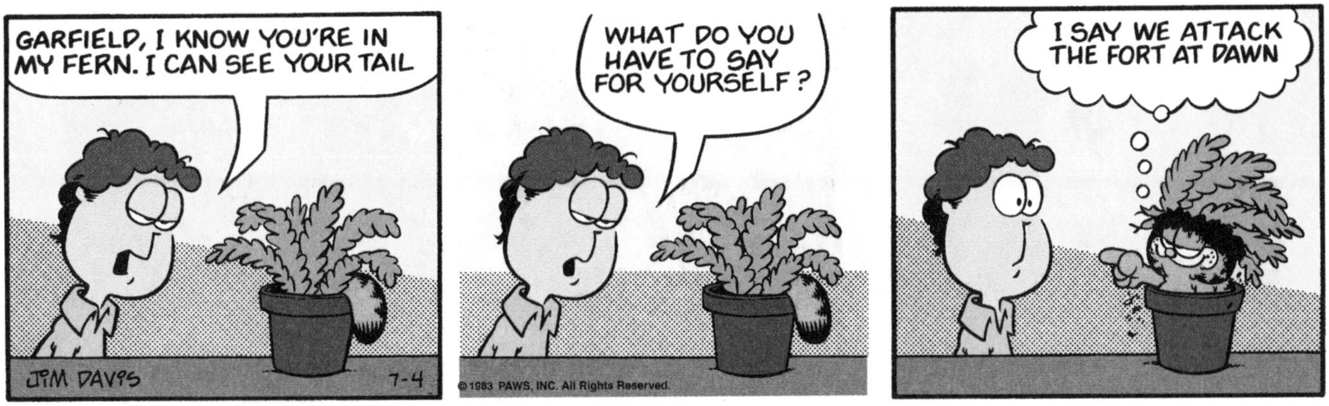
GARFIELD, I KNOW YOU'RE IN MY FERN. I CAN SEE YOUR TAIL
JIM DAVIS
7-4
© 1983 PAWS, INC. All Rights Reserved.
WHAT DO YOU HAVE TO SAY FOR YOURSELF ?
I SAY WE ATTACK THE FORT AT DAWN

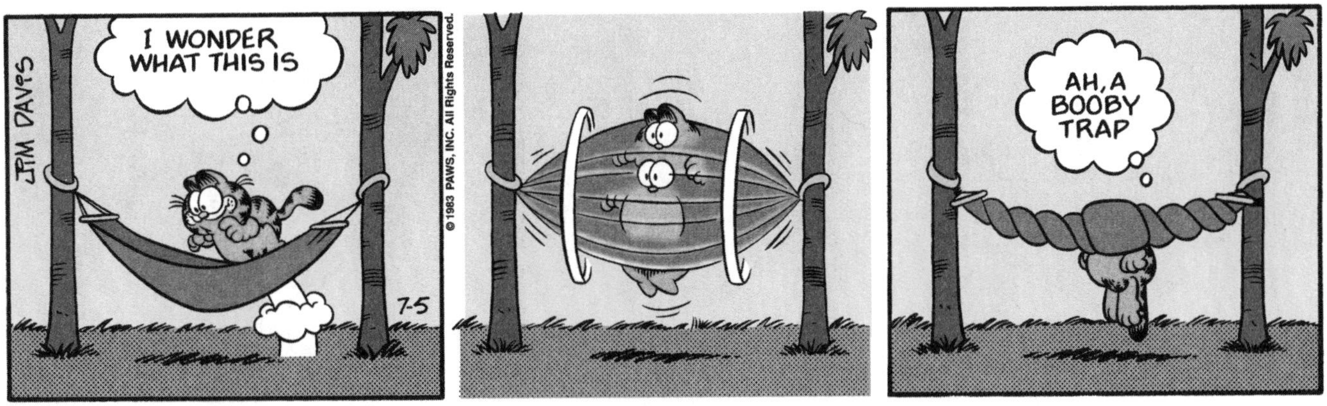
JIM DAVIS
I WONDER WHAT THIS IS
7-5
© 1983 PAWS, INC. All Rights Reserved.
AH, A BOOBY TRAP

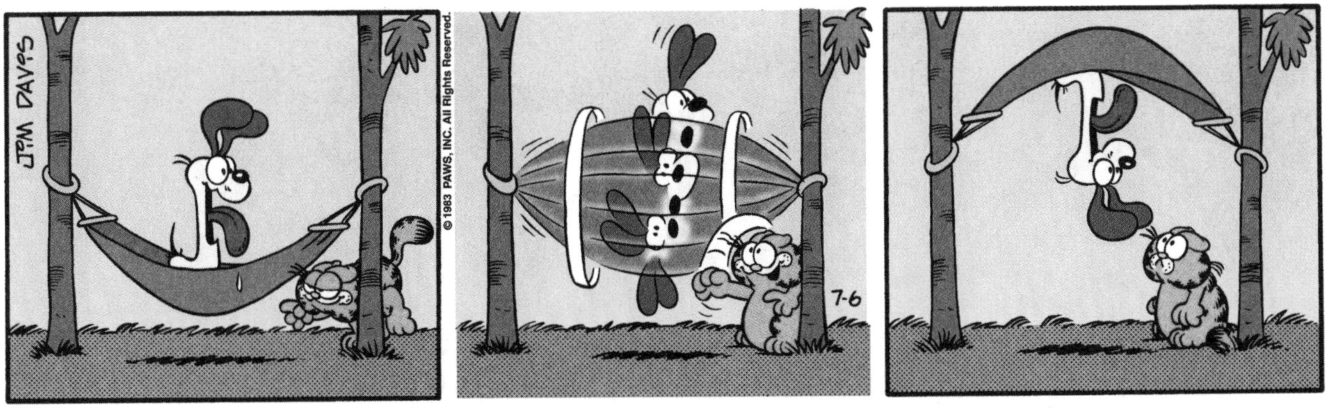
JIM DAVIS
© 1983 PAWS, INC. All Rights Reserved.
7-6

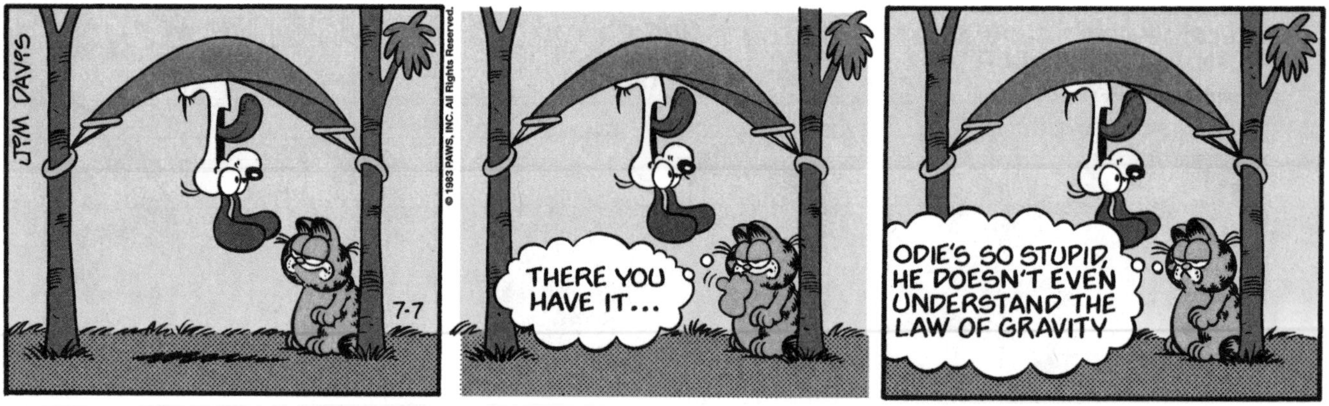
JIM DAVIS
7-7
© 1983 PAWS, INC. All Rights Reserved.
THERE YOU HAVE IT...
ODIE'S SO STUPID, HE DOESN'T EVEN UNDERSTAND THE LAW OF GRAVITY

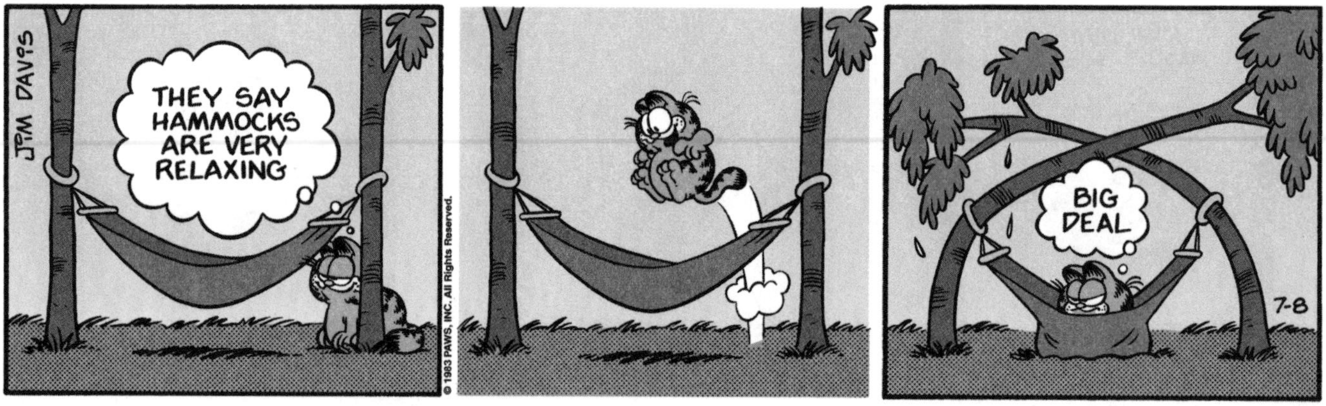
JIM DAVIS
THEY SAY HAMMOCKS ARE VERY RELAXING
© 1983 PAWS, INC. All Rights Reserved.
BIG DEAL
7-8

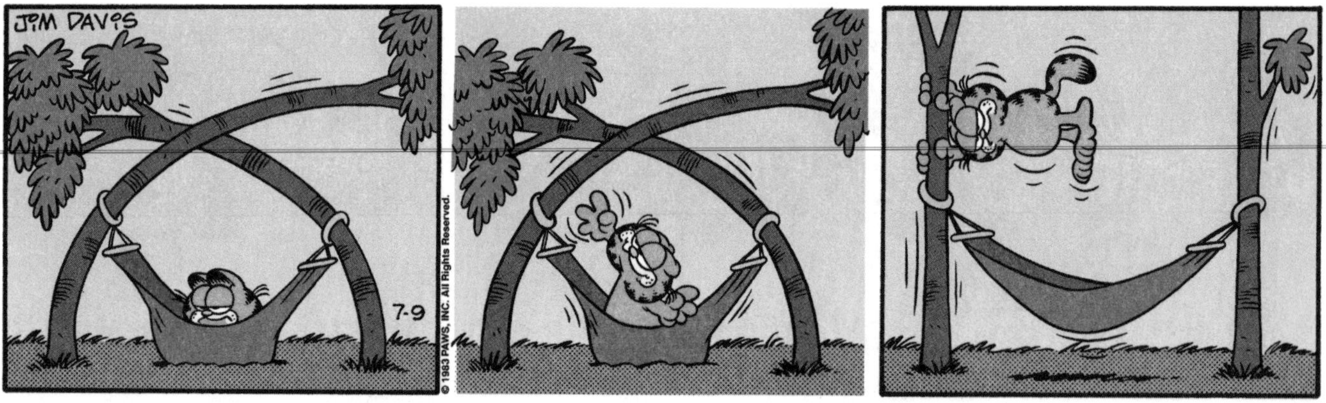
JIM DAVIS
7-9
© 1983 PAWS, INC. All Rights Reserved.

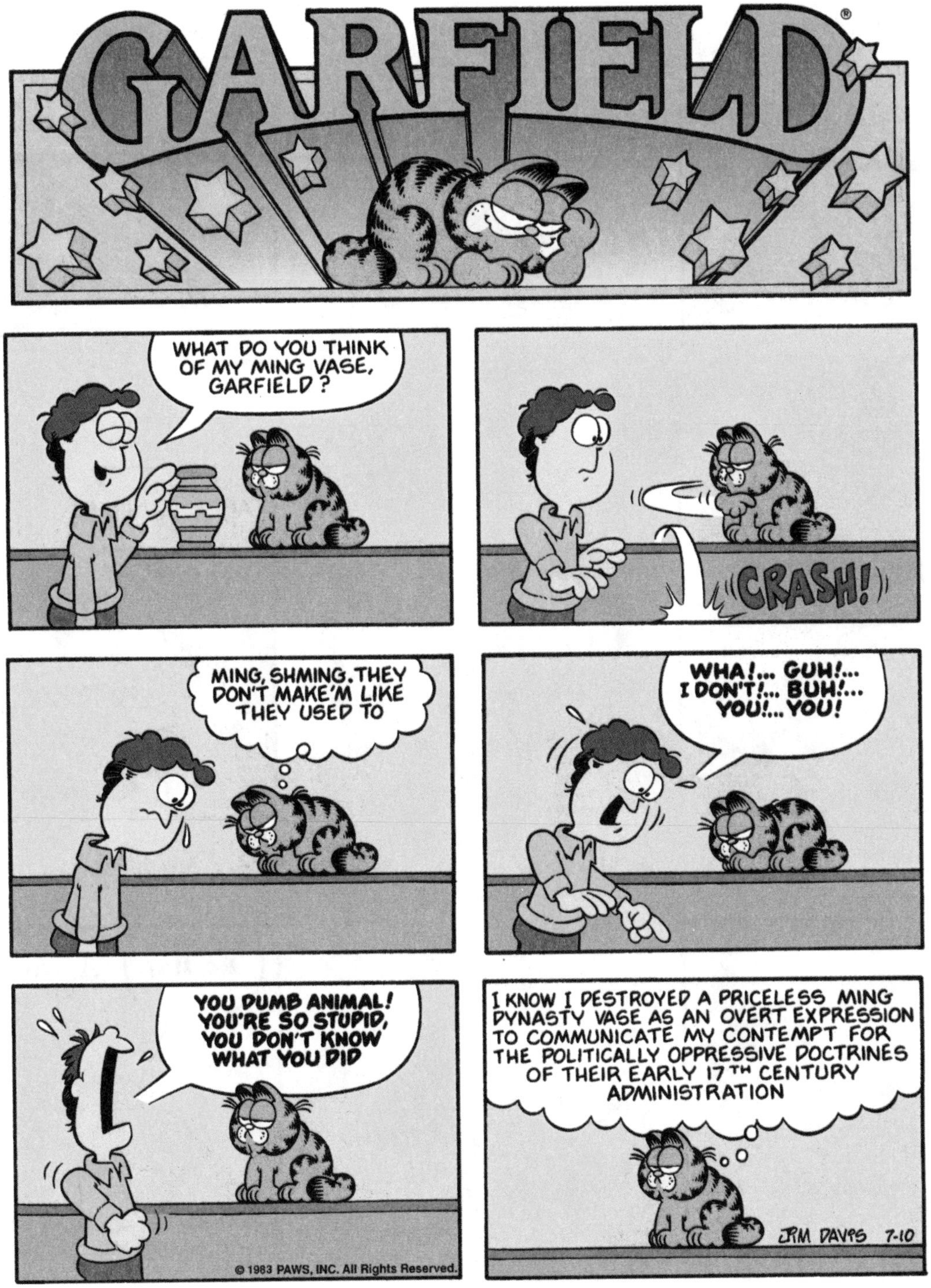
GARFIELD®
WHAT DO YOU THINK OF MY MING VASE, GARFIELD?
CRASH!
MING, SHMING. THEY DON'T MAKE'M LIKE THEY USED TO
WHA!... GUH!... I DON'T!... BUH!... YOU!... YOU!
YOU DUMB ANIMAL! YOU'RE SO STUPID, YOU DON'T KNOW WHAT YOU DID
I KNOW I DESTROYED A PRICELESS MING DYNASTY VASE AS AN OVERT EXPRESSION TO COMMUNICATE MY CONTEMPT FOR THE POLITICALLY OPPRESSIVE DOCTRINES OF THEIR EARLY 17TH CENTURY ADMINISTRATION
JIM DAVIS 7-10
© 1983 PAWS, INC. All Rights Reserved.

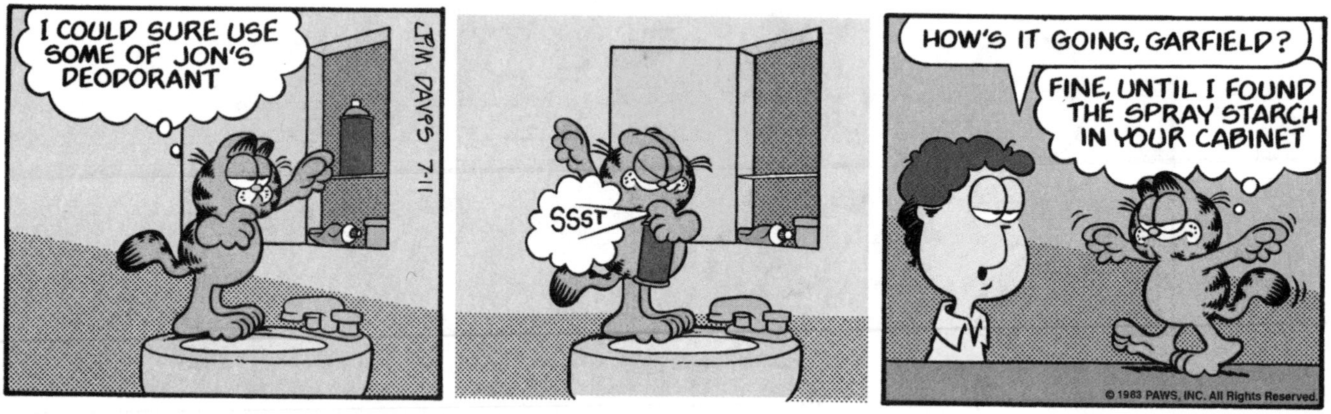
I COULD SURE USE SOME OF JON'S DEODORANT
JIM DAVIS 7-11
SSST
HOW'S IT GOING, GARFIELD?
FINE, UNTIL I FOUND THE SPRAY STARCH IN YOUR CABINET
© 1983 PAWS, INC. All Rights Reserved.

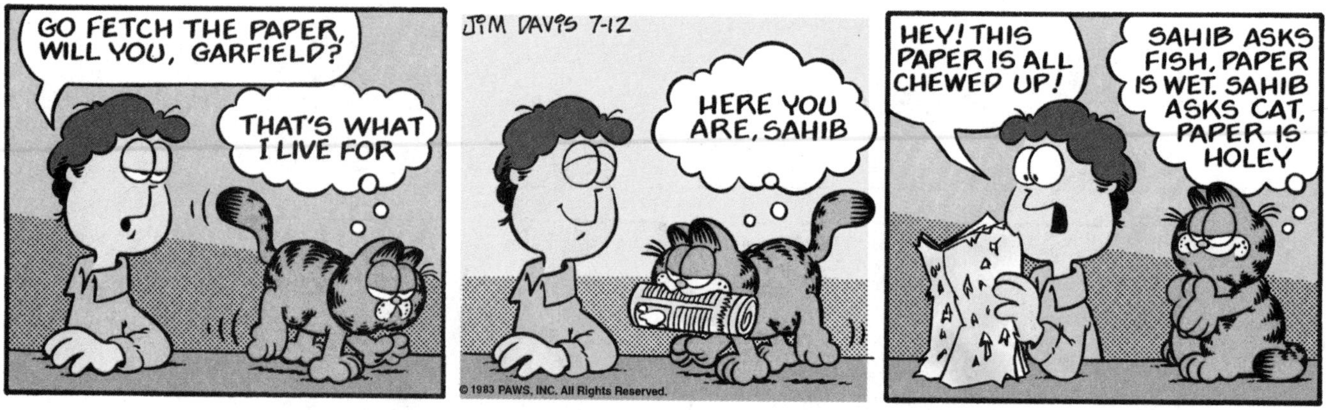
GO FETCH THE PAPER, WILL YOU, GARFIELD?
THAT'S WHAT I LIVE FOR
JIM DAVIS 7-12
HERE YOU ARE, SAHIB
© 1983 PAWS, INC. All Rights Reserved.
HEY! THIS PAPER IS ALL CHEWED UP!
SAHIB ASKS FISH, PAPER IS WET. SAHIB ASKS CAT, PAPER IS HOLEY

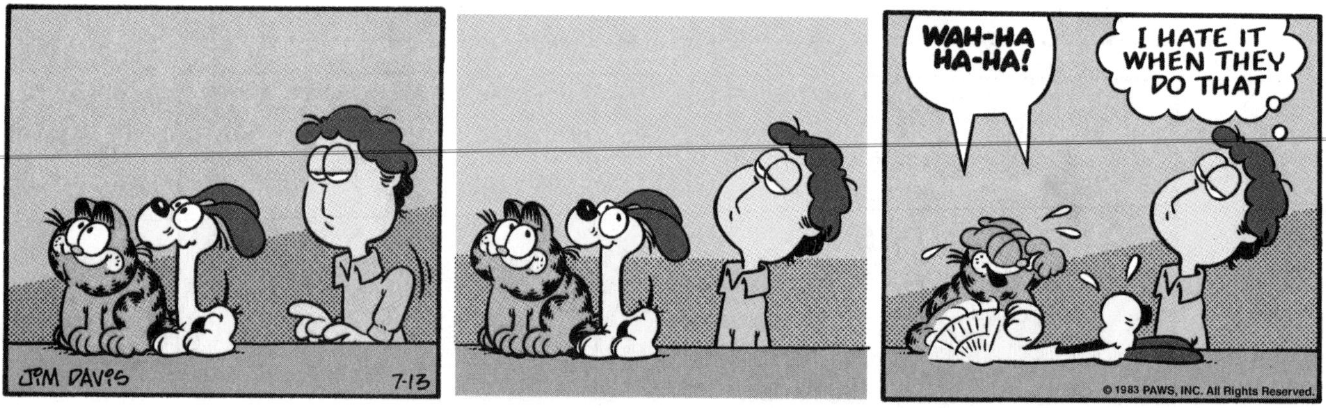
JIM DAVIS
7-13
WAH-HA HA-HA!
I HATE IT WHEN THEY DO THAT
© 1983 PAWS, INC. All Rights Reserved.

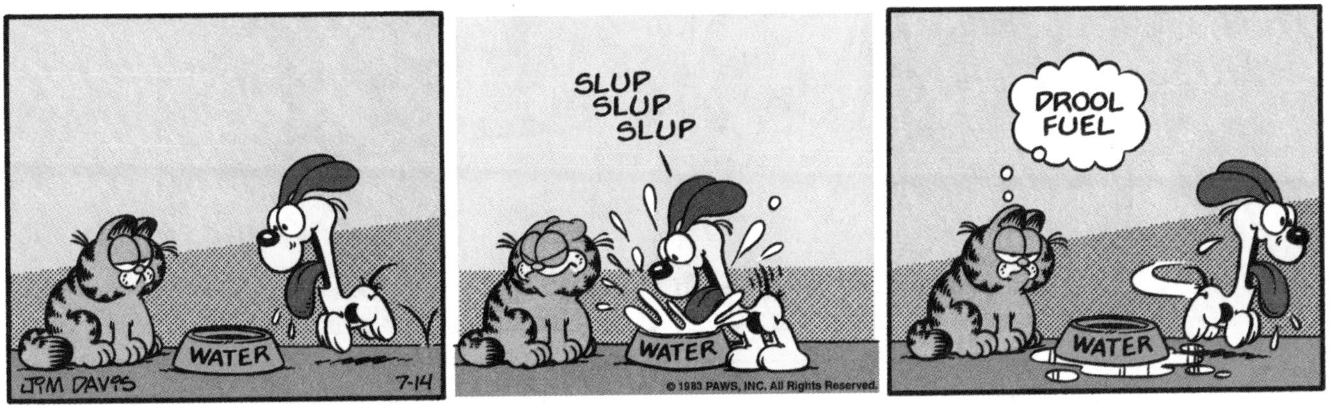
WATER
JIM DAVIS
7-14
SLUP
SLUP
SLUP
WATER
© 1983 PAWS, INC. All Rights Reserved.
DROOL FUEL
WATER

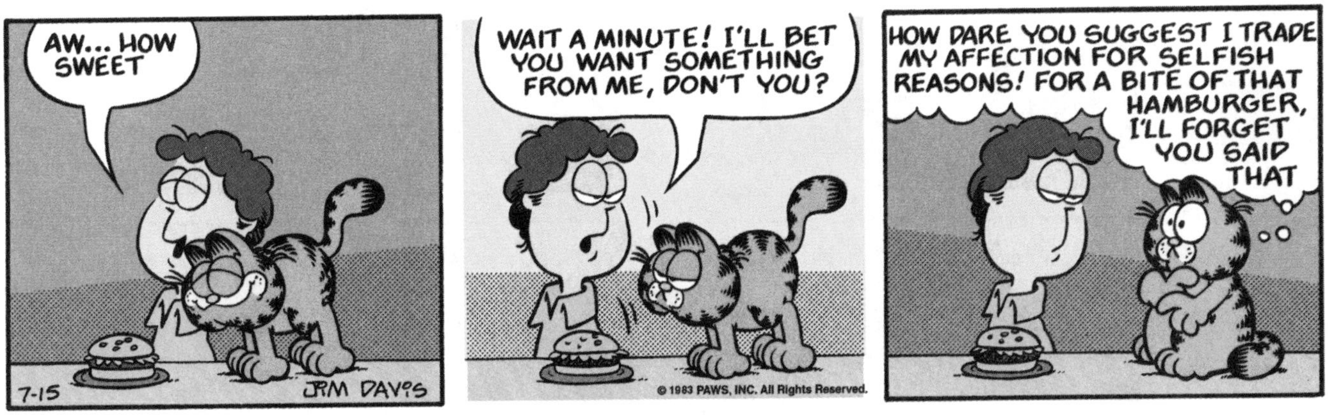
AW... HOW SWEET
7-15
JIM DAVIS
WAIT A MINUTE! I'LL BET YOU WANT SOMETHING FROM ME, DON'T YOU?
© 1983 PAWS, INC. All Rights Reserved.
HOW DARE YOU SUGGEST I TRADE MY AFFECTION FOR SELFISH REASONS! FOR A BITE OF THAT HAMBURGER, I'LL FORGET YOU SAID THAT

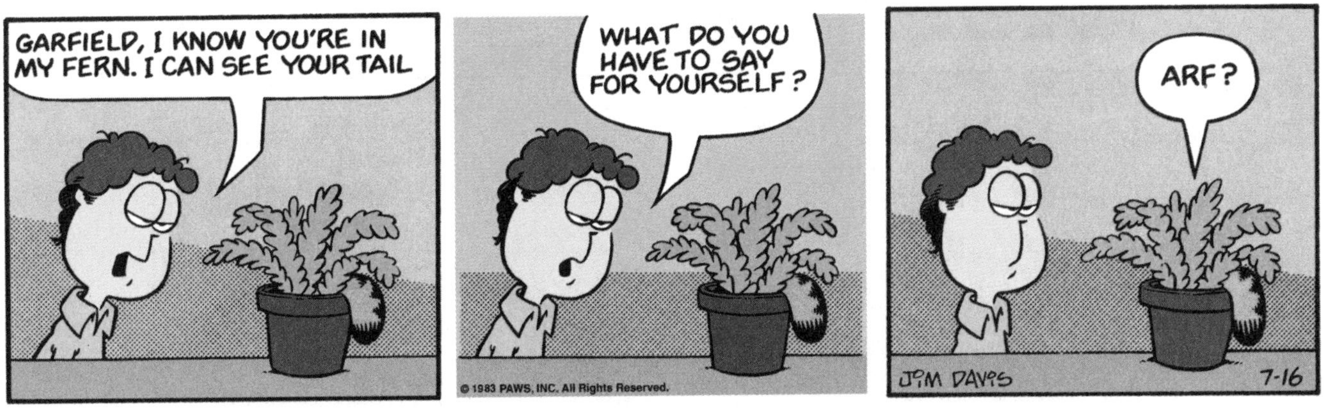
GARFIELD, I KNOW YOU'RE IN MY FERN. I CAN SEE YOUR TAIL
WHAT DO YOU HAVE TO SAY FOR YOURSELF?
© 1983 PAWS, INC. All Rights Reserved.
ARF?
JIM DAVIS
7-16

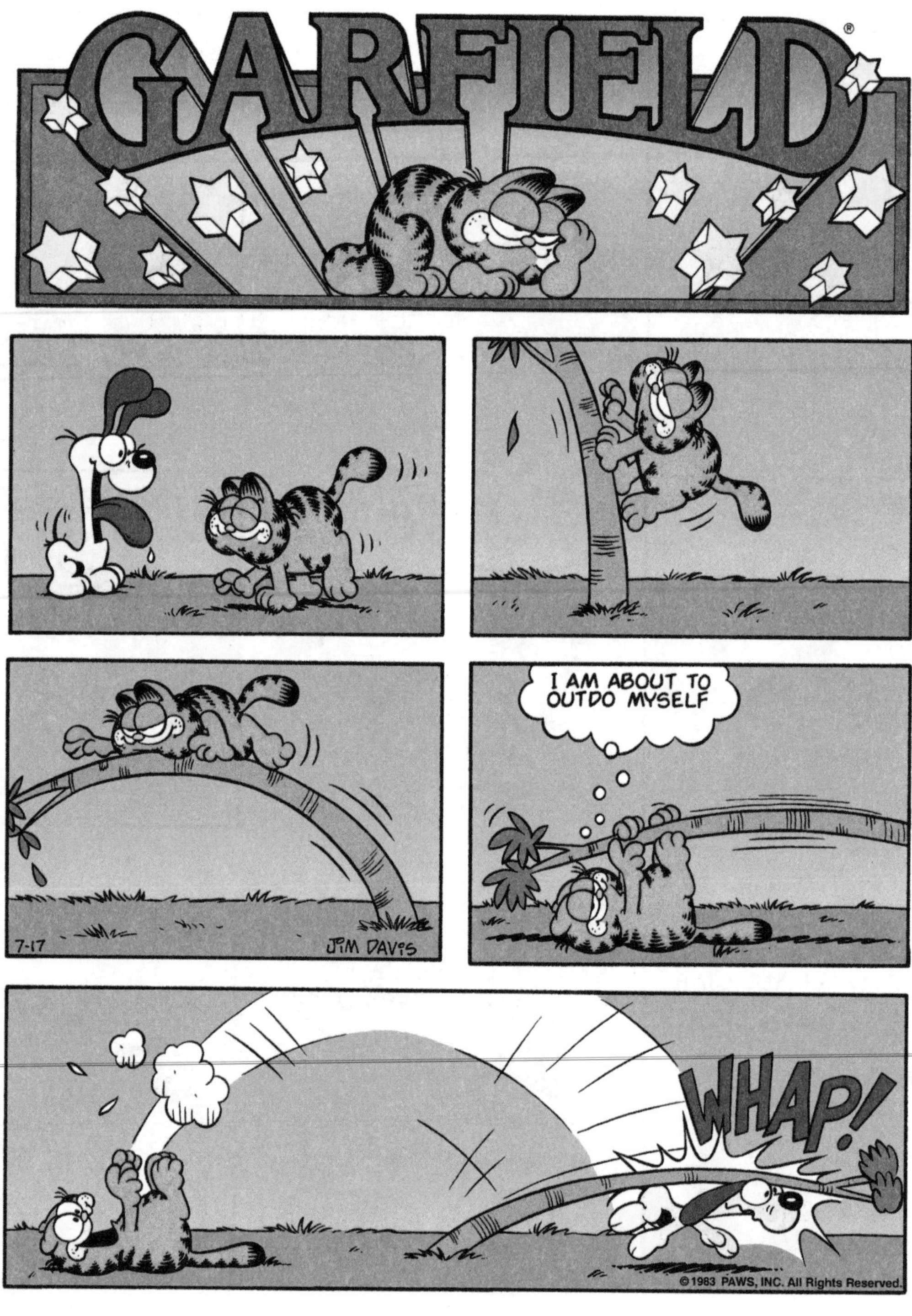
GARFIELD®
7-17
JIM DAVIS
I AM ABOUT TO OUTDO MYSELF
WHAP!
© 1983 PAWS, INC. All Rights Reserved.

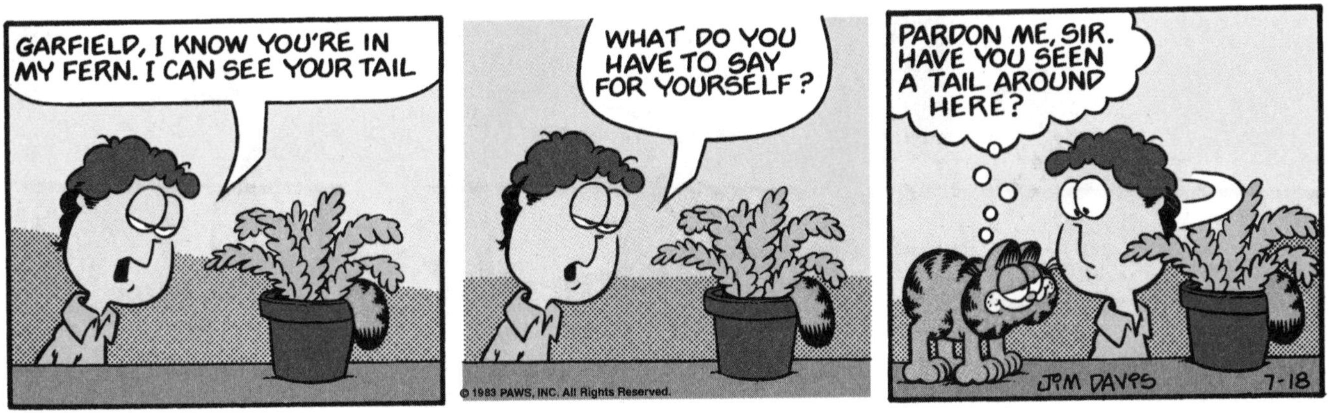
GARFIELD, I KNOW YOU'RE IN MY FERN. I CAN SEE YOUR TAIL
WHAT DO YOU HAVE TO SAY FOR YOURSELF?
© 1983 PAWS, INC. All Rights Reserved.
PARDON ME, SIR. HAVE YOU SEEN A TAIL AROUND HERE?
JIM DAVIS
7-18

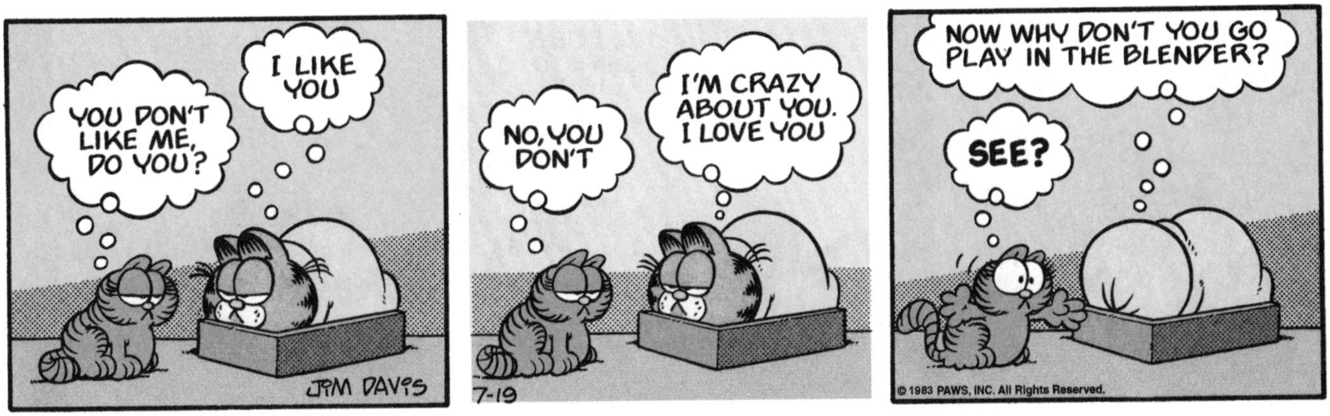
YOU DON'T LIKE ME, DO YOU?
I LIKE YOU
JIM DAVIS
NO, YOU DON'T
I'M CRAZY ABOUT YOU. I LOVE YOU
7-19
NOW WHY DON'T YOU GO PLAY IN THE BLENDER?
SEE?
© 1983 PAWS, INC. All Rights Reserved.

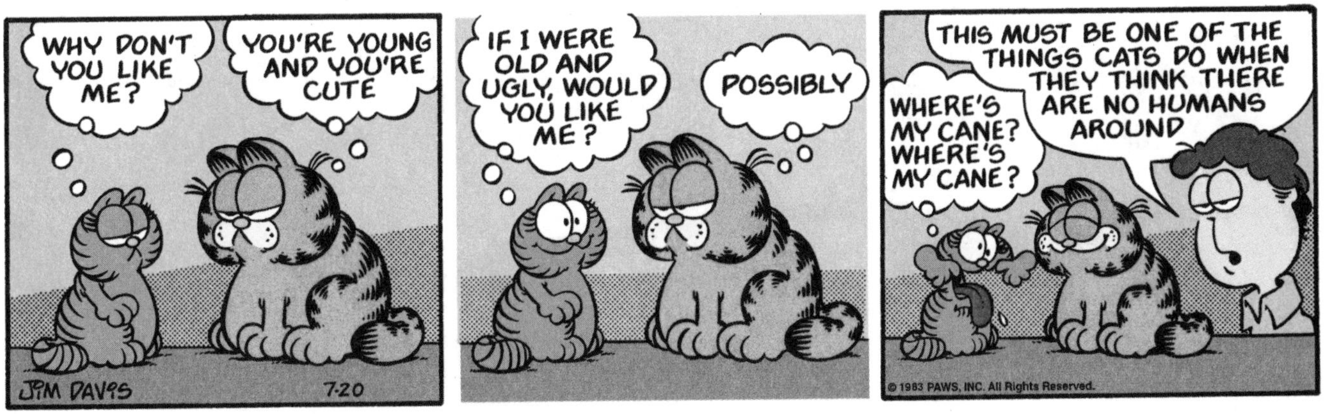
WHY DON'T YOU LIKE ME?
YOU'RE YOUNG AND YOU'RE CUTE
JIM DAVIS
7-20
IF I WERE OLD AND UGLY, WOULD YOU LIKE ME?
POSSIBLY
THIS MUST BE ONE OF THE THINGS CATS DO WHEN THEY THINK THERE ARE NO HUMANS AROUND
WHERE'S MY CANE? WHERE'S MY CANE?
© 1983 PAWS, INC. All Rights Reserved.

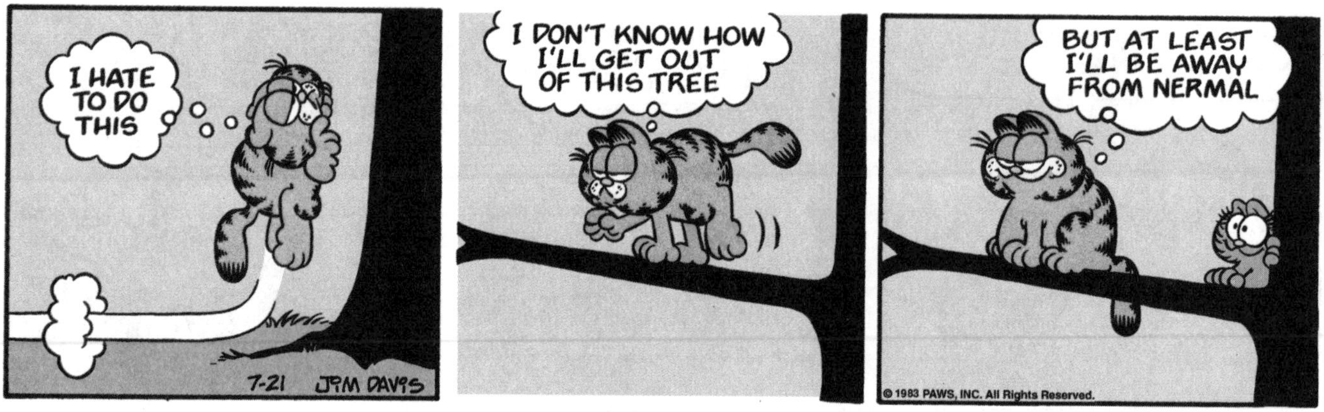
I HATE TO DO THIS
7-21 JIM DAVIS
I DON'T KNOW HOW I'LL GET OUT OF THIS TREE
BUT AT LEAST I'LL BE AWAY FROM NERMAL
© 1983 PAWS, INC. All Rights Reserved.

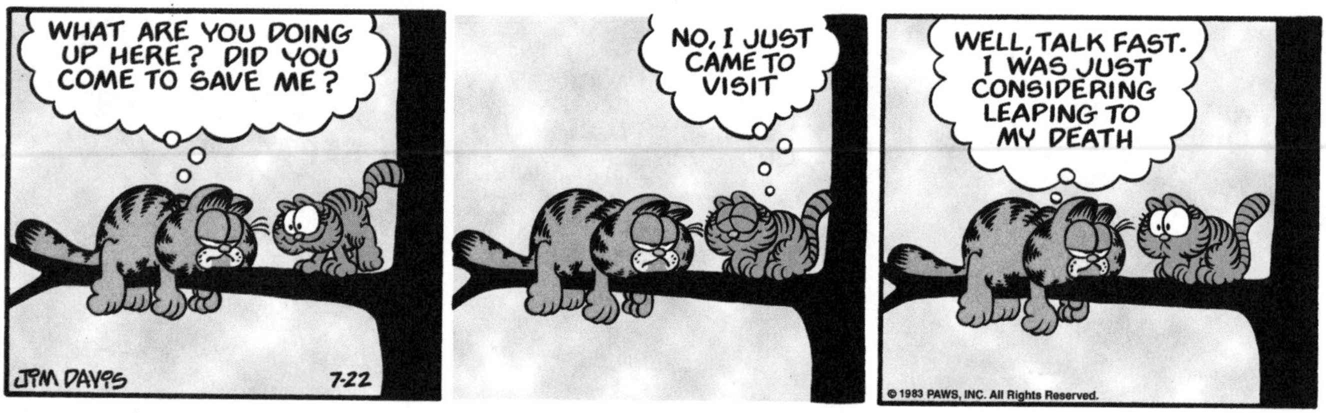
WHAT ARE YOU DOING UP HERE? DID YOU COME TO SAVE ME?
JIM DAVIS
7-22
NO, I JUST CAME TO VISIT
WELL, TALK FAST. I WAS JUST CONSIDERING LEAPING TO MY DEATH
© 1983 PAWS, INC. All Rights Reserved.

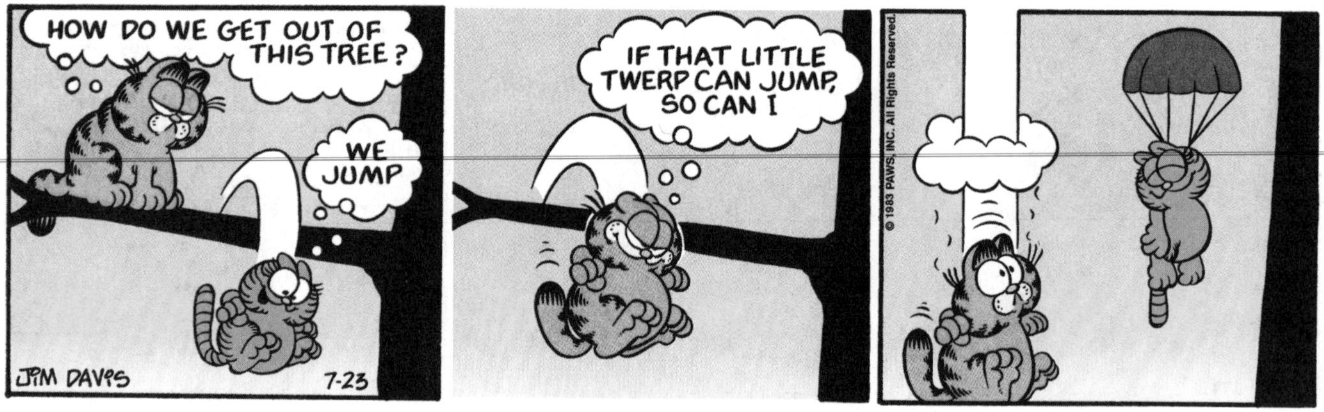
HOW DO WE GET OUT OF THIS TREE?
WE JUMP
JIM DAVIS
7-23
IF THAT LITTLE TWERP CAN JUMP, SO CAN I
© 1983 PAWS, INC. All Rights Reserved.

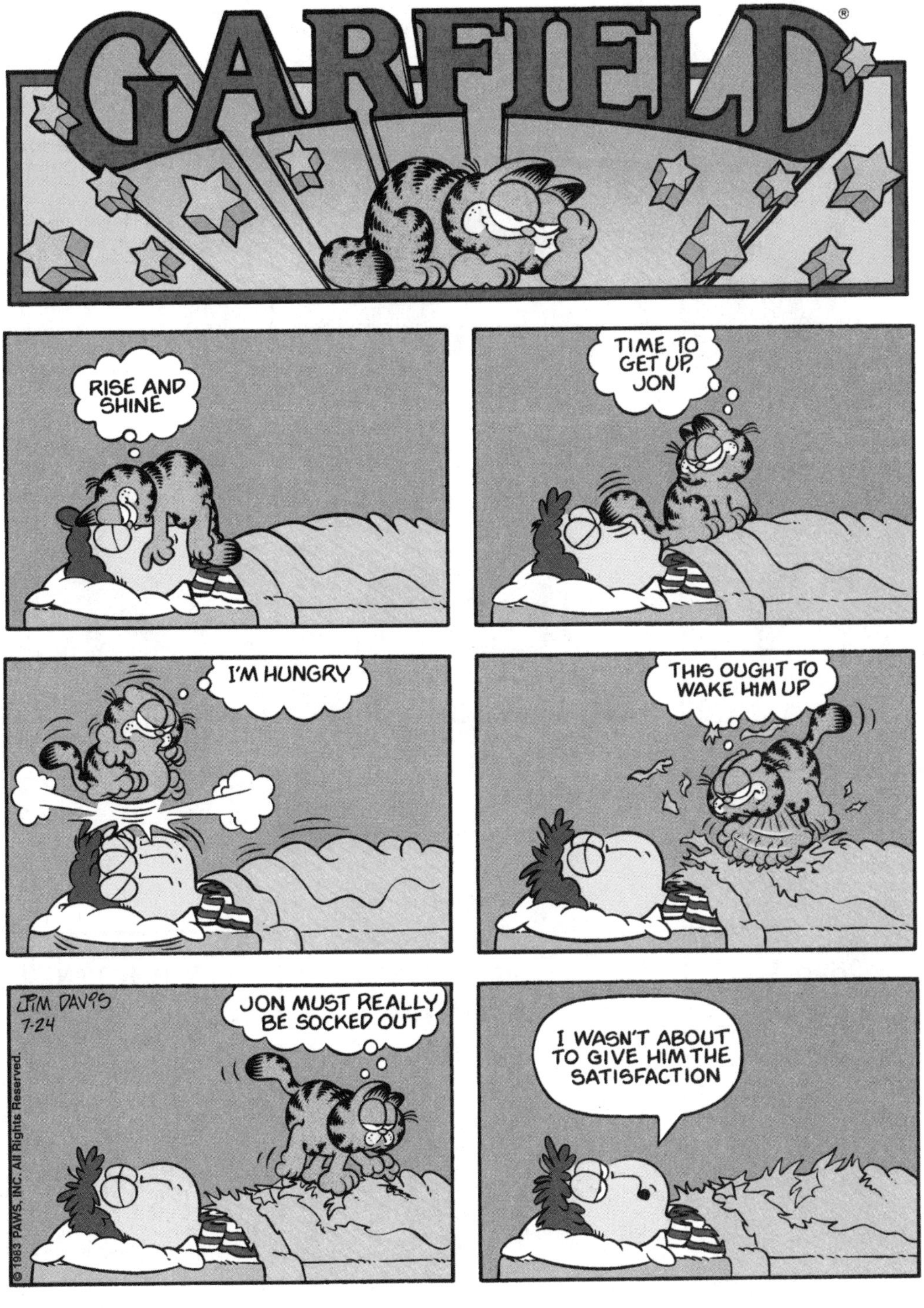
GARFIELD®
RISE AND SHINE
TIME TO GET UP, JON
I'M HUNGRY
THIS OUGHT TO WAKE HIM UP
JIM DAVIS 7-24
JON MUST REALLY BE SOCKED OUT
I WASN'T ABOUT TO GIVE HIM THE SATISFACTION

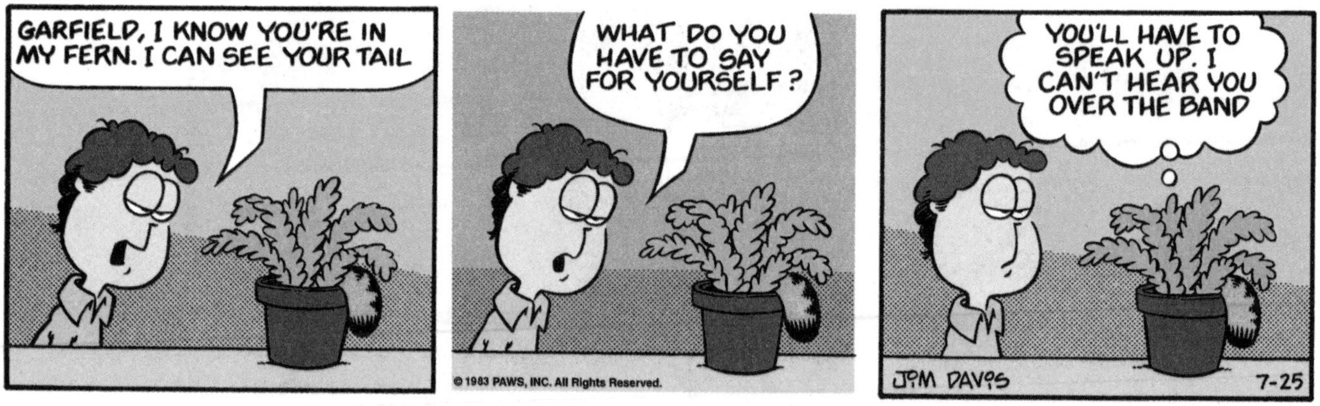
GARFIELD, I KNOW YOU'RE IN MY FERN. I CAN SEE YOUR TAIL
WHAT DO YOU HAVE TO SAY FOR YOURSELF?
© 1983 PAWS, INC. All Rights Reserved.
YOU'LL HAVE TO SPEAK UP. I CAN'T HEAR YOU OVER THE BAND
JIM DAVIS
7-25

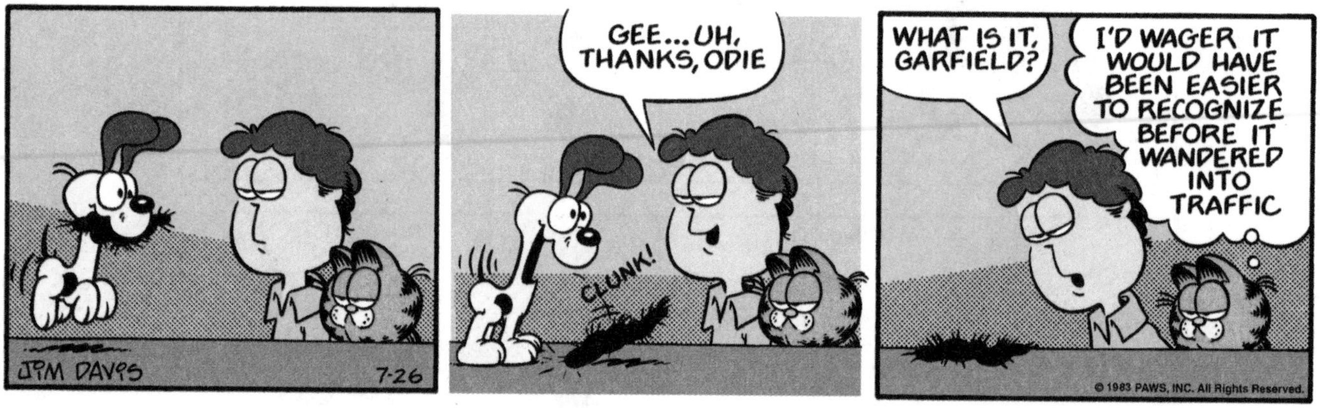
JIM DAVIS
7-26
GEE... UH, THANKS, ODIE
CLUNK!
WHAT IS IT, GARFIELD?
I'D WAGER IT WOULD HAVE BEEN EASIER TO RECOGNIZE BEFORE IT WANDERED INTO TRAFFIC
© 1983 PAWS, INC. All Rights Reserved.

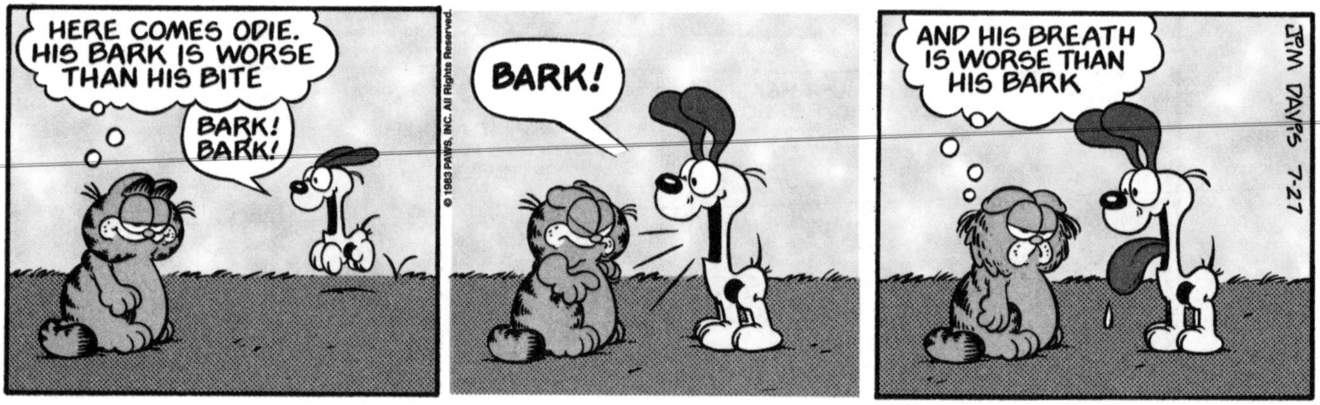
HERE COMES ODIE. HIS BARK IS WORSE THAN HIS BITE
BARK! BARK!
© 1983 PAWS, INC. All Rights Reserved.
BARK!
AND HIS BREATH IS WORSE THAN HIS BARK
JIM DAVIS 7-27

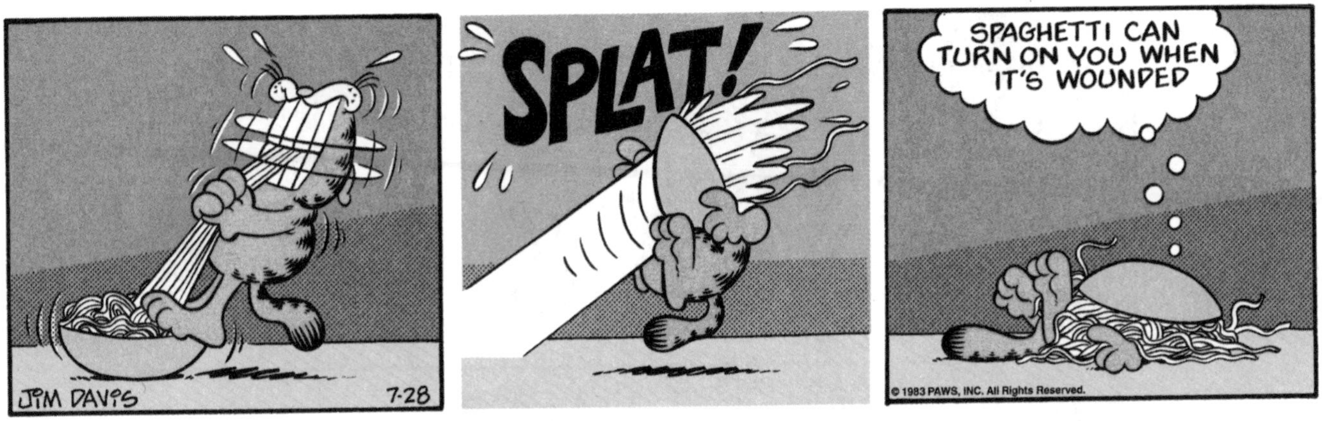
JIM DAVIS
7-28
SPLAT!
SPAGHETTI CAN TURN ON YOU WHEN IT'S WOUNDED
© 1983 PAWS, INC. All Rights Reserved.

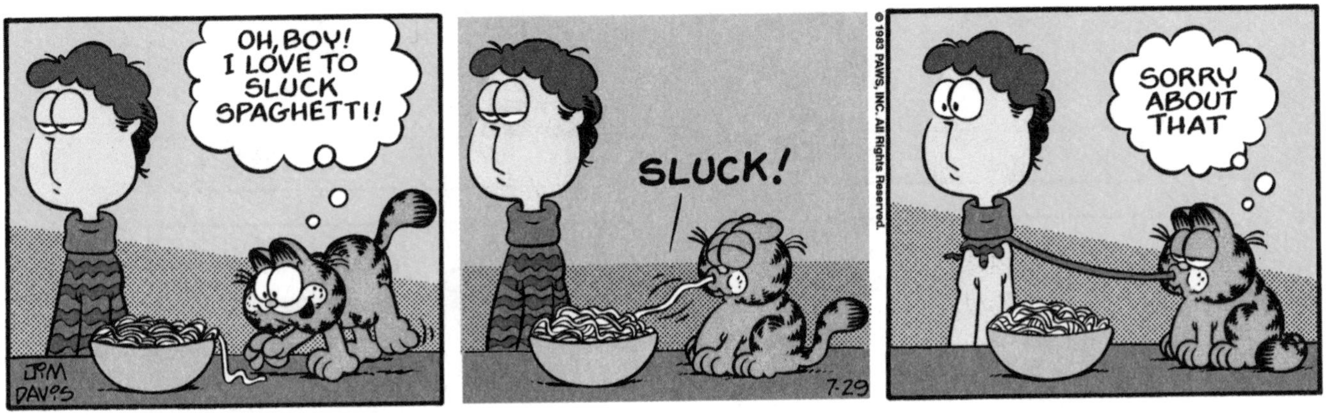
OH, BOY! I LOVE TO SLUCK SPAGHETTI!
JIM DAVIS
SLUCK!
7-29
© 1983 PAWS, INC. All Rights Reserved.
SORRY ABOUT THAT

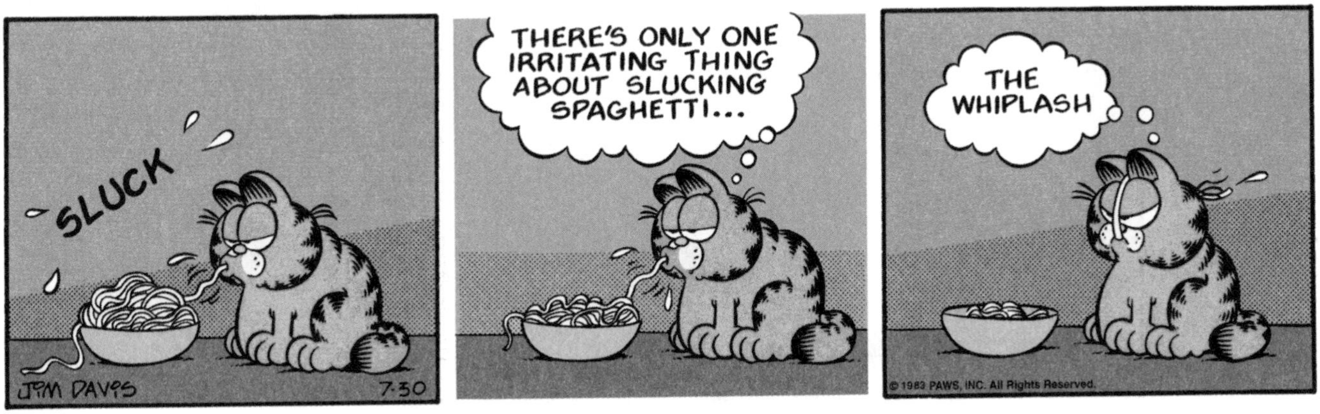
SLUCK
JIM DAVIS
7-30
THERE'S ONLY ONE IRRITATING THING ABOUT SLUCKING SPAGHETTI...
THE WHIPLASH
© 1983 PAWS, INC. All Rights Reserved.

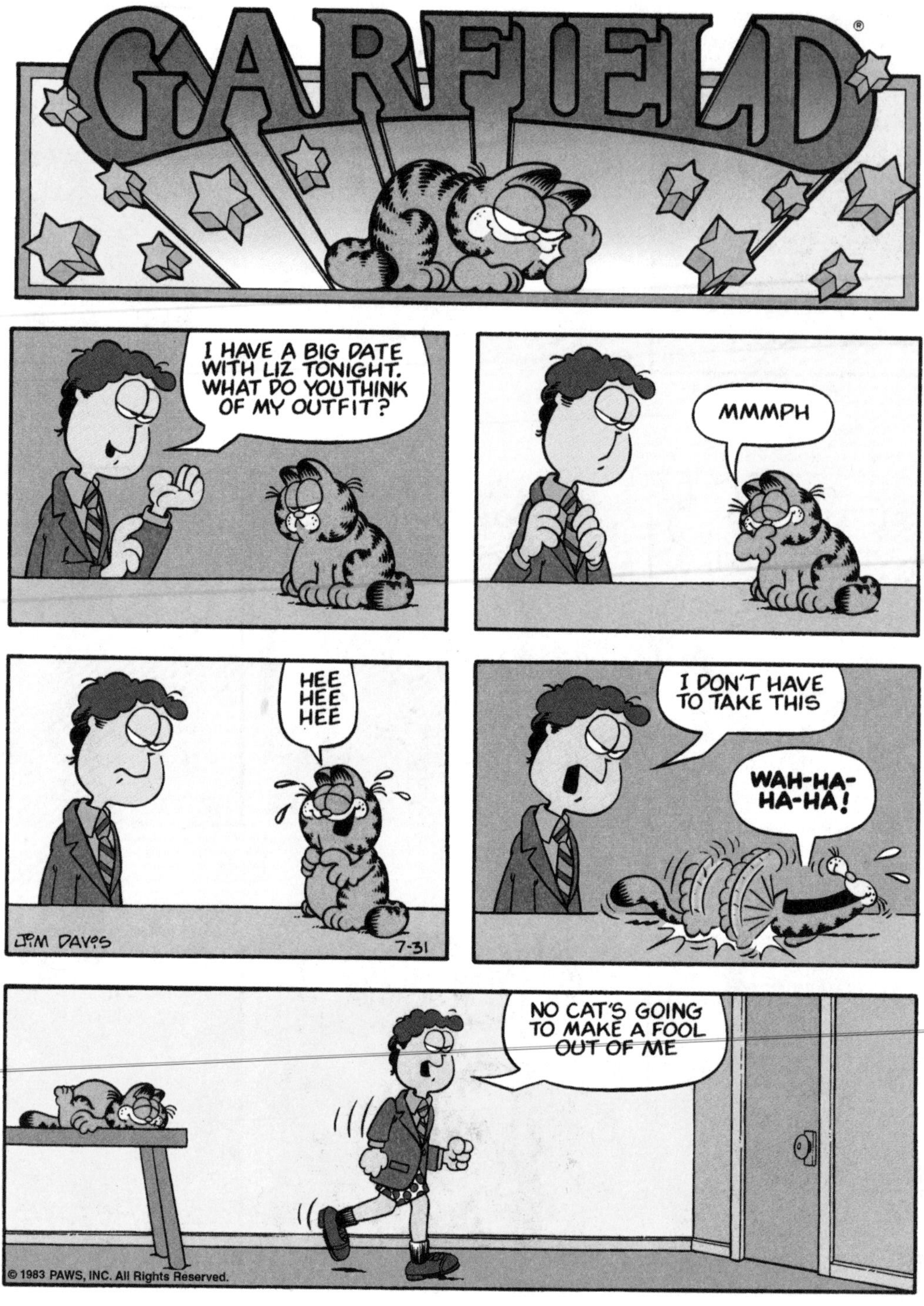
GARFIELD®
I HAVE A BIG DATE WITH LIZ TONIGHT. WHAT DO YOU THINK OF MY OUTFIT?
MMMPH
HEE HEE HEE
JIM DAVIS
7-31
I DON'T HAVE TO TAKE THIS
WAH-HA-HA-HA!
NO CAT'S GOING TO MAKE A FOOL OUT OF ME

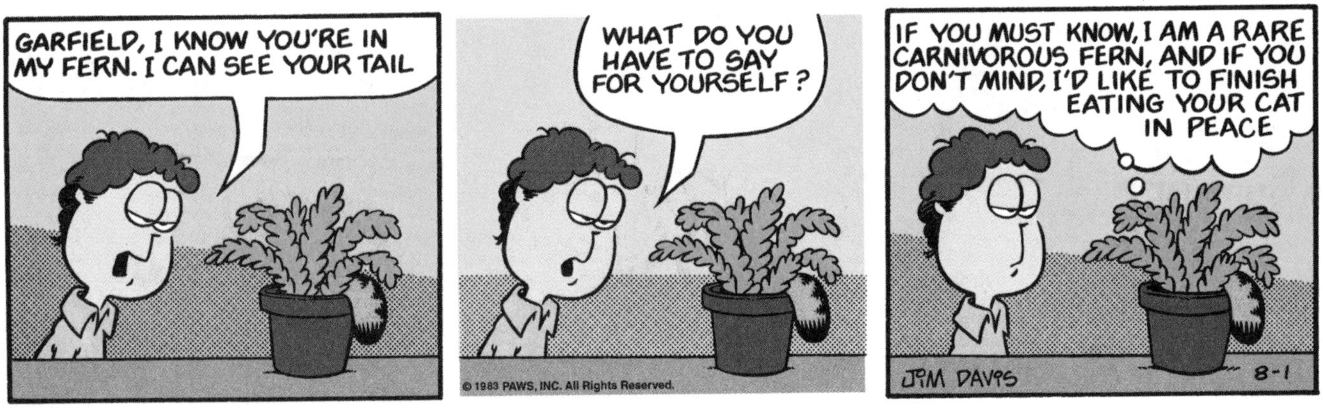
GARFIELD, I KNOW YOU'RE IN MY FERN. I CAN SEE YOUR TAIL
WHAT DO YOU HAVE TO SAY FOR YOURSELF?
© 1983 PAWS, INC. All Rights Reserved.
IF YOU MUST KNOW, I AM A RARE CARNIVOROUS FERN, AND IF YOU DON'T MIND, I'D LIKE TO FINISH EATING YOUR CAT IN PEACE
JIM DAVIS
8-1

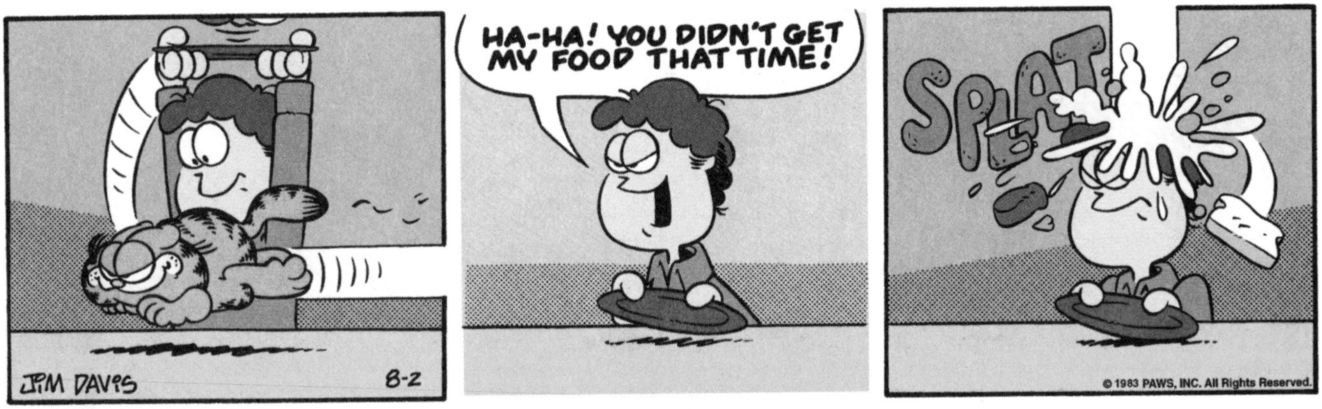
JIM DAVIS
8-2
HA-HA! YOU DIDN'T GET MY FOOD THAT TIME!
SPLAT
© 1983 PAWS, INC. All Rights Reserved.

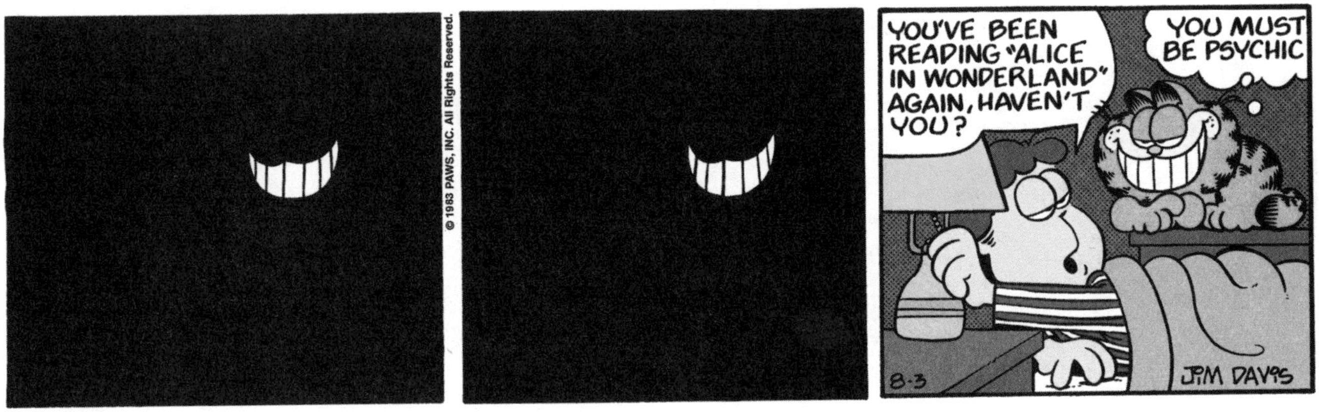
© 1983 PAWS, INC. All Rights Reserved.
YOU'VE BEEN READING "ALICE IN WONDERLAND" AGAIN, HAVEN'T YOU?
YOU MUST BE PSYCHIC
8-3
JIM DAVIS

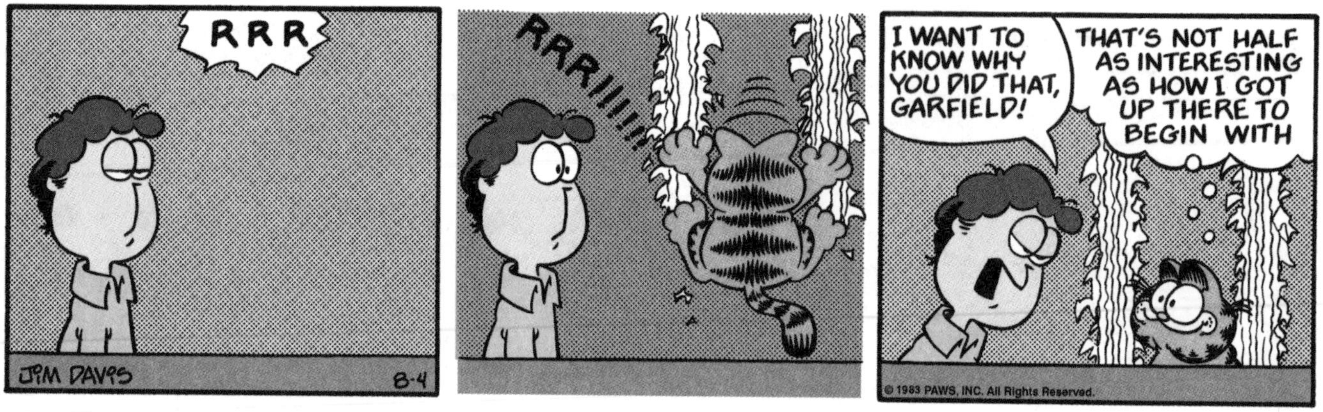
RRR
RRR
I WANT TO KNOW WHY YOU DID THAT, GARFIELD!
THAT'S NOT HALF AS INTERESTING AS HOW I GOT UP THERE TO BEGIN WITH
JIM DAVIS
8-4
© 1983 PAWS, INC. All Rights Reserved.

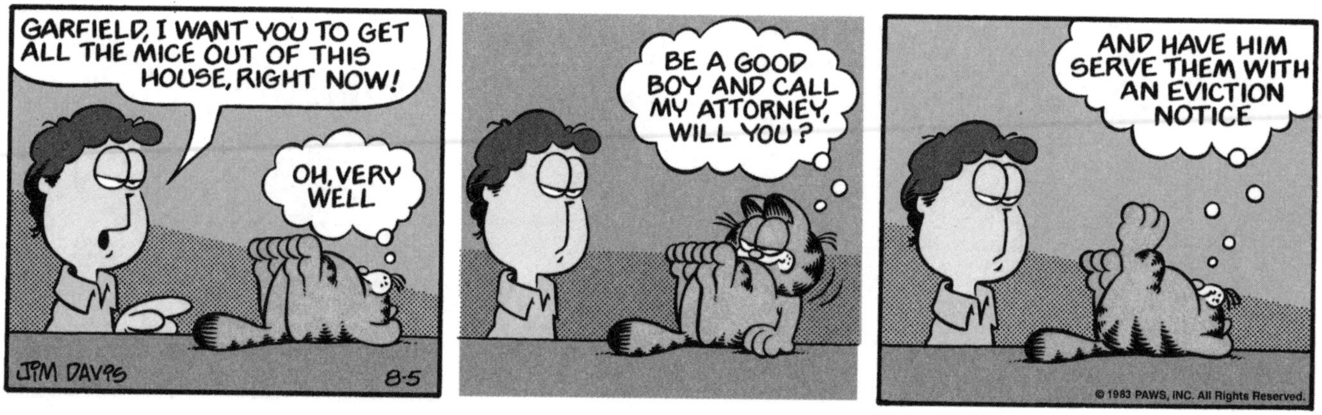
GARFIELD, I WANT YOU TO GET ALL THE MICE OUT OF THIS HOUSE, RIGHT NOW!
OH, VERY WELL
BE A GOOD BOY AND CALL MY ATTORNEY, WILL YOU?
AND HAVE HIM SERVE THEM WITH AN EVICTION NOTICE
JIM DAVIS
8-5
© 1983 PAWS, INC. All Rights Reserved.

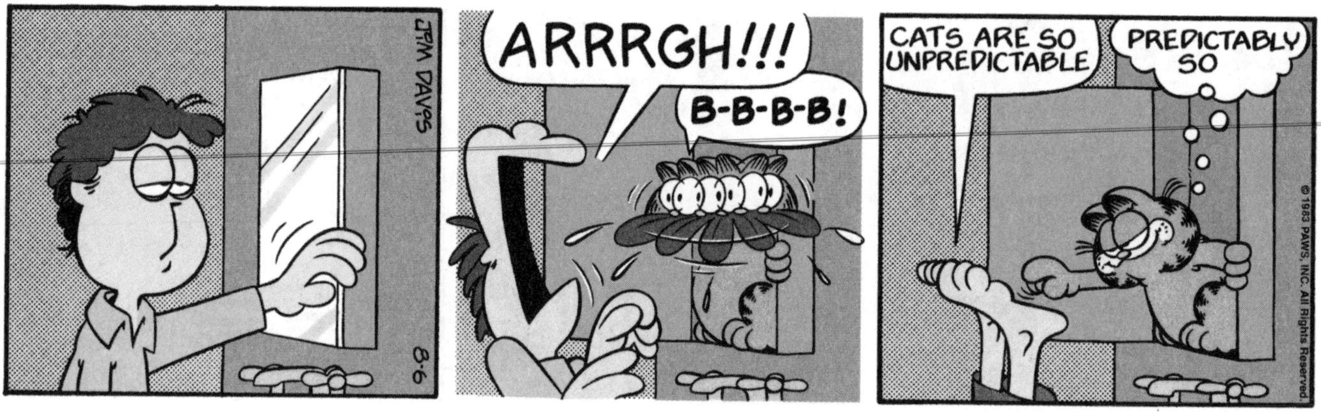
JIM DAVIS
8-6
ARRRGH!!!
B-B-B-B!
CATS ARE SO UNPREDICTABLE
PREDICTABLY SO
© 1983 PAWS, INC. All Rights Reserved.

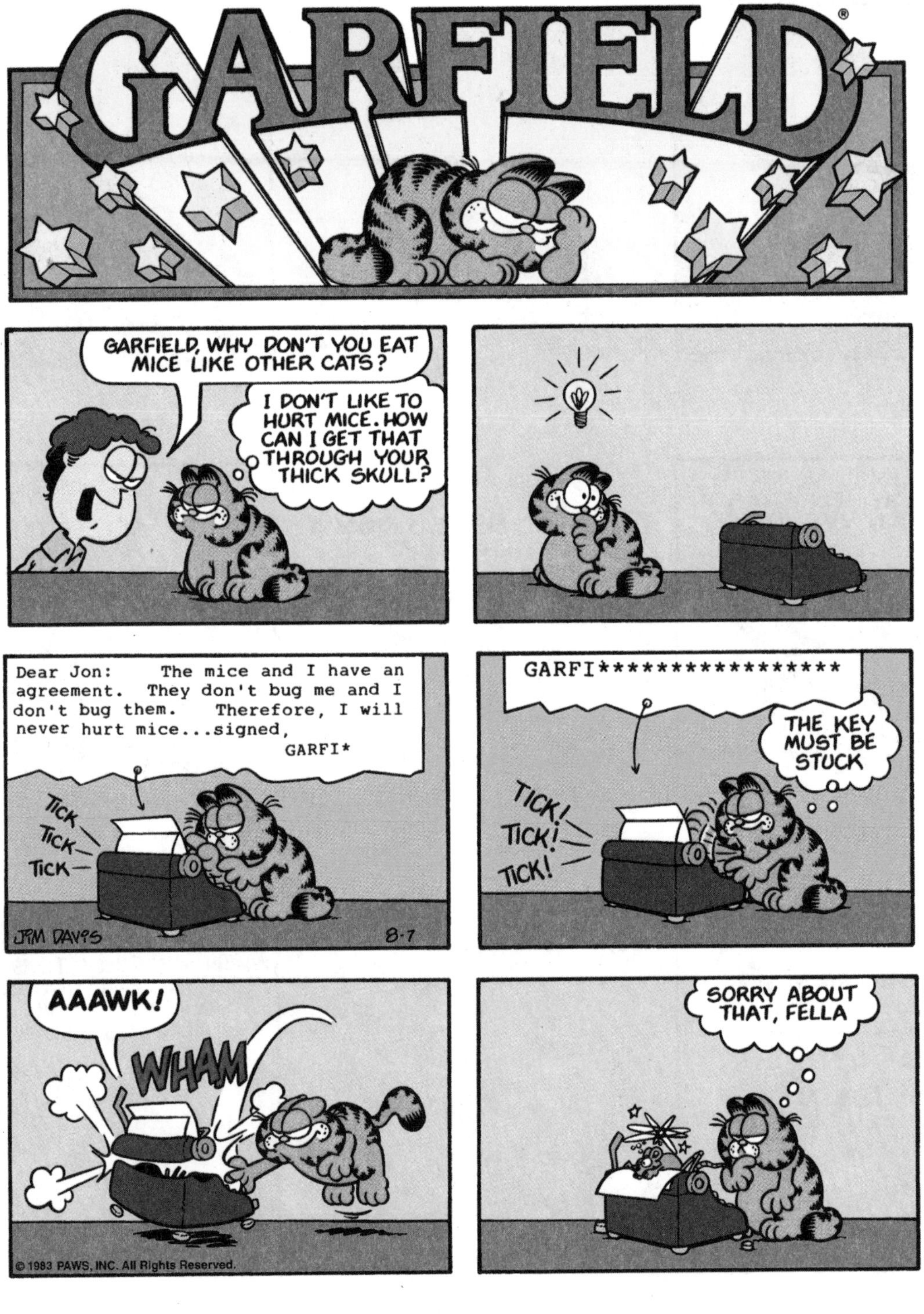
GARFIELD®
GARFIELD, WHY DON'T YOU EAT MICE LIKE OTHER CATS?
I DON'T LIKE TO HURT MICE. HOW CAN I GET THAT THROUGH YOUR THICK SKULL?
Dear Jon: The mice and I have an agreement. They don't bug me and I don't bug them. Therefore, I will never hurt mice...signed, GARFI*
TICK TICK TICK
JIM DAVIS 8-7
GARFI******************
THE KEY MUST BE STUCK
TICK! TICK! TICK!
AAAWK!
WHAM
© 1983 PAWS, INC. All Rights Reserved.
SORRY ABOUT THAT, FELLA

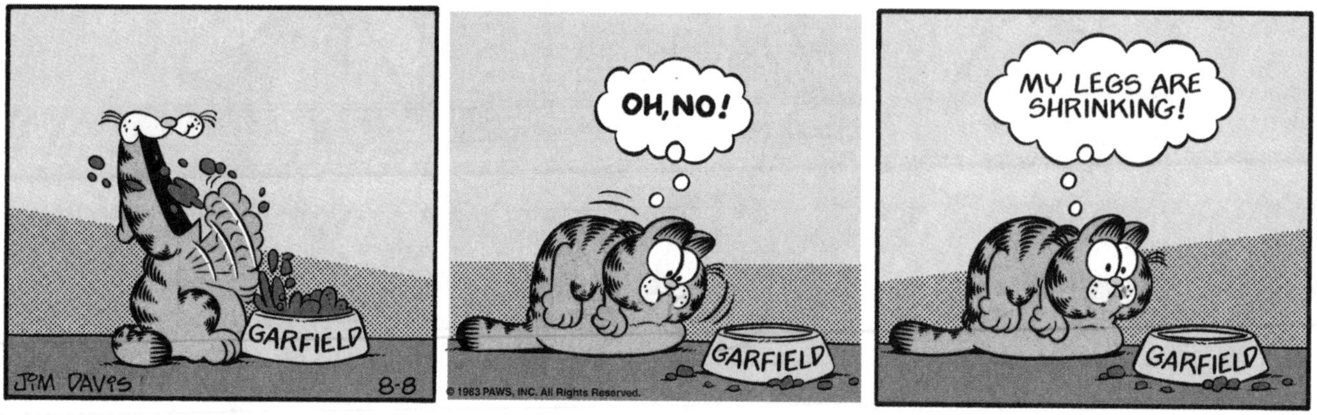
JIM DAVIS
8-8
OH, NO!
© 1983 PAWS, INC. All Rights Reserved.
MY LEGS ARE SHRINKING!
GARFIELD

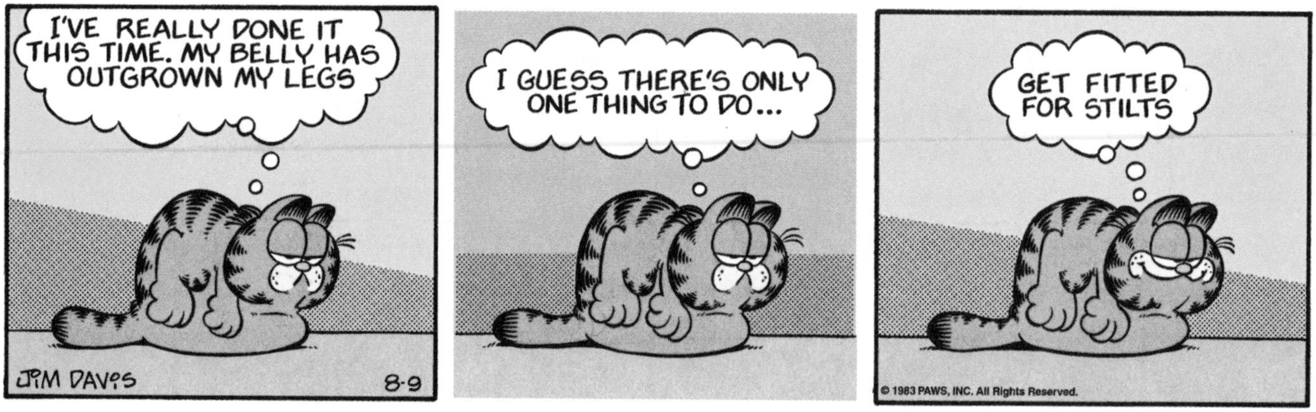
I'VE REALLY DONE IT THIS TIME. MY BELLY HAS OUTGROWN MY LEGS
JIM DAVIS
8-9
I GUESS THERE'S ONLY ONE THING TO DO...
GET FITTED FOR STILTS
© 1983 PAWS, INC. All Rights Reserved.

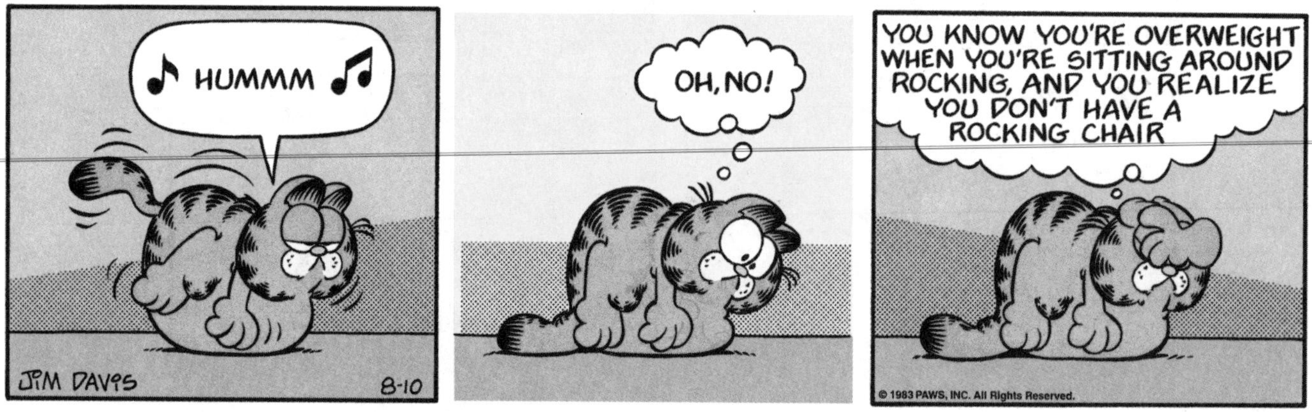
♪ HUMMM ♫
JIM DAVIS
8-10
OH, NO!
YOU KNOW YOU'RE OVERWEIGHT WHEN YOU'RE SITTING AROUND ROCKING, AND YOU REALIZE YOU DON'T HAVE A ROCKING CHAIR
© 1983 PAWS, INC. All Rights Reserved.

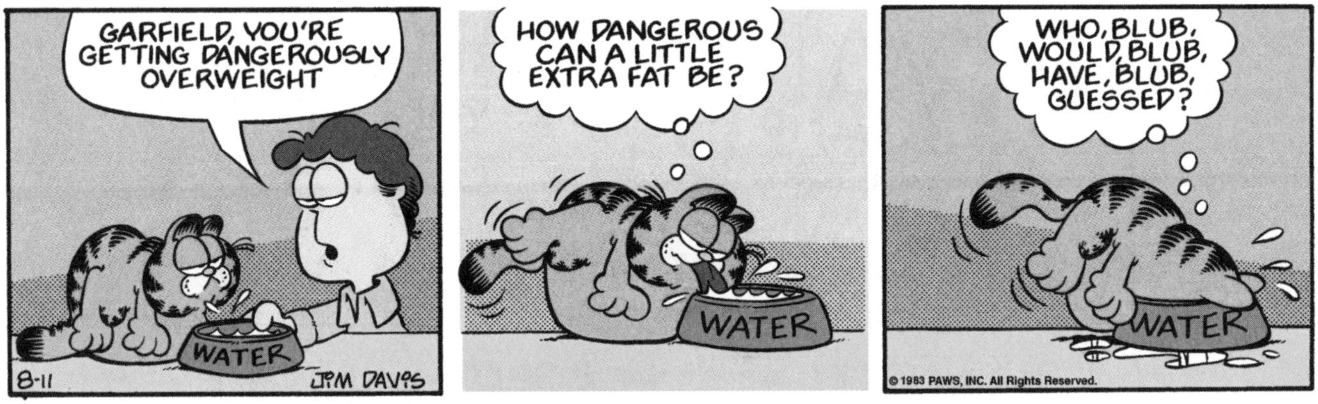
GARFIELD, YOU'RE GETTING DANGEROUSLY OVERWEIGHT
WATER
8-11
JIM DAVIS
HOW DANGEROUS CAN A LITTLE EXTRA FAT BE?
WATER
WHO, BLUB, WOULD, BLUB, HAVE, BLUB, GUESSED?
WATER
© 1983 PAWS, INC. All Rights Reserved.

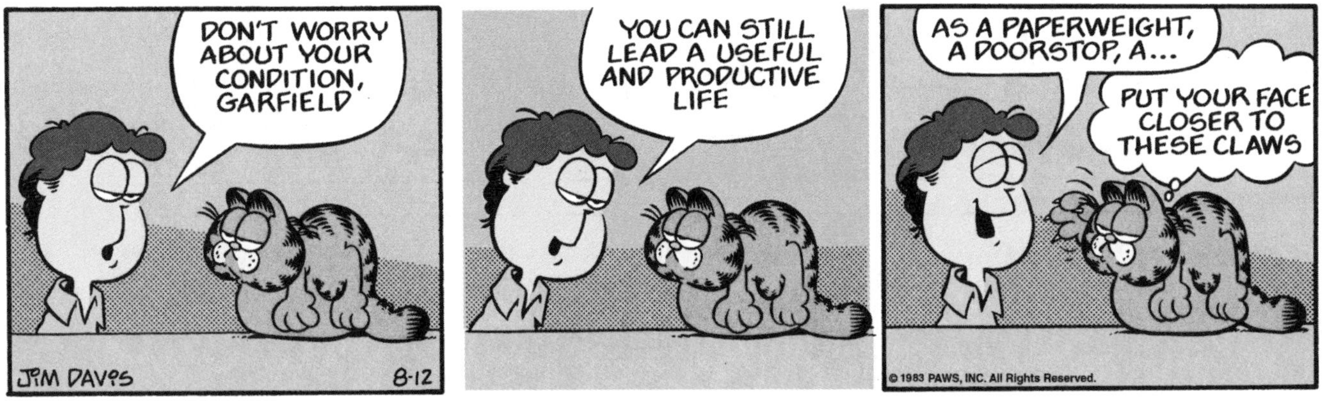
DON'T WORRY ABOUT YOUR CONDITION, GARFIELD
JIM DAVIS
8-12
YOU CAN STILL LEAD A USEFUL AND PRODUCTIVE LIFE
AS A PAPERWEIGHT, A DOORSTOP, A...
PUT YOUR FACE CLOSER TO THESE CLAWS
© 1983 PAWS, INC. All Rights Reserved.

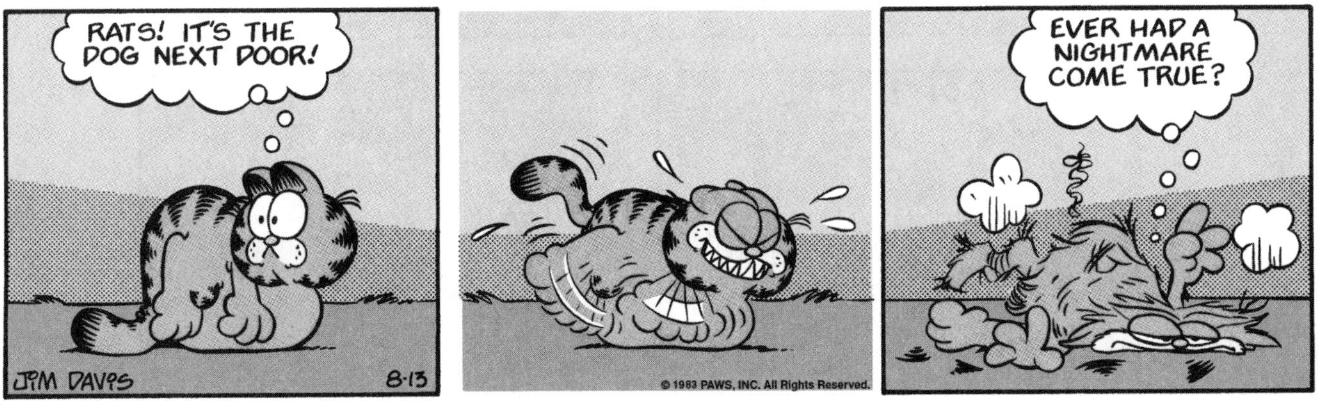
RATS! IT'S THE DOG NEXT DOOR!
JIM DAVIS
8-13
© 1983 PAWS, INC. All Rights Reserved.
EVER HAD A NIGHTMARE COME TRUE?

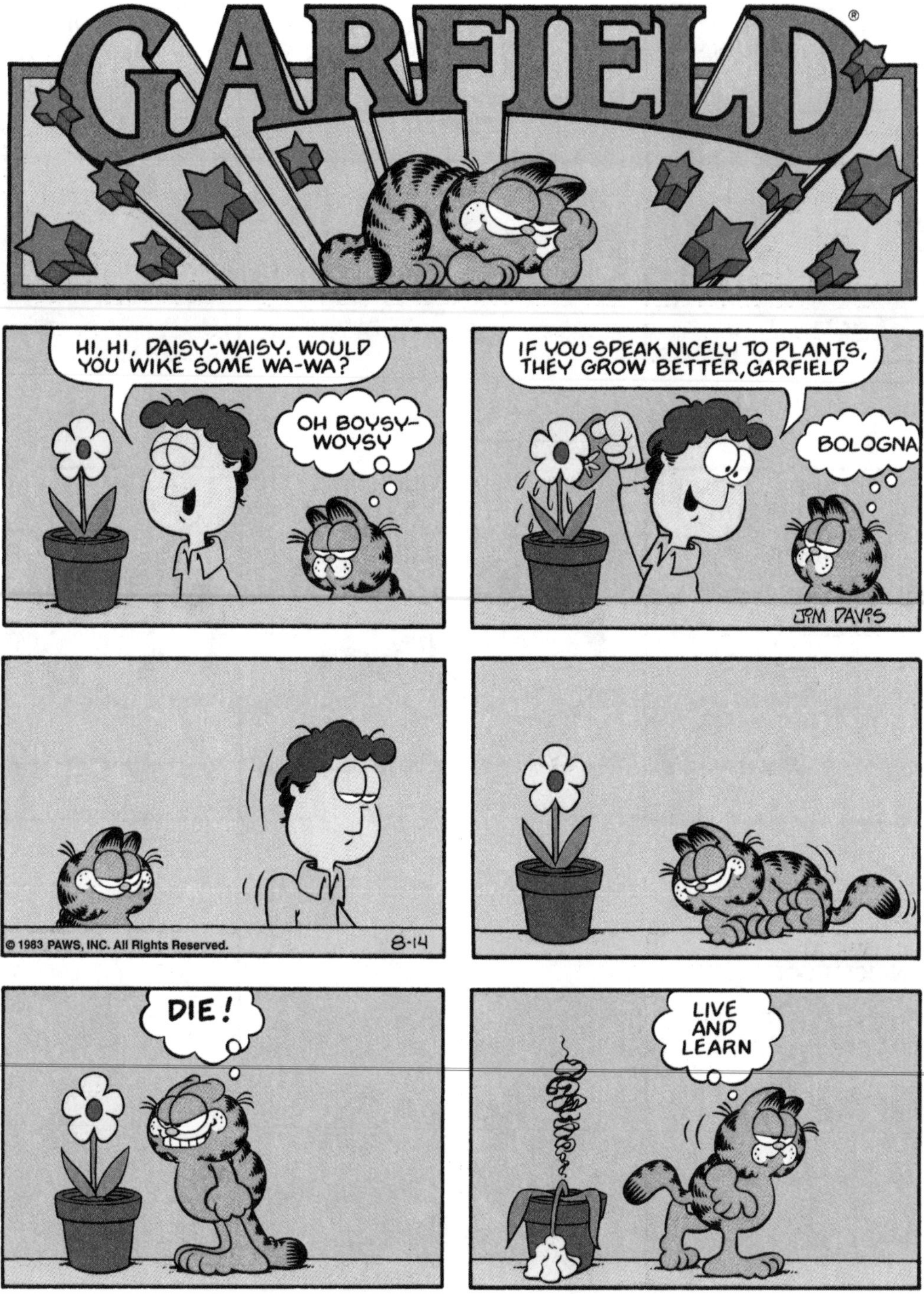
GARFIELD®
HI, HI, DAISY-WAISY. WOULD YOU WIKE SOME WA-WA?
OH BOYSY-WOYSY
IF YOU SPEAK NICELY TO PLANTS, THEY GROW BETTER, GARFIELD
BOLOGNA
JIM DAVIS
© 1983 PAWS, INC. All Rights Reserved.
8-14
DIE!
LIVE AND LEARN

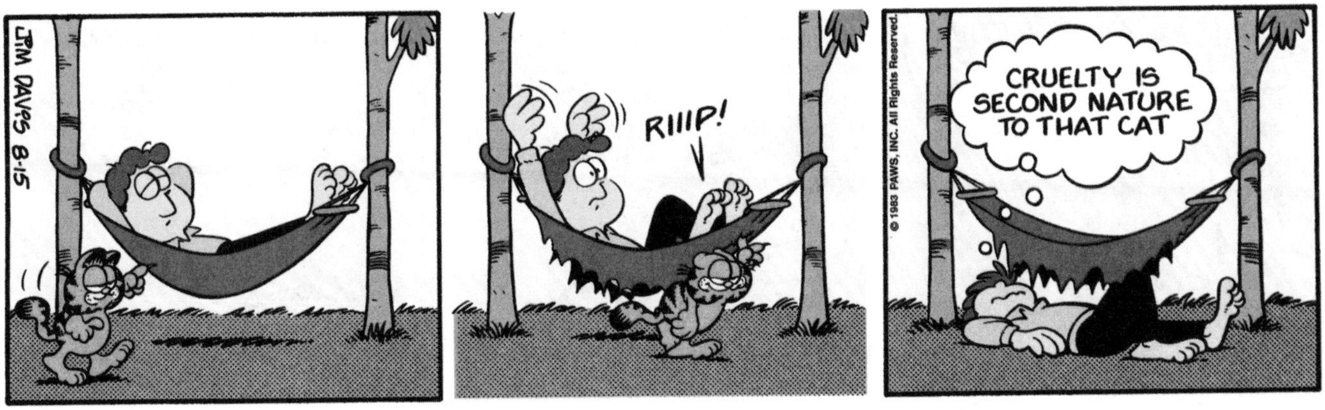
JIM DAVIS 8-15
RIIIP!
© 1983 PAWS, INC. All Rights Reserved.
CRUELTY IS SECOND NATURE TO THAT CAT

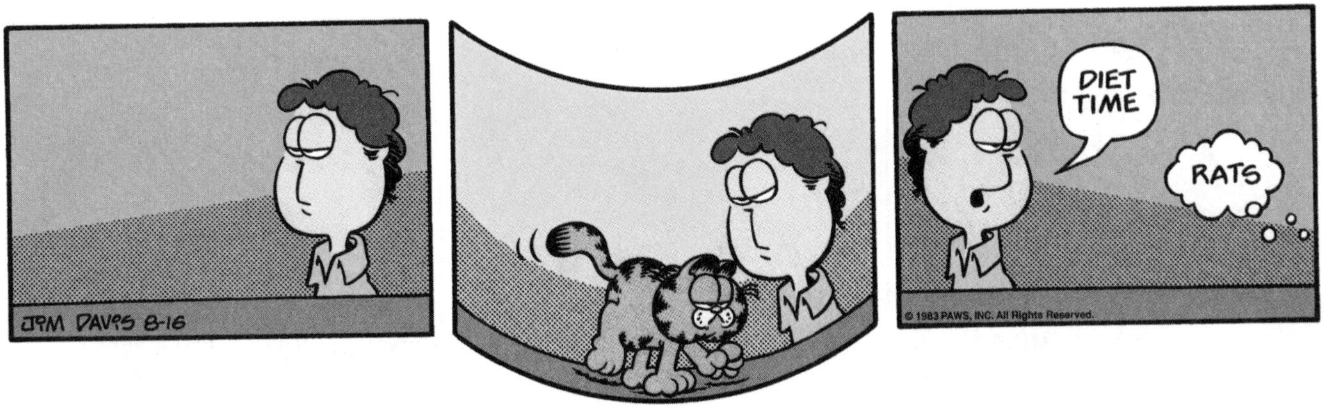
JIM DAVIS 8-16
DIET TIME
RATS
© 1983 PAWS, INC. All Rights Reserved.

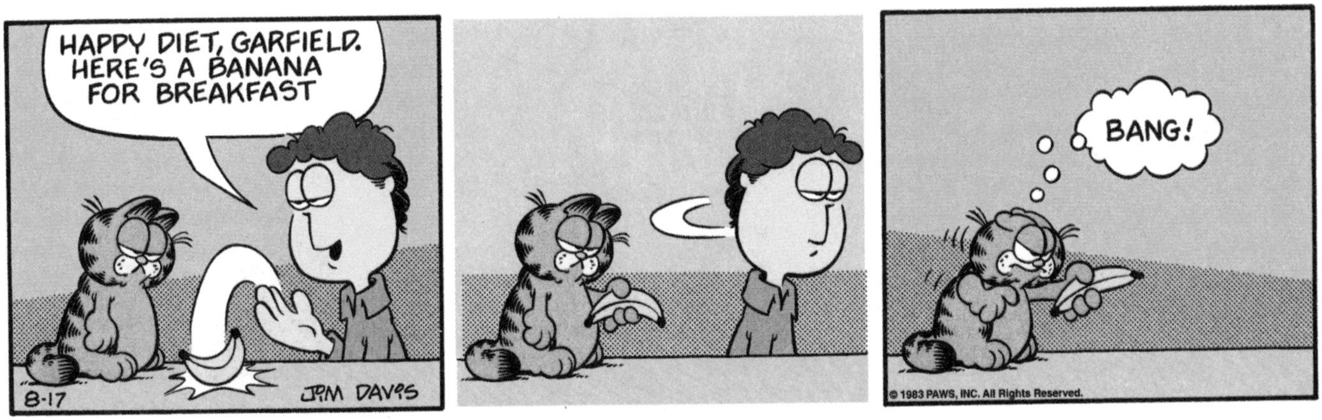
HAPPY DIET, GARFIELD. HERE'S A BANANA FOR BREAKFAST
8-17
JIM DAVIS
BANG!
© 1983 PAWS, INC. All Rights Reserved.

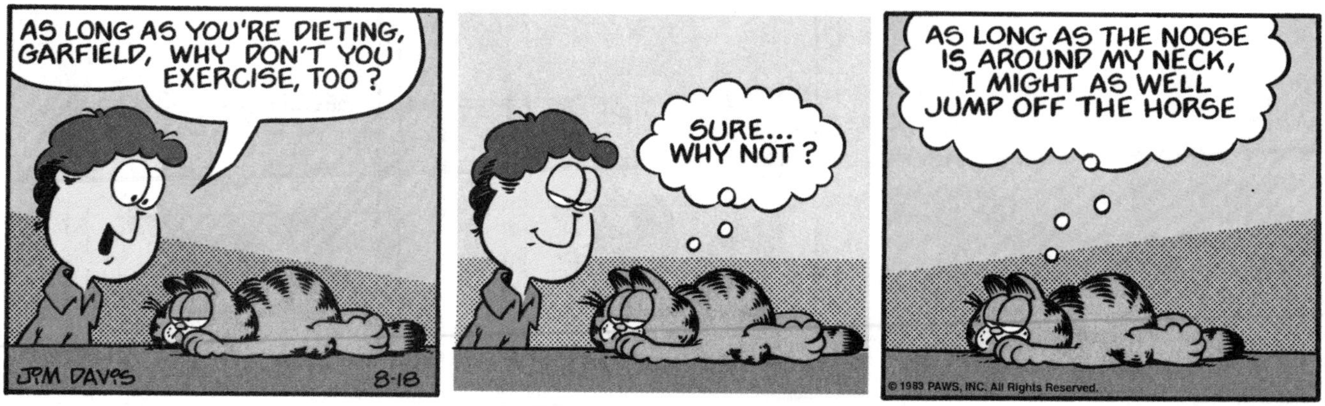
AS LONG AS YOU'RE DIETING, GARFIELD, WHY DON'T YOU EXERCISE, TOO?
JIM DAVIS
8-18
SURE... WHY NOT?
AS LONG AS THE NOOSE IS AROUND MY NECK, I MIGHT AS WELL JUMP OFF THE HORSE
© 1983 PAWS, INC. All Rights Reserved.

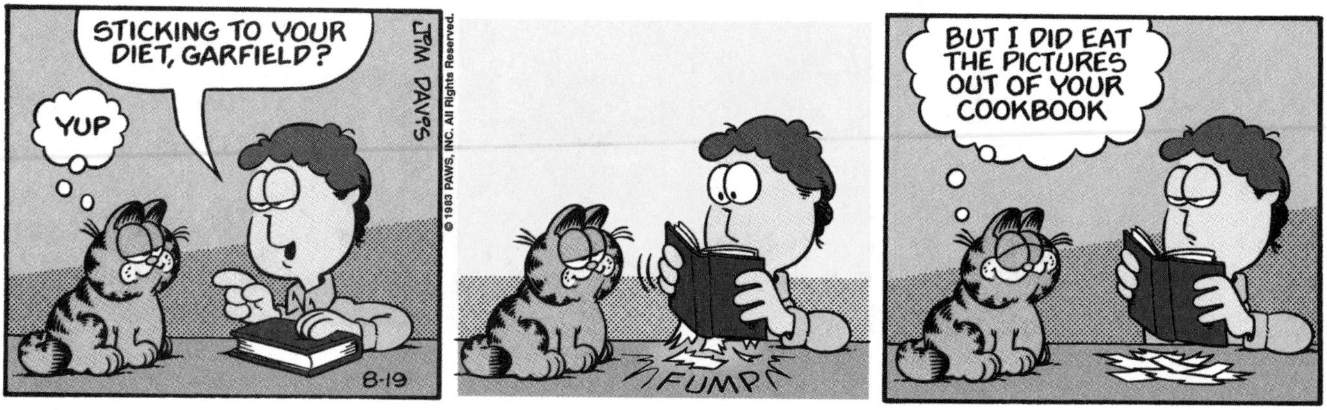
STICKING TO YOUR DIET, GARFIELD?
YUP
JIM DAVIS
8-19
© 1983 PAWS, INC. All Rights Reserved.
FUMP
BUT I DID EAT THE PICTURES OUT OF YOUR COOKBOOK

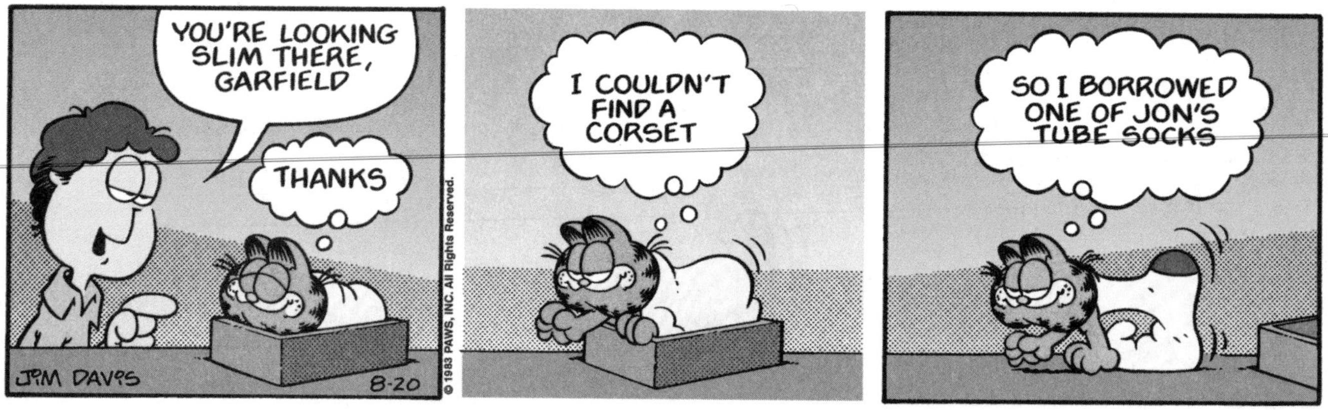
YOU'RE LOOKING SLIM THERE, GARFIELD
THANKS
JIM DAVIS
8-20
© 1983 PAWS, INC. All Rights Reserved.
I COULDN'T FIND A CORSET
SO I BORROWED ONE OF JON'S TUBE SOCKS

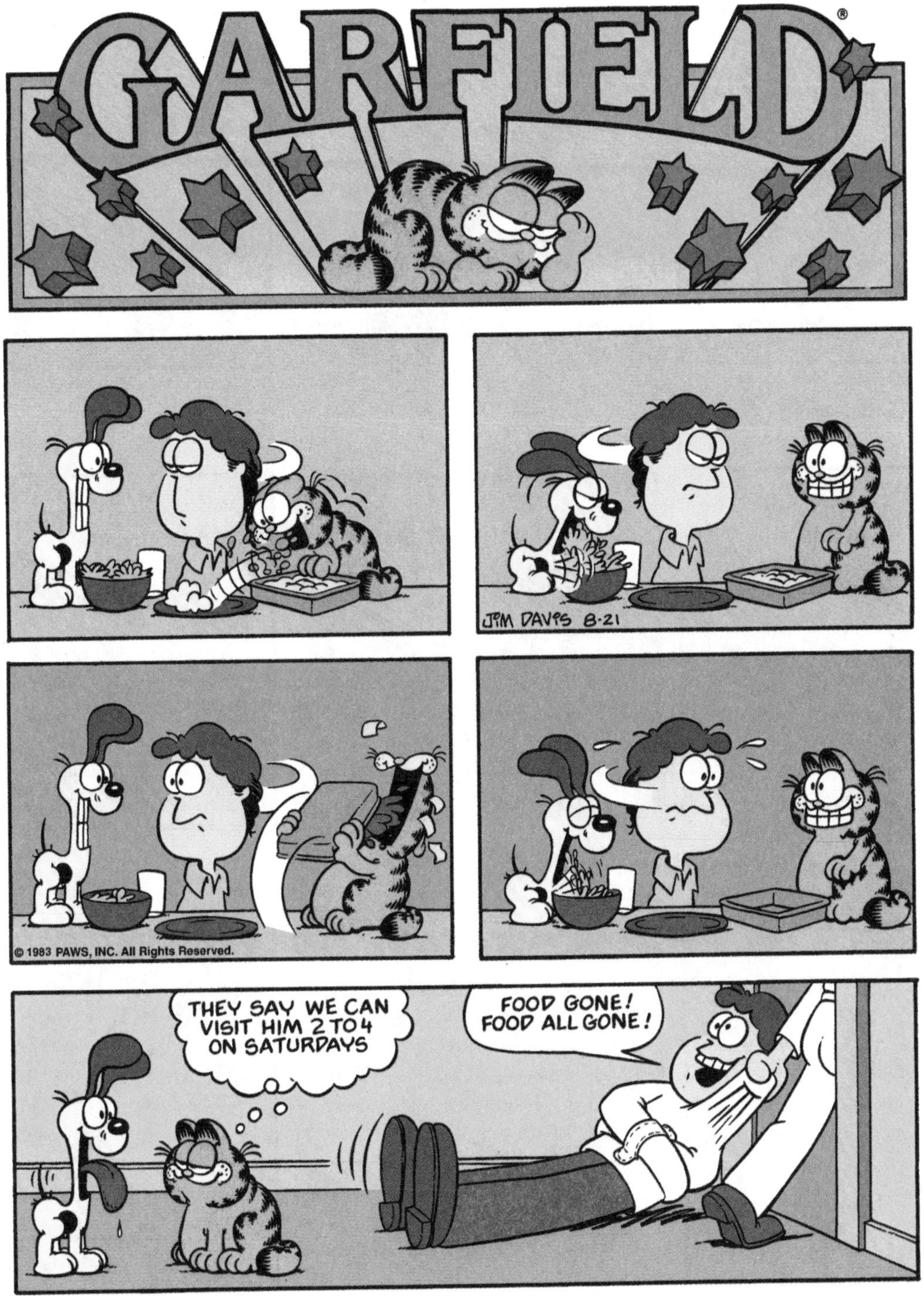
GARFIELD
JIM DAVIS 8-21
© 1983 PAWS, INC. All Rights Reserved.
THEY SAY WE CAN VISIT HIM 2 TO 4 ON SATURDAYS
FOOD GONE! FOOD ALL GONE!

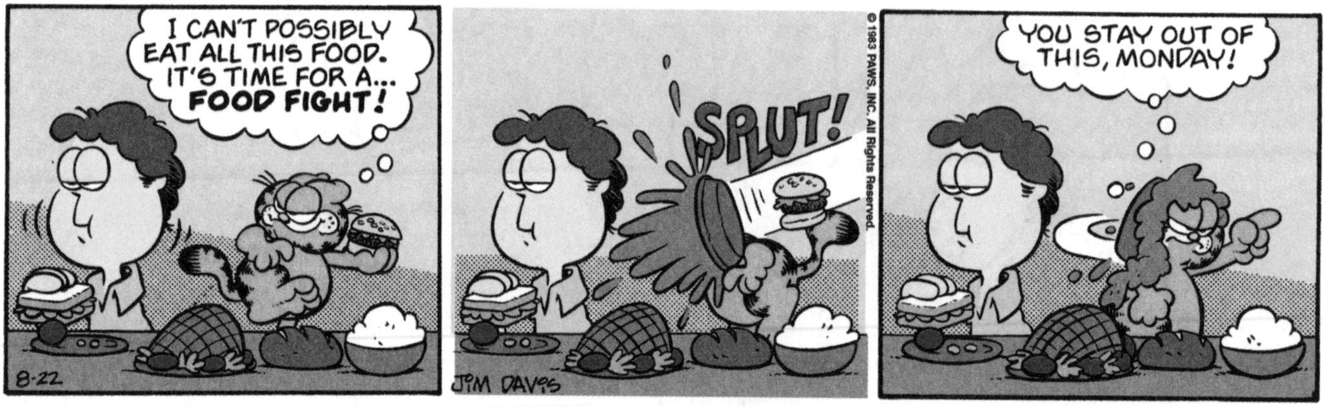
I CAN'T POSSIBLY EAT ALL THIS FOOD. IT'S TIME FOR A... **FOOD FIGHT!**
8-22
SPLUT!
JIM DAVIS
© 1983 PAWS, INC. All Rights Reserved.
YOU STAY OUT OF THIS, MONDAY!

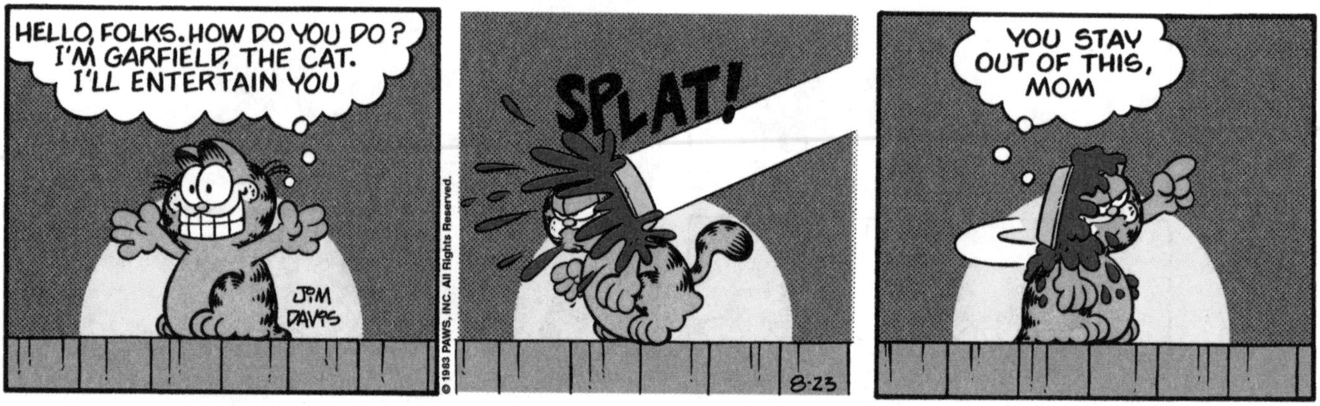
HELLO, FOLKS. HOW DO YOU DO? I'M GARFIELD, THE CAT. I'LL ENTERTAIN YOU
JIM DAVIS
© 1983 PAWS, INC. All Rights Reserved.
SPLAT!
8-23
YOU STAY OUT OF THIS, MOM

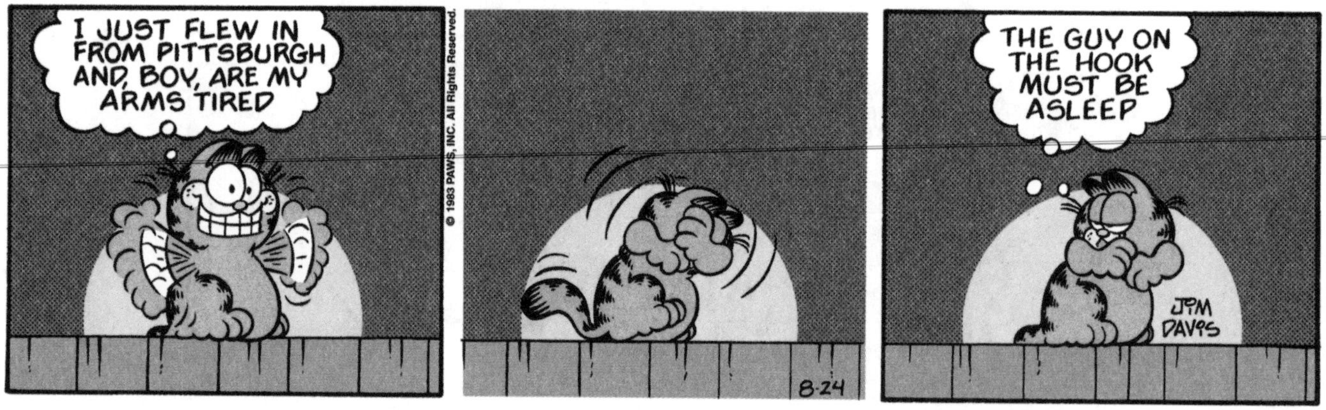
I JUST FLEW IN FROM PITTSBURGH AND, BOY, ARE MY ARMS TIRED
© 1983 PAWS, INC. All Rights Reserved.
8-24
THE GUY ON THE HOOK MUST BE ASLEEP
JIM DAVIS

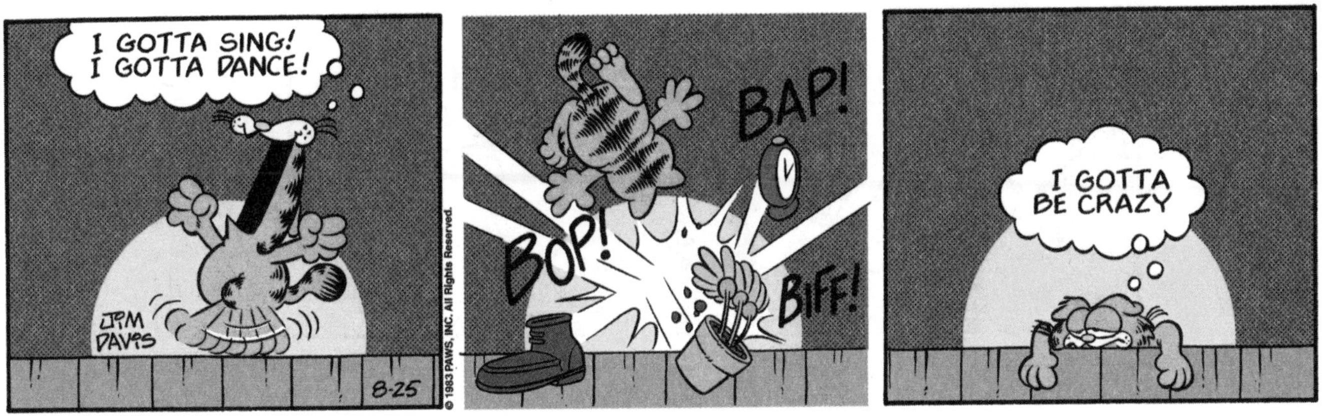
I GOTTA SING! I GOTTA DANCE!
JIM DAVIS
8-25
© 1983 PAWS, INC. All Rights Reserved.
BAP!
BOP!
BIFF!
I GOTTA BE CRAZY

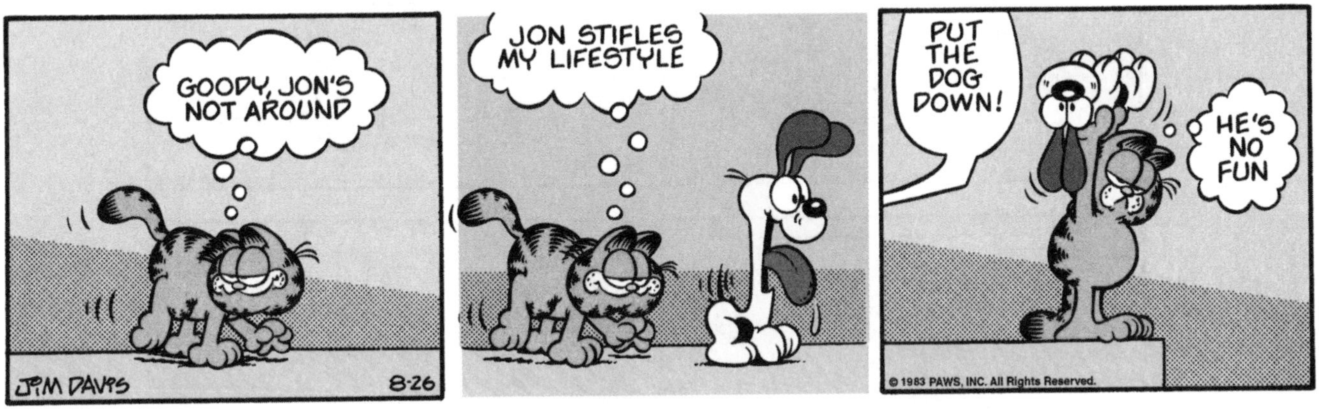
GOODY, JON'S NOT AROUND
JIM DAVIS
8-26
JON STIFLES MY LIFESTYLE
PUT THE DOG DOWN!
HE'S NO FUN
© 1983 PAWS, INC. All Rights Reserved.

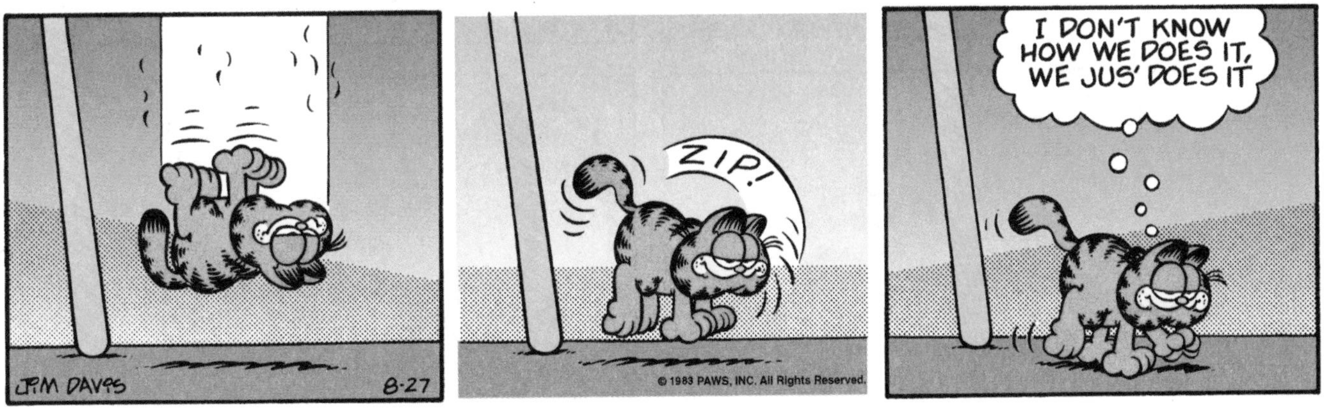
JIM DAVIS
8-27
ZIP!
© 1983 PAWS, INC. All Rights Reserved.
I DON'T KNOW HOW WE DOES IT, WE JUS' DOES IT

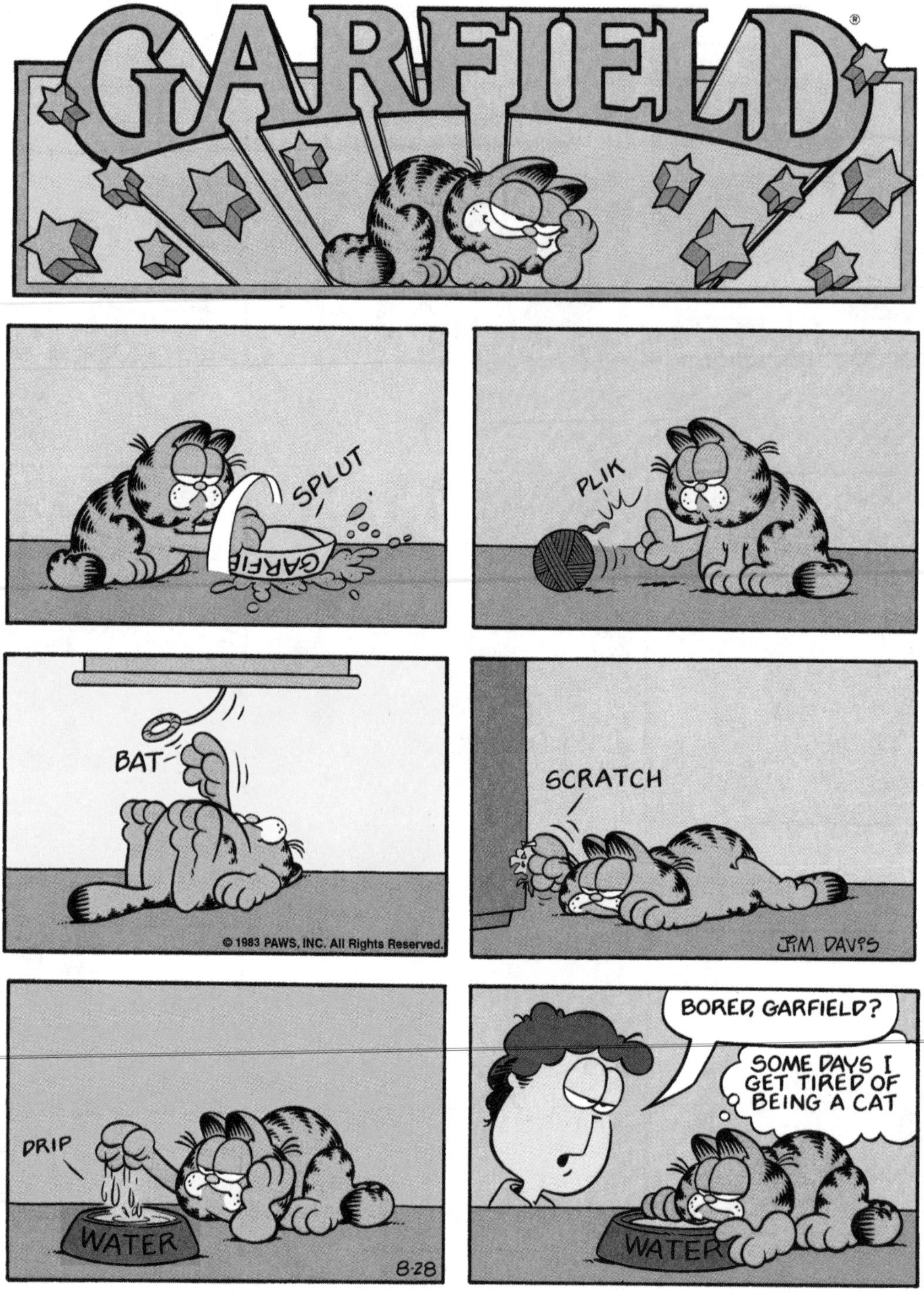
GARFIELD®
SPLUT
GARFIELD
PLIK
BAT
© 1983 PAWS, INC. All Rights Reserved.
SCRATCH
JIM DAVIS
DRIP
WATER
8-28
BORED, GARFIELD?
SOME DAYS I GET TIRED OF BEING A CAT
WATER

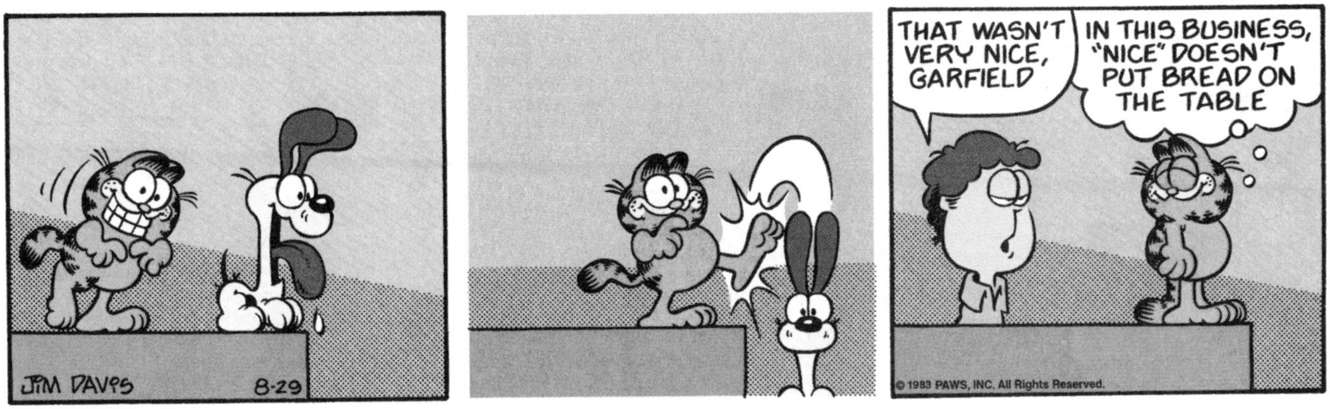
JIM DAVIS 8-29
THAT WASN'T VERY NICE, GARFIELD
IN THIS BUSINESS, "NICE" DOESN'T PUT BREAD ON THE TABLE
© 1983 PAWS, INC. All Rights Reserved.

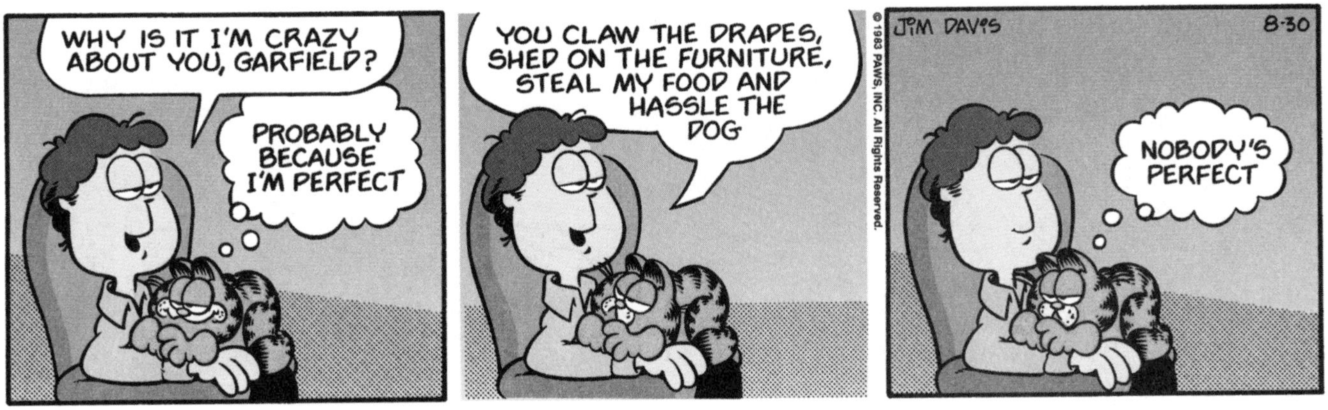
WHY IS IT I'M CRAZY ABOUT YOU, GARFIELD?
PROBABLY BECAUSE I'M PERFECT
YOU CLAW THE DRAPES, SHED ON THE FURNITURE, STEAL MY FOOD AND HASSLE THE DOG
© 1983 PAWS, INC. All Rights Reserved.
JIM DAVIS 8-30
NOBODY'S PERFECT

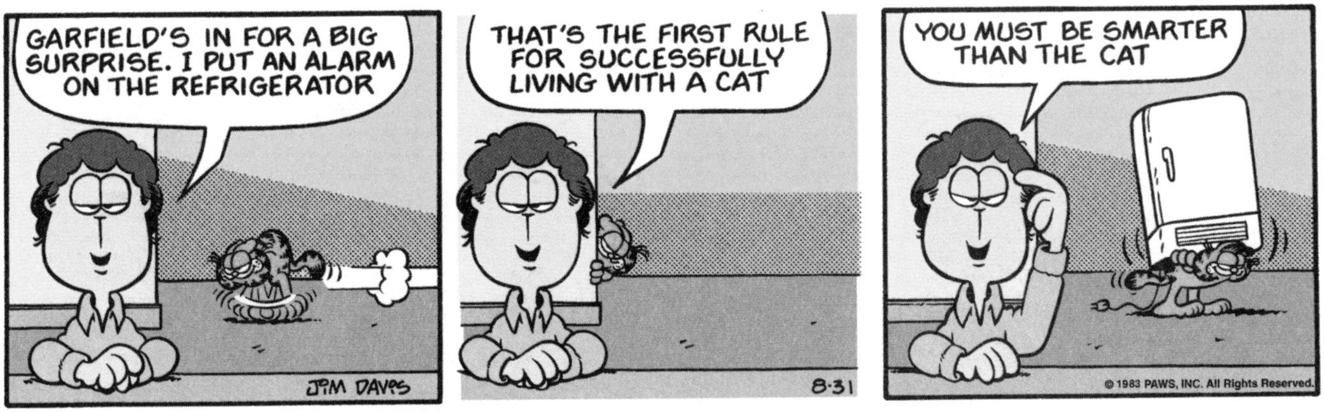
GARFIELD'S IN FOR A BIG SURPRISE. I PUT AN ALARM ON THE REFRIGERATOR
JIM DAVIS
THAT'S THE FIRST RULE FOR SUCCESSFULLY LIVING WITH A CAT
8-31
YOU MUST BE SMARTER THAN THE CAT
© 1983 PAWS, INC. All Rights Reserved.

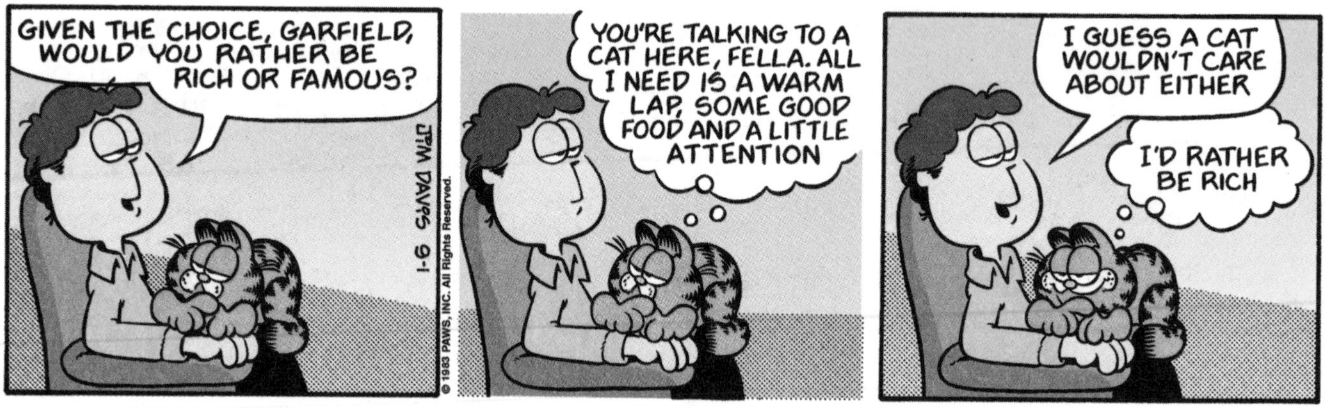
GIVEN THE CHOICE, GARFIELD, WOULD YOU RATHER BE RICH OR FAMOUS?
JIM DAVIS 9-1
© 1983 PAWS, INC. All Rights Reserved.
YOU'RE TALKING TO A CAT HERE, FELLA. ALL I NEED IS A WARM LAP, SOME GOOD FOOD AND A LITTLE ATTENTION
I GUESS A CAT WOULDN'T CARE ABOUT EITHER
I'D RATHER BE RICH

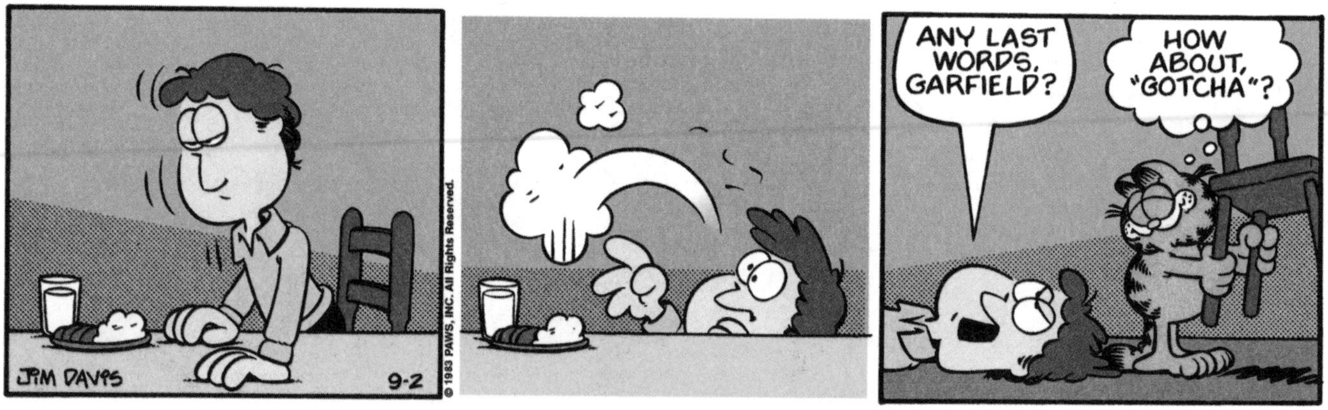
JIM DAVIS 9-2
© 1983 PAWS, INC. All Rights Reserved.
ANY LAST WORDS, GARFIELD?
HOW ABOUT, "GOTCHA"?

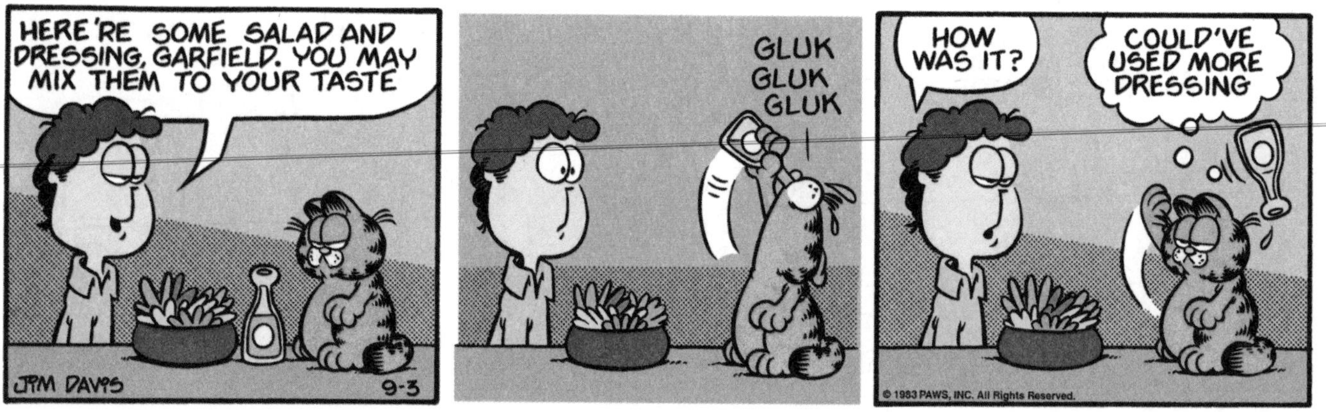
HERE'RE SOME SALAD AND DRESSING, GARFIELD. YOU MAY MIX THEM TO YOUR TASTE
JIM DAVIS 9-3
GLUK GLUK GLUK
HOW WAS IT?
COULD'VE USED MORE DRESSING
© 1983 PAWS, INC. All Rights Reserved.

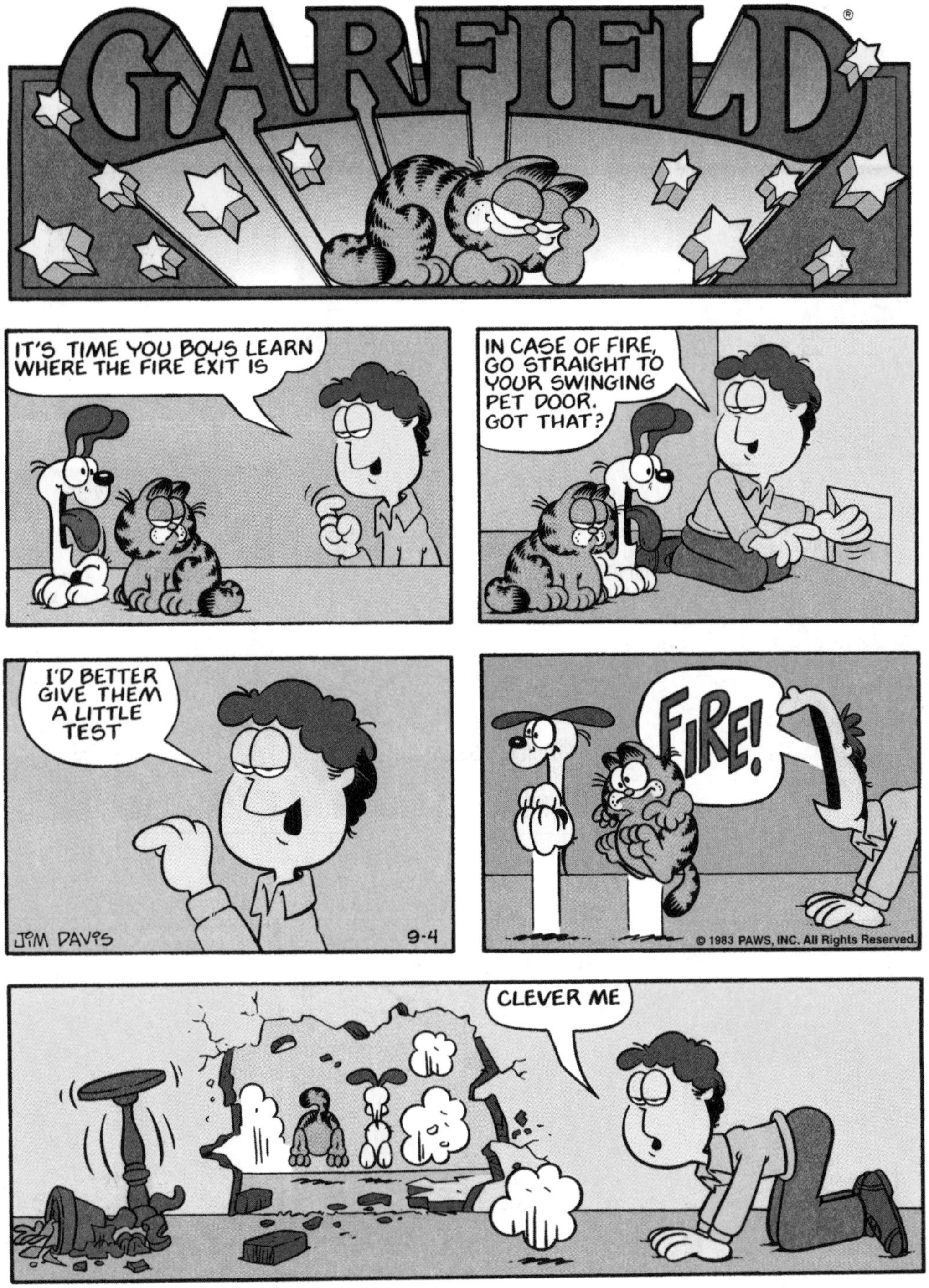
GARFIELD
IT'S TIME YOU BOYS LEARN WHERE THE FIRE EXIT IS
IN CASE OF FIRE, GO STRAIGHT TO YOUR SWINGING PET DOOR. GOT THAT?
I'D BETTER GIVE THEM A LITTLE TEST
JIM DAVIS
9-4
FIRE!
© 1983 PAWS, INC. All Rights Reserved.
CLEVER ME

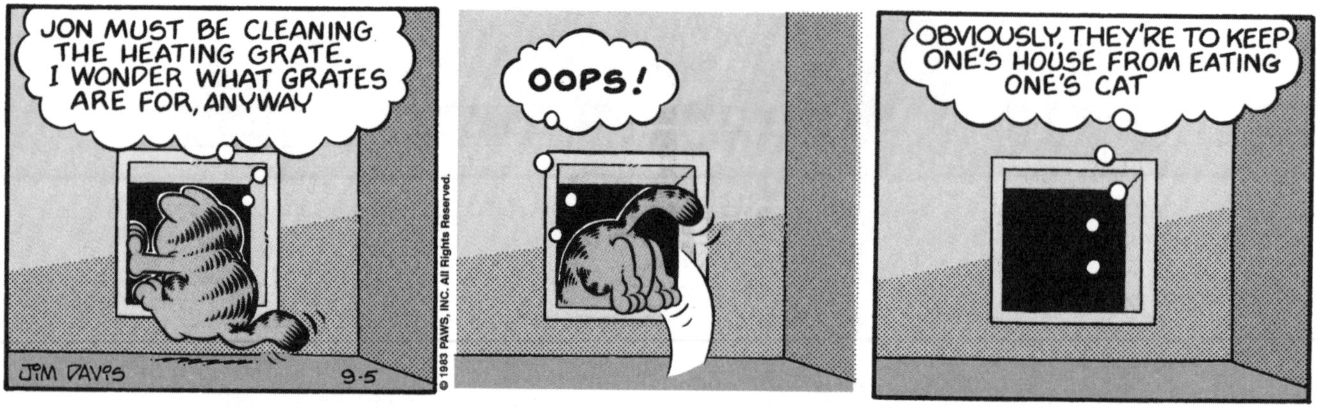
JON MUST BE CLEANING THE HEATING GRATE. I WONDER WHAT GRATES ARE FOR, ANYWAY
JIM DAVIS 9-5
© 1983 PAWS, INC. All Rights Reserved.
OOPS!
OBVIOUSLY, THEY'RE TO KEEP ONE'S HOUSE FROM EATING ONE'S CAT

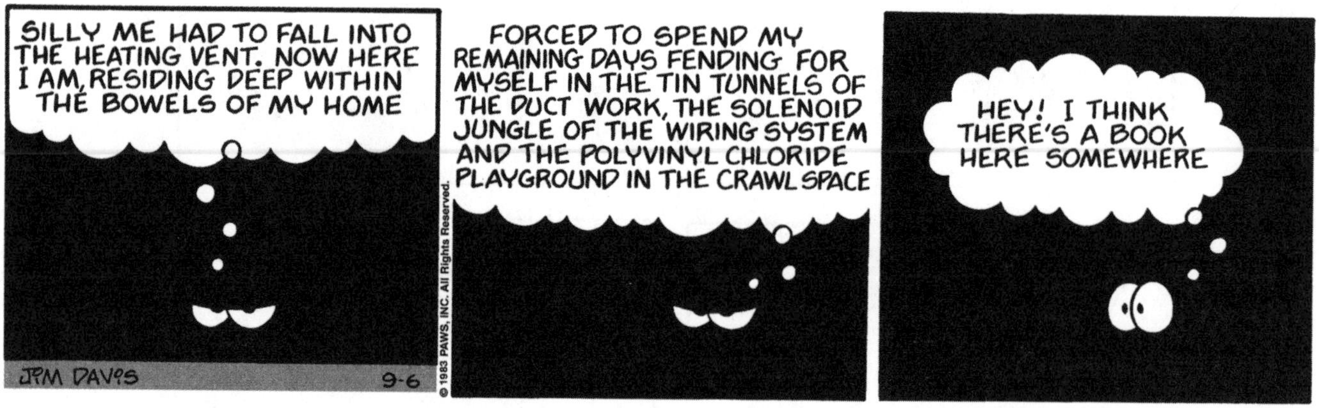
SILLY ME HAD TO FALL INTO THE HEATING VENT. NOW HERE I AM, RESIDING DEEP WITHIN THE BOWELS OF MY HOME
JIM DAVIS 9-6
© 1983 PAWS, INC. All Rights Reserved.
FORCED TO SPEND MY REMAINING DAYS FENDING FOR MYSELF IN THE TIN TUNNELS OF THE DUCT WORK, THE SOLENOID JUNGLE OF THE WIRING SYSTEM AND THE POLYVINYL CHLORIDE PLAYGROUND IN THE CRAWL SPACE
HEY! I THINK THERE'S A BOOK HERE SOMEWHERE

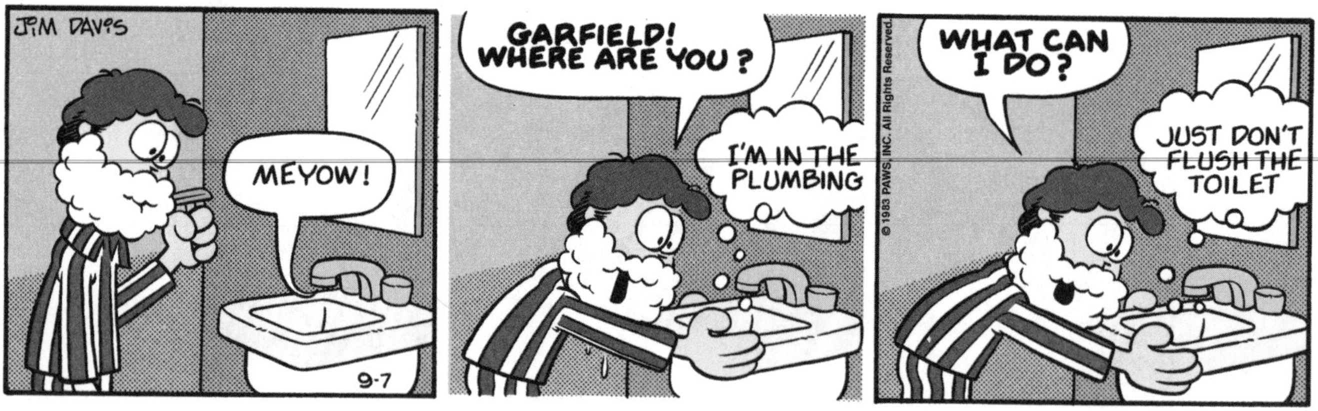
JIM DAVIS
MEYOW!
9-7
GARFIELD! WHERE ARE YOU?
I'M IN THE PLUMBING
© 1983 PAWS, INC. All Rights Reserved.
WHAT CAN I DO?
JUST DON'T FLUSH THE TOILET

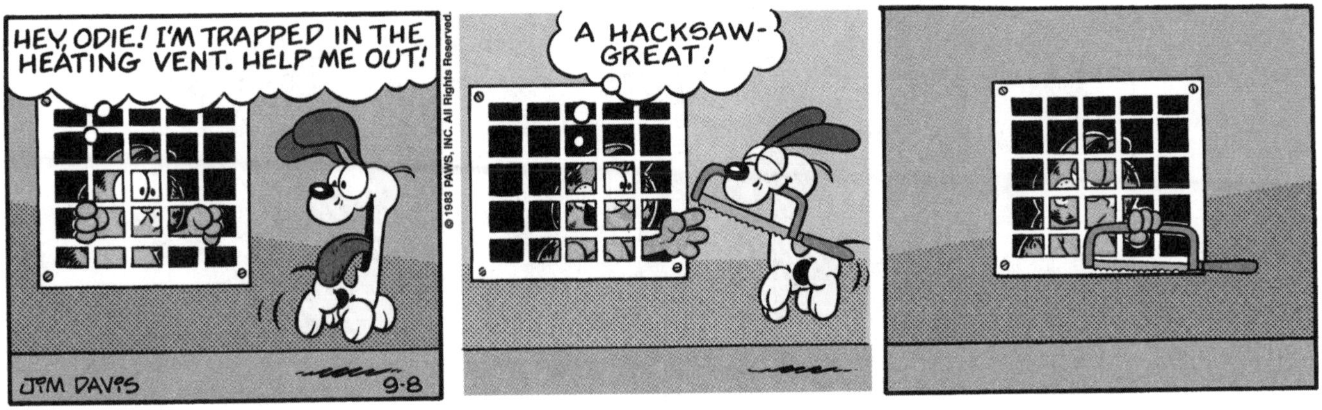
HEY, ODIE! I'M TRAPPED IN THE HEATING VENT. HELP ME OUT!
A HACKSAW- GREAT!
JIM DAVIS
9-8
© 1983 PAWS, INC. All Rights Reserved.

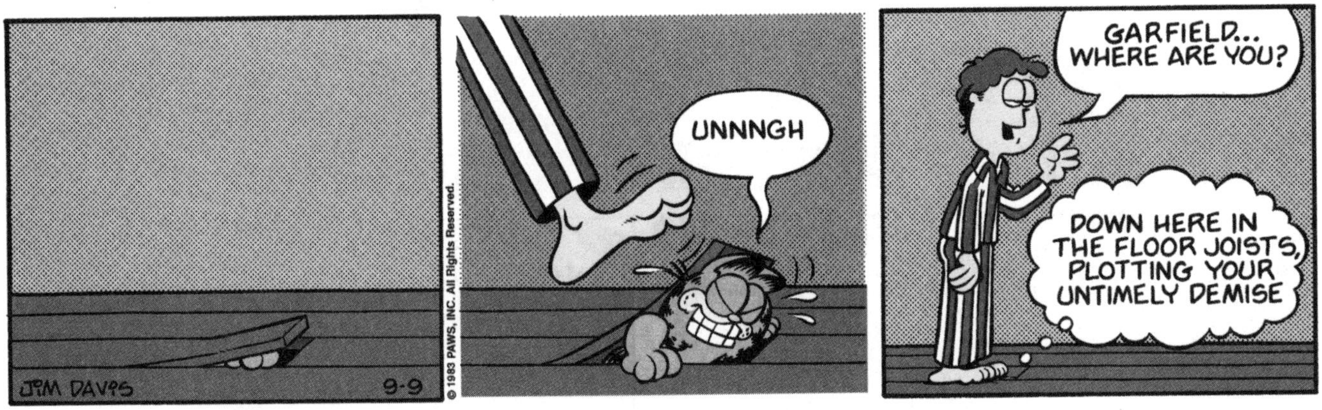
UNNNGH
GARFIELD... WHERE ARE YOU?
DOWN HERE IN THE FLOOR JOISTS, PLOTTING YOUR UNTIMELY DEMISE
JIM DAVIS
9-9
© 1983 PAWS, INC. All Rights Reserved.

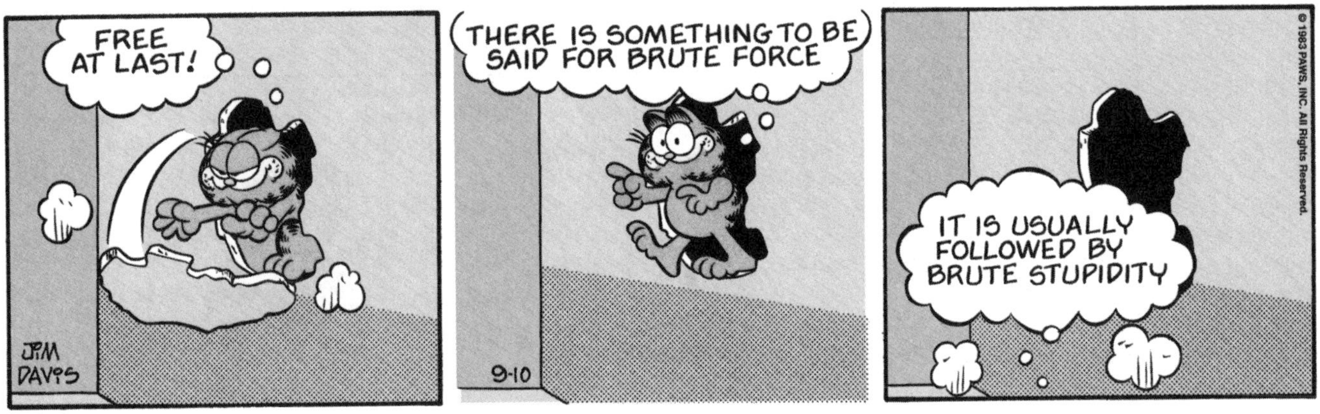
FREE AT LAST!
THERE IS SOMETHING TO BE SAID FOR BRUTE FORCE
IT IS USUALLY FOLLOWED BY BRUTE STUPIDITY
JIM DAVIS
9-10
© 1983 PAWS, INC. All Rights Reserved.

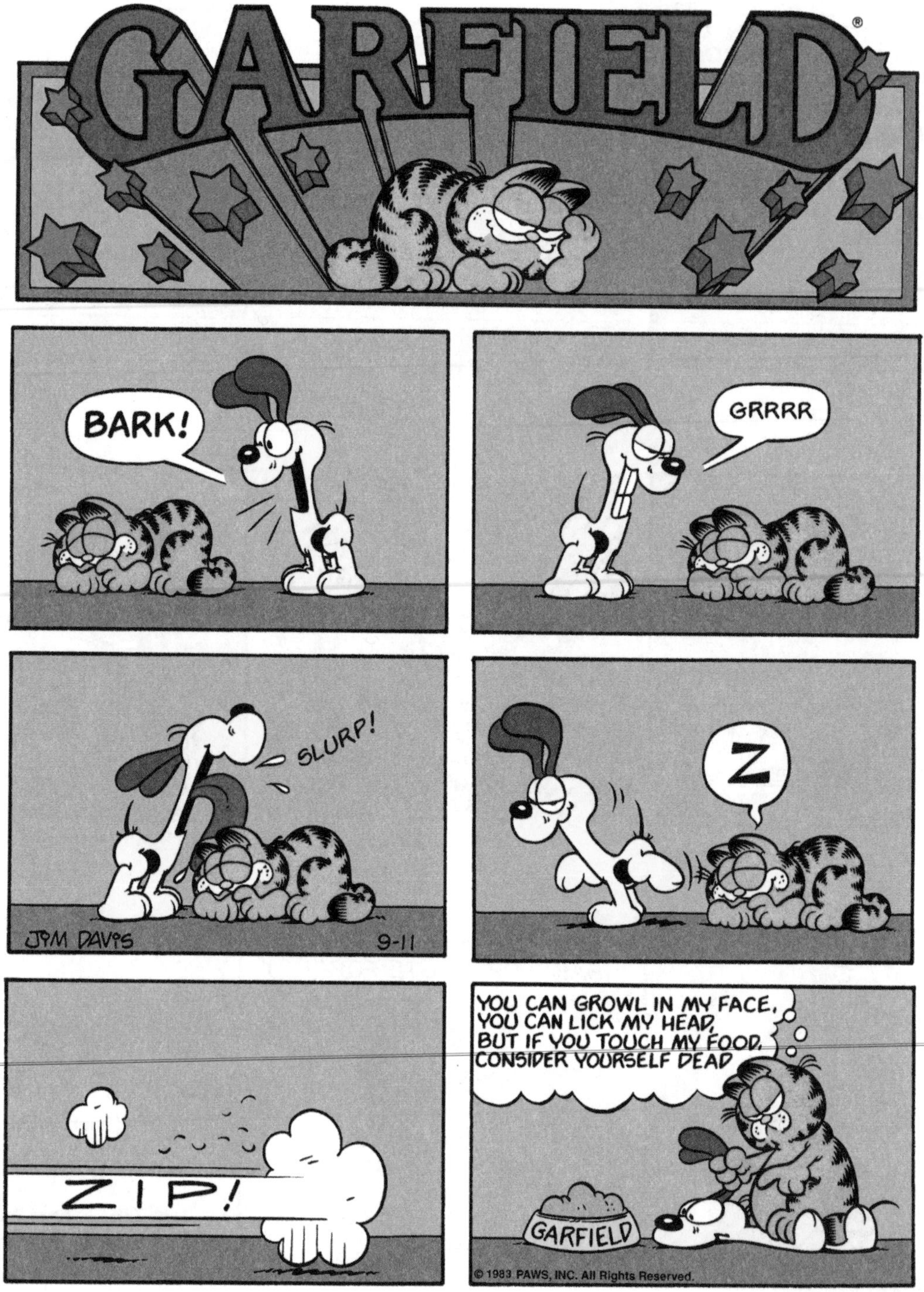
GARFIELD®
BARK!
GRRRR
SLURP!
Z
JIM DAVIS
9-11
ZIP!
YOU CAN GROWL IN MY FACE,
YOU CAN LICK MY HEAD,
BUT IF YOU TOUCH MY FOOD,
CONSIDER YOURSELF DEAD
GARFIELD
© 1983 PAWS, INC. All Rights Reserved.

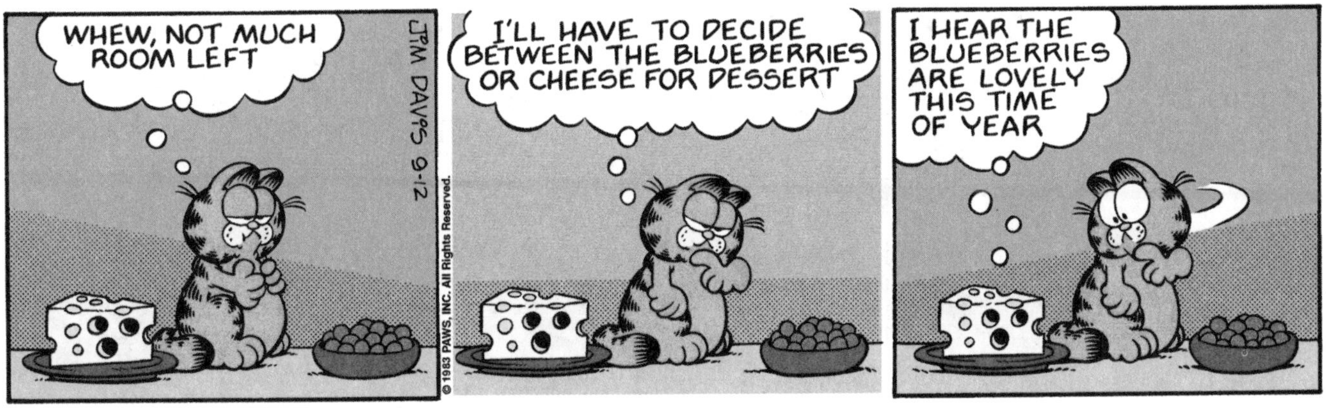
WHEW, NOT MUCH ROOM LEFT
JIM DAVIS 9-12
© 1983 PAWS, INC. All Rights Reserved.
I'LL HAVE TO DECIDE BETWEEN THE BLUEBERRIES OR CHEESE FOR DESSERT
I HEAR THE BLUEBERRIES ARE LOVELY THIS TIME OF YEAR

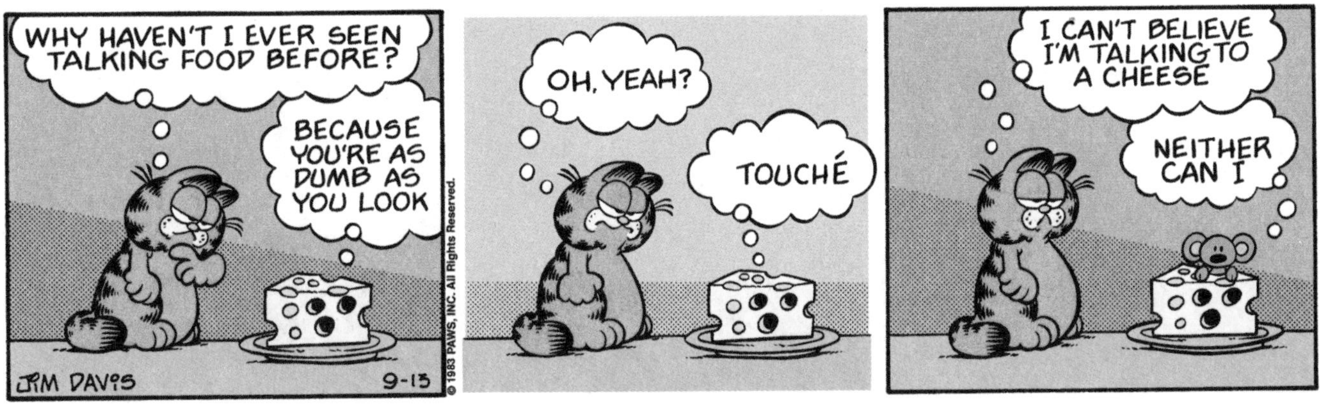
WHY HAVEN'T I EVER SEEN TALKING FOOD BEFORE?
BECAUSE YOU'RE AS DUMB AS YOU LOOK
JIM DAVIS
9-13
© 1983 PAWS, INC. All Rights Reserved.
OH, YEAH?
TOUCHÉ
I CAN'T BELIEVE I'M TALKING TO A CHEESE
NEITHER CAN I

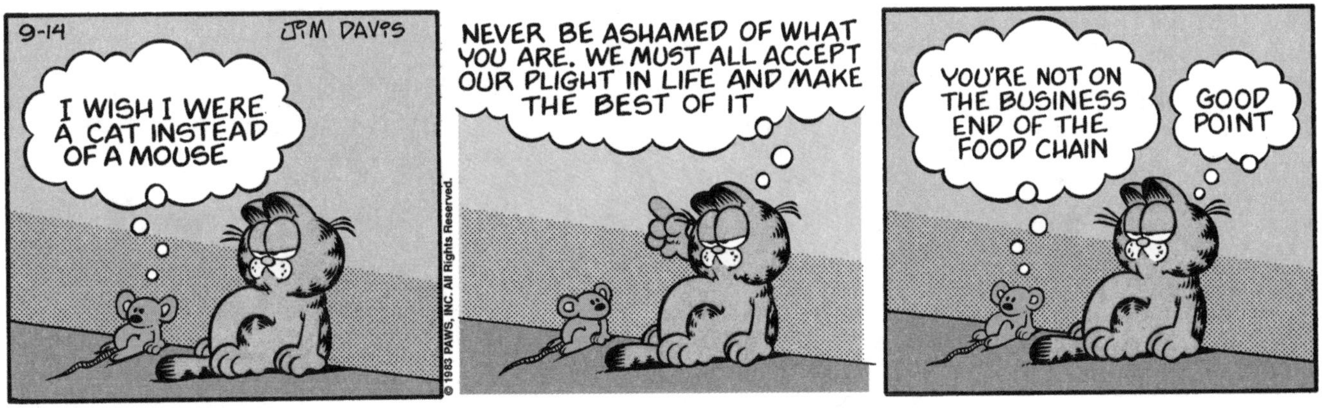
9-14
JIM DAVIS
I WISH I WERE A CAT INSTEAD OF A MOUSE
© 1983 PAWS, INC. All Rights Reserved.
NEVER BE ASHAMED OF WHAT YOU ARE. WE MUST ALL ACCEPT OUR PLIGHT IN LIFE AND MAKE THE BEST OF IT
YOU'RE NOT ON THE BUSINESS END OF THE FOOD CHAIN
GOOD POINT

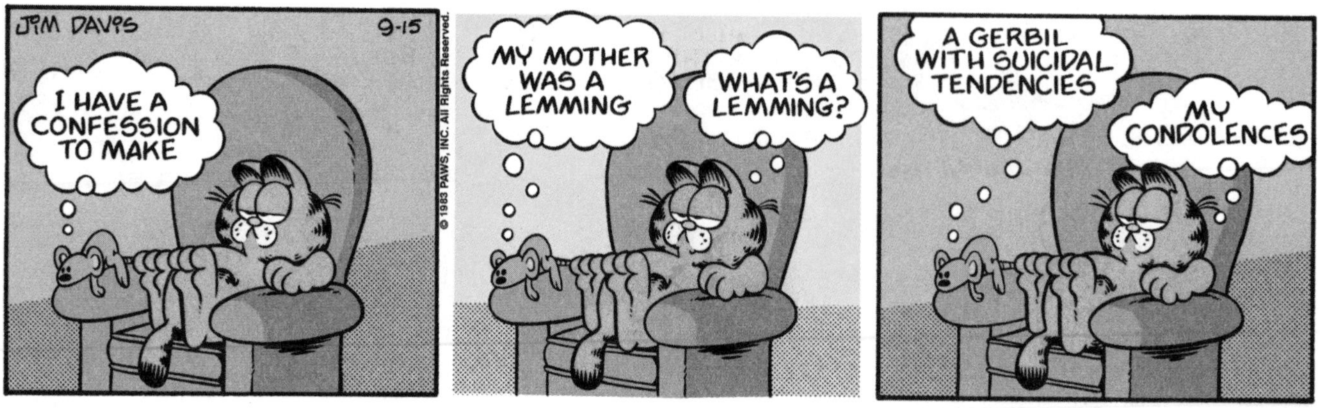
JIM DAVIS
9-15
I HAVE A CONFESSION TO MAKE
© 1983 PAWS, INC. All Rights Reserved.
MY MOTHER WAS A LEMMING
WHAT'S A LEMMING?
A GERBIL WITH SUICIDAL TENDENCIES
MY CONDOLENCES

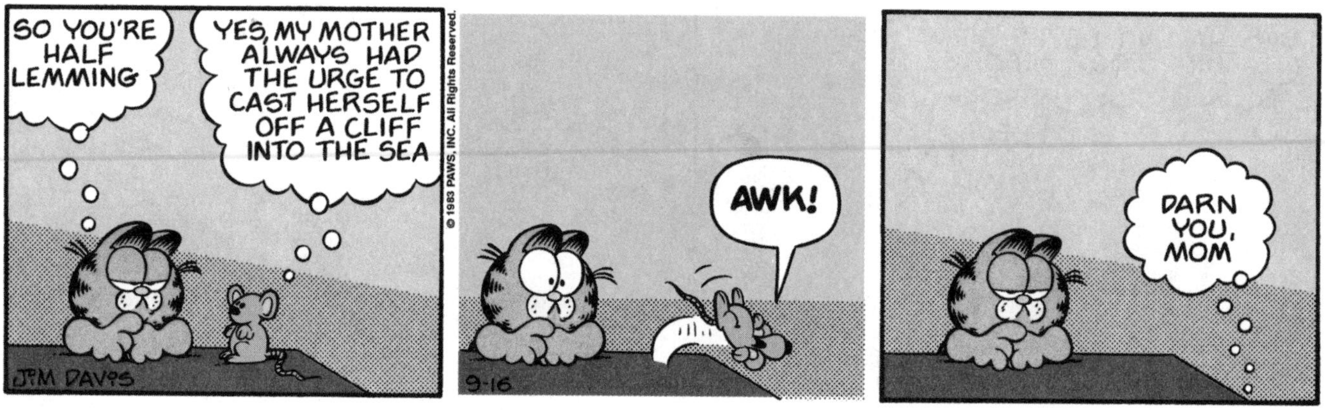
SO YOU'RE HALF LEMMING
YES, MY MOTHER ALWAYS HAD THE URGE TO CAST HERSELF OFF A CLIFF INTO THE SEA
JIM DAVIS
© 1983 PAWS, INC. All Rights Reserved.
AWK!
9-16
DARN YOU, MOM

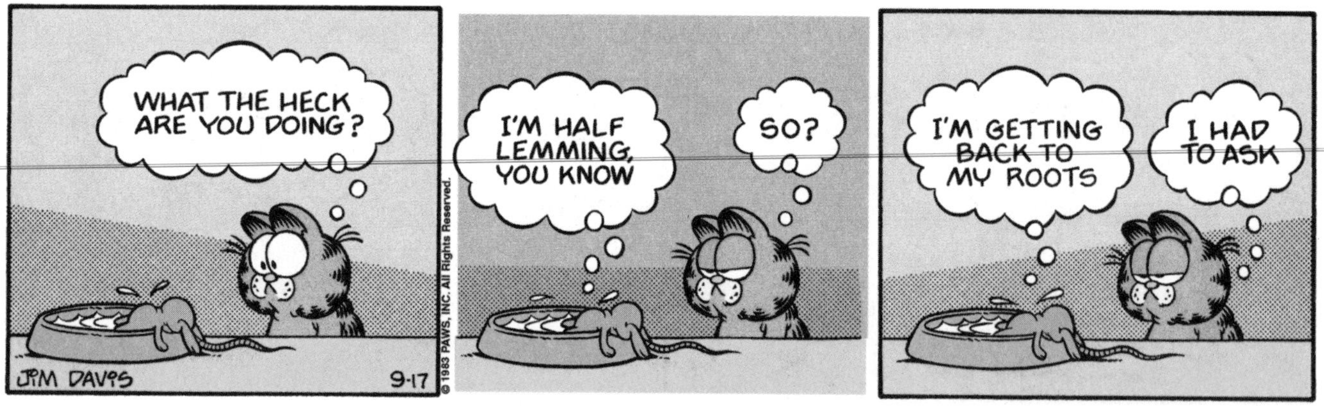
WHAT THE HECK ARE YOU DOING?
JIM DAVIS
9-17
© 1983 PAWS, INC. All Rights Reserved.
I'M HALF LEMMING, YOU KNOW
SO?
I'M GETTING BACK TO MY ROOTS
I HAD TO ASK

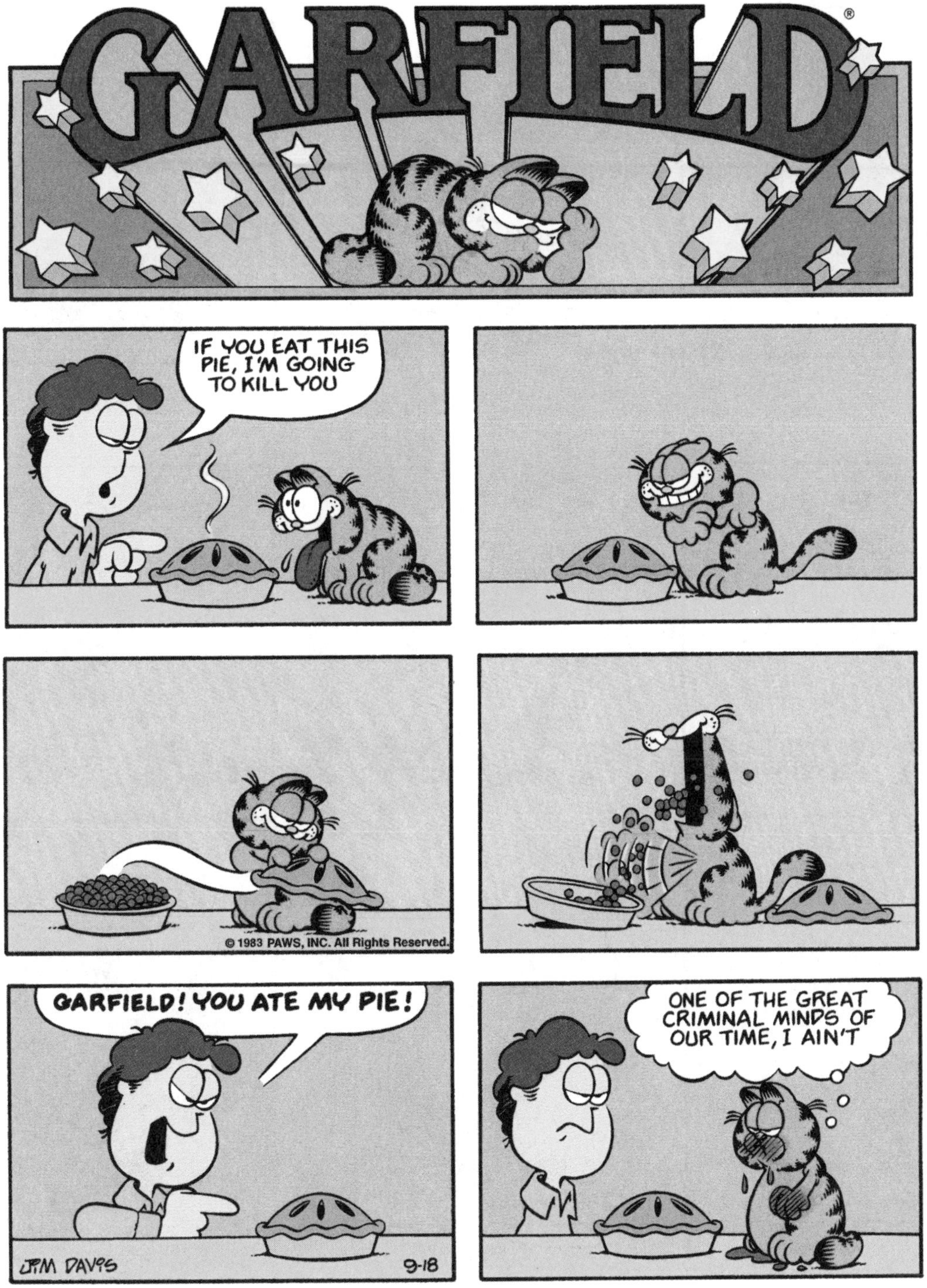
GARFIELD
IF YOU EAT THIS PIE, I'M GOING TO KILL YOU
© 1983 PAWS, INC. All Rights Reserved.
GARFIELD! YOU ATE MY PIE!
JIM DAVIS
9-18
ONE OF THE GREAT CRIMINAL MINDS OF OUR TIME, I AIN'T

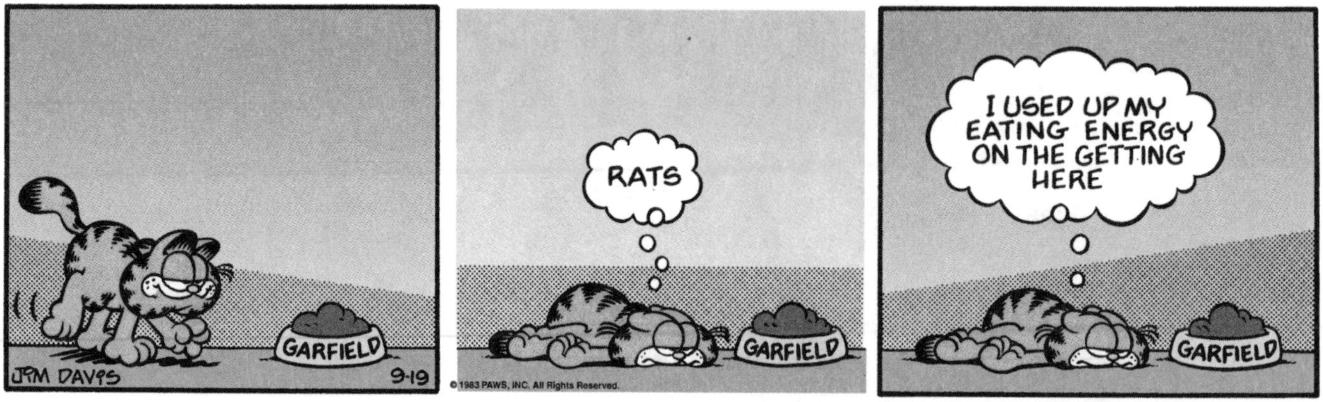
GARFIELD
JIM DAVIS
9-19
RATS
GARFIELD
© 1983 PAWS, INC. All Rights Reserved.
I USED UP MY EATING ENERGY ON THE GETTING HERE
GARFIELD

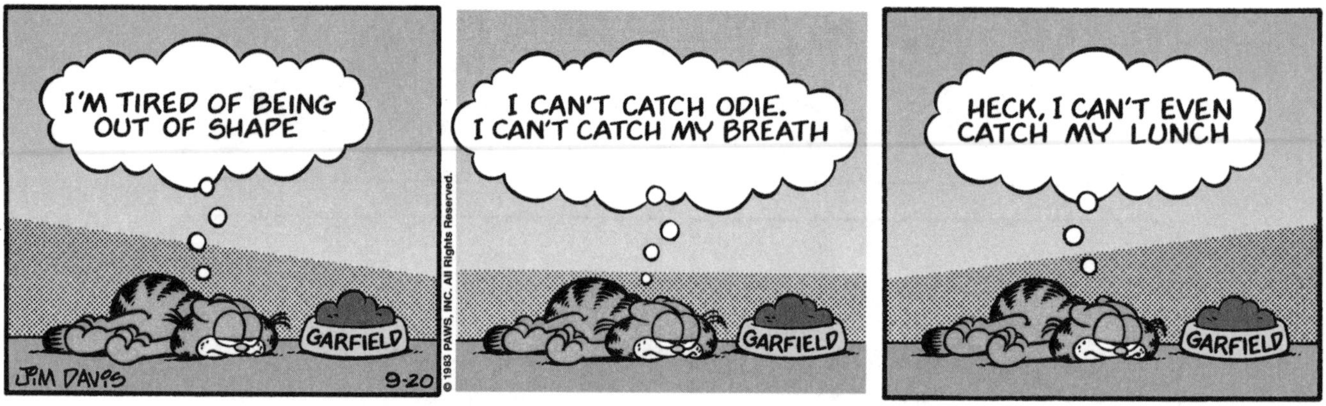
I'M TIRED OF BEING OUT OF SHAPE
GARFIELD
JIM DAVIS
9-20
© 1983 PAWS, INC. All Rights Reserved.
I CAN'T CATCH ODIE. I CAN'T CATCH MY BREATH
GARFIELD
HECK, I CAN'T EVEN CATCH MY LUNCH
GARFIELD

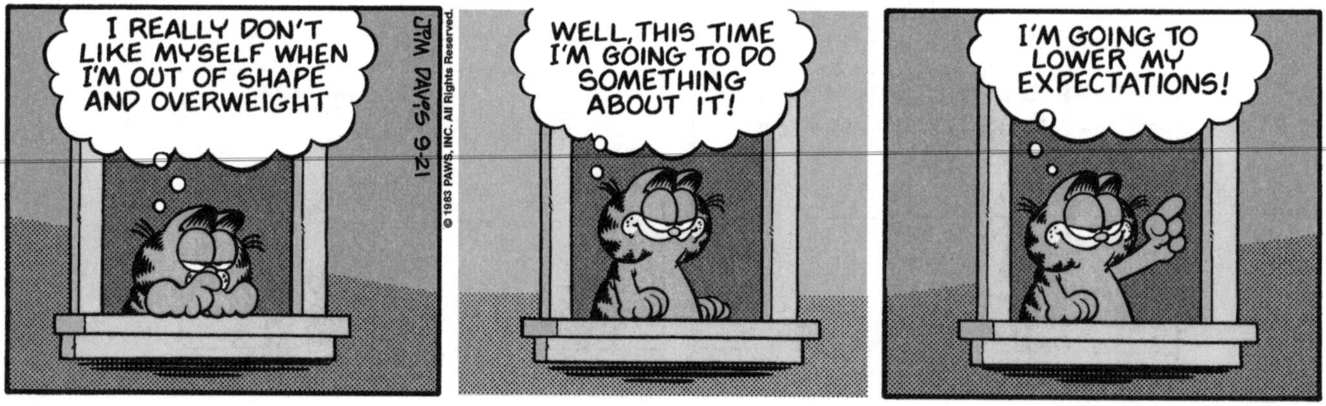
I REALLY DON'T LIKE MYSELF WHEN I'M OUT OF SHAPE AND OVERWEIGHT
JIM DAVIS 9-21
© 1983 PAWS, INC. All Rights Reserved.
WELL, THIS TIME I'M GOING TO DO SOMETHING ABOUT IT!
I'M GOING TO LOWER MY EXPECTATIONS!

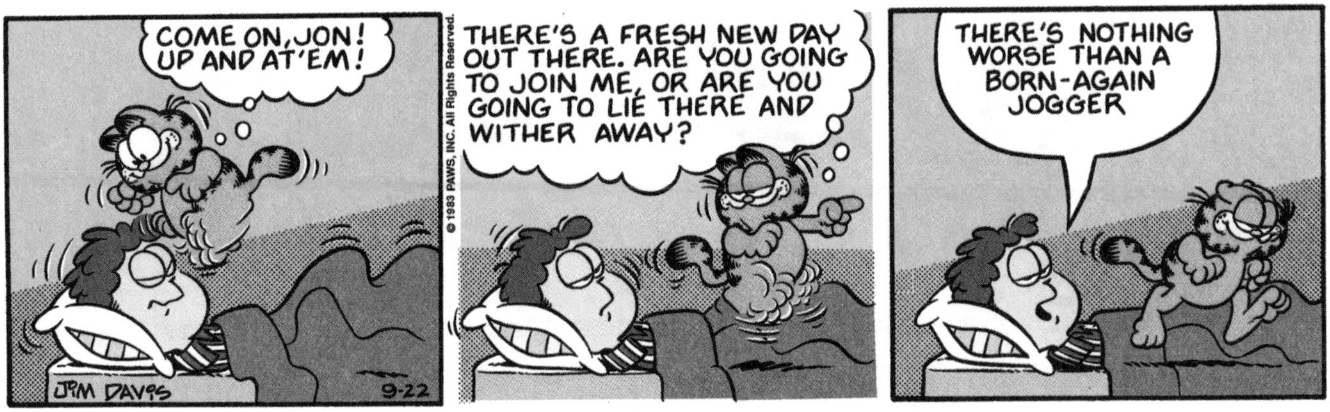
COME ON, JON! UP AND AT 'EM!
THERE'S A FRESH NEW DAY OUT THERE. ARE YOU GOING TO JOIN ME, OR ARE YOU GOING TO LIE THERE AND WITHER AWAY?
THERE'S NOTHING WORSE THAN A BORN-AGAIN JOGGER
JIM DAVIS
9-22
© 1983 PAWS, INC. All Rights Reserved.

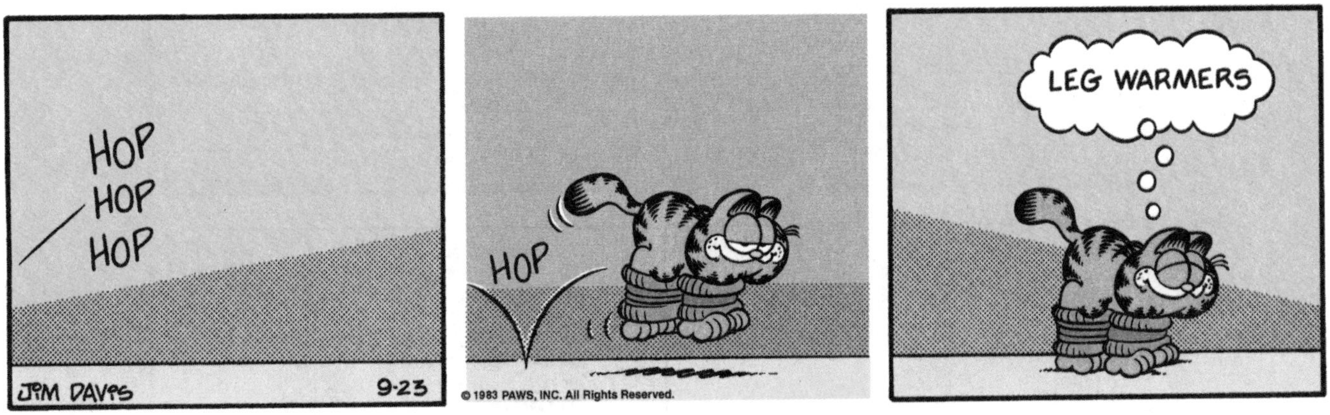
HOP
HOP
HOP
HOP
LEG WARMERS
JIM DAVIS
9-23
© 1983 PAWS, INC. All Rights Reserved.

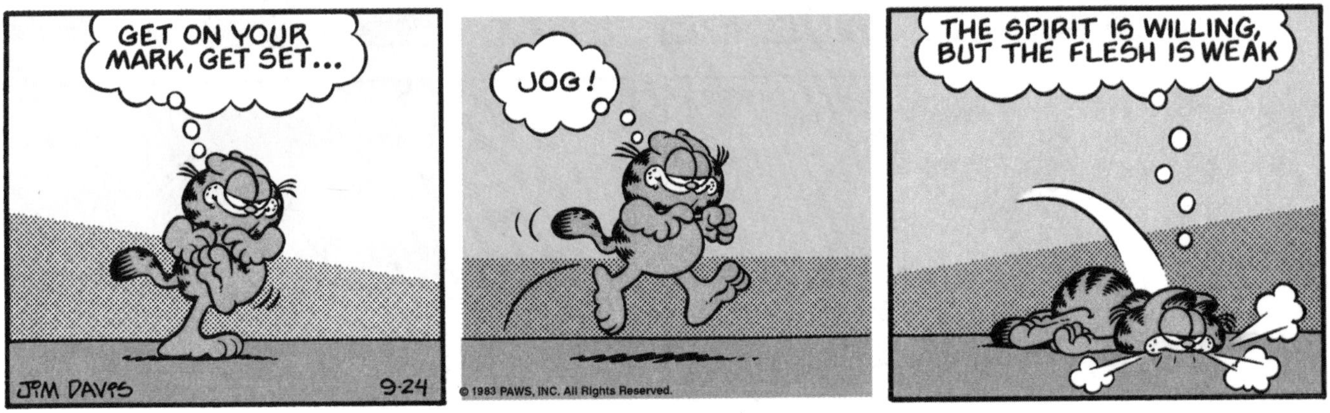
GET ON YOUR MARK, GET SET...
JOG!
THE SPIRIT IS WILLING, BUT THE FLESH IS WEAK
JIM DAVIS
9-24
© 1983 PAWS, INC. All Rights Reserved.

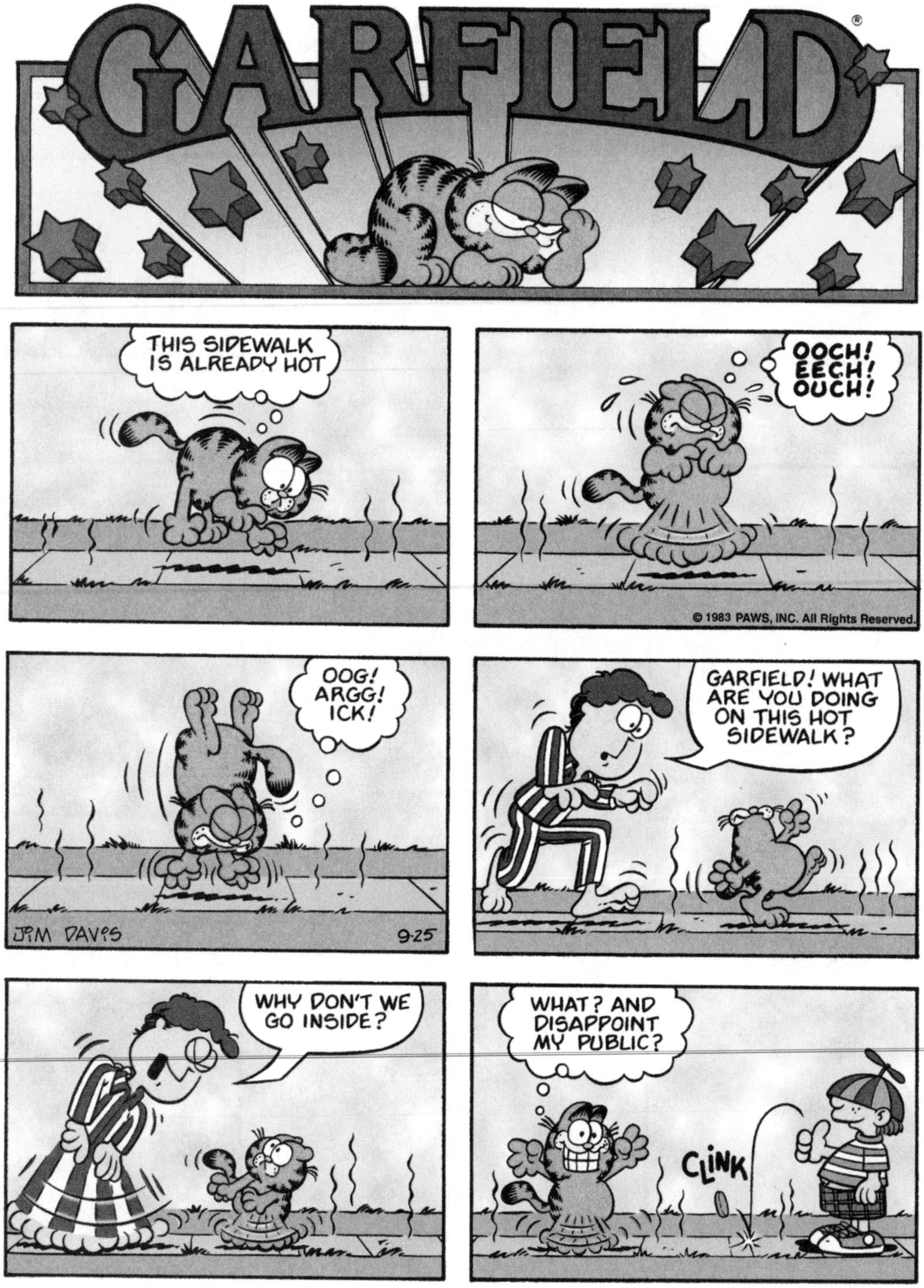
GARFIELD®
THIS SIDEWALK IS ALREADY HOT
OOCH! EECH! OUCH!
© 1983 PAWS, INC. All Rights Reserved.
OOG! ARGG! ICK!
JIM DAVIS
9-25
GARFIELD! WHAT ARE YOU DOING ON THIS HOT SIDEWALK?
WHY DON'T WE GO INSIDE?
WHAT? AND DISAPPOINT MY PUBLIC?
CLINK

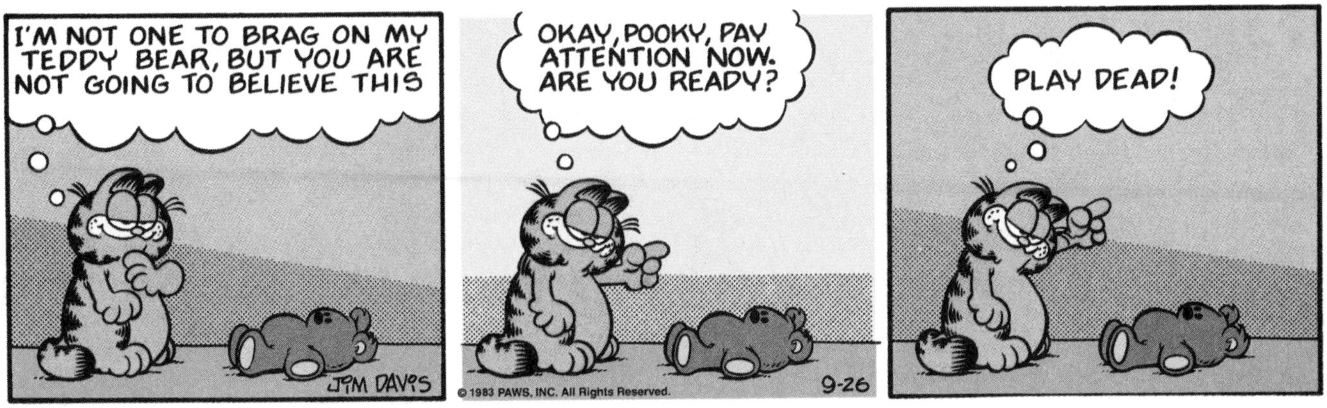
I'M NOT ONE TO BRAG ON MY TEDDY BEAR, BUT YOU ARE NOT GOING TO BELIEVE THIS
OKAY, POOKY, PAY ATTENTION NOW. ARE YOU READY?
PLAY DEAD!
JIM DAVIS
9-26
© 1983 PAWS, INC. All Rights Reserved.

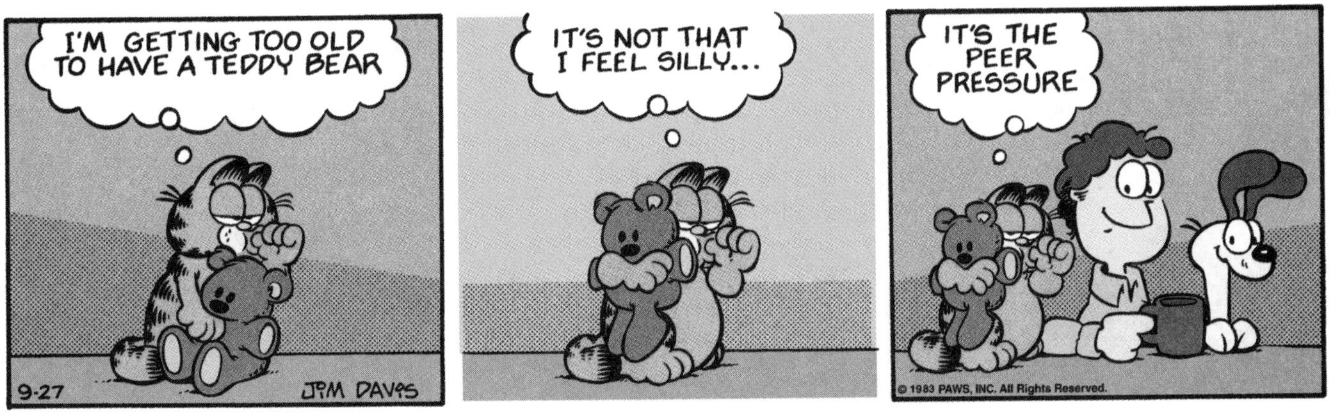
I'M GETTING TOO OLD TO HAVE A TEDDY BEAR
IT'S NOT THAT I FEEL SILLY...
IT'S THE PEER PRESSURE
9-27
JIM DAVIS
© 1983 PAWS, INC. All Rights Reserved.

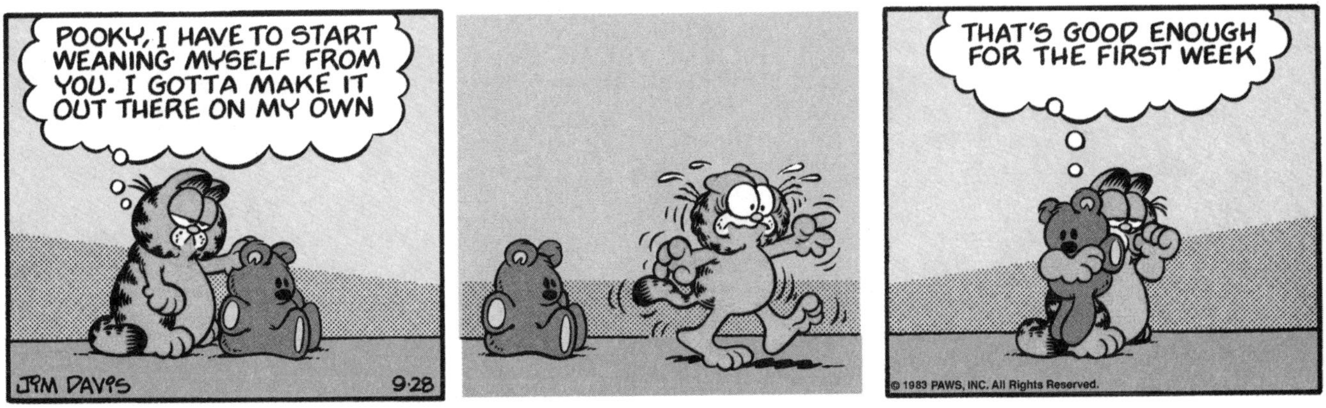
POOKY, I HAVE TO START WEANING MYSELF FROM YOU. I GOTTA MAKE IT OUT THERE ON MY OWN
THAT'S GOOD ENOUGH FOR THE FIRST WEEK
JIM DAVIS
9-28
© 1983 PAWS, INC. All Rights Reserved.

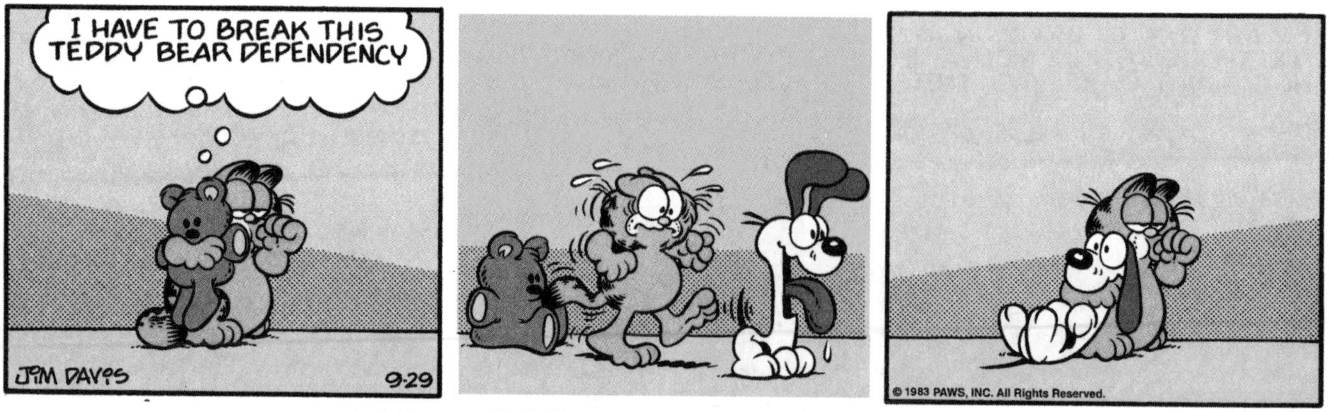
I HAVE TO BREAK THIS TEDDY BEAR DEPENDENCY
JIM DAVIS
9-29
© 1983 PAWS, INC. All Rights Reserved.

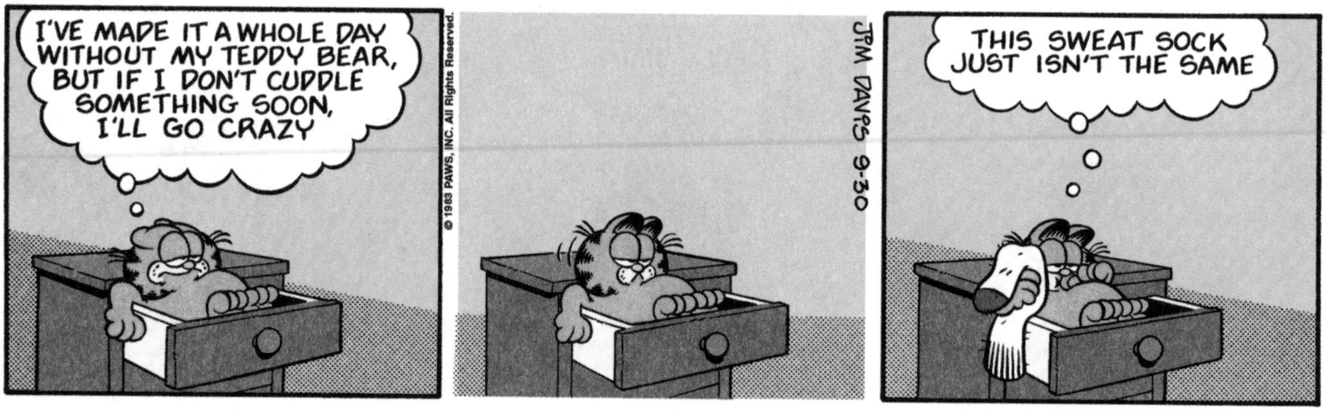
I'VE MADE IT A WHOLE DAY WITHOUT MY TEDDY BEAR, BUT IF I DON'T CUDDLE SOMETHING SOON, I'LL GO CRAZY
© 1983 PAWS, INC. All Rights Reserved.
JIM DAVIS 9-30
THIS SWEAT SOCK JUST ISN'T THE SAME

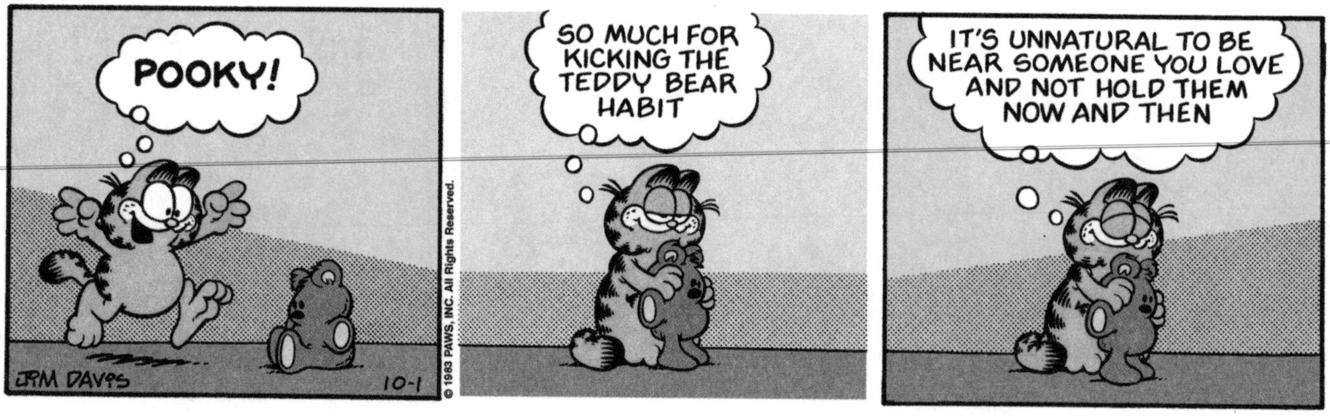
POOKY!
JIM DAVIS
10-1
© 1983 PAWS, INC. All Rights Reserved.
SO MUCH FOR KICKING THE TEDDY BEAR HABIT
IT'S UNNATURAL TO BE NEAR SOMEONE YOU LOVE AND NOT HOLD THEM NOW AND THEN

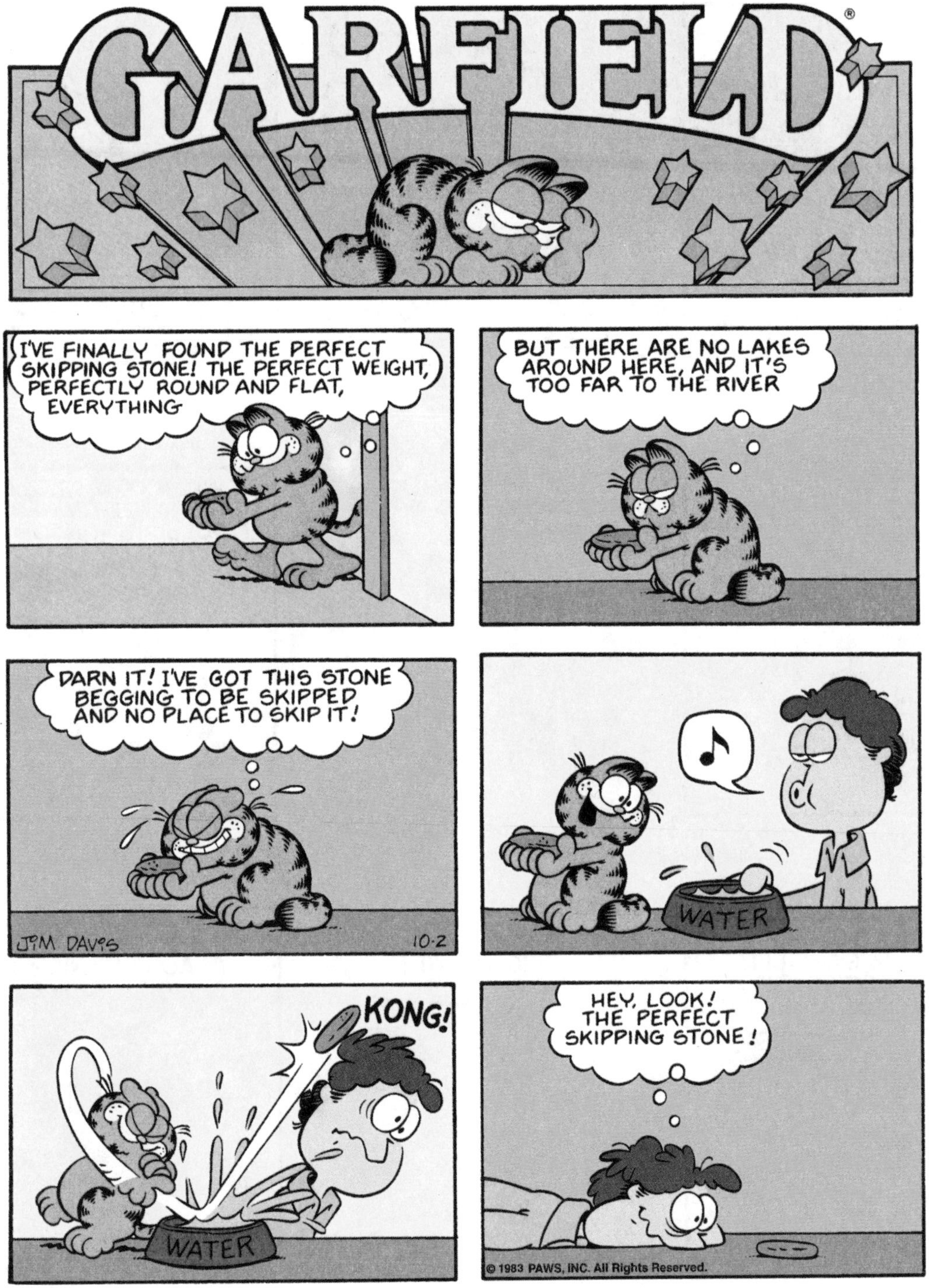
GARFIELD®
I'VE FINALLY FOUND THE PERFECT SKIPPING STONE! THE PERFECT WEIGHT, PERFECTLY ROUND AND FLAT, EVERYTHING
BUT THERE ARE NO LAKES AROUND HERE, AND IT'S TOO FAR TO THE RIVER
DARN IT! I'VE GOT THIS STONE BEGGING TO BE SKIPPED AND NO PLACE TO SKIP IT!
JIM DAVIS
10-2
♪
WATER
KONG!
WATER
HEY, LOOK! THE PERFECT SKIPPING STONE!
© 1983 PAWS, INC. All Rights Reserved.

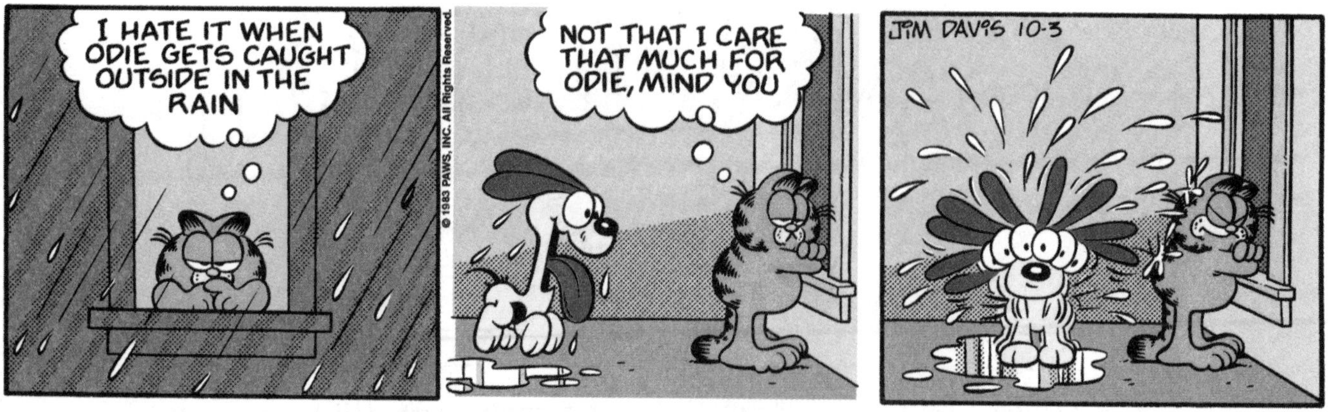
I HATE IT WHEN ODIE GETS CAUGHT OUTSIDE IN THE RAIN
© 1983 PAWS, INC. All Rights Reserved.
NOT THAT I CARE THAT MUCH FOR ODIE, MIND YOU
JIM DAVIS 10-3

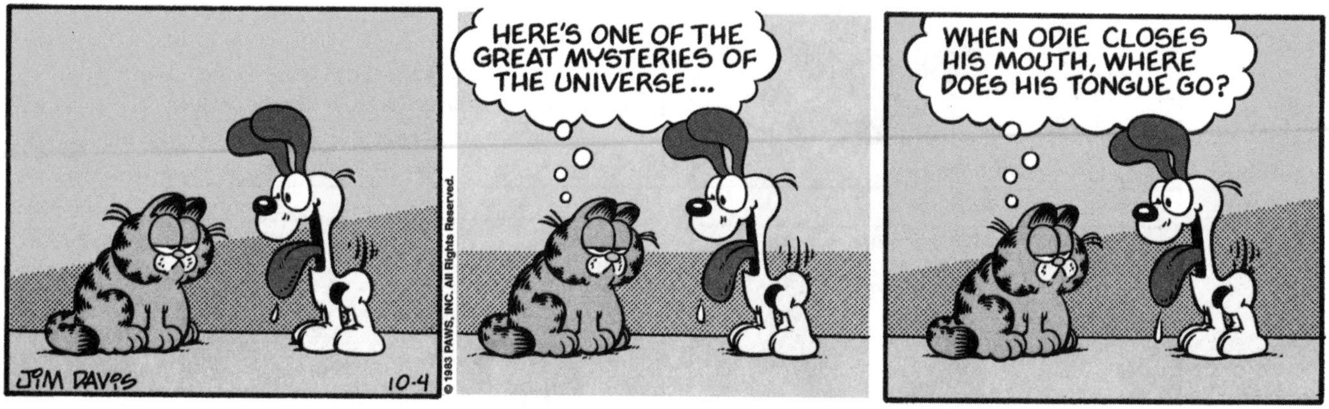
JIM DAVIS 10-4
© 1983 PAWS, INC. All Rights Reserved.
HERE'S ONE OF THE GREAT MYSTERIES OF THE UNIVERSE...
WHEN ODIE CLOSES HIS MOUTH, WHERE DOES HIS TONGUE GO?

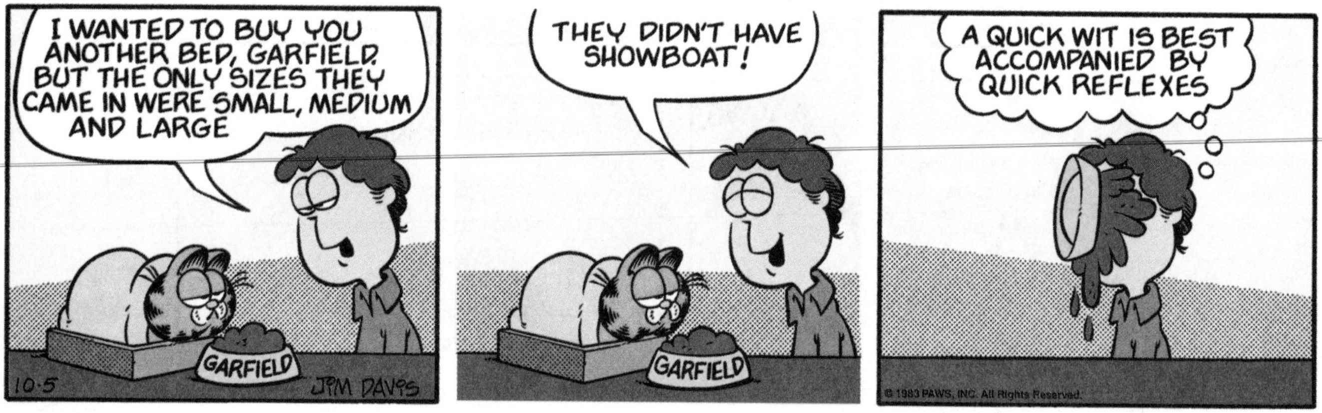
I WANTED TO BUY YOU ANOTHER BED, GARFIELD, BUT THE ONLY SIZES THEY CAME IN WERE SMALL, MEDIUM AND LARGE
GARFIELD
10-5 JIM DAVIS
THEY DIDN'T HAVE SHOWBOAT!
GARFIELD
A QUICK WIT IS BEST ACCOMPANIED BY QUICK REFLEXES
© 1983 PAWS, INC. All Rights Reserved.

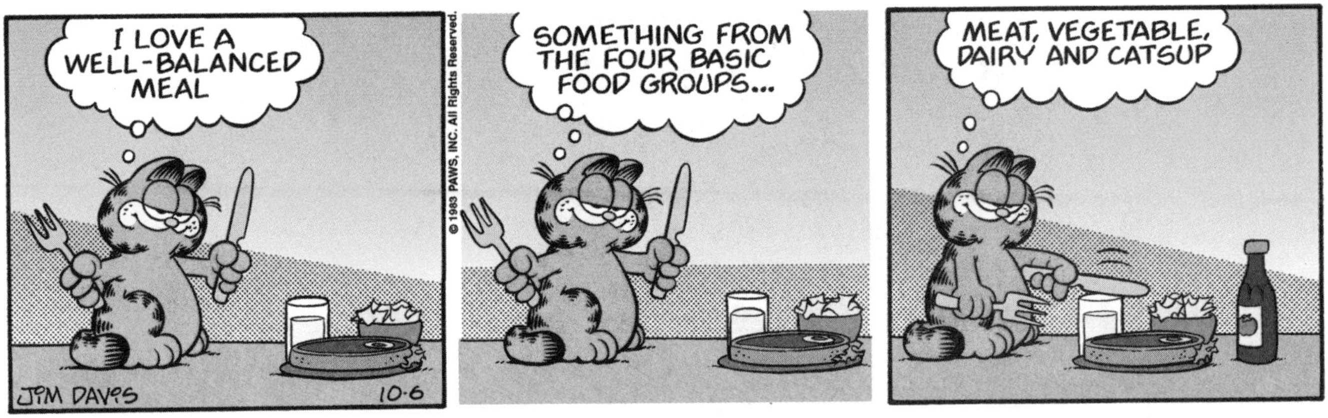
I LOVE A WELL-BALANCED MEAL
SOMETHING FROM THE FOUR BASIC FOOD GROUPS...
MEAT, VEGETABLE, DAIRY AND CATSUP
JIM DAVIS
10-6
© 1983 PAWS, INC. All Rights Reserved.

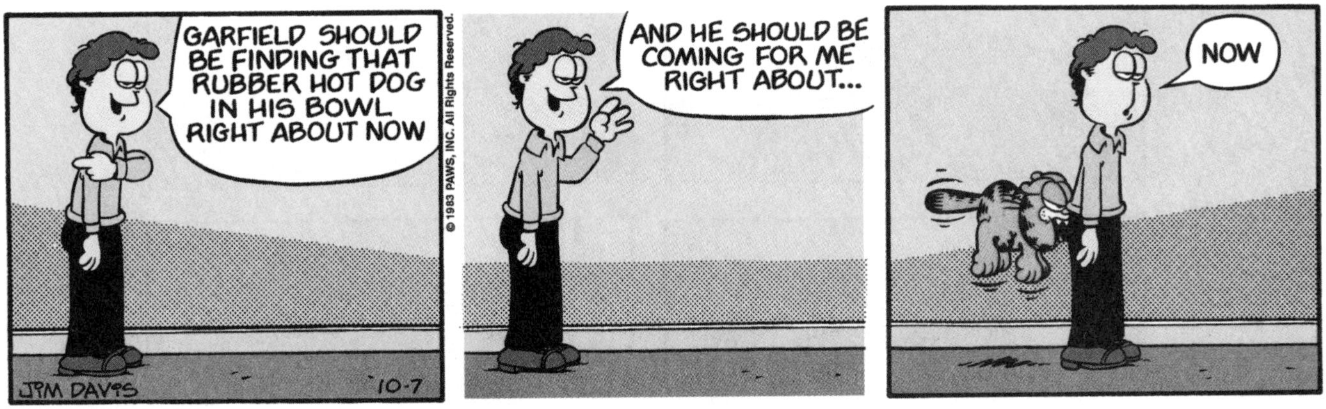
GARFIELD SHOULD BE FINDING THAT RUBBER HOT DOG IN HIS BOWL RIGHT ABOUT NOW
AND HE SHOULD BE COMING FOR ME RIGHT ABOUT...
NOW
JIM DAVIS
10-7
© 1983 PAWS, INC. All Rights Reserved.

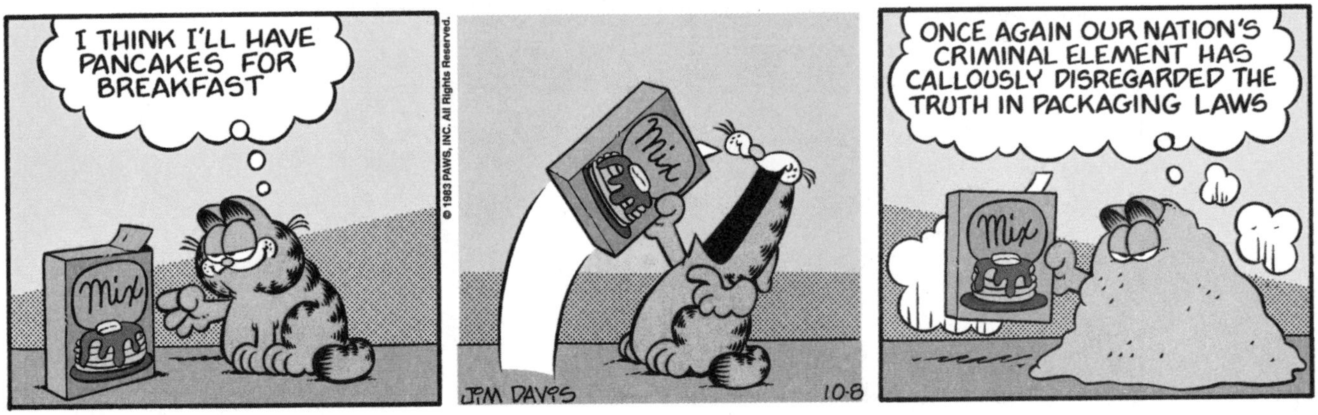
I THINK I'LL HAVE PANCAKES FOR BREAKFAST
Mix
ONCE AGAIN OUR NATION'S CRIMINAL ELEMENT HAS CALLOUSLY DISREGARDED THE TRUTH IN PACKAGING LAWS
JIM DAVIS
10-8
© 1983 PAWS, INC. All Rights Reserved.

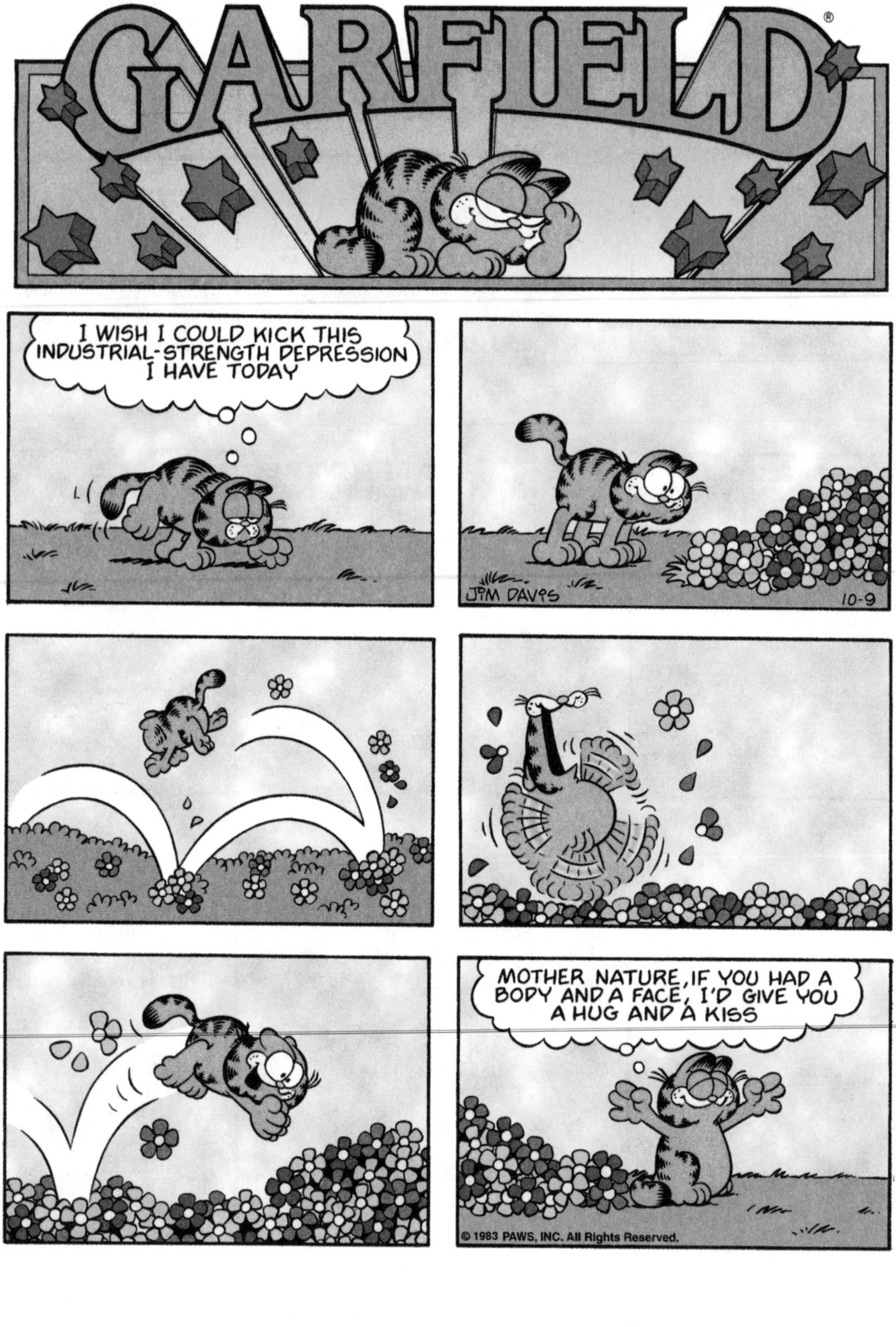
GARFIELD®
I WISH I COULD KICK THIS INDUSTRIAL-STRENGTH DEPRESSION I HAVE TODAY
JIM DAVIS
10-9
MOTHER NATURE, IF YOU HAD A BODY AND A FACE, I'D GIVE YOU A HUG AND A KISS
© 1983 PAWS, INC. All Rights Reserved.

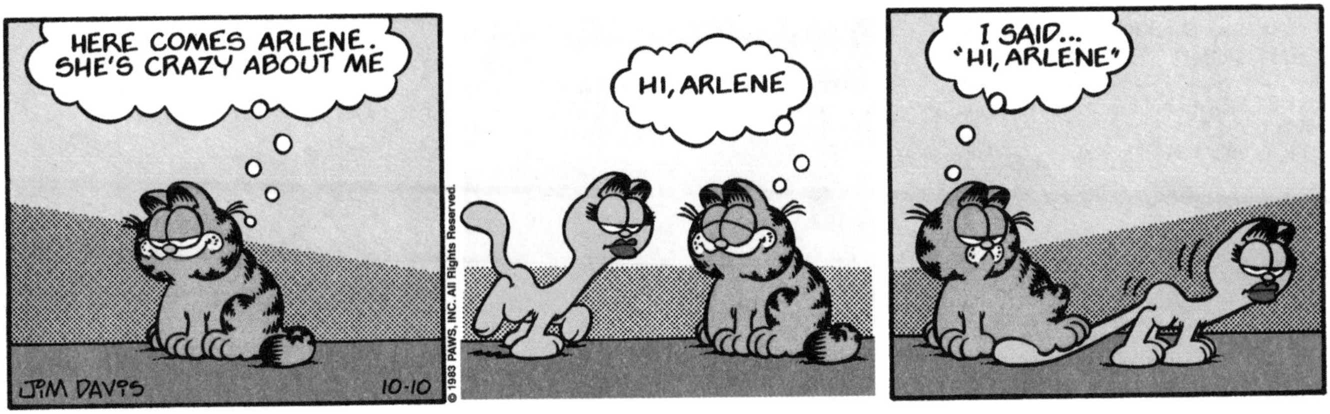
HERE COMES ARLENE. SHE'S CRAZY ABOUT ME
JIM DAVIS
10-10
© 1983 PAWS, INC. All Rights Reserved.
HI, ARLENE
I SAID... "HI, ARLENE"

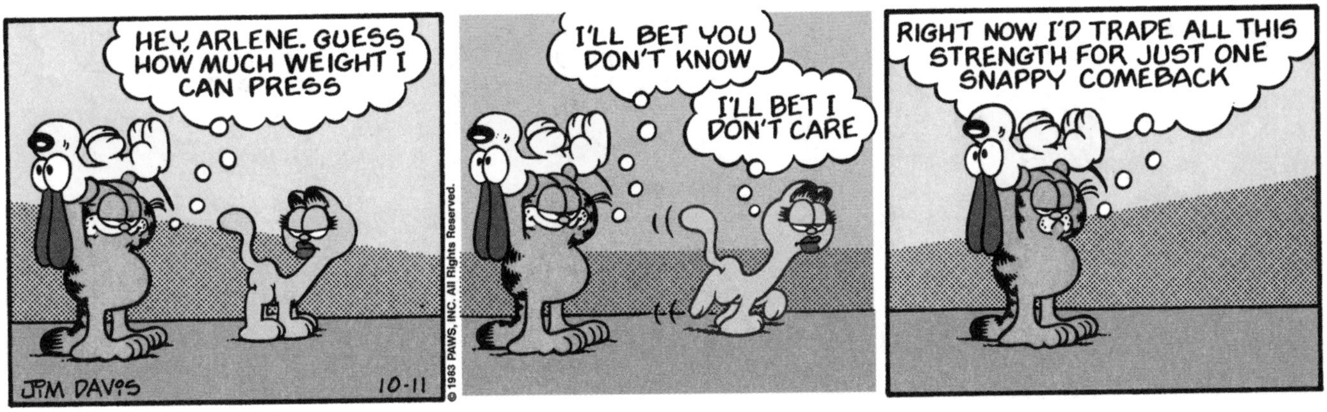
HEY, ARLENE. GUESS HOW MUCH WEIGHT I CAN PRESS
JIM DAVIS
10-11
© 1983 PAWS, INC. All Rights Reserved.
I'LL BET YOU DON'T KNOW
I'LL BET I DON'T CARE
RIGHT NOW I'D TRADE ALL THIS STRENGTH FOR JUST ONE SNAPPY COMEBACK

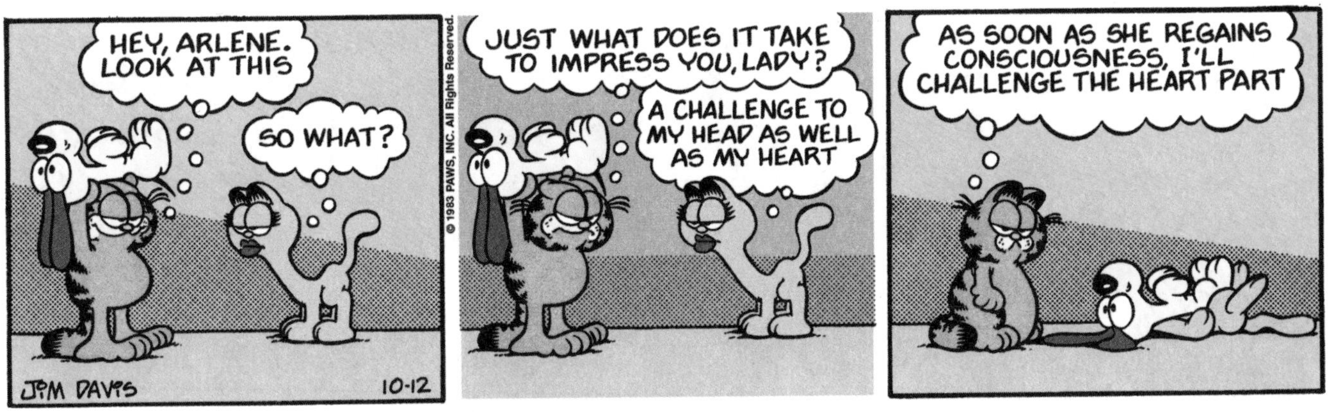
HEY, ARLENE. LOOK AT THIS
SO WHAT?
JIM DAVIS
10-12
© 1983 PAWS, INC. All Rights Reserved.
JUST WHAT DOES IT TAKE TO IMPRESS YOU, LADY?
A CHALLENGE TO MY HEAD AS WELL AS MY HEART
AS SOON AS SHE REGAINS CONSCIOUSNESS, I'LL CHALLENGE THE HEART PART

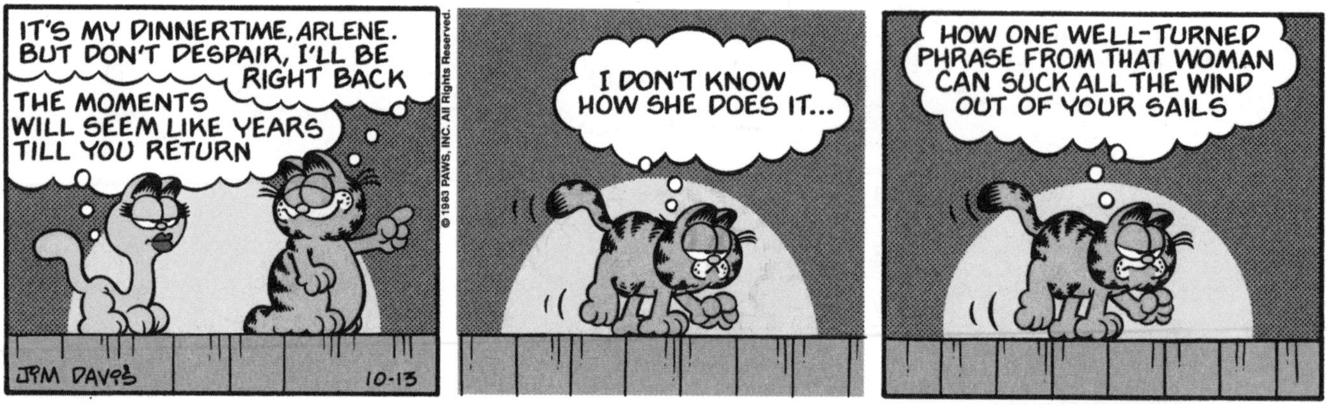
IT'S MY DINNERTIME, ARLENE. BUT DON'T DESPAIR, I'LL BE RIGHT BACK
THE MOMENTS WILL SEEM LIKE YEARS TILL YOU RETURN
JIM DAVIS
10-13
© 1983 PAWS, INC. All Rights Reserved.
I DON'T KNOW HOW SHE DOES IT...
HOW ONE WELL-TURNED PHRASE FROM THAT WOMAN CAN SUCK ALL THE WIND OUT OF YOUR SAILS

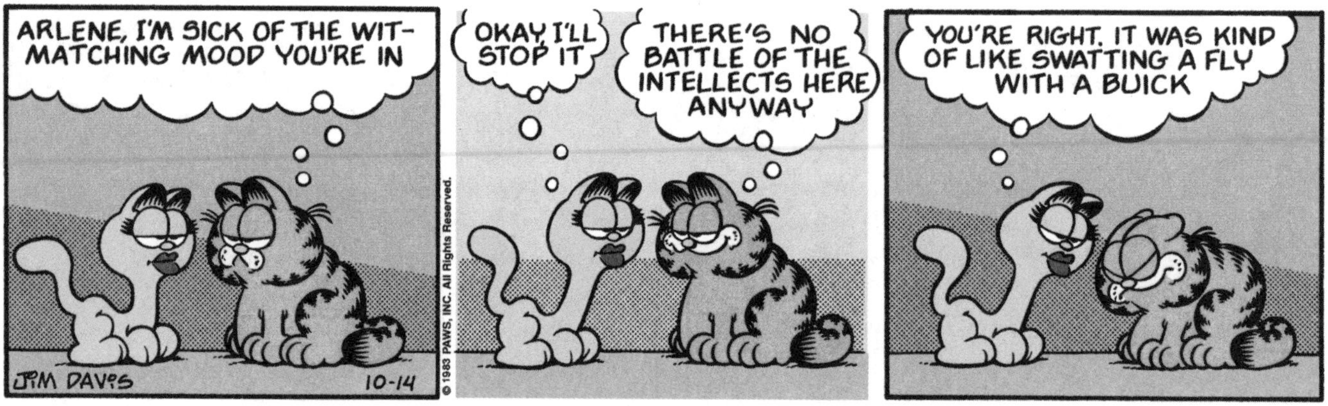
ARLENE, I'M SICK OF THE WIT-MATCHING MOOD YOU'RE IN
JIM DAVIS
10-14
© 1983 PAWS, INC. All Rights Reserved.
OKAY I'LL STOP IT
THERE'S NO BATTLE OF THE INTELLECTS HERE ANYWAY
YOU'RE RIGHT. IT WAS KIND OF LIKE SWATTING A FLY WITH A BUICK

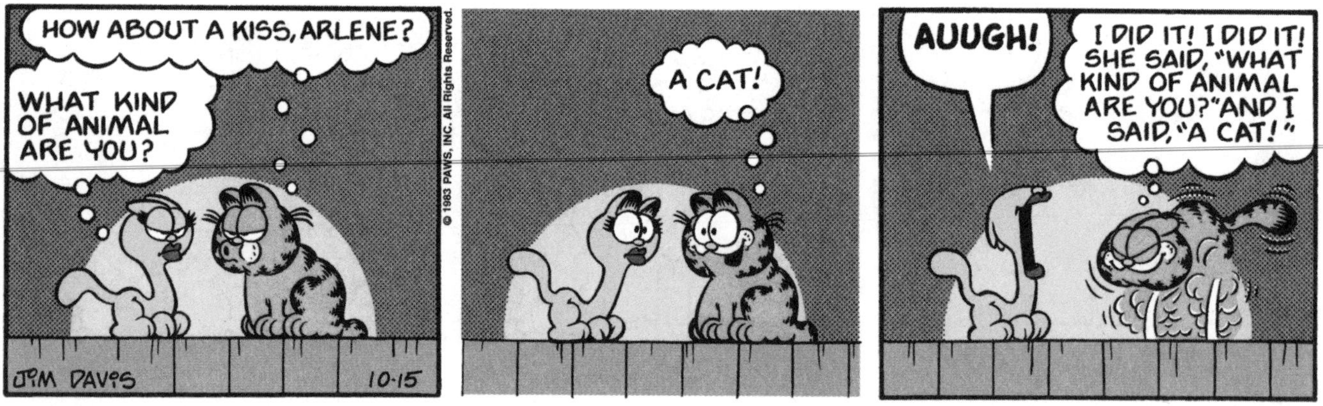
HOW ABOUT A KISS, ARLENE?
WHAT KIND OF ANIMAL ARE YOU?
JIM DAVIS
10-15
© 1983 PAWS, INC. All Rights Reserved.
A CAT!
AUUGH!
I DID IT! I DID IT! SHE SAID, "WHAT KIND OF ANIMAL ARE YOU?" AND I SAID, "A CAT!"

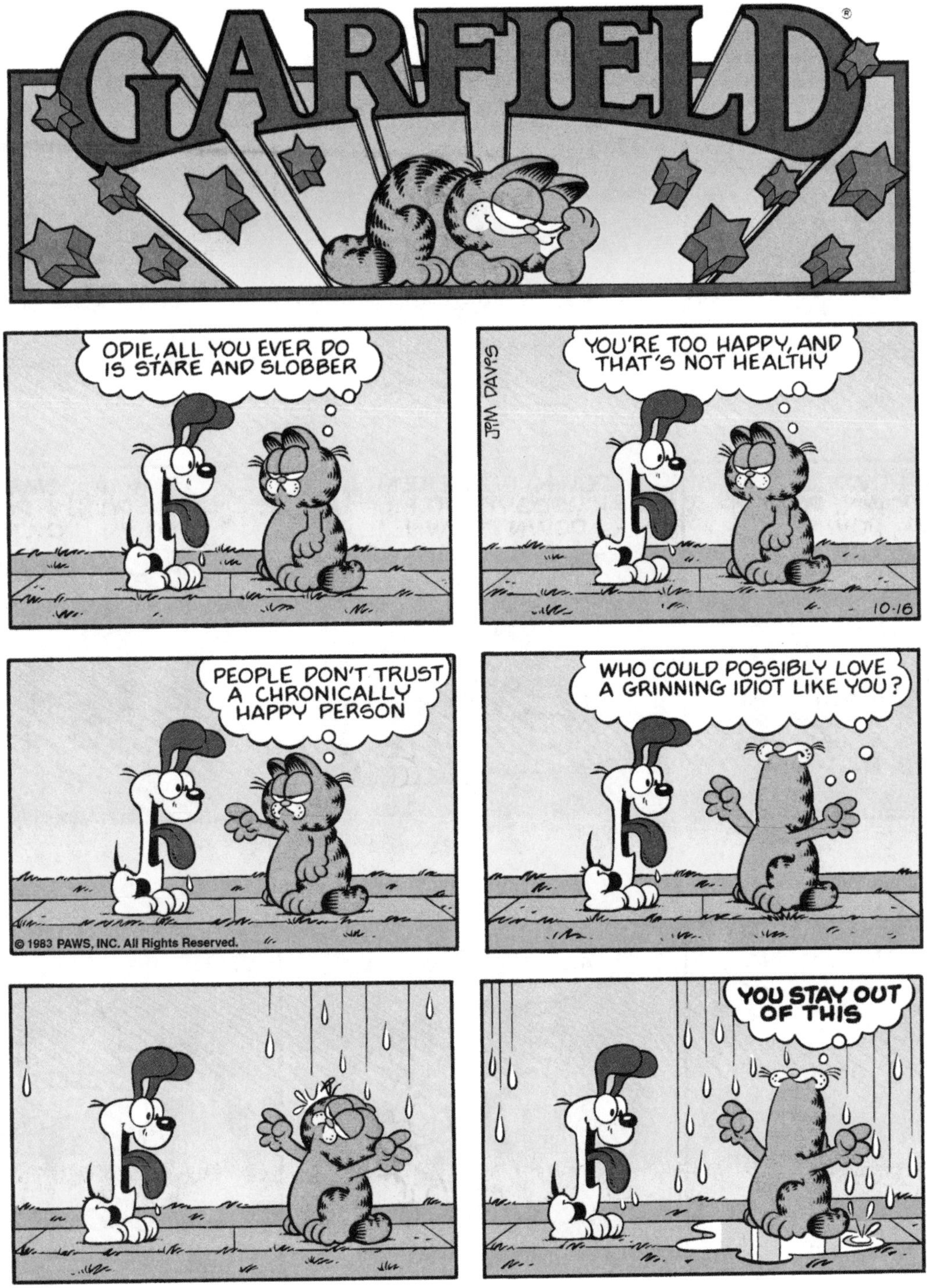
GARFIELD
ODIE, ALL YOU EVER DO IS STARE AND SLOBBER
JIM DAVIS
YOU'RE TOO HAPPY, AND THAT'S NOT HEALTHY
10-16
PEOPLE DON'T TRUST A CHRONICALLY HAPPY PERSON
© 1983 PAWS, INC. All Rights Reserved.
WHO COULD POSSIBLY LOVE A GRINNING IDIOT LIKE YOU?
YOU STAY OUT OF THIS

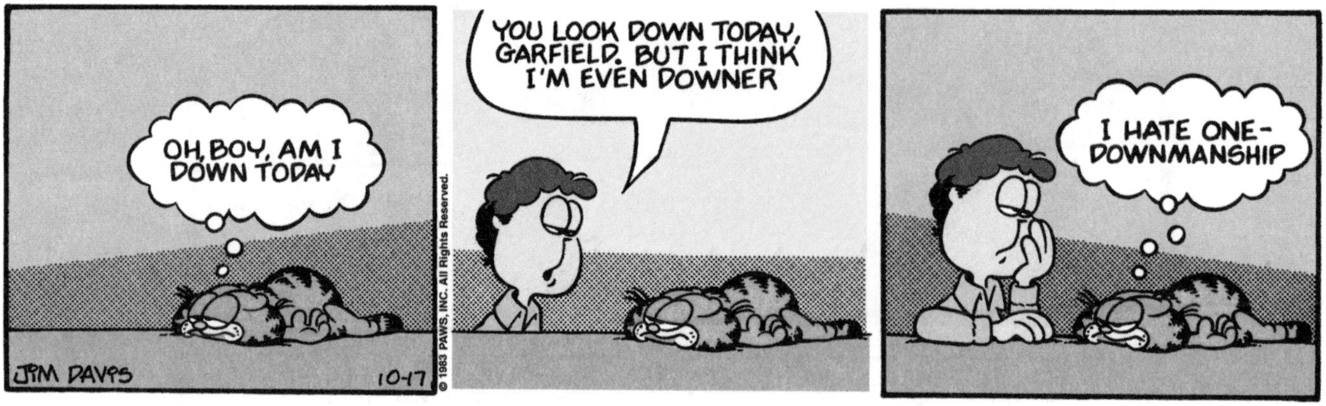
OH, BOY, AM I DOWN TODAY
YOU LOOK DOWN TODAY, GARFIELD. BUT I THINK I'M EVEN DOWNER
I HATE ONE-DOWNMANSHIP
JIM DAVIS 10-17
© 1983 PAWS, INC. All Rights Reserved.

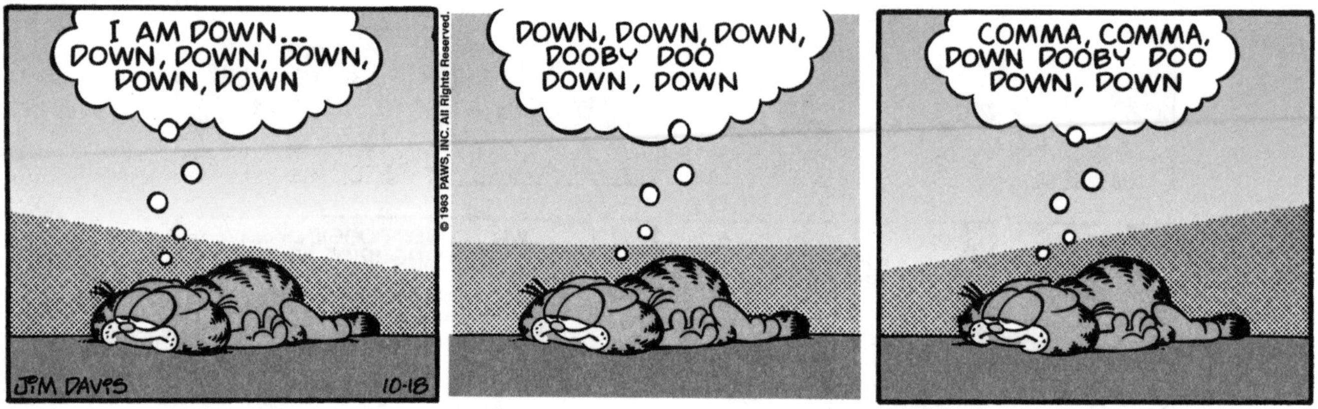
I AM DOWN... DOWN, DOWN, DOWN, DOWN, DOWN
DOWN, DOWN, DOWN, DOOBY DOO DOWN, DOWN
COMMA, COMMA, DOWN DOOBY DOO DOWN, DOWN
JIM DAVIS 10-18
© 1983 PAWS, INC. All Rights Reserved.

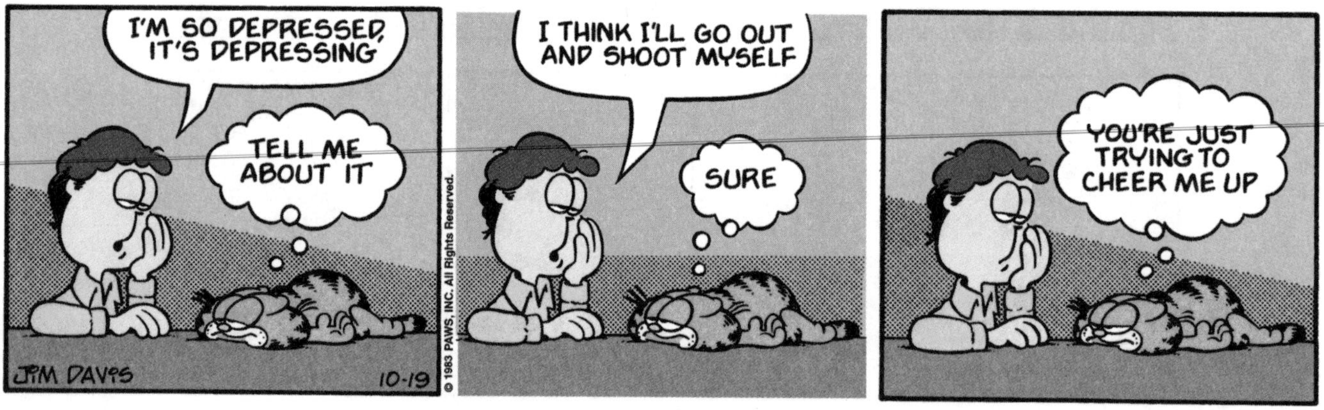
I'M SO DEPRESSED, IT'S DEPRESSING
TELL ME ABOUT IT
I THINK I'LL GO OUT AND SHOOT MYSELF
SURE
YOU'RE JUST TRYING TO CHEER ME UP
JIM DAVIS 10-19
© 1983 PAWS, INC. All Rights Reserved.

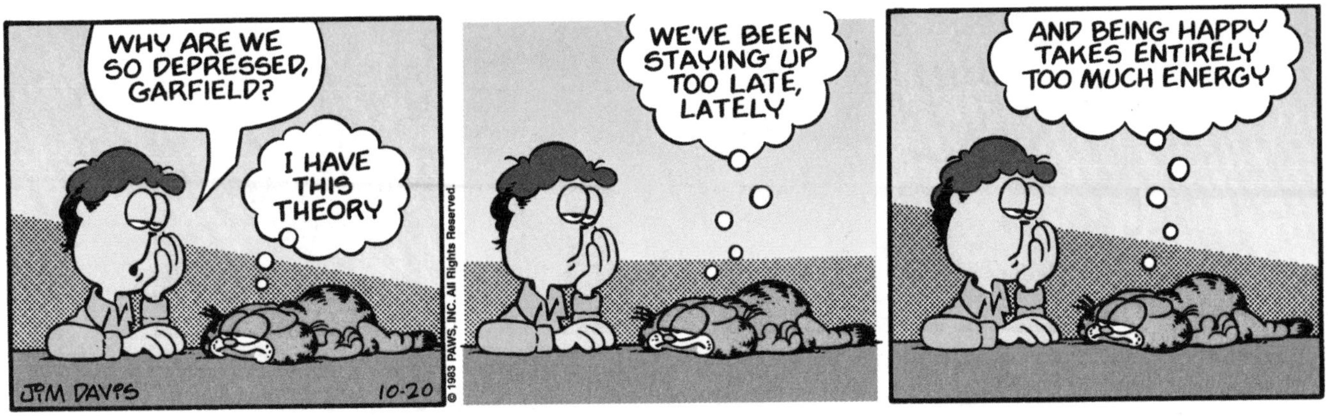
WHY ARE WE SO DEPRESSED, GARFIELD?
I HAVE THIS THEORY
JIM DAVIS
10-20
WE'VE BEEN STAYING UP TOO LATE, LATELY
AND BEING HAPPY TAKES ENTIRELY TOO MUCH ENERGY

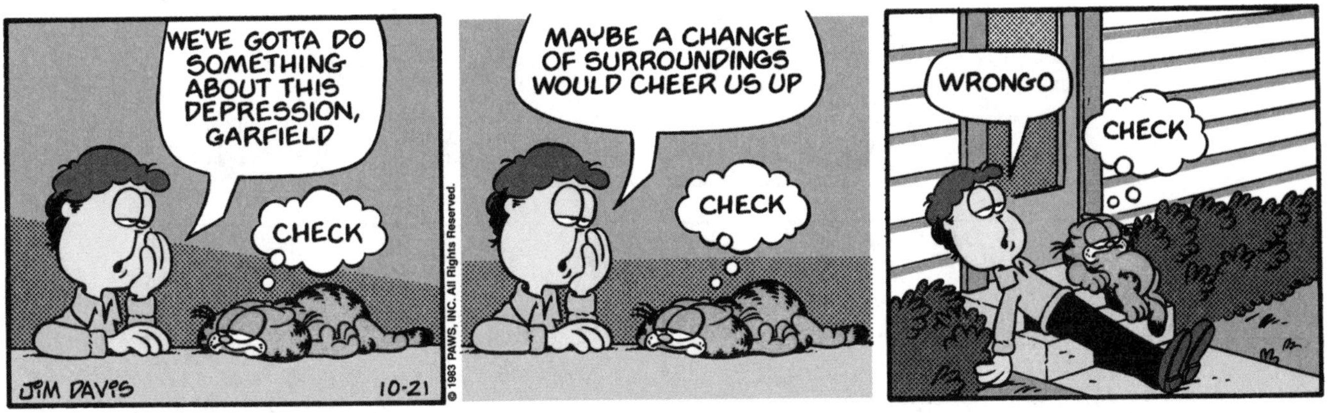
WE'VE GOTTA DO SOMETHING ABOUT THIS DEPRESSION, GARFIELD
CHECK
JIM DAVIS
10-21
MAYBE A CHANGE OF SURROUNDINGS WOULD CHEER US UP
CHECK
WRONGO
CHECK

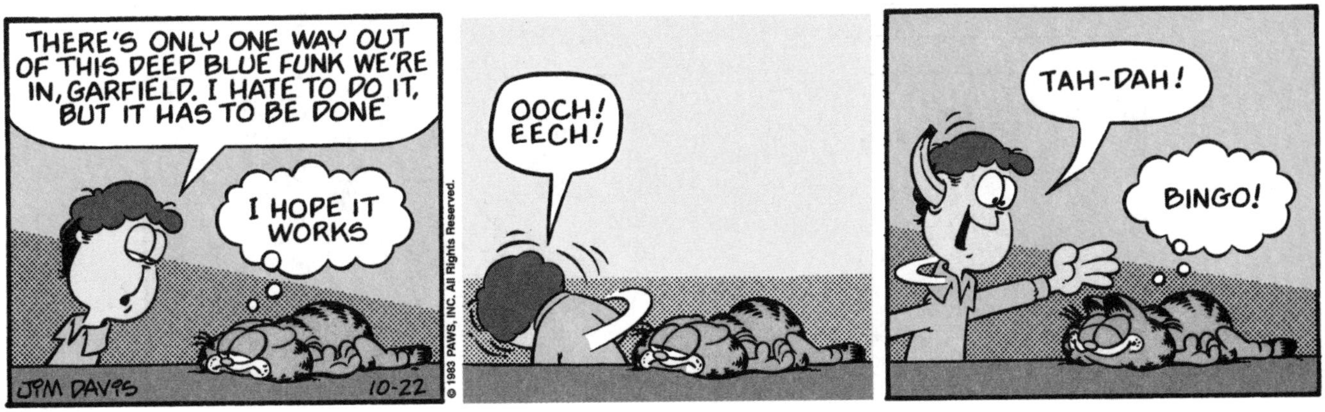
THERE'S ONLY ONE WAY OUT OF THIS DEEP BLUE FUNK WE'RE IN, GARFIELD. I HATE TO DO IT, BUT IT HAS TO BE DONE
I HOPE IT WORKS
JIM DAVIS
10-22
OOCH! EECH!
TAH-DAH!
BINGO!

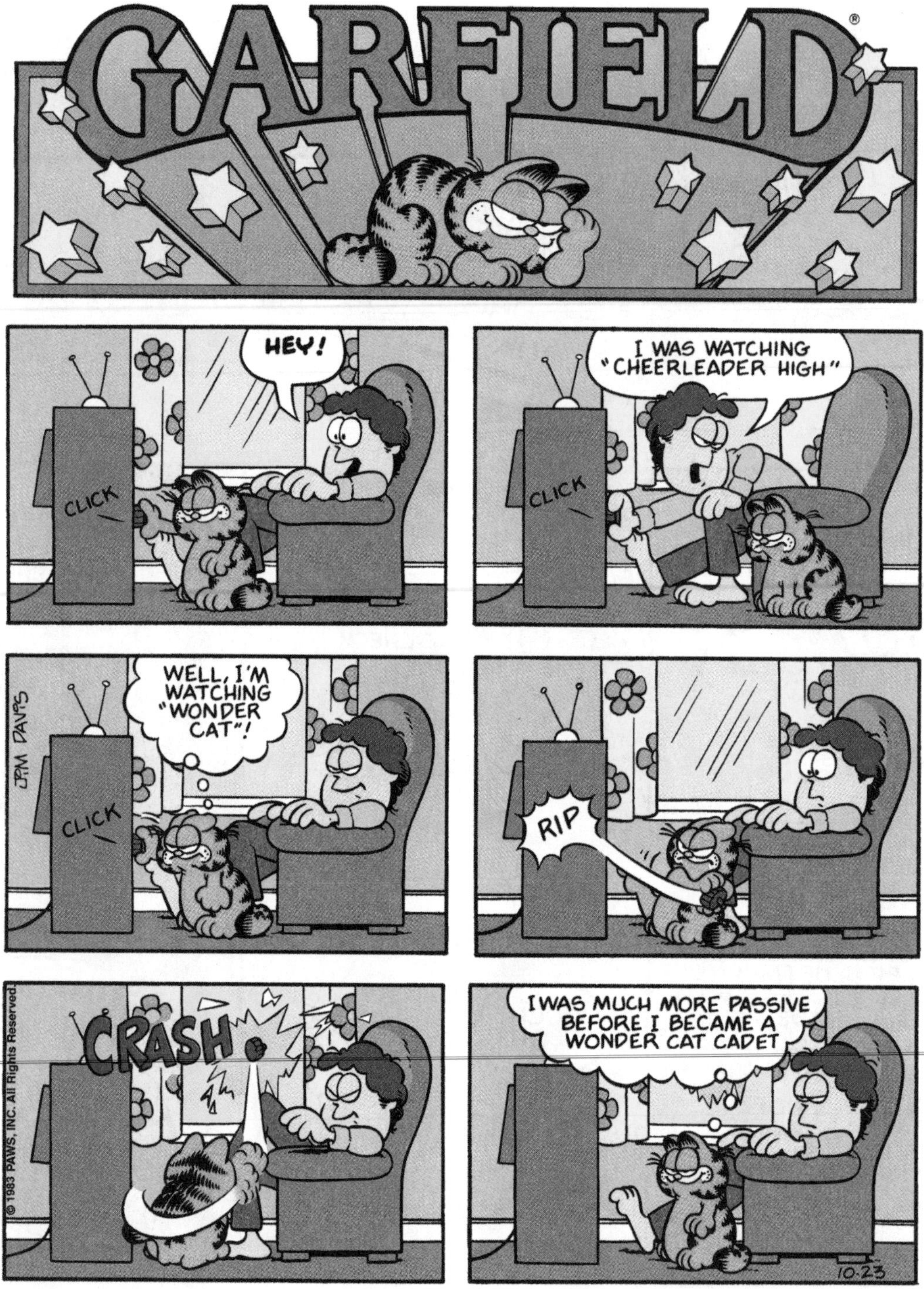
GARFIELD®
HEY!
CLICK
I WAS WATCHING "CHEERLEADER HIGH"
CLICK
JIM DAVIS
WELL, I'M WATCHING "WONDER CAT"!
CLICK
RIP
CRASH
I WAS MUCH MORE PASSIVE BEFORE I BECAME A WONDER CAT CADET
10-23

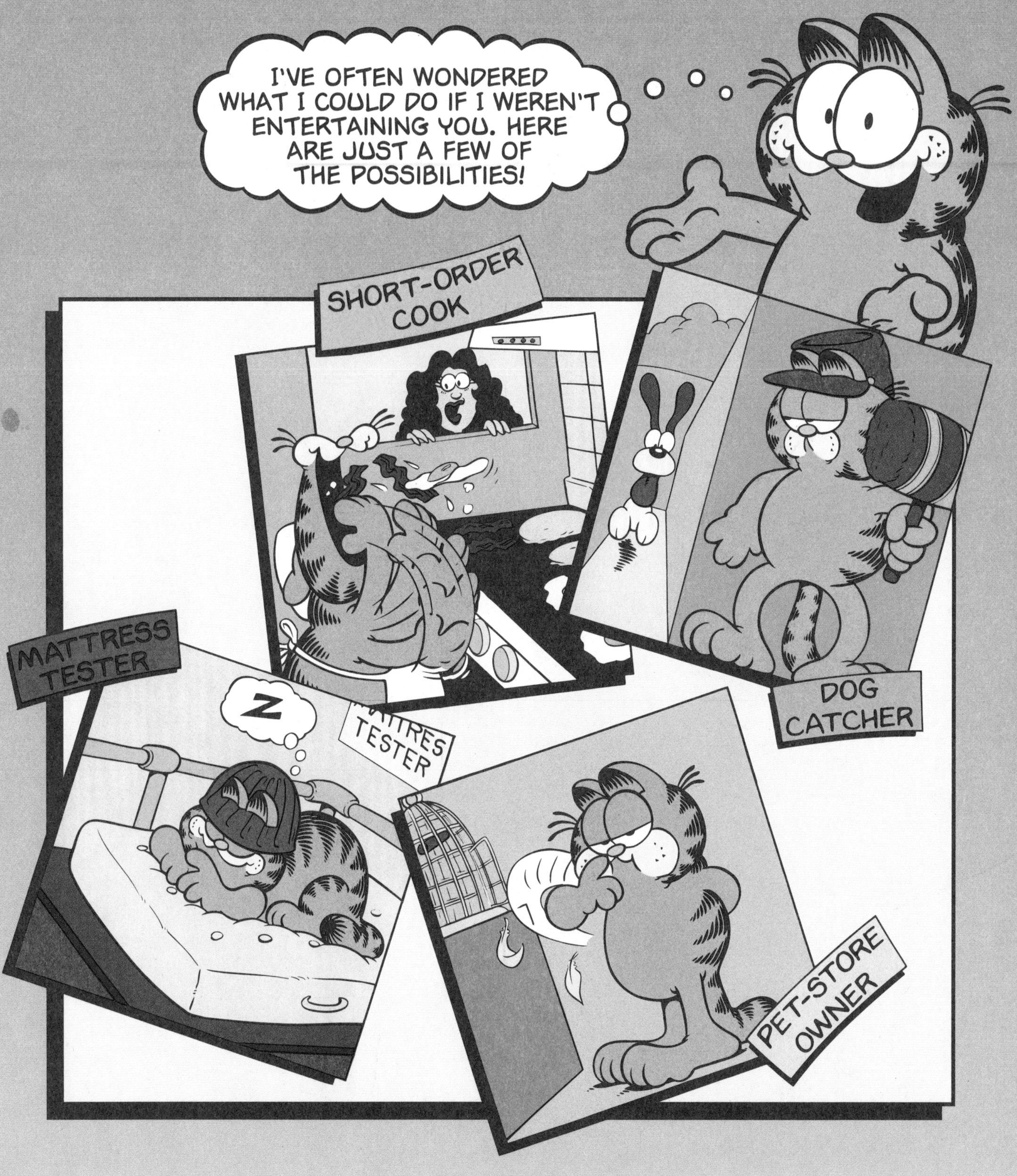
I'VE OFTEN WONDERED WHAT I COULD DO IF I WEREN'T ENTERTAINING YOU. HERE ARE JUST A FEW OF THE POSSIBILITIES!
SHORT-ORDER COOK
DOG CATCHER
MATTRESS TESTER
Z
PET-STORE OWNER

GARFIELD
CHARACTERS
THAT DIDN'T MAKE IT

When I initially designed GARFIELD,
these concepts never made it off the drawing board.
Maybe they could all be brought back in a strip
called ROGUES' GALLERY.

JIM DAVIS